Pro Spring

Fourth Edition

Chris Schaefer

Clarence Ho

Rob Harrop

Apress®

Pro Spring

ISBN-13 (pbk): 978-1-4302-6151-3

ISBN-13 (electronic): 978-1-4302-6152-0

Publisher: Heinz Weinheimer
Lead Editor: Steve Anglin
Development Editor: Matthew Moodie
Technical Reviewer: Manuel Jordan
Editorial Board: Steve Anglin, Mark Beckner, Ewan Buckingham, Gary Cornell, Louise Corrigan, James T. DeWolf, Jonathan Gennick, Robert Hutchinson, Michelle Lowman, James Markham, Matthew Moodie, Jeff Olson, Jeffrey Pepper, Douglas Pundick, Ben Renow-Clarke, Dominic Shakeshaft, Gwenan Spearing, Matt Wade, Steve Weiss
Coordinating Editor: Anamika Panchoo
Copy Editor: Sharon Wilkey
Compositor: SPi Global
Indexer: SPi Global
Artist: SPi Global
Cover Designer: Anna Ishchenko

Distributed to the book trade worldwide by Springer Science+Business Media New York, 233 Spring Street, 6th Floor, New York, NY 10013. Phone 1-800-SPRINGER, fax (201) 348-4505, e-mail orders-ny@springer-sbm.com, or visit www.springeronline.com. Apress Media, LLC is a California LLC and the sole member (owner) is Springer Science+Business Media Finance Inc (SSBM Finance Inc). SSBM Finance Inc is a Delaware corporation.

For information on translations, please e-mail rights@apress.com, or visit www.apress.com.

Apress and friends of ED books may be purchased in bulk for academic, corporate, or promotional use. eBook versions and licenses are also available for most titles. For more information, reference our Special Bulk Sales–eBook Licensing web page at www.apress.com/bulk-sales.

Any source code or other supplementary materials referenced by the author in this text is available to readers at www.apress.com. For detailed information about how to locate your book's source code, go to www.apress.com/source-code/.

I dedicate this book to my wife, son, family, friends,
and of course my cat Sally,
who shares my home office during our waking hours,
keeping me sane.

— Chris Schaefer

Contents at a Glance

Contents

About the Authors

Chris Schaefer is a software engineer primarily focused on Java and JVM-related technologies. He resides in Venice, Florida, with his wife, son, and cat. Outside of technology, he enjoys bicycling, outdoor activities in general, and astronomy.

Clarence Ho is a senior Java architect at a Hong Kong–based software consultancy firm, SkywideSoft Technology Limited (`www.skywidesoft.com`). Working in IT for over 20 years, Clarence has been the team leader on many in-house application development projects, as well as providing consultancy services on enterprise solutions to clients. Clarence started programming with Java in 2001, and since 2005 has been heavily involved in the design and development of JEE applications with technologies including EJB, Spring Framework, Hibernate, JMS, and WS. Since then, Clarence has performed as a Java enterprise architect.

Currently, Clarence is working as a consultant for an international financial institution, contributing in various areas including Java EE architectural design, education, recommendations on technology solutions, as well as application development best practices.

When he has spare time, Clarence enjoys playing sports (especially jogging, swimming, soccer, and hiking), reading, watching movies, and hanging out with friends.

Rob Harrop is a cofounder of SpringSource, the software company behind the wildly successful Spring Framework. Currently, he is CTO at First Banco. Prior to SpringSource, Rob was cofounder and CTO at Cake Solutions, a boutique consultancy in Manchester, United Kingdom. He specializes in high-volume, high-scale enterprise systems.

Rob is the author and coauthor of five books. You can follow him on Twitter at @robertharrop.

About the Technical Reviewer

Manuel Jordan Elera is an autodidactic developer and researcher who enjoys learning new technologies for his own experiments and creating new integrations.

Manuel won the 2010 Springy Award–Community Champion and Spring Champion 2013. In his little free time, he reads the Bible and composes music on his guitar. Manuel is known as dr_pompeii.

Manuel was the technical reviewer for these Apress books:

Pro SpringSource dm Server (2009)
Spring Enterprise Recipes (2009)
Spring Recipes (Second Edition, 2010)
Pro Spring Integration (2011)
Pro Spring Batch (2011)
Pro Spring 3 (2012)
Pro Spring MVC: With Web Flow (2012)
Pro Spring Security (2013)
Pro Hibernate and MongoDB (2013)
Pro JPA 2 (Second Edition, 2013)
Practical Spring LDAP (2013)

You can read his 13 detailed tutorials about many Spring technologies and contact him through his blog at www.manueljordanelera.blogspot.com, and follow him on his Twitter account, @dr_pompeii.

Introduction

Covering version 4 of the Spring Framework, this is the most comprehensive Spring reference and practical guide available for harnessing the power of this leading enterprise Java application development framework.

This edition covers core Spring and its integration with other leading Java technologies, such as Hibernate, JPA 2, and WebSocket. We share our insights and real-world experiences with enterprise application development, including remoting, transactions, the web and presentation tiers, and much more.

- With Pro Spring 4, you'll learn how to do the following:

- Use Inversion of Control (IoC) and Dependency Injection (DI)

- Use aspect-oriented programming (AOP) techniques with Spring and learn why they're important

- Build Spring-based web applications using Spring MVC and WebSocket

- Utilize the new Java 8 lambda syntax

- Work with scripting languages like Groovy to provide enhanced functionality for your applications

Arm yourself with the power to build complex Spring applications, from top to bottom. This book is for experienced Java developers who may be learning Spring for the first time or have minimal exposure to the Spring Framework. It's aimed at those who are active in or plan on getting into enterprise Java application development.

CHAPTER 1

■ ■ ■

Introducing Spring

When we think of the community of Java developers, we are reminded of the hordes of gold rush prospectors of the late 1840s, frantically panning the rivers of North America, looking for fragments of gold. As Java developers, our rivers run rife with open source projects, but, like the prospectors, finding a useful project can be time-consuming and arduous.

A common gripe with many open source Java projects is that they are conceived merely out of the need to fill the gap in the implementation of the latest buzzword-heavy technology or pattern. Having said that, many high-quality, usable projects meet and address a real need for real applications, and in the course of this book, you will meet a subset of these projects. You will get to know one in particular rather well—Spring.

Throughout this book, you will see many applications of different open source technologies, all of which are unified under the Spring Framework. When working with Spring, an application developer can use a large variety of open source tools, without needing to write reams of code and without coupling his application too closely to any particular tool.

In this chapter, as its title indicates, we introduce you to the Spring Framework, rather than presenting any solid examples or explanations. If you are already familiar with the Spring project, you might want to skip this chapter and proceed straight to Chapter 2.

What Is Spring?

Perhaps one the hardest parts of explaining Spring is classifying exactly what it is. Typically, *Spring* is described as a lightweight framework for building Java applications, but that statement brings up two interesting points.

First, you can use Spring to build any application in Java (for example, stand-alone, web, or Java Enterprise Edition (JEE) applications), unlike many other frameworks (such as Apache Struts, which is limited to web applications).

Second, the *lightweight* part of the description doesn't really refer to the number of classes or the size of the distribution, but rather defines the principle of the Spring philosophy as a whole—that is, minimal impact. Spring is lightweight in the sense that you have to make few, if any, changes to your application code to gain the benefits of the Spring core, and should you choose to stop using Spring at any point, you will find doing so quite simple.

Notice that we qualified that last statement to refer to the Spring core only—many of the extra Spring components, such as data access, require a much closer coupling to the Spring Framework. However, the benefits of this coupling are quite clear, and throughout the book we present techniques for minimizing the impact this has on your application.

Evolution of the Spring Framework

The Spring Framework originated from the book *Expert One-on-One: J2EE Design and Development* by Rod Johnson (Wrox, 2002). Over the last decade, the Spring Framework has grown dramatically in core functionality, associated projects, and community support. With the new major release of the Spring Framework, it's worthwhile to take a quick look back at important features that have come along with each milestone release of Spring, leading up to Spring Framework 4.0:

- Spring 0.9
    - The first public release of the framework, based on the book *Expert One-on-One: J2EE Design and Development*

- Spring 1.*x*
    - Spring Core: Bean container and supporting utilities
    - Spring Context: `ApplicationContext`, UI, validation, JNDI, Enterprise JavaBeans (EJB), remoting, and mail support
    - Spring DAO: Transaction infrastructure, Java Database Connectivity (JDBC) and data access object (DAO) support
    - Spring ORM: Hibernate, iBATIS and Java Data Objects (JDO) support
    - Spring AOP: An AOP Alliance–compliant aspect-oriented programming (AOP) implementation
    - Spring Web: Basic integration features such as multipart functionality, context initialization through servlet listeners, and a web-oriented application context
    - Spring Web MVC: Web-based Model-View-Controller (MVC) framework

- Spring 2.*x*
    - Easier XML configuration through use of the new XML Schema–based configuration rather than the DTD format. Notable areas of improvement include bean definitions, AOP, and declarative transactions.
    - New bean scopes for web and portal usage (request, session, and global session)
    - `@AspectJ` annotation support for AOP development
    - Java Persistence API (JPA) abstraction layer
    - Full support for asynchronous JMS message-driven POJOs (for *plain old Java objects*)
    - JDBC simplifications including `SimpleJdbcTemplate` when using Java 5+
    - JDBC named parameter support (`NamedParameterJdbcTemplate`)
    - Form tag library for Spring MVC
    - Introduction of the Portlet MVC framework
    - Dynamic language support: beans can be written in JRuby, Groovy, and BeanShell
    - Notification support and controllable MBean registration in JMX
    - `TaskExecutor` abstraction introduced for scheduling of tasks
    - Java 5 annotation support, specifically for `@Transactional`, `@Required`, in addition to `@AspectJ`

- Spring 2.5.*x*

  - New configuration annotation `@Autowired` and support for JSR-250 annotations (`@Resource`, `@PostConstruct`, `@PreDestroy`)

  - New stereotype annotations: `@Component`, `@Repository`, `@Service`, `@Controller`

  - Auto classpath scanning support to automatically detect and wire classes annotated with stereotype annotations

  - AOP updates: introduction of the bean(...) pointcut element and AspectJ load-time weaving

  - Full WebSphere transaction management support

  - In addition to the Spring MVC `@Controller` annotation, `@RequestMapping`, `@RequestParam`, and `@ModelAttribute` annotations added to support request handling through annotation configuration

  - Tiles 2 support

  - JSF 1.2 support

  - JAX-WS 2.0/2.1 support

  - Introduction of the Spring TestContext Framework, providing annotation-driven and integration testing support, agnostic of the testing framework being used

  - Ability to deploy a Spring application context as a JCA adapter

- Spring 3.0.*x*

  - Support for Java 5 features such as generics, varargs, and other improvements

  - First-class support for `Callables`, `Futures`, `ExecutorService` adapters, and `ThreadFactory` integration

  - Framework modules now managed separately with one source-tree per module JAR

  - Introduction of the Spring Expression Language (SpEL)

  - Integration of core JavaConfig features and annotations

  - General-purpose type-conversion system and field-formatting system

  - Comprehensive REST support

  - New MVC XML namespace and additional annotations such as `@CookieValue` and `@RequestHeaders` for Spring MVC

  - Validation enhancements and JSR-303 ("Bean Validation") support

  - Early support for Java EE 6: `@Async`/`@Asynchronous` annotation, JSR-303, JSF 2.0, JPA 2.0, and so on

  - Support for embedded databases such as HSQL, H2, and Derby

- Spring 3.1.*x*

  - New Cache abstraction

  - Bean definition profiles can be defined in XML as well as support for the `@Profile` annotation

- Environment abstraction for unified property management

- Annotation equivalents for common Spring XML namespace elements such as @ComponentScan, @EnableTransactionManagement, @EnableCaching, @EnableWebMvc, @EnableScheduling, @EnableAsync, @EnableAspectJAutoProxy, @EnableLoadTimeWeaving, and @EnableSpringConfigured

- Support for Hibernate 4

- Spring TestContext Framework support for @Configuration classes and bean definition profiles

- c: namespace for simplified constructor injection

- Support for Servlet 3 code-based configuration of the Servlet container

- Ability to bootstrap the JPA EntityManagerFactory without persistence.xml

- Flash and RedirectAttributes added to Spring MVC, allowing attributes to survive a redirect by using the HTTP session

- URI template variable enhancements

- Ability to annotate Spring MVC @RequestBody controller method arguments with @Valid

- Ability to annotate Spring MVC controller method arguments with the @RequestPart annotation

- Spring 3.2.*x*

  - Support for Servlet 3–based asynchronous request processing

  - New Spring MVC test framework

  - New Spring MVC annotations @ControllerAdvice, @MatrixVariable

  - Support for generic types in RestTemplate and in @RequestBody arguments

  - Jackson JSON 2 support

  - Support for Tiles 3

  - @RequestBody or an @RequestPart argument can now be followed by an Errors argument, making it possible to handle validation errors

  - Ability to exclude URL patterns by using the MVC namespace and JavaConfig configuration options

  - Support for @DateTimeFormat without Joda Time

  - Global date and time formatting

  - Concurrency refinements across the framework, minimizing locks and generally improving concurrent creation of scoped/prototyped beans

  - New Gradle-based build system

  - Migration to GitHub: https://github.com/SpringSource/spring-framework

  - Refined Java SE 7 / OpenJDK 7 support in the framework and third-party dependencies. CGLIB and ASM are now included as part of Spring. AspectJ 1.7 is supported in addition to 1.6.

- Spring 4.0

    - Improved getting-started experience via a series of Getting Started guides on the new `www.spring.io/guides` website

    - Removal of deprecated packages and methods from the prior Spring 3 version

    - Java 8 support, raising the minimum Java version to 6 update 18

    - Java EE 6 and above is now considered the baseline for Spring Framework 4.0

    - Groovy bean definition DSL allowing bean definitions to be configured via Groovy syntax

    - Core container, testing, and general web improvements

    - WebSocket, SockJS, and STOMP messaging

Inverting Control or Injecting Dependencies?

The core of the Spring Framework is based on the principle of *Inversion of Control (IoC)*. IoC is a technique that externalizes the creation and management of component dependencies. Consider an example in which class Foo depends on an instance of class Bar to perform some kind of processing. Traditionally, Foo creates an instance of Bar by using the new operator or obtains one from some kind of factory class. Using the IoC approach, an instance of Bar (or a subclass) is provided to Foo at runtime by some external process. This behavior, the injection of dependencies at runtime, led to IoC being renamed by Martin Fowler as the much more descriptive *Dependency Injection (DI)*. The precise nature of the dependencies managed by DI is discussed in Chapter 3.

■ **Note**   As you will see in Chapter 3, using the term *Dependency Injection* when referring to Inversion of Control is always correct. In the context of Spring, you can use the terms interchangeably, without any loss of meaning.

Spring's DI implementation is based on two core Java concepts: JavaBeans and interfaces. When you use Spring as the DI provider, you gain the flexibility of defining dependency configuration within your applications in different ways (for example, XML files, Java configuration classes, annotations within your code, or the new Groovy bean definition method). JavaBeans (*POJOs*) provide a standard mechanism for creating Java resources that are configurable in a number of ways, such as constructors and setter methods. In Chapter 3, you will see how Spring uses the JavaBean specification to form the core of its DI configuration model; in fact, any Spring-managed resource is referred to as a *bean*. If you are unfamiliar with JavaBeans, refer to the quick primer we present at the beginning of Chapter 3.

Interfaces and DI are technologies that are mutually beneficial. Clearly designing and coding an application to interfaces makes for a flexible application, but the complexity of wiring together an application designed using interfaces is quite high and places an additional coding burden on developers. By using DI, you reduce the amount of code you need to use an interface-based design in your application to almost zero. Likewise, by using interfaces, you can get the most out of DI because your beans can utilize any interface implementation to satisfy their dependency. The use of interfaces also allows Spring to utilize JDK dynamic proxies (Proxy Pattern) to provide powerful concepts such as AOP for crosscutting concerns.

In the context of DI, Spring acts more like a container than a framework—providing instances of your application classes with all the dependencies they need—but it does so in a much less intrusive way. Using Spring for DI relies on nothing more than following the JavaBeans naming conventions within your classes—there are no special classes from which to inherit or proprietary naming schemes to follow. If anything, the only change you make in an application that uses DI is to expose more properties on your JavaBeans, thus allowing more dependencies to be injected at runtime.

Evolution of Dependency Injection

In the past few years, thanks to the popularity gained by Spring and other DI frameworks, DI has gained wide acceptance among Java developer communities. At the same time, developers were convinced that using DI was a best practice in application development, and the benefits of using DI were also well understood.

The popularity of DI was acknowledged when the Java Community Process (JCP) adopted JSR-330, "Dependency Injection for Java" in 2009. JSR-330 had become a formal Java Specification Request, and as you might expect, one of the specification leads was Rod Johnson—the founder of the Spring Framework.

In JEE 6, JSR-330 became one of the included specifications of the entire technology stack. In the meantime, the EJB architecture (starting from version 3.0) was also revamped dramatically; it adopted the DI model in order to ease the development of various Enterprise JavaBeans apps.

Although we leave the full discussion of DI until Chapter 3, it is worth taking a look at the benefits of using DI rather than a more traditional approach:

- *Reduced glue code*: One of the biggest plus points of DI is its ability to dramatically reduce the amount of code you have to write to glue the components of your application together. Often this code is trivial, so creating a dependency involves simply creating a new instance of an object. However, the glue code can get quite complex when you need to look up dependencies in a JNDI repository or when the dependencies cannot be invoked directly, as is the case with remote resources. In these cases, DI can really simplify the glue code by providing automatic JNDI lookup and automatic proxying of remote resources.

- *Simplified application configuration*: By adopting DI, you can greatly simplify the process of configuring an application. You can use a variety of options to configure those classes that were injectable to other classes. You can use the same technique to express the dependency requirements to the "injector" for injecting the appropriate bean instance or property. In addition, DI makes it much simpler to swap one implementation of a dependency for another. Consider the case where you have a DAO component that performs data operations against a PostgreSQL database and you want to upgrade to Oracle. Using DI, you can simply reconfigure the appropriate dependency on your business objects to use the Oracle implementation rather than the PostgreSQL one.

- *Ability to manage common dependencies in a single repository*: Using a traditional approach to dependency management of common services—for example, data source connection, transaction, and remote services—you create instances (or lookup from some factory classes) of your dependencies where they are needed (within the dependent class). This will cause the dependencies to spread across the classes in your application, and changing them can prove problematic. When you use DI, all the information about those common dependencies is contained in a single repository, making the management of dependencies much simpler and less error prone.

- *Improved testability*: When you design your classes for DI, you make it possible to replace dependencies easily. This is especially handy when you are testing your application. Consider a business object that performs some complex processing; for part of this, it uses a DAO to access data stored in a relational database. For your test, you are not interested in testing the DAO; you simply want to test the business object with various sets of data. In a traditional approach, whereby the business object is responsible for obtaining an instance of the DAO itself, you have a hard time testing this, because you are unable to easily replace the DAO implementation with a mock implementation that returns your test data sets. Instead, you need to make sure your test database contains the correct data and uses the full DAO implementation for your tests. Using DI, you can create a mock implementation of the DAO object that returns the test data sets, and then you can pass this to your business object for testing. This mechanism can be extended for testing any tier of your application and is especially useful for testing web components where you can create mock implementations of `HttpServletRequest` and `HttpServletResponse`.

- *Fostering of good application design*: Designing for DI means, in general, designing against interfaces. A typical injection-oriented application is designed so that all major components are defined as interfaces, and then concrete implementations of these interfaces are created and hooked together using the DI container. This kind of design was possible in Java before the advent of DI and DI-based containers such as Spring, but by using Spring, you get a whole host of DI features for free, and you are able to concentrate on building your application logic, not a framework to support it.

As you can see from this list, DI provides a lot of benefits for your application, but it is not without its drawbacks. In particular, DI can make it difficult for someone not intimately familiar with the code to see just what implementation of a particular dependency is being hooked into which objects. Typically, this is a problem only when developers are inexperienced with DI; after becoming more experienced and following good DI coding practice (for example, putting all injectable classes within each application layer into the same package), developers will be able to discover the whole picture easily. For the most part, the massive benefits far outweigh this small drawback, but you should consider this when planning your application.

Beyond Dependency Injection

The Spring core alone, with its advanced DI capabilities, is a worthy tool, but where Spring really excels is in its myriad of additional features, all elegantly designed and built using the principles of DI. Spring provides features for all layers of an application, from helper application programming interfaces (APIs) for data access right through to advanced MVC capabilities. What is great about these features in Spring is that, although Spring often provides its own approach, you can easily integrate them with other tools in Spring, making these tools first-class members of the Spring family.

Support for Java 8

Java 8 brings many exciting features that Spring Framework 4 supports, most notably lambda expressions and method references with Spring's callback interfaces. Other Java 8 functionality includes first-class support for `java.time` (JSR-310) and parameter name discovery. While Spring Framework 4.0 supports Java 8, compatibility is still maintained back to JDK 6 update 18. The use of a more recent version of Java such as 7 or 8 is recommended for new development projects.

Aspect-Oriented Programming with Spring

AOP provides the ability to implement *crosscutting logic*—that is, logic that applies to many parts of your application—in a single place and to have that logic applied across your application automatically.

Spring's approach to AOP is creating *dynamic proxies* to the target objects and *weaving* the objects with the configured advice to execute the crosscutting logic. By the nature of JDK dynamic proxies, target objects must implement an interface declaring the method in which the AOP advice will be applied.

Another popular AOP library is the Eclipse AspectJ project (`www.eclipse.org/aspectj`), which provides more-powerful features including object construction, class loading, and stronger crosscutting capability.

However, the good news for Spring and AOP developers is that starting from version 2.0, Spring offers much tighter integration with AspectJ. The following are some highlights:

- Support for AspectJ-style pointcut expressions

- Support for `@AspectJ` annotation style, while still using Spring AOP for weaving

- Support for aspects implemented in AspectJ for DI

- Support for load-time weaving within the Spring `ApplicationContext`

Both kinds of AOP have their place, and in most cases, Spring AOP is sufficient for addressing an application's crosscutting requirements. However, for more-complicated requirements, AspectJ can be used, and both Spring AOP and AspectJ can be mixed in the same Spring-powered application.

AOP has many applications. A typical one given in many of the traditional AOP examples involves performing some kind of logging, but AOP has found uses well beyond the trivial logging applications. Indeed, within the Spring Framework itself, AOP is used for many purposes, particularly in transaction management. Spring AOP is covered in full detail in Chapter 5, where we show you typical uses of AOP within the Spring Framework and your own applications, as well as AOP performance and areas where traditional technologies are better suited than AOP.

Spring Expression Language

Expression Language (EL) is a technology to allow an application to manipulate Java objects at runtime. However, the problem with EL is that different technologies provide their own EL implementations and syntaxes. For example, Java Server Pages (JSP) and Java Server Faces (JSF) both have their own EL, and their syntaxes are different. To solve the problem, the Unified Expression Language (EL) was created.

Because the Spring Framework is evolving so quickly, there is a need for a standard expression language that can be shared among all the Spring Framework modules as well as other Spring projects. Consequently, starting in version 3.0, Spring introduced the *Spring Expression Language (SpEL)*. SpEL provides powerful features for evaluating expressions and for accessing Java objects and Spring beans at runtime. The result can be used in the application or injected into other JavaBeans.

Validation in Spring

Validation is another large topic in any kind of application. The ideal scenario is that the validation rules of the attributes within JavaBeans containing business data can be applied in a consistent way, regardless of whether the data manipulation request is initiated from the front end, a batch job, or remotely (or example Web Services, RESTful Web Services, or Remote Procedure Call (RPC)).

To address these concerns, Spring provides a built-in validation API by way of the Validator interface. This interface provides a simple, yet concise mechanism allowing you to encapsulate your validation logic into a class responsible for validating the target object. In addition to the target object, the validate method takes an Errors object, which is used to collect any validation errors that may occur.

Spring also provides a handy utility class, ValidationUtils, which provides convenience methods for invoking other validators, checking for common problems such as empty strings, and reporting errors back to the provided Errors object.

Driven by need, the JCP also developed the "Bean Validation" API specification (JSR-303), which provides a standard way of defining bean validation rules. For example, when applying the @NotNull annotation to a bean's property, it mandates that the attribute shouldn't contain a null value before being able to persist into the database.

Starting in version 3.0, Spring provides out-of-the-box support for JSR-303. To use the API, just declare a LocalValidatorFactoryBean and inject the Validator interface into any Spring-managed beans. Spring will resolve the underlying implementation for you. By default, Spring will first look for the Hibernate Validator (hibernate.org/subprojects/validator), which is a popular JSR-303 implementation. Many front-end technologies (for example, JSF 2 and Google Web Toolkit), including Spring MVC, also support the application of JSR-303 validation in the user interface. The time when developers needed to program the same validation logic in both the user interface and the back-end layer is gone. The details are discussed in Chapter 10.

■ **Note**   Starting with Spring Framework version 4.0, the 1.1 version of the Bean Validation API specification (JSR-349) is supported.

Accessing Data in Spring

Data access and persistence seem to be the most discussed topics in the Java world. Spring provides excellent integration with a choice selection of these data access tools. In addition, Spring makes plain vanilla JDBC a viable option for many projects, with its simplified wrapper APIs around the standard API.

Spring's data access module provides out-of-the-box support for JDBC, Hibernate, JDO, and the JPA.

■ **Note**   Starting with Spring Framework version 4.0, iBATIS support has been removed. The MyBatis-Spring project provides integration with Spring, and more information can be found at `http://mybatis.github.io/spring/`.

However, in the past few years, because of the explosive growth of the Internet and cloud computing, besides relational databases, a lot of other "special-purpose" databases were developed. Examples include databases based on key-value pairs to handle extremely large volumes of data (generally referred to as NoSQL), graph databases, and document databases. To help developers support those databases and to not complicate the Spring data access module, a separate project called Spring Data (`http://projects.spring.io/spring-data`) was created. The project was further split into different categories to support more-specific database access requirements.

■ **Note**   Spring's support of nonrelational databases is not covered in this book. If you are interested in this topic, the Spring Data project mentioned earlier is a good place to look. The project page details the nonrelational databases that it supports, with links to those databases' home pages.

The JDBC support in Spring makes building an application on top of JDBC a realistic undertaking, even for more-complex applications. The support for Hibernate, JDO, and JPA makes already simple APIs even simpler, thus easing the burden on developers. When using the Spring APIs to access data via any tool, you are able to take advantage of Spring's excellent transaction support. You'll find a full discussion of this in Chapter 9.

One of the nicest features in Spring is the ability to easily mix and match data access technologies within an application. For instance, you may be running an application with Oracle, using Hibernate for much of your data access logic. However, if you want to take advantage of some Oracle-specific features, it is simple to implement that part of your data access tier by using Spring's JDBC APIs.

Object/XML Mapping in Spring

Most applications need to integrate or provide services to other applications. One common requirement is to exchange data with other systems, either on a regular basis or in real time. In terms of data format, XML is the most commonly used. As a result, you will often need to transform a JavaBean into XML format, and vice versa.

Spring supports many common Java-to-XML mapping frameworks and, as usual, eliminates the need for directly coupling to any specific implementation. Spring provides common interfaces for marshalling (transforming JavaBeans into XML) and unmarshalling (transforming XML into Java objects) for DI into any Spring beans. Common libraries such as Java Architecture for XML Binding (JAXB), Castor, XStream, JiBX, and XMLBeans are supported. In Chapter 12, when we discuss remotely accessing a Spring application for business data in XML format, you will see how to use Spring's Object/XML Mapping (OXM) support in your application.

Managing Transactions

Spring provides an excellent abstraction layer for transaction management, allowing for programmatic and declarative transaction control. By using the Spring abstraction layer for transactions, you can make it simple to change the underlying transaction protocol and resource managers. You can start with simple, local, resource-specific transactions and move to global, multiresource transactions without having to change your code.

Transactions are covered in full detail in Chapter 9.

Simplifying and Integrating with JEE

With the growing acceptance of DI frameworks such as Spring, a lot of developers have chosen to construct applications by using DI frameworks in favor of the JEE's EJB approach. As a result, the JCP communities also realize the complexity of EJB. Starting in version 3.0 of the EJB specification, the API was simplified, so it now embraces many of the concepts from DI.

However, for those applications that were built on EJB or need to deploy the Spring-based applications in a JEE container and utilize the application server's enterprise services (for example, Java Transaction API (JTA) Transaction Manager, data source connection pooling, and JMS connection factories), Spring also provides simplified support for those technologies. For EJB, Spring provides a simple declaration to perform the JNDI lookup and inject into Spring beans. On the reverse side, Spring also provides simple annotation for injecting Spring beans into EJBs.

For any resources stored in a JNDI-accessible location, Spring allows you to do away with the complex lookup code and have JNDI-managed resources injected as dependencies into other objects at runtime. As a side effect of this, your application becomes decoupled from JNDI, allowing you more scope for code reuse in the future.

MVC in the Web Tier

Although Spring can be used in almost any setting, from the desktop to the Web, it provides a rich array of classes to support the creation of web-based applications. Using Spring, you have maximum flexibility when you are choosing how to implement your web front end.

For developing web applications, the MVC pattern is the most popular practice. In recent versions, Spring has gradually evolved from a simple web framework into a full-blown MVC implementation.

First, view support in Spring MVC is extensive. In addition to standard support for JSP and Java Standard Tag Library (JSTL), which is greatly bolstered by the Spring tag libraries, you can take advantage of fully integrated support for Apache Velocity, FreeMarker, Apache Tiles, and XSLT. In addition, you will find a set of base view classes that make it simple to add Microsoft Excel, PDF, and JasperReports output to your applications.

In many cases, you will find Spring MVC sufficient for your web application development needs. However, Spring can also integrate with other popular web frameworks such as Struts, JSF, Atmosphere, Google Web Toolkit (GWT), and so on.

In the past few years, the technology of web frameworks has evolved quickly. Users have required more-responsive and interactive experiences, and that has resulted in the rise of Ajax as a widely adopted technology in developing rich Internet applications (RIAs). On the other hand, users also want to be able to access their applications from any device, including smartphones and tablets. This creates a need for web frameworks that support HTML5, JavaScript, and CSS3. In Chapter 16, we discuss developing web applications by using Spring MVC.

WebSocket Support

Starting with Spring Framework 4.0, support for the Java API for WebSocket (JSR-356) is available. WebSocket defines an API for creating a persistent connection between a client and server, typically implemented in web browsers and servers. WebSocket-style development opens the door for efficient, full-duplex communication enabling real-time message exchanges for highly responsive applications. Use of WebSocket support is detailed further in Chapter 17.

Remoting Support

Accessing or exposing remote components in Java has never been the simplest of jobs. Using Spring, you can take advantage of extensive support for a wide range of remoting techniques to quickly expose and access remote services.

Spring provides support for a variety of remote access mechanisms, including Java Remote Method Invocation (RMI), JAX-WS, Caucho Hessian and Burlap, JMS, Advanced Message Queuing Protocol (AMQP), and REST. In addition to these remoting protocols, Spring also provides its own HTTP-based invoker that is based on standard Java serialization. By applying Spring's dynamic proxying capabilities, you can have a proxy to a remote resource injected as a dependency into one of your classes, thus removing the need to couple your application to a specific remoting implementation and also reducing the amount of code you need to write for your application. We discuss remote support in Spring in Chapter 12.

Mail Support

Sending e-mail is a typical requirement for many kinds of applications and is given first-class treatment within the Spring Framework. Spring provides a simplified API for sending e-mail messages that fits nicely with the Spring DI capabilities. Spring supports the standard JavaMail API.

Spring provides the ability to create a prototype message in the DI container and uses this as the base for all messages sent from your application. This allows for easy customization of mail parameters such as the subject and sender address. In addition, for customizing the message body, Spring integrates with template engines, such as Apache Velocity, which allow the mail content to be externalized from the Java code.

Job Scheduling Support

Most nontrivial applications require some kind of scheduling capability. Whether this is for sending updates to customers or performing housekeeping tasks, the ability to schedule code to run at a predefined time is an invaluable tool for developers.

Spring provides scheduling support that can fulfill most common scenarios. A task can be scheduled either for a fixed interval or by using a Unix cron expression.

On the other hand, for task execution and scheduling, Spring integrates with other scheduling libraries as well. For example, in the application server environment, Spring can delegate execution to the CommonJ library that is used by many application servers. For job scheduling, Spring also supports libraries including the JDK Timer API and Quartz, a commonly used open source scheduling library.

The scheduling support in Spring is covered in full in Chapter 11.

Dynamic Scripting Support

Starting with JDK 6, Java introduced dynamic language support, in which you can execute scripts written in other languages in a JVM environment. Examples include Groovy, JRuby, and JavaScript.

Spring also supports the execution of dynamic scripts in a Spring-powered application, or you can define a Spring bean that was written in a dynamic scripting language and injected into other JavaBeans. Spring-supported dynamic scripting languages include Groovy, JRuby, and BeanShell. In Chapter 14, we discuss the support of dynamic scripting in Spring in detail.

Simplified Exception Handling

One area where Spring really helps reduce the amount of repetitive, boilerplate code you need to write is in exception handling. The core of the Spring philosophy in this respect is that checked exceptions are overused in Java and that a framework should not force you to catch any exception from which you are unlikely to be able to recover—a point of view that we agree with wholeheartedly.

In reality, many frameworks are designed to reduce the impact of having to write code to handle checked exceptions. However, many of these frameworks take the approach of sticking with checked exceptions but artificially reducing the granularity of the exception class hierarchy. One thing you will notice with Spring is that because of the convenience afforded to the developer from using unchecked exceptions, the exception hierarchy is remarkably granular.

Throughout the book, you will see examples in which the Spring exception-handling mechanisms can reduce the amount of code you have to write and, at the same time, improve your ability to identify, classify, and diagnose errors within your application.

The Spring Project

One of the most endearing things about the Spring project is the level of activity present in the community and the amount of cross-pollination between Spring and other projects such as CGLIB, Apache Geronimo, and AspectJ. One of the most touted benefits of open source is that if the project folded tomorrow, you would be left with the code; but let's face it—you do not want to be left with a code base the size of Spring to support and improve. For this reason, it is comforting to know how well established and active the Spring community is.

Origins of Spring

As noted earlier in this chapter, the origins of Spring can be traced back to *Expert One-to-One: J2EE Design and Development*. In this book, Rod Johnson presented his own framework, called the Interface 21 Framework, which he developed to use in his own applications. Released into the open source world, this framework formed the foundation of the Spring Framework as we know it today.

Spring proceeded quickly through the early beta and release candidate stages, and the first official 1.0 release was made available March 24, 2004. Since then, Spring has undergone dramatic growth, and at the time of this writing, the latest major version of Spring Framework is 4.0.

The Spring Community

The Spring community is one of the best in any open source project we have encountered. The mailing lists and forums are always active, and progress on new features is usually rapid. The development team is truly dedicated to making Spring the most successful of all the Java application frameworks, and this shows in the quality of the code that is reproduced.

As we mentioned already, Spring also benefits from excellent relationships with other open source projects, a fact that is extremely beneficial when you consider the large amount of dependency the full Spring distribution has.

From a user's perspective, perhaps one of the best features of Spring is the excellent documentation and test suite that accompany the distribution. Documentation is provided for almost all the features of Spring, making it easy for new users to pick up the framework. The test suite Spring provides is impressively comprehensive—the development team writes tests for everything. If they discover a bug, they fix that bug by first writing a test that highlights the bug and then getting the test to pass.

Fixing bugs and creating new features is not limited just to the development team! You can contribute code through pull requests against any portfolio of Spring projects through the official GitHub repositories (http://github.com/spring-projects). Additionally, issues can be created and tracked by way of the official Spring JIRA (https://jira.springsource.org/secure/Dashboard.jspa).

What does all this mean to you? Well, put simply, it means you can be confident in the quality of the Spring Framework and confident that, for the foreseeable future, the Spring development team will continue to improve what is already an excellent framework.

The Spring Tool Suite

To ease the development of Spring-based applications in Eclipse, Spring created the Spring IDE project. Soon after that, SpringSource, the company behind Spring founded by Rod Johnson, created an integrated tool called the Spring Tool Suite (STS), which can be downloaded from `www.spring.io/tools`. Although it used to be a paid-for product, the tool is now freely available. The tool integrates the Eclipse IDE, Spring IDE, Mylyn (a task-based development environment in Eclipse), Maven for Eclipse, AspectJ Development Tools, and many other useful Eclipse plug-ins into a single package. In each new version, more features are being added, such as Groovy scripting language support, a graphical Spring configuration editor, visual development tools for projects such as Spring Batch and Spring Integration, and support for the Pivotal tc Server application server.

■ **Note** SpringSource was bought by VMWare and incorporated into Pivotal Software, Inc.

In addition to the Java-based suite, a Groovy/Grails Tool Suite is available with similar capabilities but targeted at Groovy and Grails development (`www.spring.io/tools`).

The Spring Security Project

The Spring Security project (`http://projects.spring.io/spring-security`), formerly known as the Acegi Security System for Spring, is another important project within the Spring portfolio. Spring Security provides comprehensive support for both web application and method-level security. It tightly integrates with the Spring Framework and other commonly used authentication mechanisms, such as HTTP basic authentication, form-based login, X.509 certificate, and single sign-on (SSO) products (for example, CA SiteMinder). It provides role-based access control to application resources, and in applications with more-complicated security requirements (for example, data segregations), use of an access control list (ACL) is supported. However, Spring Security is mostly used in securing web applications, which we discuss in detail in Chapter 16.

Spring Batch and Integration

Needless to say, batch job execution and integration are common use cases in applications. To cope with this need and to make it easy for developers in these areas, Spring created the Spring Batch and Spring Integration projects. Spring Batch provides a common framework and various policies for batch job implementation, reducing a lot of boilerplate code. By implementing the Enterprise Integration Patterns (EIP), Spring Integration can make integrating Spring applications with external systems easy. We discuss the details in Chapter 20.

Many Other Projects

We've covered the core modules of Spring and some of the major projects within the Spring portfolio, but there are many other projects that have been driven by the need of the community for different requirements. Some examples include Spring Boot, Spring XD, Spring for Android, Spring Mobile, Spring Social, and Spring AMQP. Some of these projects are discussed further in Chapter 20. For additional details, you can refer to the Spring by Pivotal web site (`www.spring.io/projects`).

Alternatives to Spring

Going back to our previous comments on the number of open source projects, you should not be surprised to learn that Spring is not the only framework offering Dependency Injection features or full end-to-end solutions for building applications. In fact, there are almost too many projects to mention. In the spirit of being open, we include a brief discussion of several of these frameworks here, but it is our belief that none of these platforms offers quite as comprehensive a solution as that available in Spring.

JBoss Seam Framework

Founded by Gavin King (the creator of the Hibernate ORM library), the Seam Framework (www.seamframework.org) is another full-blown DI-based framework. It supports web application front-end development (JSF), business logic layer (EJB 3), and JPA for persistence. As you can see, the main difference between Seam and Spring is that the Seam Framework is built entirely on JEE standards. JBoss also contributes the ideas in the Seam Framework back to the JCP and has become JSR-299, "Contexts and Dependency Injection for the Java EE Platform" (CDI).

Google Guice

Another popular DI framework is Google Guice (http://code.google.com/p/google-guice). Led by the search engine giant Google, Guice is a lightweight framework that focuses on providing DI for application configuration management. It was also the reference implementation of JSR-330, "Dependency Injection for Java".

PicoContainer

PicoContainer (http://picocontainer.com) is an exceptionally small DI container that allows you to use DI for your application without introducing any dependencies other than PicoContainer. Because PicoContainer is nothing more than a DI container, you may find that as your application grows, you need to introduce another framework, such as Spring, in which case you would have been better off using Spring from the start. However, if all you need is a tiny DI container, then PicoContainer is a good choice, but since Spring packages the DI container separately from the rest of the framework, you can just as easily use that and keep the flexibility for the future.

JEE 7 Container

As discussed previously, the concept of DI was widely adopted and also realized by JCP. When you are developing an application for application servers compliant with JEE 7 (JSR-342) , you can use standard DI techniques across all layers.

Summary

In this chapter, we gave you a high-level view of the Spring Framework, complete with discussions of all the major features, and we guided you to the relevant sections of the book where these features are discussed in detail. After reading this chapter, you should understand what Spring can do for you; all that remains is to see *how* it can do it.

In the next chapter, we discuss all the information you need to know to get up and running with a basic Spring application. We show you how to obtain the Spring Framework and discuss the packaging options, the test suite, and the documentation. Also, Chapter 2 introduces some basic Spring code, including the time-honored "Hello World!" example in all its DI-based glory.

CHAPTER 2

■ ■ ■

Getting Started

Often the hardest part of coming to grips with any new development tool is figuring out where to begin. Typically, this problem is worse when the tool offers as many choices as Spring. Fortunately, getting started with Spring isn't that hard if you know where to look first. In this chapter, we present you with all the basic knowledge you need to get off to a flying start. Specifically, you will look at the following:

- *Obtaining Spring:* The first logical step is to obtain or build the Spring JAR files. If you want to get up and running quickly, simply use the dependency management snippets in your build system with the provided examples located at `http://projects.spring.io/spring-framework`. However, if you want to be on the cutting edge of Spring development, check out the latest version of the source code from Spring's GitHub repository (`http://github.com/spring-projects/spring-framework`).

- *Spring packaging options:* Spring packaging is modular; it allows you to pick and choose which components you want to use in your application and to include only those components when you are distributing your application. Spring has many modules, but you need only a subset of these modules depending on your application's needs. Each module has its compiled binary code in a JAR file along with corresponding Javadoc and source JARs.

- *Spring guides:* The new Spring web site includes a Guides section located at `www.spring.io/guides`. The guides are meant to be quick, hands-on instructions for building the "Hello World" of any development task with Spring. These guides also reflect the latest Spring project releases and techniques, providing you with the most up-to-date samples available.

- *Test suite and documentation:* One of the things members of the Spring community are most proud of is their comprehensive test suite and documentation set. Testing is a big part of what the team does. The documentation set provided with the standard distribution is also excellent.

- *Putting a spring into "Hello World"* All bad punning aside, we think the best way to get started with any new programming tool is to dive right in and write some code. We present a simple example, which is a full DI-based implementation of everyone's favorite, "Hello World!" Don't be alarmed if you don't understand all the code right away; full discussions follow later in the book.

If you are already familiar with the basics of the Spring Framework, feel free to proceed straight to Chapter 3 to dive into IoC and DI in Spring. However, even if you are familiar with the basics of Spring, you may find some of the discussions in this chapter interesting, especially those on packaging and dependencies.

Obtaining the Spring Framework

Before you can get started with any Spring development, you need to obtain the Spring code. You have a couple of options for retrieving the code: you can use your build system to bring in the modules you would like to use, or you can check out and build the code from the Spring GitHub repository. Using a dependency management tool such as Maven or Gradle is often the most straightforward approach, as all you need to do is declare the dependency in the configuration file, and let the tool obtain the required libraries for you.

Quick Start

Visit the Spring Framework project page (http://projects.spring.io/spring-framework) to obtain a dependency management snippet for your build system to include the latest-release RELEASE version of Spring in your project. You can also use milestones/nightly snapshots for upcoming releases or previous versions.

Checking Spring Out of GitHub

If you want to get a grip on new features before they make their way even into the snapshots, you can check out the source code directly from Spring by Pivotal's GitHub repository. To check out the latest version of the Spring code, first install Git, which you can download from http://git-scm.com/ Then open a terminal shell and run the following command:

```
git clone git://github.com/spring-projects/spring-framework.git
```

See the README.md file in the project root for full details and requirements on how to build from source.

Understanding Spring Packaging

Spring modules are simply JAR files that package the required code for that module. After you understand the purpose of each module, you can then select the modules required in your project and include them in your code.

Understanding Spring Modules

As of Spring version 4.0.2.RELEASE, Spring comes with 20 modules, packaged into 20 JAR files. Table 2-1 describes these JAR files and their corresponding modules. The actual JAR file format is, for example, spring-aop-4.0.2.RELEASE.jar, though we have included only the specific module portion for simplicity (as in aop, for example).

Table 2-1. *Spring Modules*

JAR File	Description
aop	This module contains all the classes you need to use Spring's AOP features within your application. You also need to include this JAR in your application if you plan to use other features in Spring that use AOP, such as declarative transaction management. Moreover, classes that support integration with AspectJ are packed in this module too.
aspects	This module contains all the classes for advanced integration with the AspectJ AOP library. For example, if you are using Java classes for your Spring configuration and need AspectJ-style annotation-driven transaction management, you will need this module.
beans	This module contains all the classes for supporting Spring's manipulation of Spring beans. Most of the classes here support Spring's bean factory implementation. For example, the classes required for processing the Spring XML configuration file and Java annotations were packed into this module.
context	This module contains classes that provide many extensions to the Spring core. You will find that all classes need to use Spring's ApplicationContext feature (covered in Chapter 5), along with classes for EJB, Java Naming and Directory Interface (JNDI), and Java Management Extensions (JMX) integration. Also contained in this module are the Spring remoting classes, classes for integration with dynamic scripting languages (for example, JRuby, Groovy, and BeanShell), the Bean Validation (JSR-303) API, scheduling and task execution, and so on.
context-support	This module contains further extensions to the spring-context module. On the user-interface side, there are classes for mail support and integration with templating engines such as Velocity, FreeMarker, and JasperReports. Also, integration with various task execution and scheduling libraries including CommonJ and Quartz are packaged here.
core	This is the core module that you will need for every Spring application. In this JAR file, you will find all the classes that are shared among all other Spring modules (for example, classes for accessing configuration files). Also, in this JAR, you will find selections of extremely useful utility classes that are used throughout the Spring code base and that you can use in your own application.
expression	This module contains all support classes for Spring Expression Language (SpEL).
instrument	This module includes Spring's instrumentation agent for Java Virtual Machine (JVM) bootstrapping. This JAR file is required for using load-time weaving with AspectJ in a Spring application.
instrument-tomcat	This module includes Spring's instrumentation agent for JVM bootstrapping in the Tomcat server.
jdbc	This module includes all classes for JDBC support. You will need this module for all applications that require database access. Classes for supporting data sources, JDBC data types, JDBC templates, native JDBC connections, and so on, are packed in this module.
jms	This module includes all classes for JMS support.
messaging	This module contains key abstractions taken from the Spring Integration project to serve as a foundation for message-based applications and adds support for STOMP messages.

(*continued*)

Table 2-1. (*continued*)

JAR File	Description
orm	This module extends Spring's standard JDBC feature set with support for popular ORM tools including Hibernate, JDO, JPA, and the data mapper iBATIS. Many of the classes in this JAR depend on classes contained in the spring-jdbc JAR file, so you definitely need to include that in your application as well.
oxm	This module provides support for Object/XML Mapping (OXM). Classes for abstraction of XML marshalling and unmarshalling and support for popular tools such as Castor, JAXB, XMLBeans, and XStream are packed into this module.
test	As we mentioned earlier, Spring provides a set of mock classes to aid in testing your applications. Many of these mock classes are used within the Spring test suite, so they are well tested and make testing your applications much simpler. Certainly we have found great use for the mock HttpServletRequest and HttpServletResponse classes in unit tests for our web applications. On the other hand, Spring provides a tight integration with the JUnit unit-testing framework, and many classes that support the development of JUnit test cases are provided in this module; for example, the SpringJUnit4ClassRunner provides a simple way to bootstrap the Spring ApplicationContext in a unit test environment.
tx	This module provides all classes for supporting Spring's transaction infrastructure. You will find classes from the transaction abstraction layer to support of the Java Transaction API (JTA) and integration with application servers from major vendors.
web	This module contains the core classes for using Spring in your web applications, including classes for loading an ApplicationContext feature automatically, file upload support classes, and a bunch of useful classes for performing repetitive tasks such as parsing integer values from the query string.
webmvc	This module contains all the classes for Spring's own MVC framework. If you are using a separate MVC framework for your application, you won't need any of the classes from this JAR file. Spring MVC is covered in more detail in Chapter 16.
web-portlet	This module provides support for using Spring MVC in developing portlets for deployment to a portal server environment.
websocket	This module provides support for the Java API for WebSocket (JSR-356).

■ **Note** You no longer need an explicit dependency on the ASM module, as it is now packaged with the Spring core.

Choosing Modules for Your Application

Without a dependency management tool such as Maven or Gradle, choosing which modules to use in your application may be a bit tricky. For example, if you require Spring's bean factory and DI support only, you still need several modules including spring-core, spring-beans, spring-context, and spring-aop. If you need Spring's web application support, you then need to further add spring-web and so on. Thanks to build tool features such as Maven's transitive dependencies support, all required third-party libraries would be included automatically.

Accessing Spring Modules on the Maven Repository

Founded by Apache Software Foundation, Maven (`http://maven.apache.org`) has become one of the most popular tools in managing the dependencies for Java applications, from open source to enterprise environments.

Maven is a powerful application building, packaging, and dependency management tool. It manages the entire build cycle of an application, from resource processing and compiling, to testing and packaging. There also exists a large number of Maven plug-ins for various tasks, such as updating databases and deploying a packaged application to a specific server (for example, Tomcat, JBoss, or WebSphere).

Almost all open source projects support distribution of their library via the Maven repository. The most popular one is the Maven Central repository hosted on Apache, and you can access and search for the existence and related information of an artifact on the Maven Central web site (`http://search.maven.org`). If you download and install Maven into your development machine, you automatically gain access to the Maven Central repository. Some other open source communities (for example, JBoss and Spring by Pivotal) also provide their own Maven repository for their users. However, in order to be able to access those repositories, you need to add the repository into your Maven's setting file or in your project's Project Object Model (POM) file.

A detailed discussion of Maven is not in the scope of this book, and you can always refer to the online documentation or books that give you a detailed reference to Maven. However, since Maven is widely adopted, it's worth mentioning the structure of Spring's packaging on the Maven repository.

A group ID, artifact ID, packaging type, and version identify each Maven artifact. For example, for `log4j`, the group ID is `log4j`, the artifact ID is `log4j`, and the packaging type is `jar`. Under that, different versions are defined. For example, for version 1.2.16, the artifact's file name becomes `log4j-1.2.16.jar` under the group ID, artifact ID, and version folder.

Using Spring Documentation

One of the aspects of Spring that makes it such a useful framework for developers who are building real applications is its wealth of well-written, accurate documentation. In every release, the Spring Framework's documentation team works hard to ensure that all the documentation is finished and polished by the development team. This means that every feature of Spring is not only fully documented in the Javadoc but is also covered in the Spring reference manual included in every distribution. If you haven't yet familiarized yourself with the Spring Javadoc and the reference manual, do so now. This book is not a replacement for either of these resources; rather, it is a complementary reference, demonstrating how to build a Spring-based application from the ground up.

Putting a Spring into "Hello World!"

We hope by this point in the book you appreciate that Spring is a solid, well-supported project that has all the makings of a great tool for application development. However, one thing is missing—we haven't shown you any code yet. We are sure you are dying to see Spring in action, and because we cannot go any longer without getting into the code, let's do just that. Do not worry if you do not fully understand all the code in this section; we go into much more detail on all the topics as we proceed through the book.

Building the Sample "Hello World!" Application

Now, we are sure you are familiar with the traditional "Hello World!" example, but just in case you have been living on the moon for the past 30 years, Listing 2-1 shows the Java version in all its glory.

Listing 2-1. Typical "Hello World!" Example

```
package com.apress.prospring4.ch2;

public class HelloWorld {
    public static void main(String[] args) {
        System.out.println("Hello World!");
    }
}
```

As examples go, this one is pretty simple—it does the job, but it is not very extensible. What if we want to change the message? What if we want to output the message differently, maybe to standard error instead of standard output or enclosed in HTML tags rather than as plain text?

We are going to redefine the requirements for the sample application and say that it must support a simple, flexible mechanism for changing the message, and it must be easy to change the rendering behavior. In the basic "Hello World!" example, you can make both of these changes quickly and easily by just changing the code as appropriate. However, in a bigger application, recompiling takes time, and it requires the application to be fully tested again. A better solution is to externalize the message content and read it in at runtime, perhaps from the command-line arguments shown in Listing 2-2.

Listing 2-2. Using Command-Line Arguments with "Hello World!"

```
package com.apress.prospring4.ch2;

public class HelloWorldWithCommandLine {
    public static void main(String[] args) {
        if (args.length > 0) {
            System.out.println(args[0]);
        } else {
            System.out.println("Hello World!");
        }
    }
}
```

This example accomplishes what we wanted—we can now change the message without changing the code. However, there is still a problem with this application: the component responsible for rendering the message is also responsible for obtaining the message. Changing how the message is obtained means changing the code in the renderer. Add to this the fact that we still cannot change the renderer easily; doing so means changing the class that launches the application.

If we take this application a step further (away from the basics of "Hello World!"), a better solution is to refactor the rendering and message retrieval logic into separate components. Plus, if we really want to make our application flexible, we should have these components implement interfaces and define the interdependencies between the components and the launcher using these interfaces.

By refactoring the message retrieval logic, we can define a simple MessageProvider interface with a single method, getMessage(), as shown in Listing 2-3.

Listing 2-3. The MessageProvider Interface

```
package com.apress.prospring4.ch2;

public interface MessageProvider {
    String getMessage();
}
```

In Listing 2-4, the MessageRenderer interface is implemented by all components that can render messages.

Listing 2-4. The MessageRenderer Interface

```
package com.apress.prospring4.ch2;

public interface MessageRenderer {
    void render();
    void setMessageProvider(MessageProvider provider);
    MessageProvider getMessageProvider();
}
```

As you can see, the MessageRenderer interface has a method, render(), and also a JavaBean-style method, setMessageProvider(). Any MessageRenderer implementations are decoupled from message retrieval and delegate that responsibility to the MessageProvider with which they are supplied. Here, MessageProvider is a dependency of MessageRenderer. Creating simple implementations of these interfaces is easy, as shown in Listing 2-5.

Listing 2-5. The HelloWorldMessageProvider Class

```
package com.apress.prospring4.ch2;

public class HelloWorldMessageProvider implements MessageProvider {
    @Override
    public String getMessage() {
        return "Hello World!";
    }
}
```

You can see that we have created a simple MessageProvider that always returns "Hello World!" as the message. The StandardOutMessageRenderer class (shown in Listing 2-6) is just as simple.

Listing 2-6. The StandardOutMessageRenderer Class

```
package com.apress.prospring4.ch2;

public class StandardOutMessageRenderer implements MessageRenderer {
    private MessageProvider messageProvider;

    @Override
    public void render() {
        if (messageProvider == null) {
            throw new RuntimeException(
                "You must set the property messageProvider of class:"
                + StandardOutMessageRenderer.class.getName());
        }

        System.out.println(messageProvider.getMessage());
    }

    @Override
    public void setMessageProvider(MessageProvider provider) {
        this.messageProvider = provider;
    }
```

```
    @Override
    public MessageProvider getMessageProvider() {
        return this.messageProvider;
    }
}
```

Now all that remains is to rewrite the main() method of our entry class, as shown in Listing 2-7.

Listing 2-7. Refactored "Hello World!"

```
package com.apress.prospring4.ch2;

public class HelloWorldDecoupled {
    public static void main(String[] args) {
        MessageRenderer mr = new StandardOutMessageRenderer();
        MessageProvider mp = new HelloWorldMessageProvider();
        mr.setMessageProvider(mp);
        mr.render();
    }
}
```

The code here is fairly simple: we instantiate instances of HelloWorldMessageProvider and StandardOutMessageRenderer, although the declared types are MessageProvider and MessageRenderer, respectively. This is because we need to interact only with the methods provided by the interface in the programming logic, and HelloWorldMessageProvider and StandardOutMessageRenderer already implemented those interfaces, respectively. Then, we pass the MessageProvider to the MessageRenderer and invoke MessageRenderer.render(). If we compile and run this program, we get the expected "Hello World!" output.

Now, this example is more like what we are looking for, but there is one small problem. Changing the implementation of either the MessageRenderer or MessageProvider interface means a change to the code. To get around this, we can create a simple factory class that reads the implementation class names from a properties file and instantiates them on behalf of the application (see Listing 2-8).

Listing 2-8. The MessageSupportFactory Class

```
package com.apress.prospring4.ch2;

import java.io.FileInputStream;
import java.util.Properties;

public class MessageSupportFactory {
    private static MessageSupportFactory instance;

    private Properties props;
    private MessageRenderer renderer;
    private MessageProvider provider;

    private MessageSupportFactory() {
        props = new Properties();

        try {
            props.load(new FileInputStream("com/apress/prospring4/ch2/msf.properties"));
```

```
            String rendererClass = props.getProperty("renderer.class");
            String providerClass = props.getProperty("provider.class");

            renderer = (MessageRenderer) Class.forName(rendererClass).newInstance();
            provider = (MessageProvider) Class.forName(providerClass).newInstance();
        } catch (Exception ex) {
            ex.printStackTrace();
        }
    }

    static {
        instance = new MessageSupportFactory();
    }

    public static MessageSupportFactory getInstance() {
        return instance;
    }

    public MessageRenderer getMessageRenderer() {
        return renderer;
    }

    public MessageProvider getMessageProvider() {
        return provider;
    }
}
```

The implementation here is trivial and naïve, the error handling is simplistic, and the name of the configuration file is hard-coded, but we already have a substantial amount of code. The configuration file for this class is quite simple:

```
renderer.class=com.apress.prospring4.ch2.StandardOutMessageRenderer
provider.class=com.apress.prospring4.ch2.HelloWorldMessageProvider
```

Make a simple modification to the main() method (as shown in Listing 2-9), and we are in business.

Listing 2-9. Using MessageSupportFactory

```
package com.apress.prospring4.ch2;

public class HelloWorldDecoupledWithFactory {
    public static void main(String[] args) {
        MessageRenderer mr = MessageSupportFactory.getInstance().getMessageRenderer();
        MessageProvider mp = MessageSupportFactory.getInstance().getMessageProvider();
        mr.setMessageProvider(mp);
        mr.render();
    }
}
```

Before we move on to see how we can introduce Spring into this application, let's quickly recap what we have done. Starting with the simple "Hello World!" application, we defined two additional requirements that the application must fulfill. The first was that changing the message should be simple, and the second was that changing the rendering mechanism should also be simple. To meet these requirements, we introduced two interfaces: MessageProvider and MessageRenderer. The MessageRenderer interface depends on an implementation of the MessageProvider interface to be able to retrieve a message to render. Finally, we added a simple factory class to retrieve the names of the implementation classes and instantiate them as applicable.

Refactoring with Spring

The final example shown earlier met the goals we laid out for our sample application, but there are still problems with it. The first problem is that we had to write a lot of glue code to piece the application together, while at the same time keeping the components loosely coupled. The second problem is that we still had to provide the implementation of MessageRenderer with an instance of MessageProvider manually. We can solve both of these problems by using Spring.

To solve the problem of too much glue code, we can completely remove the MessageSupportFactory class from the application and replace it with a Spring interface, ApplicationContext. Don't worry too much about this interface; for now, it is enough to know that this interface is used by Spring for storing all the environmental information with regard to an application being managed by Spring. This interface extends another interface, ListableBeanFactory, which acts as the provider for any Spring-managed beans instance (see Listing 2-10).

Listing 2-10. Using Spring's ApplicationContext

```
package com.apress.prospring4.ch2;

import org.springframework.context.ApplicationContext;
import org.springframework.context.support.ClassPathXmlApplicationContext;

public class HelloWorldSpringDI {
    public static void main(String[] args) {
        ApplicationContext ctx = new ClassPathXmlApplicationContext
            ("META-INF/spring/app-context.xml");

        MessageRenderer mr = ctx.getBean("renderer", MessageRenderer.class);
        mr.render();
    }
}
```

In Listing 2-10, you can see that the main() method obtains an instance of ClassPathXmlApplicationContext (the application configuration information is loaded from the file META-INF/spring/app-context.xml in the project's classpath), typed as ApplicationContext, and from this, it obtains the MessageRenderer instances by using the ApplicationContext.getBean() method. Don't worry too much about the getBean() method for now; just know that this method reads the application configuration (in this case, an XML file), initializes Spring's ApplicationContext environment, and then returns the configured bean instance. This XML file (app-context.xml) serves the same purpose as the one we used for MessageSupportFactory (see Listing 2-11).

Listing 2-11. Spring XML Application Configuration

```
<?xml version="1.0" encoding="UTF-8"?>
<beans xmlns="http://www.springframework.org/schema/beans"
    xmlns:xsi="http://www.w3.org/2001/XMLSchema-instance"
    xmlns:p="http://www.springframework.org/schema/p"
    xsi:schemaLocation="http://www.springframework.org/schema/beans
        http://www.springframework.org/schema/beans/spring-beans.xsd">

    <bean id="provider" class="com.apress.prospring4.ch2.HelloWorldMessageProvider"/>

    <bean id="renderer" class="com.apress.prospring4.ch2.StandardOutMessageRenderer"
        p:messageProvider-ref="provider"/>
</beans>
```

The previous file shows a typical Spring `ApplicationContext` configuration. First, Spring's namespaces are declared, and the default namespace is beans. The beans namespace is used to declare the beans that need to be managed by Spring, and its dependency requirements (for the preceding example, the `renderer` bean's `messageProvider` property is referencing the `provider` bean) for Spring to resolve and inject those dependencies.

Afterward, we declare the bean with the ID `provider` and the corresponding implementation class. When Spring sees this bean definition during `ApplicationContext` initialization, it will instantiate the class and store it with the specified ID.

Then the `renderer` bean is declared, with the corresponding implementation class. Remember that this bean depends on the `MessageProvider` interface for getting the message to render. To inform Spring about the DI requirement, we use the p namespace attribute. The tag attribute `p:messageProvider-ref="provider"` tells Spring that the bean's property, `messageProvider`, should be injected with another bean. The bean to be injected into the property should reference a bean with the ID `provider`. When Spring sees this definition, it will instantiate the class, look up the bean's property named `messageProvider`, and inject it with the bean instance with the ID `provider`.

As you can see, upon the initialization of Spring's `ApplicationContext`, the `main()` method now just obtains the `MessageRenderer` bean by using its type-safe `getBean()` method (passing in the ID and the expected return type, which is the `MessageRenderer` interface) and calls `render()`; Spring has created the `MessageProvider` implementation and injected it into the `MessageRenderer` implementation. Notice that we didn't have to make any changes to the classes that are being wired together using Spring. In fact, these classes have no reference to Spring and are completely oblivious to its existence. However, this isn't always the case. Your classes can implement Spring-specified interfaces to interact in a variety of ways with the DI container.

With our new Spring configuration and modified `main()` method, let's see it in action. Using Maven, enter the following commands into your terminal to build the project and the root of your source code:

```
mvn clean package dependency:copy-dependencies
```

The only required Spring module to be declared in your Maven POM is `spring-context`. Maven will automatically bring in any transitive dependencies required for this module. The `dependency:copy-dependencies` goal will copy all required dependencies into a directory called dependency in the `target` directory. This path value will also be used as an appending prefix to the library files added to `MANIFEST.MF` when building the JAR. See the Chapter 2 source code (available on the Apress web site), specifically the Maven `pom.xml`, for more information if you are unfamiliar with the Maven JAR building configuration and process.

Finally, to run the Spring DI sample, enter the following commands:

```
cd target ; java -jar hello-world-4.0-SNAPSHOT.jar
```

And at this point, you should see some log statements generated by the Spring container's startup process followed by our expected "Hello World!" output.

■ **Note**   Some of the interfaces and classes defined in the "Hello World" sample may be used in later chapters. Although we showed full source code in this sample, future chapters may show condensed versions of code to be less verbose, even more so in the case of incremental code modifications. Code is also placed into a flat package structure for demonstration purposes, whereas in a real application you would want to layer your code appropriately.

Summary

In this chapter, we presented you with all the background information you need to get up and running with Spring. We showed you how to get started with Spring through dependency management systems and the current development version directly from GitHub. We described how Spring is packaged and the dependencies you need for each of Spring's features. Using this information, you can make informed decisions about which of the Spring JAR files your application needs and which dependencies you need to distribute with your application. Spring's documentation, guides, and test suite provide Spring users with an ideal base from which to start their Spring development, so we took some time to investigate what is made available by Spring. Finally, we presented an example of how, using Spring DI, it is possible to make the traditional "Hello World!" a loosely coupled, extendable message-rendering application.

The important thing to realize is that we only scratched the surface of Spring DI in this chapter, and we barely made a dent in Spring as a whole. In the next chapter, we take look at IoC and DI in Spring.

■ ■ ■

CHAPTER 3

Introducing IoC and DI in Spring

In Chapter 2, we covered the basic principles of Inversion of Control (IoC Dependency Injection (DI. Practically, DI is a specialized form of IoC, although you will often find that the two terms are used interchangeably. In this chapter, we take a much more detailed look at IoC and DI, formalizing the relationship between the two concepts and looking in great detail at how Spring fits into the picture.

After defining both and looking at Spring's relationship with them, we will explore the concepts that are essential to Spring's implementation of DI. This chapter covers only the basics of Spring's DI implementation; we discuss more-advanced DI features in Chapter 4. More specifically, this chapter covers the following topics:

- *Inversion of Control concepts*: In this section, we discuss the various kinds of IoC, including Dependency Injection and Dependency Lookup. This section presents the differences between the various IoC approaches as well as the pros and cons of each.

- *Inversion of Control in Spring*: This section looks at IoC capabilities available in Spring and how they are implemented. In particular, you'll see the Dependency Injection services that Spring offers, including Setter, Constructor, and Method Injection.

- *Dependency Injection in Spring*: This section covers Spring's implementation of the IoC container. For bean definition and DI requirements, BeanFactory is the main interface an application interacts with. However, other than the first few, the remainder of the sample code provided in this chapter focuses on using Spring's ApplicationContext interface, which is an extension of BeanFactory and provides much more powerful features. We cover the difference between BeanFactory and ApplicationContext in later sections.

- *Configuring the Spring application context*: The final part of this chapter focuses on using the XML and annotation approaches for ApplicationContext configuration. Groovy and Java configuration are further discussed in Chapter 4. This section starts with a discussion of DI configuration and moves on to present additional services provided by the BeanFactory such as bean inheritance, life-cycle management, and autowiring.

Inversion of Control and Dependency Injection

At its core, IoC, and therefore DI, aims to offer a simpler mechanism for provisioning component dependencies (often referred to as an object's *collaborators*) and managing these dependencies throughout their life cycles. A component that requires certain dependencies is often referred to as the *dependent object* or, in the case of IoC, the *target*. In general, IoC can be decomposed into two subtypes: Dependency Injection and Dependency Lookup. These subtypes are further decomposed into concrete implementations of the IoC services. From this definition, you can clearly see that when we are talking about DI, we are always talking about IoC, but when we are talking about IoC, we are not always talking about DI (for example, Dependency Lookup is also a form of IoC).

Types of Inversion of Control

You may be wondering why there are two types of IoC and why these types are split further into different implementations. There seems to be no clear answer to this question; certainly the different types provide a level of flexibility, but to us, it seems that IoC is more of a mixture of old and new ideas; the two types of IoC represent this.

Dependency Lookup is a much more traditional approach, and at first glance, it seems more familiar to Java programmers. *Dependency Injection*, although it appears counterintuitive at first, is actually much more flexible and usable than Dependency Lookup.

With Dependency Lookup-style IoC, a component must acquire a reference to a dependency, whereas with Dependency Injection, the dependencies are injected into the component by the IoC container. Dependency Lookup comes in two types: Dependency Pull and Contextualized Dependency Lookup (CDL). Dependency Injection also has two common flavors: Constructor and Setter Dependency Injection.

■ **Note**   For the discussions in this section, we are not concerned with how the fictional IoC container comes to know about all the different dependencies, just that at some point, it performs the actions described for each mechanism.

Dependency Pull

To a Java developer, *Dependency Pull* is the most familiar type of IoC. In Dependency Pull, dependencies are pulled from a registry as required. Anyone who has ever written code to access an EJB (2.1 or prior versions) has used Dependency Pull (that is, via the JNDI API to look up an EJB component). Figure 3-1 shows the scenario of Dependency Pull via the lookup mechanism.

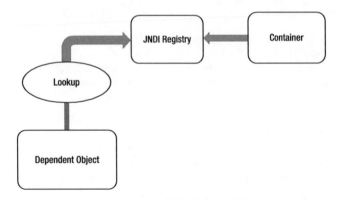

Figure 3-1. Dependency Pull via JNDI lookup

Spring also offers Dependency Pull as a mechanism for retrieving the components that the framework manages; you saw this in action in Chapter 2. Listing 3-1 shows a typical Dependency Pull lookup in a Spring-based application.

Listing 3-1. Dependency Pull in Spring

```
package com.apress.prospring4.ch3;

import org.springframework.context.ApplicationContext;
import org.springframework.context.support.ClassPathXmlApplicationContext;
```

```
public class DependencyPull {
    public static void main(String[] args) {
        ApplicationContext ctx = new ClassPathXmlApplicationContext
            ("META-INF/spring/app-context.xml");

        MessageRenderer mr = ctx.getBean("renderer", MessageRenderer.class);
        mr.render();
    }
}
```

This kind of IoC is not only prevalent in JEE-based applications (using EJB 2.1 or prior versions), which make extensive use of JNDI lookups to obtain dependencies from a registry, but also pivotal to working with Spring in many environments.

Contextualized Dependency Lookup

Contextualized Dependency Lookup (CDL) is similar, in some respects, to Dependency Pull, but in CDL, lookup is performed against the container that is managing the resource, not from some central registry, and it is usually performed at some set point. Figure 3-2 shows the CDL mechanism.

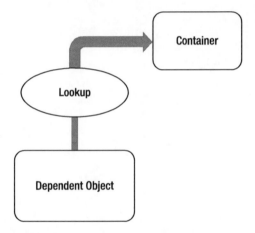

Figure 3-2. *Contextualized Dependency Lookup*

CDL works by having the component implement an interface similar to that in Listing 3-2.

Listing 3-2. Component Interface for CDL

```
package com.apress.prospring4.ch3;

public interface ManagedComponent {
    void performLookup(Container container);
}
```

By implementing this interface, a component is signaling to the container that it wants to obtain a dependency. The container is usually provided by the underlying application server or framework (for example, Tomcat or JBoss) or framework (for example, Spring). Listing 3-3 shows a simple `Container` interface that provides a Dependency Lookup service.

Listing 3-3. A Simple Container Interface

```
package com.apress.prospring4.ch3;

public interface Container {
    Object getDependency(String key);
}
```

When the container is ready to pass dependencies to a component, it calls `performLookup()` on each component in turn. The component can then look up its dependencies by using the `Container` interface, as shown in Listing 3-4.

Listing 3-4. Obtaining Dependencies in CDL

```
package com.apress.prospring4.ch3;

public class ContextualizedDependencyLookup implements ManagedComponent {
    private Dependency dependency;

    @Override
    public void performLookup(Container container) {
        this.dependency = (Dependency) container.getDependency("myDependency");
    }

    @Override
    public String toString() {
        return dependency.toString();
    }
}
```

Note that in Listing 3-4, Dependency is an empty class.

Constructor Dependency Injection

Constructor Dependency Injection occurs when a component's dependencies are provided to it in its constructor(s). The component declares a constructor or a set of constructors, taking as arguments its dependencies, and the IoC container passes the dependencies to the component when instantiation occurs, as shown in Listing 3-5.

Listing 3-5. Constructor Dependency Injection

```
package com.apress.prospring4.ch3;

public class ConstructorInjection {
    private Dependency dependency;

    public ConstructorInjection(Dependency dependency) {
        this.dependency = dependency;
    }
```

```
    @Override
    public String toString() {
        return dependency.toString();
    }
}
```

Setter Dependency Injection

In *Setter Dependency Injection*, the IoC container injects a component's dependencies via JavaBean-style setter methods. A component's setters expose the dependencies the IoC container can manage. Listing 3-6 shows a typical Setter Dependency Injection–based component.

Listing 3-6. Setter Dependency Injection

```
package com.apress.prospring4.ch3;

public class SetterInjection {
    private Dependency dependency;

    public void setDependency(Dependency dependency) {
        this.dependency = dependency;
    }

    @Override
    public String toString() {
        return dependency.toString();
    }
}
```

Within the container, the dependency requirement exposed by the setDependency() method is referred to by the JavaBeans-style name, *dependency*. In practice, Setter Injection is the most widely used injection mechanism, and it is one of the simplest IoC mechanisms to implement.

Injection vs. Lookup

Choosing which style of IoC to use—injection or lookup—is not usually a difficult decision. In many cases, the type of IoC you use is mandated by the container you are using. For instance, if you are using EJB 2.1 or prior versions, you must use lookup-style IoC (via JNDI) to obtain an EJB from the JEE container. In Spring, aside from initial bean lookups, your components and their dependencies are always wired together using injection-style IoC.

■ **Note**   When you are using Spring, you can access EJB resources without needing to perform an explicit lookup. Spring can act as an adapter between lookup and injection-style IoC systems, thus allowing you to manage all resources by using injection.

The real question is this: given the choice, which method should you use, injection or lookup? The answer is most definitely injection. If you look at the code in Listings 3-4 and 3-5, you can clearly see that using injection has zero impact on your components' code. The Dependency Pull code, on the other hand, must actively obtain a reference to the registry and interact with it to obtain the dependencies, and using CDL requires your classes to implement a specific interface and look up all dependencies manually. When you are using injection, the most your classes have to do is allow dependencies to be injected by using either constructors or setters.

Using injection, you are free to use your classes completely decoupled from the IoC container that is supplying dependent objects with their collaborators manually, whereas with lookup, your classes are always dependent on the classes and interfaces defined by the container. Another drawback with lookup is that it becomes very difficult to test your classes in isolation from the container. Using injection, testing your components is trivial, because you can simply provide the dependencies yourself by using the appropriate constructor or setter.

■ **Note** For a more complete discussion of testing by using Dependency Injection and Spring, refer to Chapter 13.

Lookup-based solutions are, by necessity, more complex than injection-based ones. Although complexity is nothing to be afraid of, we question the validity of adding unneeded complexity to a process as central to your application as dependency management.

All of these reasons aside, the biggest reason to choose injection over lookup is that it makes your life easier. You write substantially less code when you are using injection, and the code that you do write is simple and can, in general, be automated by a good IDE. You will notice that all of the code in the injection samples is passive, in that it doesn't actively try to accomplish a task. The most exciting thing you see in injection code is that objects get stored in a field only; no other code is involved in pulling the dependency from any registry or container. Therefore, the code is much simpler and less error prone. Passive code is much simpler to maintain than active code, because there is very little that can go wrong. Consider the following code taken from Listing 3-4:

```
public void performLookup(Container container) {
    this.dependency = (Dependency) container.getDependency("myDependency");
}
```

In this code, plenty could go wrong: the dependency key could change, the container instance could be null, or the returned dependency might be the incorrect type. We refer to this code as having a lot of *moving parts*, because plenty of things can break. Using Dependency Lookup might decouple the components of your application, but it adds complexity in the additional code required to couple these components back together in order to perform any useful tasks.

Setter Injection vs. Constructor Injection

Now that we have established which method of IoC is preferable, you still need to choose whether to use Setter Injection or Constructor Injection. *Constructor Injection* is particularly useful when you absolutely must have an instance of the dependency class before your component is used. Many containers, Spring included, provide a mechanism for ensuring that all dependencies are defined when you use Setter Injection, but by using Constructor Injection, you assert the requirement for the dependency in a container-agnostic manner. Constructor Injection also helps achieve the use of immutable objects.

Setter Injection is useful in a variety of cases. If the component is exposing its dependencies to the container but is happy to provide its own defaults, Setter Injection is usually the best way to accomplish this. Another benefit of Setter Injection is that it allows dependencies to be declared on an interface, although this is not as useful as you might first think. Consider a typical business interface with one business method, defineMeaningOfLife(). If, in addition to this method, you define a setter for injection such as setEncylopedia(), you are mandating that all implementations must use or at least be aware of the encyclopedia dependency. However, you don't need to define setEncylopedia() in the business interface. Instead, you can define the method in the classes implementing the business interface. While programming in this way, all recent IoC containers, Spring included, can work with the component in terms of the business interface but still provide the dependencies of the implementing class. An example of this may clarify this matter slightly. Consider the business interface in Listing 3-7.

Listing 3-7. The Oracle Interface

```
package com.apress.prospring4.ch3;

public interface Oracle {
    String defineMeaningOfLife();
}
```

Notice that the business interface does not define any setters for Dependency Injection. This interface could be implemented as shown in Listing 3-8.

Listing 3-8. Implementing the Oracle Interface

```
package com.apress.prospring4.ch3;

public class BookwormOracle implements Oracle {
    private Encyclopedia encyclopedia;

    public void setEncyclopedia(Encyclopedia encyclopedia) {
        this.encyclopedia = encyclopedia;
    }

    @Override
    public String defineMeaningOfLife() {
        return "Encyclopedias are a waste of money - use the Internet";
    }
}
```

As you can see, the BookwormOracle class not only implements the Oracle interface, but also defines the setter for Dependency Injection. Spring is more than comfortable dealing with a structure like this—there is absolutely no need to define the dependencies on the business interface. The ability to use interfaces to define dependencies is an often-touted benefit of Setter Injection, but in actuality, you should strive to keep setters used solely for injection out of your interfaces. Unless you are absolutely sure that all implementations of a particular business interface require a particular dependency, let each implementation class define its own dependencies and keep the business interface for business methods.

Although you shouldn't always place setters for dependencies in a business interface, placing setters and getters for configuration parameters in the business interface is a good idea and makes Setter Injection a valuable tool. We consider configuration parameters to be a special case for dependencies. Certainly your components depend on the configuration data, but configuration data is significantly different from the types of dependency you have seen so far. We will discuss the differences shortly, but for now, consider the business interface shown in Listing 3-9.

Listing 3-9. The NewsletterSender Interface

```
package com.apress.prospring4.ch3;

public interface NewsletterSender {
    void setSmtpServer(String smtpServer);
    String getSmtpServer();

    void setFromAddress(String fromAddress);
    String getFromAddress();

    void send();
}
```

Classes that send a set of newsletters via e-mail implement the NewsletterSender interface. The send() method is the only business method, but notice that we have defined two JavaBean properties on the interface. Why are we doing this when we just said that you shouldn't define dependencies in the business interface? The reason is that these values, the SMTP server address and the address the e-mails are sent from, are not dependencies in the practical sense; rather, they are configuration details that affect how all implementations of the NewsletterSender interface function. The question here then is this: what is the difference between a configuration parameter and any other kind of dependency? In most cases, you can clearly see whether a dependency should be classified as a configuration parameter, but if you are not sure, look for the following three characteristics that point to a configuration parameter:

- Configuration parameters are passive. In the NewsletterSender example shown in Listing 3-8, the SMTP server parameter is an example of a passive dependency. Passive dependencies are not used directly to perform an action; instead, they are used internally or by another dependency to perform their actions. In the MessageRenderer example from Chapter 2, the MessageProvider dependency was not passive—it performed a function that was necessary for the MessageRenderer to complete its task.

- Configuration parameters are usually information, not other components. By this we mean that a configuration parameter is usually some piece of information that a component needs to complete its work. Clearly, the SMTP server is a piece of information required by the NewsletterSender, but the MessageProvider is really another component that the MessageRenderer needs to function correctly.

- Configuration parameters are usually simple values or collections of simple values. This is really a by-product of the previous two points, but configuration parameters are usually simple values. In Java this means they are a primitive (or the corresponding wrapper class) or a String or collections of these values. Simple values are generally passive. This means you can't do much with a String other than manipulate the data it represents; and you almost always use these values for information purposes—for example, an int value that represents the port number that a network socket should listen on, or a String that represents the SMTP server through which an e-mail program should send messages.

When considering whether to define configuration options in the business interface, also consider whether the configuration parameter is applicable to all implementations of the business interface or just one. For instance, in the case of implementations of NewsletterSender, it is obvious that all implementations need to know which SMTP server to use when sending e-mails. However, we would probably choose to leave the configuration option that flags whether to send secure e-mail off the business interface, because not all e-mail APIs are capable of this, and it is correct to assume that many implementations will not take security into consideration at all.

■ **Note** Recall that in Chapter 2, we chose to define the dependencies in the business purposes. This was for illustration purposes and should not be treated in any way as a best practice.

Setter injection also allows you to swap dependencies for a different implementation on the fly without creating a new instance of the parent component. Spring's JMX support makes this possible. Perhaps the biggest benefit of Setter Injection is that it is the least intrusive of the injection mechanisms.

In general, you should choose an injection type based on your use case. Setter-based injection allows dependencies to be swapped out without creating new objects and also lets your class choose appropriate defaults without the need to explicitly inject an object. Constructor injection is a good choice when you want to ensure that dependencies are being passed to a component, and when designing for immutable objects. Do keep in mind that while constructor injection ensures that all dependencies are provided to a component, most containers provide a mechanism to ensure this as well but may incur a cost of coupling your code to the framework.

Inversion of Control in Spring

As we mentioned earlier, Inversion of Control is a big part of what Spring does. The core of Spring's implementation is based on Dependency Injection, although Dependency Lookup features are provided as well. When Spring provides collaborators to a dependent object automatically, it does so using Dependency Injection. In a Spring-based application, it is always preferable to use Dependency Injection to pass collaborators to dependent objects rather than have the dependent objects obtain the collaborators via lookup. Figure 3-3 shows Spring's Dependency Injection mechanism (for Dependency Lookup, please refer to Figure 3-2).

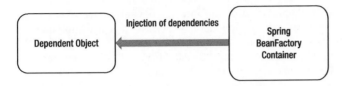

Figure 3-3. *Spring's Dependency Injection mechanism*

Although Dependency Injection is the preferred mechanism for wiring together collaborators and dependent objects, you need Dependency Lookup to access the dependent objects. In many environments, Spring cannot automatically wire up all of your application components by using Dependency Injection, and you must use Dependency Lookup to access the initial set of components. For example, in stand-alone Java applications, you need to bootstrap Spring's container in the `main()` method and obtain the dependencies (via the `ApplicationContext` interface) for processing programmatically. However, when you are building web applications by using Spring's MVC support, Spring can avoid this by gluing your entire application together automatically. Wherever it is possible to use Dependency Injection with Spring, you should do so; otherwise, you can fall back on the Dependency Lookup capabilities. You will see examples of both in action during the course of this chapter, and we will point them out when they first arise.

An interesting feature of Spring's IoC container is that it has the ability to act as an adaptor between its own Dependency Injection container and external Dependency Lookup containers. We discuss this feature later in this chapter.

Spring supports both Constructor and Setter Injection and bolsters the standard IoC feature set with a whole host of useful additions to make your life easier.

The rest of this chapter introduces the basics of Spring's DI container, complete with plenty of examples.

Dependency Injection in Spring

Spring's support for Dependency Injection is comprehensive and, as you will see in Chapter 4, goes beyond the standard IoC feature set we have discussed so far. The rest of this chapter addresses the basics of Spring's Dependency Injection container, looking at Setter, Constructor, and Method Injection, along with a detailed look at how Dependency Injection is configured in Spring.

Beans and BeanFactories

The core of Spring's Dependency Injection container is the `BeanFactory` interface. `BeanFactory` is responsible for managing components, including their dependencies as well as their life cycles. In Spring, the term *bean* is used to refer to any component managed by the container. Typically, your beans adhere, at some level, to the JavaBeans specification, but this is not required, especially if you plan to use Constructor Injection to wire your beans together.

If your application needs only DI support, you can interact with the Spring DI container via the BeanFactory interface. In this case, your application must create an instance of a class that implements the BeanFactory interface and configures it with bean and dependency information. After this is complete, your application can access the beans via BeanFactory and get on with its processing. In some cases, all of this setup is handled automatically (for example, in a web application, Spring's ApplicationContext will be bootstrapped by the web container during application startup via a Spring-provided ContextLoaderListener class declared in the web.xml descriptor file). But in many cases, you need to code the setup yourself. All of the examples in this chapter require manual setup of the BeanFactory implementation.

Although the BeanFactory can be configured programmatically, it is more common to see it configured externally using some kind of configuration file. Internally, bean configuration is represented by instances of classes that implement the BeanDefinition interface. The bean configuration stores information not only about a bean itself but also about the beans that it depends on. For any BeanFactory implementation classes that also implement the BeanDefinitionReader interface, you can read the BeanDefinition data from a configuration file, using either PropertiesBeanDefinitionReader or XmlBeanDefinitionReader. PropertiesBeanDefinitionReader reads the bean definition from properties files, while XmlBeanDefinitionReader reads from XML files.

So you can identify your beans within BeanFactory, each bean can be assigned an ID, a name, or both. A bean can also be instantiated without any ID or name (known as an *anonymous bean*) or as an inner bean within another bean. Each bean has at least one name but can have any number of names (additional names are separated by commas). Any names after the first are considered aliases for the same bean. You use bean IDs or names to retrieve a bean from BeanFactory and also to establish dependency relationships—that is, bean X depends on bean Y.

BeanFactory Implementations

The description of the BeanFactory interface may appear overly complex, but in practice, this is not the case. Take a look at a simple example.

Let's say you have an implementation that mimics an oracle that can tell you the meaning of life. Listings 3-10 and 3-11 define the interface and a simple implementation, respectively.

Listing 3-10. The Oracle Interface

```
package com.apress.prospring4.ch3;

public interface Oracle {
    String defineMeaningOfLife();
}
```

Listing 3-11. A Simple Oracle Interface Implementation

```
package com.apress.prospring4.ch3;

public class BookwormOracle implements Oracle {
    @Override
    public String defineMeaningOfLife() {
        return "Encyclopedias are a waste of money - use the Internet";
    }
}
```

Now let's see, in a stand-alone Java program, how we can initialize Spring's BeanFactory and obtain the oracle bean for processing (see Listing 3-12).

Listing 3-12. Using BeanFactory

```
package com.apress.prospring4.ch3;

import org.springframework.beans.factory.support.DefaultListableBeanFactory;
import org.springframework.beans.factory.xml.XmlBeanDefinitionReader;
import org.springframework.core.io.ClassPathResource;

public class XmlConfigWithBeanFactory {
    public static void main(String[] args) {
        DefaultListableBeanFactory factory = new DefaultListableBeanFactory();

        XmlBeanDefinitionReader rdr = new XmlBeanDefinitionReader(factory);
        rdr.loadBeanDefinitions(new
            ClassPathResource("META-INF/spring/xml-bean-factory-config.xml"));

        Oracle oracle = (Oracle) factory.getBean("oracle");

        System.out.println(oracle.defineMeaningOfLife());
    }
}
```

In Listing 3-12, you can see that we are using `DefaultListableBeanFactory`—one of the two main `BeanFactory` implementations supplied with Spring—and that we are reading in the `BeanDefinition` information from an XML file by using `XmlBeanDefinitionReader`. Once the `BeanFactory` implementation is created and configured, we retrieve the Oracle bean by using its name, `oracle`, which is configured in the XML configuration file. Listing 3-13 is the content of the XML for bootstrapping Spring's `BeanFactory` (`xml-bean-factory-config.xml`).

Listing 3-13. Simple Spring XML Configuration

```
<?xml version="1.0" encoding="UTF-8"?>

<beans xmlns="http://www.springframework.org/schema/beans"
    xmlns:xsi="http://www.w3.org/2001/XMLSchema-instance"
    xsi:schemaLocation="http://www.springframework.org/schema/beans
        http://www.springframework.org/schema/beans/spring-beans.xsd">

    <bean id="oracle" name="wiseworm" class="com.apress.prospring4.ch3.BookwormOracle"/>
</beans>
```

■ **Note** When declaring a Spring XSD location, it's a best practice to not include the version number. This resolution is already handled for you by Spring as the versioned XSD file is configured through a pointer in the `spring.schemas` file. This file resides in the `spring-beans` module defined as a dependency in your project. This also prevents you from having to modify all of your bean files when upgrading to a new version of Spring.

The previous file declares a Spring bean, gives it an ID of `oracle` and a name of `wiseworm`, and tells Spring that the underlying implementation class is `com.apress.prospring4.ch3.BookwormOracle`. Don't worry too much about the configuration at the moment; we discuss the details in later sections.

Having the configuration defined, run the program in Listing 3-12, and you will see the phrase returned by the defineMeaningOfLife() method in the console output.

In addition to XmlBeanDefinitionReader, Spring also provides PropertiesBeanDefinitionReader, which allows you to manage your bean configuration by using properties rather than XML. Although properties are ideal for small, simple applications, they can quickly become cumbersome when you are dealing with a large number of beans. For this reason, it is preferable to use the XML configuration format for all but the most trivial of applications.

Of course, you are free to define your own BeanFactory implementations, although be aware that doing so is quite involved; you need to implement a lot more interfaces than just BeanFactory to get the same level of functionality you have with the supplied BeanFactory implementations. If all you want to do is define a new configuration mechanism, create your definition reader by developing a class that extends the DefaultListableBeanFactory class, which has the BeanFactory interface implemented.

ApplicationContext

In Spring, the ApplicationContext interface is an extension to BeanFactory. In addition to DI services, ApplicationContext provides other services, such as transaction and AOP service, message source for internationalization (i18n), and application event handling, to name a few.

In developing Spring-based applications, it's recommended that you interact with Spring via the ApplicationContext interface. Spring supports the bootstrapping of ApplicationContext by manual coding (instantiate it manually and load the appropriate configuration) or in a web container environment via the ContextLoaderListener. From this point onward, all the sample code in this book uses ApplicationContext.

Configuring ApplicationContext

Having discussed the basic concepts of IoC and DI and gone through a simple example of using Spring's BeanFactory interface, let's dive into the details on how to configure a Spring application.

In the following sections, we go through various aspects of configuring Spring applications. Specifically, we focus our attention on the ApplicationContext interface, which provides many more configuration options than the traditional BeanFactory interface.

Setting Spring Configuration Options

Before we dive into the details of configuring Spring's ApplicationContext, let's take a look at the options that are available for defining an application's configuration within Spring.

Originally, Spring supported defining beans either through properties or an XML file. Since the release of JDK 5 and Spring's support of Java annotations, Spring (starting from Spring 2.5) also supports using Java annotations when configuring ApplicationContext.

So, which one is better, XML or annotations? There have been lots of debates on this topic, and you can find numerous discussions on the Internet (for example, try the Spring Community Forums at http://forum.spring.io). There is no definite answer, and each approach has its pros and cons. Using an XML file can externalize all configuration from Java code, while annotations allow the developer to define and view the DI setup from within the code. Spring also supports a mix of the two approaches in a single ApplicationContext. One common approach is to define the application infrastructure (for example, data source, transaction manager, JMS connection factory, or JMX) in an XML file, while defining the DI configuration (injectable beans and beans' dependencies) in annotations. However, no matter which option you choose, stick to it and deliver the message clearly across the entire development team. Agreeing on the style to use and keeping it consistent across the application will make ongoing development and maintenance activities much easier.

To facilitate your understanding of both the XML and annotation configuration, we provide sample code for XML and annotations side by side whenever appropriate.

Basic Configuration Overview

For XML configuration, you need to declare the required namespace base provided by Spring that your application requires. Listing 3-14 shows the most basic sample, which declares only the beans namespace for you to define the Spring beans. We refer to this configuration file as app-context-xml.xml for XML-style configuration throughout the samples.

Listing 3-14. Simple Spring XML Configuration

```xml
<?xml version="1.0" encoding="UTF-8"?>

<beans xmlns="http://www.springframework.org/schema/beans"
    xmlns:xsi="http://www.w3.org/2001/XMLSchema-instance"
    xsi:schemaLocation="http://www.springframework.org/schema/beans
        http://www.springframework.org/schema/beans/spring-beans.xsd">

</beans>
```

Besides beans, Spring provides a large number of other namespaces for different purposes. Some examples include context for ApplicationContext configuration, aop for AOP support, and tx for transactional support. Namespaces are covered in the appropriate chapters.

To use Spring's annotation support in your application, you need to declare the tags shown in Listing 3-15 in your XML configuration. We refer to this configuration file as app-context-annotation.xml for XML configuration with annotation support throughout the samples.

Listing 3-15. Spring XML Configuration with Annotation Support

```xml
<?xml version="1.0" encoding="UTF-8"?>

<beans xmlns="http://www.springframework.org/schema/beans"
    xmlns:xsi="http://www.w3.org/2001/XMLSchema-instance"
    xmlns:context="http://www.springframework.org/schema/context"
    xsi:schemaLocation="http://www.springframework.org/schema/beans
        http://www.springframework.org/schema/beans/spring-beans.xsd
        http://www.springframework.org/schema/context
        http://www.springframework.org/schema/context/spring-context.xsd">

    <context:component-scan base-package="com.apress.prospring4.ch3.annotation" />
</beans>
```

The <context:component-scan> tag tells Spring to scan the code for injectable beans annotated with @Component, @Controller, @Repository, and @Service as well as supporting the @Autowired and @Inject annotations under the package (and all its subpackages) specified. In the <context:component-scan> tag, multiple packages can be defined by using either a comma, a semicolon, or a space as the delimiter. Moreover, the tag supports inclusion and exclusion of a components scan for more fine-grained control. For example, consider the configuration in Listing 3-16.

Listing 3-16. Spring XML Configuration Component Scan

```xml
<?xml version="1.0" encoding="UTF-8"?>

<beans xmlns="http://www.springframework.org/schema/beans"
    xmlns:xsi="http://www.w3.org/2001/XMLSchema-instance"
    xmlns:context="http://www.springframework.org/schema/context"
```

```
xsi:schemaLocation="http://www.springframework.org/schema/beans
    http://www.springframework.org/schema/beans/spring-beans.xsd
    http://www.springframework.org/schema/context
    http://www.springframework.org/schema/context/spring-context.xsd">

<context:component-scan base-package="com.apress.prospring4.ch3.annotation" >
    <context:exclude-filter type="assignable" expression="com.example.NotAService"/>
</context:component-scan>
</beans>
```

The previous tag tells Spring to scan the package as specified but omit the classes that were assignable to the type as specified in the expression (can be either a class or an interface). Besides the exclude filter, you can also use an include filter. And for the type, you can use annotation, regex, assignable, AspectJ, or custom (with your own filter class that implements org.springframework.core.type.filter.TypeFilter) as the filter criteria. The expression format depends on the type you specified.

Declaring Spring Components

After you develop some kind of service class and want to use it in a Spring-base application, you need to tell Spring that those beans are eligible for injection to other beans and have Spring manage them for you. Consider the sample in Chapter 2, where MessageRender outputs the message and depends on MessageProvider to provide the message to render. Listing 3-17 recaps the interfaces and implementations of the two services.

Listing 3-17. MessageRenderer and MessageProvider

```
package com.apress.prospring4.ch3;

public interface MessageRenderer {
    void render();
    void setMessageProvider(MessageProvider provider);
    MessageProvider getMessageProvider();
}

package com.apress.prospring4.ch3;

import com.apress.prospring4.ch3.MessageProvider;
import com.apress.prospring4.ch3.MessageRenderer;

public class StandardOutMessageRenderer implements MessageRenderer {
    private MessageProvider messageProvider;

    @Override
    public void render() {
        if (messageProvider == null) {
            throw new RuntimeException(
            "You must set the property messageProvider of class:"
            + StandardOutMessageRenderer.class.getName());
        }

        System.out.println(messageProvider.getMessage());
    }
```

```java
    @Override
    public void setMessageProvider(MessageProvider provider) {
        this.messageProvider = provider;
    }

    @Override
    public MessageProvider getMessageProvider() {
        return this.messageProvider;
    }
}

package com.apress.prospring4.ch3;

public interface MessageProvider {
    String getMessage();
}

package com.apress.prospring4.ch3.xml;

import com.apress.prospring4.ch3.MessageProvider;

public class HelloWorldMessageProvider implements MessageProvider {
    @Override
    public String getMessage() {
        return "Hello World!";
    }
}
```

To declare the beans in an XML file, on top of the basic configuration (as stated earlier in Listing 3-14), you add the <bean> tags in Listing 3-18 to the file app-context-xml.xml.

Listing 3-18. Declare Spring Beans (XML)

```xml
<?xml version="1.0" encoding="UTF-8"?>

<beans xmlns="http://www.springframework.org/schema/beans"
    xmlns:xsi="http://www.w3.org/2001/XMLSchema-instance"
    xsi:schemaLocation="http://www.springframework.org/schema/beans
        http://www.springframework.org/schema/beans/spring-beans.xsd">

    <bean id="messageRenderer"
        class="com.apress.prospring4.ch3.xml.StandardOutMessageRenderer"/>

    <bean id="messageProvider"
        class="com.apress.prospring4.ch3.xml.HelloWorldMessageProvider"/>
</beans>
```

The previous tags declare two beans, one with an ID of messageProvider with the HelloWorldMessageProvider implementation, and the other with an ID of messageRenderer with the StandardOutMessageRenderer implementation.

To define the Spring beans via annotation, you don't need to modify the XML configuration file (app-context-annotation.xml) anymore; you just need to add the corresponding annotation to the service implementation classes under package com.apress.prospring4.ch3.annotation (see Listing 3-19).

41

Listing 3-19. Declare Spring Beans (Annotation)

```
package com.apress.prospring4.ch3.annotation;

import org.springframework.stereotype.Service;
import com.apress.prospring4.ch3.MessageRenderer;

@Service("messageRenderer")
public class StandardOutMessageRenderer implements MessageRenderer {
    private MessageProvider messageProvider;

    @Override
    public void render() {
        if (messageProvider == null) {
            throw new RuntimeException(
            "You must set the property messageProvider of class:"
            + StandardOutMessageRenderer.class.getName());
        }

        System.out.println(messageProvider.getMessage());
    }

    @Override
    public void setMessageProvider(MessageProvider provider) {
        this.messageProvider = provider;
    }

    @Override
    public MessageProvider getMessageProvider() {
        return this.messageProvider;
    }
}

package com.apress.prospring4.ch3.annotation;

import org.springframework.stereotype.Service;
import com.apress.prospring4.ch3.MessageProvider;

@Service("messageProvider")
public class HelloWorldMessageProvider implements MessageProvider {
    @Override
    public String getMessage() {
        return "Hello World!";
    }
}
```

From the previous code sample, you use Spring's @Service annotation to specify that the bean provides services that other beans may require, passing in the bean name as the parameter. When bootstrapping Spring's ApplicationContext with the XML configuration in Listing 3-15, Spring will seek out those components and instantiate the beans with the specified names.

Using either approach doesn't affect the way you obtain the beans from ApplicationContext. Listing 3-20 shows the example code to obtain the message provider.

Listing 3-20. Declare Spring Beans (Testing)

```
package com.apress.prospring4.ch3;

import org.springframework.context.support.GenericXmlApplicationContext;

public class DeclareSpringComponents {
    public static void main(String[] args) {
        GenericXmlApplicationContext ctx = new GenericXmlApplicationContext();
        ctx.load("classpath:app-context-xml.xml");
        ctx.refresh();

        MessageProvider messageProvider = ctx.getBean("messageProvider",
            MessageProvider.class);

        System.out.println(messageProvider.getMessage());
    }
}
```

Instead of `DefaultListableBeanFactory`, an instance of `GenericXmlApplicationContext` is instantiated. The `GenericXmlApplicationContext` class implements the `ApplicationContext` interface and is able to bootstrap Spring's `ApplicationContext` from the configurations defined in XML files.

You can swap the `app-context-xml.xml` file with `app-context-annotation.xml` in the provided source code for this chapter, and you will find that both cases produce the same result: "Hello World!" is printed.

Listing 3-21 (`app-context-xml.xml`) and Listing 3-22 (`app-context-annotation.xml`) recap the configuration file content for both XML and annotation-style configuration that we have discussed so far.

Listing 3-21. XML Configuration (`app-context-xml.xml`)

```
<?xml version="1.0" encoding="UTF-8"?>

<beans xmlns="http://www.springframework.org/schema/beans"
      xmlns:xsi="http://www.w3.org/2001/XMLSchema-instance"
      xsi:schemaLocation="http://www.springframework.org/schema/beans
          http://www.springframework.org/schema/beans/spring-beans.xsd">

    <bean id="messageProvider"
          class="com.apress.prospring4.ch3.xml.HelloWorldMessageProvider"/>
</beans>
```

Listing 3-22. Annotation Configuration (`app-context-annotation.xml`)

```
<?xml version="1.0" encoding="UTF-8"?>

<beans xmlns="http://www.springframework.org/schema/beans"
      xmlns:xsi="http://www.w3.org/2001/XMLSchema-instance"
      xmlns:context="http://www.springframework.org/schema/context"
      xsi:schemaLocation="http://www.springframework.org/schema/beans
          http://www.springframework.org/schema/beans/spring-beans.xsd
          http://www.springframework.org/schema/context
          http://www.springframework.org/schema/context/spring-context.xsd">

    <context:component-scan
          base-package="com.apress.prospring4.ch3.annotation"/>
</beans>
```

Using Setter Injection

To configure Setter Injection by using XML configuration, you need to specify `<property>` tags under the `<bean>` tag for each `<property>` into which you want to inject a dependency. For example, to assign the message provider bean to the `messageProvider` property of the `messageRenderer` bean, you simply change the `<bean>` tag for the `messageRenderer` bean, as shown in Listing 3-23.

Listing 3-23. Setter Injection (XML)

```xml
<?xml version="1.0" encoding="UTF-8"?>

<beans xmlns="http://www.springframework.org/schema/beans"
       xmlns:xsi="http://www.w3.org/2001/XMLSchema-instance"
       xsi:schemaLocation="http://www.springframework.org/schema/beans
          http://www.springframework.org/schema/beans/spring-beans.xsd">

    <bean id="messageRenderer"
        class="com.apress.prospring4.ch3.xml.StandardOutMessageRenderer">
        <property name="messageProvider" ref="messageProvider"/>
    </bean>

    <bean id="messageProvider"
        class="com.apress.prospring4.ch3.xml.HelloWorldMessageProvider"/>
</beans>
```

From this code, you can see that we are assigning the `messageProvider` bean to the `messageProvider` property. You can use the `ref` attribute to assign a bean reference to a property (discussed in more detail shortly).

If you are using Spring 2.5 or later and have the p namespace declared in your XML configuration file, you can declare the injection as shown in Listing 3-24.

Listing 3-24. Setter Injection (XML)

```xml
<?xml version="1.0" encoding="UTF-8"?>

<beans xmlns="http://www.springframework.org/schema/beans"
       xmlns:xsi="http://www.w3.org/2001/XMLSchema-instance"
       xmlns:p="http://www.springframework.org/schema/p"
       xsi:schemaLocation="http://www.springframework.org/schema/beans
          http://www.springframework.org/schema/beans/spring-beans.xsd">

    <bean id="messageRenderer"
        class="com.apress.prospring4.ch3.xml.StandardOutMessageRenderer"
        p:messageProvider-ref="messageProvider"/>

    <bean id="messageProvider"
        class="com.apress.prospring4.ch3.xml.HelloWorldMessageProvider"/>
</beans>
```

The p namespace provides a simplified way for defining Setter Injection.

■ **Note**   The p namespace is not defined in an XSD file and exists only in Spring core; therefore, no XSD is declared in the `schemaLocation` attribute.

For annotation, it's even simpler. You just need to add an @Autowired annotation to the setter method, as shown in Listing 3-25.

Listing 3-25. Setter Injection (Annotation)

```
package com.apress.prospring4.ch3.annotation;

import org.springframework.stereotype.Service;
import com.apress.prospring4.ch3.MessageRenderer;
import com.apress.prospring4.ch3.MessageProvider;

@Service("messageRenderer")
public class StandardOutMessageRenderer implements MessageRenderer {
    private MessageProvider messageProvider;

    @Override
    public void render() {
        if (messageProvider == null) {
            throw new RuntimeException(
            "You must set the property messageProvider of class:"
            + StandardOutMessageRenderer.class.getName());
        }

        System.out.println(messageProvider.getMessage());
    }

    @Override
    @Autowired
    public void setMessageProvider(MessageProvider provider) {
        this.messageProvider = provider;
    }

    @Override
    public MessageProvider getMessageProvider() {
        return this.messageProvider;
    }
}
```

Since we declared the <context:component-scan> tag in the XML configuration file, during the initialization of Spring's ApplicationContext, Spring will discover those @Autowired annotations and inject the dependency as required.

> ■ **Note**   Instead of @Autowired, you can also use @Resource(name="messageProvider") to achieve the same result.
> @Resource is one of the annotations in the JSR-250 standard that defines a common set of Java annotations for use
> on both JSE and JEE platforms. Different from @Autowired, the @Resource annotation supports the name parameter for
> more fine-grained DI requirements. Additionally, Spring supports use of the @Inject annotation introduced as part of
> JSR-299, "Contexts and Dependency Injection for the Java EE Platform" (CDI). @Inject is equivalent in behavior to
> Spring's @Autowired annotation.

Now let's verify the result by using the code in Listing 3-26.

Listing 3-26. Using Setter Injection (Testing)

```
package com.apress.prospring4.ch3;

import org.springframework.context.support.GenericXmlApplicationContext;

public class DeclareSpringComponents {
    public static void main(String[] args) {
        GenericXmlApplicationContext ctx = new GenericXmlApplicationContext();
        ctx.load("classpath:META-INF/spring/app-context-xml.xml");
        ctx.refresh();

        MessageRenderer messageRenderer = ctx.getBean("messageRenderer",
            MessageRenderer.class);

        messageRenderer.render();
    }
}
```

As in the previous section, you can swap the app-context-xml.xml file with app-context-annotation.xml in the
provided source code for this chapter, and you will find that both cases produce the same result: "Hello World!"
is printed.

Using Constructor Injection

In the previous example, the MessageProvider implementation, HelloWorldMessageProvider, returned the same
hard-coded message for each call of the getMessage() method. In the Spring configuration file, you can easily create a
configurable MessageProvider that allows the message to be defined externally, as shown in Listing 3-27.

Listing 3-27. The ConfigurableMessageProvider Class (XML)

```
package com.apress.prospring4.ch3.xml;

import com.apress.prospring4.ch3.MessageProvider;

public class ConfigurableMessageProvider implements MessageProvider {
    private String message;
```

```java
    public ConfigurableMessageProvider(String message) {
        this.message = message;
    }

    @Override
    public String getMessage() {
        return message;
    }
}
```

As you can see, it is impossible to create an instance of `ConfigurableMessageProvider` without providing a value for the message (unless you supply `null`). This is exactly what we want, and this class is ideally suited for use with Constructor Injection. Listing 3-28 shows how you can redefine the `messageProvider` bean definition to create an instance of `ConfigurableMessageProvider`, injecting the message by using Constructor Injection.

Listing 3-28. Using Constructor Injection (XML)

```xml
<?xml version="1.0" encoding="UTF-8"?>

<beans xmlns="http://www.springframework.org/schema/beans"
       xmlns:xsi="http://www.w3.org/2001/XMLSchema-instance"
       xsi:schemaLocation="http://www.springframework.org/schema/beans
           http://www.springframework.org/schema/beans/spring-beans.xsd">

    <bean id="messageProvider"
        class="com.apress.prospring4.ch3.xml.ConfigurableMessageProvider">
        <constructor-arg value="Configurable message"/>
    </bean>
</beans>
```

In this code, instead of using a `<property>` tag, we used a `<constructor-arg>` tag. Because we are not passing in another bean this time, just a `String` literal, we use the `value` attribute instead of `ref` to specify the value for the constructor argument.

When you have more than one constructor argument or your class has more than one constructor, you need to give each `<constructor-arg>` tag an `index` attribute to specify the index of the argument, starting at 0, in the constructor signature. It is always best to use the `index` attribute whenever you are dealing with constructors that have multiple arguments, to avoid confusion between the parameters and ensure that Spring picks the correct constructor.

In addition to the p namespace, as of Spring 3.1, you can also use the c namespace, as shown here:

```xml
<?xml version="1.0" encoding="UTF-8"?>

<beans xmlns="http://www.springframework.org/schema/beans"
       xmlns:xsi="http://www.w3.org/2001/XMLSchema-instance"
       xmlns:c="http://www.springframework.org/schema/c"
       xsi:schemaLocation="http://www.springframework.org/schema/beans
           http://www.springframework.org/schema/beans/spring-beans.xsd">

    <bean id="messageProvider"
        class="com.apress.prospring4.ch3.xml.ConfigurableMessageProvider"
        c:message="This is a configurable message"/>
</beans>
```

■ **Note** The c namespace is not defined in an XSD file and exists only in Spring core; therefore, no XSD is declared in the schemaLocation attribute.

To use an annotation for Constructor Injection, we also use the @Autowired annotation in the target bean's constructor method, as shown in Listing 3-29, which is an alternative option to the one using Setter Injection, as shown in Listing 3-24.

Listing 3-29. Using Constructor Injection (Annotation)

```
package com.apress.prospring4.ch3.annotation;

import org.springframework.stereotype.Service;
import org.springframework.beans.factory.annotation.Value;
import org.springframework.beans.factory.annotation.Autowired;
import com.apress.prospring4.ch3.MessageProvider;

@Service("messageProvider")
public class ConfigurableMessageProvider implements MessageProvider {
    private String message;

    @Autowired
    public ConfigurableMessageProvider(@Value("Configurable message") String message) {
        this.message = message;
    }

    @Override
    public String getMessage() {
        return this.message;
    }
}
```

From the previous listing, you can see that we use another annotation, @Value, to define the value to be injected into the constructor. This is the way in Spring you inject values into a bean. Besides simple strings, you can also use the powerful SpEL for dynamic value injection (more on this later in this chapter).

However, hard-coding the value in the code is not a good idea, since to change it, you would need to recompile the program. Even if you choose annotation-style DI, a good practice is to externalize those values for injection. To externalize the message, let's define the message as a Spring bean in the annotation configuration file, as in Listing 3-30.

Listing 3-30. Using Constructor Injection (Annotation)

```
<?xml version="1.0" encoding="UTF-8"?>

<beans xmlns="http://www.springframework.org/schema/beans"
       xmlns:xsi="http://www.w3.org/2001/XMLSchema-instance"
       xmlns:context="http://www.springframework.org/schema/context"
       xmlns:c="http://www.springframework.org/schema/c"
       xsi:schemaLocation="http://www.springframework.org/schema/beans
          http://www.springframework.org/schema/beans/spring-beans.xsd
          http://www.springframework.org/schema/context
          http://www.springframework.org/schema/context/spring-context.xsd">
```

```
<context:component-scan
        base-package="com.apress.prospring4.ch3.annotation"/>

<bean id="message" class="java.lang.String" c:_0="This is a configurable message"/>
</beans>
```

Here we define a bean with an ID of message and type of java.lang.String. Notice that we also use the c namespace for Constructor Injection to set the string value, and _0 indicates the index for the constructor argument.

Have the bean declared; we can take away the @Value annotation from the target bean, as in Listing 3-31.

Listing 3-31. Using Constructor Injection (Annotation)

```
package com.apress.prospring4.ch3.annotation;

import org.springframework.stereotype.Service;
import org.springframework.beans.factory.annotation.Autowired;
import com.apress.prospring4.ch3.MessageProvider;

@Service("messageProvider")
public class ConfigurableMessageProvider implements MessageProvider {
    private String message;

    @Autowired
    public ConfigurableMessageProvider(String message) {
        this.message = message;
    }

    @Override
    public String getMessage() {
        return this.message;
    }
}
```

Since we declare that the message bean and its ID are the same as the name of the argument specified in the constructor, Spring will detect the annotation and inject the value into the constructor method.

Now run the test by using the code in Listing 3-32 against both the XML (app-context.xml.xml) and annotation configurations (app-context-annotation.xml), and the configured message will be displayed in both cases. The following is the sample output:

```
This is a configurable message
```

Listing 3-32. Constructor Confusion

```
package com.apress.prospring4.ch3;

import org.springframework.context.support.GenericXmlApplicationContext;

public class DeclareSpringComponents {
    public static void main(String[] args) {
        GenericXmlApplicationContext ctx = new GenericXmlApplicationContext();
```

```
    ctx.load("classpath:META-INF/spring/app-context-annotation.xml");
    ctx.refresh();

    MessageProvider messageProvider = ctx.getBean("messageProvider",
        MessageProvider.class);

    System.out.println(messageProvider.getMessage());
    }
}
```

In some cases, Spring finds it impossible to tell which constructor you want it to use for Constructor Injection. This usually arises when you have two constructors with the same number of arguments and the types used in the arguments are represented in exactly the same way. Consider the code in Listing 3-33.

Listing 3-33. Constructor Confusion

```
package com.apress.prospring4.ch3.xml;

import org.springframework.context.support.GenericXmlApplicationContext;

public class ConstructorConfusion {
    private String someValue;

    public ConstructorConfusion(String someValue) {
        System.out.println("ConstructorConfusion(String) called");
        this.someValue = someValue;
    }

    public ConstructorConfusion(int someValue) {
        System.out.println("ConstructorConfusion(int) called");
        this.someValue = "Number: " + Integer.toString(someValue);
    }

    public static void main(String[] args) {
        GenericXmlApplicationContext ctx = new GenericXmlApplicationContext();
        ctx.load("classpath:META-INF/spring/app-context-xml.xml");
        ctx.refresh();

        ConstructorConfusion cc = (ConstructorConfusion) ctx.getBean("constructorConfusion");
        System.out.println(cc);
    }

    public String toString() {
        return someValue;
    }
}
```

Here, you can clearly see what this code does—it simply retrieves a bean of type ConstructorConfusion from ApplicationContext and writes the value to console output. Now look at the configuration code in Listing 3-34 (app-context-xml.xml).

Listing 3-34. Confused Constructors

```xml
<?xml version="1.0" encoding="UTF-8"?>

<beans xmlns="http://www.springframework.org/schema/beans"
    xmlns:xsi="http://www.w3.org/2001/XMLSchema-instance"
    xmlns:c="http://www.springframework.org/schema/c"
    xsi:schemaLocation="http://www.springframework.org/schema/beans
        http://www.springframework.org/schema/beans/spring-beans.xsd">

    <bean id="messageProvider"
        class="com.apress.prospring4.ch3.xml.ConfigurableMessageProvider"
        c:message="This is a configurable message"/>

    <bean id="constructorConfusion"
        class="com.apress.prospring4.ch3.xml.ConstructorConfusion">
        <constructor-arg>
            <value>90</value>
        </constructor-arg>
    </bean>
</beans>
```

Which of the constructors is called in this case? Running the example yields the following output:

```
ConstructorConfusion(String) called
90
```

This shows that the constructor with the `String` argument is called. This is not the desired effect, since we want to prefix any integer values passed in by using Constructor Injection with `Number:`, as shown in the `int` constructor. To get around this, we need to make a small modification to the configuration, shown in Listing 3-35 (`app-context-xml.xml`).

Listing 3-35. Overcoming Constructor Confusion

```xml
<?xml version="1.0" encoding="UTF-8"?>

<beans xmlns="http://www.springframework.org/schema/beans"
    xmlns:xsi="http://www.w3.org/2001/XMLSchema-instance"
    xmlns:c="http://www.springframework.org/schema/c"
    xsi:schemaLocation="http://www.springframework.org/schema/beans
        http://www.springframework.org/schema/beans/spring-beans.xsd">

    <bean id="messageProvider"
        class="com.apress.prospring4.ch3.xml.ConfigurableMessageProvider"
        c:message="This is a configurable message"/>

    <bean id="constructorConfusion"
        class="com.apress.prospring4.ch3.xml.ConstructorConfusion">
        <constructor-arg type="int">
            <value>90</value>
        </constructor-arg>
    </bean>
</beans>
```

Notice now that the <constructor-arg> tag has an additional attribute, type, that specifies the type of argument Spring should look for. Running the example again with the corrected configuration yields the correct output:

```
ConstructorConfusion(int) called
Number: 90
```

For annotation-style Construction Injection, the confusion can be avoided by applying the annotation directly to the target constructor method, as we've done in Listing 3-36.

Listing 3-36. Constructor Confusion (Annotation)

```
package com.apress.prospring4.ch3.annotation;

import org.springframework.stereotype.Service;
import org.springframework.beans.factory.annotation.Autowired;
import org.springframework.beans.factory.annotation.Value;
import org.springframework.context.support.GenericXmlApplicationContext;

@Service("constructorConfusion")
public class ConstructorConfusion {
    private String someValue;

    public ConstructorConfusion(String someValue) {
        System.out.println("ConstructorConfusion(String) called");
        this.someValue = someValue;
    }

    @Autowired
    public ConstructorConfusion(@Value("90") int someValue) {
        System.out.println("ConstructorConfusion(int) called");
        this.someValue = "Number: " + Integer.toString(someValue);
    }

    public static void main(String[] args) {
        GenericXmlApplicationContext ctx = new GenericXmlApplicationContext();
        ctx.load("classpath:META-INF/spring/app-context-annotation.xml");
        ctx.refresh();

        ConstructorConfusion cc = (ConstructorConfusion) ctx.getBean("constructorConfusion");
        System.out.println(cc);
    }

    public String toString() {
        return someValue;
    }
}
```

By applying the @Autowired annotation to the desired constructor method, Spring will use that method to instantiate the bean and inject the value as specified. As before, you should externalize the value from the configuration.

■ **Note** The @Autowired annotation can be applied to only one of the constructor methods. If you apply the annotation to more than one constructor method, Spring will complain during bootstrapping ApplicationContext.

Using Injection Parameters

In the two previous examples, you saw how to inject other components and values into a bean by using both Setter Injection and Constructor Injection. Spring supports a myriad of options for injection parameters, allowing you to inject not only other components and simple values, but also Java collections, externally defined properties, and even beans in another factory. You can use all of these injection parameter types for both Setter Injection and Constructor Injection by using the corresponding tag under the <property> and <constructor-args> tags, respectively.

Injecting Simple Values

Injecting simple values into your beans is easy. To do so, simply specify the value in the configuration tag, wrapped inside a <value> tag. By default, not only can the <value> tag read String values, but it can also convert these values to any primitive or primitive wrapper class. Listing 3-37 shows a simple bean that has a variety of properties exposed for injection.

Listing 3-37. Injecting Simple Values (XML)

```
package com.apress.prospring4.ch3.xml;

import org.springframework.context.support.GenericXmlApplicationContext;

public class InjectSimple {
    private String name;
    private int age;
    private float height;
    private boolean programmer;
    private Long ageInSeconds;

    public static void main(String[] args) {
        GenericXmlApplicationContext ctx = new GenericXmlApplicationContext();
        ctx.load("classpath:META-INF/spring/app-context-xml.xml");
        ctx.refresh();

        InjectSimple simple = (InjectSimple)ctx.getBean("injectSimple");

        System.out.println(simple);
    }

    public void setAgeInSeconds(Long ageInSeconds) {
        this.ageInSeconds = ageInSeconds;
    }

    public void setProgrammer(boolean programmer) {
        this.programmer = programmer;
    }
```

```java
    public void setAge(int age) {
        this.age = age;
    }

    public void setHeight(float height) {
        this.height = height;
    }

    public void setName(String name) {
        this.name = name;
    }

    public String toString() {
        return "Name :" + name + "\n"
            + "Age:" + age + "\n"
            + "Age in Seconds: " + ageInSeconds + "\n"
            + "Height: " + height + "\n"
            + "Is Programmer?: " + programmer;
    }
}
```

In addition to the properties, the InjectSimple class also defines the main() method that creates an ApplicationContext and then retrieves an InjectSimple bean from Spring. The property values of this bean are then written to the console output. Listing 3-38 shows the configuration (app-context-xml.xml) for this bean.

Listing 3-38. Configuring Simple Value Injection

```xml
<?xml version="1.0" encoding="UTF-8"?>

<beans xmlns="http://www.springframework.org/schema/beans"
    xmlns:xsi="http://www.w3.org/2001/XMLSchema-instance"
    xmlns:p="http://www.springframework.org/schema/p"
    xsi:schemaLocation="http://www.springframework.org/schema/beans
        http://www.springframework.org/schema/beans/spring-beans.xsd">

    <bean id="injectSimple" class="com.apress.prospring4.ch3.xml.InjectSimple"
        p:name="Chris Schaefer" p:age="32" p:height="1.778" p:programmer="true"
        p:ageInSeconds="1009843200"/>
</beans>
```

You can see from Listings 3-37 and 3-38 that it is possible to define properties on your bean that accept String values, primitive values, or primitive wrapper values and then inject values for these properties by using the <value> tag. Here is the output created by running this example as expected:

```
Name: Chris Schaefer
Age: 32
Age in Seconds: 1009843200
Height: 1.778
Is Programmer?: true
```

For annotation-style simple value injection, we can apply the @Value annotation to the bean properties. This time, instead of the setter method, we apply the annotation to the property declaration statement, as you can see in Listing 3-39. (Spring supports the annotation either at the setter method or in the properties.)

Listing 3-39. Injecting Simple Values (Annotation)

```java
package com.apress.prospring4.ch3.annotation;

import org.springframework.beans.factory.annotation.Value;
import org.springframework.context.support.GenericXmlApplicationContext;
import org.springframework.stereotype.Service;

@Service("injectSimple")
public class InjectSimple {
    @Value("Chris Schaefer")
    private String name;

    @Value("32")
    private int age;

    @Value("1.778")
    private float height;

    @Value("true")
    private boolean programmer;

    @Value("1009843200")
    private Long ageInSeconds;

    public static void main(String[] args) {
        GenericXmlApplicationContext ctx = new GenericXmlApplicationContext();
        ctx.load("classpath:META-INF/spring/app-context-annotation.xml");
        ctx.refresh();

        InjectSimple simple = (InjectSimple) ctx.getBean("injectSimple");
        System.out.println(simple);
    }

    public String toString() {
        return "Name: " + name + "\n"
            + "Age: " + age + "\n"
            + "Age in Seconds: " + ageInSeconds + "\n"
            + "Height: " + height + "\n"
            + "Is Programmer?: " + programmer;
    }
}
```

This achieves the same result as the XML configuration.

Injecting Values by Using SpEL

One powerful feature introduced into Spring 3 is the Spring Expression Language (SpEL. SpEL enables you to evaluate an expression dynamically and then use it in Spring's `ApplicationContext`. You can use the result for injection into Spring beans. In this section, we take a look at how to use SpEL to inject properties from other beans, by using the example in the preceding section.

Suppose now we want to externalize the values to be injected into a Spring bean in a configuration class, as in Listing 3-40.

Listing 3-40. Injecting Values by Using SpEL (XML)

```
package com.apress.prospring4.ch3.xml;

public class InjectSimpleConfig {
    private String name = "Chris Schaefer";
    private int age = 32;
    private float height = 1.778f;
    private boolean programmer = true;
    private Long ageInSeconds = 1009843200L;

    public String getName() {
        return name;
    }

    public void setName(String name) {
        this.name = name;
    }

    public int getAge() {
        return age;
    }

    public void setAge(int age) {
        this.age = age;
    }

    public float getHeight() {
        return height;
    }

    public void setHeight(float height) {
        this.height = height;
    }

    public boolean isProgrammer() {
        return programmer;
    }

    public void setIsProgrammer(boolean programmer) {
        this.programmer = programmer;
    }
```

```java
    public Long getAgeInSeconds() {
        return ageInSeconds;
    }

    public void setAgeInSeconds(Long ageInSeconds) {
        this.ageInSeconds = ageInSeconds;
    }
}
```

We can then define the bean in the XML configuration and use SpEL to inject the bean's properties into the dependent bean, as we have done in Listing 3-41 (app-context-xml.xml).

Listing 3-41. Injecting Values by Using SpEL (XML)

```xml
<?xml version="1.0" encoding="UTF-8"?>

<beans xmlns="http://www.springframework.org/schema/beans"
    xmlns:xsi="http://www.w3.org/2001/XMLSchema-instance"
    xmlns:p="http://www.springframework.org/schema/p"
    xsi:schemaLocation="http://www.springframework.org/schema/beans
        http://www.springframework.org/schema/beans/spring-beans.xsd">

    <bean id="injectSimpleConfig" class="com.apress.prospring4.ch3.xml.InjectSimpleConfig"/>

    <bean id="injectSimpleSpel" class="com.apress.prospring4.ch3.xml.InjectSimpleSpel"
        p:name="#{injectSimpleConfig.name}"
        p:age="#{injectSimpleConfig.age}"
        p:height="#{injectSimpleConfig.height}"
        p:programmer="#{injectSimpleConfig.programmer}"
        p:ageInSeconds="#{injectSimpleConfig.ageInSeconds}"/>
</beans>
```

Notice that we use the SpEL #{injectSimpleConfig.name} in referencing the property of the other bean. For the age, we add 1 to the value of the bean to indicate that we can use SpEL to manipulate the property as we see fit and inject it into the dependent bean. Now we can test the configuration with the program in Listing 3-42.

Listing 3-42. Injecting Values by Using SpEL (XML)

```java
package com.apress.prospring4.ch3.xml;

import org.springframework.context.support.GenericXmlApplicationContext;

public class InjectSimpleSpel {
    private String name;
    private int age;
    private float height;
    private boolean programmer;
    private Long ageInSeconds;

    public String getName() {
        return this.name;
    }
```

```java
    public void setName(String name) {
        this.name = name;
    }

    public int getAge() {
        return this.age;
    }

    public void setAge(int age) {
        this.age = age;
    }

    public float getHeight() {
        return this.height;
    }

    public void setHeight(float height) {
        this.height = height;
    }

    public boolean isProgrammer() {
        return this.programmer;
    }

    public void setProgrammer(boolean programmer) {
        this.programmer = programmer;
    }

    public Long getAgeInSeconds() {
        return this.ageInSeconds;
    }

    public void setAgeInSeconds(Long ageInSeconds) {
        this.ageInSeconds = ageInSeconds;
    }

    public String toString() {
        return "Name: " + name + "\n"
            + "Age: " + age + "\n"
            + "Age in Seconds: " + ageInSeconds + "\n"
            + "Height: " + height + "\n"
            + "Is Programmer?: " + programmer;
    }

    public static void main(String[] args) {
        GenericXmlApplicationContext ctx = new GenericXmlApplicationContext();
        ctx.load("classpath:META-INF/spring/app-context-xml.xml");
        ctx.refresh();

        InjectSimpleSpel simple = (InjectSimpleSpel)ctx.getBean("injectSimpleSpel");
        System.out.println(simple);
    }
}
```

The following is the output of the program:

```
Name: Chris Schaefer
Age:33
Age in Seconds: 1009843200
Height: 1.778
Is Programmer?: true
```

When using annotation-style value injection, we just need to substitute the value annotations with the SpEL expressions (see Listing 3-43).

Listing 3-43. Injecting Values by Using SpEL (Annotation)

```java
package com.apress.prospring4.ch3.annotation;

import org.springframework.beans.factory.annotation.Value;
import org.springframework.context.support.GenericXmlApplicationContext;
import org.springframework.stereotype.Service;

@Service("injectSimpleSpel")
public class InjectSimpleSpel {
    @Value("#{injectSimpleConfig.name}")
    private String name;

    @Value("#{injectSimpleConfig.age + 1}")
    private int age;

    @Value("#{injectSimpleConfig.height}")
    private float height;

    @Value("#{injectSimpleConfig.programmer}")
    private boolean programmer;

    @Value("#{injectSimpleConfig.ageInSeconds}")
    private Long ageInSeconds;

    public String toString() {
        return "Name: " + name + "\n"
            + "Age: " + age + "\n"
            + "Age in Seconds: " + ageInSeconds + "\n"
            + "Height: " + height + "\n"
            + "Is Programmer?: " + programmer;
    }

    public static void main(String[] args) {
        GenericXmlApplicationContext ctx = new GenericXmlApplicationContext();
        ctx.load("classpath:META-INF/spring/app-context-xml.xml");
        ctx.refresh();

        InjectSimpleSpel simple = (InjectSimpleSpel)ctx.getBean("injectSimpleSpel");
        System.out.println(simple);
    }
}
```

Listing 3-44 shows the annotation version of the InjectSimpleConfig class.

Listing 3-44. InjectSimpleConfig Class (Annotation)

```
package com.apress.prospring4.ch3.annotation;

import org.springframework.stereotype.Component;

@Component("injectSimpleConfig")
public class InjectSimpleConfig {
    private String name = "John Smith";
    private int age = 35;
    private float height = 1.78f;
    private boolean programmer = true;
    private Long ageInSeconds = 1103760000L;
}
```

In Listing 3-44, instead of the @Service annotation, @Component was used. Basically, using @Component has the same effect as @Service. Both annotations are instructing Spring that the annotated class is a candidate for autodetection using annotation-based configuration and classpath scanning. However, since the InjectSimpleConfig class is storing the application configuration, rather than providing a business service, using @Component makes more sense. Practically, @Service is a specialization of @Component, which indicates that the annotated class is providing a business service to other layers within the application.

Testing the program will produce the same result. Using SpEL, you can access any Spring-managed beans and properties and manipulate them for application use by Spring's support of sophisticated language features and syntax.

Injecting Beans in the Same XML Unit

As you have already seen, it is possible to inject one bean into another by using the ref tag. Listing 3-45 shows a class that exposes a setter to allow a bean to be injected.

Listing 3-45. Injecting Beans

```
package com.apress.prospring4.ch3.xml;

import org.springframework.context.support.GenericXmlApplicationContext;
import com.apress.prospring4.ch3.Oracle;
import com.apress.prospring4.ch3.BookwormOracle;

public class InjectRef {
    private Oracle oracle;

    public void setOracle(Oracle oracle) {
        this.oracle = oracle;
    }

    public static void main(String[] args) {
        GenericXmlApplicationContext ctx = new GenericXmlApplicationContext();
        ctx.load("classpath:META-INF/spring/app-context-xml.xml");
        ctx.refresh();
```

```
        InjectRef injectRef = (InjectRef) ctx.getBean("injectRef");
        System.out.println(injectRef);
    }

    public String toString() {
        return oracle.defineMeaningOfLife();
    }
}
```

To configure Spring to inject one bean into another, you first need to configure two beans: one to be injected and one to be the target of the injection. Once this is done, you simply configure the injection by using the <ref> tag on the target bean. Listing 3-46 shows an example of this configuration (app-context-xml.xml).

Listing 3-46. Configuring Bean Injection

```xml
<?xml version="1.0" encoding="UTF-8"?>

<beans xmlns="http://www.springframework.org/schema/beans"
    xmlns:xsi="http://www.w3.org/2001/XMLSchema-instance"
    xsi:schemaLocation="http://www.springframework.org/schema/beans
        http://www.springframework.org/schema/beans/spring-beans.xsd">

    <bean id="oracle" name="wiseworm" class="com.apress.prospring4.ch3.BookwormOracle"/>

    <bean id="injectRef" class="com.apress.prospring4.ch3.xml.InjectRef">
        <property name="oracle">
            <ref bean="oracle"/>
        </property>
    </bean>
</beans>
```

Running the class in Listing 3-46 produces the following output:

```
Encyclopedias are a waste of money - use the Internet
```

An important point to note is that the type being injected does not have to be the exact type defined on the target; the types just need to be compatible. *Compatible* means that if the declared type on the target is an interface, the injected type must implement this interface. If the declared type is a class, the injected type must be either the same type or a subtype. In this example, the InjectRef class defines the setOracle() method to receive an instance of Oracle, which is an interface, and the injected type is BookwormOracle, a class that implements Oracle. This is a point that causes confusion for some developers, but it is really quite simple. Injection is subject to the same typing rules as any Java code, so as long as you are familiar with how Java typing works, understanding typing in injection is easy.

In the previous example, the id of the bean to inject is specified by using the local attribute of the <ref> tag. As you will see later, in the section "Understanding Bean Naming," you can give a bean more than one name so that you can refer to it using a variety of aliases. When you use the local attribute, it means that the <ref> tag only looks at the bean's id and never at any of its aliases. Moreover, the bean definition should exist in the same XML configuration file. To inject a bean by any name or import one from other XML configuration files, use the bean attribute of the <ref> tag instead of the local attribute. Listing 3-47 shows an alternative configuration for the previous example, using an alternative name for the injected bean.

Listing 3-47. Injecting Using Bean Aliases

```xml
<?xml version="1.0" encoding="UTF-8"?>

<beans xmlns="http://www.springframework.org/schema/beans"
    xmlns:xsi="http://www.w3.org/2001/XMLSchema-instance"
    xsi:schemaLocation="http://www.springframework.org/schema/beans
        http://www.springframework.org/schema/beans/spring-beans.xsd">

    <bean id="oracle" name="wiseworm" class="com.apress.prospring4.ch3.BookwormOracle"/>

    <bean id="injectRef" class="com.apress.prospring4.ch3.xml.InjectRef">
        <property name="oracle">
            <ref bean="wiseworm"/>
        </property>
    </bean>
</beans>
```

In this example, the `oracle` bean is given an alias by using the `name` attribute, and then it is injected into the `injectRef` bean by using this alias in conjunction with the bean attribute of the `<ref>` tag. Don't worry too much about the naming semantics at this point—we discuss this in much more detail later in the chapter. Running the `InjectRef` class again (Listing 3-45) produces the same result as the previous example.

Injection and ApplicationContext Nesting

So far, the beans we have been injecting have been located in the same `ApplicationContext` (and hence the same `BeanFactory`) as the beans they are injected into. However, Spring supports a hierarchical structure for `ApplicationContext` so that one context (and hence the associating `BeanFactory`) is considered the parent of another. By allowing `ApplicationContext`s to be nested, Spring allows you to split your configuration into different files—a godsend on larger projects with lots of beans.

When nesting `ApplicationContext`s, Spring allows beans in what is considered the child context to reference beans in the parent context. `ApplicationContext` nesting using `GenericXmlApplicationContext` is very simple to get a grip on. To nest one `GenericXmlApplicationContext` inside another, simply call the `setParent()` method in the child `ApplicationContext`, as shown in Listing 3-48.

Listing 3-48. Nesting `GenericXmlApplicationContext`

```java
package com.apress.prospring4.ch3;

import org.springframework.context.support.GenericXmlApplicationContext;

public class HierarchicalAppContextUsage {
    public static void main(String[] args) {
        GenericXmlApplicationContext parent = new GenericXmlApplicationContext();
        parent.load("classpath:META-INF/spring/parent.xml");
        parent.refresh();

        GenericXmlApplicationContext child = new GenericXmlApplicationContext();
        child.load("classpath:META-INF/spring/app-context-xml.xml");
        child.setParent(parent);
        child.refresh();
```

```
            SimpleTarget target1 = (SimpleTarget) child.getBean("target1");
            SimpleTarget target2 = (SimpleTarget) child.getBean("target2");
            SimpleTarget target3 = (SimpleTarget) child.getBean("target3");

            System.out.println(target1.getVal());
            System.out.println(target2.getVal());
            System.out.println(target3.getVal());
    }
}
```

Listing 3-49 shows the SimpleTarget class.

Listing 3-49. The SimpleTarget Class

```
package com.apress.prospring4.ch3;

public class SimpleTarget {
    private String val;

    public void setVal(String val) {
        this.val = val;
    }

    public String getVal() {
        return val;
    }
}
```

Inside the configuration file for the child ApplicationContext, referencing a bean in the parent ApplicationContext works exactly like referencing a bean in the child ApplicationContext, unless you have a bean in the child ApplicationContext that shares the same name. In that case, you simply replace the bean attribute of the ref attribute with parent, and you are on your way. Listing 3-50 shows a sample configuration file for the parent BeanFactory (parent.xml).

Listing 3-50. Parent ApplicationContext Configuration

```
<?xml version="1.0" encoding="UTF-8"?>

<beans xmlns="http://www.springframework.org/schema/beans"
    xmlns:xsi="http://www.w3.org/2001/XMLSchema-instance"
    xmlns:c="http://www.springframework.org/schema/c"
    xsi:schemaLocation="http://www.springframework.org/schema/beans
        http://www.springframework.org/schema/beans/spring-beans.xsd">

    <bean id="injectBean" class="java.lang.String" c:_0="Bean In Parent"/>

    <bean id="injectBeanParent" class="java.lang.String" c:_0="Bean In Parent"/>
</beans>
```

As you can see, this configuration simply defines two beans: injectBean and injectBeanParent. Both are String objects with the value Bean In Parent. Listing 3-51 shows a sample configuration for the child ApplicationContext (app-context-xml.xml).

Listing 3-51. Child ApplicationContext Configuration

```xml
<?xml version="1.0" encoding="UTF-8"?>

<beans xmlns="http://www.springframework.org/schema/beans"
    xmlns:xsi="http://www.w3.org/2001/XMLSchema-instance"
    xmlns:c="http://www.springframework.org/schema/c"
    xmlns:p="http://www.springframework.org/schema/p"
    xsi:schemaLocation="http://www.springframework.org/schema/beans
        http://www.springframework.org/schema/beans/spring-beans.xsd">

    <bean id="target1" class="com.apress.prospring4.ch3.SimpleTarget"
        p:val-ref="injectBeanParent"/>

    <bean id="target2" class="com.apress.prospring4.ch3.SimpleTarget"
        p:val-ref="injectBean"/>

    <bean id="target3" class="com.apress.prospring4.ch3.SimpleTarget">
        <property name="val">
            <ref parent="injectBean"/>
        </property>
    </bean>

    <bean id="injectBean" class="java.lang.String" c:_0="Child In Bean"/>
</beans>
```

Notice that we have defined four beans here. The injectBean in this listing is similar to the injectBean in the parent except that the String it represents has a different value, indicating that it is located in the child ApplicationContext.

The target1 bean is using the bean ref attribute to reference the bean named injectBeanParent. Because this bean exists only in the parent BeanFactory, target1 receives a reference to that bean. There are two points of interest here. First, you can use the bean attribute to reference beans in both the child and the parent ApplicationContexts. This makes it easy to reference the beans transparently, allowing you to move beans between configuration files as your application grows. The second point of interest is that you can't use the local attribute to refer to beans in the parent ApplicationContext. The XML parser checks to see that the value of the local attribute exists as a valid element in the same file, preventing it from being used to reference beans in the parent context.

The target2 bean is using the bean ref attribute to reference the injectBean. Because that bean is defined in both ApplicationContexts, the target2 bean receives a reference to the injectBean in its own ApplicationContext.

The target3 bean is using the <ref> tag to reference the injectBean directly in the parent ApplicationContext. Because target3 is using the parent attribute of the <ref> tag, the injectBean declared in the child ApplicationContext is ignored completely.

■ **Note** You may have noticed that, unlike target1 and target2, the target3 bean is not using the p namespace. While the p namespace provides handy shortcuts, it does not provide all the capabilities as when using property tags, such as referencing a parent bean. While we show it as an example, its best to pick either the p namespace or property tags to define your beans, rather than mixing styles (unless absolutely necessary).

Here is the output from running the `HierarchicalAppContextUsage` class (Listing 3-48):

```
Bean In Parent
Bean In Child
Bean In Parent
```

As expected, the `target1` and `target3` beans both get a reference to beans in the parent `ApplicationContext`, whereas the `target2` bean gets a reference to a bean in the child `ApplicationContext`.

Using Collections for Injection

Often your beans need access to collections of objects rather than just individual beans or values. Therefore, it should come as no surprise that Spring allows you to inject a collection of objects into one of your beans. Using the collection is simple: you choose either `<list>`, `<map>`, `<set>`, or `<props>` to represent a `List`, `Map`, `Set`, or `Properties` instance, and then you pass in the individual items just as you would with any other injection. The `<props>` tag allows for only `Strings` to be passed in as the value, because the `Properties` class allows only for property values to be `Strings`. When using `<list>`, `<map>`, or `<set>`, you can use any tag you want when injecting into a property, even another collection tag. This allows you to pass in a `List` of `Maps`, a `Map` of `Sets`, or even a `List` of `Maps` of `Sets` of `Lists`! Listing 3-52 shows a class that can have all four of the collection types injected into it.

Listing 3-52. Collection Injection (XML)

```java
package com.apress.prospring4.ch3.xml;

import java.util.List;
import java.util.Map;
import java.util.Properties;
import java.util.Set;

import org.springframework.context.support.GenericXmlApplicationContext;

public class CollectionInjection {
    private Map<String, Object> map;
    private Properties props;
    private Set set;
    private List list;

    public static void main(String[] args) {
        GenericXmlApplicationContext ctx = new GenericXmlApplicationContext();
        ctx.load("classpath:META-INF/spring/app-context-xml.xml");
        ctx.refresh();

        CollectionInjection instance = (CollectionInjection) ctx.getBean("injectCollection");
        instance.displayInfo();
    }

    public void setList(List list) {
        this.list = list;
    }
```

```java
    public void setSet(Set set) {
        this.set = set;
    }

    public void setMap(Map <String, Object> map) {
        this.map = map;
    }

    public void setProps(Properties props) {
        this.props = props;
    }

    public void displayInfo() {
        System.out.println("Map contents:\n");

        for (Map.Entry<String, Object> entry: map.entrySet()) {
            System.out.println("Key: " + entry.getKey() + " - Value: " + entry.getValue());
        }

        System.out.println("\nProperties contents:\n");)

        for (Map.Entry<Object, Object> entry: props.entrySet()) {
            System.out.println("Key: " + entry.getKey() + " - Value: " + entry.getValue());
        }

        System.out.println("\nSet contents:\n");

        for (Object obj: set) {
            System.out.println("Value: " + obj);
        }
        System.out.println("\nList contents:\n");

        for (Object obj: list) {
            System.out.println("Value: " + obj);
        }
    }
}
```

That is quite a lot of code, but it actually does very little. The main() method retrieves a CollectionInjection bean from Spring and then calls the displayInfo() method. This method just outputs the contents of the Map, Properties, Set, and List instances that will be injected from Spring. In Listing 3-53, you can see the configuration required to inject values for each of the properties on the CollectionInjection class.

Listing 3-53. Configuring Collection Injection (XML)

```xml
<?xml version="1.0" encoding="UTF-8"?>

<beans xmlns="http://www.springframework.org/schema/beans"
    xmlns:xsi="http://www.w3.org/2001/XMLSchema-instance"
    xsi:schemaLocation="http://www.springframework.org/schema/beans
        http://www.springframework.org/schema/beans/spring-beans.xsd">
```

```xml
<bean id="oracle" name="wiseworm" class="com.apress.prospring4.ch3.xml.BookwormOracle"/>

<bean id="injectCollection" class="com.apress.prospring4.ch3.xml.CollectionInjection">
    <property name="map">
        <map>
            <entry key="someValue">
                <value>Hello World!</value>
            </entry>
            <entry key="someBean">
                <ref local="oracle"/>
            </entry>
        </map>
    </property>
    <property name="props">
        <props>
            <prop key="firstName">Chris</prop>
            <prop key="secondName">Schaefer</prop>
        </props>
    </property>
    <property name="set">
        <set>
            <value>Hello World!</value>
            <ref local="oracle"/>
        </set>
    </property>
    <property name="list">
        <list>)
            <value>Hello World!</value>
            <ref local="oracle"/>
        </list>
    </property>
</bean>
</beans>
```

Also notice the declaration of the Map<String,Object> property. For JDK 5 and newer versions, Spring also supports the strongly typed Collection declaration and will perform the conversion from the XML configuration to the corresponding type specified accordingly (app-context-xml.xml).

In this code, you can see that we have injected values into all four setters exposed on the CollectionInjection class. For the map property, we have injected a Map instance by using the <map> tag. Notice that each entry is specified using an <entry> tag, and each has a String key and then an entry value. This entry value can be any value you can inject into a property separately; this example shows the use of the <value> and <ref> tags to add a String value and a bean reference to the Map. For the props property, we use the <props> tag to create an instance of java.util.Properties and populate it using <prop> tags. Notice that although the <prop> tag is keyed in a similar manner to the <entry> tag, you can specify a String value only for each property that goes in the Properties instance.

Both the <list> and <set> tags work in exactly the same way: you specify each element by using any of the individual value tags such as <value> and <ref> that are used to inject a single value into a property. In Listing 3-52, you can see that we have added a String value and a bean reference to both the List and the Set instances.

Here is the output generated by Listing 3-52. As expected, it simply lists the elements added to the collections in the configuration file.

```
Map contents:

Key: someValue - Value: Hello World!
Key: someBean - Value: com.apress.prospring4.ch3.xml.BookwormOracle@6a4f787b

Properties contents:

Key: secondName - Value: Schaefer
Key: firstName - Value: Chris

Set contents:

Value: Hello World!
Value: com.apress.prospring4.ch3.xml.BookwormOracle@6a4f787b

List contents:

Value: Hello World!
Value: com.apress.prospring4.ch3.xml.BookwormOracle@6a4f787b
```

Remember, with the <list>, <map>, and <set> elements, you can employ any of the tags used to set the value of noncollection properties to specify the value of one of the entries in the collection. This is quite a powerful concept, because you are not limited just to injecting collections of primitive values; you can also inject collections of beans or other collections.

Using this functionality, it is much easier to modularize your application and provide different, user-selectable implementations of key pieces of application logic. Consider a system that allows corporate staff to create, proofread, and order their personalized business stationery online. In this system, the finished artwork for each order is sent to the appropriate printer when it is ready for production. The only complication is that some printers want to receive the artwork via e-mail, some via FTP, and others using Secure Copy Protocol (SCP). Using Spring's collection injection, you can create a standard interface for this functionality, as shown in Listing 3-54.

Listing 3-54. The ArtworkSender Interface

```
package com.apress.prospring4.ch3;

public interface ArtworkSender {
    void sendArtwork(String artworkPath, Recipient recipient);
    String getFriendlyName();
    String getShortName();
}
```

In Listing 3-54, the Recipient class is an empty class. From this interface, you can create multiple implementations, each of which is capable of describing itself to a human, such as the ones shown in Listing 3-55.

Listing 3-55. The FtpArtworkSender Class

```
package com.apress.prospring4.ch3;

public class FtpArtworkSender implements ArtworkSender {
    @Override
    public void sendArtwork(String artworkPath, Recipient recipient) {
        // ftp logic here...
    }
```

```
    @Override
    public String getFriendlyName() {
        return "File Transfer Protocol";
    }

    @Override
    public String getShortName() {
        return "ftp";
    }
}
```

Imagine that you then develop an ArtworkManager class that supports all available implementations of the ArtworkSender interface. With the implementations in place, you simply pass a List to your ArtworkManager class, and you are on your way. Using the getFriendlyName() method, you can display a list of delivery options for the system administrator to choose from when you are configuring each stationery template. In addition, your application can remain fully decoupled from the individual implementations if you just code to the ArtworkSender interface. We will leave the implementation of the ArtworkManager class as an exercise for you.

Besides the XML configuration, we can use annotations for collection injection. However, we would also like to externalize the values of the collections into the configuration file for easy maintenance. Listing 3-56 is the configuration of four different Spring beans that mimic the same collection properties of the previous sample (app-context-annotation.xml).

Listing 3-56. Configuring Collection Injection (Annotation)

```xml
<?xml version="1.0" encoding="UTF-8"?>

<beans xmlns="http://www.springframework.org/schema/beans"
       xmlns:xsi="http://www.w3.org/2001/XMLSchema-instance"
       xmlns:context="http://www.springframework.org/schema/context"
       xmlns:util="http://www.springframework.org/schema/util"
       xsi:schemaLocation="http://www.springframework.org/schema/beans
           http://www.springframework.org/schema/beans/spring-beans.xsd
           http://www.springframework.org/schema/context
           http://www.springframework.org/schema/context/spring-context.xsd
           http://www.springframework.org/schema/util
           http://www.springframework.org/schema/util/spring-util.xsd">

    <context:annotation-config/>

    <context:component-scan
            base-package="com.apress.prospring4.ch3.annotation"/>
    <util:map id="map" map-class="java.util.HashMap">
        <entry key="someValue">
            <value>Hello World!</value>
        </entry>
        <entry key="someBean">
            <ref bean="oracle"/>
        </entry>
    </util:map>)
```

```
        <util:properties id="props">
            <prop key="firstName">Chris</prop>
            <prop key="secondName">Schaefer</prop>
        </util:properties>

        <util:set id="set">
            <value>Hello World!</value>
            <ref bean="oracle"/>
        </util:set>

        <util:list id="list">
            <value>Hello World!</value>
            <ref bean="oracle"/>
        </util:list>
</beans>
```

Let's also develop an annotation version of the BookwormOracle class. Listing 3-57 shows the class content.

Listing 3-57. The BookwormOracle Class (Annotation)

```
package com.apress.prospring4.ch3.annotation;

import org.springframework.stereotype.Service;

import com.apress.prospring4.ch3.Oracle;

@Service("oracle")
public class BookwormOracle implements Oracle {
    @Override
    public String defineMeaningOfLife() {
        return "Encyclopedias are a waste of money - use the Internet";
    }
}
```

In the configuration in Listing 3-56, we make use of the util namespace provided by Spring to declare our beans for storing collection properties. It greatly simplifies the configuration, as compared to previous versions of Spring. In the testing class, we inject the previous beans and use the JSR-250 @Resource annotation with the name specified, as in Listing 3-58.

Listing 3-58. Configuring Collection Injection (Annotation) ";

```
package com.apress.prospring4.ch3.annotation;

import java.util.List;
import java.util.Map;
import java.util.Properties;
import java.util.Set;

import org.springframework.stereotype.Service;
import org.springframework.context.support.GenericXmlApplicationContext;

import javax.annotation.Resource;
```

```java
@Service("injectCollection")
public class CollectionInjection {
    @Resource(name="map")
    private Map<String, Object> map;

    @Resource(name="props")
    private Properties props;

    @Resource(name="set")
    private Set set;

    @Resource(name="list")
    private List list;

    public static void main(String[] args) {
        GenericXmlApplicationContext ctx = new GenericXmlApplicationContext();
        ctx.load("classpath:META-INF/spring/app-context-annotation.xml");
        ctx.refresh();

        CollectionInjection instance = (CollectionInjection) ctx.getBean("injectCollection");
        instance.displayInfo();
    }

    public void displayInfo() {
        System.out.println("Map contents:\n");

        for (Map.Entry<String, Object> entry: map.entrySet()) {
            System.out.println("Key: " + entry.getKey() + " - Value: " + entry.getValue());
        }

        System.out.println("\nProperties contents:\n");

        for (Map.Entry<Object, Object> entry: props.entrySet()) {
            System.out.println("Key: " + entry.getKey() + " - Value: " + entry.getValue());
        }

        System.out.println("\nSet contents:\n");

        for (Object obj: set) {
            System.out.println("Value: " + obj); ";
        }
        System.out.println("\nList contents:\n");

        for (Object obj: list) {
            System.out.println("Value: " + obj);
        }
    }
}
```

Run the test program, and you will get the same result as the sample using XML configuration.

■ **Note**   You may wonder why the annotation `@Resource` is used instead of `@Autowired`. It's because the `@Autowired` annotation is semantically defined in a way that it always treats arrays, collections, and maps as sets of corresponding beans, with the target bean type derived from the declared collection value type. So, for example, if a class has an attribute of type `List<Oracle>` and has the `@Autowired` annotation defined, Spring will try to inject all beans of type Oracle within the current `ApplicationContext` into that attribute (instead of the `<util:list>` declared in the configuration file), which will result in either the unexpected dependencies being injected or Spring throwing an exception if no bean of type Oracle was defined. So, for collection type injection, we have to explicitly instruct Spring to perform injection by specifying the bean name, which the `@Resource` annotation supports.

Using Method Injection

Besides Constructor and Setter Injection, another less frequently used DI feature that Spring provides is Method Injection. Spring's Method Injection capabilities come in two loosely related forms, Lookup Method Injection and Method Replacement. Lookup Method Injection provides another mechanism by which a bean can obtain one of its dependencies. Method Replacement allows you to replace the implementation of any method on a bean arbitrarily, without having to change the original source code. To provide these two features, Spring uses the dynamic bytecode enhancement capabilities of CGLIB.

Lookup Method Injection

Lookup Method Injection was added to Spring since version 1.1 to overcome the problems encountered when a bean depends on another bean with a different life cycle—specifically, when a singleton depends on a nonsingleton. In this situation, both Setter and Constructor Injection result in the singleton maintaining a single instance of what should be a nonsingleton bean. In some cases, you will want to have the singleton bean obtain a new instance of the nonsingleton every time it requires the bean in question.

Consider a scenario in which a `LockOpener` class provides the service of opening any locker. The `LockOpener` class relies on a `KeyHelper` class for opening the locker, which was injected into `LockOpener`. However, the design of the `KeyHelper` class involves some internal states that make it not suitable for reuse. Every time the `openLock()` method is called, a new `KeyHelper` instance is required. In this case, `LockOpener` will be a singleton. However, if we inject the `KeyHelper` class by using the normal mechanism, the same instance of the `KeyHelper` class (which was instantiated when Spring performed the injection the first time) will be reused. To make sure that a new instance of the `KeyHelper` instance is passed into the `openLock()` method every time it is invoked, we need to use Lookup Method Injection.

Typically, you can achieve this by having the singleton bean implement the `ApplicationContextAware` interface (we discuss this interface in next chapter). Then, using the `ApplicationContext` instance, the singleton bean can look up a new instance of the nonsingleton dependency every time it needs it. Lookup Method Injection allows the singleton bean to declare that it requires a nonsingleton dependency and that it will receive a new instance of the nonsingleton bean each time it needs to interact with it, without needing to implement any Spring-specific interfaces.

Lookup Method Injection works by having your singleton declare a method, the lookup method, which returns an instance of the nonsingleton bean. When you obtain a reference to the singleton in your application, you are actually receiving a reference to a dynamically created subclass on which Spring has implemented the lookup method. A typical implementation involves defining the lookup method, and thus the bean class, as abstract. This prevents any strange errors from creeping in when you forget to configure the Method Injection and you are working directly against the bean class with the empty method implementation instead of the Spring-enhanced subclass. This topic is quite complex and is best shown by example.

In this example, we create one nonsingleton bean and two singleton beans that both implement the same interface. One of the singletons obtains an instance of the nonsingleton bean by using "traditional" Setter Injection; the other uses Method Injection. Listing 3-59 shows the MyHelper bean, which in our example is the nonsingleton bean.

Listing 3-59. The MyHelper Bean

```
package com.apress.prospring4.ch3;

public class MyHelper {
    public void doSomethingHelpful() {
        // do something!
    }
}
```

This bean is decidedly unexciting, but it serves the purposes of this example perfectly. In Listing 3-60, you can see the DemoBean interface, which is implemented by both of the singleton beans.

Listing 3-60. The DemoBean Interface

```
package com.apress.prospring4.ch3;

public interface DemoBean {
    MyHelper getMyHelper();
    void someOperation();
}
```

This bean has two methods: getMyHelper() and someOperation(). The sample application uses the getMyHelper() method to get a reference to the MyHelper instance and, in the case of the method lookup bean, to perform the actual method lookup. The someOperation() method is a simple method that depends on the MyHelper class to do its processing.

Listing 3-61 shows the StandardLookupDemoBean class, which uses Setter Injection to obtain an instance of the MyHelper class.

Listing 3-61. The StandardLookupDemoBean Class

```
package com.apress.prospring4.ch3;

public class StandardLookupDemoBean implements DemoBean {
    private MyHelper myHelper;

    public void setMyHelper(MyHelper myHelper) {
        this.myHelper = myHelper;
    }

    @Override
    public MyHelper getMyHelper() {
        return this.myHelper;
    }
```

```
    @Override
    public void someOperation() {
        myHelper.doSomethingHelpful();
    }
}
```

This code should all look familiar, but notice that the someOperation() method uses the stored instance of MyHelper to complete its processing. In Listing 3-62, you can see the AbstractLookupDemoBean class, which uses Method Injection to obtain an instance of the MyHelper class.

Listing 3-62. The AbstractLookupDemoBean Class

```
package com.apress.prospring4.ch3;

public abstract class AbstractLookupDemoBean implements DemoBean {
    public abstract MyHelper getMyHelper();

    @Override
    public void someOperation() {
        getMyHelper().doSomethingHelpful();
    }
}
```

Notice that the getMyHelper() method is declared as abstract and that this method is called by the someOperation() method to obtain a MyHelper instance. In Listing 3-63, you can see the configuration code required for this example (app-context-xml.xml).

Listing 3-63. Configuring Lookup Method Injection

```
<?xml version="1.0" encoding="UTF-8"?>

<beans xmlns="http://www.springframework.org/schema/beans"
    xmlns:xsi="http://www.w3.org/2001/XMLSchema-instance"
    xsi:schemaLocation="http://www.springframework.org/schema/beans
        http://www.springframework.org/schema/beans/spring-beans.xsd">

    <bean id="helper" class="com.apress.prospring4.ch3.MyHelper" scope="prototype"/>

    <bean id="abstractLookupBean" class="com.apress.prospring4.ch3.AbstractLookupDemoBean">
        <lookup-method name="getMyHelper" bean="helper"/>
    </bean>

    <bean id="standardLookupBean" class="com.apress.prospring4.ch3.StandardLookupDemoBean">
        <property name="myHelper">
            <ref bean="helper"/>
        </property>
    </bean>
</beans>
```

The configuration for the helper and standardLookupBean beans should look familiar to you by now. For abstractLookupBean, you need to configure the lookup method by using the <lookup-method> tag. The name attribute of the <lookup-method> tag tells Spring the name of the method on the bean that it should override. This method must not accept any arguments, and the return type should be that of the bean you want to return from the method. In this case, the method should return a class of type MyHelper, or its subclasses. The bean attribute tells Spring which bean the lookup method should return.

Listing 3-64 shows the final piece of code for this example.

Listing 3-64. The LookupDemo Class

```
package com.apress.prospring4.ch3;

import org.springframework.context.support.GenericXmlApplicationContext;
import org.springframework.util.StopWatch;

public class LookupDemo {
    public static void main(String[] args) {
        GenericXmlApplicationContext ctx = new GenericXmlApplicationContext();
        ctx.load("classpath:META-INF/spring/app-context-xml.xml");
        ctx.refresh();

        DemoBean abstractBean = (DemoBean) ctx.getBean("abstractLookupBean");
        DemoBean standardBean = (DemoBean) ctx.getBean("standardLookupBean");

        displayInfo(standardBean);
        displayInfo(abstractBean);
    }

    public static void displayInfo(DemoBean bean) {
        MyHelper helper1 = bean.getMyHelper();
        MyHelper helper2 = bean.getMyHelper();

        System.out.println("Helper Instances the Same?: "
            + (helper1 == helper2));

        StopWatch stopWatch = new StopWatch();
        stopWatch.start("lookupDemo");

        for (int x = 0; x < 100000; x++) {
            MyHelper helper = bean.getMyHelper();
            helper.doSomethingHelpful();
        }

        stopWatch.stop();

        System.out.println("100000 gets took " + stopWatch.getTotalTimeMillis() + " ms");
    }
}
```

In this code, you can see that we retrieve the abstractLookupBean (the instantiation of the abstract class is supported only when using Lookup Method Injection, in which Spring will use CGLIB to generate a subclass of the AbstractLookupDemoBean class that overrides the method dynamically) and the standardLookupBean from the GenericXMLApplicationContext and pass each reference to the displayInfo() method. The first part of the displayInfo() method creates two local variables of MyHelper and assigns them each a value by calling getMyHelper() on the bean passed to it. Using these two variables, it writes a message to stdout indicating whether the two references point to the same object. For the abstractLookupBean class, a new instance of MyHelper should be retrieved for each call to getMyHelper(), so the references should not be the same. For standardLookupBean, a single instance of MyHelper is passed to the bean by Setter Injection, and this instance is stored and returned for every call to getMyHelper(), so the two references should be the same.

■ **Note**   The StopWatch class used in the previous example is a utility class available with Spring. You'll find StopWatch very useful when you need to perform simple performance tests and when you are testing your applications.

The final part of the displayInfo() method runs a simple performance test to see which bean is faster. Clearly, standardLookupBean should be faster because it returns the same instance each time, but it is interesting to see the difference.

We can now run the LookupDemo class (Listing 3-64) for testing. Here is the output we received from this example:

```
Helper Instances the Same?: true
100000 gets took 8 ms
Helper Instances the Same?: false
100000 gets took 1039 ms
```

As you can see, the helper instances are, as expected, the same when we use standardLookupBean and different when we use abstractLookupBean. There is a noticeable performance difference when we use standardLookupBean, but that is to be expected.

Considerations for Lookup Method Injection

Lookup Method Injection is intended for use when you want to work with two beans of different life cycles. Avoid the temptation to use Lookup Method Injection when the beans share the same life cycle, especially if they are singletons. Listing 3-64 shows a noticeable difference in performance between using Method Injection to obtain new instances of a dependency and using standard DI to obtain a single instance of a dependency. Also, make sure you don't use Lookup Method Injection needlessly, even when you have beans of different life cycles.

Consider a situation in which you have three singletons that share a dependency in common. You want each singleton to have its own instance of the dependency, so you create the dependency as a nonsingleton, but you are happy with each singleton using the same instance of the collaborator throughout its life. In this case, Setter Injection is the ideal solution; Lookup Method Injection just adds unnecessary overhead.

When you are using Lookup Method Injection, there are a few design guidelines that you should bear in mind when building your classes. In the earlier examples, we declared the lookup method in an interface. The only reason we did this was we did not have to duplicate the displayInfo() method twice for two different bean types. As we mentioned earlier, generally you do not need to pollute a business interface with unnecessary definitions that are used solely for IoC purposes. Another point to bear in mind is that although you don't have to make your lookup method abstract, doing so prevents you from forgetting to configure the lookup method and then using a blank implementation by accident.

Method Replacement

Although the Spring documentation classifies method replacement as a form of injection, it is very different from what you have seen so far. So far, we have used injection purely to supply beans with their collaborators. Using *method replacement*, you can replace the implementation of any method on any beans arbitrarily without having to change the source of the bean you are modifying. For example, you have a third-party library that you use in your Spring application, and you need to change the logic of a certain method. However, you are not able to change the source code because it was provided by a third party, so one solution is to use method replacement to just replace the logic for that method with your own implementation.

Internally, you achieve this by creating a subclass of the bean class dynamically. You use CGLIB and redirect calls to the method you want to replace to another bean that implements the MethodReplacer interface.

In Listing 3-65, you can see a simple bean that declares two overloads of the formatMessage() method.

Listing 3-65. The ReplacementTarget Class

```
package com.apress.prospring4.ch3;

public class ReplacementTarget {
    public String formatMessage(String msg) {
        return "<h1>" + msg + "</h1>";
    }

    public String formatMessage(Object msg) {
        return "<h1>" + msg + "</h1>";
    }
}
```

You can replace any of the methods on the ReplacementTarget class by using Spring's method replacement functionality. In this example, we show you how to replace the formatMessage(String) method, and we also compare the performance of the replaced method with that of the original.

To replace a method, you first need to create an implementation of the MethodReplacer interface; this is shown in Listing 3-66.

Listing 3-66. Implementing MethodReplacer

```
package com.apress.prospring4.ch3;

import java.lang.reflect.Method;

import org.springframework.beans.factory.support.MethodReplacer;

public class FormatMessageReplacer implements MethodReplacer {
    @Override
    public Object reimplement(Object argo, Method method, Object[] args)
            throws Throwable {
        if (isFormatMessageMethod(method)) {
            String msg = (String) args[0];
```

77

```
            return "<h2>" + msg + "</h2>";
        } else {
            throw new IllegalArgumentException("Unable to reimplement method "
                    + method.getName());
        }
    }

    private boolean isFormatMessageMethod(Method method) {
        if (method.getParameterTypes().length != 1) {
            return false;
        }

        if (!("formatMessage".equals(method.getName()))) {
            return false;
        }

        if (method.getReturnType() != String.class) {
            return false;
        }

        if (method.getParameterTypes()[0] != String.class) {
            return false;
        }

        return true;
    }
}
```

The MethodReplacer interface has a single method, reimplement(), that you must implement. Three arguments are passed to reimplement(): the bean on which the original method was invoked, a Method instance that represents the method that is being overridden, and the array of arguments passed to the method. The reimplement() method should return the result of your reimplemented logic, and, obviously, the type of the return value should be compatible with the return type of the method you are replacing. In Listing 3-64, the FormatMessageReplacer first checks to see whether the method that is being overridden is the formatMessage(String) method; if so, it executes the replacement logic—in this case, surrounding the message with <h2> and </h2>—and returns the formatted message to the caller. It is not necessary to check whether the message is correct, but this can be useful if you are using a few MethodReplacers with similar arguments. Using a check helps prevent a situation in which a different MethodReplacer with compatible arguments and return types is used accidentally.

Listing 3-67 shows an ApplicationContext that defines two beans of type ReplacementTarget—one has the formatMessage(String) method replaced, and the other does not (app-context-xml.xml).

Listing 3-67. Configuring Method Replacement

```xml
<?xml version="1.0" encoding="UTF-8"?>

<beans xmlns="http://www.springframework.org/schema/beans"
    xmlns:xsi="http://www.w3.org/2001/XMLSchema-instance"
    xsi:schemaLocation="http://www.springframework.org/schema/beans
        http://www.springframework.org/schema/beans/spring-beans.xsd">

    <bean id="methodReplacer" class="com.apress.prospring4.ch3.FormatMessageReplacer"/>
```

```xml
<bean id="replacementTarget" class="com.apress.prospring4.ch3.ReplacementTarget">
    <replaced-method name="formatMessage" replacer="methodReplacer">
        <arg-type>String</arg-type>
    </replaced-method>
</bean>

<bean id="standardTarget" class="com.apress.prospring4.ch3.ReplacementTarget"/>
</beans>
```

As you can see, the MethodReplacer implementation is declared as a bean in ApplicationContext. We then use the <replaced-method> tag to replace the formatMessage(String) method on the replacementTargetBean. The name attribute of the <replaced-method> tag specifies the name of the method to replace, and the replacer attribute is used to specify the name of the MethodReplacer bean that we want to replace the method implementation. In cases where there are overloaded methods such as in the ReplacementTarget class, you can use the <arg-type> tag to specify the method signature to match. The <arg-type> supports pattern matching, so String is matched to java.lang.String and also to java.lang.StringBuffer.

Listing 3-68 shows a simple demo application that retrieves both the standardTarget and replacementTarget beans from ApplicationContext, executes their formatMessage(String) methods, and then runs a simple performance test to see which is faster.

Listing 3-68. Method Replacement in Action

```java
package com.apress.prospring4.ch3;

import org.springframework.context.support.GenericXmlApplicationContext;
import org.springframework.util.StopWatch;

public class MethodReplacementExample {
    public static void main(String[] args) {
        GenericXmlApplicationContext ctx = new GenericXmlApplicationContext();
        ctx.load("classpath:META-INF/spring/app-context-xml.xml");
        ctx.refresh();

        ReplacementTarget replacementTarget = (ReplacementTarget) ctx
                .getBean("replacementTarget");
        ReplacementTarget standardTarget = (ReplacementTarget) ctx
                .getBean("standardTarget");

        displayInfo(replacementTarget);
        displayInfo(standardTarget);
    }

    private static void displayInfo(ReplacementTarget target) {
        System.out.println(target.formatMessage("Hello World!"));

        StopWatch stopWatch = new StopWatch();
        stopWatch.start("perfTest");

        for (int x = 0; x < 1000000; x++) {
            String out = target.formatMessage("foo");
        }
```

```
        stopWatch.stop();

        System.out.println("1000000 invocations took: "
                + stopWatch.getTotalTimeMillis() + " ms");
    }
}
```

You should be very familiar with this code by now, so we won't go into detail. On our machine, running this example yields the following output:

```
Hello World!</h2>
1000000 invocations took: 396 ms
Hello World!</h1>
1000000 invocations took: 18 ms
```

As expected, the output from the `replacementTarget` bean reflects the overridden implementation that the `MethodReplacer` provides. Interestingly, though, the dynamically replaced method is many times slower than the statically defined method. Removing the check for a valid method in `MethodReplacer` made a negligible difference across a number of executions, so we can conclude that most of the overhead is in the CGLIB subclass.

When to Use Method Replacement

Method replacement can prove quite useful in a variety of circumstances, especially when you want to override only a particular method for a single bean rather than all beans of the same type. With that said, we still prefer using standard Java mechanisms for overriding methods rather than depending on runtime bytecode enhancement.

If you are going to use method replacement as part of your application, we recommend you use one `MethodReplacer` per method or group of overloaded methods. Avoid the temptation to use a single `MethodReplacer` for lots of unrelated methods; this results in extra unnecessary `String` comparisons while your code works out which method it should reimplement. We have found that performing simple checks to ensure that `MethodReplacer` is working with the correct method is useful and doesn't add too much overhead to your code. If you are really concerned about performance, you can simply add a Boolean property to your `MethodReplacer`, which allows you to turn the check on and off using Dependency Injection.

Understanding Bean Naming

Spring supports quite a complex bean-naming structure that allows you the flexibility to handle many situations. Every bean must have at least one name that is unique within the containing `ApplicationContext`. Spring follows a simple resolution process to determine what name is used for the bean. If you give the <bean> tag an `id` attribute, the value of that attribute is used as the name. If no `id` attribute is specified, Spring looks for a `name` attribute, and if one is defined, it uses the first name defined in the `name` attribute. (We say the *first name* because it is possible to define multiple names within the `name` attribute; this is covered in more detail shortly.) If neither the `id` nor the `name` attribute is specified, Spring uses the bean's class name as the name, provided, of course, that no other bean is using the same class name. In case multiple beans without an ID or the name defined are using the same class name, Spring will throw an exception (of type `org.springframework.beans.factory.NoSuchBeanDefinitionException`) on injection during `ApplicationContext` initialization. Listing 3-69 shows a sample configuration that uses all three naming schemes.

Listing 3-69. Bean Naming

```
<bean id="string1" class="java.lang.String"/>
<bean name="string2" class="java.lang.String"/>
<bean class="java.lang.String"/>
```

Each of these approaches is equally valid from a technical point of view, but which is the best choice for your application? To start with, avoid using the automatic name by class behavior. This doesn't allow you much flexibility to define multiple beans of the same type, and it is much better to define your own names. That way, if Spring changes the default behavior in the future, your application continues to work. When choosing whether to use id or name, always use id to specify the bean's default name. Prior to Spring 3.1, the id attribute is the same as the XML identity (that is, xsd:ID), which places a restriction in the characters that you can use. As of Spring 3.1, Spring uses xsd:String for the id attribute, so the previous restriction on the characters that you can use is gone. However, Spring will continue to ensure that the id is unique across the entire ApplicationContext. As a general practice, you should give your bean a name by using the id attribute and then associate the bean with other names by using name aliasing, as discussed in the next section.

Bean Name Aliasing

Spring allows a bean to have more than one name. You can achieve this by specifying a space-, comma-, or semicolon-separated list of names in the name attribute of the bean's <bean> tag. You can do this in place of, or in conjunction with, using the id attribute.

Besides using the name attribute, you can use the <alias> tag for defining aliases for Spring bean names. Listing 3-70 shows a simple <bean> configuration that defines multiple names for a single bean (app-context-xml.xml).

Listing 3-70. Configuring Multiple Bean Names

```xml
<?xml version="1.0" encoding="UTF-8"?>

<beans xmlns="http://www.springframework.org/schema/beans"
    xmlns:xsi="http://www.w3.org/2001/XMLSchema-instance"
    xsi:schemaLocation="http://www.springframework.org/schema/beans
        http://www.springframework.org/schema/beans/spring-beans.xsd">

    <bean id="name1" name="name2 name3,name4;name5" class="java.lang.String"/>
    <alias name="name1" alias="name6"/>
</beans>
```

As you can see, we have defined six names: one using the id attribute and the other four as a list using all allowed bean name delimiters in the name attribute (this is just for demonstration purposes and is not recommended for real-life development). In real-life development, it's recommended you standardize on the delimiter to use for separating bean names' declarations within your application. One more alias was defined using the <alias> tag. Listing 3-71 shows a sample Java routine that grabs the same bean from the ApplicationContext six times using different names and verifies that they are the same bean.

Listing 3-71. Accessing Beans by Using Aliases

```java
package com.apress.prospring4.ch3.xml;

import org.springframework.context.support.GenericXmlApplicationContext;

public class BeanNameAliasing {
    public static void main(String[] args) {
        GenericXmlApplicationContext ctx = new GenericXmlApplicationContext();
        ctx.load("classpath:META-INF/spring/app-context-xml.xml");
        ctx.refresh();
```

```
        String s1 = (String) ctx.getBean("name1");
        String s2 = (String) ctx.getBean("name2");
        String s3 = (String) ctx.getBean("name3");
        String s4 = (String) ctx.getBean("name4");
        String s5 = (String) ctx.getBean("name5");
        String s6 = (String) ctx.getBean("name6");

        System.out.println((s1 == s2));
        System.out.println((s2 == s3));
        System.out.println((s3 == s4));
        System.out.println((s4 == s5));
        System.out.println((s5 == s6));
    }
}
```

This code prints true five times to the console output for the configuration contained in Listing 3-70, verifying that the beans accessed using different names are, in fact, the same bean.

You can retrieve a list of the bean aliases by calling ApplicationContext.getAliases(String) and passing in any one of the bean's names or ID. The list of aliases, other than the one you specified, will then be returned as a String array.

Bean name aliasing is a strange beast because it is not something you tend to use when you are building a new application. If you are going to have many other beans inject another bean, they may as well use the same name to access that bean. However, as your application goes into production and maintenance work gets carried out, modifications are made, and so on, bean name aliasing becomes more useful.

Consider the following scenario: you have an application in which 50 beans, configured using Spring, all require an implementation of the Foo interface. Twenty-five of the beans use the StandardFoo implementation with the bean name standardFoo, and the other 25 use the SuperFoo implementation with the superFoo bean name. Six months after you put the application into production, you decide to move the first 25 beans to the SuperFoo implementation. To do this, you have three options:

- The first is to change the implementation class of the standardFoo bean to SuperFoo. The drawback of this approach is that you have two instances of the SuperFoo class lying around when you really need only one. In addition, you now have two beans to make changes to when the configuration changes.

- The second option is to update the injection configuration for the 25 beans that are changing, which changes the beans' names from standardFoo to superFoo. This approach is not the most elegant way to proceed—you could perform a find and replace, but then rolling back your changes when management isn't happy means retrieving an old version of your configuration from your version control system.

- The third, and most ideal, approach is to remove (or comment out) the definition for the standardFoo bean and make standardFoo an alias to superFoo. This change requires minimal effort, and restoring the system to its previous configuration is just as simple.

Understanding Bean Instantiation Mode

By default, all beans in Spring are singletons. This means Spring maintains a single instance of the bean, all dependent objects use the same instance, and all calls to ApplicationContext.getBean() return the same instance. We demonstrated this previously in Listing 3-71, where we were able to use identity comparison (==) rather than the equals() comparison to check whether the beans were the same.

The term *singleton* is used interchangeably in Java to refer to two distinct concepts: an object that has a single instance within the application, and the Singleton design pattern. We refer to the first concept as *singleton* and to the Singleton pattern as *Singleton*. The Singleton design pattern was popularized in the seminal *Design Patterns: Elements of Reusable Object-Oriented Software* by Erich Gamma, et al. (Addison-Wesley, 1994). The problem arises when people confuse the need for singleton instances with the need to apply the Singleton pattern. Listing 3-72 shows a typical implementation of the Singleton pattern in Java.

Listing 3-72. The Singleton Design Pattern

```
package com.apress.prospring4.ch3;

public class Singleton {
    private static Singleton instance;

    static {
        instance = new Singleton();
    }

    public static Singleton getInstance() {
        return instance;
    }
}
```

This pattern achieves its goal of allowing you to maintain and access a single instance of a class throughout your application, but it does so at the expense of increased coupling. Your application code must always have explicit knowledge of the Singleton class in order to obtain the instance—completely removing the ability to code to interfaces. In reality, the Singleton pattern is actually two patterns in one. The first, and desired, pattern involves maintenance of a single instance of an object. The second, and less desirable, is a pattern for object lookup that completely removes the possibility of using interfaces. Using the Singleton pattern also makes it very difficult to swap out implementations arbitrarily, because most objects that require the Singleton instance access the Singleton object directly. This can cause all kinds of headaches when you are trying to unit test your application because you are unable to replace the Singleton with a mock for testing purposes.

Fortunately, with Spring you can take advantage of the singleton instantiation model without having to work around the Singleton design pattern. All beans in Spring are, by default, created as Singleton instances, and Spring uses the same instances to fulfill all requests for that bean. Of course, Spring is not just limited to use of the Singleton instance; it can still create a new instance of the bean to satisfy every dependency and every call to getBean(). It does all of this without any impact on your application code, and for this reason, we like to refer to Spring as being *instantiation mode agnostic*. This is a very powerful concept. If you start off with an object that is a singleton but then discover it is not really suited to multithread access, you can change it to a nonsingleton (prototype) without affecting any of your application code.

■ **Note**   Although changing the instantiation mode of your bean won't affect your application code, it does cause some problems if you rely on Spring's life-cycle interfaces. We cover this in more detail in Chapter 4.

Changing the instantiation mode from singleton to nonsingleton is simple (see Listing 3-73, the app-context-xml.xml file).

Listing 3-73. Nonsingleton Bean Configuration

```xml
<?xml version="1.0" encoding="UTF-8"?>

<beans xmlns="http://www.springframework.org/schema/beans"
    xmlns:xsi="http://www.w3.org/2001/XMLSchema-instance"
    xmlns:c="http://www.springframework.org/schema/c"
    xsi:schemaLocation="http://www.springframework.org/schema/beans
        http://www.springframework.org/schema/beans/spring-beans.xsd">

    <bean id="nonSingleton" class="java.lang.String" scope="prototype"
        c:_0="Chris Schaefer"/>
</beans>
```

As you can see, the only difference between this bean declaration and any of the declarations you have seen so far is that we add the scope attribute and set the value to prototype. Spring defaults the scope to value singleton. The prototype scope instructs Spring to instantiate a new instance of the bean every time a bean instance is requested by the application. Listing 3-74 shows the effect this setting has on your application.

Listing 3-74. Nonsingleton Beans in Action

```java
package com.apress.prospring4.ch3;

import org.springframework.context.support.GenericXmlApplicationContext;

public class NonSingleton {
    public static void main(String[] args) {
            GenericXmlApplicationContext ctx = new GenericXmlApplicationContext();
            ctx.load("classpath:META-INF/spring/app-context-xml.xml");
            ctx.refresh();

            String s1 = (String) ctx.getBean("nonSingleton");
            String s2 = (String) ctx.getBean("nonSingleton");

            System.out.println("Identity Equal?: " + (s1 ==s2));
            System.out.println("Value Equal:? " + s1.equals(s2));
            System.out.println(s1);
            System.out.println(s2);
    }
}
```

Running this example gives you the following output:

```
Identity Equal?:  false
Value Equal:? true
Chris Schaefer
Chris Schaefer
```

You can see from this that although the values of the two String objects are clearly equal, the identities are not, even though both instances were retrieved using the same bean name.

Choosing an Instantiation Mode

In most scenarios, it is quite easy to see which instantiation mode is suitable. Typically, we find that singleton is the default mode for our beans. In general, singletons should be used in the following scenarios:

- *Shared objects with no state*: You have an object that maintains no state and has many dependent objects. Because you do not need synchronization if there is no state, you do not need to create a new instance of the bean each time a dependent object needs to use it for some processing.

- *Shared object with read-only state*: This is similar to the previous point, but you have some read-only state. In this case, you still do not need synchronization, so creating an instance to satisfy each request for the bean is just adding overhead.

- *Shared object with shared state*: If you have a bean that has state that must be shared, singleton is the ideal choice. In this case, ensure that your synchronization for state writes is as granular as possible.

- *High-throughput objects with writable state*: If you have a bean that is used a great deal in your application, you may find that keeping a singleton and synchronizing all write access to the bean state allows for better performance than constantly creating hundreds of instances of the bean. When using this approach, try to keep the synchronization as granular as possible without sacrificing consistency. You will find that this approach is particularly useful when your application creates a large number of instances over a long period of time, when your shared object has only a small amount of writable state, or when the instantiation of a new instance is expensive.

You should consider using nonsingletons in the following scenarios:

- *Objects with writable state*: If you have a bean that has a lot of writable state, you may find that the cost of synchronization is greater than the cost of creating a new instance to handle each request from a dependent object.

- *Objects with private state*: In some cases, your dependent objects need a bean that has private state so that they can conduct their processing separately from other objects that depend on that bean. In this case, singleton is clearly not suitable, and you should use nonsingleton.

The main positive you gain from Spring's instantiation management is that your applications can immediately benefit from the lower memory usage associated with singletons, with very little effort on your part. Then, if you find that singleton mode does not meet the needs of your application, it is a trivial task to modify your configuration to use nonsingleton mode.

Implementing Bean Scopes

In addition to the singleton and prototype scopes, other scopes exist when defining a Spring bean for more-specific purposes. You can also implement your own custom scope and register it in Spring's `ApplicationContext`. The following bean scopes are supported as of version 4:

- *Singleton*: The default singleton scope. Only one object will be created per Spring IoC container.

- *Prototype*: A new instance will be created by Spring when requested by the application.

- *Request*: For web application use. When using Spring MVC for web applications, beans with request scope will be instantiated for every HTTP request and then destroyed when the request is completed.

- *Session*: For web application use. When using Spring MVC for web applications, beans with session scope will be instantiated for every HTTP session and then destroyed when the session is over.

- *Global session*: For portlet-based web applications. The global session scope beans can be shared among all portlets within the same Spring MVC–powered portal application.

- *Thread*: A new bean instance will be created by Spring when requested by a new thread, while for the same thread, the same bean instance will be returned. Note that this scope is not registered by default.

- *Custom*: Custom bean scope that can be created by implementing the interface `org.springframework.beans.factory.config.Scope` and registering the custom scope in Spring's configuration (for XML, use the class `org.springframework.beans.factory.config.CustomScopeConfigurer`).

Resolving Dependencies

During normal operation, Spring is able to resolve dependencies by simply looking at your configuration file or annotations in your classes. In this way, Spring can ensure that each bean is configured in the correct order so that each bean has its dependencies correctly configured. If Spring did not perform this and just created the beans and configured them in any order, a bean could be created and configured before its dependencies. This is obviously not what you want and would cause all sorts of problems within your application.

Unfortunately, Spring is not aware of any dependencies that exist between beans in your code. For instance, take one bean, called beanA, which obtains an instance of another bean, called bean B, in the constructor via a call to getBean(). For example, in the constructor of beanA, you get an instance of beanB by calling `ctx.getBean("beanB")`, without asking Spring to inject the dependency for you. In this case, Spring is unaware that beanA depends on beanB, and, as a result, it may instantiate beanA before beanB. You can provide Spring with additional information about your bean dependencies using the depends-on attribute of the <bean> tag. Listing 3-75 shows how the scenario for beanA and beanB would be configured.

Listing 3-75. Manually Defining Dependencies

```
<bean id="beanA" class="com.apress.prospring4.ch3.BeanA" depends-on="beanB"/>
<bean id="beanB" class="com.apress.prospring4.ch3.BeanB"/>
```

In this configuration, we are asserting that bean beanA depends on bean beanB. Spring takes this into consideration when instantiating the beans and ensures that beanB is created before beanA.

When developing your applications, avoid designing them to use this feature; instead, define your dependencies by means of Setter and Constructor Injection contracts. However, if you are integrating Spring with legacy code, you may find that the dependencies defined in the code require you to provide extra information to the Spring Framework.

Autowiring Your Bean

In all the examples so far, we have had to define explicitly, via the configuration file, how the individual beans are wired together. If you don't like having to wire all your components together, you can have Spring attempt to do so automatically. By default, autowiring is disabled. To enable it, you specify which method of autowiring you want to use by using the `autowire` attribute of the bean you want to autowire.

Modes of Autowiring

Spring supports five modes for autowiring: byName, byType, constructor, default, and no (which is the default). When using byName autowiring, Spring attempts to wire each property to a bean of the same name. So, if the target bean has a property named foo and a foo bean is defined in the ApplicationContext, the foo bean is assigned to the foo property of the target.

When using byType autowiring, Spring attempts to wire each of the properties on the target bean by automatically using a bean of the same type in ApplicationContext. So, if you have a property of type String on the target bean, and a bean of type String in ApplicationContext, then Spring wires the String bean to the target bean's String property. If you have more than one bean of the same type, in this case String, in the same ApplicationContext, then Spring is unable to decide which one to use for the autowiring and throws an exception (of type org.springframework.beans.factory.NoSuchBeanDefinitionException).

The constructor autowiring mode functions just like byType wiring, except that it uses constructors rather than setters to perform the injection. Spring attempts to match the greatest numbers of arguments it can in the constructor. So, if your bean has two constructors, one that accepts a String and one that accepts a String and an Integer, and you have both a String and an Integer bean in your ApplicationContext, Spring uses the two-argument constructor.

In default mode, Spring will choose between constructor and byType modes automatically. If your bean has a default (no-arguments) constructor, Spring uses byType; otherwise, it uses constructor.

Listing 3-76 shows a simple configuration that autowires three beans of the same type by using each of the modes (app-context-xml.xml).

Listing 3-76. Configuring Autowiring

```
<?xml version="1.0" encoding="UTF-8"?>

<beans xmlns="http://www.springframework.org/schema/beans"
    xmlns:xsi="http://www.w3.org/2001/XMLSchema-instance"
    xsi:schemaLocation="http://www.springframework.org/schema/beans
        http://www.springframework.org/schema/beans/spring-beans.xsd">

    <bean id="foo" class="com.apress.prospring4.ch3.Foo"/>
    <bean id="bar1" class="com.apress.prospring4.ch3.Bar"/>

    <bean id="targetByName" autowire="byName" class="com.apress.prospring4.ch3.xml.Target"
        lazy-init="true"/>

    <bean id="targetByType" autowire="byType" class="com.apress.prospring4.ch3.xml.Target"
        lazy-init="true"/>

    <bean id="targetConstructor" autowire="constructor"
        class="com.apress.prospring4.ch3.xml.Target" lazy-init="true"/>
</beans>
```

This configuration should look very familiar to you now. Foo and Bar are empty classes. Notice that each of the Target beans has a different value for the autowire attribute. Moreover, the lazy-init attribute is set to true to inform Spring to instantiate the bean only when it is first requested, rather than at startup, so that we can output the result in the correct place in the testing program. Listing 3-77 shows a simple Java application that retrieves each of the Target beans from ApplicationContext.

Listing 3-77. Autowiring Collaborators

```
package com.apress.prospring4.ch3.xml;

import org.springframework.context.support.GenericXmlApplicationContext;
import com.apress.prospring4.ch3.Foo;
import com.apress.prospring4.ch3.Bar;

public class Target {
    private Foo foo;
    private Foo foo2;
    private Bar bar;

    public Target() {
    }

    public Target(Foo foo) {
        System.out.println("Target(Foo) called");
    }

    public Target(Foo foo, Bar bar) {
        System.out.println("Target(Foo, Bar) called");
    }

    public void setFoo(Foo foo) {
        this.foo = foo;
        System.out.println("Property foo set");
    }

    public void setFoo2(Foo foo) {
        this.foo2 = foo;
        System.out.println("Property foo2 set");
    }

    public void setBar(Bar bar) {
        this.bar = bar;
        System.out.println("Property bar set");
    }

    public static void main(String[] args) {
        GenericXmlApplicationContext ctx = new GenericXmlApplicationContext();
        ctx.load("classpath:META-INF/spring/app-context-xml.xml");
        ctx.refresh();

        Target t = null;

        System.out.println("Using byName:\n");
        t = (Target) ctx.getBean("targetByName");
```

```
        System.out.println("\nUsing byType:\n");
        t = (Target) ctx.getBean("targetByType");

        System.out.println("\nUsing constructor:\n");
        t = (Target) ctx.getBean("targetConstructor");

    }
}
```

In this code, you can see that the Target class has three constructors: a no-argument constructor, a constructor that accepts a Foo instance, and a constructor that accepts a Foo and a Bar instance. In addition to these constructors, the Target bean has three properties: two of type Foo and one of type Bar. Each of these properties and constructors writes a message to console output when it is called. The main() method simply retrieves each of the Target beans declared in ApplicationContext, triggering the autowire process. Here is the output from running this example:

```
Using byName:

Property foo set

Using byType:

Property bar set
Property foo set
Property foo2 set

Using constructor:

Target(Foo, Bar) called
```

From the output, you can see that when Spring uses byName, the only property that is set is foo, because this is the only property with a corresponding bean entry in the configuration file. When using byType, Spring sets the value of all three properties. The foo and foo2 properties are set by the foo bean, and the bar property is set by the bar1 bean. When using constructor, Spring uses the two-argument constructor, because Spring can provide beans for both arguments and does not need to fall back to another constructor.

When to Use Autowiring

In most cases, the answer to the question of whether you should use autowiring is definitely no! Autowiring can save you time in small applications, but in many cases, it leads to bad practices and is inflexible in large applications. Using byName seems like a good idea, but it may lead you to give your classes artificial property names so that you can take advantage of the autowiring functionality. The whole idea behind Spring is that you can create your classes as you like and have Spring work for you, not the other way around. You may be tempted to use byType until you realize that you can have only one bean for each type in your ApplicationContext—a restriction that is problematic when you need to maintain beans with different configurations of the same type. The same argument applies to the use of constructor autowiring.

In some cases, autowiring can save you time, but it does not really take that much extra effort to define your wiring explicitly, and you benefit from explicit semantics and full flexibility on property naming and on how many instances of the same type you manage. For any nontrivial application, steer clear of autowiring at all costs.

Setting Bean Inheritance

In some cases, you many need multiple definitions of beans that are the same type or implement a shared interface. This can become problematic if you want these beans to share some configuration settings but not others. The process of keeping the shared configuration settings in sync is quite error-prone, and on large projects, doing so can be quite time-consuming. To get around this, Spring allows you to provide a `<bean>` definition that inherits its property settings from another bean in the same `ApplicationContext`. You can override the values of any properties on the child bean as required, which allows you to have full control, but the parent bean can provide each of your beans with a base configuration. Listing 3-78 shows a simple configuration with two beans, one of which is the child of the other (`app-context-xml.xml`).

Listing 3-78. Configuring Bean Inheritance

```xml
<?xml version="1.0" encoding="UTF-8"?>

<beans xmlns="http://www.springframework.org/schema/beans"
    xmlns:xsi="http://www.w3.org/2001/XMLSchema-instance"
    xmlns:p="http://www.springframework.org/schema/p"
    xsi:schemaLocation="http://www.springframework.org/schema/beans
        http://www.springframework.org/schema/beans/spring-beans.xsd">

    <bean id="inheritParent" class="com.apress.prospring4.ch3.xml.SimpleBean"
        p:name="Chris Schaefer" p:age="32"/>

    <bean id="inheritChild" class="com.apress.prospring4.ch3.xml.SimpleBean"
        parent="inheritParent" p:age="33"/>
</beans>
```

In this code, you can see that the `<bean>` tag for the `inheritChild` bean has an extra attribute, `parent`, which indicates that Spring should consider the `inheritParent` bean the parent of the bean. In case you don't want a parent bean definition to become available for lookup from `ApplicationContext`, you can add the attribute `abstract="true"` in the `<bean>` tag when declaring the parent bean. Because the `inheritChild` bean has its own value for the age property, Spring passes this value to the bean. However, `inheritChild` has no value for the name property, so Spring uses the value given to the `inheritParent` bean. Listing 3-79 shows the code for the `SimpleBean` class used in a previous configuration.

Listing 3-79. The SimpleBean Class

```java
package com.apress.prospring4.ch3.xml;

import org.springframework.context.support.GenericXmlApplicationContext;

public class SimpleBean {
    private String name;
    private int age;

    public static void main(String[] args) {
        GenericXmlApplicationContext ctx = new GenericXmlApplicationContext();
        ctx.load("classpath:META-INF/spring/app-context-xml.xml");
        ctx.refresh();
```

```
        SimpleBean parent = (SimpleBean) ctx.getBean("inheritParent");
        SimpleBean child = (SimpleBean) ctx.getBean("inheritChild");

        System.out.println("Parent:\n" + parent);
        System.out.println("Child:\n" + child);
    }

    public void setName(String name) {
        this.name = name;
    }

    public void setAge(int age) {
        this.age = age;
    }

    public String toString() {
        return "Name: " + name + "\n" + "Age: " + age;
    }
}
```

As you can see, the main() method of the SimpleBean class grabs both the inheritChild and inheritParent beans from ApplicationContext and writes the contents of their properties to stdout. Here is the output from this example:

```
Parent:
Name: Chris Schaefer
Age: 32
Child:
Name: Chris Schaefer
Age: 33
```

As expected, the inheritChild bean inherited the value for its name property from the inheritParent bean but was able to provide its own value for the age property.

Child beans inherit both constructor arguments and property values from the parent beans, so you can use both styles of injection with bean inheritance. This level of flexibility makes bean inheritance a powerful tool for building applications with more than a handful of bean definitions. If you are declaring a lot of beans of the same value with shared property values, avoid the temptation to use copy and paste to share the values; instead, set up an inheritance hierarchy in your configuration.

When you are using inheritance, remember that bean inheritance does not have to match a Java inheritance hierarchy. It is perfectly acceptable to use bean inheritance on five beans of the same type. Think of bean inheritance as more like a templating feature than an inheritance feature. Be aware, however, that if you are changing the type of the child bean, that type must be compatible with the type of the parent bean.

Summary

In this chapter, we covered a lot of ground with both the Spring core and IoC in general. We showed you examples of the types of IoC and presented the pros and cons of using each mechanism in your applications. We looked at which IoC mechanisms Spring provides and when (and when not) to use each within your applications. While exploring IoC, we introduced the Spring BeanFactory, which is the core component for Spring's IoC capabilities, and then ApplicationContext, which extends BeanFactory and provides additional functionalities. For ApplicationContext, we focused on GenericXmlApplicationContext, which allows external configuration of Spring by using XML. Another method to declare DI requirements for ApplicationContext, that is, using Java annotations, was also discussed.

This chapter also introduced you to the basics of Spring's IoC feature set including Setter Injection, Constructor Injection, Method Injection, autowiring, and bean inheritance. In the discussion of configuration, we demonstrated how you can configure your bean properties with a wide variety of values, including other beans, using both XML and annotation type configurations and `GenericXmlApplicationContext`.

This chapter only scratched the surface of Spring and Spring's IoC container. In the next chapter, you'll look at some IoC-related features specific to Spring, and you'll take a more detailed look at other functionality available in the Spring core.

CHAPTER 4

■ ■ ■

Spring Configuration in Detail

In the previous chapter, we presented a detailed look at the concept of Inversion of Control (IoC) and how it fits into the Spring Framework. However, we have really only scratched the surface of what the Spring core can do. Spring provides a wide array of services that supplement and extend its basic IoC capabilities. In this chapter, you are going to explore these in detail. Specifically, you will be looking at the following:

- *Managing the bean life cycle*: So far, all the beans you have seen have been fairly simple and completely decoupled from the Spring container. In this section, we present some strategies you can employ to enable your beans to receive notifications from the Spring container at various points throughout their life cycle. You can do this either by implementing specific interfaces laid out by Spring, by specifying methods that Spring can call via reflection, or by using JSR-250 JavaBeans life-cycle annotations.

- *Making your beans "Spring aware"*: In some cases, you want a bean to be able to interact with the `ApplicationContext` that configured it. For this reason, Spring offers two interfaces, `BeanNameAware` and `ApplicationContextAware`, that allow your bean to obtain its assigned name and reference its `ApplicationContext`, respectively. This section of the chapter covers implementing these interfaces and gives some practical considerations for using them in your application.

- *Using* `FactoryBeans`: As its name implies, the `FactoryBean` interface is meant to be implemented by any bean that acts as a factory for other beans. The `FactoryBean` interface provides a mechanism by which you can easily integrate your own factories with the Spring `BeanFactory`.

- *Working with JavaBeans* `PropertyEditors`: The `PropertyEditor` interface is a standard interface provided in the `java.beans` package. `PropertyEditors` are used to convert property values to and from `String` representations. Spring uses `PropertyEditors` extensively, mainly to read values specified in the `BeanFactory` configuration and convert them into the correct types. In this section, we discuss the set of `PropertyEditors` supplied with Spring and how you can use them within your application. We also take a look at implementing custom `PropertyEditors`.

- *Learning more about the Spring* `ApplicationContext`: As we know, `ApplicationContext` is an extension of `BeanFactory` intended for use in full applications. The `ApplicationContext` interface provides a useful set of additional functionality, including internationalized message support, resource loading, and event publishing. In this section, we present a detailed look at the features in addition to IoC that `ApplicationContext` offers. We also jump ahead of ourselves a little to show you how `ApplicationContext` simplifies the use of Spring when you are building web applications.

- *Using Java classes for configuration*: Prior to 3.0, Spring supported only the XML base configuration with annotations for beans and dependency configuration. Starting with 3.0, Spring offers another option for developers to configure the Spring `ApplicationContext` using Java classes. We take a look at this new option in Spring application configuration.

- *Using configuration enhancements*: We present features that make application configuration easier, such as profile management, environment and property source abstraction, and so on. In this section, we cover those features and show how to use them to address specific configuration needs.

- *Using Groovy for configuration*: New to Spring 4.0 is the ability to configure bean definitions in the Groovy language, which can be used as an alternative or supplement to the existing XML and Java configuration methods.

Spring's Impact on Application Portability

Most of the features discussed in this chapter are specific to Spring and, in many cases, are not available in other IoC containers. Although many IoC containers offer life-cycle management functionality, they probably do so through a different set of interfaces than Spring. If the portability of your application between different IoC containers is truly important, you might want to avoid using some of the features that couple your application to Spring.

Remember, however, that by setting a constraint—that your application is portable between IoC containers—you are losing out on the wealth of functionality Spring offers. Because you are likely to be making a strategic choice to use Spring, it makes sense that you use it to the best of its ability.

Be careful not to create a requirement for portability out of thin air. In many cases, the end users of your application do not care whether the application can run on three different IoC containers; they just want it to run. In our experience, it is often a mistake to try to build an application on the lowest common denominator of features available in your chosen technology. Doing so often sets your application at a disadvantage right from the get-go. However, if your application requires IoC container portability, do not see this as a drawback—it is a true requirement and, therefore, one your application should fulfill. In *Expert One-on-One: J2EE Development without EJB* (Wrox, 2004), Rod Johnson and Jürgen Höller describe these types of requirements as phantom requirements and provide a much more detailed discussion of them and how they can affect your project.

Although using these features may couple your application to the Spring Framework, in reality you are increasing the portability of your application in the wider scope. Consider that you are using a freely available, open source framework that has no particular vendor affiliation. An application built using Spring's IoC container runs anywhere Java runs. For Java enterprise applications, Spring opens up new possibilities for portability. Spring provides many of the same capabilities as JEE and also provides classes to abstract and simplify many other aspects of JEE. In many cases, it is possible to build a web application using Spring that runs in a simple servlet container but with the same level of sophistication as an application targeted at a full-blown JEE application server. By coupling to Spring, you can increase your application's portability by replacing many features that either are vendor-specific or rely on vendor-specific configuration with equivalent features in Spring.

Bean Life-Cycle Management

An important part of any IoC container, Spring included, is that beans can be constructed in such a way that they receive notifications at certain points in their life cycle. This enables your beans to perform relevant processing at certain points throughout their life. In general, two life-cycle events are particularly relevant to a bean: post-initialization and pre-destruction.

In the context of Spring, the *post-initialization* event is raised as soon as Spring finishes setting all the property values on the bean and finishes any dependency checks that you configured it to perform. The *pre-destruction* event is fired just before Spring destroys the bean instance. However, for beans with prototype scope, the pre-destruction event will not be fired by Spring. The design of Spring is that the initialization life-cycle callback methods will be called on objects regardless of bean scope, while for beans with prototype scope, the destruction life-cycle callback methods will not be called. Spring provides three mechanisms a bean can use to hook into each of these events and perform some additional processing: interface-based, method-based, and annotation-based mechanisms.

Using the interface-based mechanism, your bean implements an interface specific to the type of notification it wants to receive, and Spring notifies the bean via a callback method defined in the interface. For the method-based mechanism, Spring allows you to specify, in your `ApplicationContext` configuration, the name of a method to call when the bean is initialized and the name of a method to call when the bean is destroyed. For the annotation mechanism, you can use JSR-250 annotations to specify the method that Spring should call after construction or before destruction.

In the case of both events, the mechanisms achieve exactly the same goal. The interface mechanism is used extensively throughout Spring so that you don't have to remember to specify the initialization or destruction each time you use one of Spring's components. However, in your own beans, you may be better served using the method-based or annotation mechanism because your beans do not need to implement any Spring-specific interfaces. Although we stated that portability often isn't as important a requirement as many books lead you to believe, this does not mean you should sacrifice portability when a perfectly good alternative exists. That said, if you are coupling your application to Spring in other ways, using the interface method allows you to specify the callback once and then forget about it. If you are defining a lot of beans of the same type that need to take advantage of the life-cycle notifications, then using the interface mechanism can avoid the need for specifying the life-cycle callback methods for every bean in the XML configuration file. Using JSR-250 annotations is also another viable option, since it's a standard defined by the JCP and you are also not coupled to Spring's specific annotations. Just make sure that the IoC container you are running your application on supports the JSR-250 standard.

Overall, the choice of which mechanism you use for receiving life-cycle notifications depends on your application requirements. If you are concerned about portability or you are just defining one or two beans of a particular type that need the callbacks, use the method-based mechanism. If you use annotation-type configuration and are certain that you are using an IoC container that supports JSR-250, use the annotation mechanism. If you are not too concerned about portability or you are defining many beans of the same type that need the life-cycle notifications, using the interface-based mechanism is the best way to ensure that your beans always receive the notifications they are expecting. If you plan to use a bean across many different Spring projects, you almost certainly want the functionality of that bean to be as self-contained as possible, so you should definitely use the interface-based mechanism.

Figure 4-1 shows a high-level overview of how Spring manages the life cycle of the beans within its container.

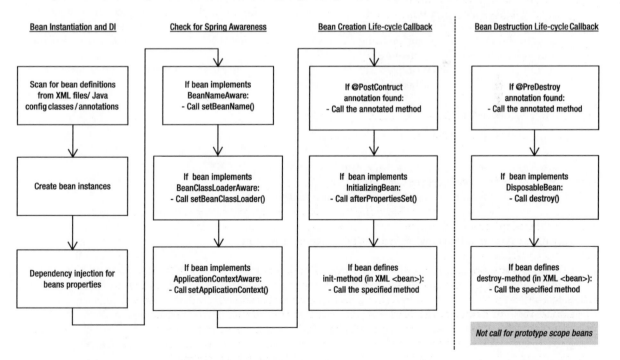

Figure 4-1. *Spring beans life cycle*

Hooking into Bean Creation

By being aware of when it is initialized, a bean can check whether all its required dependencies are satisfied. Although Spring can check dependencies for you, it is pretty much an all-or-nothing approach, and it doesn't offer any opportunities for applying additional logic to the dependency resolution procedure. Consider a bean that has four dependencies declared as setters, two of which are required and one of which has a suitable default in the event that no dependency is provided. Using an initialization callback, your bean can check for the dependencies it requires, throwing an exception or providing a default as needed.

A bean cannot perform these checks in its constructor because at this point, Spring has not had an opportunity to provide values for the dependencies it can satisfy. The initialization callback in Spring is called after Spring finishes providing the dependencies that it can and performs any dependency checks that you ask of it.

You are not limited to using the initialization callback just to check dependencies; you can do anything you want in the callback, but it is most useful for the purpose we have described. In many cases, the initialization callback is also the place to trigger any actions that your bean must take automatically in response to its configuration. For instance, if you build a bean to run scheduled tasks, the initialization callback provides the ideal place to start the scheduler—after all, the configuration data is set on the bean.

■ **Note**   You will not have to write a bean to run scheduled tasks, because this is something Spring can do automatically through its built-in scheduling feature or via integration with the Quartz scheduler. We cover this in more detail in Chapter 11.

Executing a Method When a Bean Is Created

As we mentioned previously, one way to receive the initialization callback is to designate a method on your bean as an initialization method and tell Spring to use this method as an initialization method. As discussed, this callback mechanism is useful when you have only a few beans of the same type or when you want to keep your application decoupled from Spring. Another reason for using this mechanism is to enable your Spring application to work with beans that were built previously or were provided by third-party vendors.

Specifying a callback method is simply a case of specifying the name in the init-method attribute of a bean's <bean> tag. Listing 4-1 shows a basic bean with two dependencies.

Listing 4-1. The SimpleBean Class

```
package com.apress.prospring4.ch4;

import org.springframework.beans.factory.BeanCreationException;
import org.springframework.context.ApplicationContext;
import org.springframework.context.support.GenericXmlApplicationContext;

public class SimpleBean {
    private static final String DEFAULT_NAME = "Luke Skywalker";

    private String name;
    private int age = Integer.MIN_VALUE;

    public void setName(String name) {
        this.name = name;
    }
```

```java
    public void setAge(int age) {
        this.age = age;
    }

    public void init() {
        System.out.println("Initializing bean");

        if (name == null) {
            System.out.println("Using default name");
            name = DEFAULT_NAME;
        }

        if (age == Integer.MIN_VALUE) {
            throw new IllegalArgumentException(
                    "You must set the age property of any beans of type " + SimpleBean.class);
        }
    }

    public String toString() {
        return "Name: " + name + "\nAge: " + age;
    }

    public static void main(String[] args) {
        GenericXmlApplicationContext ctx = new GenericXmlApplicationContext();
        ctx.load("classpath:META-INF/spring/app-context-xml.xml");
        ctx.refresh();

        SimpleBean simpleBean1 = getBean("simpleBean1", ctx);
        SimpleBean simpleBean2 = getBean("simpleBean2", ctx);
        SimpleBean simpleBean3 = getBean("simpleBean3", ctx);
    }

    private static SimpleBean getBean(String beanName, ApplicationContext ctx) {
        try {
            SimpleBean bean = (SimpleBean) ctx.getBean(beanName);
            System.out.println(bean);
            return bean;
        } catch (BeanCreationException ex) {
            System.out.println("An error occured in bean configuration: "
                    + ex.getMessage());
            return null;
        }
    }
}
```

Notice that we have defined a method, init(), to act as the initialization callback. The init() method checks whether the name property has been set, and if it has not, it uses the default value stored in the DEFAULT_NAME constant. The init() method also checks whether the age property is set, and throws IllegalArgumentException if it is not.

The main() method of the SimpleBean class attempts to obtain three beans from GenericXmlApplicationContext, all of type SimpleBean, using its own getBean() method. Notice that in the getBean() method, if the bean is obtained successfully, its details are written to console output. If an exception is thrown in the init() method, as will occur in this case if the age property is not set, then Spring wraps that exception in BeanCreationException. The getBean() method catches these exceptions and writes a message to the console output informing us of the error, as well as returns a null value.

Listing 4-2 shows an `ApplicationContext` configuration that defines the beans used in Listing 4-1 (app-context-xml.xml).

Listing 4-2. Configuring the `SimpleBeans`

```xml
<?xml version="1.0" encoding="UTF-8"?>

<beans xmlns="http://www.springframework.org/schema/beans"
    xmlns:xsi="http://www.w3.org/2001/XMLSchema-instance"
    xmlns:p="http://www.springframework.org/schema/p"
    xsi:schemaLocation="http://www.springframework.org/schema/beans
        http://www.springframework.org/schema/beans/spring-beans.xsd"
    default-lazy-init="true">

    <bean id="simpleBean1"
        class="com.apress.prospring4.ch4.SimpleBean"
        init-method="init" p:name="Chris Schaefer" p:age="32"/>

    <bean id="simpleBean2"
        class="com.apress.prospring4.ch4.SimpleBean"
        init-method="init" p:age="32"/>

    <bean id="simpleBean3"
        class="com.apress.prospring4.ch4.SimpleBean"
        init-method="init" p:name="Chris Schaefer"/>
</beans>
```

As you can see, the <bean> tag for each of the three beans has an `init-method` attribute that tells Spring that it should invoke the `init()` method as soon as it finishes configuring the bean. The `simpleBean1` bean has values for both the name and age properties, so it passes through the `init()` method with absolutely no changes. The `simpleBean2` bean has no value for the name property, meaning that in the `init()` method, the name property is given the default value. Finally, the `simpleBean3` bean has no value for the age property. The logic defined in the `init()` method treats this as an error, so `IllegalArgumentException` is thrown. Also note that in the <beans> tag, we added the attribute `default-lazy-init="true"` to instruct Spring to instantiate the beans defined in the configuration file only when the bean was requested from the application. If we do not specify it, Spring will try to initialize all the beans during the bootstrapping of `ApplicationContext`, and it will fail during the initialization of `simpleBean3`. Running the previous example yields the following output:

```
Initializing bean
Name: Chris Schaefer
Age: 32
Initializing bean
Using default name
Name: Luke Skywalker
Age: 32


An error occured in bean configuration: Error creating bean with name 'simpleBean3' defined in
class path resource [META-INF/spring/app-context-xml.xml]: Invocation of init method failed; nested
exception is java.lang.IllegalArgumentException: You must set the age property of any beans of type
class com.apress.prospring4.ch4.SimpleBean.
```

From this output, you can see that `simpleBean1` was configured correctly with the values that we specified in the configuration file. For `simpleBean2`, the default value for the `name` property was used because no value was specified in the configuration. Finally, for `simpleBean3`, no bean instance was created because the `init()` method raised an error because of the lack of a value for the age property.

As you can see, using the initialization method is an ideal way to ensure that your beans are configured correctly. By using this mechanism, you can take full advantage of the benefits of IoC without losing any of the control you get from manually defining dependencies. The only constraint on your initialization method is that it cannot accept any arguments. You can define any return type, although it is ignored by Spring, and you can even use a static method, but the method must accept no arguments.

The benefits of this mechanism are negated when using a static initialization method, because you cannot access any of the bean's state to validate it. If your bean is using static state as a mechanism for saving memory and you are using a static initialization method to validate this state, then you should consider moving the static state to instance state and using a nonstatic initialization method. If you use Spring's singleton management capabilities, the end effect is the same, but you have a bean that is much simpler to test, and you also have the increased effect of being able to create multiple instances of the bean with their own state when necessary. Of course, in some instances, you need to use static state shared across multiple instances of a bean, in which case you can always use a static initialization method.

Implementing the InitializingBean Interface

The `InitializingBean` interface defined in Spring allows you to define inside your bean code that you want the bean to receive notification that Spring has finished configuring it. In the same way as when you are using an initialization method, this gives you the opportunity to check the bean configuration to ensure that it is valid, providing any default values along the way. The `InitializingBean` interface defines a single method, `afterPropertiesSet()`, that serves the same purpose as the `init()` method in Listing 4-1. Listing 4-3 shows a reimplementation of the previous example using the `InitializingBean` interface in place of the initialization method.

Listing 4-3. Using the InitializingBean Interface

```
package com.apress.prospring4.ch4;

import org.springframework.beans.factory.BeanCreationException;
import org.springframework.beans.factory.InitializingBean;
import org.springframework.context.ApplicationContext;
import org.springframework.context.support.GenericXmlApplicationContext;

public class SimpleBeanWithInterface implements InitializingBean {
    private static final String DEFAULT_NAME = "Luke Skywalker";

    private String name;
    private int age = Integer.MIN_VALUE;

    public void setName(String name) {
        this.name = name;
    }

    public void setAge(int age) {
        this.age = age;
    }
```

```java
    public void myInit() {
        System.out.println("My Init");
    }

    @Override
    public void afterPropertiesSet() throws Exception {
        System.out.println("Initializing bean");

        if (name == null) {
            System.out.println("Using default name");
            name = DEFAULT_NAME;
        }

        if (age == Integer.MIN_VALUE) {
            throw new IllegalArgumentException(
                    "You must set the age property of any beans of type " +
                    SimpleBeanWithInterface.class);
        }
    }

    public String toString() {
        return "Name: " + name + "\nAge: " + age;
    }

    public static void main(String[] args) {
        GenericXmlApplicationContext ctx = new GenericXmlApplicationContext();
        ctx.load("classpath:META-INF/spring/app-context-xml.xml");
        ctx.refresh();

        SimpleBeanWithInterface simpleBean1 = getBean("simpleBean1", ctx);
        SimpleBeanWithInterface simpleBean2 = getBean("simpleBean2", ctx);
        SimpleBeanWithInterface simpleBean3 = getBean("simpleBean3", ctx);
    }

    private static SimpleBeanWithInterface getBean(String beanName,
            ApplicationContext ctx) {
        try {
            SimpleBeanWithInterface bean = (SimpleBeanWithInterface) ctx.getBean(beanName);
            System.out.println(bean);
            return bean;
        } catch (BeanCreationException ex) {
            System.out.println("An error occured in bean configuration: "
                    + ex.getMessage());
            return null;
        }
    }
}
```

As you can see, not much in this example has changed. Aside from the obvious class name change, the only differences are that this class implements InitializingBean and that the initialization logic has moved into the InitializingBean.afterPropertiesSet() method.

In Listing 4-4, you can see the configuration for this example (app-context-xml.xml).

Listing 4-4. Configuration Using InitializingBean

```xml
<?xml version="1.0" encoding="UTF-8"?>

<beans xmlns="http://www.springframework.org/schema/beans"
    xmlns:xsi="http://www.w3.org/2001/XMLSchema-instance"
    xmlns:p="http://www.springframework.org/schema/p"
    xsi:schemaLocation="http://www.springframework.org/schema/beans
        http://www.springframework.org/schema/beans/spring-beans.xsd"
    default-lazy-init="true">

    <bean id="simpleBean1"
        class="com.apress.prospring4.ch4.SimpleBeanWithInterface"
        p:name="Chris Schaefer" p:age="32"/>

    <bean id="simpleBean2"
        class="com.apress.prospring4.ch4.SimpleBeanWithInterface"
        p:age="32"/>

    <bean id="simpleBean3"
        class="com.apress.prospring4.ch4.SimpleBeanWithInterface"
        p:name="Chris Schaefer"/>
</beans>
```

Again, there's not much difference between the configuration code in Listing 4-4 and the configuration code in Listing 4-2. The noticeable difference is the omission of the init-method attribute. Because the SimpleBeanWithInterface class implements the InitializingBean interface, Spring knows which method to call as the initialization callback, thus removing the need for any additional configuration. The output from this example is shown here:

```
Initializing bean
Name: Chris Schaefer
Age: 32
Initializing bean
Using default name
Name: Luke Skywalker
Age: 32
```

```
An error occured in bean configuration: Error creating bean with name 'simpleBean3' defined in class
path resource [META-INF/spring/app-context-xml.xml]: Invocation of init method failed; nested
exception is java.lang.IllegalArgumentException: You must set the age property of any beans of type
class com.apress.prospring4.ch4.SimpleBeanWithInterface.
```

Using JSR-250 @PostConstruct Annotation

Another method that can achieve the same purpose is to use the JSR-250 life-cycle annotation, @PostConstruct. Starting from Spring 2.5, JSR-250 annotations are also supported to specify the method that Spring should call if the corresponding annotation relating to the bean's life cycle exists in the class. Listing 4-5 shows the program with the @PostConstruct annotation applied.

Listing 4-5. Using JSR-250 @PostConstruct Annotation

```java
package com.apress.prospring4.ch4;

import javax.annotation.PostConstruct;
import org.springframework.beans.factory.BeanCreationException;
import org.springframework.context.ApplicationContext;
import org.springframework.context.support.GenericXmlApplicationContext;

public class SimpleBeanWithJSR250 {
    private static final String DEFAULT_NAME = "Luke Skywalker";

    private String name;
    private int age = Integer.MIN_VALUE;

    public void setName(String name) {
        this.name = name;
    }

    public void setAge(int age) {
        this.age = age;
    }

    @PostConstruct
    public void init() throws Exception {
        System.out.println("Initializing bean");

        if (name == null) {
            System.out.println("Using default name");
            name = DEFAULT_NAME;
        }

        if (age == Integer.MIN_VALUE) {
            throw new IllegalArgumentException(
                    "You must set the age property of any beans of type " +
                    SimpleBeanWithJSR250.class);
        }
    }

    public String toString() {
        return "Name: " + name + "\nAge: " + age;
    }

    public static void main(String[] args) {
        GenericXmlApplicationContext ctx = new GenericXmlApplicationContext();
        ctx.load("classpath:META-INF/spring/app-context-annotation.xml");
        ctx.refresh();

        SimpleBeanWithJSR250 simpleBean1 = getBean("simpleBean1", ctx);
        SimpleBeanWithJSR250 simpleBean2 = getBean("simpleBean2", ctx);
        SimpleBeanWithJSR250 simpleBean3 = getBean("simpleBean3", ctx);
    }
```

```
    private static SimpleBeanWithJSR250 getBean(String beanName, ApplicationContext ctx) {
        try {
            SimpleBeanWithJSR250 bean = (SimpleBeanWithJSR250) ctx.getBean(beanName);
            System.out.println(bean);
            return bean;
        } catch (BeanCreationException ex) {
            System.out.println("An error occured in bean configuration: "
                    + ex.getMessage());
            return null;
        }
    }
}
```

The program is exactly the same as using the init-method approach; just apply the @PostConstruct annotation before the init() method. Note that you can assign any name to the method.

In terms of configuration, since we are using annotations, we need to add the <context:annotation-driven> tag from the context namespace into the configuration file:

```
<?xml version="1.0" encoding="UTF-8"?>

<beans xmlns="http://www.springframework.org/schema/beans"
       xmlns:xsi="http://www.w3.org/2001/XMLSchema-instance"
       xmlns:context="http://www.springframework.org/schema/context"
       xmlns:p="http://www.springframework.org/schema/p"
       xsi:schemaLocation="http://www.springframework.org/schema/beans
           http://www.springframework.org/schema/beans/spring-beans.xsd
           http://www.springframework.org/schema/context
           http://www.springframework.org/schema/context/spring-context.xsd"
       default-lazy-init="true">

    <context:annotation-config/>

    <bean id="simpleBean1"
        class="com.apress.prospring4.ch4.SimpleBeanWithJSR250"
        p:name="Chris Schaefer" p:age="32"/>

    <bean id="simpleBean2"
        class="com.apress.prospring4.ch4.SimpleBeanWithJSR250"
        p:age="32"/>

    <bean id="simpleBean3"
        class="com.apress.prospring4.ch4.SimpleBeanWithJSR250"
        p:name="Chris Schaefer"/>
</beans>
```

Run the program and you will see the same output as other mechanisms:

```
Initializing bean
Name: Chris Schaefer
Age: 32
Initializing bean
Using default name
Name: Luke Skywalker
Age: 32
Initializing bean
```

```
An error occured in bean configuration: Error creating bean with name 'simpleBean3' : Invocation
of init method failed; nested exception is java.lang.IllegalArgumentException: You must set the age
property of any beans of type class com.apress.prospring4.ch4.SimpleBeanWithJSR250.
```

All three approaches have their benefits and drawbacks. Using an initialization method, you have the benefit of keeping your application decoupled from Spring, but you have to remember to configure the initialization method for every bean that needs it. Using InitializingBean interface, you have the benefit of being able to specify the initialization callback once for all instances of your bean class, but you have to couple your application to do so. Using annotations, you need to apply the annotation to the method and make sure that the IoC container supports JSR-250. In the end, you should let the requirements of your application drive the decision about which approach to use. If portability is an issue, use the initialization or annotation method; otherwise, use the InitializingBean interface to reduce the amount of configuration your application needs and the chance of errors creeping into your application because of misconfiguration.

Understanding Order of Resolution

You can use all initialization mechanisms on the same bean instance. In this case, Spring invokes the method annotated with @PostConstruct first and then InitializingBean.afterPropertiesSet(), followed by your initialization method specified in the configuration file. This can be useful if you have an existing bean that performs some initialization in a specific method but you need to add some more initialization code when you use Spring.

Hooking into Bean Destruction

When using an ApplicationContext implementation that wraps the DefaultListableBeanFactory interface (such as GenericXmlApplicationContext, via the getDefaultListableBeanFactory() method), you can signal to BeanFactory that you want to destroy all singleton instances with a call to ConfigurableBeanFactory. destroySingletons(). Typically, you do this when your application shuts down, and it allows you to clean up any resources that your beans might be holding open, thus allowing your application to shut down gracefully. This callback also provides the perfect place to flush any data you are storing in memory to persistent storage and to allow your beans to end any long-running processes they may have started.

To allow your beans to receive notification that destroySingletons() has been called, you have three options, all similar to the mechanisms available for receiving an initialization callback. The destruction callback is often used in conjunction with the initialization callback. In many cases, you create and configure a resource in the initialization callback and then release the resource in the destruction callback.

Executing a Method When a Bean Is Destroyed

To designate a method to be called when a bean is destroyed, you simply specify the name of the method in the destroy-method attribute of the bean's <bean> tag. Spring calls it just before it destroys the singleton instance of the bean (Spring will not call this method for those beans with prototype scope). Listing 4-6 provides an example of using a destroy-method callback.

Listing 4-6. Using a destroy-method Callback

```java
package com.apress.prospring4.ch4;

import java.io.IOException;
import java.io.File;
import org.springframework.beans.factory.InitializingBean;
import org.springframework.context.support.GenericXmlApplicationContext;

public class DestructiveBean implements InitializingBean {
    private File file;
    private String filePath;

    @Override
    public void afterPropertiesSet() throws Exception {
        System.out.println("Initializing Bean");

        if (filePath == null) {
            throw new IllegalArgumentException(
                    "You must specify the filePath property of " + DestructiveBean.class);
        }

        this.file = new File(filePath);
        this.file.createNewFile();

        System.out.println("File exists: " + file.exists());
    }

    public void destroy() {
        System.out.println("Destroying Bean");

        if(!file.delete()) {
            System.err.println("ERROR: failed to delete file.");
        }

        System.out.println("File exists: " + file.exists());
    }

    public void setFilePath(String filePath) {
        this.filePath = filePath;
    }

    public static void main(String[] args) throws Exception {
        GenericXmlApplicationContext ctx = new GenericXmlApplicationContext();
        ctx.load("classpath:META-INF/spring/app-context-xml.xml");
        ctx.refresh();

        DestructiveBean bean = (DestructiveBean) ctx.getBean("destructiveBean");

        System.out.println("Calling destroy()");
        ctx.destroy();
        System.out.println("Called destroy()");
    }
}
```

This code defines a destroy() method, in which the file that was created gets deleted. The main() method retrieves a bean of type DestructiveBean from GenericXmlApplicationContext and then invokes its destroy() method (which will, in turn, invoke the ConfigurableBeanFactory.destroySingletons() that was wrapped by the ApplicationContext), instructing Spring to destroy all the singletons managed by it. Both the initialization and destruction callbacks write a message to console output informing us that they have been called. In Listing 4-7, you can see the configuration for the destructiveBean bean (app-context-xml.xml).

Listing 4-7. Configuring a destroy-method Callback

```xml
<?xml version="1.0" encoding="UTF-8"?>

<beans xmlns="http://www.springframework.org/schema/beans"
    xmlns:xsi="http://www.w3.org/2001/XMLSchema-instance"
    xmlns:p="http://www.springframework.org/schema/p"
    xsi:schemaLocation="http://www.springframework.org/schema/beans
        http://www.springframework.org/schema/beans/spring-beans.xsd">

    <bean id="destructiveBean"
        class="com.apress.prospring4.ch4.DestructiveBean"
        destroy-method="destroy"
        p:filePath=
        "#{systemProperties['java.io.tmpdir']}#{systemProperties['file.separator']}test.txt"/>
</beans>
```

Notice that we have specified the destroy() method as the destruction callback by using the destroy-method attribute. We build the filePath attribute by using a SpEL expression, concatenating the system properties java.io.tmpdir and file.separator before the filename test.txt to ensure cross-platform compatibility. Running this example yields the following output:

```
Initializing Bean
File exists: true
Calling destroy()
Destroying Bean
File exists: false
Called destroy()
```

As you can see, Spring first invokes the initialization callback, and the DestructiveBean instance creates the File instance and stores it. Next, during the call to destroy(), Spring iterates over the set of singletons it is managing, in this case just one, and invokes any destruction callbacks that are specified. This is where the DestructiveBean instance deletes the created file and logs messages to the screen indicating it no longer exists.

Implementing the DisposableBean Interface

As with initialization callbacks, Spring provides an interface, in this case DisposableBean, that can be implemented by your beans as a mechanism for receiving destruction callbacks. The DisposableBean interface defines a single method, destroy(), which is called just before the bean is destroyed. Using this mechanism is orthogonal to using the InitializingBean interface to receive initialization callbacks. Listing 4-8 shows a modified implementation of the DestructiveBean class that implements the DisposableBean interface.

Listing 4-8. Implementing DisposableBean

```
package com.apress.prospring4.ch4;

import java.io.IOException;
import java.io.File;
import org.springframework.beans.factory.DisposableBean;
import org.springframework.beans.factory.InitializingBean;
import org.springframework.context.support.GenericXmlApplicationContext;

public class DestructiveBeanWithInterface implements InitializingBean, DisposableBean {
    private File file;
    private String filePath;

    @Override
    public void afterPropertiesSet() throws Exception {
        System.out.println("Initializing Bean");

        if (filePath == null) {
            throw new IllegalArgumentException(
                    "You must specify the filePath property of " +
                    DestructiveBeanWithInterface.class);
        }

        this.file = new File(filePath);
        this.file.createNewFile();

        System.out.println("File exists: " + file.exists());
    }

    @Override
    public void destroy() {
        System.out.println("Destroying Bean");

        if(!file.delete()) {
            System.err.println("ERROR: failed to delete file.");
        }

        System.out.println("File exists: " + file.exists());
    }

    public void setFilePath(String filePath) {
        this.filePath = filePath;
    }

    public static void main(String[] args) throws Exception {
        GenericXmlApplicationContext ctx = new GenericXmlApplicationContext();
        ctx.load("classpath:META-INF/spring/app-context-xml.xml");
        ctx.refresh();

        DestructiveBeanWithInterface bean =
            (DestructiveBeanWithInterface) ctx.getBean("destructiveBean");
```

```
            System.out.println("Calling destroy()");
            ctx.destroy();
            System.out.println("Called destroy()");
    }
}
```

There is not much difference between the code that uses the callback method mechanism and the code that uses the callback interface mechanism. In this case, we even used the same method names. Listing 4-9 shows an amended configuration for this example (app-context-xml.xml).

Listing 4-9. Configuration Using the DisposableBean Interface

```xml
<?xml version="1.0" encoding="UTF-8"?>

<beans xmlns="http://www.springframework.org/schema/beans"
    xmlns:xsi="http://www.w3.org/2001/XMLSchema-instance"
    xmlns:p="http://www.springframework.org/schema/p"
    xsi:schemaLocation="http://www.springframework.org/schema/beans
        http://www.springframework.org/schema/beans/spring-beans.xsd">

    <bean id="destructiveBean"
        class="com.apress.prospring4.ch4.DestructiveBeanWithInterface"
        p:filePath=
        "#{systemProperties['java.io.tmpdir']}#{systemProperties['file.separator']}test.txt"/>
</beans>
```

Aside from the different class name, the only difference is the omission of the destroy-method attribute. Running this example yields the following output:

```
Initializing Bean
File exists: true
Calling destroy()
Destroying Bean
File exists: false
Called destroy()
```

Using JSR-250 @PreDestroy Annotation

The third way is to use the JSR-250 life-cycle @PreDestroy annotation, which is the inverse of the @PostConstruct annotation. Listing 4-10 is a version of DestructiveBean that uses both @PostConstruct and @PreDestroy in the same class to perform program initialization and destroy actions.

Listing 4-10. Implementing DisposableBean by Using @PreDestroy and @PostDestroy

```java
package com.apress.prospring4.ch4;

import java.io.File;
import javax.annotation.PostConstruct;
import javax.annotation.PreDestroy;
import org.springframework.context.support.GenericXmlApplicationContext;

public class DestructiveBeanWithJSR250 {
    private File file;
    private String filePath;

    @PostConstruct
    public void afterPropertiesSet() throws Exception {
        System.out.println("Initializing Bean");

        if (filePath == null) {
            throw new IllegalArgumentException(
                    "You must specify the filePath property of " +
                    DestructiveBeanWithJSR250.class);
        }

        this.file = new File(filePath);
        this.file.createNewFile();

        System.out.println("File exists: " + file.exists());
    }

    @PreDestroy
    public void destroy() {
        System.out.println("Destroying Bean");

        if(!file.delete()) {
            System.err.println("ERROR: failed to delete file.");
        }

        System.out.println("File exists: " + file.exists());
    }

    public void setFilePath(String filePath) {
        this.filePath = filePath;
    }

    public static void main(String[] args) throws Exception {
        GenericXmlApplicationContext ctx = new GenericXmlApplicationContext();
        ctx.load("classpath:META-INF/spring/app-context-annotation.xml");
        ctx.refresh();

        DestructiveBeanWithJSR250 bean =
            (DestructiveBeanWithJSR250) ctx.getBean("destructiveBean");
```

```
            System.out.println("Calling destroy()");
            ctx.destroy();
            System.out.println("Called destroy()");
        }
}
```

Listing 4-11 is the XML configuration for the bean, which adds the `<context:annotation-config>` tag (`app-context-annotation.xml`).

Listing 4-11. Configuration Using the `DisposableBean` with JSR-250 Annotation

```xml
<?xml version="1.0" encoding="UTF-8"?>

<beans xmlns="http://www.springframework.org/schema/beans"
    xmlns:xsi="http://www.w3.org/2001/XMLSchema-instance"
    xmlns:p="http://www.springframework.org/schema/p"
    xmlns:context="http://www.springframework.org/schema/context"
    xsi:schemaLocation="http://www.springframework.org/schema/beans
        http://www.springframework.org/schema/beans/spring-beans.xsd
        http://www.springframework.org/schema/context
        http://www.springframework.org/schema/context/spring-context.xsd">

    <context:annotation-config/>

    <bean id="destructiveBean"
        class="com.apress.prospring4.ch4.DestructiveBeanWithJSR250"
        p:filePath=
        "#{systemProperties['java.io.tmpdir']}#{systemProperties['file.separator']}test.txt"/>
</beans>
```

The destruction callback is an ideal mechanism for ensuring that your applications shut down gracefully and do not leave resources open or in an inconsistent state. However, you still have to decide whether to use the destruction method callback, the `DisposableBean` interface, or the `@PreDestroy` annotation. Again, let the requirements of your application drive your decision in this respect; use the method callback where portability is an issue, and use the `DisposableBean` interface or a JSR-250 annotation to reduce the amount of configuration required.

Understanding Order of Resolution

As with the case of bean creation, you can use all mechanisms on the same bean instance for bean destruction. In this case, Spring invokes the method annotated with `@PreDestroy` first and then `DisposableBean.destroy()`, followed by your destroy method configured in your XML definition.

Using a Shutdown Hook

The only drawback of the destruction callbacks in Spring is that they are not fired automatically; you need to remember to call `AbstractApplicationContext.destroy()` before your application is closed. When your application runs as a servlet, you can simply call `destroy()` in the servlet's `destroy()` method. However, in a stand-alone application, things are not quite so simple, especially if you have multiple exit points out of your application. Fortunately, there is a solution. Java allows you to create a shutdown hook, a thread that is executed just before the application shuts down. This is the perfect way to invoke the `destroy()` method of your `AbstractApplicationContext` (which was being extended by all concrete ApplicationContext implementations). The easiest way to take advantage of this mechanism is to use the AbstractApplicationContext's registerShutdownHook() method. The method automatically instructs Spring to register a shutdown hook of the underlying JVM runtime. This is shown in Listing 4-12.

Listing 4-12. Registering a Shutdown Hook

```java
package com.apress.prospring4.ch4;

import javax.annotation.PostConstruct;
import javax.annotation.PreDestroy;
import java.io.File;
import org.springframework.context.support.GenericXmlApplicationContext;

public class DestructiveBeanWithInterface {
    private File file;
    private String filePath;

    @PostConstruct
    public void afterPropertiesSet() throws Exception {
        System.out.println("Initializing Bean");

        if (filePath == null) {
            throw new IllegalArgumentException(
                    "You must specify the filePath property of " +
                    DestructiveBeanWithInterface.class);
        }

        this.file = new File(filePath);
        this.file.createNewFile();

        System.out.println("File exists: " + file.exists());
    }

    @PreDestroy
    public void destroy() {
        System.out.println("Destroying Bean");

        if(!file.delete()) {
            System.err.println("ERROR: failed to delete file.");
        }

        System.out.println("File exists: " + file.exists());
    }

    public void setFilePath(String filePath) {
        this.filePath = filePath;
    }

    public static void main(String[] args) throws Exception {
        GenericXmlApplicationContext ctx = new GenericXmlApplicationContext();
        ctx.load("classpath:META-INF/spring/app-context-annotation.xml");
        ctx.registerShutdownHook();
        ctx.refresh();
```

```
        DestructiveBeanWithInterface bean =
            (DestructiveBeanWithInterface) ctx.getBean("destructiveBean");
    }
}
```

And the corresponding XML configuration (app-context-annotation.xml):

```xml
<?xml version="1.0" encoding="UTF-8"?>

<beans xmlns="http://www.springframework.org/schema/beans"
    xmlns:xsi="http://www.w3.org/2001/XMLSchema-instance"
    xmlns:p="http://www.springframework.org/schema/p"
    xmlns:context="http://www.springframework.org/schema/context"
    xsi:schemaLocation="http://www.springframework.org/schema/beans
        http://www.springframework.org/schema/beans/spring-beans.xsd
        http://www.springframework.org/schema/context
        http://www.springframework.org/schema/context/spring-context.xsd">

    <context:annotation-config/>

    <bean id="destructiveBean"
        class="com.apress.prospring4.ch4.DestructiveBeanWithInterface"
        p:filePath=
        "#{systemProperties['java.io.tmpdir']}#{systemProperties['file.separator']}test.txt"/>
</beans>
```

Running this example results in the following output:

```
Initializing Bean
File exists: true
Destroying Bean
File exists: false
```

As you can see, the destroy() method is invoked, even though we didn't write any code to invoke it explicitly as the application was shutting down.

Making Your Beans "Spring Aware"

One of the biggest selling points of Dependency Injection over Dependency Lookup as a mechanism for achieving Inversion of Control is that your beans do not need to be aware of the implementation of the container that is managing them. To a bean that uses constructor or setter injection, the Spring container is the same as the container provided by Google Guice or PicoContainer. However, in certain circumstances, you may need a bean that is using Dependency Injection to obtain its dependencies so it can interact with the container for some other reason. An example of this may be a bean that automatically configures a shutdown hook for you, and thus it needs access to ApplicationContext. In other cases, a bean may want to know what its name is (that is, the bean name that was assigned within the current ApplicationContext) so it can perform some additional processing based on this name.

That said, this feature is really intended for internal Spring use. Giving the bean name some kind of business meaning is generally a bad idea and can lead to configuration problems as bean names have to be artificially manipulated to support their business meaning. However, we have found that being able to have a bean find out its name at runtime is really useful for logging. Say you have many beans of the same type running under different configurations. The bean name can be included in log messages to help you differentiate between the one that is generating errors and the ones that are working fine when something goes wrong.

Using the BeanNameAware Interface

The BeanNameAware interface, which can be implemented by a bean that wants to obtain its own name, has a single method: setBeanName(String). Spring calls the setBeanName() method after it has finished configuring your bean but before any life-cycle callbacks (initialization or destroy) are called (refer to Figure 4-1). In most cases, the implementation of the setBeanName() interface is just a single line that stores the value passed in by the container in a field for use later. Listing 4-13 shows a simple bean that obtains its name by using BeanNameAware and then later uses this bean name to print to the console.

Listing 4-13. Implementing BeanNameAware

```
package com.apress.prospring4.ch4;

import org.springframework.beans.factory.BeanNameAware;

public class BeanNamePrinter implements BeanNameAware {
    private String beanName;

    @Override
    public void setBeanName(String beanName) {
        this.beanName = beanName;
    }

    public void someOperation() {
        System.out.println("Bean [" + beanName + "] - someOperation()");
    }
}
```

This implementation is fairly trivial. Remember that BeanNameAware.setBeanName() is called before the first instance of the bean is returned to your application via a call to ApplicationContext.getBean(), so there is no need to check whether the bean name is available in the someOperation() method. Listing 4-14 shows a simple configuration for this example (app-context-xml.xml).

Listing 4-14. Configuring the LoggingBean Example

```
<?xml version="1.0" encoding="UTF-8"?>

<beans xmlns="http://www.springframework.org/schema/beans"
    xmlns:xsi="http://www.w3.org/2001/XMLSchema-instance"
    xsi:schemaLocation="http://www.springframework.org/schema/beans
        http://www.springframework.org/schema/beans/spring-beans.xsd">

    <bean id="beanNamePrinter" class="com.apress.prospring4.ch4.BeanNamePrinter"/>
</beans>
```

As you can see, no special configuration is required to take advantage of the BeanNameAware interface. In Listing 4-15, you can see a simple example application that retrieves the BeanNamePrinter instance from ApplicationContext and then calls the someOperation() method.

Listing 4-15. The LoggingBeanExample Class

```
package com.apress.prospring4.ch4;

import org.springframework.context.support.GenericXmlApplicationContext;

public class BeanNamePrinterExample {
    public static void main(String[] args) {
        GenericXmlApplicationContext ctx = new GenericXmlApplicationContext();
        ctx.load("classpath:META-INF/spring/app-context-xml.xml");
        ctx.refresh();

        BeanNamePrinter bean = (BeanNamePrinter) ctx.getBean("beanNamePrinter");
        bean.someOperation();
    }
}
```

This example generates the following log output—notice the inclusion of the bean name in the log message for the call to someOperation():

```
Loading XML bean definitions from class path resource [META-INF/spring/app-context-xml.xml]
...
Bean [beanNamePrinter] - someOperation()
```

Using the BeanNameAware interface is really quite simple, and it is put to good use when you are improving the quality of your log messages. Avoid being tempted to give your bean names business meaning just because you can access them; by doing so, you are coupling your classes to Spring for a feature that brings negligible benefit. If your beans need some kind of name internally, have them implement an interface such as Nameable (which is specific to your application) with a method setName() and then give each bean a name by using Dependency Injection. This way, you can keep the names you use for configuration concise, and you won't need to manipulate your configuration unnecessarily to give your beans names with business meaning.

Using the ApplicationContextAware Interface

Using the ApplicationContextAware interface, it is possible for your beans to get a reference to the ApplicationContext that configured them. The main reason this interface was created was to allow a bean to access Spring's ApplicationContext in your application—for example, to acquire other Spring beans programmatically, using getBean(). You should, however, avoid this practice and use Dependency Injection to provide your beans with their collaborators. If you use the lookup-based getBean() approach to obtain dependencies when you can use Dependency Injection, you are adding unnecessary complexity to your beans and coupling them to the Spring Framework without good reason.

Of course, ApplicationContext isn't used just to look up beans; it performs a great many other tasks. As you saw previously, one of these tasks is to destroy all singletons, notifying each of them in turn before doing so. In the previous section, you saw how to create a shutdown hook to ensure that ApplicationContext is instructed to destroy all singletons before the application shuts down. By using the ApplicationContextAware interface, you can build a bean that can be configured in ApplicationContext to create and configure a shutdown hook bean automatically. Listing 4-16 shows the code for this bean.

Listing 4-16. The ShutdownHookBean Class

```
package com.apress.prospring4.ch4;

import org.springframework.beans.BeansException;
import org.springframework.context.ApplicationContext;
import org.springframework.context.ApplicationContextAware;
import org.springframework.context.support.GenericApplicationContext;

public class ShutdownHookBean implements ApplicationContextAware {
    private ApplicationContext ctx;

    @Override
    public void setApplicationContext(ApplicationContext ctx)
        throws BeansException {

        if (ctx instanceof GenericApplicationContext) {
            ((GenericApplicationContext) ctx).registerShutdownHook();
        }
    }
}
```

Most of this code should seem familiar to you by now. The ApplicationContextAware interface defines a single method, setApplicationContext(ApplicationContext), which Spring calls to pass your bean a reference to its ApplicationContext. In Listing 4-16, the ShutdownHookBean class checks whether ApplicationContext is of type GenericApplicationContext, meaning it supports the registerShutdownHook() method; if it does, it will register a shutdown hook to ApplicationContext. Listing 4-17 shows how to configure this bean to work with the DestructiveBeanWithInterface bean (app-context-annotation.xml).

Listing 4-17. Configuring ShutdownHookBean

```
<?xml version="1.0" encoding="UTF-8"?>

<beans xmlns="http://www.springframework.org/schema/beans"
    xmlns:xsi="http://www.w3.org/2001/XMLSchema-instance"
    xmlns:p="http://www.springframework.org/schema/p"
    xmlns:context="http://www.springframework.org/schema/context"
    xsi:schemaLocation="http://www.springframework.org/schema/beans
        http://www.springframework.org/schema/beans/spring-beans.xsd
        http://www.springframework.org/schema/context
        http://www.springframework.org/schema/context/spring-context.xsd">

    <context:annotation-config/>

    <bean id="destructiveBean"
        class="com.apress.prospring4.ch4.DestructiveBeanWithInterface"
        p:filePath=
        "#{systemProperties['java.io.tmpdir']}#{systemProperties['file.separator']}test.txt"/>

    <bean id="shutdownHook"
        class="com.apress.prospring4.ch4.ShutdownHookBean"/>
</beans>
```

Notice that no special configuration is required. Listing 4-18 shows a simple example application that uses ShutdownHookBean to manage the destruction of singleton beans.

Listing 4-18. Using ShutdownHookBean

```java
package com.apress.prospring4.ch4;

import javax.annotation.PostConstruct;
import javax.annotation.PreDestroy;
import java.io.File;
import org.springframework.context.support.GenericXmlApplicationContext;

public class DestructiveBeanWithInterface {
    private File file;
    private String filePath;

    @PostConstruct
    public void afterPropertiesSet() throws Exception {
        System.out.println("Initializing Bean");

        if (filePath == null) {
            throw new IllegalArgumentException(
                    "You must specify the filePath property of " +
                    DestructiveBeanWithInterface.class);
        }

        this.file = new File(filePath);
        this.file.createNewFile();

        System.out.println("File exists: " + file.exists());
    }

    @PreDestroy
    public void destroy() {
        System.out.println("Destroying Bean");

        if(!file.delete()) {
            System.err.println("ERROR: failed to delete file.");
        }

        System.out.println("File exists: " + file.exists());
    }

    public void setFilePath(String filePath) {
        this.filePath = filePath;
    }

    public static void main(String[] args) throws Exception {
        GenericXmlApplicationContext ctx = new GenericXmlApplicationContext();
        ctx.load("classpath:META-INF/spring/app-context-annotation.xml");
        ctx.registerShutdownHook();
        ctx.refresh();

        DestructiveBeanWithInterface bean =
            (DestructiveBeanWithInterface) ctx.getBean("destructiveBean");
    }
}
```

This code should seem quite familiar to you. When Spring bootstraps the `ApplicationContext` and the `destructiveBean` is defined in the configuration, Spring passes the reference of the `ApplicationContext` to the `shutdownHook` bean for registering the shutdown hook. Running this example yields the following output, as expected:

```
Initializing Bean
File exists: true
Destroying Bean
File exists: false
```

As you can see, even though no calls to `destroy()` are in the main application, `ShutdownHookBean` is registered as a shutdown hook, and it calls `destroy()` just before the application shuts down.

Use of FactoryBeans

One of the problems that you will face when using Spring is how to create and then inject dependencies that cannot be created simply by using the `new` operator. To overcome this problem, Spring provides the `FactoryBean` interface that acts as an adaptor for objects that cannot be created and managed using the standard Spring semantics. Typically, you use `FactoryBeans` to create beans that you cannot create by using the `new` operator, such as those you access through static factory methods, although this is not always the case. Simply put, a `FactoryBean` is a bean that acts as a factory for other beans. `FactoryBeans` are configured within your `ApplicationContext` like any normal bean, but when Spring uses the `FactoryBean` interface to satisfy a dependency or lookup request, it does not return `FactoryBean`; instead, it invokes the `FactoryBean.getObject()` method and returns the result of that invocation.

`FactoryBeans` are used to great effect in Spring; the most noticeable uses are the creation of transactional proxies, which we cover in Chapter 9, and the automatic retrieval of resources from a JNDI context. However, `FactoryBeans` are useful not just for building the internals of Spring; you'll find them really useful when you build your own applications, because they allow you to manage many more resources by using IoC than would otherwise be available.

FactoryBean Example: The MessageDigestFactoryBean

Often the projects that we work on require some kind of cryptographic processing; typically, this involves generating a message digest or hash of a user's password to be stored in a database. In Java, the `MessageDigest` class provides functionality for creating a digest of any arbitrary data. `MessageDigest` itself is abstract, and you obtain concrete implementations by calling `MessageDigest.getInstance()` and passing in the name of the digest algorithm you want to use. For instance, if we want to use the MD5 algorithm to create a digest, we use the following code to create the `MessageDigest` instance:

```
MessageDigest md5 = MessageDigest.getInstance("MD5");
```

If we want to use Spring to manage the creation of the `MessageDigest` object, the best we can do without a `FactoryBean` is have a property, `algorithmName`, on our bean and then use an initialization callback to call `MessageDigest.getInstance()`. Using a `FactoryBean`, we can encapsulate this logic inside a bean. Then any beans that require a `MessageDigest` instance can simply declare a property, `messageDigest`, and use the `FactoryBean` to obtain the instance. Listing 4-19 shows an implementation of `FactoryBean` that does just this.

Listing 4-19. The MessageDigestFactoryBean Class

```java
package com.apress.prospring4.ch4;

import java.security.MessageDigest;

import org.springframework.beans.factory.FactoryBean;
import org.springframework.beans.factory.InitializingBean;

public class MessageDigestFactoryBean implements
        FactoryBean<MessageDigest>, InitializingBean {
    private String algorithmName = "MD5";

    private MessageDigest messageDigest = null;

    @Override
    public MessageDigest getObject() throws Exception {
        return messageDigest;
    }

    @Override
    public Class<MessageDigest> getObjectType() {
        return MessageDigest.class;
    }

    @Override
    public boolean isSingleton() {
        return true;
    }

    @Override
    public void afterPropertiesSet() throws Exception {
        messageDigest = MessageDigest.getInstance(algorithmName);
    }

    public void setAlgorithmName(String algorithmName) {
        this.algorithmName = algorithmName;
    }
}
```

The FactoryBean interface declares three methods: getObject(), getObjectType(), and isSingleton(). Spring calls the getObject() method to retrieve the object created by the FactoryBean. This is the actual object that is passed to other beans that use the FactoryBean as a collaborator. In Listing 4-19, you can see that MessageDigestFactoryBean passes a clone of the stored MessageDigest instance that is created in the InitializingBean.afterPropertiesSet() callback.

The getObjectType() method allows you to tell Spring what type of object your FactoryBean will return. This can be null if the return type is unknown in advance (for example, the FactoryBean creates different types of objects depending on the configuration, which will be determined only after the FactoryBean is initialized), but if you specify a type, Spring can use it for autowiring purposes. We return MessageDigest as our type (in this case, a class, but try to return an interface type and have the FactoryBean instantiate the concrete implementation class, unless necessary). The reason is that we do not know what concrete type will be returned (not that it matters, because all beans will define their dependencies by using MessageDigest anyway).

The isSingleton() property allows you to inform Spring whether the FactoryBean is managing a singleton instance. Remember that by setting the singleton attribute of the FactoryBean's <bean> tag, you tell Spring about the singleton status of the FactoryBean itself, not the objects it is returning.

Now let's see how the FactoryBean is employed in an application. In Listing 4-20, you can see a simple bean that maintains two MessageDigest instances and then displays the digests of a message passed to its digest() method.

Listing 4-20. The MessageDigester Class

```
package com.apress.prospring4.ch4;

import java.security.MessageDigest;

public class MessageDigester {
    private MessageDigest digest1;
    private MessageDigest digest2;

    public void setDigest1(MessageDigest digest1) {
        this.digest1 = digest1;
    }

    public void setDigest2(MessageDigest digest2) {
        this.digest2 = digest2;
    }

    public void digest(String msg) {
        System.out.println("Using digest1");
        digest(msg, digest1);

        System.out.println("Using digest2");
        digest(msg, digest2);
    }

    private void digest(String msg, MessageDigest digest) {
        System.out.println("Using alogrithm: " + digest.getAlgorithm());
        digest.reset();
        byte[] bytes = msg.getBytes();
        byte[] out = digest.digest(bytes);
        System.out.println(out);
    }
}
```

Listing 4-21 shows an example configuration for two MessageDigestFactoryBeans, one for the SHA1 algorithm, the other using the default (MD5) algorithm (app-context-xml.xml).

Listing 4-21. Configuring FactoryBeans

```
<?xml version="1.0" encoding="UTF-8"?>

<beans xmlns="http://www.springframework.org/schema/beans"
    xmlns:xsi="http://www.w3.org/2001/XMLSchema-instance"
    xmlns:p="http://www.springframework.org/schema/p"
    xsi:schemaLocation="http://www.springframework.org/schema/beans
        http://www.springframework.org/schema/beans/spring-beans.xsd">
```

```
<bean id="shaDigest" class="com.apress.prospring4.ch4.MessageDigestFactoryBean"
    p:algorithmName="SHA1"/>

<bean id="defaultDigest"
    class="com.apress.prospring4.ch4.MessageDigestFactoryBean"/>

<bean id="digester"
    class="com.apress.prospring4.ch4.MessageDigester"
    p:digest1-ref="shaDigest"
    p:digest2-ref="defaultDigest"/>
</beans>
```

As you can see, not only have we configured the two MessageDigestFactoryBeans, but we have also configured a MessageDigester, using the two MessageDigestFactoryBeans, to provide values for the digest1 and digest2 properties. For the defaultDigest bean, since the algorithmName property was not specified, no injection will happen, and the default algorithm (MD5) that was coded in the class will be used. In Listing 4-22, you see a basic example class that retrieves the MessageDigester bean from the BeanFactory and creates the digest of a simple message.

Listing 4-22. Using MessageDigester

```
package com.apress.prospring4.ch4;

import org.springframework.context.support.GenericXmlApplicationContext;

public class MessageDigestExample {
    public static void main(String[] args) {
        GenericXmlApplicationContext ctx = new GenericXmlApplicationContext();
        ctx.load("classpath:META-INF/spring/app-context-xml.xml");
        ctx.refresh();

        MessageDigester digester = (MessageDigester) ctx.getBean("digester");
        digester.digest("Hello World!");
    }
}
```

Running this example gives the following output:

```
Using digest1
Using alogrithm: SHA1
[B@77cd7a0
Using digest2
Using alogrithm: MD5
[B@204f30ec
```

As you can see, the MessageDigest bean is provided with two MessageDigest implementations, SHA1 and MD5, even though no MessageDigest beans are configured in the BeanFactory. This is the FactoryBean at work.

FactoryBeans are the perfect solution when you are working with classes that cannot be created by using the new operator. If you work with objects that are created by using a factory method and you want to use these classes in a Spring application, create a FactoryBean to act as an adaptor, allowing your classes to take full advantage of Spring's IoC capabilities.

Accessing a FactoryBean Directly

Given that Spring automatically satisfies any references to a FactoryBean by the objects produced by that FactoryBean, you may be wondering whether you can actually access the FactoryBean directly. The answer is yes.

Accessing FactoryBean is simple: you prefix the bean name with an ampersand in the call to getBean(), as shown in Listing 4-23.

Listing 4-23. Accessing FactoryBeans Directly

```
package com.apress.prospring4.ch4;

import java.security.MessageDigest;

import org.springframework.context.support.GenericXmlApplicationContext;

public class AccessingFactoryBeans {
    public static void main(String[] args) {
        GenericXmlApplicationContext ctx = new GenericXmlApplicationContext();
        ctx.load("classpath:META-INF/spring/app-context-xml.xml");
        ctx.refresh();

        MessageDigest digest = (MessageDigest) ctx.getBean("shaDigest");

        MessageDigestFactoryBean factoryBean =
            (MessageDigestFactoryBean) ctx.getBean("&shaDigest");

        try {
            MessageDigest shaDigest = factoryBean.getObject();
            System.out.println(shaDigest.digest("Hello world".getBytes()));
        } catch (Exception ex) {
            ex.printStackTrace();
        }
    }
}
```

Running this program generates the following output:

```
[B@77cd7a0
```

This feature is used in a few places in the Spring code, but your application should really have no reason to use it. The intention of FactoryBean is to be used as a piece of supporting infrastructure to allow you to use more of your application's classes in an IoC setting. Avoid accessing FactoryBean directly and invoking its getObject() manually, and let Spring do it for you; if you do this manually, you are making extra work for yourself and are unnecessarily coupling your application to a specific implementation detail that could quite easily change in the future.

Using the factory-bean and factory-method Attributes

Sometimes you need to instantiate JavaBeans that were provided by a non-Spring-powered third-party application. You don't know how to instantiate that class, but you know that the third-party application provides a class that can be used to get an instance of the JavaBean that your Spring application needs. In this case, Spring bean's factory-bean and factory-method attributes in the <bean> tag can be used.

To take a look at how it works, Listing 4-24 shows another version of the MessageDigestFactory that provides a method to return a MessageDigest bean.

Listing 4-24. The MessageDigestFactory Class

```java
package com.apress.prospring4.ch4;

import java.security.MessageDigest;

public class MessageDigestFactory {
    private String algorithmName = "MD5";

    public MessageDigest createInstance() throws Exception {
        return MessageDigest.getInstance(algorithmName);
    }

    public void setAlgorithmName(String algorithmName) {
        this.algorithmName = algorithmName;
    }
}
```

Listing 4-25 shows how to configure the factory method for getting the corresponding MessageDigest bean instance (app-context-xml.xml).

Listing 4-25. Configuring MessageDigestFactory

```xml
<?xml version="1.0" encoding="UTF-8"?>

<beans xmlns="http://www.springframework.org/schema/beans"
    xmlns:xsi="http://www.w3.org/2001/XMLSchema-instance"
    xmlns:p="http://www.springframework.org/schema/p"
    xsi:schemaLocation="http://www.springframework.org/schema/beans
        http://www.springframework.org/schema/beans/spring-beans.xsd">

    <bean id="shaDigestFactory"
        class="com.apress.prospring4.ch4.MessageDigestFactory"
        p:algorithmName="SHA1"/>

    <bean id="defaultDigestFactory"
        class="com.apress.prospring4.ch4.MessageDigestFactory"/>

    <bean id="shaDigest"
        factory-bean="shaDigestFactory"
        factory-method="createInstance">
    </bean>

    <bean id="defaultDigest"
        factory-bean="defaultDigestFactory"
        factory-method="createInstance"/>

    <bean id="digester"
        class="com.apress.prospring4.ch4.MessageDigester"
        p:digest1-ref="shaDigest"
        p:digest2-ref="defaultDigest"/>
</beans>
```

Notice that two digest factory beans were defined, one using SHA1 and the other using the default algorithm. Then for the beans shaDigest and defaultDigest, we instructed Spring to instantiate the beans by using the corresponding message digest factory bean via the factory-bean attribute, and we specified the method to use to obtain the bean instance via the factory-method attribute. Listing 4-26 shows the testing class.

Listing 4-26. MessageDigestFactory in Action

```
package com.apress.prospring4.ch4;

import org.springframework.context.support.GenericXmlApplicationContext;

public class MessageDigestFactoryExample {
    public static void main(String[] args) {
        GenericXmlApplicationContext ctx = new GenericXmlApplicationContext();
        ctx.load("classpath:META-INF/spring/app-context-xml.xml");
        ctx.refresh();

        MessageDigester digester = (MessageDigester) ctx.getBean("digester");
        digester.digest("Hello World!");
    }
}
```

Running the program generates the following output:

```
Using digest1
Using alogrithm: SHA1
[B@1e397ed7
Using digest2
Using alogrithm: MD5
[B@490ab905
```

JavaBeans PropertyEditors

If you are not entirely familiar with JavaBeans concepts, a PropertyEditor is an interface that converts a property's value to and from its native type representation into a String. Originally, this was conceived as a way to allow property values to be entered, as String values, into an editor and have them transformed into the correct type. However, because PropertyEditors are inherently lightweight classes, they have found uses in many settings, including Spring.

Because a good portion of property values in a Spring-based application start life in the BeanFactory configuration file, they are essentially Strings. However, the property that these values are set on may not be String-typed. So, to save you from having to create a load of String-typed properties artificially, Spring allows you to define PropertyEditors to manage the conversion of String-based property values into the correct types.

Using the Built-in PropertyEditors

As of version 4, Spring comes with 13 built-in PropertyEditor implementations that are preregistered with BeanFactory. Listing 4-27 shows a simple bean that declares 13 properties, one for each of the types supported by the built-in PropertyEditors.

Listing 4-27. Using the Built-in PropertyEditors

```java
package com.apress.prospring4.ch4;

import java.io.File;
import java.io.InputStream;
import java.net.URL;
import java.util.Date;
import java.util.List;
import java.util.Locale;
import java.util.Properties;
import java.util.regex.Pattern;
import java.text.SimpleDateFormat;
import org.springframework.beans.PropertyEditorRegistrar;
import org.springframework.beans.PropertyEditorRegistry;
import org.springframework.beans.propertyeditors.CustomDateEditor;
import org.springframework.beans.propertyeditors.StringTrimmerEditor;

import org.springframework.context.support.GenericXmlApplicationContext;

public class PropertyEditorBean {
    private byte[] bytes;              // ByteArrayPropertyEditor
    private Class cls;                 // ClassEditor
    private Boolean trueOrFalse;       // CustomBooleanEditor
    private List<String> stringList;   // CustomCollectionEditor
    private Date date;                 // CustomDateEditor
    private Float floatValue;          // CustomNumberEditor
    private File file;                 // FileEditor
    private InputStream stream;        // InputStreamEditor
    private Locale locale;             // LocaleEditor
    private Pattern pattern;           // PatternEditor
    private Properties properties;     // PropertiesEditor
    private String trimString;         // StringTrimmerEditor
    private URL url;                   // URLEditor

    public void setCls(Class cls) {
        System.out.println("Setting class: " + cls.getName());
        this.cls = cls;
    }

    public void setFile(File file) {
        System.out.println("Setting file: " + file.getName());
        this.file = file;
    }
    public void setLocale(Locale locale) {
        System.out.println("Setting locale: " + locale.getDisplayName());
        this.locale = locale;
    }

    public void setProperties(Properties properties) {
        System.out.println("Loaded " + properties.size() + " properties");
        this.properties = properties;
    }
```

```java
public void setUrl(URL url) {
    System.out.println("Setting URL: " + url.toExternalForm());
    this.url = url;
}

public void setBytes(byte[] bytes) {
    System.out.println("Adding " + bytes.length + " bytes");
    this.bytes = bytes;
}

public void setTrueOrFalse(Boolean trueOrFalse) {
    System.out.println("Setting Boolean: " + trueOrFalse);
    this.trueOrFalse = trueOrFalse;
}

public void setStringList(List<String> stringList) {
    System.out.println("Setting string list with size: "
        + stringList.size());

    this.stringList = stringList;

    for (String string: stringList) {
        System.out.println("String member: " + string);
    }
}

public void setDate(Date date) {
    System.out.println("Setting date: " + date);
    this.date = date;
}

public void setFloatValue(Float floatValue) {
    System.out.println("Setting float value: " + floatValue);
    this.floatValue = floatValue;
}

public void setStream(InputStream stream) {
    System.out.println("Setting stream: " + stream);
    this.stream = stream;
}

public void setPattern(Pattern pattern) {
    System.out.println("Setting pattern: " + pattern);
    this.pattern = pattern;
}

public void setTrimString(String trimString) {
    System.out.println("Setting trim string: " + trimString);
    this.trimString = trimString;
}
```

```
    public static class CustomPropertyEditorRegistrar implements PropertyEditorRegistrar {
        @Override
        public void registerCustomEditors(PropertyEditorRegistry registry) {
            SimpleDateFormat dateFormatter = new SimpleDateFormat("MM/dd/yyyy");
            registry.registerCustomEditor(Date.class,
                    new CustomDateEditor(dateFormatter, true));

            registry.registerCustomEditor(String.class, new StringTrimmerEditor(true));
        }
    }

    public static void main(String[] args) throws Exception {
        File file = File.createTempFile("test", "txt");
        file.deleteOnExit();

        GenericXmlApplicationContext ctx = new GenericXmlApplicationContext();
        ctx.load("classpath:META-INF/spring/app-context-xml.xml");
        ctx.refresh();

        PropertyEditorBean bean =
            (PropertyEditorBean) ctx.getBean("builtInSample");
    }
}
```

In Listing 4-27, you can see that PropertyEditorBean has 13 properties, each corresponding to one of the built-in PropertyEditors. In Listing 4-28, you can see an example configuration specifying values for all of these properties (app-config-xml.xml).

Listing 4-28. Configuration Using PropertyEditors

```xml
<?xml version="1.0" encoding="UTF-8"?>

<beans xmlns="http://www.springframework.org/schema/beans"
    xmlns:xsi="http://www.w3.org/2001/XMLSchema-instance"
    xmlns:util="http://www.springframework.org/schema/util"
    xmlns:p="http://www.springframework.org/schema/p"
    xsi:schemaLocation="http://www.springframework.org/schema/beans
        http://www.springframework.org/schema/beans/spring-beans.xsd
        http://www.springframework.org/schema/util
        http://www.springframework.org/schema/util/spring-util.xsd">

    <bean id="customEditorConfigurer"
        class="org.springframework.beans.factory.config.CustomEditorConfigurer"
        p:propertyEditorRegistrars-ref="propertyEditorRegistrarsList"/>

    <util:list id="propertyEditorRegistrarsList">
        <bean class="com.apress.prospring4.ch4.PropertyEditorBean$CustomPropertyEditorRegistrar"/>
    </util:list>
```

```
    <bean id="builtInSample" class="com.apress.prospring4.ch4.PropertyEditorBean"
        p:bytes="Hello World"
        p:cls="java.lang.String"
        p:trueOrFalse="true"
        p:stringList-ref="stringList"
        p:stream="test.txt"
        p:floatValue="123.45678"
        p:date="05/03/13"
  p:file="#{systemProperties['java.io.tmpdir']}#{systemProperties['file.separator']}test.txt"
        p:locale="en_US"
        p:pattern="a*b"
        p:properties="name=Chris age=32"
        p:trimString="    String need trimming      "
        p:url="http://www.springframework.org"
    />

    <util:list id="stringList">
        <value>String member 1</value>
        <value>String member 2</value>
    </util:list>
</beans>>
```

As you can see, although all the properties on the PropertyEditorBean are not Strings, the values for the properties are specified as simple Strings. Also note that we registered the CustomDateEditor and StringTrimmerEditor, since those two editors were not registered by default in Spring. Running this example yields the following output:

```
Adding 11 bytes
Setting class: java.lang.String
Setting date: Wed May 03 00:00:00 EST 13
Setting file: test.txt
Setting float value: 123.45678
Setting locale: English (United States)
Setting pattern: a*b
Loaded 1 properties
Setting stream: sun.net.www.protocol.jar.JarURLConnection$JarURLInputStream@57e1b0c
Setting string list with size: 2
String member: String member 1
String member: String member 2
Setting trim string: String need trimming
Setting Boolean: true
Setting URL: http://www.springframework.org
```

As you can see, Spring has, using the built-in PropertyEditors, converted the String representations of the various properties to the correct types. Table 4-1 summarizes the built-in PropertyEditors available in Spring.

Table 4-1. *Spring PropertyEditors*

PropertyEditor	Description
ByteArrayPropertyEditor	Converts a String value into an array of bytes.
ClassEditor	Converts from a fully qualified class name into a Class instance. When using this PropertyEditor, be careful not to include any extraneous spaces on either side of the class name when using GenericXmlApplicationContext, because this results in a ClassNotFoundException.
CustomBooleanEditor	Converts a string into a Java Boolean type.
CustomCollectionEditor	Converts a source collection (e.g., represented by the util namespace in Spring) into the target Collection type.
CustomDateEditor	Converts a string representation of a date into a java.util.Date value. You need to register the CustomDateEditor in Spring's ApplicationContext with the desired date format.
CustomNumberEditor	Converts a string into the target number value, which can be Integer, Long, Float, or Double.
FileEditor	Converts a String file path into a File instance. Spring does not check whether the file exists.
InputStreamEditor	Converts a string representation of a resource (e.g., file resource using file:D:/temp/test.txt or classpath:test.txt) into an input stream property.
LocaleEditor	Converts the String representation of a locale, such as en-GB, into a java.util.Locale instance.
Pattern	Converts a string into the JDK Pattern object or the other way round.
PropertiesEditor	Converts a String in the format key1=value1 key2=value2 keyn=valuen into an instance of java.util.Properties with the corresponding properties configured.
StringTrimmerEditor	Performs trimming on the string values before injection. You need to explicitly register this editor.
URLEditor	Converts a String representation of a URL into an instance of java.net.URL.

This set of PropertyEditors provides a good base for working with Spring and makes configuring your application with common components such as files and URLs much simpler.

Creating a Custom PropertyEditor

Although the built-in PropertyEditors cover some of the standard cases of property type conversion, there may come a time when you need to create your own PropertyEditor to support a class or a set of classes you are using in your application. Spring has full support for registering custom PropertyEditors; the only downside is that the java.beans.PropertyEditor interface has a lot of methods, many of which are irrelevant to the task at hand—converting property types. Thankfully, JDK 5 or newer provides the PropertyEditorSupport class, which your own PropertyEditors can extend, leaving you to implement only a single method: setAsText().

Let's consider a simple example to see implementing a custom property editor in action. Suppose we have a Name class with just two properties, first name and last name. Listing 4-29 shows the class.

Listing 4-29. The Name Class

```
package com.apress.prospring4.ch4;

public class Name {
    private String firstName;
    private String lastName;

    public Name(String firstName, String lastName) {
        this.firstName = firstName;
        this.lastName = lastName;
    }

    public String getFirstName() {
        return firstName;
    }

    public void setFirstName(String firstName) {
        this.firstName = firstName;
    }

    public String getLastName() {
        return lastName;
    }

    public void setLastName(String lastName) {
        this.lastName = lastName;
    }

    public String toString() {
        return "First name: " + firstName + " - Last name: " + lastName;
    }
}
```

To simplify the application configuration, let's develop a custom editor that converts a string with a space separator into the Name class's first name and last name, respectively. Listing 4-30 shows the custom property editor.

Listing 4-30. The NamePropertyEditor Class

```
package com.apress.prospring4.ch4;

import java.beans.PropertyEditorSupport;

public class NamePropertyEditor extends PropertyEditorSupport {
    @Override
    public void setAsText(String text) throws IllegalArgumentException {
        String[] name = text.split("\\s");

        setValue(new Name(name[0], name[1]));
    }
}
```

The editor is very simple. It extends JDK's PropertyEditorSupport class and implements the setAsText() method. In the method, we simply split the String into a string array with a space as the delimiter. Afterward, an instance of the Name class is instantiated, passing in the String before the space character as the first name and passing the String after the space character as the last name. Finally, the converted value is returned by calling the setValue() method with the result.

To use the NamePropertyEditor in our application, we need to register the editor in Spring's ApplicationContext. Listing 4-31 shows an ApplicationContext configuration of a CustomEditorConfigurer and the NamePropertyEditor (app-context-xml.xml).

Listing 4-31. Using CustomEditorConfigurer

```xml
<?xml version="1.0" encoding="UTF-8"?>

<beans xmlns="http://www.springframework.org/schema/beans"
    xmlns:xsi="http://www.w3.org/2001/XMLSchema-instance"
    xmlns:p="http://www.springframework.org/schema/p"
    xsi:schemaLocation="http://www.springframework.org/schema/beans
        http://www.springframework.org/schema/beans/spring-beans.xsd">

    <bean name="customEditorConfigurer"
            class="org.springframework.beans.factory.config.CustomEditorConfigurer">
        <property name="customEditors">
            <map>
                <entry key="com.apress.prospring4.ch4.Name"
                        value="com.apress.prospring4.ch4.NamePropertyEditor"/>
            </map>
        </property>
    </bean>

    <bean id="exampleBean" class="com.apress.prospring4.ch4.CustomEditorExample"
        p:name="Chris Schaefer"/>
</beans>
```

You should notice two points in this configuration. First, custom PropertyEditors get injected into the CustomEditorConfigurer class by using the Map-typed customEditors property. Second, each entry in the Map represents a single PropertyEditor, with the key of the entry being the name of the class for which the PropertyEditor is used. As you can see, the key for the NamePropertyEditor is com.apress.prospring4.ch4.Name, which signifies that this is the class for which the editor should be used.

Listing 4-32 shows the code for the CustomEditorExample class that is registered as a bean in Listing 4-31.

Listing 4-32. The CustomEditorExample Class

```java
package com.apress.prospring4.ch4;

import org.springframework.context.support.GenericXmlApplicationContext;

public class CustomEditorExample {
    private Name name;

    public Name getName() {
        return name;
    }
```

```
    public void setName(Name name) {
        this.name = name;
    }

    public static void main(String[] args) {
        GenericXmlApplicationContext ctx = new GenericXmlApplicationContext();
        ctx.load("classpath:META-INF/spring/app-context-xml.xml");
        ctx.refresh();

        CustomEditorExample bean =
            (CustomEditorExample) ctx.getBean("exampleBean");

        System.out.println(bean.getName());
    }
}
```

The previous code is nothing special. Run the example, and you will see the following output:

```
First name: Chris - Last name: Schaefer
```

This is the output from the toString() method we implemented in the Name class, and you can see that the first name and last name of the Name object were correctly populated by Spring by using the configured NamePropertyEditor.

Starting from version 3, Spring introduced the Type Conversion and Field Formatting Service Provider interface (SPI), which provide a simpler and well-structured API in performing type conversion and field formatting. It's especially useful for web application development. Both the Type Conversion SPI and the Field Formatting API are discussed in detail in Chapter 10.

More Spring ApplicationContext Configuration

So far, although we are discussing Spring's ApplicationContext, most of the features that we covered mainly surround the BeanFactory interface wrapped by ApplicationContext. In Spring, various implementations of the BeanFactory interface are responsible for bean instantiation, providing Dependency Injection and life-cycle support for beans managed by Spring. However, as stated earlier, being an extension of the BeanFactory, ApplicationContext provides other useful functionalities as well.

The main function of ApplicationContext is to provide a much richer framework on which to build your applications. ApplicationContext is much more aware of the beans (compared to BeanFactory) that you configure within it, and in the case of many of the Spring infrastructure classes and interfaces, such as BeanFactoryPostProcessor, it interacts with them on your behalf, reducing the amount of code you need to write in order to use Spring.

The biggest benefit of using ApplicationContext is that it allows you to configure and manage Spring and Spring-managed resources in a completely declarative way. This means that wherever possible, Spring provides support classes to load ApplicationContext into your application automatically, thus removing the need for you to write any code to access ApplicationContext. In practice, this feature is currently available only when you are building web applications with Spring, which allows you to initialize Spring's ApplicationContext in the web application deployment descriptor. When using a stand-alone application, you can also initialize Spring's ApplicationContext by simple coding.

In addition to providing a model that is focused more on declarative configuration, `ApplicationContext` supports the following features:

- Internationalization

- Event publication

- Resource management and access

- Additional life-cycle interfaces

- Improved automatic configuration of infrastructure components

In the following sections, we discuss some of the most important features in `ApplicationContext` besides DI.

Internationalization with the MessageSource

One area where Spring really excels is in support for internationalization (i18n). Using the `MessageSource` interface, your application can access `String` resources, called *messages*, stored in a variety of languages. For each language you want to support in your application, you maintain a list of messages that are keyed to correspond to messages in other languages. For instance, if I wanted to display "The quick brown fox jumped over the lazy dog" in English and in Czech, I would create two messages, both keyed as `msg`; the one for English would read, "The quick brown fox jumped over the lazy dog," and the one for Czech would read, "Príšerne žlutoucký kun úpel dábelské ódy."

Although you don't need to use `ApplicationContext` to use `MessageSource`, the `ApplicationContext` interface extends `MessageSource` and provides special support for loading messages and for making them available in your environment. The automatic loading of messages is available in any environment, but automatic access is provided only in certain Spring-managed scenarios, such as when you are using Spring's MVC framework to build a web application. Although any class can implement `ApplicationContextAware` and thus access the automatically loaded messages, we suggest a better solution later in this chapter, in the section "Using MessageSource in Stand-Alone Applications."

Before we continue, if you are unfamiliar with i18n support in Java, we suggest that you at least check out the Javadocs (`http://download.java.net/jdk8/docs/api/index.html`).

Using ApplicationContext and MessageSource

Aside from `ApplicationContext`, Spring provides three `MessageSource` implementations: `ResourceBundleMessageSource`, `ReloadableResourceBundleMessageSource`, and `StaticMessageSource`. The `StaticMessageSource` implementation should not be used in a production application because you can't configure it externally, and this is generally one of the main requirements when you are adding i18n capabilities to your application. `ResourceBundleMessageSource` loads messages by using a Java `ResourceBundle`. `ReloadableResourceBundleMessageSource` is essentially the same, except it supports scheduled reloading of the underlying source files.

All three `MessageSource` implementations also implement another interface called `HierarchicalMessageSource`, which allows for many `MessageSource` instances to be nested. This is key to the way `ApplicationContext` works with `MessageSources`.

To take advantage of `ApplicationContext`'s support for `MessageSource`, you must define a bean in your configuration of type `MessageSource` and with the name `messageSource`. `ApplicationContext` takes this `MessageSource` and nests it within itself, allowing you to access the messages by using `ApplicationContext`. This can be hard to visualize, so take a look at the following example.

Listing 4-33 shows a simple application that accesses a set of messages for both the English and Czech locales.

Listing 4-33. Exploring MessageSource Usage

```
package com.apress.prospring4.ch4;

import java.util.Locale;

import org.springframework.context.support.GenericXmlApplicationContext;

public class MessageSourceDemo {
    public static void main(String[] args) {
        GenericXmlApplicationContext ctx = new GenericXmlApplicationContext();
        ctx.load("classpath:META-INF/spring/app-context-xml.xml");
        ctx.refresh();

        Locale english = Locale.ENGLISH;
        Locale czech = new Locale("cs", "CZ");

        System.out.println(ctx.getMessage("msg", null, english));
        System.out.println(ctx.getMessage("msg", null, czech));

        System.out.println(ctx.getMessage("nameMsg", new Object[] { "Chris",
                "Schaefer" }, english));
    }
}
```

Don't worry about the calls to getMessage() just yet; we return to those shortly. For now, just know that they retrieve a keyed message for the locale specified. In Listing 4-34, you can see the configuration used by this application (app-context-xml.xml).

Listing 4-34. Configuring a MessageSource Bean

```xml
<?xml version="1.0" encoding="UTF-8"?>

<beans xmlns="http://www.springframework.org/schema/beans"
    xmlns:xsi="http://www.w3.org/2001/XMLSchema-instance"
    xmlns:p="http://www.springframework.org/schema/p"
    xmlns:util="http://www.springframework.org/schema/util"
    xsi:schemaLocation="http://www.springframework.org/schema/beans
        http://www.springframework.org/schema/beans/spring-beans.xsd
        http://www.springframework.org/schema/util
        http://www.springframework.org/schema/util/spring-util.xsd">

    <bean id="messageSource"
            class="org.springframework.context.support.ResourceBundleMessageSource"
        p:basenames-ref="basenames"/>

    <util:list id="basenames">
        <value>buttons</value>
        <value>labels</value>
    </util:list>
</beans>
```

Here we define a ResourceBundleMessageSource bean with the name messageSource as required and configure it with a set of names to form the base of its file set. A Java ResourceBundle, which is used by

ResourceBundleMessageSource, works on a set of properties files that are identified by base names. When looking for a message for a particular Locale, the ResourceBundle looks for a file that is named as a combination of the base name and the locale name. For instance, if the base name is foo and we are looking for a message in the en-GB (British English) locale, ResourceBundle looks for a file called foo_en_GB.properties.

For the previous example, the content of the properties files for English (labels_en.properties) and Czech (labels_cs_CZ.properties) are shown in Listing 4-35 and Listing 4-36, respectively.

Listing 4-35. labels_en.properties File

```
msg=The quick brown fox jumped over the lazy dog
nameMsg=My name is {0} {1}
```

Listing 4-36. labels_cs_CZ.properties File

```
msg=Príšerne žlutoucký kun úpel dábelské ódy
```

Running the MessageSourceDemo class in Listing 4-33 yields the following output:

```
The quick brown fox jumped over the lazy dog
Príšerne žlutoucký kun úpel dábelské ódy
My name is Chris Schaefer
```

Now this example just raises even more questions. What did those calls to getMessage() mean? Why did we use ApplicationContext.getMessage() rather than access the ResourceBundleMessageSource bean directly? We'll answer each of these questions in turn.

Using the getMessage() Method

The MessageSource interface defines three overloads for the getMessage() method. These are described in Table 4-2.

Table 4-2. *Overloads for MessageSource.getMessage()*

Method Signature	Description
getMessage (String, Object[], Locale)	This is the standard getMessage() method. The String argument is the key of the message corresponding to the key in the properties file. In Listing 4-33, the first call to getMessage() used msg as the key, and this corresponded to the following entry in the properties file for the en locale: msg=The quick brown fox jumped over the lazy dog. The Object[] array argument is used for replacements in the message. In the third call to getMessage() in Listing 4-33, we passed in an array of two Strings. The message keyed as nameMsg was My name is {0} {1}. The numbers in braces are placeholders, and each one is replaced with the corresponding entry in the argument array. The final argument, Locale, tells ResourceBundleMessageSource which properties file to look in. Even though the first and second calls to getMessage() in the example used the same key, they returned different messages that correspond to the Locale that was passed in to getMessage().
getMessage (String, Object[], String, Locale)	This overload works in the same way as getMessage(String, Object[], Locale), other than the second String argument, which allows you to pass in a default value in case a message for the supplied key is not available for the supplied Locale.
getMessage (MessageSourceResolvable, Locale)	This overload is a special case. We discuss it in further detail in the section "The MessageSourceResolvable Interface."

Why Use ApplicationContext As a MessageSource?

To answer this question, we need to jump a little ahead of ourselves and look at the web application support in Spring. The answer, in general, is that you shouldn't use ApplicationContext as a MessageSource because doing so couples your bean to ApplicationContext unnecessarily (this is discussed in more detail in the next section). You should use ApplicationContext when you are building a web application by using Spring's MVC framework.

The core interface in Spring MVC is Controller. Unlike frameworks such as Struts that require you to implement your controllers by inheriting from a concrete class, Spring simply requires that you implement the Controller interface (or annotate your controller class with the @Controller annotation). Having said that, Spring provides a collection of useful base classes that you will use to implement your own controllers. Each of these base classes are themselves subclasses (directly or indirectly) of the ApplicationObjectSupport class, which is a convenient superclass for any application objects that want to be aware of ApplicationContext.

Remember that in a web application setting, ApplicationContext is loaded automatically. ApplicationObjectSupport accesses this ApplicationContext, wraps it in a MessageSourceAccessor object, and makes that available to your controller via the protected getMessageSourceAccessor() method. MessageSourceAccessor provides a wide array of convenient methods for working with MessageSources. This form of *autoinjection* is quite beneficial; it removes the need for all of your controllers to expose a MessageSource property.

However, this is not the best reason for using ApplicationContext as a MessageSource in your web application. The main reason to use ApplicationContext rather than a manually defined MessageSource bean is that Spring does, where possible, expose ApplicationContext, as a MessageSource, to the view tier. This means that when you are using Spring's JSP tag library, the <spring:message> tag automatically reads messages from ApplicationContext, and when you are using JSTL, the <fmt:message> tag does the same.

All of these benefits mean that it is better to use the MessageSource support in ApplicationContext when you are building a web application, rather than manage an instance of MessageSource separately. This is especially true when you consider that all you need to do to take advantage of this feature is configure a MessageSource bean with the name messageSource.

Using MessageSource in Stand-Alone Applications

When you are using MessageSource in stand-alone applications, where Spring offers no additional support other than to nest the MessageSource bean automatically in ApplicationContext, it is best to make the MessageSource available by using Dependency Injection. You can opt to make your bean ApplicationContextAware, but doing so precludes its use in a BeanFactory context. Add to this that you complicate testing without any discernible benefit, and it is clear that you should stick to using Dependency Injection to access MessageSource objects in a stand-alone setting.

The MessageSourceResolvable Interface

You can use an object that implements MessageSourceResolvable in place of a key and a set of arguments when you are looking up a message from a MessageSource. This interface is most widely used in the Spring validation libraries to link Error objects to their internationalized error messages.

Application Events

Another feature of ApplicationContext not present in BeanFactory is the ability to publish and receive events by using ApplicationContext as a broker. In this section, you will take a look at its usage.

Using Application Events

An event is class-derived from ApplicationEvent, which itself derives from java.util.EventObject. Any bean can listen for events by implementing the ApplicationListener<T> interface; ApplicationContext automatically registers any bean that implements this interface as a listener when it is configured. Events are published using the ApplicationEventPublisher.publishEvent() method, so the publishing class must have knowledge of ApplicationContext (which extends the ApplicationEventPublisher interface). In a web application, this is simple because many of your classes are derived from Spring Framework classes that allow access to ApplicationContext through a protected method. In a stand-alone application, you can have your publishing bean implement ApplicationContextAware to enable it to publish events.

Listing 4-37 shows an example of a basic event class.

Listing 4-37. Creating an Event Class

```
package com.apress.prospring4.ch4;

import org.springframework.context.ApplicationEvent;

public class MessageEvent extends ApplicationEvent {
    private String msg;

    public MessageEvent(Object source, String msg) {
        super(source);
        this.msg = msg;
    }

    public String getMessage() {
        return msg;
    }
}
```

This code is quite basic; the only point of note is that ApplicationEvent has a single constructor that accepts a reference to the source of the event. This is reflected in the constructor for MessageEvent. In Listing 4-38, you can see the code for the listener.

Listing 4-38. The MessageEventListener Class

```
package com.apress.prospring4.ch4;

import org.springframework.context.ApplicationListener;

public class MessageEventListener implements ApplicationListener<MessageEvent> {
    @Override
    public void onApplicationEvent(MessageEvent event) {
        MessageEvent msgEvt = (MessageEvent) event;
        System.out.println("Received: " + msgEvt.getMessage());
    }
}
```

The ApplicationListener interface defines a single method, onApplicationEvent, that is called by Spring when an event is raised. MessageEventListener shows its interest only in events of type MessageEvent (or its subclasses) by implementing the strongly typed ApplicationListener interface. If a MessageEvent was received, it writes the message to stdout. Publishing events is simple; it is just a matter of creating an instance of the event class and passing it to the ApplicationEventPublisher .publishEvent() method, as shown in Listing 4-39.

Listing 4-39. Publishing an Event

```java
package com.apress.prospring4.ch4;

import org.springframework.beans.BeansException;
import org.springframework.context.ApplicationContext;
import org.springframework.context.ApplicationContextAware;
import org.springframework.context.support.ClassPathXmlApplicationContext;

public class Publisher implements ApplicationContextAware {
    private ApplicationContext ctx;

    @Override
    public void setApplicationContext(ApplicationContext applicationContext)
            throws BeansException {
        this.ctx = applicationContext;
    }

    public void publish(String message) {
        ctx.publishEvent(new MessageEvent(this, message));
    }

    public static void main(String[] args) {
        ApplicationContext ctx = new ClassPathXmlApplicationContext(
                "classpath:META-INF/spring/app-context-xml.xml");

        Publisher pub = (Publisher) ctx.getBean("publisher");
        pub.publish("Hello World!");
        pub.publish("The quick brown fox jumped over the lazy dog");
    }
}
```

Here you can see that the Publisher class retrieves an instance of itself from ApplicationContext and then, using the publish() method, publishes two MessageEvents to ApplicationContext. The Publisher bean instance accesses the ApplicationContext by implementing ApplicationContextAware. Listing 4-40 shows the configuration for this example (app-context-xml.xml).

Listing 4-40. Configuring ApplicationListener Beans

```xml
<?xml version="1.0" encoding="UTF-8"?>

<beans xmlns="http://www.springframework.org/schema/beans"
    xmlns:xsi="http://www.w3.org/2001/XMLSchema-instance"
    xsi:schemaLocation="http://www.springframework.org/schema/beans
        http://www.springframework.org/schema/beans/spring-beans.xsd">

    <bean id="publisher" class="com.apress.prospring4.ch4.Publisher"/>

    <bean id="messageEventListener"
        class="com.apress.prospring4.ch4.MessageEventListener"/>
</beans>
```

137

Notice that you do not need special configuration to register `MessageEventListener` with `ApplicationContext`; it is picked up automatically by Spring. Running this example results in the following output:

```
Received: Hello World!
Received: The quick brown fox jumped over the lazy dog
```

Considerations for Event Usage

In many cases in an application, certain components need to be notified of certain events. Often you do this by writing code to notify each component explicitly or by using a messaging technology such as JMS. The drawback of writing code to notify each component in turn is that you are coupling those components to the publisher, in many cases unnecessarily.

Consider a situation whereby you cache product details in your application to avoid trips to the database. Another component allows product details to be modified and persisted to the database. To avoid making the cache invalid, the update component explicitly notifies the cache that the user details have changed. In this example, the update component is coupled to a component that, really, has nothing to do with its business responsibility. A better solution would be to have the update component publish an event every time a product's details are modified and then have interested components, such as the cache, listen for that event. This has the benefit of keeping the components decoupled, which makes it simple to remove the cache if needed, or to add another listener that is interested in knowing when a product's details change.

Using JMS in this case would be overkill, because the process of invalidating the product's entry in the cache is quick and is not business critical. The use of the Spring event infrastructure adds very little overhead to your application.

Typically, we use events for reactionary logic that executes quickly and is not part of the main application logic. In the previous example, the invalidation of a product in cache happens in reaction to the updating of product details, it executes quickly (or it should), and it is not part of the main function of the application. For processes that are long running and form part of the main business logic, it is recommended to use JMS or similar messaging systems such as RabbitMQ. The main benefits of using JMS are that it is more suited to long-running processes, and as the system grows, you can, if necessary, factor the JMS-driven processing of messages containing business information onto a separate machine.

Accessing Resources

Often an application needs to access a variety of resources in different forms. You might need to access some configuration data stored in a file in the file system, some image data stored in a JAR file on the classpath, or maybe some data on a server elsewhere. Spring provides a unified mechanism for accessing resources in a protocol-independent way. This means your application can access a file resource in the same way, whether it is stored in the file system, in the classpath, or on a remote server.

At the core of Spring's resource support is the `org.springframework.core.io.Resource` interface. The `Resource` interface defines ten self-explanatory methods: `contentLength()`, `exists()`, `getDescription()`, `getFile()`, `getFileName()`, `getURI()`, `getURL()`, `isOpen()`, `isReadable()`, and `lastModified()`. In addition to these ten methods, there is one that is not quite so self-explanatory: `createRelative()`. The `createRelative()` method creates a new `Resource` instance by using a path that is relative to the instance on which it is invoked. You can provide your own `Resource` implementations, although that is outside the scope of this chapter, but in most cases, you use one of the built-in implementations for accessing a file (the `FileSystemResource` class), a classpath (the `ClassPathResource` class), or URL resources (the `UrlResource` class).

Internally, Spring uses another interface, `ResourceLoader`, and the default implementation, `DefaultResourceLoader`, to locate and create `Resource` instances. However, you generally won't interact with `DefaultResourceLoader`, instead using another `ResourceLoader` implementation—`ApplicationContext`.

Listing 4-41 shows a sample application that accesses three resources by using `ApplicationContext`.

Listing 4-41. Accessing Resources

```
package com.apress.prospring4.ch4;

import java.io.File;
import org.springframework.context.ApplicationContext;
import org.springframework.context.support.ClassPathXmlApplicationContext;
import org.springframework.core.io.Resource;

public class ResourceDemo {
    public static void main(String[] args) throws Exception{
        ApplicationContext ctx = new ClassPathXmlApplicationContext();

        File file = File.createTempFile("test", "txt");
        file.deleteOnExit();

        System.out.println(file.getPath());
        Resource res1 = ctx.getResource("file://" + file.getPath());
        displayInfo(res1);

        Resource res2 = ctx.getResource("classpath:test.txt");
        displayInfo(res2);

        Resource res3 = ctx.getResource("http://www.google.com");
        displayInfo(res3);
    }

    private static void displayInfo(Resource res) throws Exception{
        System.out.println(res.getClass());
        System.out.println(res.getURL().getContent());
        System.out.println("");
    }
}
```

Notice that in each call to getResource(), we pass in a URI for each resource. You will recognize the common file: and http: protocols that we pass in for res1 and res3. The classpath: protocol we use for res2 is Spring-specific and indicates that ResourceLoader should look in the classpath for the resource. Running this example results in the following output:

```
class org.springframework.core.io.UrlResource
java.io.BufferedInputStream@6a024a67

class org.springframework.core.io.ClassPathResource
sun.net.www.content.text.PlainTextInputStream@4de8b406

class org.springframework.core.io.UrlResource
sun.net.www.protocol.http.HttpURLConnection$HttpInputStream@48eff760
```

Notice that for both the file: and http: protocols, Spring returns a UrlResource instance. Spring does include a FileSystemResource class, but the DefaultResourceLoader does not use this class at all. It's because Spring's default resource-loading strategy treats the URL and file as the same type of resource with difference protocols (file: and http:). If an instance of FileSystemResource is required, use FileSystemResourceLoader. Once a Resource instance is obtained, you are free to access the contents as you see fit, using getFile(), getInputStream(), or getURL(). In some cases, such as when you are using the http: protocol, the call to getFile() results in a FileNotFoundException. For this reason, we recommend that you use getInputStream() to access resource contents because it is likely to function for all possible resource types.

Configuration Using Java Classes

Besides XML and property file configuration, you can use Java classes to configure Spring's ApplicationContext. Spring JavaConfig used to be a separate project, but starting with Spring 3.0, its major features for configuration using Java classes was merged into the core Spring Framework.

In this section, we show how to use Java classes to configure Spring's ApplicationContext and its equivalent when using XML configuration.

ApplicationContext Configuration in Java

Let's see how we can configure Spring's ApplicationContext by using Java classes, by referring to the same example for message provider and renderer that we presented in Chapter 3. Listing 4-42 recaps the message provider interface and a configurable message provider.

Listing 4-42. MessageProvider and ConfigurableMessageProvider

```
package com.apress.prospring4.ch4;

public class ConfigurableMessageProvider implements MessageProvider {
    private String message = "Default message";

    public ConfigurableMessageProvider() {

    }

    public ConfigurableMessageProvider(String message) {
        this.message = message;
    }

    public void setMessage(String message) {
        this.message = message;
    }

    @Override
    public String getMessage() {
        return message;
    }
}
```

Listing 4-43 shows the MessageRenderer interface and the StandardOutMessageRenderer implementation.

Listing 4-43. MessageRenderer and StandardOutMessageRenderer

```
package com.apress.prospring4.ch4;

public interface MessageRenderer {
    void render();
    void setMessageProvider(MessageProvider provider);
    MessageProvider getMessageProvider();
}

package com.apress.prospring4.ch4;

public class StandardOutMessageRenderer implements MessageRenderer {
    private MessageProvider messageProvider;

    @Override
    public void render() {
        if (messageProvider == null) {
            throw new RuntimeException(
                "You must set the property messageProvider of class:"
                    + StandardOutMessageRenderer.class.getName());
        }

        System.out.println(messageProvider.getMessage());
    }

    @Override
    public void setMessageProvider(MessageProvider provider){
        this.messageProvider = provider;
    }

    @Override
    public MessageProvider getMessageProvider() {
        return this.messageProvider;
    }
}
```

Listing 4-44 shows the XML configuration for the Spring ApplicationContext (app-context-xml.xml).

Listing 4-44. XML Configuration

```
<?xml version="1.0" encoding="UTF-8"?>

<beans xmlns="http://www.springframework.org/schema/beans"
    xmlns:xsi="http://www.w3.org/2001/XMLSchema-instance"
    xmlns:p="http://www.springframework.org/schema/p"
    xmlns:c="http://www.springframework.org/schema/c"
    xsi:schemaLocation="http://www.springframework.org/schema/beans
        http://www.springframework.org/schema/beans/spring-beans.xsd">
```

```
    <bean id="messageRenderer"
        class="com.apress.prospring4.ch4.StandardOutMessageRenderer"
        p:messageProvider-ref="messageProvider"/>

    <bean id="messageProvider"
        class="com.apress.prospring4.ch4.ConfigurableMessageProvider"
        c:message="This is a configurable message"/>
</beans>
```

Listing 4-45 shows the testing program.

Listing 4-45. XML Configuration Testing Program

```
package com.apress.prospring4.ch4;

import org.springframework.context.ApplicationContext;
import org.springframework.context.support.ClassPathXmlApplicationContext;

public class JavaConfigXMLExample {
    public static void main(String[] args) {
        ApplicationContext ctx = new
            ClassPathXmlApplicationContext("classpath:META-INF/spring/app-context-xml.xml");

        MessageRenderer renderer =
            ctx.getBean("messageRenderer", MessageRenderer.class);

        renderer.render();
    }
}
```

Running this program produces the following output:

```
This is a configurable message
```

When using a Java class instead of XML to configure the previous message provider and renderer, we just need to implement a normal JavaBean as usual, with the appropriate annotations for Spring's Java configuration. Listing 4-46 shows the Java class, which is equivalent to the XML configuration shown in Listing 4-44.

Listing 4-46. Java Configuration

```
package com.apress.prospring4.ch4;

import org.springframework.context.annotation.Bean;
import org.springframework.context.annotation.Configuration;

@Configuration
public class AppConfig {
    @Bean
    public MessageProvider messageProvider() {
        return new ConfigurableMessageProvider();
    }
```

```
    @Bean
    public MessageRenderer messageRenderer() {
        MessageRenderer renderer = new StandardOutMessageRenderer();
        renderer.setMessageProvider(messageProvider());

        return renderer;
    }
}
```

In the `AppConfig` class, you can see that we first use the `@Configuration` annotation to inform Spring that this is a Java-based configuration file. Afterward, the `@Bean` annotation is used to declare a Spring bean and the DI requirements. The `@Bean` annotation is equivalent to the `<bean>` tag, the method name is equivalent to the `id` attribute within the `<bean>` tag, and when instantiating the `MessageRender` bean, setter injection is achieved by calling the corresponding method to get the message provider, which is the same as using the `<ref>` attribute in the XML configuration. Listing 4-47 shows how to initialize the `ApplicationContext` from the Java configuration file.

Listing 4-47. Java Configuration Testing

```
package com.apress.prospring4.ch4;

import org.springframework.context.ApplicationContext;
import org.springframework.context.annotation.AnnotationConfigApplicationContext;

public class JavaConfigSimpleExample {
    public static void main(String[] args) {
        ApplicationContext ctx = new
            AnnotationConfigApplicationContext(AppConfig.class);

        MessageRenderer renderer =
            ctx.getBean("messageRenderer", MessageRenderer.class);

        renderer.render();
    }
}
```

From the previous listing, we use the `AnnotationConfigApplicationContext` class, passing in the configuration class as the constructor argument (you can pass multiple configuration classes to it via the JDK varargs feature). Afterward, you can use `ApplicationContext` returned as usual.

Running the program gives the following result:

```
Default message
```

Having seen the basic usage of a Java configuration class, let's proceed to more configuration options. For the message provider, let's say we want to externalize the message into a properties file (`message.properties`) and then inject it into `ConfigurableMessageProvider` by using Constructor Injection. The content of `message.properties` is as follows:

```
message=Hello from Spring Java Configuration
```

Let's see the revised testing program, which loads the properties files by using the `@PropertySource` annotation and then injects them into the message provider implementation. In Listing 4-48, we also added a lot of various annotations that Spring supports for a base Java configuration and their XML equivalents. Note that for the

@EnableTransactionManagement annotation to work, we need to add the dependency on the spring-tx module to the project (see Table 4-3).

Table 4-3. *Dependency for Spring Transaction Support*

Group ID	Artifact ID	Version	Description
org.springframework	spring-tx	4.0.2.RELEASE	Spring module for transaction support

Listing 4-48. Java Configuration Class AppConfig (Revised)

```
package com.apress.prospring4.ch4;

import org.springframework.beans.factory.annotation.Autowired;
import org.springframework.context.annotation.Bean;
import org.springframework.context.annotation.ComponentScan;
import org.springframework.context.annotation.Configuration;
import org.springframework.context.annotation.DependsOn;
import org.springframework.context.annotation.Import;
import org.springframework.context.annotation.ImportResource;
import org.springframework.context.annotation.Lazy;
import org.springframework.context.annotation.PropertySource;
import org.springframework.context.annotation.Scope;
import org.springframework.core.env.Environment;
import org.springframework.transaction.annotation.EnableTransactionManagement;

@Configuration
@ImportResource(value="classpath:META-INF/spring/app-context-xml.xml")
@PropertySource(value="classpath:message.properties")
@ComponentScan(basePackages={"com.apress.prospring4.ch4"})
@EnableTransactionManagement
public class AppConfig {
    @Autowired
    Environment env;

    @Bean
    @Lazy(value=true)
    public MessageProvider messageProvider() {
        return new ConfigurableMessageProvider(env.getProperty("message"));
    }

    @Bean(name="messageRenderer")
    @Scope(value="prototype")
    @DependsOn(value="messageProvider")
    public MessageRenderer messageRenderer() {
        MessageRenderer renderer = new StandardOutMessageRenderer();
        renderer.setMessageProvider(messageProvider());

        return renderer;
    }
}
```

In the listing, you can see a lot of common annotations for configuration in Java classes. The following are some special points about Listing 4-48:

- The @PropertySource annotation is used to load properties files into the Spring ApplicationContext, which accepts the location as the argument (more than one location can be provided). For XML, <context:property-placeholder> serves the same purpose.

- @ImportResource can also be used to import configuration from XML files, which means you can use XML and Java configuration classes in a mix-and-match way, although we do not recommend doing that. Mixing XML and Java configurations will make your application harder to maintain, because you need to scan through both XML files and Java classes to search for a specific bean.

- Besides @ImportResource, the @Import annotation can import other configuration classes, which means you can also have multiple Java configuration classes for various configurations (for example, one class can be dedicated to DAO beans declaration, one for the Service beans declaration, and so forth).

- @ComponentScan defines the packages that Spring should scan for annotations for bean definitions. It's the same as the <context:component-scan> tag in the XML configuration.

- The other annotations are quite self-explanatory. The @Lazy annotation instructs Spring to instantiate the bean only when requested (same as lazy-init="true" in XML), and @DependsOn tells Spring that a certain bean depends on some other beans, so Spring will make sure that those beans are instantiated first. The @Scope annotation is to define the bean's scope.

- Application infrastructure services can also be defined in Java classes. For example, @EnableTransactionManagement defines that we will use Spring's transaction management feature, which is discussed further in Chapter 9.

- You may also notice the @Autowired property of the env variable, which is of the Environment type. This is the Environment abstraction feature that Spring provides. We discuss it later in this chapter.

Running the testing program again yields the following output:

```
Hello from Spring Java Configuration
```

This is the message defined in the message.properties file.

Java or XML Configuration?

As you already saw, using Java classes can achieve the same level of ApplicationContext configuration as XML. So, which one should you use? The consideration is quite like the one of whether to use XML or Java annotations for DI configuration. Each approach has its own pros and cons. However, the recommendation is the same; that is, when you and your team decide on the approach to use, stick to it and keep the configuration style persistent, instead of scattered around between Java class and XML files. Using one approach will make the maintenance work much easier.

Profiles

Another interesting feature that Spring provides is the concept of configuration profiles. Basically, a *profile* instructs Spring to configure only the ApplicationContext that was defined when the specified profile was active. In this section, we demonstrate the usage of profiles in a simple program.

An Example of Using the Spring Profiles Feature

Let's say there is a service called FoodProviderService that is responsible for providing food to schools, including kindergarten and high school. The FoodProviderService interface has only one method called provideLunchSet(), which produces the lunch set to each student for the calling school. A lunch set is a list of Food objects, which is a very simple class that has only a name attribute. Listing 4-49 shows the Food class.

Listing 4-49. The Food Class

```
package com.apress.prospring4.ch4;

public class Food {
    private String name;

    public Food() {
    }

    public Food(String name) {
        this.name = name;
    }

    public String getName() {
        return name;
    }

    public void setName(String name) {
        this.name = name;
    }
}
```

Listing 4-50 shows the FoodProviderService interface.

Listing 4-50. The FoodProviderService Interface

```
package com.apress.prospring4.ch4;

import java.util.List;

public interface FoodProviderService {
    List<Food> provideLunchSet();
}
```

Now suppose that there are two providers for the lunch set, one for kindergarten and one for high school. The lunch set produced by them is different, although the service they provide is the same—that is, to provide lunch to students. So, now let's create two implementations of the FoodProviderService, using the same name but putting them into different packages to identify their target school. Listings 4-51 and 4-52 show the two classes.

Listing 4-51. The Kindergarten FoodProviderService Implementation

```
package com.apress.prospring4.ch4.kindergarten;

import java.util.ArrayList;
import java.util.List;

import com.apress.prospring4.ch4.Food;
import com.apress.prospring4.ch4.FoodProviderService;

public class FoodProviderServiceImpl implements FoodProviderService {
    @Override
    public List<Food> provideLunchSet() {
        List<Food> lunchSet = new ArrayList<Food>();
        lunchSet.add(new Food("Milk"));
        lunchSet.add(new Food("Biscuits"));

        return lunchSet;
    }
}
```

Listing 4-52. The High-School FoodProviderService Implementation

```
package com.apress.prospring4.ch4.highschool;

import java.util.ArrayList;
import java.util.List;

import com.apress.prospring4.ch4.Food;
import com.apress.prospring4.ch4.FoodProviderService;

public class FoodProviderServiceImpl implements FoodProviderService {
    @Override
    public List<Food> provideLunchSet() {
        List<Food> lunchSet = new ArrayList<Food>();
        lunchSet.add(new Food("Coke"));
        lunchSet.add(new Food("Hamburger"));
        lunchSet.add(new Food("French Fries"));

        return lunchSet;
    }
}
```

From the previous listings, you can see that the two implementations provide the same FoodProviderService interface but produce different combinations of food in the lunch set. So, now suppose a kindergarten wants the provider to deliver the lunch set for their students; let's see how we can use Spring's profile configuration to achieve this. We will run through the XML configuration first.

We will create two XML configuration files, one for the kindergarten profile and the other for the high-school profile. Listings 4-53 and 4-54 show the configuration for kindergarten and high-school food providers, respectively.

Listing 4-53. XML Configuration for Kindergarten (`kindergarten-config.xml`)

```xml
<?xml version="1.0" encoding="UTF-8"?>

<beans xmlns="http://www.springframework.org/schema/beans"
    xmlns:xsi="http://www.w3.org/2001/XMLSchema-instance"
    xsi:schemaLocation="http://www.springframework.org/schema/beans
        http://www.springframework.org/schema/beans/spring-beans.xsd"
        profile="kindergarten">

    <bean id="foodProviderService"
      class="com.apress.prospring4.ch4.kindergarten.FoodProviderServiceImpl"/>
</beans>
```

Listing 4-54. XML Configuration for High School (`highschool-config.xml`)

```xml
<?xml version="1.0" encoding="UTF-8"?>

<beans xmlns="http://www.springframework.org/schema/beans"
    xmlns:xsi="http://www.w3.org/2001/XMLSchema-instance"
    xsi:schemaLocation="http://www.springframework.org/schema/beans
        http://www.springframework.org/schema/beans/spring-beans.xsd"
        profile="highschool">

    <bean id="foodProviderService"
      class="com.apress.prospring4.ch4.highschool.FoodProviderServiceImpl"/>
</beans>
```

In the previous two configurations, notice the usage of profile="kindergarten" and profile="highschool", respectively, within the <beans> tag. It actually tells Spring that those beans in the file should be instantiated only when the specified profile is active. Now let's see how to activate the correct profile when using Spring's ApplicationContext in a stand-alone application. Listing 4-55 shows the testing program.

Listing 4-55. Profile XML Configuration Example

```java
package com.apress.prospring4.ch4;

import java.util.List;
import org.springframework.context.support.GenericXmlApplicationContext;

public class ProfileXmlConfigExample {
    public static void main(String[] args) {
        GenericXmlApplicationContext ctx = new GenericXmlApplicationContext();
        ctx.load("classpath:META-INF/spring/*-config.xml");
        ctx.refresh();

        FoodProviderService foodProviderService =
            ctx.getBean("foodProviderService", FoodProviderService.class);

        List<Food> lunchSet = foodProviderService.provideLunchSet();
```

```
        for (Food food: lunchSet) {
            System.out.println("Food: " + food.getName());
        }
    }
}
```

The ctx.load() method will load both kindergarten-config.xml and highschool-config.xml, since we pass the method the wildcard as the prefix. In this example, only the beans in the file kindergarten-config.xml will be instantiated by the Spring base on the profile attribute, which is activated by passing the JVM argument -Dspring.profiles.active="kindergarten". Running the program with this JVM argument produces the following output:

```
Food: Milk
Food: Biscuits
```

This is exactly what the implementation of the kindergarten provider will produce for the lunch set. Now change the profile argument from the previous listing to highschool (-Dspring.profiles.active="highschool"), and the output will change to the following:

```
Food: Coke
Food: Hamburger
Food: French Fries
```

So, now you see the usage. You can also programmatically set the profile to use in your code by calling ctx.getEnvironment().setActiveProfiles("kindergarten"). Additionally you can also register classes to be enabled by profiles using JavaConfig by simply adding the @Profile annotation to your class.

Considerations for Using Profiles

The profiles feature in Spring creates another way for developers to manage the application's running configuration, which used to be done in build tools (for example, Maven's profile support). Build tools rely on the arguments passed into the tool to pack the correct configuration/property files into the Java archive (JAR or WAR, depending on the application type) and then deploy to the target environment. Spring's profile feature lets us as application developers define the profiles by ourselves and activate them either programmatically or by passing in the JVM argument. By using Spring's profile support, you can now use the same application archive and deploy to all environments, by passing in the correct profiles as an argument during JVM startup. For example, you can have applications with different profiles such as (dev, hibernate), (prd, jdbc), and so on, with each combination representing the running environment (development or production) and the data access library to use (Hibernate or JDBC). It brings application profile management into the programming side.

But this approach also has its drawbacks. For example, some may argue that putting all the configuration for different environments into application configuration files or Java classes and bundling them together will be error prone if not handled carefully (for example, the administrator may forget to set the correct JVM argument in the application server environment). Packing files for all profiles together will also make the package a bit larger than usual. Again, let the application and configuration requirements drive you to select the approach that best fits your project.

Environment and PropertySource Abstraction

To set the active profile, we need to access the Environment interface. The Environment interface is an abstraction layer that serves to encapsulate the environment of the running Spring application.

Besides the profile, other key pieces of information encapsulated by the Environment interface are properties. Properties are used to store the application's underlying environment configuration, such as the location of the application folder, database connection information, and so on.

The Environment and PropertySource abstraction features in Spring assist us as developers in accessing various configuration information from the running platform. Under the abstraction, all system properties, environment variables, and application properties are served by the Environment interface, which Spring populates when bootstrapping ApplicationContext. Listing 4-56 shows a simple example.

Listing 4-56. Spring Environment Abstraction Example

```
package com.apress.prospring4.ch4;

import java.util.HashMap;
import java.util.Map;

import org.springframework.context.support.GenericXmlApplicationContext;
import org.springframework.core.env.ConfigurableEnvironment;
import org.springframework.core.env.MapPropertySource;
import org.springframework.core.env.MutablePropertySources;

public class EnvironmentSample {
    public static void main(String[] args) {
        GenericXmlApplicationContext ctx = new GenericXmlApplicationContext();
        ctx.refresh();

        ConfigurableEnvironment env = ctx.getEnvironment();
        MutablePropertySources propertySources = env.getPropertySources();
        Map appMap = new HashMap();
        appMap.put("application.home", "application_home");
        propertySources.addLast(new MapPropertySource("PROSPRING4_MAP", appMap));

        System.out.println("user.home: " + System.getProperty("user.home"));
        System.out.println("JAVA_HOME: " + System.getenv("JAVA_HOME"));

        System.out.println("user.home: " + env.getProperty("user.home"));
        System.out.println("JAVA_HOME: " + env.getProperty("JAVA_HOME"));
        System.out.println("application.home: " + env.getProperty("application.home"));
    }
}
```

In Listing 4-56, after the ApplicationContext initialization, we get a reference to the ConfigurableEnvironment interface. Via the interface, a handle to MutablePropertySources (a default implementation of the PropertySources interface, which allows manipulation of the contained property sources) is obtained. Afterward, we construct a map, put the application properties into the map, and then construct a MapPropertySource class (a PropertySource subclass that reads keys and values from a Map instance) with the map. Finally, the MapPropertySource class is added to the MutablePropertySources via the addLast() method.

Run the program, and the following prints:

```
user.home: /home/chris
JAVA_HOME: /home/chris/bin/java
user.home: /home/chris
JAVA_HOME: /home/chris/bin/java
application.home: application_home
```

For the first two lines, the JVM system property user.home and the environment variable JAVA_HOME are retrieved, as before (by using the JVM's System class). However, for the last three lines, you can see that all the system properties, environment variables, and application properties can be accessed via the Environment interface. You can see how the Environment abstraction can help us manage and access all the various properties within the application's running environment.

For the PropertySource abstraction, Spring will access the properties in the following default order:

- System properties for the running JVM

- Environment variables

- Application-defined properties

So, for example, suppose we define the same application property, user.home, and add it to the Environment interface via the MutablePropertySources class. If you run the program, you will still see that user.home is retrieved from the JVM properties, not yours. However, Spring allows you to control the order in which Environment retrieves the properties. Let's revise Listing 4-56 a bit and see how it works. Listing 4-57 shows the revised version (the differences are highlighted in bold).

Listing 4-57. Spring Environment Abstraction Example (Revised)

```java
package com.apress.prospring4.ch4;

import java.util.HashMap;
import java.util.Map;

import org.springframework.context.support.GenericXmlApplicationContext;
import org.springframework.core.env.ConfigurableEnvironment;
import org.springframework.core.env.MapPropertySource;
import org.springframework.core.env.MutablePropertySources;

public class EnvironmentSample {
    public static void main(String[] args) {
        GenericXmlApplicationContext ctx = new GenericXmlApplicationContext();
        ctx.refresh();

        ConfigurableEnvironment env = ctx.getEnvironment();
        MutablePropertySources propertySources = env.getPropertySources();

        Map appMap = new HashMap();
        appMap.put("user.home", "application_home");

        propertySources.addFirst(new MapPropertySource("PROSPRING4_MAP", appMap));

        System.out.println("user.home: " + System.getProperty("user.home"));
        System.out.println("JAVA_HOME: " + System.getenv("JAVA_HOME"));
```

```
            System.out.println("user.home: " + env.getProperty("user.home"));
            System.out.println("JAVA_HOME: " + env.getProperty("JAVA_HOME"));
    }
}
```

In Listing 4-57, we have defined an application property also called user.home and added it as the first one to search for via the addFirst() method of the MutablePropertySources class. When you run the program, you will see the following output:

```
user.home: /home/chris
JAVA_HOME: /home/chris/bin/java
user.home: application_home
JAVA_HOME: /home/chris/bin/java
```

The first two lines remain the same, because we still use the getProperty() and getenv() methods of the JVM System class to retrieve them. However, when using the Environment interface, you will see that the user.home property we defined takes precedence, since we defined it as the first one to search for property values.

In real life, you seldom need to interact directly with the Environment interface but will use a property placeholder in the form of ${} (for example, ${application.home}) and inject the resolved value into Spring beans. Let's see this in action.

Suppose we had a class to store all the application properties loaded from a property file. Listing 4-58 shows the AppProperty class.

Listing 4-58. Spring Property Placeholder Example

```
package com.apress.prospring4.ch4;

public class AppProperty {
    private String applicationHome;
    private String userHome;

    public String getApplicationHome() {
        return applicationHome;
    }

    public void setApplicationHome(String applicationHome) {
        this.applicationHome = applicationHome;
    }

    public String getUserHome() {
        return userHome;
    }

    public void setUserHome(String userHome) {
        this.userHome = userHome;
    }
}
```

Listing 4-59 is the application.properties file that stores the running application's properties.

Listing 4-59. `application.properties` File

```
application.home=application_home
user.home=/home/chris-new
```

Note that the property file also declares the `user.home` property. Let's take a look at the Spring XML configuration (see Listing 4-60, the `app-context-xml.xml` file).

Listing 4-60. Spring Property Placeholder Configuration

```xml
<?xml version="1.0" encoding="UTF-8"?>

<beans xmlns="http://www.springframework.org/schema/beans"
    xmlns:xsi="http://www.w3.org/2001/XMLSchema-instance"
    xmlns:context="http://www.springframework.org/schema/context"
    xsi:schemaLocation="http://www.springframework.org/schema/beans
        http://www.springframework.org/schema/beans/spring-beans.xsd
        http://www.springframework.org/schema/context
        http://www.springframework.org/schema/context/spring-context.xsd">

    <context:property-placeholder location="classpath:application.properties"/>

    <bean id="appProperty" class="com.apress.prospring4.ch4.AppProperty">
        <property name="applicationHome" value="${application.home}"/>
        <property name="userHome" value="${user.home}"></property>
    </bean>
</beans>
```

We use the `<context:property-placeholder>` tag to load the properties into Spring's `Environment`, which is wrapped into the `ApplicationContext` interface. We also use the placeholders to inject the values into the `AppProperty` bean. Listing 4-61 shows the testing program.

Listing 4-61. Spring Property Placeholder Testing

```java
package com.apress.prospring4.ch4;

import org.springframework.context.support.GenericXmlApplicationContext;

public class PlaceHolderSample {
    public static void main(String[] args) {
        GenericXmlApplicationContext ctx = new GenericXmlApplicationContext();
        ctx.load("classpath:META-INF/spring/app-context-xml.xml");
        ctx.refresh();

        AppProperty appProperty = ctx.getBean("appProperty", AppProperty.class);

        System.out.println("application.home: " + appProperty.getApplicationHome());
        System.out.println("user.home: " + appProperty.getUserHome());
    }
}
```

Let's run the program, and you will see the following output:

```
application.home: application_home
user.home: /home/chris
```

You will see the `application.home` placeholder is properly resolved, while the `user.home` property is still retrieved from the JVM properties, which is correct because it's the default behavior for the `PropertySource` abstraction. To instruct Spring to give precedence for the values in the `application.properties` file, we add the attribute `local-override="true"` to the `<context:property-placeholder>` tag.

```
<context:property-placeholder local-override="true"
    location="classpath:env/application.properties"/>
```

The `local-override` attribute instructs Spring to override the existing properties with the properties defined in this placeholder. Run the program, and you will see that now the `user.home` property from the `application. properties` file is retrieved.

```
application.home: application_home
user.home: /home/chris-new
```

Configuration Using JSR-330 Annotations

As we discussed in Chapter 1, JEE 6 provides support for JSR-330 ("Dependency Injection for Java"), which is a collection of annotations for expressing an application's DI configuration within a JEE container or other compatible IoC framework. Spring also supports and recognizes those annotations, so although you may not be running your application in a JEE 6 container, you can still use JSR-330 annotations within Spring. Using JSR-330 annotations can help you ease the migration to the JEE 6 container or other compatible IoC container (for example, Google Guice) away from Spring.

Again, let's take the message renderer and message provider as an example and implement it using JSR-330 annotations. To support JSR-330 annotations, you need to add a dependency to the project, as shown in Table 4-4.

Table 4-4. *Dependency for JSR-330 Support*

Group ID	Artifact ID	Version	Description
javax.inject	javax.inject	1	JSR-330 standard library

Listing 4-62 shows the `MessageProvider` and `ConfigurableMessageProvider` implementation.

Listing 4-62. `ConfigurableMessageProvider` (JSR-330)

```
package com.apress.prospring4.ch4;

public interface MessageProvider {
    String getMessage();
}

package com.apress.prospring4.ch4;

import javax.inject.Inject;
import javax.inject.Named;
```

```
@Named("messageProvider")
public class ConfigurableMessageProvider implements MessageProvider {
    private String message = "Default message";

    public ConfigurableMessageProvider() {
    }

    @Inject
    @Named("message")
    public ConfigurableMessageProvider(String message) {
        this.message = message;
    }

    public void setMessage(String message) {
        this.message = message;
    }

    @Override
    public String getMessage() {
        return message;
    }
}
```

You will notice that all annotations belong to the javax.inject package, which is the JSR-330 standard. This class used @Named in two places. First, it can be used to declare an injectable bean (the same as the @Component or @Service annotation in Spring). In the listing, the @Named("messageProvider") annotation specifies that the ConfigurableMessageProvider is an injectable bean and gives it the name messageProvider, which is the same as the name attribute in Spring's <bean> tag. Second, we use constructor injection by using the @Inject annotation before the constructor that accepts a string value. Then, we use @Named to specify that we want to inject the value that had the name message assigned. Let's move on to see the MessageRenderer interface and StandardOutMessageRenderer implementation in Listing 4-63.

Listing 4-63. StandardOutMessageRenderer (JSR-330)

```
package com.apress.prospring4.ch4;

public interface MessageRenderer {
    void render();
    void setMessageProvider(MessageProvider provider);
    MessageProvider getMessageProvider();
}

package com.apress.prospring4.ch4;

import javax.inject.Inject;
import javax.inject.Named;
import javax.inject.Singleton;

@Named("messageRenderer")
@Singleton
public class StandardOutMessageRenderer implements MessageRenderer {
    @Inject
```

```java
@Named("messageProvider")
private MessageProvider messageProvider = null;

@Override
public void render() {
    if (messageProvider == null) {
        throw new RuntimeException(
            "You must set the property messageProvider of class:"
            + StandardOutMessageRenderer.class.getName());
    }

    System.out.println(messageProvider.getMessage());
}

@Override
public void setMessageProvider(MessageProvider provider) {
    this.messageProvider = provider;
}

@Override
public MessageProvider getMessageProvider() {
    return this.messageProvider;
}
}
```

In Listing 4-63, we used @Named to define that it's an injectable bean. Notice the @Singleton annotation. It's worth noting that in the JSR-330 standard, a bean's default scope is nonsingleton, which is like Spring's prototype scope. So, in a JSR-330 environment, if you want your bean to be a singleton, you need to use the @Singleton annotation. However, using this annotation in Spring actually doesn't have any effect, because Spring's default scope for bean instantiation is already singleton. We just put it here for a demonstration, and it's worth noting the difference between Spring and other JSR-330-compatible containers.

For the messageProvider property, we use @Inject for setter injection this time and specify that a bean with the name messageProvider should be used for injection.

Listing 4-64 defines a simple Spring XML configuration for the application (app-context-annotation.xml).

Listing 4-64. Spring XML Configuration (JSR-330)

```xml
<?xml version="1.0" encoding="UTF-8"?>

<beans xmlns="http://www.springframework.org/schema/beans"
    xmlns:xsi="http://www.w3.org/2001/XMLSchema-instance"
    xmlns:context="http://www.springframework.org/schema/context"
    xsi:schemaLocation="http://www.springframework.org/schema/beans
      http://www.springframework.org/schema/beans/spring-beans.xsd
      http://www.springframework.org/schema/context
      http://www.springframework.org/schema/context/spring-context.xsd">

    <context:component-scan base-package="com.apress.prospring4.ch4"/>
```

```xml
    <bean id="message" class="java.lang.String">
        <constructor-arg value="You are running JSR330!"/>
    </bean>
</beans>
```

You don't need any special tags to use JSR-330; just configure your application like a normal Spring application. We use `<context:component-scan>` to instruct Spring to scan for the DI-related annotations, and Spring will recognize those JSR-330 annotations. We also declare a Spring bean called `message` for Constructor Injection into the `ConfigurableMessageProvider` class. Listing 4-65 shows the testing program.

Listing 4-65. JSR-330 Example

```java
package com.apress.prospring4.ch4;

import org.springframework.context.support.GenericXmlApplicationContext;

public class Jsr330Example {
    public static void main(String[] args) {
        GenericXmlApplicationContext ctx = new GenericXmlApplicationContext();
        ctx.load("classpath:META-INF/spring/app-context-annotation.xml");
        ctx.refresh();

        MessageRenderer renderer = ctx.getBean("messageRenderer", MessageRenderer.class);
        renderer.render();
    }
}
```

Running the program yields the following output:

```
You are running JSR330!
```

By using JSR-330, you can ease the migration into other JSR-330-compatible IoC containers (for example, JEE 6–compatible application servers or other DI containers such as Google Guice). However, Spring's annotations are much more feature rich and flexible than JSR-330 annotations. Some main differences are highlighted here:

- When using Spring's @Autowired annotation, you can specify a `required` attribute to indicate that the DI must be fulfilled (you can also use Spring's @Required annotation to declare this requirement), while for JSR-330's @Inject annotation, there is no such equivalent. Moreover, Spring provides the @Qualifier annotation, which allows more fine-grained control for Spring to perform autowiring of dependencies based on qualifier name.

- JSR-330 supports only singleton and nonsingleton bean scopes, while Spring supports more scopes, which is very useful for web applications.

- In Spring, you can use the @Lazy annotation to instruct Spring to instantiate the bean only when requested by the application. There's no such equivalent in JSR-330.

You can also mix and match Spring and JSR-330 annotations in the same application. However, it is recommended that you settle on either one to maintain a consistent style for your application. One possible way is to use JSR-330 annotations as much as possible and use Spring annotations when required. However, this brings you fewer benefits, because you still need to do quite a bit of work in migrating to another DI container. In conclusion, Spring's annotations approach is recommended over JSR-330 annotations, because Spring's annotations are much more powerful, unless there is a requirement that your application should be IoC container independent.

Configuration Using Groovy

New to Spring Framework 4.0 is the ability to configure your bean definitions and ApplicationContext by using the Groovy language. This provides developers another choice in configuration to either replace or supplement XML- and/or annotation-based bean configuration. A Spring ApplicationContext can be created directly in a Groovy script or loaded from Java, both by way of the GenericGroovyApplicationContext class. First let's dive into the details by showing how to create bean definitions from an external Groovy script and loading them from Java. Listing 4-66 shows our sample Contact POJO.

Listing 4-66. Sample Contact POJO Class

```
package com.apress.prospring4.ch4;

public class Contact {
    private String firstName;
    private String lastName;
    private int age;

    public void setFirstName(String firstName) {
        this.firstName = firstName;
    }

    public String getFirstName() {
        return firstName;
    }

    public void setLastName(String lastName) {
        this.lastName = lastName;
    }

    public String getLastName() {
        return lastName;
    }

    public void setAge(int age) {
        this.age = age;
    }

    public int getAge() {
        return age;
    }

    @Override
    public String toString() {
        return "First name: " + firstName + ", Last name: " + lastName + ", Age: " + age;
    }
}
```

As you can see, this is just a normal Java class with a couple of properties about a contact. We use a simple Java class here to show that just because you configure your beans in Groovy doesn't mean your entire code base needs to be rewritten in Groovy. With our class created, let's create the Groovy script (beans.groovy) that will be used to create the bean definition, as shown in Listing 4-67.

Listing 4-67. External Groovy Bean Configuration Script

```
package com.apress.prospring4.ch4

beans {
    contact(Contact, firstName: 'Chris', lastName: 'Schaefer', age: 32)
}
```

This Groovy script starts with a top-level closure called beans, which provides bean definitions to Spring. First, we specify the bean name (contact), and then as arguments we provide the class type (Contact) followed by the property names and values that we would like to set. Next, let's create a simple test driver in Java, loading bean definitions from the Groovy script, as shown in Listing 4-68.

Listing 4-68. Loading Groovy Bean Definitions from Java

```
package com.apress.prospring4.ch4;

import org.springframework.context.ApplicationContext;
import org.springframework.context.support.GenericGroovyApplicationContext;

public class GroovyBeansFromJava {
    public static void main(String[] args) {
        ApplicationContext context = new GenericGroovyApplicationContext("classpath:beans.groovy");
        Contact contact = context.getBean("contact", Contact.class);
        System.out.println(contact);
    }
}
```

As you can see, creation of ApplicationContext is carried out in typical fashion, but by using the GenericGroovyApplicationContext class and providing your Groovy script that builds the bean definitions.

Before you can run the samples in this section, you need to add the dependency outlined in Table 4-5.

Table 4-5. Dependency for Groovy Support

Group ID	Artifact ID	Version	Description
org.codehaus.groovy	groovy-all	2.2.2	The Groovy library

Running the sample code in Listing 4-68 yields the following output:

```
First name: Chris, Last name: Schaefer, Age: 32
```

Now that you have seen how to load bean definitions from Java via an external Groovy script, how can we go about creating the ApplicationContext and bean definitions from a Groovy script alone? Let's take a look at the Groovy code (GroovyConfig.groovy) shown in Listing 4-69.

Listing 4-69. Creating ApplicationContext and Bean Definitions in Groovy

```
package com.apress.prospring4.ch4

import org.springframework.context.support.GenericApplicationContext
import org.springframework.beans.factory.groovy.GroovyBeanDefinitionReader

def ctx = new GenericApplicationContext()
def reader = new GroovyBeanDefinitionReader(ctx)

reader.beans {
    contact(Contact, firstName: 'Chris', lastName: 'Schaefer', age: 32)
}

ctx.refresh()

println ctx.getBean("contact")
```

When we run this sample, we get familiar output:

```
First name: Chris, Last name: Schaefer, Age: 32
```

This time we create an instance of a typical GenericApplicationContext, but use GroovyBeanDefinitionReader, which will be used to pass bean definitions to. Then as in the previous sample, we create a bean from our simple POJO, refresh ApplicationContext and print the string representation of the Contact bean. It doesn't get any easier than that!

As you probably can tell, we are only scratching the surface of what can be done with the Groovy support in Spring 4. Since the developer has the full power of the Groovy language, all sorts of interesting things can be done when creating bean definitions. As you have full access to ApplicationContext, you can not only configure beans, but also work with profile support, property files, and so on. Just keep in mind, with great power comes great responsibility.

Summary

In this chapter, you saw a wide range of Spring-specific features that complement the core IoC capabilities. You saw how to hook into the life cycle of a bean and to make it aware of the Spring environment. We introduced FactoryBeans as a solution for IoC, enabling a wider set of classes. We also showed how you can use PropertyEditors to simplify application configuration and to remove the need for artificial String-typed properties. Moreover, we finished with an in-depth look at some additional features offered by ApplicationContext, including i18n, event publication, and resource access.

We also covered features such as using Java classes and the new Groovy syntax instead of XML configuration, profiles support, and the environment and property source abstraction layer. Finally, we discussed using JSR-330 standard annotations in Spring.

So far, we have covered the main concepts of the Spring Framework and its features as a DI container as well as other services that the core Spring Framework provides. In the next chapter and onward, we discuss using Spring in specific areas such as AOP, data access, transaction support, and web application support.

CHAPTER 5

■ ■ ■

Introducing Spring AOP

Besides Dependency Injection (DI), another core feature that the Spring Framework offers is support for aspect-oriented programming (AOP. AOP is often referred to as a tool for implementing crosscutting concerns. The term *crosscutting concerns* refers to logic in an application that cannot be decomposed from the rest of the application and may result in code duplication and tight coupling. By using AOP for modularizing individual pieces of logic, known as *concerns*, you can apply these to many parts of an application without duplicating the code or creating hard dependencies. Logging and security are typical examples of crosscutting concerns that are present in many applications. Consider an application that logs the start and end of every method for debugging purposes. You will probably refactor the logging code into a special class, but you still have to call methods on that class twice per method in your application in order to perform the logging. Using AOP, you can simply specify that you want the methods on your logging class to be invoked before and after each method call in your application.

It is important to understand that AOP complements object-oriented programming (OOP), rather than competing with it. OOP is very good at solving a wide variety of problems that we, as programmers, encounter. However, if you look at the logging example again, it is obvious to see where OOP is lacking when it comes to implementing crosscutting logic on a large scale. Using AOP on its own to develop an entire application is practically impossible, given that AOP functions on top of OOP. Likewise, although it is certainly possible to develop entire applications by using OOP, you can work smarter by employing AOP to solve certain problems that involve crosscutting logic.

This chapter covers the following topics:

- *AOP basics*: Before discussing Spring's AOP implementation, we cover the basics of AOP as a technology. Most of the concepts covered in this section are not specific to Spring and can be found in any AOP implementation. If you are already familiar with another AOP implementation, feel free to skip this section.

- *Types of AOP*: There are two distinct types of AOP: static and dynamic. In static AOP, like that provided by AspectJ's (http://eclipse.org/aspectj/) compile-time weaving mechanisms, the crosscutting logic is applied to your code at compile time, and you cannot change it without modifying the code and recompiling. With dynamic AOP, such as Spring AOP, crosscutting logic is applied dynamically at runtime. This allows you to make changes to the AOP configuration without having to recompile the application. These types of AOP are complementary, and, when used together, they form a powerful combination that you can use in your applications.

- *Spring AOP architecture*: Spring AOP is only a subset of the full AOP feature set found in other implementations such as AspectJ. In this section, we take a high-level look at which features are present in Spring, how they are implemented, and why some features are excluded from the Spring implementation.

- *Proxies\ in Spring AOP*: Proxies are a huge part of how Spring AOP works, and you must understand them to get the most out of Spring AOP. In this section, we look at the two kinds of proxy: the JDK dynamic proxy and the CGLIB proxy. In particular, we look at the different scenarios in which Spring uses each proxy, the performance of the two proxy types, and some simple guidelines to follow in your application to get the most from Spring AOP.

- *Using Spring AOP*: In this section, we present some practical examples of AOP usage. We start off with a simple "Hello World" example to ease you into Spring's AOP code, and we continue with a detailed description of the AOP features that are available in Spring, complete with examples.

- *Advanced use of pointcuts*: We explore the `ComposablePointcut` and `ControlFlowPointcut` classes, introductions, and the appropriate techniques you should employ when using pointcuts in your application.

- *AOP framework services*: The Spring Framework fully supports configuring AOP transparently and declaratively. We look at three ways (the `ProxyFactoryBean` class, the aop namespace, and @AspectJ-style annotations) to inject declaratively defined AOP proxies into your application objects as collaborators, thus making your application completely unaware that it is working with advised objects.

- *Integrating AspectJ*: AspectJ is a fully featured AOP implementation. The main difference between AspectJ and Spring AOP is that AspectJ applies advice to target objects via weaving (either compile-time or load-time weaving), while Spring AOP is based on proxies. The feature set of AspectJ is much greater than that of Spring AOP, but it is much more complicated to use than Spring. AspectJ is a good solution when you find that Spring AOP lacks a feature you need.

AOP Concepts

As with most technologies, AOP comes with its own specific set of concepts and terms, and it's important to understand what they mean. The following are the core concepts of AOP:

- *Joinpoints*: A joinpoint is a well-defined point during the execution of your application. Typical examples of joinpoints include a call to a method, the method invocation itself, class initialization, and object instantiation. Joinpoints are a core concept of AOP and define the points in your application at which you can insert additional logic using AOP.

- *Advice*: The code that is executed at a particular joinpoint is the advice, defined by a method in your class. There are many types of advice, such as *before*, which executes before the joinpoint, and *after*, which executes after it.

- *Pointcuts*: A pointcut is a collection of joinpoints that you use to define when advice should be executed. By creating pointcuts, you gain fine-grained control over how you apply advice to the components in your application. As mentioned previously, a typical joinpoint is a method invocation, or the collection of all method invocations in a particular class. Often you can compose pointcuts in complex relationships to further constrain when advice is executed.

- *Aspects*: An aspect is the combination of advice and pointcuts encapsulated in a class. This combination results in a definition of the logic that should be included in the application and where it should execute.

- *Weaving*: This is the process of inserting aspects into the application code at the appropriate point. For compile-time AOP solutions, this weaving is generally done at build time. Likewise, for runtime AOP solutions, the weaving process is executed dynamically at runtime. AspectJ supports another weaving mechanism called *load-time weaving* (LTW), in which it intercepts the underlying JVM class loader and provides weaving to the bytecode when it is being loaded by the class loader.

- *Target*: An object whose execution flow is modified by an AOP process is referred to as the target object. Often you see the target object referred to as the *advised object.*

- *Introduction*: This is the process by which you can modify the structure of an object by introducing additional methods or fields to it. You can use introduction AOP to make any object implement a specific interface without needing the object's class to implement that interface explicitly.

Don't worry if you find these concepts confusing; this will all become clear when you see some examples. Also, be aware that you are shielded from many of these concepts in Spring AOP, and some are not relevant because of Spring's choice of implementation. We will discuss each of these features in the context of Spring as we progress through the chapter.

Types of AOP

As we mentioned earlier, there are two distinct types of AOP: static and dynamic. The difference between them is really the point at which the weaving process occurs and how this process is achieved.

Using Static AOP

In *static AOP*, the weaving process forms another step in the build process for an application. In Java terms, you achieve the weaving process in a static AOP implementation by modifying the actual bytecode of your application, changing and extending the application code as necessary. This is a well-performing way of achieving the weaving process because the end result is just Java bytecode, and you do not perform any special tricks at runtime to determine when advice should be executed.

The drawback of this mechanism is that any modifications you make to the aspects, even if you simply want to add another joinpoint, require you to recompile the entire application. AspectJ's compile-time weaving is an excellent example of a static AOP implementation.

Using Dynamic AOP

Dynamic AOP implementations, such as Spring AOP, differ from static AOP implementations in that the weaving process is performed dynamically at runtime. How this is achieved is implementation-dependent, but as you will see, Spring's approach is to create proxies for all advised objects, allowing for advice to be invoked as required. The drawback of dynamic AOP is that, typically, it does not perform as well as static AOP, but the performance is steadily increasing. The major benefit of dynamic AOP implementations is the ease with which you can modify the entire aspect set of an application without needing to recompile the main application code.

Choosing an AOP Type

Choosing whether to use static or dynamic AOP is quite a hard decision. Both have their own benefits, and you are not restricted to using only one type. In general, static AOP implementations have been around longer and tend to have more feature-rich implementations, with a greater number of available joinpoints. Typically, if performance is absolutely critical or you need an AOP feature that is not implemented in Spring, you will want to use AspectJ. In most other cases, Spring AOP is ideal. Keep in mind that many AOP-based solutions such as transaction management are already provided for you by Spring, so check the framework capabilities before rolling your own!

As always, let the requirements of your application drive your choice of AOP implementation, and don't restrict yourself to a single implementation if a combination of technologies would better suit your application. In general, Spring AOP is less complex than AspectJ, so it tends to be an ideal first choice.

AOP in Spring

Spring's AOP implementation can be viewed as two logical parts. The first part is the AOP core, which provides fully decoupled, purely programmatic AOP functionality (also known as the *Spring AOP API*). The second part of the AOP implementation is the set of framework services that make AOP easier to use in your applications. On top of this, other components of Spring, such as the transaction manager and EJB helper classes, provide AOP-based services to simplify the development of your application.

The AOP Alliance

The AOP Alliance (http://aopalliance.sourceforge.net/) is a joint effort among representatives of many open source AOP projects to define a standard set of interfaces for AOP implementations. Wherever applicable, Spring uses the AOP Alliance interfaces rather than defining its own. This allows you to reuse certain advice across multiple AOP implementations that support the AOP Alliance interfaces.

"Hello World!" in AOP

Before we dive into discussing the Spring AOP implementation in detail, let's take a look at an example. We will take a simple class that outputs the message "World," and then using AOP, transform an instance of this class at runtime to output "Hello World!" instead. Listing 5-1 shows the basic MessageWriter class.

Listing 5-1. The MessageWriter Class

```
package com.apress.prospring4.ch5;

public class MessageWriter {
    public void writeMessage() {
        System.out.print("World");
    }
}
```

With our message-printing method implemented, let's *advise*—which in AOP terms means *add advice to*—this method so that writeMessage() prints "Hello World!" instead.

To do this, we need to execute code prior to the existing body executing (to write "Hello"), and we need to execute code after that method body executes (to write "!"). In AOP terms, what we need is *around* advice, which executes around a joinpoint. In this case, the joinpoint is the invocation of the writeMessage() method. Listing 5-2 shows the code of the MessageDecorator class, which acts as our around-advice implementation.

Listing 5-2. Implementing Around Advice

```
package com.apress.prospring4.ch5;

import org.aopalliance.intercept.MethodInterceptor;
import org.aopalliance.intercept.MethodInvocation;
```

```
public class MessageDecorator implements MethodInterceptor {
    @Override
    public Object invoke(MethodInvocation invocation) throws Throwable {
        System.out.print("Hello ");
        Object retVal = invocation.proceed();
        System.out.println("!");
        return retVal;
    }
}
```

The MethodInterceptor interface is a standard AOP Alliance interface for implementing around advice for method invocation joinpoints. The MethodInvocation object represents the method invocation that is being advised, and using this object, we control when the method invocation is allowed to proceed. Because this is around advice, we are capable of performing actions before the method is invoked as well as after it is invoked but before it returns. In Listing 5-2, we simply write "Hello" to console output, invoke the method with a call to MethodInvocation.proceed(), and then write "!" to console output.

The final step in this sample is to weave the MessageDecorator advice (more specifically, the invoke() method) into the code. To do this, we create an instance of MessageWriter, the target, and then create a proxy of this instance, instructing the proxy factory to weave in the MessageDecorator advice. This is shown in Listing 5-3.

Listing 5-3. Weaving the MessageDecorator Advice

```
package com.apress.prospring4.ch5;

import org.springframework.aop.framework.ProxyFactory;

public class HelloWorldAOPExample {
    public static void main(String[] args) {
        MessageWriter target = new MessageWriter();

        ProxyFactory pf = new ProxyFactory();
        pf.addAdvice(new MessageDecorator());
        pf.setTarget(target);

        MessageWriter proxy = (MessageWriter) pf.getProxy();

        target.writeMessage();
        System.out.println("");
        proxy.writeMessage();
    }
}
```

The important part here is that we use the ProxyFactory class to create the proxy of the target object, weaving in the advice at the same time. We pass the MessageDecorator advice to the ProxyFactory with a call to addAdvice() and specify the target for weaving with a call to setTarget(). Once the target is set and some advice is added to the ProxyFactory, we generate the proxy with a call to getProxy(). Finally, we call writeMessage() on both the original target object and the proxy object.

Running the code from Listing 5-3 results in the following output:

```
World
Hello World!
```

As you can see, calling writeMessage() on the untouched target object results in a standard method invocation, and no extra content is written to console output. However, the invocation of the proxy causes the code in MessageDecorator to execute, creating the desired "Hello World!" output. From this example, you can see that the advised class had no dependencies on Spring or the AOP Alliance interfaces; the beauty of Spring AOP, and indeed AOP in general, is that you can advise almost any class, even if that class was created without AOP in mind. The only restriction, in Spring AOP at least, is that you can't advise final classes, because they cannot be overridden and therefore cannot be proxied.

Spring AOP Architecture

The core architecture of Spring AOP is based around proxies. When you want to create an advised instance of a class, you must use ProxyFactory to create a proxy instance of that class, first providing ProxyFactory with all the aspects that you want to be woven into the proxy. Using ProxyFactory is a purely programmatic approach to creating AOP proxies. For the most part, you don't need to use this in your application; instead, you can rely on the declarative AOP configuration mechanisms provided by Spring (the ProxyFactoryBean class, the aop namespace, and @AspectJ-style annotations) to take advantage of declarative proxy creation. However, it is important to understand how proxy creation works, so we will first use the programmatic approach to proxy creation and then dive into Spring's declarative AOP configurations.

At runtime, Spring analyzes the crosscutting concerns defined for the beans in ApplicationContext and generates proxy beans (which wrap the underlying target bean) dynamically. Instead of calling the target bean directly, callers are injected with the proxied bean. The proxy bean then analyzes the running condition (that is, joinpoint, pointcut, or advice) and weaves in the appropriate advice accordingly. Figure 5-1 shows a high-level view of a Spring AOP proxy in action.

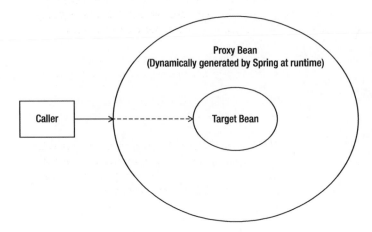

Figure 5-1. *Spring AOP proxy in action*

Internally, Spring has two proxy implementations: JDK dynamic proxies and CGLIB proxies. By default, when the target object to be advised implements an interface, Spring will use a JDK dynamic proxy to create proxy instances of the target. However, when the advised target object doesn't implement an interface (for example, it's a concrete class), CGLIB will be used for proxy instance creation. One major reason is that JDK dynamic proxy supports only the proxying of interfaces. We discuss proxies in detail in the section "Understanding Proxies."

Joinpoints in Spring

One of the more noticeable simplifications in Spring AOP is that it supports only one joinpoint type: method invocation. At first glance, this might seem like a severe limitation if you are familiar with other AOP implementations such as AspectJ, which supports many more joinpoints, but in fact this makes Spring more accessible.

The Method Invocation joinpoint is by far the most useful joinpoint available, and using it, you can achieve many of the tasks that make AOP useful in day-to-day programming. Remember that if you need to advise some code at a joinpoint other than a method invocation, you can always use Spring and AspectJ together.

Aspects in Spring

In Spring AOP, an aspect is represented by an instance of a class that implements the Advisor interface. Spring provides convenience Advisor implementations that you can reuse in your applications, thus removing the need for you to create custom Advisor implementations. There are two subinterfaces of Advisor: PointcutAdvisor and IntroductionAdvisor.

The PointcutAdvisor interface is implemented by all Advisor implementations that use pointcuts to control the advice applied to joinpoints. In Spring, introductions are treated as special kinds of advice, and by using the IntroductionAdvisor interface, you can control those classes to which an introduction applies.

We discuss PointcutAdvisor implementations in detail in the upcoming section "Advisors and Pointcuts in Spring."

About the ProxyFactory Class

The ProxyFactory class controls the weaving and proxy creation process in Spring AOP. Before you can create a proxy, you must specify the advised or target object. You can do this, as you saw earlier, by using the setTarget() method. Internally, ProxyFactory delegates the proxy creation process to an instance of DefaultAopProxyFactory, which in turn delegates to either Cglib2AopProxy or JdkDynamicAopProxy, depending on the settings of your application. We discuss proxy creation in more detail later in this chapter.

The ProxyFactory class provides the addAdvice() method that you saw in Listing 5-3 for cases where you want advice to apply to the invocation of all methods in a class, not just a selection. Internally, addAdvice() wraps the advice you pass it in an instance of DefaultPointcutAdvisor, which is the standard implementation of PointcutAdvisor, and configures it with a pointcut that includes all methods by default. When you want more control over the Advisor that is created, or when you want to add an introduction to the proxy, create the Advisor yourself and use the addAdvisor() method of the ProxyFactory.

You can use the same ProxyFactory instance to create many proxies, each with different aspects. To help with this, ProxyFactory has removeAdvice() and removeAdvisor() methods, which allow you to remove any advice or Advisors from the ProxyFactory that you previously passed to it. To check whether a ProxyFactory has particular advice attached to it, call adviceIncluded(), passing in the advice object for which you want to check.

Creating Advice in Spring

Spring supports six flavors of advice, described in Table 5-1.

Table 5-1. *Advice Types in Spring*

Advice Name	Interface	Description
Before	org.springframework.aop .MethodBeforeAdvice	Using before advice, you can perform custom processing before a joinpoint executes. Because a joinpoint in Spring is always a method invocation, this essentially allows you to perform preprocessing before the method executes. Before advice has full access to the target of the method invocation as well as the arguments passed to the method, but it has no control over the execution of the method itself. In case the before advice throws an exception, further execution of the interceptor chain (as well as the target method) will be aborted, and the exception will propagate back up the interceptor chain.
After-returning	org.springframework.aop .AfterReturningAdvice	After-returning advice is executed after the method invocation at the joinpoint has finished executing and has returned a value. The after-returning advice has access to the target of the method invocation, the arguments passed to the method, and the return value as well. Because the method has already executed when the after-returning advice is invoked, it has no control over the method invocation at all. In case the target method throws an exception, the after-returning advice will not be run, and the exception will be propagated up to the call stack as usual.
After (finally)	org.springframework.aop .AfterAdvice	After-returning advice is executed only when the advised method completes normally. However, the after (finally) advice will be executed no matter the result of the advised method. The advice is executed even when the advised method fails and an exception is thrown.
Around	org.aopalliance.intercept .MethodInterceptor	In Spring, around advice is modeled using the AOP Alliance standard of a method interceptor. Your advice is allowed to execute before and after the method invocation, and you can control the point at which the method invocation is allowed to proceed. You can choose to bypass the method altogether if you want, providing your own implementation of the logic.
Throws	org.springframework.aop .ThrowsAdvice	Throws advice is executed after a method invocation returns, but only if that invocation threw an exception. It is possible for throws advice to catch only specific exceptions, and if you choose to do so, you can access the method that threw the exception, the arguments passed into the invocation, and the target of the invocation.
Introduction	org.springframework.aop .IntroductionInterceptor	Spring models introductions as special types of interceptors. Using an introduction interceptor, you can specify the implementation for methods that are being introduced by the advice.

Interfaces for Advice

From our previous discussion of the ProxyFactory class, recall that advice is added to a proxy either directly, by using the addAdvice() method, or indirectly, by using Advisor with the addAdvisor() method. The main difference between Advice and Advisor is that Advisor carries Advice with the associated Pointcut, which provides more fine-grained control on which joinpoints the Advice will intercept. With regard to advice, Spring has created a well-defined hierarchy for advice interfaces. This hierarchy is based on the AOP Alliance interfaces and is shown in detail in Figure 5-2.

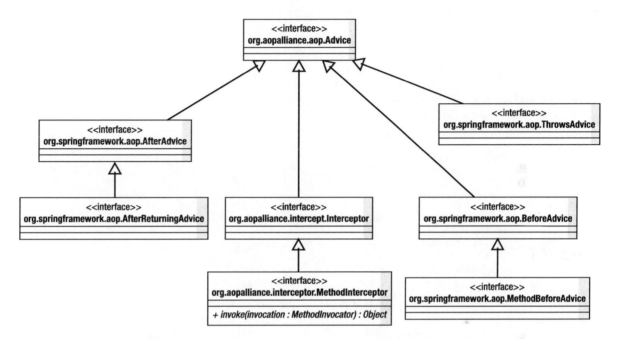

Figure 5-2. *Interfaces for Spring advice types*

This kind of hierarchy has the benefit of not only being sound OO design but also enabling you to deal with advice types generically, such as by using a single addAdvice() method on the ProxyFactory, and you can add new advice types easily without having to modify the ProxyFactory class.

Creating Before Advice

Before advice is one of the most useful advice types available in Spring. This advice can modify the arguments passed to a method and can prevent the method from executing by raising an exception. In this section, we show you two simple examples of using before advice: one that writes a message to console output containing the name of the method before the method executes, and another that you can use to restrict access to methods on an object.

In Listing 5-4, you can see the code for the SimpleBeforeAdvice class.

Listing 5-4. The SimpleBeforeAdvice Class

```java
package com.apress.prospring4.ch5;

import java.lang.reflect.Method;

import org.springframework.aop.MethodBeforeAdvice;
import org.springframework.aop.framework.ProxyFactory;

public class SimpleBeforeAdvice implements MethodBeforeAdvice {
    public static void main(String[] args) {
        MessageWriter target = new MessageWriter();

        ProxyFactory pf = new ProxyFactory();
        pf.addAdvice(new SimpleBeforeAdvice());
        pf.setTarget(target);

        MessageWriter proxy = (MessageWriter) pf.getProxy();

        proxy.writeMessage();
    }

    @Override
    public void before(Method method, Object[] args, Object target)
            throws Throwable {
        System.out.println("Before method: " + method.getName());
    }
}
```

In this code, you can see that we have advised an instance of the MessageWriter class that we created earlier with an instance of the SimpleBeforeAdvice class. The MethodBeforeAdvice interface, which is implemented by SimpleBeforeAdvice, defines a single method, before(), which the AOP framework calls before the method at the joinpoint is invoked. Remember that, for now, we are using the default pointcut provided by the addAdvice() method, which matches all methods in a class. The before() method is passed three arguments: the method that is to be invoked, the arguments that will be passed to that method, and the Object that is the target of the invocation. The SimpleBeforeAdvice class uses the Method argument of the before() method to write a message to console output containing the name of the method to be invoked. Running this example gives us the following output:

```
Before method: writeMessage
World
```

As you can see, the output from the call to writeMessage() is shown, but just before it, you can see the output generated by SimpleBeforeAdvice.

Securing Method Access by Using Before Advice

In this section, we are going to implement before advice that checks user credentials before allowing the method invocation to proceed. If the user credentials are invalid, an exception is thrown by the advice, thus preventing the method from executing. The example in this section is simplistic. It allows users to authenticate with any password, and it also allows only a single, hard-coded user access to the secured methods. However, it does illustrate how easy it is to use AOP to implement a crosscutting concern such as security.

> ■ **Note**   This is just an example demonstrating the use of before advice. For securing the method execution of Spring beans, the Spring Security project already provides comprehensive support; you don't need to implement the features by yourself.

Listing 5-5 shows the SecureBean class. This is the class that we will be securing using AOP.

Listing 5-5. The SecureBean Class

```
package com.apress.prospring4.ch5;

public class SecureBean {
    public void writeSecureMessage() {
        System.out.println("Every time I learn something new, "
            + "it pushes some old stuff out of my brain");
    }
}
```

The SecureBean class imparts a small pearl of wisdom from Homer Simpson, wisdom that we don't want everyone to see. Because this example requires users to authenticate, we are somehow going to need to store their details. Listing 5-6 shows the UserInfo class we use to store a user's credentials.

Listing 5-6. The UserInfo Class

```
package com.apress.prospring4.ch5;

public class UserInfo {
    private String userName;
    private String password;

    public UserInfo(String userName, String password) {
        this.userName = userName;
        this.password = password;
    }

    public String getPassword() {
        return password;
    }

    public String getUserName() {
        return userName;
    }
}
```

This class simply holds data about the user so that we can do something useful with it. Listing 5-7 shows the SecurityManager class, which is responsible for authenticating users and storing their credentials for later retrieval.

Listing 5-7. The SecurityManager Class

```
package com.apress.prospring4.ch5;

public class SecurityManager {
    private static ThreadLocal<UserInfo> threadLocal = new ThreadLocal<UserInfo>();

    public void login(String userName, String password) {
        threadLocal.set(new UserInfo(userName, password));
    }

    public void logout() {
        threadLocal.set(null);
    }

    public UserInfo getLoggedOnUser() {
        return threadLocal.get();
    }
}
```

The application uses the SecurityManager class to authenticate a user and, later, to retrieve the details of the currently authenticated user. The application authenticates a user by using the login() method. In a real application, the login() method would probably check the supplied credentials against a database or LDAP directory, but here we assume that all users are allowed to authenticate. The login() method creates a UserInfo object for the user and stores it on the current thread by using ThreadLocal. The logout() method sets any value that might be stored in ThreadLocal to null. Finally, the getLoggedOnUser() method returns the UserInfo object for the currently authenticated user. This method returns null if no user is authenticated.

To check whether a user is authenticated and, if so, whether the user is permitted to access the methods on SecureBean, we need to create advice that executes before the method and checks the UserInfo object returned by SecurityManager.getLoggedOnUser() against the set of credentials for allowed users. The code for this advice, SecurityAdvice, is shown in Listing 5-8.

Listing 5-8. The SecurityAdvice Class

```
package com.apress.prospring4.ch5;

import java.lang.reflect.Method;

import org.springframework.aop.MethodBeforeAdvice;

public class SecurityAdvice implements MethodBeforeAdvice {
    private SecurityManager securityManager;

    public SecurityAdvice() {
        this.securityManager = new SecurityManager();
    }

    @Override
    public void before(Method method, Object[] args, Object target)
            throws Throwable {
        UserInfo user = securityManager.getLoggedOnUser();
```

```
        if (user == null) {
            System.out.println("No user authenticated");
            throw new SecurityException(
                "You must login before attempting to invoke the method: "
                + method.getName());
        } else if ("chris".equals(user.getUserName())) {
            System.out.println("Logged in user is chris - OKAY!");
        } else {
            System.out.println("Logged in user is " + user.getUserName()
                + " NOT GOOD :(");
            throw new SecurityException("User " + user.getUserName()
                + " is not allowed access to method " + method.getName());
        }
    }
}
```

The SecurityAdvice class creates an instance of SecurityManager in its constructor and then stores this instance in a field. You should note that the application and SecurityAdvice don't need to share the same SecurityManager instance, because all data is stored with the current thread by using ThreadLocal. In the before() method, we perform a simple check to see whether the username of the authenticated user is chris. If so, we allow the user access; otherwise, an exception is raised. Also notice that we check for a null UserInfo object, which indicates that the current user is not authenticated.

In Listing 5-9, you can see a sample application that uses the SecurityAdvice class to secure the SecureBean class.

Listing 5-9. The SecurityExample Class

```
package com.apress.prospring4.ch5;

import org.springframework.aop.framework.ProxyFactory;

public class SecurityExample {
    public static void main(String[] args) {
        SecurityManager mgr = new SecurityManager();

        SecureBean bean = getSecureBean();

        mgr.login("chris", "pwd");
        bean.writeSecureMessage();
        mgr.logout();

        try {
            mgr.login("invaliduser", "pwd");
            bean.writeSecureMessage();
        } catch(SecurityException ex) {
            System.out.println("Exception Caught: " + ex.getMessage());
        } finally {
            mgr.logout();
        }
```

```
        try {
            bean.writeSecureMessage();
        } catch(SecurityException ex) {
            System.out.println("Exception Caught: " + ex.getMessage());
        }
    }

    private static SecureBean getSecureBean() {
        SecureBean target = new SecureBean();

        SecurityAdvice advice = new SecurityAdvice();

        ProxyFactory factory = new ProxyFactory();
        factory.setTarget(target);
        factory.addAdvice(advice);

        SecureBean proxy = (SecureBean)factory.getProxy();

        return proxy;
    }
}
```

In the getSecureBean() method, we create a proxy of the SecureBean class that is advised using an instance of SecurityAdvice. This proxy is returned to the caller. When the caller invokes any method on this proxy, the call is first routed to the instance of SecurityAdvice for a security check. In the main() method, we test three scenarios, invoking the SecureBean.writeSecureMessage() method with two sets of user credentials and then no user credentials at all. Because SecurityAdvice allows method calls to proceed only if the currently authenticated user is chris, we expect that the only successful scenario in Listing 5-9 is the first. Running this example gives the following output:

```
Logged in user is chris - OKAY!
Every time I learn something new, it pushes some old stuff out of my brain
Logged in user is invaliduser NOT GOOD :(

Exception Caught: User invaliduser is not allowed access to method writeSecureMessage
No user authenticated
Exception Caught: You must login before attempting to invoke the method: writeSecureMessage
```

As you can see, only the first invocation of SecureBean.writeSecureMessage() was allowed to proceed. The remaining invocations were prevented by the SecurityException exception thrown by SecurityAdvice.

This example is simple, but it does highlight the usefulness of before advice. Security is a typical example of before advice, but we also find it useful when a scenario demands the modification of arguments passed to the method.

Creating After-Returning Advice

After-returning advice is executed after the method invocation at the joinpoint returns. Given that the method has already executed, you can't change the arguments that are passed to it. Although you can read these arguments, you can't change the execution path, and you can't prevent the method from executing. These restrictions are expected; what is not expected, however, is that you cannot modify the return value in the after-returning advice. When using after-returning advice, you are limited to adding processing. Although after-returning advice cannot modify the return value of a method invocation, it can throw an exception that can be sent up the stack instead of the return value.

In this section, we look at two examples of using after-returning advice in an application. The first example simply writes a message to console output after the method has been invoked. The second example shows how you can use after-returning advice to add error checking to a method. Consider a class, KeyGenerator, which generates keys for cryptographic purposes. Many cryptographic algorithms suffer from the problem that a small number of keys are considered weak. A *weak key* is any key whose characteristics make it significantly easier to derive the original message without knowing the key. For the DES algorithm, there are a total of 256 possible keys. From this key-space, 4 keys are considered weak, and another 12 are considered semi-weak. Although the chance of one of these keys being generated randomly is small (1 in 252), testing for the keys is so simple that it's worthwhile to do so. In the second example of this section, we build after-returning advice that checks for weak keys generated by the KeyGenerator, raising an exception if one is found.

■ **Note**   For more information on weak keys and cryptography at large, we recommend you read *Applied Cryptography* by Bruce Schneier (Wiley, 1996).

In Listing 5-10, you can see the SimpleAfterReturningAdvice class, which demonstrates the use of after-returning advice by writing a message to console output after a method has returned.

Listing 5-10. The SimpleAfterReturningAdvice Class

```java
package com.apress.prospring4.ch5;

import java.lang.reflect.Method;

import org.springframework.aop.AfterReturningAdvice;
import org.springframework.aop.framework.ProxyFactory;

public class SimpleAfterReturningAdvice implements AfterReturningAdvice {
    public static void main(String[] args) {
        MessageWriter target = new MessageWriter();

        ProxyFactory pf = new ProxyFactory();

        pf.addAdvice(new SimpleAfterReturningAdvice());
        pf.setTarget(target);

        MessageWriter proxy = (MessageWriter) pf.getProxy();
        proxy.writeMessage();
    }

    @Override
    public void afterReturning(Object returnValue, Method method,
            Object[] args, Object target) throws Throwable {
        System.out.println("");
        System.out.println("After method: " + method.getName());
    }
}
```

Notice that the AfterReturningAdvice interface declares a single method, afterReturning(), which is passed the return value of method invocation, a reference to the method that was invoked, the arguments that were passed to the method, and the target of the invocation. Running this example results in the following output:

```
World
After method: writeMessage
```

The output is very similar to that of the before-advice example except that, as expected, the message written by the advice appears after the message written by the writeMessage() method.

A good use of after-returning advice is to perform some additional error checking when it is possible for a method to return an invalid value. In the scenario we described earlier, it is possible for a cryptographic key generator to generate a key that is considered weak for a particular algorithm. Ideally, the key generator would check for these weak keys, but since the chance of these keys arising is often very small, many generators do not check. By using after-returning advice, we can advise the method that generates the key and performs this additional check. Listing 5-11 shows an extremely primitive key generator.

Listing 5-11. The KeyGenerator Class

```java
package com.apress.prospring4.ch5;

import java.util.Random;

public class KeyGenerator {
    protected static final long WEAK_KEY = 0xFFFFFFFF0000000L;
    protected static final long STRONG_KEY = 0xACDF03F590AE56L;

    private Random rand = new Random();

    public long getKey() {
        int x = rand.nextInt(3);

        if (x == 1) {
            return WEAK_KEY;
        }

        return STRONG_KEY;
    }
}
```

This key generator should not be considered secure. It's purposely simple for this example and has a one-in-three chance of producing a weak key. In Listing 5-12, you can see the WeakKeyCheckAdvice that checks to see whether the result of the getKey() method is a weak key.

Listing 5-12. Checking for Weak Keys

```java
package com.apress.prospring4.ch5;

import java.lang.reflect.Method;
import org.springframework.aop.AfterReturningAdvice;

public class WeakKeyCheckAdvice implements AfterReturningAdvice {
    @Override
```

```
    public void afterReturning(Object returnValue, Method method,
            Object[] args,Object target) throws Throwable {

        if ((target instanceof KeyGenerator
                && ("getKey".equals(method.getName())))) {
            long key = ((Long) returnValue).longValue();

            if (key == KeyGenerator.WEAK_KEY) {
                throw new SecurityException(
                    "Key Generator generated a weak key. Try again");
            }
        }
    }
}
```

In the afterReturning() method, we check first to see whether the method that was executed at the joinpoint was the getKey() method. If so, we then check the result value to see whether it was the weak key. If we find that the result of the getKey() method was a weak key, then we throw a SecurityException to inform the calling code of this. Listing 5-13 shows a simple application that demonstrates the use of this advice.

Listing 5-13. Testing the WeakKeyCheckAdvice Class

```
package com.apress.prospring4.ch5;

import org.springframework.aop.framework.ProxyFactory;

public class AfterAdviceExample {
    private static KeyGenerator getKeyGenerator() {
        KeyGenerator target = new KeyGenerator();

        ProxyFactory factory = new ProxyFactory();
        factory.setTarget(target);
        factory.addAdvice(new WeakKeyCheckAdvice());

        return (KeyGenerator)factory.getProxy();
    }

    public static void main(String[] args) {
        KeyGenerator keyGen = getKeyGenerator();

        for(int x = 0; x < 10; x++) {
            try {
                long key = keyGen.getKey();
                System.out.println("Key: " + key);
            } catch(SecurityException ex) {
                System.out.println("Weak Key Generated!");
            }
        }
    }
}
```

177

After creating an advised proxy of the KeyGenerator target, the AfterAdviceExample class attempts to generate ten keys. If a SecurityException is thrown during a single generation, a message is written to the console, informing the user that a weak key was generated; otherwise, the generated key is displayed. A single run of this on our machine generated the following output:

```
Key: 48658904092028502
Key: 48658904092028502
Key: 48658904092028502
Weak Key Generated!
Key: 48658904092028502
Key: 48658904092028502
Key: 48658904092028502
Weak Key Generated!
Key: 48658904092028502
Key: 48658904092028502
```

As you can see, the KeyGenerator class sometimes generates weak keys, as expected, and WeakKeyCheckAdvice ensures that SecurityException is raised whenever a weak key is encountered.

Creating Around Advice

Around advice functions like a combination of before and after advice, with one big difference—you can modify the return value. Not only that, but you can prevent the method from executing. This means that by using around advice, you can essentially replace the entire implementation of a method with new code. Around advice in Spring is modeled as an interceptor using the MethodInterceptor interface. There are many uses for around advice, and you will find that many features of Spring are created by using method interceptors, such as the remote proxy support and the transaction management features. Method interception is also a good mechanism for profiling the execution of your application, and it forms the basis of the example in this section.

We are not going to build a simple example for method interception; instead, we refer to the first example in Listing 5-2, which shows how to use a basic method interceptor to write a message on either side of a method invocation. Notice from this earlier example that the invoke() method of the MethodInterceptor class does not provide the same set of arguments as MethodBeforeAdvice and AfterReturningAdvice. The method is not passed the target of the invocation, the method that was invoked, nor the arguments used. However, you can access this data by using the MethodInvocation object that is passed to invoke(). You will see a demonstration of this in the following example.

For this example, we want to achieve some way to advise a class so we get basic information about the runtime performance of its methods. Specifically, we want to know how long the method took to execute. To achieve this, we can use the StopWatch class included in Spring, and we clearly need a MethodInterceptor, because we need to start StopWatch before the method invocation and stop it right afterward.

Listing 5-14 shows the WorkerBean class that we are going to profile by using the StopWatch class and around advice.

Listing 5-14. The WorkerBean Class

```
package com.apress.prospring4.ch5;

public class WorkerBean {
    public void doSomeWork(int noOfTimes) {
        for(int x = 0; x < noOfTimes; x++) {
            work();
        }
    }
}
```

```
    private void work() {
        System.out.print("");
    }
}
```

This is a simple class. The doSomeWork() method accepts a single argument, noOfTimes, and calls the work() method exactly the number of times specified by this method. The work() method simply has a dummy call to System.out.print(), which passes in an empty String. This prevents the compiler from optimizing out the work() method and thus the call to work().

In Listing 5-15, you can see the ProfilingInterceptor class that uses the StopWatch class to profile method invocation times. We use this interceptor to profile the WorkerBean class shown in Listing 5-14.

Listing 5-15. The ProfilingInterceptor Class

```
package com.apress.prospring4.ch5;

import java.lang.reflect.Method;

import org.aopalliance.intercept.MethodInterceptor;
import org.aopalliance.intercept.MethodInvocation;
import org.springframework.util.StopWatch;

public class ProfilingInterceptor implements MethodInterceptor {
    @Override
    public Object invoke(MethodInvocation invocation) throws Throwable {
        StopWatch sw = new StopWatch();
        sw.start(invocation.getMethod().getName());

        Object returnValue = invocation.proceed();

        sw.stop();
        dumpInfo(invocation, sw.getTotalTimeMillis());
        return returnValue;
    }

    private void dumpInfo(MethodInvocation invocation, long ms) {
        Method m = invocation.getMethod();
        Object target = invocation.getThis();
        Object[] args = invocation.getArguments();

        System.out.println("Executed method: " + m.getName());
        System.out.println("On object of type: " +
                target.getClass().getName());

        System.out.println("With arguments:");
        for (int x = 0; x < args.length; x++) {
            System.out.print("        > " + args[x]);
        }
        System.out.print("\n");

        System.out.println("Took: " + ms + " ms");
    }
}
```

In the invoke() method, which is the only method in the MethodInterceptor interface, we create an instance of StopWatch and then start it running immediately, allowing the method invocation to proceed with a call to MethodInvocation.proceed(). As soon as the method invocation has ended and the return value has been captured, we stop StopWatch and pass the total number of milliseconds taken, along with the MethodInvocation object, to the dumpInfo() method. Finally, we return the Object returned by MethodInvocation.proceed() so that the caller obtains the correct return value. In this case, we did not want to disrupt the call stack in any way; we were simply acting as an eavesdropper on the method invocation. If we had wanted, we could have changed the call stack completely, redirecting the method call to another object or a remote service, or we could simply have reimplemented the method logic inside the interceptor and returned a different return value.

The dumpInfo() method simply writes some information about the method call to console output, along with the time taken for the method to execute. In the first three lines of dumpInfo(), you can see how you can use the MethodInvocation object to determine the method that was invoked, the original target of the invocation, and the arguments used.

Listing 5-16 shows the ProfilingExample class that first advises an instance of WorkerBean with a ProfilingInterceptor and then profiles the doSomeWork() method.

Listing 5-16. The ProfilingExample Class

```
package com.apress.prospring4.ch5;

import org.springframework.aop.framework.ProxyFactory;

public class ProfilingExample {
    public static void main(String[] args) {
        WorkerBean bean = getWorkerBean();
        bean.doSomeWork(10000000);
    }

    private static WorkerBean getWorkerBean() {
        WorkerBean target = new WorkerBean();

        ProxyFactory factory = new ProxyFactory();
        factory.setTarget(target);
        factory.addAdvice(new ProfilingInterceptor());

        return (WorkerBean)factory.getProxy();
    }
}
```

Running this example on our machine produces the following output:

```
Executed method: doSomeWork
On object of type: com.apress.prospring4.ch5.WorkerBean
With arguments:
    > 10000000
Took: 477 ms
```

From this output, you can see which method was executed, what the class of the target was, what arguments were passed in, and how long the invocation took.

Creating Throws Advice

Throws advice is similar to after-returning advice in that it executes after the joinpoint, which is always a method invocation, but throws advice executes only if the method throws an exception. Throws advice is also similar to after-returning advice in that it has little control over program execution. If you are using throws advice, you can't choose to ignore the exception that was raised and return a value for the method instead. The only modification you can make to the program flow is to change the type of exception that is thrown. This is quite a powerful concept and can make application development much simpler. Consider a situation where you have an API that throws an array of poorly defined exceptions. Using throws advice, you can advise all classes in that API and reclassify the exception hierarchy into something more manageable and descriptive. Of course, you can also use throws advice to provide centralized error logging across your application, thus reducing the amount of error-logging code that is spread across your application.

As you saw from the diagram in Figure 5-2, throws advice is implemented by the ThrowsAdvice interface. Unlike the interfaces you have seen so far, ThrowsAdvice does not define any methods; instead, it is simply a marker interface used by Spring. The reason for this is that Spring allows typed throws advice, which allows you to define exactly which Exception types your throws advice should catch. Spring achieves this by detecting methods with certain signatures using reflection. Spring looks for two distinct method signatures. This is best demonstrated with a simple example. Listing 5-17 shows a simple bean with two methods that both simply throw exceptions of different types.

Listing 5-17. The ErrorBean Class

```
package com.apress.prospring4.ch5;

public class ErrorBean {
    public void errorProneMethod() throws Exception {
        throw new Exception("Foo");
    }

    public void otherErrorProneMethod() throws IllegalArgumentException {
        throw new IllegalArgumentException("Bar");
    }
}
```

In Listing 5-18, you can see the SimpleThrowsAdvice class that demonstrates both of the method signatures that Spring looks for on throws advice.

Listing 5-18. The SimpleThrowsAdvice Class

```
package com.apress.prospring4.ch5;

import java.lang.reflect.Method;

import org.springframework.aop.ThrowsAdvice;
import org.springframework.aop.framework.ProxyFactory;

public class SimpleThrowsAdvice implements ThrowsAdvice {
    public static void main(String[] args) throws Exception {
        ErrorBean errorBean = new ErrorBean();

        ProxyFactory pf = new ProxyFactory();
        pf.setTarget(errorBean);
        pf.addAdvice(new SimpleThrowsAdvice());
```

```
        ErrorBean proxy = (ErrorBean) pf.getProxy();

        try {
            proxy.errorProneMethod();
        } catch (Exception ignored) {

        }

        try {
            proxy.otherErrorProneMethod();
        } catch (Exception ignored) {

        }
    }

    @Override
    public void afterThrowing(Exception ex) throws Throwable {
        System.out.println("***");
        System.out.println("Generic Exception Capture");
        System.out.println("Caught: " + ex.getClass().getName());
        System.out.println("***\n");
    }

    @Override
    public void afterThrowing(Method method, Object[] args, Object target,
            IllegalArgumentException ex) throws Throwable {
        System.out.println("***");
        System.out.println("IllegalArgumentException Capture");
        System.out.println("Caught: " + ex.getClass().getName());
        System.out.println("Method: " + method.getName());
        System.out.println("***\n");
    }
}
```

The first thing Spring looks for in throws advice is one or more public methods called afterThrowing(). The return type of the methods is unimportant, although we find it best to stick with void because this method can't return any meaningful value. The first afterThrowing() method in the SimpleThrowsAdvice class has a single argument of type Exception. You can specify any type of Exception as the argument, and this method is ideal when you are not concerned about the method that threw the exception or the arguments that were passed to it. Note that this method catches Exception and any subtypes of Exception unless the type in question has its own afterThrowing() method.

In the second afterThrowing() method, we declared four arguments to catch the Method that threw the exception, the arguments that were passed to the method, and the target of the method invocation. The order of the arguments in this method is important, and you must specify all four. Notice that the second afterThrowing() method catches exceptions of type IllegalArgumentException (or its subtype). Running this example produces the following output:

```
***
Generic Exception Capture
Caught: java.lang.Exception
***
```

```
***
IllegalArgumentException Capture
Caught: java.lang.IllegalArgumentException
Method: otherErrorProneMethod
***
```

As you can see, when a plain old `Exception` is thrown, the first `afterThrowing()` method is invoked, but when an `IllegalArgumentException` is thrown, the second `afterThrowing()` method is invoked. Spring invokes a single `afterThrowing()` method only for each `Exception`, and as you saw from the example in Listing 5-18, Spring uses the method whose signature contains the best match for the `Exception` type. In the situation where your after-throwing advice has two `afterThrowing()` methods, both declared with the same `Exception` type but one with a single argument and the other with four arguments, Spring invokes the four-argument `afterThrowing()` method.

After-throwing advice is useful in a variety of situations; it allows you to reclassify entire `Exception` hierarchies as well as build centralized `Exception` logging for your application. We have found that after-throwing advice is particularly useful when we are debugging a live application, because it allows us to add extra logging code without needing to modify the application's code.

Choosing an Advice Type

In general, choosing an advice type is driven by the requirements of your application, but you should choose the most specific advice type for your need. That is to say, don't use around advice when before advice will do. In most cases, around advice can accomplish everything that the other three advice types can, but it may be overkill for what you are trying to achieve. By using the most specific type of advice, you are making the intention of your code clearer, and you are also reducing the possibility of errors. Consider advice that counts method calls. When you are using before advice, all you need to code is the counter, but with around advice, you need to remember to invoke the method and return the value to the caller. These small things can allow spurious errors to creep into your application. By keeping the advice type as focused as possible, you reduce the scope for errors.

Advisors and Pointcuts in Spring

Thus far, all the examples you have seen have used the `ProxyFactory.addAdvice()` method to configure advice for a proxy. This method delegates to `addAdvisor()` behind the scenes, creating an instance of `DefaultPointcutAdvisor` and configuring it with a pointcut that points to all methods. In this way, the advice is deemed to apply to all methods on the target. In some cases, such as when you are using AOP for logging purposes, this may be desirable, but in other cases you may want to limit the methods to which the advice applies.

Of course, you could simply perform the checking in the advice itself that the method being advised is the correct one, but this approach has several drawbacks. First, hard-coding the list of acceptable methods into the advice reduces the advice's reusability. By using pointcuts, you can configure the methods to which an advice applies, without needing to put this code inside the advice; this clearly increases the reuse value of the advice. Other drawbacks with hard-coding the list of methods into the advice are performance related. To inspect the method being advised in the advice, you need to perform the check each time any method on the target is invoked. This clearly reduces the performance of your application. When you use pointcuts, the check is performed once for each method, and the results are cached for later use. The other performance-related drawback of not using pointcuts to restrict the list-advised methods is that Spring can make optimizations for nonadvised methods when creating a proxy, which results in faster invocations on nonadvised methods. These optimizations are covered in greater detail when we discuss proxies later in the chapter.

We strongly recommend that you avoid the temptation to hard-code method checks into your advice and instead use pointcuts wherever possible to govern the applicability of advice to methods on the target. That said, in some cases it is necessary to hard-code the checks into your advice. Consider the earlier example of the after-returning advice designed to catch weak keys generated by the `KeyGenerator` class. This kind of advice is closely coupled to the class it is advising, and it is wise to check inside the advice to ensure that it is applied to the correct type. We refer to this coupling between advice and target as *target affinity*. In general, you should use pointcuts when your advice has little or no target affinity—that is, it can apply to any type or a wide range of types. When your advice has strong target affinity, try to check that the advice is being used correctly in the advice itself; this helps reduce head-scratching errors when advice is misused. We also recommend you avoid advising methods needlessly. As you will see, this results in a noticeable drop in invocation speed that can have a large impact on the overall performance of your application.

The Pointcut Interface

Pointcuts in Spring are created by implementing the Pointcut interface, as shown in Listing 5-19.

Listing 5-19. The Pointcut Interface

```
package org.springframework.aop;

public interface Pointcut {
    ClassFilter getClassFilter ();
    MethodMatcher getMethodMatcher();
}
```

As you can see from this code, the Pointcut interface defines two methods, getClassFilter() and getMethodMatcher(), which return instances of ClassFilter and MethodMatcher, respectively. Obviously, if you choose to implement the Pointcut interface, you will need to implement these methods. Thankfully, as you will see in the next section, this is usually unnecessary because Spring provides a selection of Pointcut implementations that cover most, if not all, of your use cases.

When determining whether a Pointcut applies to a particular method, Spring first checks to see whether the Pointcut applies to the method's class by using the ClassFilter instance returned by Pointcut.getClassFilter(). Listing 5-20 shows the ClassFilter interface.

Listing 5-20. The ClassFilter Interface

```
org.springframework.aop;

public interface ClassFilter {
    boolean matches(Class<?> clazz);
}
```

As you can see, the ClassFilter interface defines a single method, matches(), that is passed an instance of Class that represents the class to be checked. As you have no doubt determined, the matches() method returns true if the pointcut applies to the class and false otherwise.

The MethodMatcher interface is more complex than the ClassFilter interface, as shown in Listing 5-21.

Listing 5-21. The MethodMatcher Interface

```
package org.springframework.aop;

public interface MethodMatcher {
    boolean matches(Method m, Class<?> targetClass);
    boolean isRuntime();
    boolean matches(Method m, Class<?> targetClass, Object[] args);
}
```

Spring supports two types of `MethodMatcher`, static and dynamic, which are determined by the return value of `isRuntime()`. Before using `MethodMatcher`, Spring calls `isRuntime()` to determine whether `MethodMatcher` is static, indicated by a return value of `false`, or dynamic, indicated by a return value of `true`.

For a static pointcut, Spring calls the `matches(Method, Class<T>)` method of the `MethodMatcher` once for every method on the target, caching the return value for subsequent invocations of those methods. In this way, the check for method applicability is performed only once for each method, and subsequent invocations of a method do not result in an invocation of `matches()`.

With dynamic pointcuts, Spring still performs a static check by using `matches(Method, Class<T>)` the first time a method is invoked to determine the overall applicability of a method. However, in addition to this and provided that the static check returned `true`, Spring performs a further check for each invocation of a method by using the `matches(Method, Class<T>, Object[])` method. In this way, a dynamic `MethodMatcher` can determine whether a pointcut should apply based on a particular invocation of a method, not just on the method itself. For example, a pointcut needs to be applied only when the argument is an `Integer` with a value larger than 100. In this case, the `matches(Method, Class<T>, Object[])` method can be coded to perform further checking on the argument for each invocation.

Clearly, static pointcuts perform much better than dynamic pointcuts because they avoid the need for an additional check per invocation. Dynamic pointcuts provide a greater level of flexibility for deciding whether to apply advice. In general, we recommend you use static pointcuts wherever you can. However, in cases where your advice adds substantial overhead, it may be wise to avoid any unnecessary invocations of your advice by using a dynamic pointcut.

In general, you rarely create your own `Pointcut` implementations from scratch because Spring provides abstract base classes for both static and dynamic pointcuts. We look at these base classes, along with other `Pointcut` implementations, over the next few sections.

Available Pointcut Implementations

As of version 4.0, Spring provides eight implementations of the `Pointcut` interface: two abstract classes intended as convenience classes for creating static and dynamic pointcuts, and six concrete classes, one for each of the following:

- Composing multiple pointcuts together

- Handling control flow pointcuts

- Performing simple name-based matching

- Defining pointcuts using regular expressions

- Defining pointcuts using AspectJ expressions

- Defining pointcuts that look for specific annotations at the class or method level

Table 5-2 summarizes the eight `Pointcut` interface implementations.

Table 5-2. *Summary of Spring Pointcut Implementations*

Implementation Class	Description
org.springframework.aop.support.annotation.AnnotationMatchingPointcut	Pointcut that looks for specific Java annotation on a class or method. This class requires JDK 5 or higher.
org.springframework.aop.aspectj.AspectJExpressionPointcut	Pointcut that uses AspectJ weaver to evaluate a pointcut expression in AspectJ syntax.
org.springframework.aop.support.ComposablePointcut	The ComposablePointcut class is used to compose two or more pointcuts together with operations such as union() and intersection().
org.springframework.aop.support.ControlFlowPointcut	The ControlFlowPointcut is a special case pointcut that matches all methods within the control flow of another method—that is, any method that is invoked either directly or indirectly as the result of another method being invoked.
org.springframework.aop.support.DynamicMethodMatcherPointcut	The DynamicMethodMatcherPointcut is intended as a base class for building dynamic pointcuts.
org.springframework.aop.support.JdkRegexpMethodPointcut	The JdkRexepMethodPointcut allows you to define pointcuts using JDK 1.4 regular expression support. This class requires JDK 1.4 or newer.
org.springframework.aop.support.NameMatchMethodPointcut	Using the NameMatchMethodPointcut, you can create a pointcut that performs simple matching against a list of method names.
org.springframework.aop.support.StaticMethodMatcherPointcut	The StaticMethodMatcherPointcut class is intended as a base for building static pointcuts.

Figure 5-3 shows the Unified Modeling Language (UML) diagram for the Pointcut implementation classes.

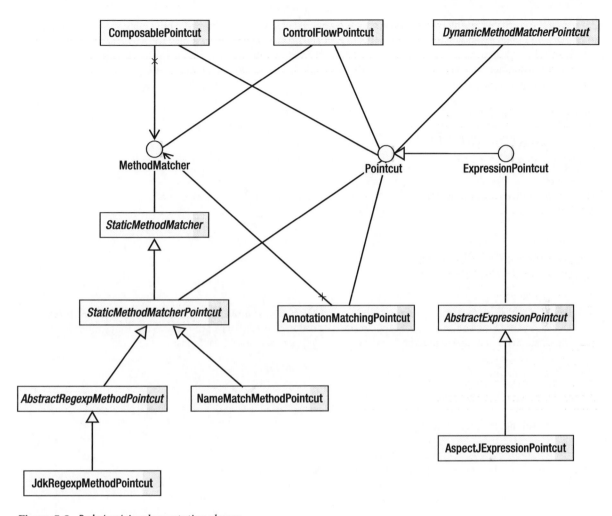

Figure 5-3. *Pointcut implementation classes*

Using DefaultPointcutAdvisor

Before you can use any Pointcut implementation, you must first create an instance of the Advisor interface, or more specifically a PointcutAdvisor interface. Remember from our earlier discussions that an Advisor is Spring's representation of an aspect (in the previous section "Aspects in Spring"), a coupling of advice and pointcuts that governs which methods should be advised and how they should be advised. Spring provides a number of implementations of PointcutAdvisor, but for now we concern ourselves with just one, DefaultPointcutAdvisor. DefaultPointcutAdvisor is a simple PointcutAdvisor for associating a single Pointcut with a single Advice.

Creating a Static Pointcut by Using StaticMethodMatcherPointcut

In this section, we will create a simple static pointcut by extending the abstract StaticMethodMatcherPointcut class. Since the StaticMethodMatcherPointcut class extends the StaticMethodMatcher class (an abstract class too), which implements the MethodMatcher interface, you are required to implement the method matches(Method, Class<?>);

the rest of the Pointcut implementation is handled automatically. Although this is the only method you are required to implement (when extending the StaticMethodMatcherPointcut class), you may also want to override the getClassFilter() method as we do in this example to ensure that only methods of the correct type get advised.

For this example, we have two classes, BeanOne and BeanTwo, with identical methods defined in both. Listing 5-22 shows the BeanOne class.

Listing 5-22. The BeanOne Class

```
package com.apress.prospring4.ch5;

public class BeanOne {
    public void foo() {
        System.out.println("foo");
    }

    public void bar() {
        System.out.println("bar");
    }
}
```

The BeanTwo class has identical methods to BeanOne. With this example, we want to be able to create a proxy of both classes by using the same DefaultPointcutAdvisor but have the advice apply only to the foo() method of the BeanOne class. To do this, we created the SimpleStaticPointcut class, as shown in Listing 5-23.

Listing 5-23. The SimpleStaticPointcut Class

```
package com.apress.prospring4.ch5;

import java.lang.reflect.Method;

import org.springframework.aop.ClassFilter;
import org.springframework.aop.support.StaticMethodMatcherPointcut;

public class SimpleStaticPointcut extends StaticMethodMatcherPointcut {
    @Override
    public boolean matches(Method method, Class<?> cls) {
        return ("foo".equals(method.getName()));
    }

    @Override
    public ClassFilter getClassFilter() {
        return new ClassFilter() {
            public boolean matches(Class<?> cls) {
                return (cls == BeanOne.class);
            }
        };
    }
}
```

Here you can see that we implemented the matches(Method, Class<?>) method as required by the StaticMethodMatcher abstract class. The implementation simply returns true if the name of the method is foo; otherwise, it returns false. Notice that we have also overridden the getClassFilter() method to return a

ClassFilter instance whose matches() method returns true only for the BeanOne class. With this static pointcut, we are saying that only methods of the BeanOne class will be matched, and furthermore, only the foo() method of that class will be matched.

Listing 5-24 shows the SimpleAdvice class that simply writes out a message on either side of the method invocation.

Listing 5-24. The SimpleAdvice Class

```
package com.apress.prospring4.ch5;

import org.aopalliance.intercept.MethodInterceptor;
import org.aopalliance.intercept.MethodInvocation;

public class SimpleAdvice implements MethodInterceptor {
    @Override
    public Object invoke(MethodInvocation invocation) throws Throwable {
        System.out.println(">>Invoking " + invocation.getMethod().getName());
        Object retVal = invocation.proceed();
        System.out.println(">>Done");
        return retVal;
    }
}
```

In Listing 5-25, you can see a simple driver application for this example that creates an instance of DefaultPointcutAdvisor by using the SimpleAdvice and SimpleStaticPointcut classes.

Listing 5-25. The StaticPointcutExample Class

```
package com.apress.prospring4.ch5;

import org.aopalliance.aop.Advice;
import org.springframework.aop.Advisor;
import org.springframework.aop.Pointcut;
import org.springframework.aop.framework.ProxyFactory;
import org.springframework.aop.support.DefaultPointcutAdvisor;

public class StaticPointcutExample {
    public static void main(String[] args) {
        BeanOne one = new BeanOne();
        BeanTwo two = new BeanTwo();

        BeanOne proxyOne;
        BeanTwo proxyTwo;

        Pointcut pc = new SimpleStaticPointcut();
        Advice advice = new SimpleAdvice();
        Advisor advisor = new DefaultPointcutAdvisor(pc, advice);

        ProxyFactory pf = new ProxyFactory();
        pf.addAdvisor(advisor);
        pf.setTarget(one);
        proxyOne = (BeanOne)pf.getProxy();
```

```
        pf = new ProxyFactory();
        pf.addAdvisor(advisor);
        pf.setTarget(two);
        proxyTwo = (BeanTwo)pf.getProxy();

        proxyOne.foo();
        proxyTwo.foo();

        proxyOne.bar();
        proxyTwo.bar();
    }
}
```

Notice that the DefaultPointcutAdvisor instance is then used to create two proxies: one for an instance of BeanOne and one for an instance of BeanTwo. Finally, both the foo() and bar() methods are invoked on the two proxies. Running this example results in the following output:

```
>> Invoking foo
foo
>> Done
foo
bar
bar
```

As you can see, the only method for which SimpleAdvice was actually invoked was the foo() method for the BeanOne class, exactly as expected. Restricting the methods to which advice applies is quite simple and, as you will see when we discuss proxy options, is key to getting the best performance out of your application.

Creating a Dynamic Pointcut by Using DyanmicMethodMatcherPointcut

Creating a dynamic pointcut is not much different from creating a static one, so for this example, we create a dynamic pointcut for the class shown in Listing 5-26.

Listing 5-26. The SampleBean Class

```
package com.apress.prospring4.ch5;

public class SampleBean {
    public void foo(int x) {
        System.out.println("Invoked foo() with: " + x);
    }

    public void bar() {
        System.out.println("Invoked bar()");
    }
}
```

For this example, we want to advise only the foo() method, but unlike the previous example, we want to advise this method only if the int argument passed to it is greater or less than 100.

As with static pointcuts, Spring provides a convenient base class for creating dynamic pointcuts—DynamicMethodMatcherPointcut. The DynamicMethodMatcherPointcut class has a single abstract method, matches(Method, Class<?>, Object[]) (via the MethodMatcher interface that it implements), that you must implement, but as you will see, it is also prudent to implement the matches(Method, Class<?>) method to control the behavior of the static checks. Listing 5-27 shows the SimpleDynamicPointcut class.

Listing 5-27. The SimpleDynamicPointcut Class

```
package com.apress.prospring4.ch5;

import java.lang.reflect.Method;

import org.springframework.aop.ClassFilter;
import org.springframework.aop.support.DynamicMethodMatcherPointcut;

public class SimpleDynamicPointcut extends DynamicMethodMatcherPointcut {
    @Override
    public boolean matches(Method method, Class<?> cls) {
        System.out.println("Static check for " + method.getName());
        return ("foo".equals(method.getName()));
    }

    @Override
    public boolean matches(Method method, Class<?> cls, Object[] args) {
        System.out.println("Dynamic check for " + method.getName());

        int x = ((Integer) args[0]).intValue();

        return (x != 100);
    }

    @Override
    public ClassFilter getClassFilter() {
        return new ClassFilter() {
            public boolean matches(Class<?> cls) {
                return (cls == SampleBean.class);
            }
        };
    }
}
```

As you can see from the code in Listing 5-27, we override the getClassFilter() method in a similar manner to the previous example shown in Listing 5-23. This removes the need to check the class in the method-matching methods—something that is especially important for the dynamic check. Although we are required to implement only the dynamic check, we implement the static check as well. The reason for this is that we know the bar() method will never be advised. By indicating this by using the static check, Spring never has to perform a dynamic check for this method. This is because when the static check method is implemented, Spring will first check against it, and if the checking result is a not a match, Spring will stop doing any further dynamic checking. Moreover, the result of the static check will be cached for better performance. But if we neglect the static check, Spring performs a dynamic check each time the bar() method is invoked. As a recommended practice, perform the class checking in the getClassFilter() method, method checking in the matches(Method, Class<?>) method, and argument checking in the matches(Method, Class<?>, Object[]) method. This will make your pointcut much easier to understand and maintain, and performance will be better too.

In the matches(Method, Class<?>, Object[]) method, you can see that we return false if the value of the int argument passed to the foo() method is not equal to 100; otherwise, we return true. Note that in the dynamic check, we know that we are dealing with the foo() method, because no other method makes it past the static check.

In Listing 5-28, you can see an example of this pointcut in action.

Listing 5-28. The DynamicPointcutExample Class

```
package com.apress.prospring4.ch5;

import org.springframework.aop.Advisor;
import org.springframework.aop.framework.ProxyFactory;
import org.springframework.aop.support.DefaultPointcutAdvisor;

public class DynamicPointcutExample {
    public static void main(String[] args) {
        SampleBean target = new SampleBean();

        Advisor advisor = new DefaultPointcutAdvisor(
            new SimpleDynamicPointcut(), new SimpleAdvice());

        ProxyFactory pf = new ProxyFactory();
        pf.setTarget(target);
        pf.addAdvisor(advisor);
        SampleBean proxy = (SampleBean)pf.getProxy();

        proxy.foo(1);
        proxy.foo(10);
        proxy.foo(100);

        proxy.bar();
        proxy.bar();
        proxy.bar();
    }
}
```

Notice that we have used the same advice class as in the static pointcut example. However, in this example, only the first two calls to foo() should be advised. The dynamic check prevents the third call to foo() from being advised, and the static check prevents the bar() method from being advised. Running this example yields the following output:

```
Static check for foo
Static check for bar
Static check for toString
Static check for clone
Static check for foo
Dynamic check for foo
>> Invoking foo
Invoked foo() with: 1
>> Done
Dynamic check for foo
>> Invoking foo
Invoked foo() with: 10
```

```
>> Done
Dynamic check for foo
Invoked foo() with: 100
Static check for bar
Invoked bar()
Invoked bar()
Invoked bar()
```

As we expected, only the first two invocations of the foo() method were advised. Notice that none of the bar() invocations is subject to a dynamic check, thanks to the static check on bar(). An interesting point to note here is that the foo() method is subject to two static checks: one during the initial phase when all methods are checked and another when it is first invoked.

As you can see, dynamic pointcuts offer a greater degree of flexibility than static pointcuts, but because of the additional runtime overhead they require, you should use a dynamic pointcut only when absolutely necessary.

Using Simple Name Matching

Often when creating a pointcut, you want to match based on just the name of the method, ignoring method signature and return type. In this case, you can avoid needing to create a subclass of StaticMethodMatcherPointcut and use the NameMatchMethodPointcut (which is a subclass of StaticMethodMatcherPointcut) to match against a list of method names instead. When you are using NameMatchMethodPointcut, no consideration is given to the signature of the method, so if you have methods foo() and foo(int), they are both matched for the name foo.

Listing 5-29 shows a simple class with four methods.

Listing 5-29. The NameBean Class

```
package com.apress.prospring4.ch5;

public class NameBean {
    public void foo() {
        System.out.println("foo");
    }

    public void foo(int x) {
        System.out.println("foo " + x);
    }

    public void bar() {
        System.out.println("bar");
    }

    public void yup() {
        System.out.println("yup");
    }
}
```

For this example, we want to match the foo(), foo(int), and bar() methods by using NameMatchMethodPointcut; this translates to matching the names foo and bar. This is shown in Listing 5-30.

Listing 5-30. Using NameMatchMethodPointcut

```
package com.apress.prospring4.ch5;

import org.springframework.aop.Advisor;
import org.springframework.aop.framework.ProxyFactory;
import org.springframework.aop.support.DefaultPointcutAdvisor;
import org.springframework.aop.support.NameMatchMethodPointcut;

public class NamePointcutExample {
    public static void main(String[] args) {
        NameBean target = new NameBean();

        NameMatchMethodPointcut pc = new NameMatchMethodPointcut();
        pc.addMethodName("foo");
        pc.addMethodName("bar");
        Advisor advisor = new DefaultPointcutAdvisor(pc, new SimpleAdvice());

        ProxyFactory pf = new ProxyFactory();
        pf.setTarget(target);
        pf.addAdvisor(advisor);
        NameBean proxy = (NameBean)pf.getProxy();

        proxy.foo();
        proxy.foo(999);
        proxy.bar();
        proxy.yup();
    }
}
```

There is no need to create a class for the pointcut; you can simply create an instance of NameMatchMethodPointcut, and you are on your way. Notice that we have added two names to the pointcut, foo and bar, using the addMethodName() method. Running this example results in the following output:

```
>> Invoking foo
foo
>> Done
>> Invoking foo
foo 999
>> Done
>> Invoking bar
bar
>> Done
yup
```

As expected, the foo(), foo(int), and bar() methods are advised, thanks to the pointcut, but the yup() method is left unadvised.

Creating Pointcuts with Regular Expressions

In the previous section, we discussed how to perform simple matching against a predefined list of methods. But what if you don't know all of the methods' names in advance, and instead you know the pattern that the names follow? For instance, what if you want to match all methods whose names starts with get? In this case, you can use the regular expression pointcut JdkRegexpMethodPointcut to match a method name based on a regular expression.

Listing 5-31 shows a simple class with three methods.

Listing 5-31. The RegexpBean Class

```
package com.apress.prospring4.ch5;

public class RegexpBean {
    public void foo1() {
        System.out.println("foo1");
    }

    public void foo2() {
        System.out.println("foo2");
    }

    public void bar() {
        System.out.println("bar");
    }
}
```

Using a regular expression–based pointcut, we can match all methods in this class whose name starts with foo. This is shown in Listing 5-32.

Listing 5-32. Using Regular Expressions for Pointcuts

```
package com.apress.prospring4.ch5;

import org.springframework.aop.Advisor;
import org.springframework.aop.framework.ProxyFactory;
import org.springframework.aop.support.DefaultPointcutAdvisor;
import org.springframework.aop.support.JdkRegexpMethodPointcut;

public class RegexpPointcutExample {
    public static void main(String[] args) {
        RegexpBean target = new RegexpBean();

        JdkRegexpMethodPointcut pc = new JdkRegexpMethodPointcut();
        pc.setPattern(".*foo.*");
        Advisor advisor = new DefaultPointcutAdvisor(pc, new SimpleAdvice());

        ProxyFactory pf = new ProxyFactory();
        pf.setTarget(target);
        pf.addAdvisor(advisor);
        RegexpBean proxy = (RegexpBean) pf.getProxy();
```

```
        proxy.foo1();
        proxy.foo2();
        proxy.bar();
    }
}
```

Notice we do not need to create a class for the pointcut; instead, we just create an instance of JdkRegexpMethodPointcut and specify the pattern to match, and we are finished. The interesting thing to note is the pattern. When matching method names, Spring matches the fully qualified name of the method, so for foo1(), Spring is matching against com.apress.prospring4.ch5.RegexpBean.foo1, which is why there's the leading .* in the pattern. This is a powerful concept because it allows you to match all methods within a given package, without needing to know exactly which classes are in that package and what the names of the methods are. Running this example yields the following output:

```
>> Invoking foo1
foo1
>> Done
>> Invoking foo2
foo2
>> Done
bar
```

As you would expect, only the foo1() and foo2() methods have been advised, because the bar() method does not match the regular expression pattern.

Creating Pointcuts with AspectJ Pointcut Expression

Besides JDK regular expressions, you can use AspectJ's pointcut expression language for pointcut declaration. Later in this chapter, you will see that when we declare the pointcut in XML configuration by using the aop namespace, Spring defaults to use AspectJ's pointcut language. Moreover, when using Spring's @AspectJ annotation-style AOP support, you also need to use AspectJ's pointcut language. So when declaring pointcuts by using expression language, using an AspectJ pointcut expression is the best way to go. Spring provides the class AspectJExpressionPointcut for defining pointcuts via AspectJ's expression language. To use AspectJ pointcut expressions with Spring, you need to include two AspectJ library files, aspectjrt.jar and aspectjweaver.jar, in your project's classpath. Simply add the dependencies shown in Table 5-3 to your project.

Table 5-3. *Maven Dependencies for AspectJ*

Group ID	Artifact ID	Version	Description
org.aspectj	aspectjrt	1.7.4 (1.8.0.M1 for Java 8)	AspectJ runtime library
org.aspectj	aspectjweaver	1.7.4 (1.8.0.M1 for Java 8)	AspectJ weaving library

Let's take the previous example using JDK regular expressions again and see how to use AspectJ expressions to achieve the same result. Listing 5-33 shows the bean that was the same as the one in Listing 5-31; just the class name is different.

Listing 5-33. The AspectJexpBean Class

```
package com.apress.prospring4.ch5;

public class AspectjexpBean {
    public void foo1() {
        System.out.println("foo1");
    }

    public void foo2() {
        System.out.println("foo2");
    }

    public void bar() {
        System.out.println("bar");
    }
}
```

Using an AspectJ expression–based pointcut, we also can easily match all methods in this class whose names start with foo. This is shown in Listing 5-34.

Listing 5-34. Using AspectJ Expressions for Pointcuts

```
package com.apress.prospring4.ch5;

import org.springframework.aop.Advisor;
import org.springframework.aop.aspectj.AspectJExpressionPointcut;
import org.springframework.aop.framework.ProxyFactory;
import org.springframework.aop.support.DefaultPointcutAdvisor;

public class AspectjexpPointcutExample {
    public static void main(String[] args) {
        AspectjexpBean target = new AspectjexpBean();

        AspectJExpressionPointcut pc = new AspectJExpressionPointcut();
        pc.setExpression("execution(* foo*(..))");
        Advisor advisor = new DefaultPointcutAdvisor(pc, new SimpleAdvice());

        ProxyFactory pf = new ProxyFactory();
        pf.setTarget(target);
        pf.addAdvisor(advisor);
        AspectjexpBean proxy = (AspectjexpBean) pf.getProxy();

        proxy.foo1();
        proxy.foo2();
        proxy.bar();
    }
}
```

Note that we use the AspectJExpressionPointcut's setExpression() method to set the matching criteria. The expression "execution(* foo*(..))" means that the advice should apply to the execution of any methods that start with foo, with any arguments, and return any types. Running the program will get the same result as the previous example using JDK regular expressions.

Creating Annotation Matching Pointcuts

If your application is annotation-based, you may want to use your own specified annotations for defining pointcuts, that is, apply the advice logic to all methods or types with specific annotations. Spring provides the class AnnotationMatchingPointcut for defining pointcuts using annotations. Again, let's reuse the previous example and see how we did it when using an annotation as a pointcut.

First we define an annotation called AdviceRequired, which is an annotation that we will use for declaring a pointcut. Listing 5-35 shows the annotation class.

Listing 5-35. Using an Annotation for Pointcuts

```
package com.apress.prospring4.ch5;

import java.lang.annotation.ElementType;
import java.lang.annotation.Retention;
import java.lang.annotation.RetentionPolicy;
import java.lang.annotation.Target;

@Retention(RetentionPolicy.RUNTIME)
@Target({ElementType.TYPE, ElementType.METHOD})
public @interface AdviceRequired {
}
```

In the previous listing, you can see that we declare the interface as an annotation by using @interface as the type, and the @Target annotation defines that the annotation can apply at either the type or method level.

Listing 5-36 shows a simple bean with our annotation on it.

Listing 5-36. The SampleAnnotationBean Class

```
package com.apress.prospring4.ch5;

public class SampleAnnotationBean {
    @AdviceRequired
    public void foo(int x) {
        System.out.println("Invoked foo() with: "  +x);
    }

    public void bar() {
        System.out.println("Invoked bar()");
    }
}
```

For the previous bean, the foo() method was annotated with @AdviceRequired, to which we want the advice to be applied.

Listing 5-37 shows the testing program.

Listing 5-37. Testing Pointcut by Using Annotation

```
package com.apress.prospring4.ch5;

import org.springframework.aop.Advisor;
import org.springframework.aop.framework.ProxyFactory;
import org.springframework.aop.support.DefaultPointcutAdvisor;
import org.springframework.aop.support.annotation.AnnotationMatchingPointcut;
```

```
public class AnnotationPointcutExample {
    public static void main(String[] args) {
        SampleAnnotationBean target = new SampleAnnotationBean();

        AnnotationMatchingPointcut pc = AnnotationMatchingPointcut
            .forMethodAnnotation(AdviceRequired.class);
        Advisor advisor = new DefaultPointcutAdvisor(pc, new SimpleAdvice());

        ProxyFactory pf = new ProxyFactory();
        pf.setTarget(target);
        pf.addAdvisor(advisor);
        SampleAnnotationBean proxy = (SampleAnnotationBean) pf.getProxy();

        proxy.foo(100);
        proxy.bar();
    }
}
```

In the previous listing, an instance of AnnotationMatchingPointcut is acquired by calling its static method forMethodAnnotation() and passing in the annotation type. This indicates that we want to apply the advice to all the methods annotated with the given annotation. It's also possible to specify annotations applied at the type level by calling the forClassAnnotation() method. The following shows the output when the program runs:

```
>> Invoking foo
Invoked foo() with: 100
>> Done
Invoked bar()
```

As you can see, since we annotated the foo() method, only that method was advised.

Convenience Advisor Implementations

For many of the Pointcut implementations, Spring also provides a convenience Advisor implementation that acts as the Pointcut. For instance, instead of using NameMatchMethodPointcut coupled with DefaultPointcutAdvisor in the previous example, we could simply have used NameMatchMethodPointcutAdvisor, as shown in Listing 5-38.

Listing 5-38. Using NameMatchMethodPointcutAdvisor

```
package com.apress.prospring4.ch5;

import org.springframework.aop.framework.ProxyFactory;
import org.springframework.aop.support.NameMatchMethodPointcutAdvisor;

import com.apress.prospring4.ch5.staticpc.SimpleAdvice;

public class NamePointcutUsingAdvisor {
    public static void main(String[] args) {
        NameBean target = new NameBean();
```

```
NameMatchMethodPointcutAdvisor advisor = new
    NameMatchMethodPointcutAdvisor(new SimpleAdvice());
advisor.addMethodName("foo");
advisor.addMethodName("bar");

ProxyFactory pf = new ProxyFactory();
pf.setTarget(target);
pf.addAdvisor(advisor);
NameBean proxy = (NameBean) pf.getProxy();

proxy.foo();
proxy.foo(999);
proxy.bar();
proxy.yup();
    }
}
```

Notice that rather than creating an instance of NameMatchMethodPointcut, we configure the pointcut details on the instance of NameMatchMethodPointcutAdvisor. In this way, NameMatchMethodPointcutAdvisor is acting as both the Advisor and the Pointcut.

You can find full details of the different Advisor implementations by exploring the Javadoc for the org.springframework.aop.support package. There is no noticeable performance difference between the two approaches, and aside from there being slightly less code in the second example, there is very little difference in the actual coding approach. We prefer to stick with the first approach because we feel the intent is slightly clearer in the code. At the end of the day, the style you choose comes down to personal preference.

Understanding Proxies

So far, we have taken only a cursory look at the proxies generated by ProxyFactory. We mentioned that two types of proxy are available in Spring: JDK proxies created by using the JDK Proxy class and CGLIB-based proxies created by using the CGLIB Enhancer class. You may be wondering exactly what the difference between the two proxies is and why Spring needs two types of proxy. In this section, we take a detailed look at the differences between the proxies.

The core goal of a proxy is to intercept method invocations and, where necessary, execute chains of advice that apply to a particular method. The management and invocation of advice is largely proxy independent and is managed by the Spring AOP framework. However, the proxy is responsible for intercepting calls to all methods and passing them as necessary to the AOP framework for the advice to be applied.

In addition to this core functionality, the proxy must support a set of additional features. It is possible to configure the proxy to expose itself via the AopContext class (which is an abstract class) so that you can retrieve the proxy and invoke advised methods on the proxy from the target object. The proxy is responsible for ensuring that when this option is enabled via ProxyFactory.setExposeProxy(), the proxy class is appropriately exposed. In addition, all proxy classes implement the Advised interface by default, which allows for, among other things, the advice chain to be changed after the proxy has been created. A proxy must also ensure that any methods that return this(that is, return the proxied target) do in fact return the proxy and not the target.

As you can see, a typical proxy has quite a lot of work to perform, and all of this logic is implemented in both the JDK and CGLIB proxies.

Using JDK Dynamic Proxies

JDK proxies are the most basic type of proxy available in Spring. Unlike the CGLIB proxy, the JDK proxy can generate proxies only of interfaces, not classes. In this way, any object you want to proxy must implement at least one interface. In general, it is good design to use interfaces for your classes, but it is not always possible, especially when you are working with third-party or legacy code. In this case, you must use the CGLIB proxy.

When you are using the JDK proxy, all method calls are intercepted by the JVM and routed to the invoke() method of the proxy. This method then determines whether the method in question is advised (by the rules defined by the pointcut), and if so, it invokes the advice chain and then the method itself by using reflection. In addition to this, the invoke() method performs all the logic discussed in the previous section.

The JDK proxy makes no determination between methods that are advised and unadvised until it is in the invoke() method. This means that for unadvised methods on the proxy, the invoke() method is still called, all the checks are still performed, and the method is still invoked by using reflection. Obviously, this incurs runtime overhead each time the method is invoked, even though the proxy often performs no additional processing other than to invoke the unadvised method via reflection.

You can instruct ProxyFactory to use a JDK proxy by specifying the list of interfaces to proxy by using setInterfaces() (in the AdvisedSupport class that the ProxyFactory class extends indirectly).

Using CGLIB Proxies

With the JDK proxy, all decisions about how to handle a particular method invocation are handled at runtime each time the method is invoked. When you use CGLIB, CGLIB dynamically generates the bytecode for a new class on the fly for each proxy, reusing already generated classes wherever possible.

When a *CGLIB proxy* is first created, CGLIB asks Spring how it wants to handle each method. This means that many of the decisions that are performed in each call to invoke() on the JDK proxy are performed just once for the CGLIB proxy. Because CGLIB generates actual bytecode, there is also a lot more flexibility in the way you can handle methods. For instance, the CGLIB proxy generates the appropriate bytecode to invoke any unadvised methods directly, reducing the overhead introduced by the proxy. In addition, the CGLIB proxy determines whether it is possible for a method to return this; if not, it allows the method call to be invoked directly, again reducing the runtime overhead.

The CGLIB proxy also handles fixed-advice chains differently than the JDK proxy. A *fixed-advice chain* is one that you guarantee will not change after the proxy has been generated. By default, you are able to change the advisors and advice on a proxy even after it is created, although this is rarely a requirement. The CGLIB proxy handles fixed-advice chains in a particular way, reducing the runtime overhead for executing an advice chain.

Comparing Proxy Performance

So far, all we have done is discuss in loose terms the differences in implementation between the proxy types. In this section, we are going to run a simple test to compare the performance of the CGLIB proxy with the JDK proxy.

Let's create a SimpleBean interface and its implementation class, DefaultSimpleBean, which we will use as the target object for proxying. Listing 5-39 and Listing 5-40 show the SimpleBean interface and DefaultSimpleBean class, respectively.

Listing 5-39. The SimpleBean Interface

```
package com.apress.prospring4.ch5;

public interface SimpleBean {
    void advised();
    void unadvised();
}
```

Listing 5-40. The DefaultSimpleBean Class

```
package com.apress.prospring4.ch5;

public class DefaultSimpleBean implements SimpleBean {
    private long dummy = 0;

    @Override
    public void advised() {
        dummy = System.currentTimeMillis();
    }

    @Override
    public void unadvised() {
        dummy = System.currentTimeMillis();
    }
}
```

Listing 5-41 shows the TestPointcut class, which provides static checking on the method to advise.

Listing 5-41. The TestPointcut Class

```
package com.apress.prospring4.ch5;

import java.lang.reflect.Method;

import org.springframework.aop.support.StaticMethodMatcherPointcut;

public class TestPointcut extends StaticMethodMatcherPointcut {
    @Override
    public boolean matches(Method method, Class cls) {
        return ("advised".equals(method.getName()));
    }
}
```

Listing 5-42 shows the NoOpBeforeAdvice class, which is just simple before advice without any operation.

Listing 5-42. The NoOpBeforeAdvice Class

```
package com.apress.prospring4.ch5;

import java.lang.reflect.Method;

import org.springframework.aop.MethodBeforeAdvice;

public class NoOpBeforeAdvice implements MethodBeforeAdvice {
    @Override
    public void before(Method method, Object[] args, Object target)
      throws Throwable {
        // no-op
    }
}
```

Listing 5-43 shows the code for the performance test.

Listing 5-43. Testing Proxy Performance

```
package com.apress.prospring4.ch5;

import org.springframework.aop.Advisor;
import org.springframework.aop.framework.Advised;
import org.springframework.aop.framework.ProxyFactory;
import org.springframework.aop.support.DefaultPointcutAdvisor;

public class ProxyPerfTest {
    public static void main(String[] args) {
        SimpleBean target = new DefaultSimpleBean();

        Advisor advisor = new DefaultPointcutAdvisor(new TestPointcut(),
                new NoOpBeforeAdvice());

        runCglibTests(advisor, target);
        runCglibFrozenTests(advisor, target);
        runJdkTests(advisor, target);
    }

    private static void runCglibTests(Advisor advisor, SimpleBean target) {
        ProxyFactory pf = new ProxyFactory();
        pf.setProxyTargetClass(true);
        pf.setTarget(target);
        pf.addAdvisor(advisor);

        SimpleBean proxy = (SimpleBean)pf.getProxy();
        System.out.println("Running CGLIB (Standard) Tests");
        test(proxy);
    }

    private static void runCglibFrozenTests(Advisor advisor, SimpleBean target) {
        ProxyFactory pf = new ProxyFactory();
        pf.setProxyTargetClass(true);
        pf.setTarget(target);
        pf.addAdvisor(advisor);
        pf.setFrozen(true);

        SimpleBean proxy = (SimpleBean)pf.getProxy();
        System.out.println("Running CGLIB (Frozen) Tests");
        test(proxy);
    }

    private static void runJdkTests(Advisor advisor, SimpleBean target) {
        ProxyFactory pf = new ProxyFactory();
        pf.setTarget(target);
        pf.addAdvisor(advisor);
        pf.setInterfaces(new Class[]{SimpleBean.class});
```

```
        SimpleBean proxy = (SimpleBean)pf.getProxy();
        System.out.println("Running JDK Tests");
        test(proxy);
    }

    private static void test(SimpleBean bean) {
        long before = 0;
        long after = 0;

        System.out.println("Testing Advised Method");
        before = System.currentTimeMillis();
        for(int x = 0; x < 500000; x++) {
            bean.advised();
        }
        after = System.currentTimeMillis();

        System.out.println("Took " + (after - before) + " ms");

        System.out.println("Testing Unadvised Method");
        before = System.currentTimeMillis();
        for(int x = 0; x < 500000; x++) {
            bean.unadvised();
        }
        after = System.currentTimeMillis();

        System.out.println("Took " + (after - before) + " ms");

        System.out.println("Testing equals() Method");
        before = System.currentTimeMillis();
        for(int x = 0; x < 500000; x++) {
            bean.equals(bean);
        }
        after = System.currentTimeMillis();

        System.out.println("Took " + (after - before) + " ms");

        System.out.println("Testing hashCode() Method");
        before = System.currentTimeMillis();
        for(int x = 0; x < 500000; x++) {
            bean.hashCode();
        }
        after = System.currentTimeMillis();

        System.out.println("Took " + (after - before) + " ms");

        Advised advised = (Advised)bean;

        System.out.println("Testing Advised.getProxyTargetClass() Method");
        before = System.currentTimeMillis();
        for(int x = 0; x < 500000; x++) {
            advised.getTargetClass();
        }
```

```
        after = System.currentTimeMillis();

        System.out.println("Took " + (after - before) + " ms");

        System.out.println(">>>\n");
    }
}
```

In this code, you can see that we are testing three kinds of proxies: a standard CGLIB proxy, a CGLIB proxy with a frozen advice chain (that is, when a proxy is frozen by calling the setFrozen() method in the ProxyConfig class that ProxyFactory extends indirectly, CGLIB will perform further optimization; however, further advice change will not be allowed), and a JDK proxy. For each proxy type, we run the following five test cases:

- *Advised method (test 1)*: A method that is advised. The advice type used in the test is before advice that performs no processing, so it reduces the effects of the advice on the performance tests.

- *Unadvised method (test 2)*: A method on the proxy that is unadvised. Often your proxy has many methods that are not advised. This test looks at how well unadvised methods perform for the different proxies.

- *The equals() method (test 3)*: This test looks at the overhead of invoking the equals() method. This is especially important when you use proxies as keys in a HashMap or similar collection.

- *The hashCode() method (test 4)*: As with the *equals()* method, the hashCode() method is important when you are using HashMaps or similar collections.

- *Executing methods on the Advised interface (test 5)*: As we mentioned earlier, a proxy implements the Advised interface by default, allowing you to modify the proxy after creation and to query information about the proxy. This test looks at how fast methods on the Advised interface can be accessed using the different proxy types.

The results of these tests are shown in Table 5-4.

Table 5-4. *Proxy Performance Test Results (ms)*

	CGLIB (Standard)	CGLIB (Frozen)	JDK
Advised method	245	135	224
Unadvised method	92	42	78
equals()	9	6	77
hashCode()	29	13	23
Advised.getProxyTargetClass()	9	6	15

As you can see, the performance between standard CGLIB and JDK dynamic proxy for both advised and unadvised methods doesn't differ much. As always, these numbers will vary based on hardware and the JDK being used.

However, there is a noticeable difference when you are using a CGLIB proxy with a frozen advice chain. Similar figures apply to the equals() and hashCode() methods, which are noticeably faster when you are using the CGLIB proxy. For methods on the Advised interface, you will notice that they are also faster on the CGLIB frozen proxy. The reason for this is that Advised methods are handled early on in the intercept() method so they avoid much of the logic that is required for other methods.

Choosing a Proxy to Use

Deciding which proxy to use is typically easy. The CGLIB proxy can proxy both classes and interfaces, whereas JDK proxies can proxy only interfaces. In terms of performance, there is no significant difference between JDK and CGLIB standard mode (at least in running both advised and unadvised methods), unless you use CGLIB in frozen mode, in which case the advice chain can't be changed and CGLIB performs further optimization when in frozen mode. When proxying a class, the CGLIB proxy is the default choice because it is the only proxy capable of generating a proxy of a class. To use the CGLIB proxy when proxying an interface, you must set the value of the `optimize` flag in the ProxyFactory to `true` by using the `setOptimize()` method.

Advanced Use of Pointcuts

Earlier in the chapter, we looked at six basic `Pointcut` implementations Spring provides; for the most part, we found that these meet the needs of our applications. However, sometimes you need more flexibility when defining pointcuts. Spring provides two additional `Pointcut` implementations, `ComposablePointcut` and `ControlFlowPointcut`, which provide exactly the flexibility you need.

Using Control Flow Pointcuts

Spring control flow pointcuts, implemented by the `ControlFlowPointcut` class, are similar to the `cflow` construct available in many other AOP implementations, although they are not quite as powerful. Essentially, a *control flow pointcut* in Spring pointcuts all method calls below a given method or below all methods in a class. This is quite hard to visualize and is better explained using an example.

Listing 5-44 shows a `SimpleBeforeAdvice` class that writes out a message describing the method it is advising.

Listing 5-44. The `SimpleBeforeAdvice` Class

```
package com.apress.prospring4.ch5;

import java.lang.reflect.Method;

import org.springframework.aop.MethodBeforeAdvice;

public class SimpleBeforeAdvice implements MethodBeforeAdvice {
    @Override
    public void before(Method method, Object[] args, Object target)
            throws Throwable {
        System.out.println("Before method: " + method);
    }
}
```

This advice class allows us to see which methods are being pointcut by the `ControlFlowPointcut`. In Listing 5-45, you can see a simple class with one method—the method that we want to advise.

Listing 5-45. The `TestBean` Class

```
package com.apress.prospring4.ch5;

public class TestBean {
    public void foo() {
        System.out.println("foo()");
    }
}
```

You can see the simple foo() method that we want to advise. We have, however, a special requirement—we want to advise this method only when it is called from another, specific method. Listing 5-46 shows a simple driver program for this example.

Listing 5-46. Using the ControlFlowPointcut Class

```
package com.apress.prospring4.ch5;

import org.springframework.aop.Advisor;
import org.springframework.aop.Pointcut;
import org.springframework.aop.framework.ProxyFactory;
import org.springframework.aop.support.ControlFlowPointcut;
import org.springframework.aop.support.DefaultPointcutAdvisor;

public class ControlFlowExample {
    public static void main(String[] args) {
        ControlFlowExample ex = new ControlFlowExample();
        ex.run();
    }

    public void run() {
        TestBean target = new TestBean();

        Pointcut pc = new ControlFlowPointcut(ControlFlowExample.class,
            "test");
        Advisor advisor = new DefaultPointcutAdvisor(pc,
            new SimpleBeforeAdvice());

        ProxyFactory pf = new ProxyFactory();
        pf.setTarget(target);
        pf.addAdvisor(advisor);

        TestBean proxy = (TestBean) pf.getProxy();

        System.out.println("Trying normal invoke");
        proxy.foo();
        System.out.println("Trying under ControlFlowExample.test()");
        test(proxy);
    }

    private void test(TestBean bean) {
        bean.foo();
    }
}
```

In Listing 5-46, the advised proxy is assembled with ControlFlowPointcut and then the foo() method is invoked twice: once directly from the run() method and once from the test() method. Here is the line of particular interest:

```
Pointcut pc = new ControlFlowPointcut(ControlFlowExample.class, "test");
```

In this line, we are creating a `ControlFlowPointcut` instance for the `test()` method of the `ControlFlowExample` class. Essentially, this says, "Pointcut all methods that are called from the `ControlFlowExample.test()` method." Note that although we said "Pointcut all methods," in fact, this really means "Pointcut all methods on the proxy object that is advised using the `Advisor` corresponding to this instance of `ControlFlowPointcut`."

Running the example in Listing 5-46 yields the following output:

```
Trying normal invoke
foo()
Trying under ControlFlowExample.test()
Before method: public void com.apress.prospring4.ch5.TestBean.foo()
foo()
```

As you can see, when the `foo()` method is first invoked outside of the control flow of the `test()` method, it is unadvised. When it executes for a second time, this time inside the control flow of the `test()` method, the `ControlFlowPointcut` indicates that its associated advice applies to the method, and thus the method is advised. Note that if we had called another method from within the `test()` method, one that was not on the advised proxy, it would not have been advised.

Control flow pointcuts can be extremely useful, allowing you to advise an object selectively only when it is executed in the context of another. However, be aware that you take a substantial performance hit for using control flow pointcut over other pointcuts.

Let's consider an example. Suppose we have a transaction processing system, which contains a `TransactionService` interface as well as an `AccountService` interface. We would like to apply after advice so that when the `AccountService.updateBalance()` method is called by `TransactionService.reverseTransaction()`, an e-mail notification is sent to the customer, after the account balance is updated. However, e-mail will not be sent under any other circumstances. In this case, the control flow pointcut will be useful. Figure 5-4 shows the UML sequence diagram for this scenario.

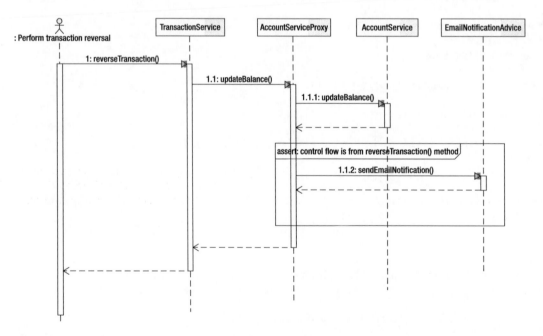

Figure 5-4. *UML sequence diagram for a control flow pointcut*

Using a Composable Pointcut

In previous pointcut examples, we used just a single pointcut for each `Advisor`. In most cases, this is usually enough, but in some cases, you may need to compose two or more pointcuts together to achieve the desired goal. Say you want to pointcut all getter and setter methods on a bean. You have a pointcut for getters and a pointcut for setters, but you don't have one for both. Of course, you could just create another pointcut with the new logic, but a better approach is to combine the two pointcuts into a single pointcut by using `ComposablePointcut`.

`ComposablePointcut` supports two methods: `union()` and `intersection()`. By default, `ComposablePointcut` is created with a `ClassFilter` that matches all classes and a `MethodMatcher` that matches all methods, although you can supply your own initial `ClassFilter` and `MethodMatcher` during construction. The `union()` and `intersection()` methods are both overloaded to accept `ClassFilter` and `MethodMatcher` arguments.

The `ComposablePointcut.union()` method can be called by passing in an instance of either the `ClassFilter`, `MethodMatcher`, or `Pointcut` interface. The result of a union operation is that `ComposablePointcut` will add an or condition into its call chain for matching with the joinpoints. It's the same for the `ComposablePointcut.intersection()` method, but this time an and condition will be added instead, which means that all `ClassFilter`, `MethodMatcher`, and `Pointcut` definitions within the `ComposablePointcut` should be matched for applying an advice. You can imagine it as the `WHERE` clause in a SQL query, with the `union()` method like the or operator and the `intersection()` method like the and operator.

As with control flow pointcuts, this is quite difficult to visualize, and it is much easier to understand with an example. Listing 5-47 shows a simple bean with three methods.

Listing 5-47. The SampleBean Class

```
package com.apress.prospring4.ch5;

public class SampleBean {
    public String getName() {
        return "Chris Schaefer";
    }

    public void setName(String name) {
    }

    public int getAge() {
        return 32;
    }
}
```

With this example, we are going to generate three proxies by using the same `ComposablePointcut` instance, but each time, we are going to modify `ComposablePointcut` by using either the `union()` or `intersection()` method. Following this, we will invoke all three methods on the `SampleBean` proxy and look at which ones have been advised. Listing 5-48 shows the code for this.

Listing 5-48. Investigating `ComposablePointcut`

```
package com.apress.prospring4.ch5;

import java.lang.reflect.Method;

import org.springframework.aop.Advisor;
import org.springframework.aop.ClassFilter;
import org.springframework.aop.framework.ProxyFactory;
```

```java
import org.springframework.aop.support.ComposablePointcut;
import org.springframework.aop.support.DefaultPointcutAdvisor;
import org.springframework.aop.support.StaticMethodMatcher;

public class ComposablePointcutExample {
    public static void main(String[] args) {
        SampleBean target = new SampleBean();

        ComposablePointcut pc = new ComposablePointcut(ClassFilter.TRUE,
            new GetterMethodMatcher());

        System.out.println("Test 1");
        SampleBean proxy = getProxy(pc, target);
        testInvoke(proxy);

        System.out.println("Test 2");
        pc.union(new SetterMethodMatcher());
        proxy = getProxy(pc, target);
        testInvoke(proxy);

        System.out.println("Test 3");
        pc.intersection(new GetAgeMethodMatcher());
        proxy = getProxy(pc, target);
        testInvoke(proxy);
    }

    private static SampleBean getProxy(ComposablePointcut pc,
            SampleBean target) {
        Advisor advisor = new DefaultPointcutAdvisor(pc,
            new SimpleBeforeAdvice());

        ProxyFactory pf = new ProxyFactory();
        pf.setTarget(target);
        pf.addAdvisor(advisor);
        return (SampleBean) pf.getProxy();
    }

    private static void testInvoke(SampleBean proxy) {
        proxy.getAge();
        proxy.getName();
        proxy.setName("Chris Schaefer");
    }

    private static class GetterMethodMatcher extends StaticMethodMatcher {
        @Override
        public boolean matches(Method method, Class<?> cls) {
            return (method.getName().startsWith("get"));
        }
    }
}
```

```
    private static class GetAgeMethodMatcher extends StaticMethodMatcher {
        @Override
        public boolean matches(Method method, Class<?> cls) {
            return "getAge".equals(method.getName());
        }
    }

    private static class SetterMethodMatcher extends StaticMethodMatcher {
        @Override
        public boolean matches(Method method, Class<?> cls) {
            return (method.getName().startsWith("set"));
        }
    }
}
```

The first thing to notice in this example is the set of three private MethodMatcher implementations. GetterMethodMatcher matches all methods that start with get. This is the default MethodMatcher that we use to assemble ComposablePointcut. Because of this, we expect that the first round of invocations on the SampleBean methods will result in only the getAge() and getName() methods being advised.

SetterMethodMatcher matches all methods that start with set, and it is combined with ComposablePointcut by using union() for the second round of invocations. At this point, we have a union of two MethodMatchers: one that matches all methods starting with get and one that matches all methods starting with set. We now expect that all invocations during the second round will be advised.

GetAgeMethodMatcher is very specific and matches only the getAge() method. This MethodMatcher is combined with ComposablePointcut by using intersection() for the third round for invocations. Because GetAgeMethodMatcher is being composed by using intersection(), the only method that we expect to be advised in the third round of invocations is getAge(), because this is the only method that matches all the composed MethodMatchers.

Running this example results in the following output:

```
Test 1
Before method: public int com.apress.prospring4.ch5.SampleBean.getAge()
Before method: public java.lang.String com.apress.prospring4.ch5.SampleBean.getName()
Test 2
Before method: public int com.apress.prospring4.ch5.SampleBean.getAge()
Before method: public java.lang.String com.apress.prospring4.ch5.SampleBean.getName()
Before method: public void com.apress.prospring4.ch5.SampleBean.setName(java.lang.String)
Test 3
Before method: public int com.apress.prospring4.ch5.SampleBean.getAge()
```

As expected, the first round of invocations on the proxy saw only the getAge() and getName() methods being advised. For the second round, when the SetterMethodMatcher had been composed with the union() method, all methods were advised. In the final round, as a result of the intersection of the GetAgeMethodMatcher, only the getAge() method was advised.

Although this example demonstrated the use of MethodMatchers only in the composition process, it is just as simple to use ClassFilter when you are building the pointcut. Indeed, you can use a combination of MethodMatchers and ClassFilters when building your composite pointcut.

Composition and the Pointcut Interface

In the previous section, you saw how to create a composite pointcut by using multiple MethodMatchers and ClassFilters. You can also create composite pointcuts by using other objects that implement the Pointcut interface.

Another way for constructing a composite pointcut is to use the org.springframework.aop.support.Pointcuts class. The class provides three static methods. The intersection() and union() methods both take two pointcuts as arguments to construct a composite pointcut. On the other hand, a matches(Pointcut, Method, Class, Object[]) method also is provided for performing a quick check on whether a pointcut matches with the provided method, class, and method arguments.

The Pointcuts class supports operations on only two pointcuts. So, if you need to combine MethodMatcher and ClassFilter with Pointcut, you need to use the ComposablePointcut class. However, when you need to combine just two pointcuts, the Pointcuts class will be more convenient.

Pointcut Summary

Spring offers a powerful set of Pointcut implementations that should meet most, if not all, of your application's requirements. Remember that if you can't find a pointcut to suit your needs, you can create your own implementation from scratch by implementing Pointcut, MethodMatcher, and ClassFilter.

You can use two patterns to combine pointcuts and advisors. The first pattern, the one we have used so far, involves having the pointcut implementation decoupled from the advisor. In the code we have seen up to this point, we created instances of Pointcut implementations and then used the DefaultPointcutAdvisor to add advice along with the Pointcut to the proxy.

The second option, one that is adopted by many of the examples in the Spring documentation, is to encapsulate the Pointcut inside your own Advisor implementation. This way, you have a class that implements both Pointcut and PointcutAdvisor, with the PointcutAdvisor.getPointcut() method simply returning this. This is an approach many classes, such as StaticMethodMatcherPointcutAdvisor, use in Spring.

We find that the first approach is the most flexible, allowing you to use different Pointcut implementations with different Advisor implementations. However, the second approach is useful in situations where you are going to be using the same combination of Pointcut and Advisor in different parts of your application, or, indeed, across many applications. The second approach is useful when each Advisor must have a separate instance of a Pointcut; by making the Advisor responsible for creating the Pointcut, you can ensure that this is the case.

If you recall the discussion on proxy performance from the previous chapter, you will remember that unadvised methods perform much better than methods that are advised. For this reason, you should ensure that, by using Pointcuts, you advise only the methods that are absolutely necessary. This way, you reduce the amount of unnecessary overhead added to your application by using AOP.

Getting Started with Introductions

Introductions are an important part of the AOP feature set available in Spring. By using introductions, you can introduce new functionality to an existing object dynamically. In Spring, you can introduce an implementation of any interface to an existing object. You may well be wondering exactly why this is useful—why would you want to add functionality dynamically at runtime when you can simply add that functionality at development time? The answer to this question is easy. You add functionality dynamically when the functionality is crosscutting and is not easily implemented using traditional advice.

Introduction Basics

Spring treats *introductions* as a special type of advice, more specifically, as a special type of around advice. Because introductions apply solely at the class level, you cannot use pointcuts with introductions; semantically, the two don't match. An introduction adds new interface implementations to a class, and a pointcut defines which methods the advice applies. You create an introduction by implementing the `IntroductionInterceptor` interface, which extends the `MethodInterceptor` and the `DynamicIntroductionAdvice` interfaces. Figure 5-5 shows this structure along with the methods of both interfaces.

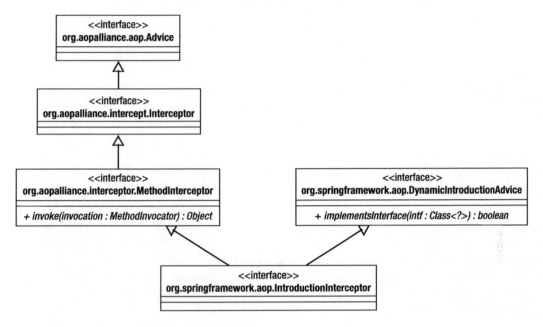

Figure 5-5. *Interface structure for introductions*

As you can see, the `MethodInterceptor` interface defines an `invoke()` method. Using this method, you provide the implementation for the interfaces that you are introducing and perform interception for any additional methods as required. Implementing all methods for an interface inside a single method can prove troublesome, and it is likely to result in an awful lot of code that you will have to wade through just to decide which method to invoke. Thankfully, Spring provides a default implementation of `IntroductionInterceptor`, `DelegatingIntroductionInterceptor`, which makes creating introductions much simpler. To build an introduction by using `DelegatingIntroductionInterceptor`, you create a class that both inherits from `DelegatingIntroductionInterceptor` and implements the interfaces you want to introduce. The `DelegatingIntroductionInterceptor` then simply delegates all calls to introduced methods to the corresponding method on itself. Don't worry if this seems a little unclear; you will see an example of it in the next section.

Just as you need to use `PointcutAdvisor` when you are working with pointcut advice, you need to use `IntroductionAdvisor` to add introductions to a proxy. The default implementation of `IntroductionAdvisor` is `DefaultIntroductionAdvisor`, which should suffice for most, if not all, of your introduction needs. You should be aware that adding an introduction by using `ProxyFactory.addAdvice()` is not permitted and results in `AopConfigException` being thrown. Instead, you should use the `addAdvisor()` method and pass an instance of the `IntroductionAdvisor` interface.

When using standard advice—that is, not introductions—it is possible for the same advice instance to be used for many objects. The Spring documentation refers to this as the *per-class life cycle*, although you can use a single advice instance for many classes. For introductions, the introduction advice forms part of the state of the advised object, and as a result, you must have a distinct advice instance for every advised object. This is called the *per-instance life cycle*. Because you must ensure that each advised object has a distinct instance of the introduction, it is often preferable to create a subclass of `DefaultIntroductionAdvisor` that is responsible for creating the introduction advice. This way, you need to ensure only that a new instance of your advisor class is created for each object, because it will automatically create a new instance of the introduction.

213

For example, we want to apply before advice to the setFirstName() method on all instances of the Contact class. Figure 5-6 shows the same advice that applies to all objects of the Contact type.

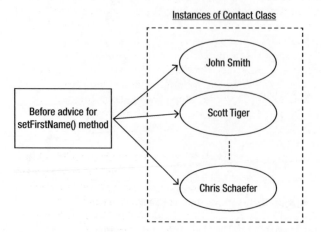

Figure 5-6. *Per-class life cycle of advice*

Now let's say we want to mix an introduction into all instances of the Contact class, and the introduction will carry information for each Contact instance (for example, an attribute isModified that indicates whether the specific instance was modified). In this case, the introduction will be created for each instance of Contact and tied to that specific instance, as shown in Figure 5-7.

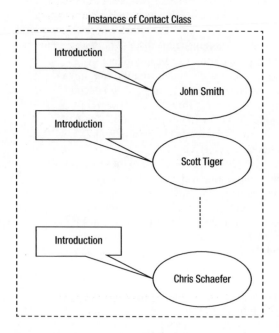

Figure 5-7. *Per-instance introduction*

That covers the basics of introduction creation. We will now discuss how you can use introductions to solve the problem of object modification detection.

Object Modification Detection with Introductions

Object modification detection is a useful technique for many reasons. Typically, you apply modification detection to prevent unnecessary database access when you are persisting object data. If an object is passed to a method for modification but it comes back unmodified, there is little point in issuing an update statement to the database. Using a modification check in this way can really increase application throughput, especially when the database is already under a substantial load or is located on a remote network, making communication an expensive operation.

Unfortunately, this kind of functionality is difficult to implement by hand because it requires you to add to every method that can modify object state to check whether the object state is actually being modified. When you consider all the null checks that have to be made and the checks to see whether the value is actually changing, you are looking at around eight lines of code per method. You could refactor this into a single method, but you still have to call this method every time you need to perform the check. Spread this across a typical application with many classes that require modification checks, and you have a disaster waiting to happen.

This is clearly a place where introductions will help. We don't want to have each class that requires modification checks inherit from some base implementation, losing its only chance for inheritance as a result, nor do we really want to be adding checking code to each and every state-changing method. Using introductions, we can provide a flexible solution to the modification detection problem without having to write a bunch of repetitive, error-prone code.

In this example, we are going to build a full modification check framework using introductions. The modification check logic is encapsulated by the IsModified interface, an implementation of which will be introduced into the appropriate objects, along with interception logic to perform modification checks automatically. For the purposes of this example, we use JavaBeans conventions, in that we consider a modification to be any call to a setter method. Of course, we don't just treat all calls to a setter method as a modification—we check to see whether the value being passed to the setter is different from the one currently stored in the object. The only flaw with this solution is that setting an object back to its original state will still reflect a modification if any one of the values on the object changed. For example, you have a Contact object with the firstName attribute. Let's say that during processing, the firstName attribute was changed from Peter to John. As a result, the object was marked as modified. However, it will still be marked as modified, even if the value is then changed back from John to its original value Peter in later processing. One way to keep track of such changes is to store the full history of changes in the object's entire life cycle. However, the implementation here is nontrivial and suffices for most requirements. Implementing the more complete solution would result in an overly complex example.

Using the IsModified Interface

Central to the modification check solution is the IsModified interface, which our fictional application uses to make intelligent decisions about object persistence. We do not look at how the application would use IsModified; instead, we focus on the implementation of the introduction. Listing 5-49 shows the IsModified interface.

Listing 5-49. The IsModified Interface

```
package com.apress.prospring4.ch5;

public interface IsModified {
    boolean isModified();
}
```

There's nothing special here—just a single method, isModified(), indicating whether an object has been modified.

Creating a Mixin

The next step is to create the code that implements IsModified and that is introduced to the objects;
this is referred to as a *mixin*. As we mentioned earlier, it is much simpler to create mixins by subclassing
DelegatingIntroductionInterceptor than to create one by directly implementing the IntroductionInterceptor
interface. Our mixin class, IsModifiedMixin, subclasses DelegatingIntroductionInterceptor and also implements
the IsModified interface. This is shown in Listing 5-50.

Listing 5-50. The IsModifiedMixin Class

```
package com.apress.prospring4.ch5;

import java.lang.reflect.Method;
import java.util.HashMap;
import java.util.Map;

import org.aopalliance.intercept.MethodInvocation;
import org.springframework.aop.support.DelegatingIntroductionInterceptor;

public class IsModifiedMixin extends DelegatingIntroductionInterceptor
        implements IsModified {
    private boolean isModified = false;

    private Map<Method, Method> methodCache = new HashMap<Method, Method>();

    @Override
    public boolean isModified() {
        return isModified;
    }

    @Override
    public Object invoke(MethodInvocation invocation) throws Throwable {
        if (!isModified) {
            if ((invocation.getMethod().getName().startsWith("set"))
                && (invocation.getArguments().length == 1)) {

                Method getter = getGetter(invocation.getMethod());

                if (getter != null) {
                    Object newVal = invocation.getArguments()[0];
                    Object oldVal = getter.invoke(invocation.getThis(), null);

                    if((newVal == null) && (oldVal == null)) {
                        isModified = false;
                    } else if((newVal == null) && (oldVal != null)) {
                        isModified = true;
                    } else if((newVal != null) && (oldVal == null)) {
                        isModified = true;
```

```
                } else {
                    isModified = (!newVal.equals(oldVal));
                }
            }
        }
    }

    return super.invoke(invocation);
}

private Method getGetter(Method setter) {
    Method getter = null;

    getter = (Method) methodCache.get(setter);

    if (getter != null) {
        return getter;
    }

    String getterName = setter.getName().replaceFirst("set", "get");

    try {
        getter = setter.getDeclaringClass().getMethod(getterName, null);

        synchronized (methodCache) {
            methodCache.put(setter, getter);
        }

        return getter;
    } catch (NoSuchMethodException ex) {
        return null;
    }
}
}
```

The first thing to notice here is the implementation of IsModified, which consists of the private modified field and the isModified() method. This example highlights why you must have one mixin instance per advised object—the mixin introduces not only methods to the object but also state. If you share a single instance of this mixin across many objects, then you are also sharing the state, which means all objects show as modified the first time a single object becomes modified.

You do not actually have to implement the invoke() method for a mixin, but in this case, doing so allows us to detect automatically when a modification occurs. We start by performing the check only if the object is still unmodified; we do not need to check for modifications once we know that the object has been modified. Next, we check to see whether the method is a setter, and if it is, we retrieve the corresponding getter method. Note that we cache the getter/setter pairs for quicker future retrieval. Finally, we compare the value returned by the getter with that passed to the setter to determine whether a modification has occurred. Notice that we check for the different possible combinations of null and set the modifications appropriately. It is important to remember that when you are using DelegatingIntroductionInterceptor, you must call super.invoke() when overriding invoke() because it is the DelegatingIntroductionInterceptor that dispatches the invocation to the correct location, either the advised object or the mixin itself.

You can implement as many interfaces as you like in your mixin, each of which is automatically introduced into the advised object.

Creating an Advisor

The next step is to create an Advisor to wrap the creation of the mixin class. This step is optional, but it does help ensure that a new instance of the mixin is being used for each advised object. Listing 5-51 shows the IsModifiedAdvisor class.

Listing 5-51. Creating an Advisor for Your Mixin

```
package com.apress.prospring4.ch5;

import org.springframework.aop.support.DefaultIntroductionAdvisor;

public class IsModifiedAdvisor extends DefaultIntroductionAdvisor {
    public IsModifiedAdvisor() {
        super(new IsModifiedMixin());
    }
}
```

Notice that we have extended DefaultIntroductionAdvisor to create our IsModifiedAdvisor. The implementation of this advisor is trivial and self-explanatory.

Putting It All Together

Now that we have a mixin class and an Advisor class, we can test the modification check framework. Listing 5-52 shows a simple class that we use to test IsModifiedMixin.

Listing 5-52. The TargetBean Class

```
package com.apress.prospring4.ch5;

public class TargetBean {
    private String name;

    public void setName(String name) {
        this.name = name;
    }

    public String getName() {
        return name;
    }
}
```

This bean has a single property, name, that we use when we are testing the modification check mixin. Listing 5-53 shows how to assemble the advised proxy and then tests the modification check code.

Listing 5-53. Using IsModifiedMixin

```
package com.apress.prospring4.ch5;

import org.springframework.aop.IntroductionAdvisor;
import org.springframework.aop.framework.ProxyFactory;
```

```java
public class IntroductionExample {
    public static void main(String[] args) {
        TargetBean target = new TargetBean();
        target.setName("Chris Schaefer");

        IntroductionAdvisor advisor = new IsModifiedAdvisor();

        ProxyFactory pf = new ProxyFactory();
        pf.setTarget(target);
        pf.addAdvisor(advisor);
        pf.setOptimize(true);

        TargetBean proxy = (TargetBean) pf.getProxy();
        IsModified proxyInterface = (IsModified)proxy;

        System.out.println("Is TargetBean?: " + (proxy instanceof TargetBean));
        System.out.println("Is IsModified?: " + (proxy instanceof IsModified));

        System.out.println("Has been modified?: " +
            proxyInterface.isModified());

        proxy.setName("Chris Schaefer");

        System.out.println("Has been modified?: " +
            proxyInterface.isModified());

        proxy.setName("Chris Schaefer");

        System.out.println("Has been modified?: " +
            proxyInterface.isModified());
    }
}
```

Notice that when we are creating the proxy, we set the optimize flag to true to force the use of the CGLIB proxy. The reason for this is that when you are using the JDK proxy to introduce a mixin, the resulting proxy will not be an instance of the object class (in this case TargetBean); the proxy implements only the mixin interfaces, not the original class. With the CGLIB proxy, the original class is implemented by the proxy along with the mixin interfaces.

Notice in the code that we test first to see whether the proxy is an instance of TargetBean and then to see whether it is an instance of IsModified. Both tests return true when you are using the CGLIB proxy, but only the IsModified test returns true for the JDK proxy. Finally, we test the modification check code by first setting the name property to its current value and then to a new value, checking the value of the isModified flag each time. Running this example results in the following output:

```
Is TargetBean?: true
Is IsModified?: true
Has been modified?: false
Has been modified?: false
Has been modified?: true
```

As expected, both `instanceof` tests return `true`. Notice that the first call to `isModified()`, before any modification occurred, returns `false`. The next call, after we set the value of `name` to the same value, also returns `false`. For the final call, however, after we set the value of `name` to a new value, the `isModified()` method returns `true`, indicating that the object has in fact been modified.

Introduction Summary

Introductions are one of the most powerful features of Spring AOP; they allow you not only to extend the functionality of existing methods, but also to extend the set of interfaces and object implementations dynamically. Using introductions is the perfect way to implement crosscutting logic that your application interacts with through well-defined interfaces. In general, this is the kind of logic that you want to apply declaratively rather than programmatically. By using the `IsModifiedMixin` defined in this example and the framework services discussed in the next section, we can declaratively define which objects are capable of modification checks, without needing to modify the implementations of those objects.

Obviously, because introductions work via proxies, they add a certain amount of overhead. All methods on the proxy are considered advised since pointcuts cannot be used in conjunction with introductions. However, in the case of many of the services that you can implement by using introductions such as the object modification check, this performance overhead is a small price to pay for the reduction in code required to implement the service, as well as the increase in stability and maintainability that comes from fully centralizing the service logic.

Framework Services for AOP

Up to now, we have had to write a lot of code to advise objects and generate the proxies for them. Although this in itself is not a huge problem, it does mean that all advice configuration is hard-coded into your application, removing some of the benefits of being able to advise a method implementation transparently. Thankfully, Spring provides additional framework services that allow you to create an advised proxy in your application configuration and then inject this proxy into a target bean just like any other dependencies.

Using the declarative approach to AOP configuration is preferable to the manual, programmatic mechanism. When you use the declarative mechanism, not only do you externalize the configuration of advice, but you also reduce the chance of coding errors. You can also take advantage of DI and AOP combined to enable AOP so it can be used in a completely transparent environment.

Configuring AOP Declaratively

When using declarative configuration of Spring AOP, three options exist:

- *Using* `ProxyFactoryBean`: In Spring AOP, `ProxyFactoryBean` provides a declarative way for configuring Spring's `ApplicationContext` (and hence the underlying `BeanFactory`) in creating AOP proxies based on defined Spring beans.

- *Using the Spring aop namespace*: Introduced in Spring 2.0, the aop namespace provides a simplified way (when compared to `ProxyFactoryBean`) for defining aspects and their DI requirements in Spring applications. However, the aop namespace also uses `ProxyFactoryBean` behind the scenes.

- *Using @AspectJ-style annotations*: Besides the XML-based aop namespace, you can use the @ AspectJ-style annotations within your classes for configuring Spring AOP. Although the syntax it uses is based on AspectJ and you need to include some AspectJ libraries when using this option, Spring still uses the proxy mechanism (that is, creates proxied objects for the targets) when bootstrapping `ApplicationContext`.

Using ProxyFactoryBean

The `ProxyFactoryBean` class is an implementation of `FactoryBean` that allows you to specify a bean to target, and it provides a set of advice and advisors for that bean that are eventually merged into an AOP proxy. Because you can use both advisor and advice with `ProxyFactoryBean`, you can configure not only the advice declaratively but the pointcuts as well.

`ProxyFactoryBean` shares a common interface (the `org.springframework.aop.framework.Advised` interface) with `ProxyFactory` (both classes extend the `org.springframework.aop.framework.AdvisedSupport` class indirectly, which implements the `Advised` interface), and as a result, it exposes many of the same flags such as `frozen`, `optimize`, and `exposeProxy`. The values for these flags are passed directly to the underlying `ProxyFactory`, which allows you to configure the factory declaratively as well.

ProxyFactoryBean in Action

Using `ProxyFactoryBean` is very simple. You define a bean that will be the target bean, and then using `ProxyFactoryBean`, you define the bean that your application will access, using the target bean as the proxy target. Where possible, define the target bean as an anonymous bean inside the proxy bean declaration. This prevents your application from accidentally accessing the unadvised bean. However, in some cases, such as the sample we are about to show you, you may want to create more than one proxy for the same bean, so you should use a normal top-level bean for this case.

Listings 5-54 and 5-55 show two classes, one of which has a dependency on the other.

Listing 5-54. The `MyDependency` Class

```
package com.apress.prospring4.ch5;

public class MyDependency {
    public void foo() {
        System.out.println("foo()");
    }

    public void bar() {
        System.out.println("bar()");
    }
}
```

Listing 5-55. The `MyBean` Class

```
package com.apress.prospring4.ch5;

public class MyBean {
    private MyDependency dep;

    public void execute() {
        dep.foo();
        dep.bar();
    }

    public void setDep(MyDependency dep) {
        this.dep = dep;
    }
}
```

For this example, we are going to create two proxies for a single MyDependency instance, both with the same basic advice shown in Listing 5-56.

Listing 5-56. The MyAdvice Class

```
package com.apress.prospring4.ch5;

import java.lang.reflect.Method;
import org.springframework.aop.MethodBeforeAdvice;

public class MyAdvice implements MethodBeforeAdvice { @Override
    public void before(Method method, Object[] args, Object target)
            throws Throwable {
        System.out.println("Executing: " + method);
    }
}
```

The first proxy will just advise the target by using the advice directly; thus, all methods will be advised. For the second proxy, we will configure AspectJExpressionPointcut and DefaultPointcutAdvisor so that only the foo() method of the MyDependency class is advised. To test the advice, we will create two bean definitions of type MyBean, each of which will be injected with a different proxy. Then we will invoke the execute() method on each of these beans and observe what happens when the advised methods on the dependency are invoked.

Listing 5-57 shows the configuration for this example (app-context-xml.xml).

Listing 5-57. Declarative AOP Configuration

```
<?xml version="1.0" encoding="UTF-8"?>

<beans xmlns="http://www.springframework.org/schema/beans"
        xmlns:xsi="http://www.w3.org/2001/XMLSchema-instance"
        xsi:schemaLocation="http://www.springframework.org/schema/beans
          http://www.springframework.org/schema/beans/spring-beans.xsd">

    <bean id="myBean1" class="com.apress.prospring4.ch5.MyBean">
        <property name="dep">
            <ref bean="myDependency1"/>
        </property>
    </bean>

    <bean id="myBean2" class="com.apress.prospring4.ch5.MyBean">
        <property name="dep">
            <ref bean="myDependency2"/>
        </property>
    </bean>

    <bean id="myDependencyTarget" class="com.apress.prospring4.ch5.MyDependency"/>

    <bean id="myDependency1" class="org.springframework.aop.framework.ProxyFactoryBean">
        <property name="target">
            <ref bean="myDependencyTarget"/>
        </property>
```

```xml
        <property name="interceptorNames">
            <list>
                <value>advice</value>
            </list>
        </property>
    </bean>

    <bean id="myDependency2" class="org.springframework.aop.framework.ProxyFactoryBean">
        <property name="target">
            <ref bean="myDependencyTarget"/>
        </property>
        <property name="interceptorNames">
            <list>
                <value>advisor</value>
            </list>
        </property>
    </bean>

    <bean id="advice" class="com.apress.prospring4.ch5.MyAdvice"/>

    <bean id="advisor" class="org.springframework.aop.support.DefaultPointcutAdvisor">
        <property name="advice">
            <ref bean="advice"/>
        </property>
        <property name="pointcut">
            <bean class="org.springframework.aop.aspectj.AspectJExpressionPointcut">
                <property name="expression">
                    <value>execution(* foo*(..))</value>
                </property>
            </bean>
        </property>
    </bean>
</beans>
```

In the example, we are simply setting the properties that we set in code using Spring's DI capabilities. The only points of interest are that we use an anonymous bean for the pointcut and we use the ProxyFactoryBean class. We prefer to use anonymous beans for pointcuts when they are not being shared because it keeps the set of beans that are directly accessible as small and as application-relevant as possible. The important point to realize when you are using ProxyFactoryBean is that the ProxyFactoryBean declaration is the one to expose to your application and the one to use when you are fulfilling dependencies. The underlying target bean declaration is not advised, so you should use this bean only when you want to bypass the AOP framework, although in general, your application should not be aware of the AOP framework and thus should not want to bypass it. For this reason, you should use anonymous beans wherever possible to avoid accidental access from the application.

Listing 5-58 shows a simple class that obtains the two MyBean instances from ApplicationContext and then runs the execute() method for each one.

Listing 5-58. The ProxyFactoryBeanExample Class

```
package com.apress.prospring4.ch5;

import org.springframework.context.support.GenericXmlApplicationContext;

public class ProxyFactoryBeanExample {
    public static void main(String[] args) {
        GenericXmlApplicationContext ctx = new GenericXmlApplicationContext();
        ctx.load("classpath:META-INF/spring/app-context-xml.xml");
        ctx.refresh();

        MyBean bean1 = (MyBean)ctx.getBean("myBean1");
        MyBean bean2 = (MyBean)ctx.getBean("myBean2");

        System.out.println("Bean 1");
        bean1.execute();

        System.out.println("\nBean 2");
        bean2.execute();
    }
}
```

Running the example in Listing 5-58 results in the following output:

```
Bean 1
Executing: public void com.apress.prospring4.ch5.MyDependency.foo()
foo()
Executing: public void com.apress.prospring4.ch5.MyDependency.bar()
bar()

Bean 2
Executing: public void com.apress.prospring4.ch5.MyDependency.foo()
foo()
bar()
```

As expected, both the foo() and bar() methods in the first proxy are advised, because no pointcut was used in its configuration. For the second proxy, however, only the foo() method was advised because of the pointcut used in the configuration.

Using ProxyFactoryBean for Introductions

You are not limited in using the ProxyFactoryBean class for just advising an object but also for introducing mixins to your objects. Remember from our earlier discussion on introductions that you must use an IntroductionAdvisor to add an introduction; you cannot add an introduction directly. The same rule applies when you are using ProxyFactoryBean with introductions. When you are using ProxyFactoryBean, it becomes much easier to configure your proxies if you created a custom Advisor for your mixin. Listing 5-59 shows a sample configuration for the IsModifiedMixin introduction from earlier in the chapter (app-context-xml.xml).

Listing 5-59. Configuring Introductions with ProxyFactoryBean

```xml
<?xml version="1.0" encoding="UTF-8"?>

<beans xmlns="http://www.springframework.org/schema/beans"
    xmlns:xsi="http://www.w3.org/2001/XMLSchema-instance"
    xsi:schemaLocation="http://www.springframework.org/schema/beans
    http://www.springframework.org/schema/beans/spring-beans.xsd">

    <bean id="bean" class="org.springframework.aop.framework.ProxyFactoryBean">
        <property name="target">
            <bean class="com.apress.prospring4.ch5.TargetBean">
                <property name="name">
                    <value>Chris Schaefer</value>
                </property>
            </bean>
        </property>
        <property name="interceptorNames">
            <list>
                <value>advisor</value>
            </list>
        </property>
        <property name="proxyTargetClass">
            <value>true</value>
        </property>
    </bean>

    <bean id="advisor" class="com.apress.prospring4.ch5.IsModifiedAdvisor"/>
</beans>
```

As you can see from the configuration, we use the IsModifiedAdvisor class as the advisor for the ProxyFactoryBean, and because we do not need to create another proxy of the same target object, we use an anonymous declaration for the target bean. Listing 5-60 shows a modification of the previous introduction example that obtains the proxy from ApplicationContext.

Listing 5-60. The IntroductionConfigExample Class

```java
package com.apress.prospring4.ch5;

import org.springframework.context.support.GenericXmlApplicationContext;

public class IntroductionConfigExample {
    public static void main(String[] args) {
        GenericXmlApplicationContext ctx = new GenericXmlApplicationContext();
        ctx.load("classpath:META-INF/spring/app-context-xml.xml");
        ctx.refresh();

        TargetBean bean = (TargetBean) ctx.getBean("bean");
        IsModified mod = (IsModified) bean;

        System.out.println("Is TargetBean?: " + (bean instanceof TargetBean));
        System.out.println("Is IsModified?: " + (bean instanceof IsModified));

        System.out.println("Has been modified?: " + mod.isModified());
        bean.setName("Chris Schaefer");
```

```
        System.out.println("Has been modified?: " + mod.isModified());
        bean.setName("Chris Schaefer");

        System.out.println("Has been modified?: " + mod.isModified());
    }
}
```

Running this example yields exactly the same output as the previous introduction example, but this time the proxy is obtained from ApplicationContext and no configuration is present in the application code.

ProxyFactoryBean Summary

When you use ProxyFactoryBean, you can configure AOP proxies that provide all the flexibility of the programmatic method without needing to couple your application to the AOP configuration. Unless you need to perform decisions at runtime as to how your proxies should be created, it is best to use the declarative method of proxy configuration over the programmatic method. Let's move on to see the other two options for declarative Spring AOP, which are both preferred options for applications based on Spring 2.0 or newer with JDK 5 or newer.

Using the aop Namespace

The aop namespace provides a greatly simplified syntax for declarative Spring AOP configurations. To show you how it works, let's reuse the previous ProxyFactoryBean example, with a slightly modified version in order to demonstrate its usage.

Listings 5-61 and 5-62 show the MyDependency and MyBean classes, with some modifications.

Listing 5-61. The MyDependency Class

```
package com.apress.prospring4.ch5;

public class MyDependency {
    public void foo(int intValue) {
        System.out.println("foo(int): " + intValue);
    }

    public void bar() {
        System.out.println("bar()");
    }
}
```

Listing 5-62. The MyBean Class

```
package com.apress.prospring4.ch5;

public class MyBean {
    private MyDependency dep;

    public void execute() {
        dep.foo(100);
        dep.foo(101);
        dep.bar();
    }
```

```
    public void setDep(MyDependency dep) {
        this.dep = dep;
    }
}
```

In the previous listing, we modified the foo() method of the MyDependency class to accept an integer value as an argument. And in the MyBean class, the foo() method was called twice with different parameters.

Let's see what the advice class looks like. Listing 5-63 shows the revised MyAdvice class.

Listing 5-63. The MyAdvice Class

```
package com.apress.prospring4.ch5;

import org.aspectj.lang.JoinPoint;

public class MyAdvice {
    public void simpleBeforeAdvice(JoinPoint joinPoint) {
        System.out.println("Executing: " +
                joinPoint.getSignature().getDeclaringTypeName() + " "
                + joinPoint.getSignature().getName());
    }
}
```

You will see that the advice class no longer needs to implement the MethodBeforeAdvice interface. Also, the before advice accepts the JoinPoint as an argument but not the method, object, and arguments. Actually, for the advice class, this argument is optional, so you can leave the method with no argument. However, if in the advice you need to access the information of the joinpoint being advised (in this case, we want to dump the information of the calling type and method name), then we need to define the acceptance of the argument. When the argument is defined for the method, Spring will automatically pass the joinpoint into the method for your processing.

Listing 5-64 shows the Spring XML configuration with the aop namespace (app-context-xml.xml).

Listing 5-64. Configuring Spring AOP with the aop Namespace

```
<?xml version="1.0" encoding="UTF-8"?>

<beans xmlns="http://www.springframework.org/schema/beans"
    xmlns:xsi="http://www.w3.org/2001/XMLSchema-instance"
    xmlns:aop="http://www.springframework.org/schema/aop"
    xsi:schemaLocation="http://www.springframework.org/schema/beans
        http://www.springframework.org/schema/beans/spring-beans.xsd
        http://www.springframework.org/schema/aop
        http://www.springframework.org/schema/aop/spring-aop.xsd">

    <aop:config>
        <aop:pointcut id="fooExecution"
            expression="execution(* com.apress.prospring4.ch5..foo*(int))"/>

        <aop:aspect ref="advice">
            <aop:before pointcut-ref="fooExecution"
                method="simpleBeforeAdvice"/>
        </aop:aspect>
    </aop:config>
```

```
        <bean id="advice" class="com.apress.prospring4.ch5.MyAdvice"/>

        <bean id="myDependency"
            class="com.apress.prospring4.ch5.MyDependency"/>

        <bean id="myBean" class="com.apress.prospring4.ch5.MyBean">
            <property name="dep" ref="myDependency"/>
        </bean>
</beans>
```

First, we need to declare the aop namespace in the <beans> tags. Second, all the Spring AOP configuration was put under the tag <aop:config>. Under <aop:config>, you can then define the pointcut, aspects, advisors, and so on, and reference other Spring beans as usual.

From the previous configuration, we defined a pointcut with the ID fooExecution. The expression "execution(* com.apress.prospring4.ch5..foo*(int))" means that we want to advise all methods with the prefix foo, and the classes are defined under the package com.apress.prospring4.ch5 (including all the subpackages). Also, the foo() method should receive one argument with the integer type. Afterward, for the aspect, it was declared by using the <aop:aspect> tag, and the advice class is referencing the Spring bean with the ID "advice", which is the MyAdvice class. The pointcut-ref is referencing the defined pointcut with the ID fooExecution, and the before advice (declared by using the <aop:before> tag) is the method simpleBeforeAdvice() within the advice bean.

Listing 5-65 shows the testing program.

Listing 5-65. The AopNamespaceExample Class

```
package com.apress.prospring4.ch5;

import org.springframework.context.support.GenericXmlApplicationContext;

public class AopNamespaceExample {
    public static void main(String[] args) {
        GenericXmlApplicationContext ctx = new GenericXmlApplicationContext();
        ctx.load("classpath:META-INF/spring/app-context-xml.xml");
        ctx.refresh();

        MyBean myBean = (MyBean) ctx.getBean("myBean");
        myBean.execute();
    }
}
```

In this example, we simply initialize the ApplicationContext as usual, retrieve the bean, and call its execute() method. Running the program will yield the following output:

```
Executing: com.apress.prospring4.ch5.MyDependency foo
foo(int): 100
Executing: com.apress.prospring4.ch5.MyDependency foo
foo(int): 101
bar()
```

As you can see, the two calls to the foo() method were advised but not the bar() method. It exactly works as we expected, and you can see the configuration was greatly simplified when compared to the ProxyFactoryBean configuration.

Let's further revise the previous sample into a bit more complicated case. Suppose now we want to advise only those methods with Spring beans with an ID starting with myDependency and an integer argument that is not equal to 100.

To run the advice only when the argument is not 100, we need to modify the advice slightly. Listing 5-66 shows the revised MyAdvice class.

Listing 5-66. The MyAdvice Class (Revised for Argument Checking)

```
package com.apress.prospring4.ch5;

import org.aspectj.lang.JoinPoint;

public class MyAdvice {
    public void simpleBeforeAdvice(JoinPoint joinPoint, int intValue) {
        if (intValue != 100) {
            System.out.println("Executing: " +
                joinPoint.getSignature().getDeclaringTypeName() + " "
                + joinPoint.getSignature().getName()
                + " argument: " + intValue);
        }
    }
}
```

Two places were modified. First, the argument intValue was added into the signature of the before advice. Second, in the advice, we check and execute the logic only when the argument does not equal 100.

To pass the argument to the advice, we also need to revise the XML configuration a bit. In this case, we need to modify the point expression. The modified pointcut expression is shown here:

```
<aop:pointcut id="fooExecution" expression="execution(* foo*(int))
    and args(intValue) and bean(myDependency*)"/>
```

Two more directives were added to the pointcut expression. First, the args(intValue) instructs Spring to also pass the argument with the name intValue into the before advice. Second, the bean(myDependency*) directive instructs Spring to advise only the beans with an ID that has myDependency as the prefix. This is a powerful feature; if you have a well-defined structure of Spring beans naming, you can easily advise the objects that you want. For example, you can have advice that applies to all DAO beans by using bean(*DAO*) or all service layer beans using bean(*Service*), instead of using the fully qualified class name for matching.

Running the same testing program (AopNamespaceExample) produces the following output:

```
foo(int): 100
Executing: com.apress.prospring4.ch5.MyDependency foo argument: 101
foo(int): 101
bar()
```

You can see that only the foo() method with arguments not equal to 100 are advised.

Let's see one more example of using the aop namespace for around advice. Instead of creating another class to implement the MethodInterceptor interface, we can simply add a new method to the MyAdvice class. Listing 5-67 shows the new method, simpleAroundAdvice(), in the revised MyAdvice class.

Listing 5-67. The MyAdvice Class (Revised for Argument Checking)

```
package com.apress.prospring4.ch5;

import org.aspectj.lang.JoinPoint;
import org.aspectj.lang.ProceedingJoinPoint;
```

```java
public class MyAdvice {
    public void simpleBeforeAdvice(JoinPoint joinPoint, int intValue) {
        if (intValue != 100) {
            System.out.println("Executing: " +
                joinPoint.getSignature().getDeclaringTypeName() + " "
                + joinPoint.getSignature().getName()
                + " argument: " + intValue);
        }
    }

    public Object simpleAroundAdvice(ProceedingJoinPoint pjp, int intValue)
            throws Throwable {
        System.out.println("Before execution: " +
            pjp.getSignature().getDeclaringTypeName() + " "
            + pjp.getSignature().getName()
            + " argument: " + intValue);

        Object retVal = pjp.proceed();

        System.out.println("After execution: " +
            pjp.getSignature().getDeclaringTypeName() + " "
            + pjp.getSignature().getName() + " argument: " + intValue);

        return retVal;
    }
}
```

The newly added simpleAroundAdvice() method needs to take at least one argument of type ProceedingJoinPoint so that it can proceed with the invocation of the target object. We also added the intValue argument to display the value in the advice.

Listing 5-68 shows XML configuration.

Listing 5-68. Configuring Spring AOP with the aop Namespace (Around Advice)

```xml
<?xml version="1.0" encoding="UTF-8"?>

<beans xmlns="http://www.springframework.org/schema/beans"
    xmlns:xsi="http://www.w3.org/2001/XMLSchema-instance"
    xmlns:aop="http://www.springframework.org/schema/aop"
    xsi:schemaLocation="http://www.springframework.org/schema/beans
        http://www.springframework.org/schema/beans/spring-beans.xsd
        http://www.springframework.org/schema/aop
        http://www.springframework.org/schema/aop/spring-aop.xsd">

    <aop:config>
        <aop:pointcut id="fooExecution"
            expression="execution(* com.apress.prospring4.ch5..foo*(int))"/>

        <aop:aspect ref="advice">
            <aop:before pointcut-ref="fooExecution"
                method="simpleBeforeAdvice"/>
            <aop:around pointcut-ref="fooExecution"
                method="simpleAroundAdvice"/>
        </aop:aspect>
```

```
        </aop:config>

        <bean id="advice" class="com.apress.prospring4.ch5.MyAdvice"/>

        <bean id="myDependency"
            class="com.apress.prospring4.ch5.MyDependency"/>

        <bean id="myBean" class="com.apress.prospring4.ch5.MyBean">
            <property name="dep" ref="myDependency"/>
        </bean>
</beans
```

We just added a new tag `<aop:around>` to declare the around advice and reference the same pointcut. Run the testing program again, and you will have the following output:

```
Before execution: com.apress.prospring4.ch5.MyDependency foo argument: 100
foo(int): 100
After execution: com.apress.prospring4.ch5.MyDependency foo argument: 100
Executing: com.apress.prospring4.ch5.MyDependency foo argument: 101
Before execution: com.apress.prospring4.ch5.MyDependency foo argument: 101
foo(int): 101
After execution: com.apress.prospring4.ch5.MyDependency foo argument: 101
bar()
```

There are two interesting points here. First, you see that the around advice was applied to both invocations of the foo() method, since it doesn't check the argument. Second, for the foo() method with 101 as an argument, both the before and around advice were executed, and by default the before advice takes precedence.

■ **Note** When using the aop namespace or the @AspectJ style, there are two types of after advice. The *after-returning advice* (using the `<aop:after-returning>` tag) applies only when the target method is completed normally. Another one is the *after advice* (using the `<aop:after>` tag), which takes place whether the method was completed normally or the method runs into an error and an exception is thrown. If you need advice that executes regardless of the execution result of the target method, you should use after advice.

Using @AspectJ-Style Annotations

When using Spring AOP with JDK 5 or above, you can also use the @AspectJ-style annotations to declare your advice. However, as stated before, Spring still uses its own proxying mechanism for advising the target methods, not AspectJ's weaving mechanism.

In this section, we will go through how to implement the same aspects as the one in the aop namespace, by using @AspectJ-style annotations. For the examples in this section, we will use annotation for other Spring beans as well.

Listings 5-69 and 5-70 show the MyDependency and MyBean classes with Spring's DI annotations.

Listing 5-69. The MyDependency Class

```
package com.apress.prospring4.ch5;

import org.springframework.stereotype.Component;

@Component("myDependency")
public class MyDependency {
    public void foo(int intValue) {
        System.out.println("foo(int): " + intValue);
    }

    public void bar() {
        System.out.println("bar()");
    }
}
```

Listing 5-70. The MyBean Class

```
package com.apress.prospring4.ch5;

import org.springframework.beans.factory.annotation.Autowired;
import org.springframework.stereotype.Component;

@Component("myBean")
public class MyBean {
    private MyDependency myDependency;

    public void execute() {
        myDependency.foo(100);
        myDependency.foo(101);
        myDependency.bar();
    }

    @Autowired
    public void setDep(MyDependency myDependency) {
        this.myDependency = myDependency;
    }
}
```

We annotate both classes with the @Component annotation and assign them with the corresponding name. In the MyBean class, the setter method of the property myDependency was annotated with @Autowired for automatic injection by Spring.

Now let's see the MyAdvice class using @AspectJ-style annotations. We will implement the pointcuts, before advice, and around advice altogether in one shot. Listing 5-71 shows the MyAdvice class.

Listing 5-71. The MyAdvice Class

```java
package com.apress.prospring4.ch5;

import org.aspectj.lang.JoinPoint;
import org.aspectj.lang.ProceedingJoinPoint;
import org.aspectj.lang.annotation.Around;
import org.aspectj.lang.annotation.Aspect;
import org.aspectj.lang.annotation.Before;
import org.aspectj.lang.annotation.Pointcut;
import org.springframework.stereotype.Component;

@Component
@Aspect
public class MyAdvice {
    @Pointcut("execution(* com.apress.prospring4.ch5..foo*(int)) && args(intValue)")
    public void fooExecution(int intValue) {
    }

    @Pointcut("bean(myDependency*)")
    public void inMyDependency() {
    }

    @Before("fooExecution(intValue) && inMyDependency()")
    public void simpleBeforeAdvice(JoinPoint joinPoint, int intValue) {
        if (intValue != 100) {
        System.out.println("Executing: " +
            joinPoint.getSignature().getDeclaringTypeName() + " "
            + joinPoint.getSignature().getName() + " argument: " + intValue);
        }
    }

    @Around("fooExecution(intValue) && inMyDependency()")
    public Object simpleAroundAdvice(ProceedingJoinPoint pjp, int intValue) throws Throwable {
        System.out.println("Before execution: " +
            pjp.getSignature().getDeclaringTypeName() + " "
            + pjp.getSignature().getName()
            + " argument: " + intValue);

        Object retVal = pjp.proceed();

        System.out.println("After execution: " +
            pjp.getSignature().getDeclaringTypeName() + " "
            + pjp.getSignature().getName()
            + " argument: " + intValue);

        return retVal;
    }
}
```

You will notice that the code structure is quite like the one we used in the aop namespace, just in this case we used annotations instead. However, there are still a few points worth noting:

- We used both @Component and @Aspectto annotate the MyAdvice class. The @Aspect is used to declare that it's an aspect class. To allow Spring to scan the component when we use the `<context:component-scan>` tag in the XML configuration, we also need to annotate the class with @Component.

- The pointcuts were defined as methods that return void. In the class, we defined two pointcuts; both are annotated with @Pointcut. We intentionally split the pointcut expression in the aop namespace example in two. The first one (indicated by the method fooExecution(int intValue)) defines the pointcut for execution of foo*() methods within all classes under the package com.apress.prospring4.ch5 with an integer argument, and the argument (intValue) will also be passed into the advice. The other one (indicated by the method inMyDependency()) is to define another pointcut that defines all method executions with Spring beans' names prefixed by myDependency. Also note that we need to use && to define the and condition in the pointcut expression, while for the aop namespace, we need to use the and operator.

- The before-advice method was annotated with @Before, while the around advice was annotated with @Around. For both advice types, we pass in the value that uses the two pointcuts defined in the class. The value "fooExecution(intValue) && inMyDependency()" means the condition of both pointcuts should be matched for applying the advice, which is the same as the intersection operation in the ComposablePointcut.

- The before-advice and around-advice logic is the same as the one in the aop namespace example.

With all the annotations in place, the XML configuration becomes very simple. Listing 5-72 shows the configuration for this example (app-config-annotation.xml).

Listing 5-72. Configuring Spring AOP with @AspectJ Annotations

```xml
<?xml version="1.0" encoding="UTF-8"?>

<beans xmlns="http://www.springframework.org/schema/beans"
    xmlns:xsi="http://www.w3.org/2001/XMLSchema-instance"
    xmlns:aop="http://www.springframework.org/schema/aop"
    xmlns:context="http://www.springframework.org/schema/context"
    xsi:schemaLocation="http://www.springframework.org/schema/aop
      http://www.springframework.org/schema/aop/spring-aop.xsd
      http://www.springframework.org/schema/beans
      http://www.springframework.org/schema/beans/spring-beans.xsd
      http://www.springframework.org/schema/context
      http://www.springframework.org/schema/context/spring-context.xsd">

    <aop:aspectj-autoproxy/>

    <context:component-scan base-package="com.apress.prospring4.ch5"/>
</beans>
```

Only two tags were declared. The `<aop:aspect-autoproxy>` is to inform Spring to scan for @AspectJ-style annotations, while the `<context:component-scan>` was still required for Spring to scan for Spring beans within the package that the advice resides. We also need to annotate the advice class with @Component to indicate that it's a Spring component.

The `<aop:aspectj-autoproxy>` tag carries an attribute called `proxy-target-class`. The default is `false`, which means that Spring will create standard interface-based proxies using a JDK dynamic proxy. If set to `true`, Spring will use CGLIB to create class-based proxies.

Listing 5-73 shows the testing program, the `AspectJAnnotationExample` class.

Listing 5-73. Testing AspectJ Annotation

```
package com.apress.prospring4.ch5;

import org.springframework.context.support.GenericXmlApplicationContext;

public class AspectJAnnotationExample {
    public static void main(String[] args) {
        GenericXmlApplicationContext ctx = new GenericXmlApplicationContext();
        ctx.load("classpath:META-INF/spring/app-context-xml.xml");
        ctx.refresh();

        MyBean myBean = (MyBean) ctx.getBean("myBean");
        myBean.execute();
    }
}
```

Running the program yields the same results as the aop namespace example:

```
Before execution: com.apress.prospring4.ch5.MyDependency foo argument: 100
foo(int): 100
After execution: com.apress.prospring4.ch5.MyDependency foo argument: 100
Before execution: com.apress.prospring4.ch5.MyDependency foo argument: 101
Executing: com.apress.prospring4.ch5.MyDependency foo argument: 101
foo(int): 101
After execution: com.apress.prospring4.ch5.MyDependency foo argument: 101
bar()
```

Considerations for Declarative Spring AOP Configuration

So far, we have discussed three ways of declaring Spring AOP configuration, including the `ProxyFactoryBean`, the aop namespace, and @AspectJ-style annotations. We believe you will agree that the aop namespace is much simpler than `ProxyFactoryBean`. So, the general question is, do you use the aop namespace or @AspectJ-style annotations?

If your Spring application is XML configuration–based, using the aop namespace approach is a natural choice, because it keeps the AOP and DI configuration styles consistent. On the other hand, if your application is mainly annotation based, use the @AspectJ annotation. Again, let the requirements of your application drive the configuration approach and make your best effort to be consistent.

Moreover, there are some other differences between the aop namespace and @AspectJ annotation approaches:

- The pointcut expression syntax has some minor differences (for example, in the previous discussions, we need to use and in the aop namespace, but && in @AspectJ annotation).

- The aop namespace approach supports only the "singleton" aspect instantiation model.

- In the aop namespace, you can't "combine" multiple pointcut expressions. In the example using @AspectJ, we can combine the two pointcut definitions (that is, `fooExecution(intValue)` `&& inMyDependency()`) in the before and around advice. When using the aop namespace, and you need to create a new pointcut expression that combines the matching conditions.

AspectJ Integration

AOP provides a powerful solution to many of the common problems that arise with OOP-based applications. When using Spring AOP, you can take advantage of a select subset of AOP functionality that, in most cases, enables you to solve problems you encounter in your application. However, in some cases, you may want to use some AOP features that are outside the scope of Spring AOP.

From the joinpoint perspective, Spring AOP supports only pointcuts matching on the execution of public nonstatic methods. However, in some cases, you may need to apply advice to protected/private methods, during object construction or field access, and so on.

In those cases, you need to look at an AOP implementation with a fuller feature set. Our preference, in this case, is to use AspectJ, and because you can now configure AspectJ aspects using Spring, AspectJ forms the perfect complement to Spring AOP.

About AspectJ

AspectJ is a fully featured AOP implementation that uses a weaving process (either compile-time or load-time weaving) to introduce aspects into your code. In AspectJ, aspects and pointcuts are built using a Java-like syntax, which reduces the learning curve for Java developers. We are not going to spend too much time looking at AspectJ and how it works because that is outside the scope of this book. Instead, we present some simple AspectJ examples and show you how to configure them using Spring. For more information on AspectJ, you should definitely read *AspectJ in Action: Enterprise AOP with Spring Applications,* 2nd Edition, by Ramnivas Laddad (Manning, 2009).

■ **Note**   We are not going to cover how to weave AspectJ aspects into your application. Refer to the AspectJ documentation for details or take a look at the provided Maven build in the Chapter 5 aspectj-aspects book code sample.

Using Singleton Aspects

By default, AspectJ aspects are singletons, meaning you get a single instance per class loader. The problem Spring faces with any AspectJ aspect is that it cannot create the aspect instance, as this is already handled by AspectJ itself. However, each aspect exposes a method, org.aspectj.lang.Aspects.aspectOf() that can be used to access the aspect instance. Using the aspectOf() method and a special feature of Spring configuration, you can have Spring configure the aspect for you. With this support, you can take full advantage of AspectJ's powerful AOP feature set without losing out on Spring's excellent DI and configuration abilities. This also means you do not need two separate configuration methods for your application; you can use the same Spring ApplicationContext approach for all your Spring-managed beans and for your AspectJ aspects.

In Listing 5-74, you can see a basic class, MessageWriter, that we will advise using AspectJ.

Listing 5-74. The MessageWriter Class

```
package com.apress.prospring4.ch5;

public class MessageWriter {
    public void writeMessage() {
        System.out.println("foobar!");
    }

    public void foo() {
        System.out.println("foo");
    }
}
```

For this example, we are going to use AspectJ to advise the `writeMessage()` method and write out a message before and after the method invocation. These messages will be configurable using Spring.

Listing 5-75 shows the `MessageWrapper` aspect (the filename is `MessageWrapper.aj`, which is an AspectJ file instead of a standard Java class).

Listing 5-75. `MessageWrapper` Aspect

```
package com.apress.prospring4.ch5;

public aspect MessageWrapper {
    private String prefix;
    private String suffix;

    public void setPrefix(String prefix) {
        this.prefix = prefix;
    }

    public String getPrefix() {
        return this.prefix;
    }

    public void setSuffix(String suffix) {
        this.suffix = suffix;
    }

    public String getSuffix() {
        return this.suffix;
    }

    pointcut doWriting() :
        execution(*
            com.apress.prospring4.ch5.MessageWriter.writeMessage());

    before() : doWriting() {
        System.out.println(prefix);
    }

    after() : doWriting()
        System.out.println(suffix);
    }
}
```

Essentially, we create an aspect called `MessageWrapper`, and, just as with a normal Java class, we give the aspect two properties, `suffix` and `prefix`, which we will use when advising the `writeMessage()` method. Next, we define a named pointcut, `doWriting()`, for a single joinpoint, in this case, the execution of the `writeMessage()` method. AspectJ has a large number of joinpoints, but coverage of those is outside the scope of this example. Finally, we define two bits of advice: one that executes before the `doWriting()` pointcut and one that executes after it. Listing 5-76 shows how this aspect is configured in Spring (`app-config-xml.xml`).

Listing 5-76. Configuring an AspectJ Aspect

```xml
<?xml version="1.0" encoding="UTF-8"?>

<beans xmlns="http://www.springframework.org/schema/beans"
    xmlns:xsi="http://www.w3.org/2001/XMLSchema-instance"
    xsi:schemaLocation="http://www.springframework.org/schema/beans
      http://www.springframework.org/schema/beans/spring-beans.xsd">

    <bean id="aspect" class="com.apress.prospring4.ch5.MessageWrapper"
        factory-method="aspectOf">
        <property name="prefix">
            <value>The Prefix</value>
        </property>
        <property name="suffix">
            <value>The Suffix</value>
        </property>
    </bean>
</beans>
```

As you can see, much of the configuration of the aspect bean is very similar to standard bean configuration. The only difference is the use of the factory-method attribute of the <bean> tag. The factory-method attribute is intended to allow classes that follow a traditional Factory pattern to be integrated seamlessly into Spring. For instance, if you have a class Foo with a private constructor and then a static factory method, getInstance(), using factory-method allows a bean of this class to be managed by Spring. The aspectOf() method exposed by every AspectJ aspect allows you to access the instance of the aspect and thus allows Spring to set the properties of the aspect. Listing 5-77 shows a simple driver application for this example.

Listing 5-77. AspectJ Configuration in Action

```java
package com.apress.prospring4.ch5;

import org.springframework.context.support.GenericXmlApplicationContext;

public class AspectJExample {
    public static void main(String[] args) {
        GenericXmlApplicationContext ctx = new GenericXmlApplicationContext();
        ctx.load(new String[] {"classpath:META-INF/spring/app-context-xml.xml"});
        ctx.refresh();

        MessageWriter writer = new MessageWriter();
        writer.writeMessage();
        writer.foo();
    }
}
```

Notice that first we load ApplicationContext to allow Spring to configure the aspect. Next we create an instance of MessageWriter and then invoke the writeMessage() and foo() methods. The output from this example is as follows:

```
The Prefix
foobar!
The Suffix
foo
```

As you can see, the advice in the `MessageWrapper` aspect was applied to the `writeMessage()` method, and the `prefix` and `suffix` values specified in the `ApplicationContext` configuration were used by the advice when writing out the before and after messages.

Summary

In this chapter we covered a large number of AOP core concepts and looked at how these concepts translate into the Spring AOP implementation. We discussed the features that are (and are not) implemented in Spring AOP, and we pointed to AspectJ as an AOP solution for those features that Spring does not implement. We spent some time explaining the details of the advice types available in Spring, and you saw examples of the four types in action. We also looked at how you limit the methods to which advice applies by using pointcuts. In particular, we looked at the six basic pointcut implementations available with Spring. We also covered the details of how the AOP proxies are constructed, the different options, and what makes them different. We compared performance among three proxy types and highlighted some major differences and restrictions for choosing between a JDK vs. CGLIB proxy. We looked at the advanced options for pointcutting, as well as how to extend the set of interfaces implemented by an object using introductions. We explored Spring Framework services to configure AOP declaratively, thus avoiding the need to hard-code AOP proxy construction logic into your code. We spent some time looking at how Spring and AspectJ are integrated to allow you to use the added power of AspectJ without losing any of the flexibility of Spring. That's certainly a lot of AOP!

In the next chapter, we move on to a completely different topic—how we can use Spring's JDBC support to radically simplify the creation of JDBC-based data access code.

CHAPTER 6

■ ■ ■

Spring JDBC Support

By now you have seen how easy it is to build a fully Spring-managed application. You have a solid understanding of bean configuration and aspect-oriented programming (AOP). However, one part of the puzzle is missing: how do you get the data that drives the application?

Apart from simple throwaway command-line utilities, almost every application needs to persist data to some sort of data store. The most usual and convenient data store is a relational database.

The most notable open source relational databases are perhaps MySQL (`www.mysql.com`) and PostgreSQL (`www.postgresql.org`). MySQL is generally more widely used for web application development, especially on the Linux platform. On the other side, PostgreSQL is friendlier to Oracle developers, because its procedural language, PL/pgSQL, is very close to Oracle's PL/SQL language.

Even if you choose the fastest and most reliable database, you cannot afford to lose its speed and flexibility by using a poorly designed and implemented data access layer. Applications tend to use the data access layer very frequently; thus, any unnecessary bottlenecks in the data access code impact the entire application, no matter how well designed it is.

In this chapter, we show you how you can use Spring to simplify the implementation of data access code using JDBC. We start by looking at the large and repetitive amount of code you would normally need to write without Spring and then compare it to a class implemented using Spring's data access classes. The result is truly amazing, as Spring allows you to use the full power of human-tuned SQL queries while minimizing the amount of support code you need to implement. Specifically, we discuss the following:

- *Comparing traditional JDBC code and Spring JDBC support*: We explore how Spring simplifies the old-style JDBC code while keeping the same functionality. You will also see how Spring accesses the low-level JDBC API and how this low-level API is mapped into convenient classes such as `JdbcTemplate`.

- *Connecting to the database*: Even though we do not go into every little detail of database connection management, we do show you the fundamental differences between a simple `Connection` and a `DataSource`. Naturally, we discuss how Spring manages the data sources and which data sources you can use in your applications.

- *Retrieving and mapping the data to Java objects*: We show you how to retrieve data and then how to effectively map the selected data to Java objects. You also learn that Spring JDBC is a viable alternative to object-relational mapping (ORM) tools.

- *Inserting, updating, and deleting data*: Finally, we discuss how you can implement the insert, update, and delete operations by using Spring to execute these types of queries.

Introducing Lambda Expressions

The release of Java version 8 brings lambda expression support, among many other features. Lambda expressions make a great replacement for anonymous inner class usage and an ideal candidate for working with Spring's JDBC support. The usage of lambda expressions *requires* the use of Java 8. This book was written during the pre-release versions of Java 8 and now the first General Availability version, so we understand not everybody will be using Java 8 yet. Given that, the chapter code samples and source code download show both flavors where applicable. Lambda expressions are suitable in most places of the Spring API where templates or callbacks are used, not just limited to JDBC. This chapter does not cover lambda expressions themselves, as they are a Java language feature, and the reader should be familiar with lambda concepts and syntax. Please refer to the Java Lambda Expressions tutorial at `http://docs.oracle.com/javase/tutorial/java/javaOO/lambdaexpressions.html` for more information.

Sample Data Model for Example Code

Before proceeding with the discussion, we would like to introduce a simple data model that is used for the examples throughout this chapter, as well as the next few chapters when discussing other data access techniques (we will expand the model accordingly to fulfill the needs of each topic as we go).

The model is a simple contact database. There are two tables. The first one is the CONTACT table, which stores a contact person's information, and the other table is CONTACT_TEL_DETAIL, which stores the telephone details of a contact. Each contact can have zero or more telephone numbers; in other words, it's a one-to-many relationship between CONTACT and CONTACT_TEL_DETAIL. A contact's information includes their first and last name, date of birth, telephone type, and the corresponding phone number. Figure 6-1 shows the entity-relationship (ER) diagram of the database.

Figure 6-1. *Simple data model for the example code*

As you can see, both tables have an ID column that will be automatically assigned by the database during insertion. For the CONTACT_TEL_DETAIL table, there is a foreign-key relation to the CONTACT table, which is linked by the column CONTACT_ID with the primary key of the CONTACT table (that is, the ID column).

■ **Note** In this chapter, we use the open source database MySQL to show interactions with a real database in some examples. This will require you to have an instance of MySQL available to use. We do not cover how to install MySQL. You may use another database of your choice, but you may need to modify the schema and function definitions. We also cover embedded database usage, which does not require a MySQL database.

Listing 6-1 shows the database creation script (MySQL compatible).

Listing 6-1. Simple Data Model Creation Script (`schema.sql`)

```
CREATE TABLE CONTACT (
        ID INT NOT NULL AUTO_INCREMENT
      , FIRST_NAME VARCHAR(60) NOT NULL
      , LAST_NAME VARCHAR(40) NOT NULL
      , BIRTH_DATE DATE
      , UNIQUE UQ_CONTACT_1 (FIRST_NAME, LAST_NAME)
      , PRIMARY KEY (ID)
);

CREATE TABLE CONTACT_TEL_DETAIL (
        ID INT NOT NULL AUTO_INCREMENT
      , CONTACT_ID INT NOT NULL
      , TEL_TYPE VARCHAR(20) NOT NULL
      , TEL_NUMBER VARCHAR(20) NOT NULL
      , UNIQUE UQ_CONTACT_TEL_DETAIL_1 (CONTACT_ID, TEL_TYPE)
      , PRIMARY KEY (ID)
      , CONSTRAINT FK_CONTACT_TEL_DETAIL_1 FOREIGN KEY (CONTACT_ID)
                  REFERENCES CONTACT (ID)
);
```

Listing 6-2 shows the script that populates some sample data into the CONTACT and CONTACT_TEL_DETAIL tables.

Listing 6-2. Simple Data Population Script (`test-data.sql`)

```
insert into contact (first_name, last_name, birth_date) values
  ('Chris', 'Schaefer', '1981-05-03');
insert into contact (first_name, last_name, birth_date) values
  ('Scott', 'Tiger', '1990-11-02');
insert into contact (first_name, last_name, birth_date) values
  ('John', 'Smith', '1964-02-28');
insert into contact_tel_detail (contact_id, tel_type, tel_number) values
  (1, 'Mobile', '1234567890');
insert into contact_tel_detail (contact_id, tel_type, tel_number) values
  (1, 'Home', '1234567890');
insert into contact_tel_detail (contact_id, tel_type, tel_number) values
  (2, 'Home', '1234567890');
```

In later sections of this chapter, you will see examples of retrieving the data via JDBC from the database and directly mapping the result set into Java objects (that is, POJOs). Listings 6-3 and 6-4 show the Contact and ContactTelDetail domain classes, respectively.

Listing 6-3. The Contact Domain Object

```
package com.apress.prospring4.ch6;

import java.io.Serializable;
import java.sql.Date;
import java.util.List;
```

```java
public class Contact implements Serializable {
    private Long id;
    private String firstName;
    private String lastName;
    private Date birthDate;
    private List<ContactTelDetail> contactTelDetails;

    public void setId(Long id) {
        this.id = id;
    }

    public Long getId() {
        return this.id;
    }

    public void setFirstName(String firstName) {
        this.firstName = firstName;
    }

    public String getFirstName() {
        return this.firstName;
    }

    public void setLastName(String lastName) {
        this.lastName = lastName;
    }

    public String getLastName() {
        return this.lastName;
    }

    public void setContactTelDetails(List<ContactTelDetail> contactTelDetails) {
        this.contactTelDetails = contactTelDetails;
    }

    public List<ContactTelDetail> getContactTelDetails() {
        return contactTelDetails;
    }

    public void setBirthDate(Date birthDate) {
        this.birthDate = birthDate;
    }

    public Date getBirthDate() {
        return birthDate;
    }
    public String toString() {
        return "Contact - Id: " + id + ", First name: " + firstName
            + ", Last name: " + lastName + ", Birthday: " + birthDate;
    }
```

Listing 6-4. The ContactTelDetail Domain Object

```
package com.apress.prospring4.ch6;

import java.io.Serializable; }

public class ContactTelDetail implements Serializable {
    private Long id;
    private Long contactId;
    private String telType;
    private String telNumber;

    public void setId(Long id) {
        this.id = id;
    }

    public Long getId() {
        return this.id;
    }

    public void setContactId(Long contactId) {
        this.contactId = contactId;
    }

    public Long getContactId() {
        return this.contactId;
    }

    public void setTelType(String telType) {
        this.telType = telType;
    }

    public String getTelType() {
        return this.telType;
    }

    public void setTelNumber(String telNumber) {
        this.telNumber = telNumber;
    }

    public String getTelNumber() {}

        return this.telNumber;
    }

    @Override
    public String toString() {
        return "Contact Tel Detail - Id: " + id + ", Contact id: " + contactId
            + ", Type: " + telType + ", Number: " + telNumber;
    }
}
```

Let's start with a simple interface for `ContactDao` that encapsulates all the data access services for contact information. Listing 6-5 shows the `ContactDao` interface.

Listing 6-5. The `ContactDao` Interface

```
package com.apress.prospring4.ch6;

import java.util.List;

public interface ContactDao {
    List<Contact> findAll();
    List<Contact> findByFirstName(String firstName);
    String findLastNameById(Long id);
    String findFirstNameById(Long id);
    void insert(Contact contact);
    void update(Contact contact);
    void delete(Long contactId);
}
```

In the previous interface, we define two finder methods and the insert, update, and delete methods, respectively. They correspond to the CRUD terms (create, read, update, delete).

Finally, to facilitate testing, let's modify the `log4j` properties to turn the log level to `DEBUG` for all classes. At the `DEBUG` level, the Spring JDBC module will output all the underlying SQL statements being fired to the database so you know what exactly is going on; this is especially useful for troubleshooting SQL statement syntax errors. Listing 6-6 shows the `log4j.properties` file (residing under `src/main/resources` with the source code files for the Chapter 6 project) with the `DEBUG` level turned on.

Listing 6-6. The `log4j.properties` File

```
log4j.rootCategory=DEBUG, stdout

log4j.appender.stdout=org.apache.log4j.ConsoleAppender
log4j.appender.stdout.layout=org.apache.log4j.PatternLayout
log4j.appender.stdout.layout.ConversionPattern=%d{ABSOLUTE} %5p %40.40c:%4L - %m%n
```

Exploring the JDBC Infrastructure

JDBC provides a standard way for Java applications to access data stored in a database. The core of the JDBC infrastructure is a driver that is specific to each database; it is this driver that allows Java code to access the database.

Once a driver is loaded, it registers itself with a `java.sql.DriverManager` class. This class manages a list of drivers and provides static methods for establishing connections to the database. The `DriverManager`'s `getConnection()` method returns a driver-implemented `java.sql.Connection` interface. This interface allows you to run SQL statements against the database.

The JDBC framework is quite complex and well tested; however, with this complexity comes difficulty in development. The first level of complexity lies in making sure your code manages the connections to the database. A connection is a scarce resource and is very expensive to establish. Generally, the database creates a thread or spawns a child process for each connection. Also, the number of concurrent connections is usually limited, and an excessive number of open connections will slow down the database.

We will show you how Spring helps manage this complexity, but before we can proceed any further, we need to show you how to select, delete, and update data in pure JDBC.

Let's create a plain form of implementation of the ContactDao interface for interacting with the database via pure JDBC. Keeping in mind what we already know about database connections, we take the cautious and expensive (in terms of performance) approach of creating a connection for each statement. This greatly degrades the performance of Java and adds extra stress to the database, because a connection has to be established for each query. However, if we kept a connection open, we could bring the database server to a halt. Listing 6-7 shows the code required for managing a JDBC connection, using MySQL as an example.

Listing 6-7. Managing a JDBC Connection

```
package com.apress.prospring4.ch6;

public class PlainContactDao implements ContactDao {
    static {
        try {
            Class.forName("com.mysql.jdbc.Driver");
        } catch (ClassNotFoundException ex) {
            ex.printStackTrace();
        }
    }

    private Connection getConnection() throws SQLException {
        return DriverManager.getConnection(
            "jdbc:mysql://localhost:3306/prospring4_ch6",
            "prospring4", "prospring4");
    }

...

    private void closeConnection(Connection connection) {
        if (connection == null) {
            return;
        }

        try {
            connection.close();
        } catch (SQLException ex) {
            ex.printStackTrace();
        }
    }
}
```

This code is far from complete, but it gives you an idea of the steps you need in order to manage a JDBC connection. This code does not even deal with connection pooling, which is a common technique for managing connections to the database more effectively. We do not discuss connection pooling at this point (connection pooling is discussed in the "Database Connections and DataSources" section later in this chapter); instead, in Listing 6-8, we show an implementation of the findAll(), insert(), and delete() methods of the ContactDao interface using plain JDBC.

Listing 6-8. Plain JDBC DAO Implementation

```java
package com.apress.prospring4.ch6;

import java.sql.Connection;
import java.sql.DriverManager;
import java.sql.PreparedStatement;
import java.sql.ResultSet;
import java.sql.SQLException;
import java.sql.Statement;
import java.util.ArrayList;
import java.util.List;

public class PlainContactDao implements ContactDao {
    static {
        try {
            Class.forName("com.mysql.jdbc.Driver");
        } catch (ClassNotFoundException ex) {
            ex.printStackTrace();
        }
    }

    private Connection getConnection() throws SQLException {
        return DriverManager.getConnection(
            "jdbc:mysql://localhost:3306/prospring4_ch6",
            "prospring4", "prospring4");
    }

    private void closeConnection(Connection connection) {
        if (connection == null) {
            return;
        }

        try {
            connection.close();
        } catch (SQLException ex) {
            ex.printStackTrace();
        }
    }

    @Override
    public List<Contact> findAll() {
        List<Contact> result = new ArrayList<Contact>();

        Connection connection = null;

        try {
            connection = getConnection();

            PreparedStatement statement =
                connection.prepareStatement("select * from contact");.
```

```java
            ResultSet resultSet = statement.executeQuery();

            while (resultSet.next()) {
                Contact contact = new Contact();
                contact.setId(resultSet.getLong("id"));
                contact.setFirstName(resultSet.getString("first_name"));
                contact.setLastName(resultSet.getString("last_name"));
                contact.setBirthDate(resultSet.getDate("birth_date"));

                result.add(contact);
            }
        } catch (SQLException ex) {
            ex.printStackTrace();
        } finally {
            closeConnection(connection);
        }

        return result;
    }

    @Override
    public void insert(Contact contact) {
        Connection connection = null;

        try {
            connection = getConnection();

            PreparedStatement statement = connection.prepareStatement(
              "insert into Contact (first_name, last_name, birth_date) values (?, ?, ?)"
              , Statement.RETURN_GENERATED_KEYS);
            statement.setString(1, contact.getFirstName());
            statement.setString(2, contact.getLastName());
            statement.setDate(3, contact.getBirthDate());
            statement.execute();

            ResultSet generatedKeys = statement.getGeneratedKeys();.

            if (generatedKeys.next()) {
                contact.setId(generatedKeys.getLong(1));
            }
        } catch (SQLException ex) {
            ex.printStackTrace();
        } finally {
            closeConnection(connection);
        }
    }

    @Override
    public void delete(Long contactId) {
        Connection connection = null;
```

```java
        try {
            connection = getConnection();

            PreparedStatement statement =
                connection.prepareStatement("delete from contact where id=?");
            statement.setLong(1, contactId);
            statement.execute();
        } catch (SQLException ex) {
            ex.printStackTrace();
        } finally {
            closeConnection(connection);
        }
    }

    @Override
    public List<Contact> findByFirstName(String firstName) {
        return null;
    }

    @Override
    public String findFirstNameById(Long id) {
        return null;
    }

    @Override
    public String findLastNameById(Long id) {
        return null;
    }

    @Override
    public void update(Contact contact) {.
    }
}
```

Listing 6-9 shows a main testing program with the previous DAO implementation in action

Listing 6-9. Pure JDBC Implementation Testing

```java
package com.apress.prospring4.ch6;

import java.sql.Date;
import java.util.GregorianCalendar;
import java.util.List;

public class PlainJdbcSample {
    private static ContactDao contactDao = new PlainContactDao();

    public static void main(String[] args) {
        System.out.println("Listing initial contact data:");

        listAllContacts();
```

```
            System.out.println();
            System.out.println("Insert a new contact");

            Contact contact = new Contact();
            contact.setFirstName("Jacky");
            contact.setLastName("Chan");
            contact.setBirthDate(new Date(
                (new GregorianCalendar(2001, 10, 1)).getTime().getTime()));
            contactDao.insert(contact);

            System.out.println("Listing contact data after new contact created:");

            listAllContacts();

            System.out.println();
            System.out.println("Deleting the previous created contact");

            contactDao.delete(contact.getId());.

            System.out.println("Listing contact data after new contact deleted:");

            listAllContacts();
        }

    private static void listAllContacts() {
        List<Contact> contacts = contactDao.findAll();

        for (Contact contact: contacts) {
            System.out.println(contact);
        }
    }
}
```

To run the program, you need to add the dependency for MySQL Java into your project, as shown in Table 6-1.

Table 6-1. *Dependency for MySQL*

Group ID	Artifact ID	Version	Description
mysql	mysql-connector-java	5.1.29	MySQL Java driver library

Running the program in Listing 6-9 yields the following result (assuming you have a locally installed MySQL database called prospring4_ch6 that has a username and password set to prospring4; it should be able to access the database schema, and you should run the scripts schema.sql and test-data.sql against the database to create the tables and populate the initial data):

```
Listing initial contact data:
Contact - Id: 1, First name: Chris, Last name: Schaefer, Birthday: 1981-05-03
Contact - Id: 2, First name: Scott, Last name: Tiger, Birthday: 1990-11-02
Contact - Id: 3, First name: John, Last name: Smith, Birthday: 1964-02-28
```

```
Insert a new contact
Listing contact data after new contact created:
Contact - Id: 1, First name: Chris, Last name: Schaefer, Birthday: 1981-05-03
Contact - Id: 2, First name: Scott, Last name: Tiger, Birthday: 1990-11-02
Contact - Id: 3, First name: John, Last name: Smith, Birthday: 1964-02-28
Contact - Id: 4, First name: Jacky, Last name: Chan, Birthday: 2001-11-01

Deleting the previous created contact
Listing contact data after new contact deleted:
Contact - Id: 1, First name: Chris, Last name: Schaefer, Birthday: 1981-05-03
Contact - Id: 2, First name: Scott, Last name: Tiger, Birthday: 1990-11-02
Contact - Id: 3, First name: John, Last name: Smith, Birthday: 1964-02-28
```

As shown in the output, the first block of lines shows the initial data. The second block of lines shows that the new record was added. The final block of lines shows that the newly created contact was deleted.

As you can see in Listing 6-8 shown previously, a lot of code needs to be moved to a helper class, or even worse, duplicated in each DAO class. This is the main disadvantage of JDBC from the application programmer's point of view—you just do not have time to write repetitive code in every DAO class. Instead, you want to concentrate on writing code that actually does what you need the DAO class to do: select, update, and delete the data. The more helper code you need to write, the more checked exceptions you need to handle, and the more bugs you may introduce in your code.

This is where a DAO framework and Spring come in. A framework eliminates the code that does not actually perform any custom logic and allows you to forget about all the housekeeping that needs to be performed. In addition, Spring's extensive JDBC support makes your life a lot easier.

Spring JDBC Infrastructure

The code we discussed in the first part of the chapter is not very complex, but it is tedious, and because there is so much of it to write, the likelihood of coding errors is quite high. It is time to take a look at how Spring makes things easier and more elegant.

Overview and Used Packages

JDBC support in Spring is divided into the five packages detailed in Table 6-2; each handles different aspects of JDBC access.

Table 6-2. *Spring JDBC Packages*

Package	Description
org.springframework.jdbc.core	Contains the foundations of JDBC classes in Spring. It includes the core JDBC class, JdbcTemplate, which simplifies programming database operations with JDBC. Several subpackages provide support of JDBC data access with more-specific purposes (e.g., a JdbcTemplate class that supports named parameters) and related support classes as well.
org.springframework.jdbc.datasource	Contains helper classes and DataSource implementations that you can use to run JDBC code outside a JEE container. Several subpackages provide support for embedded databases, database initialization, and various data source lookup mechanisms.
org.springframework.jdbc.object	Contains classes that help convert the data returned from the database into objects or lists of objects. These objects and lists are plain Java objects and therefore are disconnected from the database.
org.springframework.jdbc.support	The most important class in this package is SQLException translation support. This allows Spring to recognize error codes used by the database and map them to higher-level exceptions.
org.springframework.jdbc.config	Contains classes that support JDBC configuration within Spring's ApplicationContext. For example, it contains a handler class for the jdbc namespace (e.g., <jdbc:embedded-database> tags).

Let's start the discussion of Spring JDBC support by looking at the lowest-level functionality. The first thing that needs to be done before running SQL queries is establishing a connection to the database.

Database Connections and DataSources

You can use Spring to manage the database connection for you by providing a bean that implements javax.sql. DataSource. The difference between a DataSource and a Connection is that a DataSource provides and manages Connections.

DriverManagerDataSource (under the package org.springframework.jdbc.datasource) is the simplest implementation of a DataSource. By looking at the class name, you can guess that it simply calls DriverManager to obtain a connection. The fact that DriverManagerDataSource doesn't support database connection pooling makes this class unsuitable for anything other than testing. The configuration of DriverManagerDataSource is quite simple, as you can see in Listing 6-10; you just need to supply the driver class name, a connection URL, a username, and a password (datasource-drivermanager.xml).

Listing 6-10. Spring-Managed DriverManagerDataSource dataSource Bean

```xml
<?xml version="1.0" encoding="UTF-8"?>

<beans xmlns="http://www.springframework.org/schema/beans"
    xmlns:xsi="http://www.w3.org/2001/XMLSchema-instance"
    xmlns:context="http://www.springframework.org/schema/context"
    xmlns:p="http://www.springframework.org/schema/p"
    xsi:schemaLocation="http://www.springframework.org/schema/beans
        http://www.springframework.org/schema/beans/spring-beans.xsd
        http://www.springframework.org/schema/context
        http://www.springframework.org/schema/context/spring-context.xsd">
```

```xml
<bean id="dataSource"
  class="org.springframework.jdbc.datasource.DriverManagerDataSource"
  p:driverClassName="${jdbc.driverClassName}"
  p:url="${jdbc.url}"
  p:username="${jdbc.username}"
  p:password="${jdbc.password}"/>

<context:property-placeholder location="classpath:META-INF/config/jdbc.properties"/>
</beans>
```

You most likely recognize the properties in the listing. They represent the values you normally pass to JDBC to obtain a Connection interface. The database connection information typically is stored in a properties file for easy maintenance and substitution in different deployment environments. Listing 6-11 shows a sample jdbc.properties from which Spring's property placeholder will load the connection information.

Listing 6-11. The jdbc.properties File

```
jdbc.driverClassName=com.mysql.jdbc.Driver
jdbc.url=jdbc:mysql://localhost:3306/prospring4_ch6
jdbc.username=prospring4
jdbc.password=prospring4
```

In real-world applications, you can use the Apache Commons BasicDataSource (http://commons.apache.org/dbcp/) or a DataSource implemented by a JEE application server (for example, JBoss, WebSphere, WebLogic, or GlassFish), which may further increase the performance of the application. You could use a DataSource in the plain JDBC code and get the same pooling benefits; however, in most cases, you would still miss a central place to configure the DataSource. Spring, on the other hand, allows you to declare a dataSource bean and set the connection properties in the ApplicationContext definition files (see Listing 6-12; the file name is datasource-dbcp.xml).

Listing 6-12. Spring-Managed dataSource Bean

```xml
<?xml version="1.0" encoding="UTF-8"?>

<beans xmlns="http://www.springframework.org/schema/beans"
    xmlns:xsi="http://www.w3.org/2001/XMLSchema-instance"
    xmlns:context="http://www.springframework.org/schema/context"
    xmlns:p="http://www.springframework.org/schema/p"
    xsi:schemaLocation="http://www.springframework.org/schema/beans
        http://www.springframework.org/schema/beans/spring-beans.xsd
        http://www.springframework.org/schema/context
        http://www.springframework.org/schema/context/spring-context.xsd">

    <bean id="dataSource"
      class="org.apache.commons.dbcp.BasicDataSource"
      destroy-method="close"
      p:driverClassName="${jdbc.driverClassName}"
      p:url="${jdbc.url}"
      p:username="${jdbc.username}"
      p:password="${jdbc.password}"/>

    <context:property-placeholder location="classpath:META-INF/config/jdbc.properties"/>
</beans>
```

■ **Note**   Besides the Apache Commons `BasicDataSource`, other popular open source database connection pool libraries include C3PO (`www.mchange.com/projects/c3p0/index.html`) and BoneCP (`http://jolbox.com/`).

This particular Spring-managed `DataSource` is implemented in `org.apache.commons.dbcp.BasicDataSource`. The most important bit is that the `dataSource` bean implements `javax.sql.DataSource`, and you can immediately start using it in your data access classes.

Another way to configure a `dataSource` bean is to use JNDI. If the application you are developing is going to run in a JEE container, you can take advantage of the container-managed connection pooling. To use a JNDI-based data source, you need to change the `dataSource` bean declaration, as shown in Listing 6-13 (`datasource-jndi.xml`).

Listing 6-13. Spring-Managed JNDI dataSource Bean

```
<?xml version="1.0" encoding="UTF-8"?>

<beans xmlns="http://www.springframework.org/schema/beans"
    xmlns:xsi="http://www.w3.org/2001/XMLSchema-instance"
    xsi:schemaLocation="http://www.springframework.org/schema/beans
        http://www.springframework.org/schema/beans/spring-beans.xsd">

    <bean id="dataSource" class="org.springframework.jndi.JndiObjectFactoryBean").
        p:jndiName="java:comp/env/jdbc/prospring4ch6"/>
</beans>
```

In the previous example, we use Spring's `JndiObjectFactoryBean` to obtain the data source by JNDI lookup. Starting from version 2.5, Spring provides the jee namespace, which further simplifies the configuration. Listing 6-14 shows the same JNDI data source configuration using the jee namespace (`datasource-jee.xml`).

Listing 6-14. Spring-Managed JNDI dataSource Bean (Using the jee Namespace)

```
<?xml version="1.0" encoding="UTF-8"?>

<beans xmlns="http://www.springframework.org/schema/beans"
    xmlns:xsi="http://www.w3.org/2001/XMLSchema-instance"
    xmlns:jee="http://www.springframework.org/schema/jee"
    xsi:schemaLocation="http://www.springframework.org/schema/beans
        http://www.springframework.org/schema/beans/spring-beans.xsd
        http://www.springframework.org/schema/jee
        http://www.springframework.org/schema/jee/spring-jee.xsd">

    <jee:jndi-lookup jndi-name="java:comp/env/jdbc/prospring4ch6"/>
</beans>
```

In the previous listing, we declare the jee namespace in the `<beans>` tag and then the `<jee:jndi-lookup>` tag to declare the data source.

If you take the JNDI approach, you must not forget to add a resource reference (`resource-ref`) in the application descriptor file (see Listing 6-15).

Listing 6-15. A Resource Reference in Descriptor Files

```
<root-node>
    <resource-ref>
        <res-ref-name>jdbc/prospring4ch6</res-ref-name>
        <res-type>javax.sql.DataSource</res-type>
        <res-auth>Container</res-auth>
    </resource-ref>
</root-node>
```

The `<root-node>` is a placeholder value; you need to change it depending on how your module is packaged. For example, it becomes `<web-app>` in the web deployment descriptor (`WEB-INF/web.xml`) if the application is a web module. Most likely, you will need to configure the `resource-ref` in an application server–specific descriptor file as well. However, notice that the `resource-ref` element configures the `jdbc/prospring4ch6` reference name and that the `dataSource` bean's `jndiName` is set to `java:comp/env/jdbc/prospring4ch6`.

As you can see, Spring allows you to configure the `DataSource` in almost any way you like, and it hides the actual implementation or location of the data source from the rest of the application's code. In other words, your DAO classes do not know and do not need to know where the `DataSource` points.

The connection management is also delegated to the `dataSource` bean, which in turn performs the management itself or uses the JEE container to do all the work.

Embedded Database Support

Starting from version 3.0, Spring also offers embedded database support, which automatically starts an embedded database and exposes it as a `DataSource` for the application. Listing 6-16 shows the configuration of an embedded database (`app-context-xml.xml`).

Listing 6-16. Spring Embedded Database Support

```xml
<?xml version="1.0" encoding="UTF-8"?>

<beans xmlns="http://www.springframework.org/schema/beans"
    xmlns:xsi="http://www.w3.org/2001/XMLSchema-instance"
    xmlns:jdbc="http://www.springframework.org/schema/jdbc"
    xsi:schemaLocation="http://www.springframework.org/schema/beans
        http://www.springframework.org/schema/beans/spring-beans.xsd
        http://www.springframework.org/schema/jdbc
        http://www.springframework.org/schema/jdbc/spring-jdbc.xsd">

    <jdbc:embedded-database id="dataSource" type="H2">
        <jdbc:script location="classpath:META-INF/sql/schema.sql"/>
        <jdbc:script location="classpath:META-INF/sql/test-data.sql"/>
    </jdbc:embedded-database>
</beans>
```

In the previous listing, we first declare the `jdbc` namespace in the `<beans>` tag. Afterward, we use the `<jdbc:embedded-database>` to declare the embedded database and assign it an ID of `dataSource`. Within the tag, we also instruct Spring to execute the scripts specified to create the database schema and populate testing data accordingly. Note that the order of the scripts is important, and the file that contains Data Definition Language (DDL) should always appear first, followed by the file with Data Manipulation Language (DML). For the type attribute, we specify the type of embedded database to use. As of version 4.0, Spring supports HSQL (the default), H2, and DERBY.

The embedded database support is extremely useful for local development or unit testing. Throughout the rest of this chapter, we use the embedded database to run the sample code, so your machine doesn't require a database to be installed in order to run the samples.

You can not only utilize the embedded database support via the JDBC namespace but also initialize a database instance running elsewhere, such as MySQL, Oracle, and so on. Rather than specifying type and embedded-database, simply use initialize-database, and your scripts will execute against the intended dataSource just as they would with an embedded database.

Using DataSources in DAO Classes

Let's create a ContactDao interface to implement for our sample, as shown in Listing 6-17.

Listing 6-17. ContactDao Interface

```
package com.apress.prospring4.ch6;

public interface ContactDao {
    String findLastNameById(Long id);
}
```

For the simple implementation, first we will add a dataSource property to the JdbcContactDao implementation class. The reason we want to add the dataSource property to the implementation class rather than the interface should be quite obvious: the interface does not need to know how the data is going to be retrieved and updated. By adding DataSource mutator methods to the interface, in the best-case scenario this forces the implementations to declare the getter and setter stubs. Clearly, this is not a very good design practice. Take a look at the simple JdbcContactDao class in Listing 6-18.

Listing 6-18. JdbcUserDao with the dataSource Property

```
package com.apress.prospring4.ch6;

import javax.sql.DataSource;

public class JdbcContactDao implements ContactDao {
    private DataSource dataSource;

    public void setDataSource(DataSource dataSource) {
        this.dataSource = dataSource;
    }

    ...
}
```

We can now instruct Spring to configure our contactDao bean by using the JdbcContactDao implementation and set the dataSource property (see Listing 6-19 for the enhanced app-context-xml.xml configuration).

Listing 6-19. Spring Application Context File with dataSource and contactDao Beans

```xml
<?xml version="1.0" encoding="UTF-8"?>

<beans xmlns="http://www.springframework.org/schema/beans"
    xmlns:xsi="http://www.w3.org/2001/XMLSchema-instance"
    xmlns:jdbc="http://www.springframework.org/schema/jdbc"
    xsi:schemaLocation="http://www.springframework.org/schema/beans
        http://www.springframework.org/schema/beans/spring-beans.xsd
        http://www.springframework.org/schema/jdbc
        http://www.springframework.org/schema/jdbc/spring-jdbc.xsd">

    <jdbc:embedded-database id="dataSource" type="H2">
        <jdbc:script location="classpath:META-INF/sql/schema.sql"/>
        <jdbc:script location="classpath:META-INF/sql/test-data.sql"/>
    </jdbc:embedded-database>

    <bean id="contactDao" class="com.apress.prospring4.ch6.JdbcContactDao"
      p:dataSource-ref="dataSource"/>
</beans>
```

To support the H2 database, we need to add the dependency on the H2 database into the project, as shown in Table 6-3.

Table 6-3. *Dependency for the H2 Database*

Group ID	Artifact ID	Version	Description
com.h2database	h2	1.3.172	H2 database Java library

Spring now creates the contactDao bean by instantiating the JdbcContactDao class with the dataSource property set to the dataSource bean.

It is good practice to make sure that all required properties on a bean have been set. The easiest way to do this is to implement the InitializingBean interface and provide an implementation for the afterPropertiesSet() method (see Listing 6-20). This way, you make sure that all required properties have been set on your JdbcContactDao. For further discussion of bean initialization, refer to Chapter 4.

Listing 6-20. JdbcContactDao Implementation with InitializingBean

```java
package com.apress.prospring4.ch6;

import javax.sql.DataSource;

import org.springframework.beans.factory.BeanCreationException;
import org.springframework.beans.factory.InitializingBean;

public class JdbcContactDao implements ContactDao, InitializingBean {
    private DataSource dataSource;

    public void setDataSource(DataSource dataSource) {
        this.dataSource = dataSource;
    }

    ...
```

```
    @Override
    public void afterPropertiesSet() throws Exception {
        if (dataSource == null) {
            throw new BeanCreationException("Must set dataSource on ContactDao");
        }
    }
}
```

The code we have looked at so far uses Spring to manage the data source and introduces the ContactDao interface and its JDBC implementation. We also set the dataSource property on the JdbcContactDao class in the Spring ApplicationContext file. Now we expand the code by adding the actual DAO operations to the interface and implementation.

Exception Handling

Because Spring advocates using runtime exceptions rather than checked exceptions, you need a mechanism to translate the checked SQLException into a runtime Spring JDBC exception. Because Spring's SQL exceptions are runtime exceptions, they can be much more granular than checked exceptions. By definition, this is not a feature of runtime exceptions, but it is very inconvenient to have to declare a long list of checked exceptions in the throws clause; hence, checked exceptions tend to be much more coarse-grained than their runtime equivalents.

Spring provides a default implementation of the SQLExceptionTranslator interface, which takes care of translating the generic SQL error codes into Spring JDBC exceptions. In most cases, this implementation is sufficient enough, but we can extend Spring's default implementation and set our new SQLExceptionTranslator implementation to be used in JdbcTemplate, as shown in Listing 6-21.

Listing 6-21. Custom SQLExceptionTranslator

```
package com.apress.prospring4.ch6;

import java.sql.SQLException;

import org.springframework.dao.DataAccessException;
import org.springframework.dao.DeadlockLoserDataAccessException;
import org.springframework.jdbc.support.SQLErrorCodeSQLExceptionTranslator;

public class MySQLErrorCodesTranslator extends
                                    SQLErrorCodeSQLExceptionTranslator {
    @Override
    protected DataAccessException customTranslate(String task,
            String sql, SQLException sqlex) {
        if (sqlex.getErrorCode() == -12345) {
            return new DeadlockLoserDataAccessException(task, sqlex);
        }

        return null;
    }
}
```

At the same time, we need to add the dependency on spring-jdbc into the project, as shown in Table 6-4.

Table 6-4. *Dependency for spring-jdbc*

Group ID	Artifact ID	Version	Description
org.springframework	spring-jdbc	4.0.2.RELEASE	Spring JDBC module

To use the custom translator, we need to pass it into JdbcTemplate in the DAO classes. Listing 6-22 shows a sample code snippet from the enhanced JdbcContactDao.setDataSource() method to illustrate its usage.

Listing 6-22. Using Custom SQLExceptionTranslator in Spring Jdbc

```
public void setDataSource(DataSource dataSource) {
    this.dataSource = dataSource;

    JdbcTemplate jdbcTemplate = new JdbcTemplate();
    jdbcTemplate.setDataSource(dataSource);

    MySQLErrorCodesTranslator errorTranslator =
        new MySQLErrorCodesTranslator();

    errorTranslator.setDataSource(dataSource);

    jdbcTemplate.setExceptionTranslator(errorTranslator);

    this.jdbcTemplate = jdbcTemplate;
}
```

Having the custom SQL exception translator in place, Spring will invoke it upon SQL exceptions detected when executing SQL statements against the database, and custom exception translation will happen when the error code is -12345. For other errors, Spring will fall back to its default mechanism for exception translation.

Obviously, nothing can stop you from creating SQLExceptionTranslator as a Spring-managed bean and using the JdbcTemplate bean in your DAO classes. Don't worry if you don't remember reading about the JdbcTemplate class; we are going to discuss it in more detail.

The JdbcTemplate Class

This class represents the core of Spring's JDBC support. It can execute all types of SQL statements. In the most simplistic view, you can classify the data definition and data manipulation statements. *Data definition statements* cover creating various database objects (tables, views, stored procedures, and so on). *Data manipulation statements* manipulate the data and can be classified as select and update statements. A *select statement* generally returns a set of rows; each row has the same set of columns. An *update statement* modifies the data in the database but does not return any results.

The JdbcTemplate class allows you to issue any type of SQL statement to the database and return any type of result.

In this section, we will go through several common use cases for JDBC programming in Spring with the JdbcTemplate class.

Initializing JdbcTemplate in a DAO Class

Before we discuss how to use JdbcTemplate, let's take a look at how to prepare JdbcTemplate for use in the DAO class. It's very straightforward; most of the time you just need to construct the class by passing in the data source object (which should be injected by Spring into the DAO class). Listing 6-23 shows the code snippet that will initialize the JdbcTemplate object.

Listing 6-23. Initializing JdbcTemplate

```
private JdbcTemplate jdbcTemplate;

private DataSource dataSource;

public void setDataSource(DataSource dataSource) {
    this.dataSource = dataSource;
    this.jdbcTemplate = new JdbcTemplate(dataSource);
}
```

The general practice is to initialize JdbcTemplate within the setDataSource method so that once the data source is injected by Spring, JdbcTemplate will also be initialized and ready for use.

Once configured, JdbcTemplate is thread safe. That means you can also choose to initialize a single instance of JdbcTemplate in Spring's XML configuration and have it inject into all DAO beans.

■ **Note** In the Spring Jdbc module, there is a class called JdbcDaoSupport. It wraps the JdbcTemplate class, and you can have your DAO classes extend the JdbcDaoSupport class. In this case, when the DAO class is injected with the data source, the JdbcTemplate will be initialized automatically.

Retrieving a Single-Value by Using JdbcTemplate

Let's start with a simple query that returns a single value. For example, we want to be able to retrieve the first name of a contact by its ID. Using JdbcTemplate, we can retrieve the value easily. Listing 6-24 shows the implementation of the findFirstNameById() method in the JdbcContactDao class. For other methods, empty implementations were created.

Listing 6-24. Using JdbcTemplate to Retrieve a Single Value

```
package com.apress.prospring4.ch6;

import javax.sql.DataSource;
import java.util.List;

import org.springframework.beans.factory.BeanCreationException;
import org.springframework.beans.factory.InitializingBean;
import org.springframework.jdbc.core.JdbcTemplate;

public class JdbcContactDao implements ContactDao, InitializingBean {
    private DataSource dataSource;
    private JdbcTemplate jdbcTemplate;
```

```java
    @Override
    public String findFirstNameById(Long id) {
        return jdbcTemplate.queryForObject(
                "select first_name from contact where id = ?",
                new Object[]{id}, String.class);
    }

    public void setDataSource(DataSource dataSource) {
        this.dataSource = dataSource;

        JdbcTemplate jdbcTemplate = new JdbcTemplate();
        jdbcTemplate.setDataSource(dataSource);

        MySQLErrorCodesTranslator errorTranslator =
            new MySQLErrorCodesTranslator();

        errorTranslator.setDataSource(dataSource);

        jdbcTemplate.setExceptionTranslator(errorTranslator);

        this.jdbcTemplate = jdbcTemplate;
    }

    @Override
    public void afterPropertiesSet() throws Exception {
        if (dataSource == null) {
            throw new BeanCreationException("Must set dataSource on ContactDao");
        }

        if (jdbcTemplate == null) {
            throw new BeanCreationException("Null JdbcTemplate on ContactDao");
        }
    }
}
```

In the previous listing, we use the queryForObject() method of JdbcTemplate to retrieve the value of the first name. The first argument is the SQL string, and the second argument consists of the parameters to be passed to the SQL for parameter binding in object array format. The last argument is the type to be returned, which is String in this case. Besides Object, you can also query for other types such as Long and Integer. Let's take a look at the outcome. Listing 6-25 shows the testing program.

Listing 6-25. Selecting Data Using JdbcTemplate

```java
package com.apress.prospring4.ch6;

import org.springframework.context.support.GenericXmlApplicationContext;

public class JdbcContactDaoSample {
    public static void main(String[] args) {
        GenericXmlApplicationContext ctx = new GenericXmlApplicationContext();
        ctx.load("classpath:META-INF/spring/app-context-xml.xml");
        ctx.refresh();
```

```
        ContactDao contactDao = ctx.getBean("contactDao", ContactDao.class);

        System.out.println("First name for contact id 1 is: " +
            contactDao.findFirstNameById(1l));
    }
}
```

As expected, running the program yields the following output:

```
First name for contact id 1 is: Chris
```

Using Named Parameters with NamedParameterJdbcTemplate

In the previous example, we are using the normal placeholder (the ? character) as a query parameter, and we need to pass the parameter values as an Object array. When using a normal placeholder, the order is important, and the order that you put the parameters into the array should be the same as the order of the parameters in the query.

Some developers prefer to use named parameters to ensure that each parameter is being bound exactly as intended. In Spring, a variant of JdbcTemplate, called NamedParameterJdbcTemplate (under the package org.springframework.jdbc.core.namedparam), provides support for this.

The initialization of NamedParameterJdbcTemplate is the same as JdbcTemplate, so we just need to declare a variable with type NamedParameterJdbcTemplate and create a new instance of it in the setDataSource() method, as shown in Listing 6-26.

Listing 6-26. JdbcContactDao Using NamedParameterJdbcTemplate to find Last Name By ID

```
package com.apress.prospring4.ch6;

import javax.sql.DataSource;
import java.util.List;
import java.util.Map;
import java.util.HashMap;

import org.springframework.beans.factory.BeanCreationException;
import org.springframework.beans.factory.InitializingBean;
import org.springframework.jdbc.core.namedparam.NamedParameterJdbcTemplate;

public class JdbcContactDao implements ContactDao, InitializingBean {
    private DataSource dataSource;
    private NamedParameterJdbcTemplate namedParameterJdbcTemplate;

    @Override
    public String findLastNameById(Long id) {
        String sql = "select last_name from contact where id = :contactId";

        Map<String, Object> namedParameters = new HashMap<String, Object>();
        namedParameters.put("contactId", id);

        return namedParameterJdbcTemplate.queryForObject(sql,
            namedParameters, String.class);
    }
```

```
    public void setDataSource(DataSource dataSource) {
        this.dataSource = dataSource;

        NamedParameterJdbcTemplate namedParameterJdbcTemplate =
            new NamedParameterJdbcTemplate(dataSource);

        this.namedParameterJdbcTemplate = namedParameterJdbcTemplate;
    }

    @Override
    public void afterPropertiesSet() throws Exception {
        if (dataSource == null) {
            throw new BeanCreationException("Must set dataSource on ContactDao");
        }

        if (namedParameterJdbcTemplate == null) {
            throw new BeanCreationException("Null NamedParameterJdbcTemplate on ContactDao");
        }
    }
}
```

You will see that instead of the ? placeholder, the named parameter (prefixed by a semicolon) is used instead. Listing 6-27 shows our updated test program.

Listing 6-27. Updated JdbcContactDaoSample Test Program Using Named Parameters

```
package com.apress.prospring4.ch6;

import org.springframework.context.support.GenericXmlApplicationContext;

public class JdbcContactDaoSample {
    public static void main(String[] args) {
        GenericXmlApplicationContext ctx = new GenericXmlApplicationContext();
        ctx.load("classpath:META-INF/spring/app-context-xml.xml");
        ctx.refresh();

        ContactDao contactDao = ctx.getBean("contactDao", ContactDao.class);

        System.out.println("Last name for contact id 1 is: " +
            contactDao.findLastNameById(11));
    }
}
```

Let's run this program again, now using named parameters, and you should see the following output printed to the console:

```
Last name for contact id 1 is: Schaefer
```

Retrieving Domain Objects with RowMapper<T>

Rather than retrieving a single value, most of the time you will want to query one or more rows and then transform each row into the corresponding domain object. Spring's RowMapper<T> interface (under the package org.springframework.jdbc.core) provides a simple way for you to perform mapping from a JDBC result set to POJOs. Let's see it in action by implementing the findAll() method of the ContactDao using the RowMapper<T> interface. Listing 6-28 shows the implementation of the findAll() method.

Listing 6-28. Use RowMapper<T> to Query Domain Objects

```
package com.apress.prospring4.ch6;

import javax.sql.DataSource;
import java.sql.SQLException;
import java.sql.ResultSet;

import java.util.List;
import java.util.Map;
import java.util.HashMap;

import org.springframework.beans.factory.BeanCreationException;
import org.springframework.beans.factory.InitializingBean;
import org.springframework.jdbc.core.namedparam.NamedParameterJdbcTemplate;
import org.springframework.jdbc.core.RowMapper;

public class JdbcContactDao implements ContactDao, InitializingBean {
    private DataSource dataSource;
    private NamedParameterJdbcTemplate namedParameterJdbcTemplate;

    @Override
    public String findLastNameById(Long id) {
        String sql = "select last_name from contact where id = :contactId";

        Map<String, Object> namedParameters = new HashMap<String, Object>();
        namedParameters.put("contactId", id);

        return namedParameterJdbcTemplate.queryForObject(sql,
            namedParameters, String.class);
    }

    @Override
    public List<Contact> findAll() {
        String sql = "select id, first_name, last_name, birth_date from contact";
        return namedParameterJdbcTemplate.query(sql, new ContactMapper());
    }

    public void setDataSource(DataSource dataSource) {
        this.dataSource = dataSource;

        NamedParameterJdbcTemplate namedParameterJdbcTemplate =
            new NamedParameterJdbcTemplate(dataSource);

        this.namedParameterJdbcTemplate = namedParameterJdbcTemplate;
    }
```

```java
@Override
public void afterPropertiesSet() throws Exception {>
    if (dataSource == null) {
        throw new BeanCreationException("Must set dataSource on ContactDao");
    }

    if (namedParameterJdbcTemplate == null) {
        throw new BeanCreationException("Null NamedParameterJdbcTemplate on ContactDao");
    }
}

private static final class ContactMapper implements RowMapper<Contact> {
    @Override
    public Contact mapRow(ResultSet rs, int rowNum) throws SQLException {
        Contact contact = new Contact();
        contact.setId(rs.getLong("id"));
        contact.setFirstName(rs.getString("first_name"));
        contact.setLastName(rs.getString("last_name"));
        contact.setBirthDate(rs.getDate("birth_date"));

        return contact;
    }
}
}
```

In the previous listing, we define a static inner class called ContactMapper that implements the RowMapper<T> interface. The class needs to provide the mapRow() implementation, which transforms the values in a specific record of the ResultSet into the domain object you want. Making it a static inner class allows you to share the RowMapper<T> among multiple finder methods.

REFACTORING USING LAMBDA

When using Java 8, rather than creating the ContactMapper class as shown previously, a lambda expression can be used:

```java
@Override
public List<Contact> findAll() {
    String sql = "select id, first_name, last_name, birth_date from contact";
    return namedParameterJdbcTemplate.query(sql, (rs, rowNum) -> {
        Contact contact = new Contact();
        contact.setId(rs.getLong("id"));
        contact.setFirstName(rs.getString("first_name"));
        contact.setLastName(rs.getString("last_name"));
        contact.setBirthDate(rs.getDate("birth_date"));

        return contact; >
    });
}
```

Afterward, the findAll() method just needs to invoke the query method and pass in the query string and the row mapper. In case the query requires parameters, the query() method provides an overloaded method that accepts the query parameters.

Let's create our JdbcContactDaoSample as shown in Listing 6-29 to find all contacts.

Listing 6-29. Listing Contacts

```
package com.apress.prospring4.ch6;

import java.util.List;
import org.springframework.context.support.GenericXmlApplicationContext;

public class JdbcContactDaoSample {
    public static void main(String[] args) {
        GenericXmlApplicationContext ctx = new GenericXmlApplicationContext();
        ctx.load("classpath:META-INF/spring/app-context-xml.xml");
        ctx.refresh();>

        ContactDao contactDao = ctx.getBean("contactDao", ContactDao.class);

        List<Contact> contacts = contactDao.findAll();

        for (Contact contact: contacts) {
            System.out.println(contact);

            if (contact.getContactTelDetails() != null) {
                for (ContactTelDetail contactTelDetail:
                    contact.getContactTelDetails()) {
                    System.out.println("---" + contactTelDetail);
                }
            }

            System.out.println();
        }
    }>
}
```

Running the program yields the following result (other outputs were omitted):

```
Contact - Id: 1, First name: Chris, Last name: Schaefer, Birthday: 1981-05-03

Contact - Id: 2, First name: Scott, Last name: Tiger, Birthday: 1990-11-02

Contact - Id: 3, First name: John, Last name: Smith, Birthday: 1964-02-28
```

Retrieving Nested Domain Objects with ResultSetExtractor

Let's proceed to a somewhat more complicated example, in which we need to retrieve the data from the parent (CONTACT) and child (CONTACT_TEL_DETAIL) tables with a join and then transform the data back into the nested object (ContactTelDetail within Contact) accordingly.

The previously mentioned RowMapper<T> is suitable only for row mapping to a single domain object. For a more complicated object structure, we need to use the ResultSetExtractor interface. To demonstrate its use, let's add one more method, findAllWithDetail(), into the ContactDao interface. The method should populate the list of contacts with their telephone details.

Listing 6-30 shows the addition of the findAllWithDetail() method to the interface and the implementation of the method using ResultSetExtractor.

Listing 6-30. Using ResultSetExtractor to Query Domain Objects

```
package com.apress.prospring4.ch6;

import java.util.List;

public interface ContactDao {
    String findLastNameById(Long id);
    List<Contact> findAllWithDetail();
}

package com.apress.prospring4.ch6;

import javax.sql.DataSource;
import java.util.List;
import java.util.Map;
import java.util.HashMap;
import java.util.ArrayList;
import java.sql.ResultSet;
import java.sql.SQLException;

import org.springframework.dao.DataAccessException;
import org.springframework.jdbc.core.ResultSetExtractor;
import org.springframework.beans.factory.BeanCreationException;
import org.springframework.beans.factory.InitializingBean;
import org.springframework.jdbc.core.namedparam.NamedParameterJdbcTemplate;

public class JdbcContactDao implements ContactDao, InitializingBean {
    private DataSource dataSource;
    private NamedParameterJdbcTemplate namedParameterJdbcTemplate;

    @Override
    public String findLastNameById(Long id) {
        String sql = "select last_name from contact where id = :contactId";

        Map<String, Object> namedParameters = new HashMap<String, Object>();
        namedParameters.put("contactId", id);

        return namedParameterJdbcTemplate.queryForObject(sql,
            namedParameters, String.class);
    }
```

```java
    @Override
    public List<Contact> findAllWithDetail() {
        String sql = "select c.id, c.first_name, c.last_name, c.birth_date" +
                    ", t.id as contact_tel_id, t.tel_type, t.tel_number from contact c " +
                    "left join contact_tel_detail t on c.id = t.contact_id";

        return namedParameterJdbcTemplate.query(sql, new ContactWithDetailExtractor());
    }

    public void setDataSource(DataSource dataSource) {
        this.dataSource = dataSource;

        NamedParameterJdbcTemplate namedParameterJdbcTemplate =
            new NamedParameterJdbcTemplate(dataSource);

        this.namedParameterJdbcTemplate = namedParameterJdbcTemplate;
    }

    @Override
    public void afterPropertiesSet() throws Exception {
        if (dataSource == null) {
            throw new BeanCreationException("Must set dataSource on ContactDao");
        }

        if (namedParameterJdbcTemplate == null) {
            throw new BeanCreationException("Null NamedParameterJdbcTemplate on ContactDao");
        }
    }

    private static final class ContactWithDetailExtractor implements
                                                ResultSetExtractor<List<Contact>> {
        @Override
        public List<Contact> extractData(ResultSet rs) throws SQLException,
                                                DataAccessException {
            Map<Long, Contact> map = new HashMap<Long, Contact>();
            Contact contact = null;

            while (rs.next()) {
                Long id = rs.getLong("id");
                contact = map.get(id);

                if (contact == null) {
                    contact = new Contact();
                    contact.setId(id);
                    contact.setFirstName(rs.getString("first_name"));
                    contact.setLastName(rs.getString("last_name"));
                    contact.setBirthDate(rs.getDate("birth_date"));
                    contact.setContactTelDetails(new ArrayList<ContactTelDetail>());
                    map.put(id, contact);
                }

                Long contactTelDetailId = rs.getLong("contact_tel_id");
```

269

```
                if (contactTelDetailId > 0) {
                    ContactTelDetail contactTelDetail = new ContactTelDetail();
                    contactTelDetail.setId(contactTelDetailId);
                    contactTelDetail.setContactId(id);
                    contactTelDetail.setTelType(rs.getString("tel_type"));
                    contactTelDetail.setTelNumber(rs.getString("tel_number"));
                    contact.getContactTelDetails().add(contactTelDetail);
                }
            }

            return new ArrayList<Contact> (map.values());
        }
    }
}
```

The code looks quite like the RowMapper sample, but this time we declare an inner class that implements ResultSetExtractor. Then we implement the extractData() method to transform the result set into a list of Contact objects accordingly. For the findAllWithDetail() method, the query uses a left join to join the two tables so that contacts with no telephones will also be retrieved. The result is a Cartesian product of the two tables. Finally, we use the JdbcTemplate.query() method, passing in the query string and the result set extractor.

REFACTORING USING LAMBDA

When using Java 8, rather than creating the ContactWithDetailExtractor class as shown previously, a lambda expression can be used:

```
@Override
public List<Contact> findAllWithDetail() {
    String sql = "select c.id, c.first_name, c.last_name, c.birth_date" +
                ", t.id as contact_tel_id, t.tel_type, t.tel_number from contact c " +
                "left join contact_tel_detail t on c.id = t.contact_id";

    return namedParameterJdbcTemplate.query(sql, (ResultSet rs) -> {
        Map<Long, Contact> map = new HashMap<Long, Contact>();
        Contact contact = null;

        while (rs.next()) {
            Long id = rs.getLong("id");
            contact = map.get(id);

            if (contact == null) {
                contact = new Contact();
                contact.setId(id);
                contact.setFirstName(rs.getString("first_name"));
                contact.setLastName(rs.getString("last_name"));
                contact.setBirthDate(rs.getDate("birth_date"));
                contact.setContactTelDetails(new ArrayList<ContactTelDetail>());
                map.put(id, contact);
            }
```

```
            Long contactTelDetailId = rs.getLong("contact_tel_id");

            if (contactTelDetailId > 0) {
                ContactTelDetail contactTelDetail = new ContactTelDetail();
                contactTelDetail.setId(contactTelDetailId);
                contactTelDetail.setContactId(id);
                contactTelDetail.setTelType(rs.getString("tel_type"));
                contactTelDetail.setTelNumber(rs.getString("tel_number"));
                contact.getContactTelDetails().add(contactTelDetail);
            }
        }

        return new ArrayList<Contact> (map.values());
        });
    }
```

Listing 6-31 shows the new JdbcContactDaoSample used to list contacts with details.

Listing 6-31. Listing Contacts with Details

```
package com.apress.prospring4.ch6;

import java.util.List;
import org.springframework.context.support.GenericXmlApplicationContext;

public class JdbcContactDaoSample {
    public static void main(String[] args) {
        GenericXmlApplicationContext ctx = new GenericXmlApplicationContext();
        ctx.load("classpath:META-INF/spring/app-context-xml.xml");
        ctx.refresh();

        ContactDao contactDao = ctx.getBean("contactDao", ContactDao.class);

        List<Contact> contactsWithDetail = contactDao.findAllWithDetail();

        for (Contact contact: contactsWithDetail) {
            System.out.println(contact);

            if (contact.getContactTelDetails() != null) {
                for (ContactTelDetail contactTelDetail: contact.getContactTelDetails()) {
                    System.out.println("---" + contactTelDetail);
                }
            }

            System.out.println();
        }
    }
}
```

Run the testing program again, and it yields the following output:

```
Contact - Id: 2, First name: Scott, Last name: Tiger, Birthday: 1990-11-02
---Contact Tel Detail - Id: 3, Contact id: 2, Type: Home, Number: 1234567890
Contact - Id: 3, First name: John, Last name: Smith, Birthday: 1964-02-28
Contact - Id: 1, First name: Chris, Last name: Schaefer, Birthday: 1981-05-03
---Contact Tel Detail - Id: 2, Contact id: 1, Type: Home, Number: 1234567890
---Contact Tel Detail - Id: 1, Contact id: 1, Type: Mobile, Number: 1234567890
```

You can see the contacts and their telephone details are listed accordingly. The data is based on the data population script in Listing 6-2.

So far, you have seen how to use JdbcTemplate to perform some common query operations. JdbcTemplate (and the NamedParameterJdbcTemplate class too) also provides a number of overloading update() methods that support data update operations, including insert, update, delete, and so on. However, the update() method is quite self-explanatory, so we leave it as an exercise for you to explore. On the other side, as you will see in later sections, we will use the Spring-provided SqlUpdate class to perform data update operations.

Spring Classes That Model JDBC Operations

In the preceding section, you saw how JdbcTemplate and the related data mapper utility classes greatly simplify the programming model in developing data access logic with JDBC. Built on top of JdbcTemplate, Spring also provides a number of useful classes that model JDBC data operations and let developers maintain the query and transformation logic from ResultSet to domain objects in a more object-oriented fashion. Specifically, this section presents the following classes:

- MappingSqlQuery<T>: The MappingSqlQuery<T> class allows you to wrap the query string together with the mapRow() method into a single class.

- SqlUpdate: The SqlUpdate class allows you to wrap any SQL update statement into it. It also provides a lot of useful functions for you to bind SQL parameters, retrieve the RDBMS-generated key after a new record is inserted, and so on.

- BatchSqlUpdate: As its name indicates, this class allows you to perform batch update operations. For example, you can loop through a Java List object and have the BatchSqlUpdate queue up the records and submit the update statements for you in a batch. You can set the batch size and flush the operation anytime as you want.

- SqlFunction<T>: The SqlFunction<T> class allows you to call stored functions in the database with argument and return types. Another class, StoredProcedure, also exists that helps you invoke stored procedures.

- Setting Up JDBC DAO by Using Annotations

First let's take a look at how to set up the DAO implementation class by using annotations. The following example code implements the ContactDao interface method by method until we have a full ContactDao implementation. Listing 6-32 shows the ContactDao interface class with a complete listing of the data access services it provides.

Listing 6-32. ContactDao Interface

```
package com.apress.prospring4.ch6;

import java.util.List;

public interface ContactDao {
    List<Contact> findAll();
    List<Contact> findByFirstName(String firstName);
    String findFirstNameById(Long id);
    List<Contact> findAllWithDetail();
    void insert(Contact contact);
    void insertWithDetail(Contact contact);
    void update(Contact contact);
}
```

In Listing 6-33, the initial declaration and injection of the data source property using the JSR-250 annotation is shown.

Listing 6-33. Declaring JdbcContactDao by Using Annotations

```
package com.apress.prospring4.ch6;

import javax.annotation.Resource;
import javax.sql.DataSource;

import org.apache.commons.logging.Log;
import org.apache.commons.logging.LogFactory;
import org.springframework.stereotype.Repository;

@Repository("contactDao")
public class JdbcContactDao implements ContactDao {
    private Log log = LogFactory.getLog(JdbcContactDao.class);

    private DataSource dataSource;

    @Resource(name="dataSource")
    public void setDataSource(DataSource dataSource) {
        this.dataSource = dataSource;
    }

    public DataSource getDataSource() {
        return dataSource;
    }

    ...
}
```

In the previous listing, we use @Repository to declare the Spring bean with a name of contactDao, and since the class contains data access code, @Repository also instructs Spring to perform database-specific SQL exceptions to the more application-friendly DataAccessException hierarchy in Spring.

We also declare the log variable by using Apache commons-logging to log the message within the program. We use JSR-250's @Resource for the dataSource property to let Spring inject the data source with a name of dataSource.

Listing 6-34 shows the XML configuration for Spring using annotations (app-context-annotation.xml).

Listing 6-34. Spring Configuration Using Annotations

```xml
<?xml version="1.0" encoding="UTF-8"?>

<beans xmlns="http://www.springframework.org/schema/beans"
    xmlns:xsi="http://www.w3.org/2001/XMLSchema-instance"
    xmlns:context="http://www.springframework.org/schema/context"
    xmlns:jdbc="http://www.springframework.org/schema/jdbc"
    xsi:schemaLocation="http://www.springframework.org/schema/beans
        http://www.springframework.org/schema/beans/spring-beans.xsd
        http://www.springframework.org/schema/context
        http://www.springframework.org/schema/context/spring-context.xsd
        http://www.springframework.org/schema/jdbc
        http://www.springframework.org/schema/jdbc/spring-jdbc.xsd">

    <context:component-scan base-package="com.apress.prospring4.ch6"/>

    <jdbc:embedded-database id="dataSource" type="H2">
        <jdbc:script location="classpath:META-INF/sql/schema.sql"/>
        <jdbc:script location="classpath:META-INF/sql/test-data.sql"/>
    </jdbc:embedded-database>
</beans>).
```

In this configuration, we declare the embedded database by using H2 and use <context:component-scan> for automatic Spring bean discovery. Having the infrastructure in place, we can now proceed to the implementation of JDBC operations.

Querying Data by Using MappingSqlQuery<T>

Spring provides the MappingSqlQuery<T> class for modeling query operations. Basically, we construct a MappingSqlQuery<T> class by using the data source and the query string. We then implement the mapRow() method to map each ResultSet record into the corresponding domain object.

Let's begin by creating the SelectAllContacts class (which represents the query operation for selecting all contacts) that extends the MappingSqlQuery<T> abstract class. Listing 6-35 shows the SelectAllContacts class.

Listing 6-35. The SelectAllContacts Class

```java
package com.apress.prospring4.ch6;

import java.sql.ResultSet;
import java.sql.SQLException;

import javax.sql.DataSource;

import org.springframework.jdbc.object.MappingSqlQuery;

public class SelectAllContacts extends MappingSqlQuery<Contact> {
    private static final String SQL_SELECT_ALL_CONTACT =
        "select id, first_name, last_name, birth_date from contact";
```

```
    public SelectAllContacts(DataSource dataSource) {
        super(dataSource, SQL_SELECT_ALL_CONTACT);
    }

    protected Contact mapRow(ResultSet rs, int rowNum) throws SQLException {
        Contact contact = new Contact();

        contact.setId(rs.getLong("id"));
        contact.setFirstName(rs.getString("first_name"));
        contact.setLastName(rs.getString("last_name"));
        contact.setBirthDate(rs.getDate("birth_date"));

        return contact;
    }
}
```

Within the SelectAllContacts class, the SQL for selecting all contacts is declared. In the class constructor, the super() method is called to construct the class, using the DataSource as well as the SQL statement. Moreover, the MappingSqlQuery<T>.mapRow() method is implemented to provide the mapping of the result set to the Contact domain object.

Having the SelectAllContacts class in place, we can implement the findAll() method in the JdbcContactDao class. Listing 6-36 shows the class.

Listing 6-36. Implementing the findAll() Method

```
package com.apress.prospring4.ch6;

import java.util.List;

import javax.annotation.Resource;
import javax.sql.DataSource;

import org.apache.commons.logging.Log;
import org.apache.commons.logging.LogFactory;
import org.springframework.stereotype.Repository;

@Repository("contactDao")
public class JdbcContactDao implements ContactDao {
    private static final Log LOG = LogFactory.getLog(JdbcContactDao.class);

    private DataSource dataSource;
    private SelectAllContacts selectAllContacts;

    @Override
    public List<Contact> findAll() {
        return selectAllContacts.execute();
    }

    @Override
    public List<Contact> findByFirstName(String firstName) {
        return null;
    }
```

```java
    @Override
    public String findFirstNameById(Long id) {.
        return null;
    }

    @Override
    public void insert(Contact contact) {
    }

    @Override
    public void update(Contact contact) {
    }

    @Resource(name="dataSource")
    public void setDataSource(DataSource dataSource) {
        this.dataSource = dataSource;
        this.selectAllContacts = new SelectAllContacts(dataSource);
    }

    public DataSource getDataSource() {
        return dataSource;
    }
}
```

In the setDataSource() method, upon the injection of the DataSource, an instance of the SelectAllContacts class is constructed. In the findAll() method, we simply invoke the SelectAllContacts.execute() method, which is inherited from the SqlQuery<T> abstract class indirectly. That's all we need to do. Listing 6-37 shows the sample program to test the logic.

Listing 6-37. Testing MappingSqlQuery

```java
package com.apress.prospring4.ch6;

import java.util.List;
import org.springframework.context.support.GenericXmlApplicationContext;

public class AnnotationJdbcDaoSample {
    public static void main(String[] args) {
        GenericXmlApplicationContext ctx = new GenericXmlApplicationContext();
        ctx.load("classpath:META-INF/spring/app-context-annotation.xml");
        ctx.refresh();

        ContactDao contactDao = ctx.getBean("contactDao", ContactDao.class);

        List<Contact> contacts = contactDao.findAll();
        listContacts(contacts);
    }

    private static void listContacts(List<Contact> contacts) {
        for (Contact contact: contacts) {
            System.out.println(contact);
```

```
            if (contact.getContactTelDetails() != null) {
                for (ContactTelDetail contactTelDetail: contact.getContactTelDetails()) {
                    System.out.println("---" + contactTelDetail);
                }
            }

            System.out.println();
        }
    }
}
```

Running the testing program yields the following output:

```
Contact - Id: 1, First name: Chris, Last name: Schaefer, Birthday: 1981-05-03

Contact - Id: 2, First name: Scott, Last name: Tiger, Birthday: 1990-11-02

Contact - Id: 3, First name: John, Last name: Smith, Birthday: 1964-02-28
```

Since we set the logging properties to the DEBUG level, from the console output, you will also see the query that was submitted by Spring, as shown here:

```
JdbcTemplate: 663 - Executing prepared SQL query
JdbcTemplate: 597 - Executing prepared SQL statement [select id, first_name, last_name, birth_date
from contact].
```

Let's proceed to implement the findByFirstName() method, which takes one named parameter. As in the previous sample, we create the class SelectContactByFirstName for the operation, which is shown in Listing 6-38.

Listing 6-38. The SelectContactByFirstName Class

```
package com.apress.prospring4.ch6;

import java.sql.ResultSet;
import java.sql.SQLException;
import java.sql.Types;

import javax.sql.DataSource;

import org.springframework.jdbc.object.MappingSqlQuery;
import org.springframework.jdbc.core.SqlParameter;

public class SelectContactByFirstName extends MappingSqlQuery<Contact> {
    private static final String SQL_FIND_BY_FIRST_NAME =
        "select id, first_name, last_name, birth_date from contact where first_name = :first_name";

    public SelectContactByFirstName(DataSource dataSource) {
        super(dataSource, SQL_FIND_BY_FIRST_NAME);
        super.declareParameter(new SqlParameter("first_name", Types.VARCHAR));
    }
```

```
        protected Contact mapRow(ResultSet rs, int rowNum) throws SQLException {
            Contact contact = new Contact();

            contact.setId(rs.getLong("id"));
            contact.setFirstName(rs.getString("first_name"));
            contact.setLastName(rs.getString("last_name"));
            contact.setBirthDate(rs.getDate("birth_date"));

            return contact;
        }
}
```

The SelectContactByFirstName class is similar to the SelectAllContacts class. First, the SQL statement is different and carries a named parameter called first_name. In the constructor method, the declareParameter() method is called (which is inherited from the org.springframework.jdbc.object.RdbmsOperation abstract class indirectly). Let's proceed to implement the findByFirstName() method in the JdbcContactDao class. Listing 6-39 shows the updated code.

Listing 6-39. Implementing the findByFirstName() Method

```
package com.apress.prospring4.ch6;

import java.util.List;
import java.util.Map;
import java.util.HashMap;

import javax.annotation.Resource;
import javax.sql.DataSource;

import org.apache.commons.logging.Log;
import org.apache.commons.logging.LogFactory;
import org.springframework.stereotype.Repository;

@Repository("contactDao")
public class JdbcContactDao implements ContactDao {
    private static final Log LOG = LogFactory.getLog(JdbcContactDao.class);

    private DataSource dataSource;
    private SelectAllContacts selectAllContacts;
    private SelectContactByFirstName selectContactByFirstName;

    @Override
    public List<Contact> findAll() {
        return selectAllContacts.execute();
    }

    @Override
    public List<Contact> findByFirstName(String firstName) {
        Map<String, Object> paramMap = new HashMap<String, Object>();
        paramMap.put("first_name", firstName);

        return selectContactByFirstName.executeByNamedParam(paramMap);
    }
```

```
    @Override
    public String findFirstNameById(Long id) {
        return null;
    }

    @Override
    public void insert(Contact contact) {
    }

    @Override
    public void update(Contact contact) {.
    }

    @Resource(name="dataSource")
    public void setDataSource(DataSource dataSource) {
        this.dataSource = dataSource;
        this.selectAllContacts = new SelectAllContacts(dataSource);
        this.selectContactByFirstName = new SelectContactByFirstName(dataSource);
    }

    public DataSource getDataSource() {
        return dataSource;
    }
}
```

Upon data source injection, an instance of SelectContactByFirstName is constructed. Afterward, in the findByFirstName() method, a HashMap is constructed with the named parameters and values. Finally, the executeByNamedParam() method (inherited from SqlQuery<T> abstract class indirectly) is called. Let's test this method by executing the code in Listing 6-40.

Listing 6-40. Testing the findByFirstName() Method

```
package com.apress.prospring4.ch6;

import java.util.List;
import org.springframework.context.support.GenericXmlApplicationContext;

public class AnnotationJdbcDaoSample {
    public static void main(String[] args) {
        GenericXmlApplicationContext ctx = new GenericXmlApplicationContext();
        ctx.load("classpath:META-INF/spring/app-context-annotation.xml");
        ctx.refresh();

        ContactDao contactDao = ctx.getBean("contactDao", ContactDao.class);

        List<Contact> contacts = contactDao.findByFirstName("Chris");
        listContacts(contacts);
    }

    private static void listContacts(List<Contact> contacts) {
        for (Contact contact: contacts) {
            System.out.println(contact);
```

```
            if (contact.getContactTelDetails() != null) {
                for (ContactTelDetail contactTelDetail: contact.getContactTelDetails()) {
                    System.out.println("---" + contactTelDetail);
                }
            }

            System.out.println();.
        }
    }
}
```

Running the program produces the following output from the findByFirstName() method:

```
Contact - Id: 1, First name: Chris, Last name: Schaefer, Birthday: 1981-05-03
```

One point worth noting here is that MappingSqlQuery<T> is suitable only for mapping a single row to a domain object. For a nested object, you still need to use JdbcTemplate with ResultSetExtractor, like the example method findAllWithDetail() presented in the JdbcTemplate class section.

Updating Data by Using SqlUpdate

For updating data, Spring provides the SqlUpdate class. Listing 6-41 shows the UpdateContact class that extends the SqlUpdate class for update operations.

Listing 6-41. The UpdateContact Class

```java
package com.apress.prospring4.ch6;

import java.sql.Types;

import javax.sql.DataSource;

import org.springframework.jdbc.core.SqlParameter;
import org.springframework.jdbc.object.SqlUpdate;

public class UpdateContact extends SqlUpdate {
    private static final String SQL_UPDATE_CONTACT =
        "update contact set first_name=:first_name, last_name=:last_name, birth_date=:birth_date
where id=:id";

    public UpdateContact(DataSource dataSource) {
        super(dataSource, SQL_UPDATE_CONTACT);
        super.declareParameter(new SqlParameter("first_name", Types.VARCHAR));
        super.declareParameter(new SqlParameter("last_name", Types.VARCHAR));
        super.declareParameter(new SqlParameter("birth_date", Types.DATE));
        super.declareParameter(new SqlParameter("id", Types.INTEGER));
    }
}
```

The preceding listing should be familiar to you now. An instance of the SqlUpdate class is constructed with the query, and the named parameters are declared too.

Listing 6-42 shows the implementation of the update() method in the JdbcContactDao class.

Listing 6-42. Using SqlUpdate

```
package com.apress.prospring4.ch6;

import java.util.List;
import java.util.Map;
import java.util.HashMap;

import javax.annotation.Resource;
import javax.sql.DataSource;

import org.apache.commons.logging.Log;
import org.apache.commons.logging.LogFactory;
import org.springframework.stereotype.Repository;

@Repository("contactDao")
public class JdbcContactDao implements ContactDao {
    private static final Log LOG = LogFactory.getLog(JdbcContactDao.class);

    private DataSource dataSource;
    private SelectAllContacts selectAllContacts;
    private SelectContactByFirstName selectContactByFirstName;
    private UpdateContact updateContact;

    @Override
    public List<Contact> findAll() {
        return selectAllContacts.execute();
    }

    @Override
    public List<Contact> findByFirstName(String firstName) {
        Map<String, Object> paramMap = new HashMap<String, Object>();
        paramMap.put("first_name", firstName);

        return selectContactByFirstName.executeByNamedParam(paramMap);
    }

    @Override
    public String findFirstNameById(Long id) {
        return null;
    }

    @Override
    public void insert(Contact contact) {
    }

    @Override
    public void update(Contact contact) {
        Map<String, Object> paramMap = new HashMap<String, Object>();
        paramMap.put("first_name", contact.getFirstName());
```

```
            paramMap.put("last_name", contact.getLastName());
            paramMap.put("birth_date", contact.getBirthDate());
            paramMap.put("id", contact.getId());

            updateContact.updateByNamedParam(paramMap);

            LOG.info("Existing contact updated with id: " + contact.getId());
        }

    @Resource(name="dataSource")
    public void setDataSource(DataSource dataSource) {
        this.dataSource = dataSource;
        this.selectAllContacts = new SelectAllContacts(dataSource);
        this.selectContactByFirstName = new SelectContactByFirstName(dataSource);
        this.updateContact = new UpdateContact(dataSource);
    }

    public DataSource getDataSource() {
        return dataSource;
    }
}
```

Upon data source injection, an instance of UpdateContact is constructed. In the update() method, a HashMap of named parameters is constructed from the passed-in Contact object, and then the updateByNamedParam() is called to update the contact record. To test the operation, let's update the AnnotationJdbcDaoSample class, as shown in Listing 6-43.

Listing 6-43. Testing the update() Method

```
package com.apress.prospring4.ch6;

import java.util.List;
import java.util.GregorianCalendar;
import java.sql.Date;
import org.springframework.context.support.GenericXmlApplicationContext;

public class AnnotationJdbcDaoSample {
    public static void main(String[] args) {
        GenericXmlApplicationContext ctx = new GenericXmlApplicationContext();
        ctx.load("classpath:META-INF/spring/app-context-annotation.xml");
        ctx.refresh();

        ContactDao contactDao = ctx.getBean("contactDao", ContactDao.class);

        Contact contact = new Contact();
        contact.setId(1l);
        contact.setFirstName("Chris");
        contact.setLastName("John");
        contact.setBirthDate(new Date(
            (new GregorianCalendar(1977, 10, 1)).getTime().getTime()));
```

```
        contactDao.update(contact);

        listContacts(contactDao.findAll());
    }

    private static void listContacts(List<Contact> contacts) {
        for (Contact contact: contacts) {
            System.out.println(contact);

            if (contact.getContactTelDetails() != null) {
                for (ContactTelDetail contactTelDetail: contact.getContactTelDetails()) {
                    System.out.println("---" + contactTelDetail);
                }
            }

            System.out.println();
        }
    }
}
```

Here we simply construct a Contact object and then invoke the update() method. Running the program produces the following output from the last listContacts() method:

```
INFO com.apress.prospring4.ch6.JdbcContactDao:  60 - Existing contact updated with id: 1
Contact - Id: 1, First name: Chris, Last name: John, Birthday: 1977-11-01

Contact - Id: 2, First name: Scott, Last name: Tiger, Birthday: 1990-11-02

Contact - Id: 3, First name: John, Last name: Smith, Birthday: 1964-02-28
```

In the output, you can see that the contact with an ID of 1 is updated accordingly.

Inserting Data and Retrieving the Generated Key

For inserting data, we can also use the SqlUpdate class. One interesting point is how the primary key is generated (which is typically the id column). This value is available only after the insert statement has completed, as the RDBMS generates the identity value for the record on insert. The column ID is declared with the attribute AUTO_INCREMENT and is the primary key, and this value will be assigned by the RDBMS during the insert operation. If you are using Oracle, you will probably get a unique ID first from an Oracle sequence and then execute an insert statement with the query result.

In old versions of JDBC, the method is a bit tricky. For example, if we are using MySQL, we need to execute the SQL select last_insert_id() and select @@IDENTITY statements for Microsoft SQL Server.

Luckily, starting from JDBC version 3.0, a new feature was added that allows the retrieval of an RDBMS-generated key in a unified fashion. Listing 6-44 shows the implementation of the insert() method, which also retrieves the generated key for the inserted contact record. It will work in most databases (if not all); just make sure you are using a JDBC driver that is compatible with JDBC 3.0 or newer.

We start by creating the InsertContact class for the insert operation, which extends the SqlUpdate class. Listing 6-44 shows the class.

Listing 6-44. The InsertContact Class

```
package com.apress.prospring4.ch6;

import java.sql.Types;

import javax.sql.DataSource;

import org.springframework.jdbc.core.SqlParameter;
import org.springframework.jdbc.object.SqlUpdate;

public class InsertContact extends SqlUpdate {
    private static final String SQL_INSERT_CONTACT =
        "insert into contact (first_name, last_name, birth_date) values (:first_name,
        :last_name, :birth_date)";

    public InsertContact(DataSource dataSource) {
        super(dataSource, SQL_INSERT_CONTACT);
        super.declareParameter(new SqlParameter("first_name", Types.VARCHAR));
        super.declareParameter(new SqlParameter("last_name", Types.VARCHAR));
        super.declareParameter(new SqlParameter("birth_date", Types.DATE));
        super.setGeneratedKeysColumnNames(new String[] {"id"});
        super.setReturnGeneratedKeys(true);
    }

} JDBC operations:inserting data and generated key
```

The InsertContact class is almost the same as the UpdateContact class; we need to do just two more things. When constructing the InsertContact class, we call the method SqlUpdate.setGeneratedKeysColumnNames() to declare the name of the ID column. The method SqlUpdate.setReturnGeneratedKeys() then instructs the underlying JDBC driver to retrieve the generated key.

Listing 6-45 shows the implementation of the insert() method in the JdbcContactDao class.

Listing 6-45. Using SqlUpdate for the Insert Operation

```
package com.apress.prospring4.ch6;

import java.util.List;
import java.util.Map;
import java.util.HashMap;

import javax.annotation.Resource;
import javax.sql.DataSource;

import org.apache.commons.logging.Log;
import org.apache.commons.logging.LogFactory;
import org.springframework.stereotype.Repository;
import org.springframework.jdbc.support.GeneratedKeyHolder;
import org.springframework.jdbc.support.KeyHolder;
```

```java
@Repository("contactDao")
public class JdbcContactDao implements ContactDao {
    private static final Log LOG = LogFactory.getLog(JdbcContactDao.class);

    private DataSource dataSource;
    private SelectAllContacts selectAllContacts;
    private SelectContactByFirstName selectContactByFirstName;
    private UpdateContact updateContact;
    private InsertContact insertContact;

    @Override
    public List<Contact> findAll() {
        return selectAllContacts.execute();
    }

    @Override
    public List<Contact> findByFirstName(String firstName) {
        Map<String, Object> paramMap = new HashMap<String, Object>();
        paramMap.put("first_name", firstName);

        return selectContactByFirstName.executeByNamedParam(paramMap);
    }

    @Override
    public String findFirstNameById(Long id) {
        return null;
    }

    @Override
    public void insert(Contact contact) {
        Map<String, Object> paramMap = new HashMap<String, Object>();
        paramMap.put("first_name", contact.getFirstName());
        paramMap.put("last_name", contact.getLastName());
        paramMap.put("birth_date", contact.getBirthDate());

        KeyHolder keyHolder = new GeneratedKeyHolder();

        insertContact.updateByNamedParam(paramMap, keyHolder);

        contact.setId(keyHolder.getKey().longValue());

        LOG.info("New contact inserted with id: " + contact.getId());
    }

    @Override
    public void update(Contact contact) {
        Map<String, Object> paramMap = new HashMap<String, Object>();
        paramMap.put("first_name", contact.getFirstName());
        paramMap.put("last_name", contact.getLastName());
        paramMap.put("birth_date", contact.getBirthDate());
        paramMap.put("id", contact.getId());
```

```
        updateContact.updateByNamedParam(paramMap);

        LOG.info("Existing contact updated with id: " + contact.getId());
    }

    @Resource(name="dataSource")
    public void setDataSource(DataSource dataSource) {
        this.dataSource = dataSource;
        this.selectAllContacts = new SelectAllContacts(dataSource);
        this.selectContactByFirstName = new SelectContactByFirstName(dataSource);
        this.updateContact = new UpdateContact(dataSource);
        this.insertContact = new InsertContact(dataSource);
    }

    public DataSource getDataSource() {
        return dataSource;
    }
}
```

Upon data source injection, an instance of InsertContact is constructed. In the insert() method, we also use the SqlUpdate.updateByNamedParam() method. Additionally, we pass in an instance of KeyHolder to the method, which will have the generated ID stored in it. After the data is inserted, we can then retrieve the generated key from the KeyHolder.

Listing 6-46 shows the updated AnnotationJdbcDaoSample class.

Listing 6-46. Testing the insert() Method

```
package com.apress.prospring4.ch6;

import java.util.List;
import java.util.GregorianCalendar;
import java.sql.Date;
import org.springframework.context.support.GenericXmlApplicationContext;

public class AnnotationJdbcDaoSample {
    public static void main(String[] args) {
        GenericXmlApplicationContext ctx = new GenericXmlApplicationContext();
        ctx.load("classpath:META-INF/spring/app-context-annotation.xml");
        ctx.refresh();

        ContactDao contactDao = ctx.getBean("contactDao", ContactDao.class);

        Contact contact = new Contact();
        contact.setFirstName("Rod");
        contact.setLastName("Johnson");
        contact.setBirthDate(new Date((new GregorianCalendar(2001, 10, 1)).getTime().getTime()));

        contactDao.insert(contact);

        listContacts(contactDao.findAll());
    }
```

```
    private static void listContacts(List<Contact> contacts) {
        for (Contact contact: contacts) {
            System.out.println(contact);

            if (contact.getContactTelDetails() != null) {
                for (ContactTelDetail contactTelDetail: contact.getContactTelDetails()) {
                    System.out.println("---" + contactTelDetail);
                }
            }

            System.out.println();JDBC operations:inserting data and generated key
        }
    }
}
```

Running the program produces the following output from the last `listContacts()` method:

```
INFO com.apress.prospring4.ch6.JdbcContactDao:  62 - New contact inserted with id: 4
Contact - Id: 1, First name: Chris, Last name: Schaefer, Birthday: 1981-05-03

Contact - Id: 2, First name: Scott, Last name: Tiger, Birthday: 1990-11-02

Contact - Id: 3, First name: John, Last name: Smith, Birthday: 1964-02-28

Contact - Id: 4, First name: Rod, Last name: Johnson, Birthday: 2001-11-01
```

You can see that the new contact is inserted with an ID of 4 and retrieved correctly.

Batching Operations with BatchSqlUpdate

For batch operations, we use the `BatchSqlUpdate` class. The new `insertWithDetail()` method will insert both the contact and its telephone details into the database.

In order to be able to insert the telephone detail record, we need to create the `InsertContactTelDetail` class, which is shown in Listing 6-47.

Listing 6-47. The InsertContactTelDetail Class

```
package com.apress.prospring4.ch6;

import java.sql.Types;

import javax.sql.DataSource;

import org.springframework.jdbc.core.SqlParameter;
import org.springframework.jdbc.object.BatchSqlUpdate;

public class InsertContactTelDetail extends BatchSqlUpdate {
    private static final String SQL_INSERT_CONTACT_TEL =
        "insert into contact_tel_detail (contact_id, tel_type, tel_number) values
        (:contact_id, :tel_type, :tel_number)";
```

```
    private static final int BATCH_SIZE = 10;

    public InsertContactTelDetail(DataSource dataSource) {
        super(dataSource, SQL_INSERT_CONTACT_TEL);

        declareParameter(new SqlParameter("contact_id", Types.INTEGER));
        declareParameter(new SqlParameter("tel_type", Types.VARCHAR));
        declareParameter(new SqlParameter("tel_number", Types.VARCHAR));

        setBatchSize(BATCH_SIZE);
    }
}
```

Note that in the constructor, we call the BatchSqlUpdate.setBatchSize() method to set the batch size for the JDBC insert operation.

Listing 6-48 shows the implementation of the insertWithDetail() method in the JdbcContactDao class.

Listing 6-48. Batch SQL Update Operation

```java
package com.apress.prospring4.ch6;

import java.util.List;
import java.util.ArrayList;
import java.util.Map;
import java.util.HashMap;

import java.sql.ResultSet;
import java.sql.SQLException;

import javax.annotation.Resource;
import javax.sql.DataSource;

import org.apache.commons.logging.Log;
import org.apache.commons.logging.LogFactory;
import org.springframework.stereotype.Repository;
import org.springframework.jdbc.core.JdbcTemplate;
import org.springframework.jdbc.support.GeneratedKeyHolder;
import org.springframework.jdbc.support.KeyHolder;
import org.springframework.jdbc.core.ResultSetExtractor;
import org.springframework.dao.DataAccessException;

@Repository("contactDao")
public class JdbcContactDao implements ContactDao {
    private static final Log LOG = LogFactory.getLog(JdbcContactDao.class);

    private DataSource dataSource;
    private SelectAllContacts selectAllContacts;
    private SelectContactByFirstName selectContactByFirstName;
    private UpdateContact updateContact;
    private InsertContact insertContact;
    private InsertContactTelDetail insertContactTelDetail;
```

```java
@Override
public List<Contact> findAll() {
    return selectAllContacts.execute();
}

@Override
public List<Contact> findByFirstName(String firstName) {
    Map<String, Object> paramMap = new HashMap<String, Object>();
    paramMap.put("first_name", firstName);

    return selectContactByFirstName.executeByNamedParam(paramMap);
}

@Override
public String findFirstNameById(Long id) {
    return null;
}

@Override
public void insert(Contact contact) {
    Map<String, Object> paramMap = new HashMap<String, Object>();
    paramMap.put("first_name", contact.getFirstName());
    paramMap.put("last_name", contact.getLastName());
    paramMap.put("birth_date", contact.getBirthDate());

    KeyHolder keyHolder = new GeneratedKeyHolder();

    insertContact.updateByNamedParam(paramMap, keyHolder);

    contact.setId(keyHolder.getKey().longValue());

    LOG.info("New contact inserted with id: " + contact.getId());
}

@Override
public void insertWithDetail(Contact contact) {
    insertContactTelDetail = new InsertContactTelDetail(dataSource);

    Map<String, Object> paramMap = new HashMap<String, Object>();
    paramMap.put("first_name", contact.getFirstName());
    paramMap.put("last_name", contact.getLastName());
    paramMap.put("birth_date", contact.getBirthDate());

    KeyHolder keyHolder = new GeneratedKeyHolder();

    insertContact.updateByNamedParam(paramMap, keyHolder);

    contact.setId(keyHolder.getKey().longValue());

    LOG.info("New contact inserted with id: " + contact.getId());
```

```java
            List<ContactTelDetail> contactTelDetails =
                contact.getContactTelDetails();

            if (contactTelDetails != null) {
                for (ContactTelDetail contactTelDetail: contactTelDetails) {
                    paramMap = new HashMap<String, Object>();
                    paramMap.put("contact_id", contact.getId());
                    paramMap.put("tel_type", contactTelDetail.getTelType());
                    paramMap.put("tel_number", contactTelDetail.getTelNumber());
                    insertContactTelDetail.updateByNamedParam(paramMap);
                }
            }

            insertContactTelDetail.flush();
        }

    @Override
    public List<Contact> findAllWithDetail() {
        JdbcTemplate jdbcTemplate = new JdbcTemplate(getDataSource());

        String sql = "select c.id, c.first_name, c.last_name, c.birth_date" +
", t.id as contact_tel_id, t.tel_type, t.tel_number from contact c " +
"left join contact_tel_detail t on c.id = t.contact_id";

        return jdbcTemplate.query(sql, new ContactWithDetailExtractor());
    }

    @Override
    public void update(Contact contact) {
        Map<String, Object> paramMap = new HashMap<String, Object>();
        paramMap.put("first_name", contact.getFirstName());
        paramMap.put("last_name", contact.getLastName());
        paramMap.put("birth_date", contact.getBirthDate());
        paramMap.put("id", contact.getId());

        updateContact.updateByNamedParam(paramMap);

        LOG.info("Existing contact updated with id: " + contact.getId());
    }

    @Resource(name="dataSource")
    public void setDataSource(DataSource dataSource) {
        this.dataSource = dataSource;
        this.selectAllContacts = new SelectAllContacts(dataSource);
        this.selectContactByFirstName = new SelectContactByFirstName(dataSource);
        this.updateContact = new UpdateContact(dataSource);
        this.insertContact = new InsertContact(dataSource);
    }

    public DataSource getDataSource() {
        return dataSource;
    }
```

```java
    private static final class ContactWithDetailExtractor
        implements ResultSetExtractor<List<Contact>> {

        @Override
        public List<Contact> extractData(ResultSet rs) throws
            SQLException, DataAccessException {

            Map<Long, Contact> map = new HashMap<Long, Contact>();
            Contact contact = null;

            while (rs.next()) {
                Long id = rs.getLong("id");
                contact = map.get(id);

                if (contact == null) {
                    contact = new Contact();
                    contact.setId(id);
                    contact.setFirstName(rs.getString("first_name"));
                    contact.setLastName(rs.getString("last_name"));
                    contact.setBirthDate(rs.getDate("birth_date"));
                    contact.setContactTelDetails(new ArrayList<ContactTelDetail>());

                    map.put(id, contact);
                }

                Long contactTelDetailId = rs.getLong("contact_tel_id");

                if (contactTelDetailId > 0) {
                    ContactTelDetail contactTelDetail = new ContactTelDetail();
                    contactTelDetail.setId(contactTelDetailId);
                    contactTelDetail.setContactId(id);
                    contactTelDetail.setTelType(rs.getString("tel_type"));
                    contactTelDetail.setTelNumber(rs.getString("tel_number"));
                    contact.getContactTelDetails().add(contactTelDetail);
                }
            }

            return new ArrayList<Contact> (map.values());
        }
    }
}
```

Each time the insertWithDetail() method is called, a new instance of InsertContactTelDetail is constructed, as the BatchSqlUpdate class is not thread safe. Then we use it just like SqlUpdate. One main difference is that the BatchSqlUpdate class will queue up the insert operations and submit them to the database in batch. Every time the number of records equals the batch size, Spring will execute a bulk insert operation to the database for the pending records. On the other hand, upon completion, we call the BatchSqlUpdate.flush() method to instruct Spring to flush all pending operations (that is, the insert operations being queued that still haven't reached the batch size yet). Finally, we loop through the list of ContactTelDetail objects in the Contact object and invoke the BatchSqlUpdate.updateByNamedParam() method.

To facilitate testing, the findAllWithDetail() method is also implemented.

REFACTORING WITH LAMBDA

When using Java 8, rather than creating the ContactWithDetailExtractor class as shown previously, a lambda expression can be used:

```java
@Override
public List<Contact> findAllWithDetail() {
    JdbcTemplate jdbcTemplate = new JdbcTemplate(getDataSource());

    String sql = "select c.id, c.first_name, c.last_name, c.birth_date" +
", t.id as contact_tel_id, t.tel_type, t.tel_number from contact c " +
"left join contact_tel_detail t on c.id = t.contact_id";

    return jdbcTemplate.query(sql, (ResultSet rs) -> {
        Map<Long, Contact> map = new HashMap<Long, Contact>();
        Contact contact = null;

        while (rs.next()) {
            Long id = rs.getLong("id");
            contact = map.get(id);

            if (contact == null) {
                contact = new Contact();
                contact.setId(id);
                contact.setFirstName(rs.getString("first_name"));
                contact.setLastName(rs.getString("last_name"));
                contact.setBirthDate(rs.getDate("birth_date"));
                contact.setContactTelDetails(new ArrayList<ContactTelDetail>());

                map.put(id, contact);
            }

            Long contactTelDetailId = rs.getLong("contact_tel_id");

            if (contactTelDetailId > 0) {
                ContactTelDetail contactTelDetail = new ContactTelDetail();
                contactTelDetail.setId(contactTelDetailId);
                contactTelDetail.setContactId(id);
                contactTelDetail.setTelType(rs.getString("tel_type"));
                contactTelDetail.setTelNumber(rs.getString("tel_number"));
                contact.getContactTelDetails().add(contactTelDetail);
            }
        }

        return new ArrayList<Contact> (map.values());
    });
}
```

Listing 6-49 shows the updated AnnotationJdbcDaoSample class for testing the batch insert operation.

Listing 6-49. Testing the insertWithDetail() Method

```java
package com.apress.prospring4.ch6;

import java.util.List;
import java.util.ArrayList;
import java.util.GregorianCalendar;
import java.sql.Date;
import org.springframework.context.support.GenericXmlApplicationContext;

public class AnnotationJdbcDaoSample {
    public static void main(String[] args) {
        GenericXmlApplicationContext ctx = new GenericXmlApplicationContext();
        ctx.load("classpath:META-INF/spring/app-context-annotation.xml");
        ctx.refresh();

        ContactDao contactDao = ctx.getBean("contactDao", ContactDao.class);

        Contact contact = new Contact();
        contact.setFirstName("Michael");
        contact.setLastName("Jackson");
        contact.setBirthDate(new Date((new GregorianCalendar(1964, 10, 1)).getTime().getTime()));

        List<ContactTelDetail> contactTelDetails = new ArrayList<ContactTelDetail>();

        ContactTelDetail contactTelDetail = new ContactTelDetail();
        contactTelDetail.setTelType("Home");
        contactTelDetail.setTelNumber("11111111");

        contactTelDetails.add(contactTelDetail);

        contactTelDetail = new ContactTelDetail();
        contactTelDetail.setTelType("Mobile");
        contactTelDetail.setTelNumber("22222222");

        contactTelDetails.add(contactTelDetail);

        contact.setContactTelDetails(contactTelDetails);

        contactDao.insertWithDetail(contact);

        listContacts(contactDao.findAllWithDetail());
    }

    private static void listContacts(List<Contact> contacts) {
        for (Contact contact: contacts) {
            System.out.println(contact);
```

```
            if (contact.getContactTelDetails() != null) {
                for (ContactTelDetail contactTelDetail: contact.getContactTelDetails()) {
                    System.out.println("---" + contactTelDetail);
                }
            }

            System.out.println();
        }
    }
}
```

Running the program produces the following output from the last listContacts() method:

```
Contact - Id: 1, First name: Chris, Last name: Schaefer, Birthday: 1981-05-03
---Contact Tel Detail - Id: 2, Contact id: 1, Type: Home, Number: 1234567890
---Contact Tel Detail - Id: 1, Contact id: 1, Type: Mobile, Number: 1234567890

Contact - Id: 2, First name: Scott, Last name: Tiger, Birthday: 1990-11-02
---Contact Tel Detail - Id: 3, Contact id: 2, Type: Home, Number: 1234567890

Contact - Id: 3, First name: John, Last name: Smith, Birthday: 1964-02-28

Contact - Id: 4, First name: Michael, Last name: Jackson, Birthday: 1964-11-01
---Contact Tel Detail - Id: 4, Contact id: 4, Type: Home, Number: 11111111
---Contact Tel Detail - Id: 5, Contact id: 4, Type: Mobile, Number: 22222222
```

You can see that the new contacts with the telephone details are all inserted into the database.

Calling Stored Functions by Using SqlFunction

Spring also provides classes to simplify the execution of stored procedures/functions using JDBC. In this section, we show you how to execute a simple function by using the SqlFunction class. We will use MySQL for the database, create a stored function, and call it by using the SqlFunction<T> class.

We're assuming you have a MySQL database with a schema called prospring4_ch6, with a username and password both equaling prospring4 (the same as the example in the section "Exploring the JDBC Infrastructure"). Let's create a stored function called getFirstNameById(), which accepts the contact's ID and returns the first name of the contact. Listing 6-50 shows the script to create the stored function in MySQL (stored-function.sql). Run the script against the MySQL database.

Listing 6-50. Stored Function for MySQL

```
DELIMITER //
CREATE FUNCTION getFirstNameById(in_id INT)
    RETURNS VARCHAR(60)
BEGIN
    RETURN (SELECT first_name FROM contact WHERE id = in_id);
END //
DELIMITER ;
```

The stored function simply accepts the ID and returns the first name of the contact record with the ID.

Next we create a StoredFunctionFirstNameById class to represent the stored function operation, which extends the SqlFunction<T> class. Listing 6-51 shows the class.

Listing 6-51. The StoredFunctionFirstNameById Class

```
package com.apress.prospring4.ch6;

import java.sql.Types;

import javax.sql.DataSource;

import org.springframework.jdbc.core.SqlParameter;
import org.springframework.jdbc.object.SqlFunction;

public class StoredFunctionFirstNameById extends SqlFunction<String> {
    private static final String SQL = "select getfirstnamebyid(?)";

    public StoredFunctionFirstNameById (DataSource dataSource) {
        super(dataSource, SQL);
        declareParameter(new SqlParameter(Types.INTEGER));
        compile();
    }
}
```

Here the class extends SqlFunction<T> and passes in the type String, which indicates the return type of the function. Then we declare the SQL to call the stored function in MySQL. Afterward, in the constructor, the parameter is declared, and we compile the operation. The class is now ready for use in the implementation class. Listing 6-52 shows the updated JdbcContactDao class to use the stored function.

Listing 6-52. The JdbcContactDao Class Using the Stored Function

```
package com.apress.prospring4.ch6;

import java.util.List;
import java.util.ArrayList;
import java.util.Map;
import java.util.HashMap;

import java.sql.ResultSet;
import java.sql.SQLException;

import javax.annotation.Resource;
import javax.sql.DataSource;

import org.apache.commons.logging.Log;
import org.apache.commons.logging.LogFactory;
import org.springframework.stereotype.Repository;
import org.springframework.jdbc.core.JdbcTemplate;
import org.springframework.jdbc.support.GeneratedKeyHolder;
import org.springframework.jdbc.support.KeyHolder;
import org.springframework.jdbc.core.ResultSetExtractor;
import org.springframework.dao.DataAccessException;

@Repository("contactDao")
public class JdbcContactDao implements ContactDao {
    private static final Log LOG = LogFactory.getLog(JdbcContactDao.class);
```

```java
    private DataSource dataSource;
    private SelectAllContacts selectAllContacts;
    private SelectContactByFirstName selectContactByFirstName;
    private UpdateContact updateContact;
    private InsertContact insertContact;
    private InsertContactTelDetail insertContactTelDetail;
    private StoredFunctionFirstNameById storedFunctionFirstNameById;

    @Override
    public List<Contact> findAll() {
        return selectAllContacts.execute();
    }

    @Override
    public List<Contact> findByFirstName(String firstName) {
        Map<String, Object> paramMap = new HashMap<String, Object>();
        paramMap.put("first_name", firstName);

        return selectContactByFirstName.executeByNamedParam(paramMap);
    }

    @Override
    public String findFirstNameById(Long id) {
        List<String> result = storedFunctionFirstNameById.execute(id);
        return result.get(0);
    }

    @Override
    public void insert(Contact contact) {
        Map<String, Object> paramMap = new HashMap<String, Object>();
        paramMap.put("first_name", contact.getFirstName());
        paramMap.put("last_name", contact.getLastName());
        paramMap.put("birth_date", contact.getBirthDate());

        KeyHolder keyHolder = new GeneratedKeyHolder();

        insertContact.updateByNamedParam(paramMap, keyHolder);

        contact.setId(keyHolder.getKey().longValue());

        LOG.info("New contact inserted with id: " + contact.getId());
    }

    @Override
    public void insertWithDetail(Contact contact) {
        insertContactTelDetail = new InsertContactTelDetail(dataSource);

        Map<String, Object> paramMap = new HashMap<String, Object>();
        paramMap.put("first_name", contact.getFirstName());
        paramMap.put("last_name", contact.getLastName());
        paramMap.put("birth_date", contact.getBirthDate());
```

```
        KeyHolder keyHolder = new GeneratedKeyHolder();

        insertContact.updateByNamedParam(paramMap, keyHolder);

        contact.setId(keyHolder.getKey().longValue());

        LOG.info("New contact inserted with id: " + contact.getId());

        List<ContactTelDetail> contactTelDetails =
            contact.getContactTelDetails();

        if (contactTelDetails != null) {
            for (ContactTelDetail contactTelDetail: contactTelDetails) {
                paramMap = new HashMap<String, Object>();
                paramMap.put("contact_id", contact.getId());
                paramMap.put("tel_type", contactTelDetail.getTelType());
                paramMap.put("tel_number", contactTelDetail.getTelNumber());
                insertContactTelDetail.updateByNamedParam(paramMap);
            }
        }

        insertContactTelDetail.flush();
    }

    @Override
    public List<Contact> findAllWithDetail() {
        JdbcTemplate jdbcTemplate = new JdbcTemplate(getDataSource());

        String sql = "select c.id, c.first_name, c.last_name, c.birth_date" +
", t.id as contact_tel_id, t.tel_type, t.tel_number from contact c " +
"left join contact_tel_detail t on c.id = t.contact_id";

        return jdbcTemplate.query(sql, new ContactWithDetailExtractor());
    }

    @Override
    public void update(Contact contact) {
        Map<String, Object> paramMap = new HashMap<String, Object>();
        paramMap.put("first_name", contact.getFirstName());
        paramMap.put("last_name", contact.getLastName());
        paramMap.put("birth_date", contact.getBirthDate());
        paramMap.put("id", contact.getId());

        updateContact.updateByNamedParam(paramMap);

        LOG.info("Existing contact updated with id: " + contact.getId());
    }

    @Resource(name="dataSource")
    public void setDataSource(DataSource dataSource) {
        this.dataSource = dataSource;
```

```java
        this.selectAllContacts = new SelectAllContacts(dataSource);
        this.selectContactByFirstName = new SelectContactByFirstName(dataSource);
        this.updateContact = new UpdateContact(dataSource);
        this.insertContact = new InsertContact(dataSource);
        this.storedFunctionFirstNameById = new StoredFunctionFirstNameById(dataSource);
    }

    public DataSource getDataSource() {
        return dataSource;
    }

    private static final class ContactWithDetailExtractor
        implements ResultSetExtractor<List<Contact>> {

        @Override
        public List<Contact> extractData(ResultSet rs) throws
            SQLException, DataAccessException {

            Map<Long, Contact> map = new HashMap<Long, Contact>();
            Contact contact = null;

            while (rs.next()) {
                Long id = rs.getLong("id");
                contact = map.get(id);

                if (contact == null) {
                    contact = new Contact();
                    contact.setId(id);
                    contact.setFirstName(rs.getString("first_name"));
                    contact.setLastName(rs.getString("last_name"));
                    contact.setBirthDate(rs.getDate("birth_date"));
                    contact.setContactTelDetails(new ArrayList<ContactTelDetail>());

                    map.put(id, contact);
                }

                Long contactTelDetailId = rs.getLong("contact_tel_id");

                if (contactTelDetailId > 0) {
                    ContactTelDetail contactTelDetail = new ContactTelDetail();
                    contactTelDetail.setId(contactTelDetailId);
                    contactTelDetail.setContactId(id);
                    contactTelDetail.setTelType(rs.getString("tel_type"));
                    contactTelDetail.setTelNumber(rs.getString("tel_number"));
                    contact.getContactTelDetails().add(contactTelDetail);
                }
            }

            return new ArrayList<Contact> (map.values());
        }
    }
}
```

Upon data source injection, an instance of StoredFunctionFirstNameById is constructed. Then in the findFirstNameById() method, its execute() method is called, passing in the contact ID. The method will return a list of Strings, and we need only the first one, because there should be only one record returned in the result set.

REFACTORING WITH LAMBDA

When using Java 8, rather than creating the ContactWithDetailExtractor class as shown previously, a lambda expression can be used:

```java
@Override
public List<Contact> findAllWithDetail() {
    JdbcTemplate jdbcTemplate = new JdbcTemplate(getDataSource());

    String sql = "select c.id, c.first_name, c.last_name, c.birth_date" +
", t.id as contact_tel_id, t.tel_type, t.tel_number from contact c " +
"left join contact_tel_detail t on c.id = t.contact_id";

    return jdbcTemplate.query(sql, (ResultSet rs) -> {
        Map<Long, Contact> map = new HashMap<Long, Contact>();
        Contact contact = null;

        while (rs.next()) {
            Long id = rs.getLong("id");
            contact = map.get(id);

            if (contact == null) {
                contact = new Contact();
                contact.setId(id);
                contact.setFirstName(rs.getString("first_name"));
                contact.setLastName(rs.getString("last_name"));
                contact.setBirthDate(rs.getDate("birth_date"));
                contact.setContactTelDetails(new ArrayList<ContactTelDetail>());

                map.put(id, contact);
            }

            Long contactTelDetailId = rs.getLong("contact_tel_id");

            if (contactTelDetailId > 0) {
                ContactTelDetail contactTelDetail = new ContactTelDetail();
                contactTelDetail.setId(contactTelDetailId);
                contactTelDetail.setContactId(id);
                contactTelDetail.setTelType(rs.getString("tel_type"));
                contactTelDetail.setTelNumber(rs.getString("tel_number"));
                contact.getContactTelDetails().add(contactTelDetail);
            }
        }

        return new ArrayList<Contact> (map.values());
    });
}
```

Listing 6-53 shows the updated Spring configuration file for connecting to MySQL (app-context-annotation.xml

Listing 6-53. Spring Configuration for MySQL

```xml
<?xml version="1.0" encoding="UTF-8"?>

<beans xmlns="http://www.springframework.org/schema/beans"
    xmlns:xsi="http://www.w3.org/2001/XMLSchema-instance"
    xmlns:context="http://www.springframework.org/schema/context"
    xsi:schemaLocation="http://www.springframework.org/schema/beans
        http://www.springframework.org/schema/beans/spring-beans.xsd
        http://www.springframework.org/schema/context
        http://www.springframework.org/schema/context/spring-context.xsd">

    <import resource="classpath:META-INF/spring/datasource-dbcp.xml"/>

    <context:component-scan base-package="com.apress.prospring4.ch6"/>
</beans>
```

The file datasource-dbcp.xml is imported, which holds the data source configuration to the MySQL database. To run the program, the dependency on commons-dbcp should be added to the project, as shown in Table 6-5

Table 6-5. *Dependency for commons-dbcp*

Group ID	Artifact ID	Version	Description
commons-dbcp	commons-dbcp	1.4	Apache commons-dbcp database connection pool library

Listing 6-54 shows the updated testing program.

Listing 6-54. Testing the Stored Function in MySQL

```java
package com.apress.prospring4.ch6;

import org.springframework.context.support.GenericXmlApplicationContext;

public class AnnotationJdbcDaoSample {
    public static void main(String[] args) {
        GenericXmlApplicationContext ctx = new GenericXmlApplicationContext();
        ctx.load("classpath:META-INF/spring/app-context-annotation.xml");
        ctx.refresh();

        ContactDao contactDao = ctx.getBean("contactDao", ContactDao.class);

        System.out.println(contactDao.findFirstNameById(1l));
    }
}
```

In the program, we pass an ID of 1 into the stored function. This will return Chris as the first name if you ran the `test-data.sql` against the MySQL database. Running the program produces the following output:

```
JdbcTemplate: 663 - Executing prepared SQL query
JdbcTemplate: 597 - Executing prepared SQL statement [select getfirstnamebyid(?)]
DataSourceUtils: 110 - Fetching JDBC Connection from DataSource
DataSourceUtils: 327 - Returning JDBC Connection to DataSource
Chris
```

You can see that the first name is retrieved correctly. What is presented here is just a simple sample to demonstrate the Spring JDBC module's function capabilities. Spring also provides other classes (for example, `StoredProcedure`) for you to invoke complex stored procedures that return complex data types. We recommend you refer to Spring's reference manual in case you need to access stored procedures using JDBC.

Spring Data Project: JDBC Extensions

In recent years, database technology has evolved so quickly with the rise of so many purpose-specific databases, nowadays an RDBMS is not the only choice for an application's back-end database. In response to this database technology evolution and the developer community's needs, Spring created the Spring Data project (`www.springsource.org/spring-data`). The major objective of the project is to provide useful extensions on top of Spring's core data access functionality to interact with databases other than traditional RDBMSs.

The Spring Data project comes with various extensions. One that we would like to mention here is JDBC Extensions (`www.springsource.org/spring-data/jdbc-extensions`). As its name implies, the extension provides some advanced features to facilitate the development of JDBC applications using Spring.

The main features that JDBC Extensions provides are listed here:

- *QueryDSL support*: QueryDSL (`www.querydsl.com`) is a domain-specific language that provides a framework for developing type-safe queries. Spring Data's JDBC Extensions provides `QueryDslJdbcTemplate` to facilitate the development of JDBC applications using QueryDSL instead of SQL statements.

- *Advanced support for Oracle Database*: The extension provides advanced features for Oracle Database users. On the database connection side, it supports Oracle-specific session settings, as well as Fast Connection Failover technology when working with Oracle RAC. Also, classes that integrate with Oracle Advanced Queueing are provided. On the data-type side, native support for Oracle's XML types, `STRUCT` and `ARRAY`, and so on, are provided.

If you are developing JDBC applications using Spring with Oracle Database, JDBC Extensions is really worth a look.

Considerations for Using JDBC

With this rich feature set, you can see how Spring can make your life much easier when using JDBC to interact with the underlying RDBMS. However, there is still quite a lot of code you need to develop, especially when transforming the result set into the corresponding domain objects.

On top of JDBC, a lot of open source libraries have been developed to help close the gap between the relational data structure and Java's OO model. For example, iBATIS is a popular `DataMapper` framework that is also based on SQL mapping. iBATIS lets you map objects with stored procedures or queries to an XML descriptor file. Like Spring, iBATIS provides a declarative way to query object mapping, greatly saving you the time it takes to maintain SQL queries that may be scattered around various DAO classes.

There are also many other ORM frameworks that focus on the object model, rather than the query. Popular ones include Hibernate, EclipseLink (also known as TopLink), and OpenJPA. All of them comply with the JCP's JPA specification.

In recent years, these ORM tools and mapping frameworks have become much more mature so that most developers will settle on one of them, instead of using JDBC directly. However, in cases where you need to have absolute control over the query that will be submitted to the database for performance purposes (for example, using a hierarchical query in Oracle), Spring JDBC is really a viable option. And when using Spring, one great advantage is that you can mix and match different data access technologies. For example, you can use Hibernate as the main ORM and then JDBC as a supplement for some of the complex query logic or batch operations; you can mix and match them in a single business operation and then wrap them under the same database transaction. Spring will help you handle those situations easily.

Summary

This chapter showed you how to use Spring to simplify JDBC programming. You learned how to connect to a database and perform selects, updates, deletes, and inserts, as well as call database stored functions. Using the core Spring JDBC class, JdbcTemplate, was discussed in detail. In addition, we covered other Spring classes that are built on top of JdbcTemplate and that help you model various JDBC operations. We also showed how to use the new lambda expressions from Java 8 where appropriate. In the next couple of chapters, we will discuss how to use Spring with popular ORM technologies when developing data access logic.

CHAPTER 7

■ ■ ■

Using Hibernate in Spring

In the previous chapter, you saw how to use JDBC in Spring applications. However, even though Spring goes a long way toward simplifying JDBC development, you still have a lot of code to write. In this chapter, we cover one of the object-relational mapping (ORM) libraries called Hibernate.

If you have experience developing data access applications using EJB entity beans (prior to EJB 3.0), you may remember the painful process. Tedious configuration of mappings, transaction demarcation, and much boilerplate code in each bean to manage its life cycle greatly reduced productivity when developing enterprise Java applications.

Just like Spring was developed to embrace POJO-based development and declarative configuration management rather than EJB's heavy and clumsy setup, the developer community realized that a simpler, lightweight, and POJO-based framework could ease the development of data access logic. Since then, many libraries have appeared; they are generally referred to as *ORM libraries*. The main objectives of an ORM library are to close the gap between the relational data structure in the relational database management system (RDBMS) and the object oriented (OO) model in Java so that developers can focus on programming with the object model and at the same time easily perform actions related to persistence.

Out of the ORM libraries available in the open source community, Hibernate is one of the most successful. Its features, such as a POJO-based approach, ease of development, and support of sophisticated relationship definitions, have won the heart of the mainstream Java developer community.

Hibernate's popularity has also influenced the JCP, which developed the Java Data Objects (JDO) specification as one of the standard ORM technologies in Java EE. Starting from EJB 3.0, the EJB entity bean was even replaced with the Java Persistence API (JPA). JPA has a lot of concepts that were influenced by popular ORM libraries such as Hibernate, TopLink, and JDO.

The relationship between Hibernate and JPA is also very close. Gavin King, the founder of Hibernate, represented JBoss as one of the JCP expert group members in defining the JPA specification. Starting from version 3.2, Hibernate provides an implementation of JPA. That means when you develop applications with Hibernate, you can choose to use either Hibernate's own API or the JPA API with Hibernate as the persistence service provider.

Having offered a rough history of Hibernate, this chapter will cover how to use Spring with Hibernate when developing data access logic. Hibernate is such an extensive ORM library that covering every aspect in just one chapter is simply not possible, and numerous books are dedicated to discussing Hibernate.

This chapter covers the basic ideas and main use cases of Hibernate in Spring. In particular, we discuss the following topics:

- *Configuring the Hibernate* SessionFactory: The core concept of Hibernate revolves around the Session interface, which is managed by SessionFactory. We show how to configure Hibernate's session factory to work in a Spring application.

- *Major concepts of ORMs using Hibernate*: We go through the major concepts of how to use Hibernate to map a POJO to the underlying relational database structure. Some commonly used relationships, including one-to-many and many-to-many, are also discussed.

- *Data operations*: We present examples of how to perform data operations (query, insert, update, delete) by using Hibernate in the Spring environment. When working with Hibernate, its Session interface is the main interface that we will interact with.

303

■ **Note** When defining object-to-relational mappings, Hibernate supports two configuration styles. One is configuring the mapping information in XML files, and the other is using Java annotations within the entity classes (in the ORM or JPA world, a Java class that is mapped to the underlying relational database structure is called an *entity class*). This chapter focuses on using the annotation approach for object-relational mapping. For the mapping annotation, we use the JPA standards (for example, under the `javax.persistence` package), because they are interchangeable with Hibernate's own annotations and will help you with future migrations to a JPA environment.

Sample Data Model for Example Code

Figure 7-1 shows the data model used in this chapter.

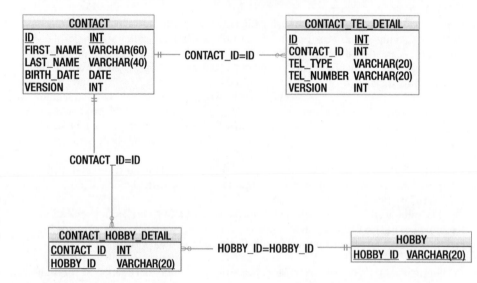

Figure 7-1. *Sample data model for Hibernate*

As shown in this data model, two new tables were added, namely, HOBBY and CONTACT_HOBBY_DETAIL (the join table), which models the many-to-many relationships between the CONTACT and HOBBY tables. On the other hand, a VERSION column was added to the CONTACT and CONTACT_TEL_DETAIL tables for optimistic locking, which we discuss in detail later. In the examples in this chapter, we use the embedded H2 database, so the database name is not required.

Listings 7-1 and 7-2 show the scripts for schema creation and sample data population.

Listing 7-1. Sample Data Model Creation Script (`schema.sql`)

```
CREATE TABLE CONTACT (
    ID INT NOT NULL AUTO_INCREMENT
    , FIRST_NAME VARCHAR(60) NOT NULL
    , LAST_NAME VARCHAR(40) NOT NULL
    , BIRTH_DATE DATE
    , VERSION INT NOT NULL DEFAULT 0
```

```
     , UNIQUE UQ_CONTACT_1 (FIRST_NAME, LAST_NAME)
     , PRIMARY KEY (ID)
);

CREATE TABLE HOBBY (
     HOBBY_ID VARCHAR(20) NOT NULL
     , PRIMARY KEY (HOBBY_ID)
);

CREATE TABLE CONTACT_TEL_DETAIL (
ID INT NOT NULL AUTO_INCREMENT
     , CONTACT_ID INT NOT NULL
     , TEL_TYPE VARCHAR(20) NOT NULL
     , TEL_NUMBER VARCHAR(20) NOT NULL
     , VERSION INT NOT NULL DEFAULT 0
     , UNIQUE UQ_CONTACT_TEL_DETAIL_1 (CONTACT_ID, TEL_TYPE)
     , PRIMARY KEY (ID)
     , CONSTRAINT FK_CONTACT_TEL_DETAIL_1 FOREIGN KEY (CONTACT_ID)
        REFERENCES CONTACT (ID)
);

CREATE TABLE CONTACT_HOBBY_DETAIL (
     CONTACT_ID INT NOT NULL
     , HOBBY_ID VARCHAR(20) NOT NULL
     , PRIMARY KEY (CONTACT_ID, HOBBY_ID)
     , CONSTRAINT FK_CONTACT_HOBBY_DETAIL_1 FOREIGN KEY (CONTACT_ID)
        REFERENCES CONTACT (ID) ON DELETE CASCADE
     , CONSTRAINT FK_CONTACT_HOBBY_DETAIL_2 FOREIGN KEY (HOBBY_ID)
     REFERENCES HOBBY (HOBBY_ID)
);
```

Listing 7-2. Data Population Script (test-data.sql)

```
insert into contact (first_name, last_name, birth_date) values ('Chris', 'Schaefer', '1981-05-03');
insert into contact (first_name, last_name, birth_date) values ('Scott', 'Tiger', '1990-11-02');
insert into contact (first_name, last_name, birth_date) values ('John', 'Smith', '1964-02-28');

insert into contact_tel_detail (contact_id, tel_type, tel_number) values (1, 'Mobile',
'1234567890');
insert into contact_tel_detail (contact_id, tel_type, tel_number) values (1, 'Home', '1234567890');
insert into contact_tel_detail (contact_id, tel_type, tel_number) values (2, 'Home', '1234567890');

insert into hobby (hobby_id) values ('Swimming');
insert into hobby (hobby_id) values ('Jogging');
insert into hobby (hobby_id) values ('Programming');
insert into hobby (hobby_id) values ('Movies');
insert into hobby (hobby_id) values ('Reading');

insert into contact_hobby_detail(contact_id, hobby_id) values (1, 'Swimming');
insert into contact_hobby_detail(contact_id, hobby_id) values (1, 'Movies');
insert into contact_hobby_detail(contact_id, hobby_id) values (2, 'Swimming');
```

Configuring Hibernate SessionFactory

As mentioned earlier in this chapter, the core concept of Hibernate is based on the Session interface, which is obtained from SessionFactory. Spring provides classes to support the configuration of Hibernate's session factory as a Spring bean with the desired properties. In order to use Hibernate, you must add the Hibernate dependency, as shown in Table 7-1.

Table 7-1. *Dependency for Hibernate*

Group ID	Artifact ID	Version	Description
org.hibernate	hibernate-entitymanager	4.2.3.Final	Hibernate 4 library

Listing 7-3 shows the corresponding XML configuration file (app-context-annotation.xml).

Listing 7-3. Spring Configuration for Hibernate's SessionFactory

```xml
<?xml version="1.0" encoding="UTF-8"?>

<beans xmlns="http://www.springframework.org/schema/beans"
    xmlns:xsi="http://www.w3.org/2001/XMLSchema-instance"
    xmlns:context="http://www.springframework.org/schema/context"
    xmlns:tx="http://www.springframework.org/schema/tx"
    xmlns:p="http://www.springframework.org/schema/p"
    xmlns:jdbc="http://www.springframework.org/schema/jdbc"
    xmlns:util="http://www.springframework.org/schema/util"
    xsi:schemaLocation="
      http://www.springframework.org/schema/jdbc
      http://www.springframework.org/schema/jdbc/spring-jdbc.xsd
      http://www.springframework.org/schema/beans
      http://www.springframework.org/schema/beans/spring-beans.xsd
      http://www.springframework.org/schema/tx
      http://www.springframework.org/schema/tx/spring-tx.xsd
      http://www.springframework.org/schema/util
      http://www.springframework.org/schema/util/spring-util.xsd
      http://www.springframework.org/schema/context
      http://www.springframework.org/schema/context/spring-context.xsd">

    <jdbc:embedded-database id="dataSource" type="H2">
        <jdbc:script location="classpath:META-INF/sql/schema.sql"/>
        <jdbc:script location="classpath:META-INF/sql/test-data.sql"/>
    </jdbc:embedded-database>

    <bean id="transactionManager"
      class="org.springframework.orm.hibernate4.HibernateTransactionManager"
        p:sessionFactory-ref="sessionFactory"/>

    <tx:annotation-driven/>

    <context:component-scan base-package="com.apress.prospring4.ch7"/>
```

```
<bean id="sessionFactory"
    class="org.springframework.orm.hibernate4.LocalSessionFactoryBean"
        p:dataSource-ref="dataSource"
        p:packagesToScan="com.apress.prospring4.ch7"
        p:hibernateProperties-ref="hibernateProperties"/>

<util:properties id="hibernateProperties">
    <prop key="hibernate.dialect">org.hibernate.dialect.H2Dialect</prop>
    <prop key="hibernate.max_fetch_depth">3</prop>
    <prop key="hibernate.jdbc.fetch_size">50</prop>
    <prop key="hibernate.jdbc.batch_size">10</prop>
    <prop key="hibernate.show_sql">true</prop>
</util:properties>
</beans>
```

In the previous configuration, several beans were declared in order to be able to support Hibernate's session factory. The main configurations are listed here:

- *The* dataSource *bean*: We declared the data source with an embedded database by using H2.

- *The* transactionManager *bean*: The Hibernate session factory requires a transaction manager for transactional data access. Spring provides a transaction manager specifically for Hibernate 4 (org.springframework.orm.hibernate4.HibernateTransactionManager). The bean was declared with the ID transactionManager assigned. By default, Spring will look up the bean with the name transactionManager within its ApplicationContext whenever transaction management is required. We discuss transactions in detail in Chapter 9. In addition, we declare the tag <tx:annotation-driven> to support the declaration of transaction demarcation requirements using annotations.

- *Component scan*: This tag should be familiar to you. We instruct Spring to scan the components under the package com.apress.prospring4.ch7.

- *Hibernate* SessionFactory *bean*: The sessionFactory bean is the most important part. Within the bean, several properties are provided. First we need to inject the data source bean into the session factory. Second, we instruct Hibernate to scan for the domain objects under the package com.apress.prospring4.ch7. Finally, the hibernateProperties property provides configuration details for Hibernate. There are many configuration parameters, and we define only a few important properties that should be provided for every application. Table 7-2 lists the main configuration parameters for the Hibernate session factory.

Table 7-2. *Main Hibernate Configurations*

Property	Description
hibernate.dialect	The database dialect for the queries that Hibernate should use. Hibernate supports the SQL dialects for many databases. Those dialects are subclasses of org.hibernate.dialect.Dialect. Major dialects include H2Dialect, Oracle10gDialect, PostgreSQLDialect, MySQLDialect, SQLServerDialect, and so on.
hibernate.max_fetch_depth	Declares the "depth" for outer joins when the mapping objects have associations with other mapped objects. This setting prevents Hibernate from fetching too much data with a lot of nested associations. A commonly used value is 3.
hibernate.jdbc.fetch_size	The number of records from the underlying JDBC ResultSet that Hibernate should use to retrieve the records from the database for each fetch. For example, a query was submitted to the database, and the ResultSet contains 500 records. If the fetch size is 50, Hibernate will need to fetch 10 times to get all the data.
hibernate.jdbc.batch_size	Instructs Hibernate on the number of update operations that should be grouped together into a batch. This is very useful for performing batch job operations in Hibernate. Obviously, when we are doing a batch job updating hundreds of thousands of records, we would like Hibernate to group the queries in batches, rather than submit the updates one by one.
hibernate.show_sql	Indicates whether Hibernate should output the SQL queries to the log file or console. You should turn this on in a development environment, which can greatly help in the testing and troubleshooting process.

For the full list of properties that Hibernate supports, please refer to Hibernate's reference manual on configuration (http://docs.jboss.org/hibernate/core/4.3/manual/en-US/html/ch03.html).

ORM Mapping Using Hibernate Annotations

Having the configuration in place, the next step is to model the Java POJO entity classes and their mapping to the underlying relational data structure.

There are two approaches to the mapping. The first one is to design the object model and then generate the DB scripts based on the object model. For example, for the session factory configuration, you can pass in the Hibernate property hibernate.hbm2ddl.auto to have Hibernate automatically export the schema DDL to the database. The second approach is to start with the data model and then model the POJOs with the desired mappings. We prefer the latter approach, because we can have more control of the data model, which is very useful in optimizing the performance of data access. Based on the data model, Figure 7-2 shows the corresponding OO model with a class diagram.

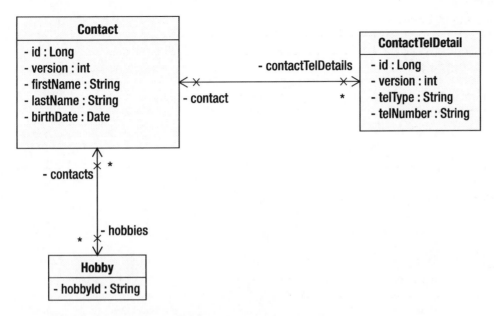

Figure 7-2. *Class diagram for the sample data model*

You can see there is a one-to-many relationship between Contact and ContactTelDetail, while there's a many-to-many relationship between the Contact and Hobby objects.

Simple Mappings

First let's start by mapping the simple attributes of the class. Listing 7-4 shows the Contact class with the mapping annotations.

Listing 7-4. The Contact Class

```
package com.apress.prospring4.ch7;

import static javax.persistence.GenerationType.IDENTITY;

import java.io.Serializable;
import java.util.Date;
import java.util.HashSet;
import java.util.Set;
import javax.persistence.Entity;
import javax.persistence.Table;
import javax.persistence.Id;
import javax.persistence.GeneratedValue;
import javax.persistence.Column;
import javax.persistence.Version;
import javax.persistence.Temporal;
import javax.persistence.TemporalType;
```

```java
@Entity
@Table(name = "contact")
public class Contact implements Serializable {
    private Long id;
    private int version;
    private String firstName;
    private String lastName;
    private Date birthDate;

    @Id
    @GeneratedValue(strategy = IDENTITY)
    @Column(name = "ID")
    public Long getId() {
        return this.id;
    }

    public void setId(Long id) {
        this.id = id;
    }

    @Version
    @Column(name = "VERSION")
    public int getVersion() {
        return this.version;
    }

    public void setVersion(int version) {
        this.version = version;
    }

    @Column(name = "FIRST_NAME")
    public String getFirstName() {
        return this.firstName;
    }

    public void setFirstName(String firstName) {
        this.firstName = firstName;
    }

    @Column(name = "LAST_NAME")
    public String getLastName() {
        return this.lastName;
    }

    public void setLastName(String lastName) {
        this.lastName = lastName;
    }
```

```
@Temporal(TemporalType.DATE)
@Column(name = "BIRTH_DATE")
public Date getBirthDate() {
    return this.birthDate;
}

public void setBirthDate(Date birthDate) {
    this.birthDate = birthDate;
}

public String toString() {
    return "Contact - Id: " + id + ", First name: " + firstName
        + ", Last name: " + lastName + ", Birthday: " + birthDate;
}
}
```

First, we annotate the type with @Entity, which means that this is a mapped entity class. The @Table annotation defines the table name in the database that this entity is being mapped to. For each mapped attribute, we annotate it with the @Column annotation, with the column names provided. You can skip the table and column names if the type and attribute names are exactly the same as the table and column names.

About the mappings, we would like to highlight a few points:

- For the birth date attribute, we annotate it with @Temporal, using the TemporalType.DATE value. This means we would like to map the data type from the Java date type (java.util. Date) to the SQL date type (java.sql.Date). This allows us to access the attribute birthDate in the Contact object by using java.util.Date as usual in our application.

- For the id attribute, we annotate it with @Id. This means it's the primary key of the object. Hibernate will use it as the unique identifier when managing the contact entity instances within its session. Additionally, the @GeneratedValue annotation tells Hibernate how the id value was generated. The IDENTITY strategy means that the id was generated by the backend during insert.

- For the version attribute, we annotate it with @Version. This instructs Hibernate that we would like to use an optimistic locking mechanism, using the version attribute as a control. Every time Hibernate updates a record, it compares the version of the entity instance to that of the record in the database. If both versions are the same, it means that no one updated the data before, and Hibernate will update the data and increment the version column. However, if the version is not the same, it means that someone has updated the record before, and Hibernate will throw a StaleObjectStateException exception, which Spring will translate to HibernateOptimisticLockingFailureException. In the example, we used an integer for version control. Instead of an integer, Hibernate also supports using a timestamp. However, using an integer for version control is recommended since Hibernate will always increment the version number by 1 after each update. When using a timestamp, Hibernate will update the latest timestamp after each update. A timestamp is slightly less safe, because two concurrent transactions may both load and update the same item in the same millisecond.

Another mapped object is ContactTelDetail, which is shown in Listing 7-5.

Listing 7-5. The ContactTelDetail Class

```java
package com.apress.prospring4.ch7;

import static javax.persistence.GenerationType.IDENTITY;

import java.io.Serializable;
import javax.persistence.Entity;
import javax.persistence.Table;
import javax.persistence.Id;
import javax.persistence.GeneratedValue;
import javax.persistence.Column;
import javax.persistence.Version;

@Entity
@Table(name = "contact_tel_detail")
public class ContactTelDetail implements Serializable {
    private Long id;
    private int version;
    private String telType;
    private String telNumber;

    public ContactTelDetail() {
    }

    public ContactTelDetail(String telType, String telNumber) {
        this.telType = telType;
        this.telNumber = telNumber;
    }

    @Id
    @GeneratedValue(strategy = IDENTITY)
    @Column(name = "ID")
    public Long getId() {
        return this.id;
    }

    public void setId(Long id) {
        this.id = id;
    }

    @Version
    @Column(name = "VERSION")
    public int getVersion() {
        return this.version;
    }

    public void setVersion(int version) {
        this.version = version;
    }
```

```
    @Column(name = "TEL_TYPE")
    public String getTelType() {
        return this.telType;
    }

    public void setTelType(String telType) {
        this.telType = telType;
    }

    @Column(name = "TEL_NUMBER")
    public String getTelNumber() {
        return this.telNumber;
    }

    public void setTelNumber(String telNumber) {
        this.telNumber = telNumber;
    }
}
```

Listing 7-6 shows the Hobby class.

Listing 7-6. The Hobby Class

```
package com.apress.prospring4.ch7;

import java.io.Serializable;
import javax.persistence.Entity;
import javax.persistence.Table;
import javax.persistence.Column;
import javax.persistence.Id;

@Entity
@Table(name = "hobby")
public class Hobby implements Serializable {
    private String hobbyId;

    @Id
    @Column(name = "HOBBY_ID")
    public String getHobbyId() {
        return this.hobbyId;
    }

    public void setHobbyId(String hobbyId) {
        this.hobbyId = hobbyId;
    }

    public String toString() {
        return "Hobby :" + getHobbyId();
    }
}
```

One-to-Many Mappings

Hibernate has the capability to model many kinds of associations. The most common associations are one-to-many and many-to-many. Each Contact will have zero or more telephone numbers, so it's a one-to-many association (in ORM terms, the one-to-many association is used to model both zero-to-many and one-to-many relationships within the data structure). Listing 7-7 shows the updated Contact class for mapping with the ContactTelDetail class.

Listing 7-7. One-to-Many Association

```
package com.apress.prospring4.ch7;

import static javax.persistence.GenerationType.IDENTITY;

import java.io.Serializable;
import java.util.Date;
import java.util.HashSet;
import java.util.Set;
import javax.persistence.Entity;
import javax.persistence.Table;
import javax.persistence.Id;
import javax.persistence.GeneratedValue;
import javax.persistence.Column;
import javax.persistence.Version;
import javax.persistence.Temporal;
import javax.persistence.TemporalType;
import javax.persistence.CascadeType;
import javax.persistence.OneToMany;

@Entity
@Table(name = "contact")
public class Contact implements Serializable {
    private Long id;
    private int version;
    private String firstName;
    private String lastName;
    private Date birthDate;
    private Set<ContactTelDetail> contactTelDetails = new HashSet<ContactTelDetail>();

    @Id
    @GeneratedValue(strategy = IDENTITY)
    @Column(name = "ID")
    public Long getId() {
        return this.id;
    }

    public void setId(Long id) {
        this.id = id;
    }

    @Version
    @Column(name = "VERSION")
```

```java
public int getVersion() {
    return this.version;
}

public void setVersion(int version) {
    this.version = version;
}

@Column(name = "FIRST_NAME")
public String getFirstName() {
    return this.firstName;
}

public void setFirstName(String firstName) {
    this.firstName = firstName;
}

@Column(name = "LAST_NAME")
public String getLastName() {
    return this.lastName;
}

public void setLastName(String lastName) {
    this.lastName = lastName;
}

@Temporal(TemporalType.DATE)
@Column(name = "BIRTH_DATE")
public Date getBirthDate() {
    return this.birthDate;
}

public void setBirthDate(Date birthDate) {
    this.birthDate = birthDate;
}

@OneToMany(mappedBy = "contact", cascade=CascadeType.ALL,
    orphanRemoval=true)
public Set<ContactTelDetail> getContactTelDetails() {
    return this.contactTelDetails;
}

public void setContactTelDetails(Set<ContactTelDetail> contactTelDetails) {
 this.contactTelDetails = contactTelDetails;
}

public void addContactTelDetail(ContactTelDetail contactTelDetail) {
    contactTelDetail.setContact(this);
    getContactTelDetails().add(contactTelDetail);
}
```

```java
    public void removeContactTelDetail(ContactTelDetail contactTelDetail) {
        getContactTelDetails().remove(contactTelDetail);
    }

    public String toString() {
        return "Contact - Id: " + id + ", First name: " + firstName
            + ", Last name: " + lastName + ", Birthday: " + birthDate;
    }
}
```

The getter method of the attribute contactTelDetails is annotated with @OneToMany, which indicates the one-to-many relationship with the ContactTelDetail class. Several attributes are passed to the annotation. The mappedBy attribute indicates the property in the ContactTelDetail class that provides the association (that is, linked up by the foreign-key definition in the CONTACT_TEL_DETAIL table). The cascade attribute means that the update operation should cascade to the child. The orphanRemoval attribute means that after the contact telephone details have been updated, those entries that no longer exist in the set should be deleted from the database. Listing 7-8 shows the updated code in the ContactTelDetail class for the association mapping.

Listing 7-8. One-to-Many Mapping in ContactTelDetail

```java
package com.apress.prospring4.ch7;

import static javax.persistence.GenerationType.IDENTITY;

import java.io.Serializable;
import javax.persistence.Entity;
import javax.persistence.Table;
import javax.persistence.Id;
import javax.persistence.GeneratedValue;
import javax.persistence.Column;
import javax.persistence.Version;
import javax.persistence.ManyToOne;
import javax.persistence.JoinColumn;

@Entity
@Table(name = "contact_tel_detail")
public class ContactTelDetail implements Serializable {
    private Long id;
    private int version;
    private String telType;
    private String telNumber;
    private Contact contact;

    public ContactTelDetail() {
    }

    public ContactTelDetail(String telType, String telNumber) {
        this.telType = telType;
        this.telNumber = telNumber;
    }
```

```java
@Id
@GeneratedValue(strategy = IDENTITY)
@Column(name = "ID")
public Long getId() {
    return this.id;
}

public void setId(Long id) {
    this.id = id;
}

@Version
@Column(name = "VERSION")
public int getVersion() {
    return this.version;
}

public void setVersion(int version) {
    this.version = version;
}

@Column(name = "TEL_TYPE")
public String getTelType() {
    return this.telType;
}

public void setTelType(String telType) {
    this.telType = telType;
}

@Column(name = "TEL_NUMBER")
public String getTelNumber() {
    return this.telNumber;
}

public void setTelNumber(String telNumber) {
    this.telNumber = telNumber;
}

@ManyToOne
@JoinColumn(name = "CONTACT_ID")
public Contact getContact() {
    return this.contact;
}

public void setContact(Contact contact) {
    this.contact = contact;
}
```

```
    public String toString() {
    return "Contact Tel Detail - Id: " + id + ", Contact id: "
            + getContact().getId() + ", Type: "
            + telType + ", Number: " + telNumber;
    }
}
```

We annotate the getter method of the contact attribute with @ManyToOne, which indicates it's the other side of the association from Contact. We also specify the @JoinColumn annotation for the underlying foreign-key column name. Finally, the toString() method is overridden to facilitate testing output the example code later.

Many-to-Many Mappings

Every contact has zero or more hobbies, and each hobby is also associated with zero or more contacts, which means it's a many-to-many mapping. A many-to-many mapping requires a join table, which is the CONTACT_HOBBY_DETAIL table in Figure 7-2. Listing 7-9 shows the updated code in the Contact class to model the relationship.

Listing 7-9. Many-to-Many Association

```
package com.apress.prospring4.ch7;

import static javax.persistence.GenerationType.IDENTITY;

import java.io.Serializable;
import java.util.Date;
import java.util.HashSet;
import java.util.Set;
import javax.persistence.Entity;
import javax.persistence.Table;
import javax.persistence.Id;
import javax.persistence.GeneratedValue;
import javax.persistence.Column;
import javax.persistence.Version;
import javax.persistence.Temporal;
import javax.persistence.TemporalType;
import javax.persistence.OneToMany;
import javax.persistence.ManyToMany;
import javax.persistence.JoinTable;
import javax.persistence.JoinColumn;
import javax.persistence.CascadeType;

@Entity
@Table(name = "contact")
public class Contact implements Serializable {
    private Long id;
    private int version;
    private String firstName;
    private String lastName;
    private Date birthDate;
    private Set<ContactTelDetail> contactTelDetails = new HashSet<ContactTelDetail>();
    private Set<Hobby> hobbies = new HashSet<Hobby>();
```

```java
@Id
@GeneratedValue(strategy = IDENTITY)
@Column(name = "ID")
public Long getId() {
    return this.id;
}

public void setId(Long id) {
    this.id = id;
}

@Version
@Column(name = "VERSION")
public int getVersion() {
    return this.version;
}

public void setVersion(int version) {
    this.version = version;
}

@Column(name = "FIRST_NAME")
public String getFirstName() {
    return this.firstName;
}

public void setFirstName(String firstName) {
    this.firstName = firstName;
}

@Column(name = "LAST_NAME")
public String getLastName() {
    return this.lastName;
}

public void setLastName(String lastName) {
    this.lastName = lastName;
}

@Temporal(TemporalType.DATE)
@Column(name = "BIRTH_DATE")
public Date getBirthDate() {
    return this.birthDate;
}

public void setBirthDate(Date birthDate) {
    this.birthDate = birthDate;
}
```

```
@OneToMany(mappedBy = "contact", cascade=CascadeType.ALL,
    orphanRemoval=true)
public Set<ContactTelDetail> getContactTelDetails() {
    return this.contactTelDetails;
}

public void setContactTelDetails(Set<ContactTelDetail> contactTelDetails) {
  this.contactTelDetails = contactTelDetails;
}

public void addContactTelDetail(ContactTelDetail contactTelDetail) {
    contactTelDetail.setContact(this);
    getContactTelDetails().add(contactTelDetail);
}

public void removeContactTelDetail(ContactTelDetail contactTelDetail) {
    getContactTelDetails().remove(contactTelDetail);
}

@ManyToMany
@JoinTable(name = "contact_hobby_detail",
    joinColumns = @JoinColumn(name = "CONTACT_ID"),
    inverseJoinColumns = @JoinColumn(name = "HOBBY_ID"))
public Set<Hobby> getHobbies() {
    return this.hobbies;
}

public void setHobbies(Set<Hobby> hobbies) {
    this.hobbies = hobbies;
}

public String toString() {
    return "Contact - Id: " + id + ", First name: " + firstName
        + ", Last name: " + lastName + ", Birthday: " + birthDate;
}
}
```

The getter method of the attribute hobbies in the Contact class is annotated with @ManyToMany. We also provide @JoinTable to indicate the underlying join table that Hibernate should look for. The name is the join table's name, the joinColumns defines the column that is the foreign key to the CONTACT table, and inverseJoinColumns defines the column that is the foreign key to the other side of the association (that is, the HOBBY table). Listing 7-10 shows the updated code in the Hobby class.

Listing 7-10. Many-to-Many Mapping in the Hobby Class

```
package com.apress.prospring4.ch7;

import java.io.Serializable;
import javax.persistence.Entity;
import javax.persistence.Table;
import javax.persistence.Column;
import javax.persistence.Id;
```

```java
import javax.persistence.ManyToMany;
import javax.persistence.JoinTable;
import javax.persistence.JoinColumn;
import java.util.Set;
import java.util.HashSet;

@Entity
@Table(name = "hobby")
public class Hobby implements Serializable {
    private String hobbyId;
    private Set<Contact> contacts = new HashSet<Contact>();

    @Id
    @Column(name = "HOBBY_ID")
    public String getHobbyId() {
        return this.hobbyId;
    }

    public void setHobbyId(String hobbyId) {
        this.hobbyId = hobbyId;
    }

    @ManyToMany
    @JoinTable(name = "contact_hobby_detail",
        joinColumns = @JoinColumn(name = "HOBBY_ID"),
        inverseJoinColumns = @JoinColumn(name = "CONTACT_ID"))
    public Set<Contact> getContacts() {
        return this.contacts;
    }

    public void setContacts(Set<Contact> contacts) {
        this.contacts = contacts;
    }

    @Override
    public String toString() {
        return "Hobby :" + getHobbyId();
    }
}
```

The mapping is more or less the same as Listing 7-9, but the joinColumns and inverseJoinColumns attributes are reversed to reflect the association.

The Hibernate Session Interface

In Hibernate, when interacting with the database, the main interface you need to deal with is the Session interface, which is obtained from SessionFactory.

Listing 7-11 shows the ContactDaoImpl class used in the samples in this chapter and has the configured Hibernate SessionFactory injected into the class.

Listing 7-11. Injecting Hibernate SessionFactory

```
package com.apress.prospring4.ch7;

import org.springframework.transaction.annotation.Transactional;
import org.springframework.stereotype.Repository;
import org.apache.commons.logging.Log;
import org.apache.commons.logging.LogFactory;
import org.hibernate.SessionFactory;
import javax.annotation.Resource;

@Transactional
@Repository("contactDao")
public class ContactDaoImpl implements ContactDao {
    private static final Log LOG = LogFactory.getLog(ContactDaoImpl.class);

    private SessionFactory sessionFactory;

    public SessionFactory getSessionFactory() {
        return sessionFactory;
    }

    ...

    @Resource(name="sessionFactory")
    public void setSessionFactory(SessionFactory sessionFactory) {
        this.sessionFactory = sessionFactory;
    }
}
```

As usual, we declare the DAO class as a Spring bean by using the @Repository annotation. The @Transactional annotation defines the transaction requirements that we discuss further in Chapter 9. The sessionFactory attribute is injected by using the @Resource annotation.

Database Operations with Hibernate

Listing 7-12 shows the ContactDao interface, which outlines the contract of contact data access services we are going to provide for contacts.

Listing 7-12. The ContactDao Interface

```
package com.apress.prospring4.ch7;

import java.util.List;

public interface ContactDao {
    List<Contact> findAll();
    List<Contact> findAllWithDetail();
    Contact findById(Long id);
    Contact save(Contact contact);
    void delete(Contact contact);
}
```

The interface is very simple; it has just three finder methods, one save method, and one delete method. The save() method will perform both the insert and update operations.

Querying Data by Using Hibernate Query Language

Hibernate, together with other ORM tools such as JDO and JPA, is engineered around the object model. So, after the mappings are defined, we don't need to construct SQL to interact with the database. Instead, for Hibernate, we use the Hibernate Query Language (HQL) to define our queries. When interacting with the database, Hibernate will translate the queries into SQL statements on our behalf.

When coding HQL queries, the syntax is quite like SQL. However, you need to think on the object side rather than database side. We go through several examples in the following sections.

Simple Query with Lazy Fetching

Let's begin by implementing the findAll() method, which simply retrieves all the contacts from the database. Listing 7-13 shows the updated code for this functionality.

Listing 7-13. Implementing the findAll Method

```
package com.apress.prospring4.ch7;

import org.springframework.transaction.annotation.Transactional;
import org.springframework.stereotype.Repository;
import org.apache.commons.logging.Log;
import org.apache.commons.logging.LogFactory;
import org.hibernate.SessionFactory;
import javax.annotation.Resource;
import java.util.List;

@Transactional
@Repository("contactDao")
public class ContactDaoImpl implements ContactDao {
    private static final Log LOG = LogFactory.getLog(ContactDaoImpl.class);

    private SessionFactory sessionFactory;

    @Override
    @Transactional(readOnly=true)
    public List<Contact> findAll() {
        return sessionFactory.getCurrentSession().createQuery("from Contact c").list();
    }

    @Override
    public List<Contact> findAllWithDetail() {
        return null;
    }

    @Override
    public Contact findById(Long id) {
        return null;
    }
```

```
    @Override
    public Contact save(Contact contact) {
        return null;
    }

    @Override
    public void delete(Contact contact) {

    }

    public SessionFactory getSessionFactory() {
        return sessionFactory;
    }

    @Resource(name="sessionFactory")
    public void setSessionFactory(SessionFactory sessionFactory) {
        this.sessionFactory = sessionFactory;
    }
}
```

The method SessionFactory.getCurrentSession() gets hold of Hibernate's Session interface. Then, the Session.createQuery() method is called, passing in the HQL statement. The statement from Contact c simply retrieves all contacts from the database. An alternative syntax for the statement is "select c from Contact c". The @Transactional(readOnly=true) annotation means we want the transaction to be set as read-only. Setting that attribute for read only methods will result in better performance.

Listing 7-14 shows a simple testing program for ContactDaoImpl.

Listing 7-14. Testing the ContactDaoImpl Class

```
package com.apress.prospring4.ch7;

import java.util.List;

import org.springframework.context.support.GenericXmlApplicationContext;

public class SpringHibernateSample {
    public static void main(String[] args) {
        GenericXmlApplicationContext ctx = new GenericXmlApplicationContext();
        ctx.load("classpath:META-INF/spring/app-context-annotation.xml");
        ctx.refresh();

        ContactDao contactDao = ctx.getBean("contactDao", ContactDao.class);

        listContacts(contactDao.findAll());
    }

    private static void listContacts(List<Contact> contacts) {
        System.out.println("");
        System.out.println("Listing contacts without details:");
```

```
        for (Contact contact: contacts) {
            System.out.println(contact);
            System.out.println();
        }
    }
}
```

Running the previous class yields the following output:

```
Listing contacts without details:
Contact - Id: 1, First name: Chris, Last name: Schaefer, Birthday: 1981-05-03

Contact - Id: 2, First name: Scott, Last name: Tiger, Birthday: 1990-11-02

Contact - Id: 3, First name: John, Last name: Smith, Birthday: 1964-02-28
```

Although the contact records were retrieved, what about the telephone and hobby details? Let's modify the testing class to print the details information. Listing 7-15 shows the updated class to do so.

Listing 7-15. Testing the ContactDaoImpl Class

```
package com.apress.prospring4.ch7;

import java.util.List;

import org.springframework.context.support.GenericXmlApplicationContext;

public class SpringHibernateSample {
    public static void main(String[] args) {
        GenericXmlApplicationContext ctx = new GenericXmlApplicationContext();
        ctx.load("classpath:META-INF/spring/app-context-annotation.xml");
        ctx.refresh();

        ContactDao contactDao = ctx.getBean("contactDao", ContactDao.class);

        listContactsWithDetail(contactDao.findAll());
    }

    private static void listContactsWithDetail(List<Contact> contacts) {
        System.out.println("");
        System.out.println("Listing contacts with details:");

        for (Contact contact: contacts) {
            System.out.println(contact);

            if (contact.getContactTelDetails() != null) {
                for (ContactTelDetail contactTelDetail:
                        contact.getContactTelDetails()) {
                    System.out.println(contactTelDetail);
                }
            }
```

```
            if (contact.getHobbies() != null) {
                for (Hobby hobby: contact.getHobbies()) {
                    System.out.println(hobby);
                }
            }

            System.out.println();
        }
    }
}
```

If you run the program again, you will see the following exception:

```
Listing contacts with details:
Contact - Id: 1, First name: Chris, Last name: Schaefer, Birthday: 1981-05-03
Exception in thread "main" org.hibernate.LazyInitializationException:
...
```

You will see Hibernate throw the LazyInitializationException when you try to access the associations. It's because, by default, Hibernate will fetch the associations "lazily," which means that Hibernate will not join the association tables (that is, CONTACT_TEL_DETAIL) for records. The rationale behind this is for performance, since as you can imagine, if a query is retrieving thousands of records and all the associations are retrieved, the massive amount of data transfer will degrade performance.

Query with Associations Fetching

To have Hibernate fetch the data from associations, there are two options. First, you can define the association with the fetch mode EAGER, for example: @ManyToMany(fetch=FetchType.EAGER). This tells Hibernate to fetch the associated records in every query. However, as discussed, this will impact data retrieval performance.

The other option is to force Hibernate to fetch the associated records in the query when required. If you use the Criteria query, you can call the function Criteria.setFetchMode() to instruct Hibernate to eagerly fetch the association. When using NamedQuery, you can use the "fetch" operator to instruct Hibernate to fetch the association eagerly.

Let's take a look at the implementation of the findAllWithDetail() method, which will retrieve all contact information together with their telephone details and hobbies. In this example, we will use the NamedQuery approach. NamedQuery can be externalized into an XML file or declared using an annotation on the entity class. Listing 7-16 shows the revised Contact domain object with the named query defined using annotations.

Listing 7-16. Using NamedQuery

```
package com.apress.prospring4.ch7;

import static javax.persistence.GenerationType.IDENTITY;

import java.io.Serializable;
import java.util.Date;
import java.util.HashSet;
import java.util.Set;
import javax.persistence.Entity;
import javax.persistence.Table;
import javax.persistence.Id;
```

```java
import javax.persistence.GeneratedValue;
import javax.persistence.Column;
import javax.persistence.Version;
import javax.persistence.Temporal;
import javax.persistence.TemporalType;
import javax.persistence.OneToMany;
import javax.persistence.ManyToMany;
import javax.persistence.JoinTable;
import javax.persistence.JoinColumn;
import javax.persistence.CascadeType;
import javax.persistence.NamedQueries;
import javax.persistence.NamedQuery;

@Entity
@Table(name = "contact")
@NamedQueries({
@NamedQuery(name="Contact.findAllWithDetail",
query="select distinct c from Contact c left join fetch c.contactTelDetails t left join fetch
c.hobbies h")
})
public class Contact implements Serializable {
    private Long id;
    private int version;
    private String firstName;
    private String lastName;
    private Date birthDate;
    private Set<ContactTelDetail> contactTelDetails = new HashSet<ContactTelDetail>();
    private Set<Hobby> hobbies = new HashSet<Hobby>();

    @Id
    @GeneratedValue(strategy = IDENTITY)
    @Column(name = "ID")
    public Long getId() {
        return this.id;
    }

    public void setId(Long id) {
        this.id = id;
    }

    @Version
    @Column(name = "VERSION")
    public int getVersion() {
        return this.version;
    }

    public void setVersion(int version) {
        this.version = version;
    }
```

```java
@Column(name = "FIRST_NAME")
public String getFirstName() {
    return this.firstName;
}

public void setFirstName(String firstName) {
    this.firstName = firstName;
}

@Column(name = "LAST_NAME")
public String getLastName() {
    return this.lastName;
}

public void setLastName(String lastName) {
    this.lastName = lastName;
}

@Temporal(TemporalType.DATE)
@Column(name = "BIRTH_DATE")
public Date getBirthDate() {
    return this.birthDate;
}

public void setBirthDate(Date birthDate) {
    this.birthDate = birthDate;
}

@OneToMany(mappedBy = "contact", cascade=CascadeType.ALL,
    orphanRemoval=true)
public Set<ContactTelDetail> getContactTelDetails() {
    return this.contactTelDetails;
}

public void setContactTelDetails(Set<ContactTelDetail> contactTelDetails) {
 this.contactTelDetails = contactTelDetails;
}

public void addContactTelDetail(ContactTelDetail contactTelDetail) {
    contactTelDetail.setContact(this);
    getContactTelDetails().add(contactTelDetail);
}

public void removeContactTelDetail(ContactTelDetail contactTelDetail) {
    getContactTelDetails().remove(contactTelDetail);
}

@ManyToMany
@JoinTable(name = "contact_hobby_detail",
    joinColumns = @JoinColumn(name = "CONTACT_ID"),
    inverseJoinColumns = @JoinColumn(name = "HOBBY_ID"))
```

```
public Set<Hobby> getHobbies() {
    return this.hobbies;
}

public void setHobbies(Set<Hobby> hobbies) {
    this.hobbies = hobbies;
}

@Override
public String toString() {
    return "Contact - Id: " + id + ", First name: " + firstName
        + ", Last name: " + lastName + ", Birthday: " + birthDate;
}
}
```

A NamedQuery called Contact.findAllWithDetail is defined. Then we define the query in HQL. Pay attention to the left join fetch clause, which instructs Hibernate to fetch the association eagerly. You also need to use select distinct; otherwise, Hibernate will return duplicate objects (two contact objects will be returned if a single contact has two telephone details).

Listing 7-17 shows the implementation of the findAllWithDetail() method.

Listing 7-17. Implementing the findAllWithDetail Method

```
package com.apress.prospring4.ch7;

import org.springframework.transaction.annotation.Transactional;
import org.springframework.stereotype.Repository;
import org.apache.commons.logging.Log;
import org.apache.commons.logging.LogFactory;
import org.hibernate.SessionFactory;
import javax.annotation.Resource;
import java.util.List;

@Transactional
@Repository("contactDao")
public class ContactDaoImpl implements ContactDao {
    private static final Log LOG = LogFactory.getLog(ContactDaoImpl.class);

    private SessionFactory sessionFactory;

    @Override
    @Transactional(readOnly=true)
    public List<Contact> findAll() {
        return sessionFactory.getCurrentSession().createQuery("from Contact c").list();
    }

    @Override
    @Transactional(readOnly=true)
    public List<Contact> findAllWithDetail() {
        return sessionFactory.getCurrentSession().
            getNamedQuery("Contact.findAllWithDetail").list();
    }
```

```
    @Override
    public Contact findById(Long id) {
        return null;
    }

    @Override
    public Contact save(Contact contact) {
        return null;
    }

    @Override
    public void delete(Contact contact) {

    }

    public SessionFactory getSessionFactory() {
        return sessionFactory;
    }

    @Resource(name="sessionFactory")
    public void setSessionFactory(SessionFactory sessionFactory) {
        this.sessionFactory = sessionFactory;
    }
}
```

This time we use the Session.getNamedQuery() method, passing in the name of the NamedQuery. Modifying the testing program (SpringHibernateSample) to call ContactDao.findAllWithDetail() will yield the following output:

```
Listing contacts with details:
Contact - Id: 1, First name: Chris, Last name: Schaefer, Birthday: 1981-05-03
Contact Tel Detail - Id: 1, Contact id: 1, Type: Mobile, Number: 1234567890
Contact Tel Detail - Id: 2, Contact id: 1, Type: Home, Number: 1234567890
Hobby :Movies
Hobby :Swimming

Contact - Id: 3, First name: John, Last name: Smith, Birthday: 1964-02-28

Contact - Id: 2, First name: Scott, Last name: Tiger, Birthday: 1990-11-02
Contact Tel Detail - Id: 3, Contact id: 2, Type: Home, Number: 1234567890
Hobby :Swimming
```

Now all the contacts with details were retrieved correctly. Let's see another example with NamedQuery with parameters. This time, we will implement the findById() method and would like to fetch the associations as well. Listing 7-18 shows the Contact class with the new named query added.

Listing 7-18. Using NamedQuery with Parameters

```java
package com.apress.prospring4.ch7;

import static javax.persistence.GenerationType.IDENTITY;

import java.io.Serializable;
import java.util.Date;
import java.util.HashSet;
import java.util.Set;
import javax.persistence.Entity;
import javax.persistence.Table;
import javax.persistence.Id;
import javax.persistence.GeneratedValue;
import javax.persistence.Column;
import javax.persistence.Version;
import javax.persistence.Temporal;
import javax.persistence.TemporalType;
import javax.persistence.OneToMany;
import javax.persistence.ManyToMany;
import javax.persistence.JoinTable;
import javax.persistence.JoinColumn;
import javax.persistence.CascadeType;
import javax.persistence.NamedQueries;
import javax.persistence.NamedQuery;

@Entity
@Table(name = "contact")
@NamedQueries({
@NamedQuery(name="Contact.findById",
query="select distinct c from Contact c left join fetch c.contactTelDetails t left join fetch
c.hobbies h where c.id = :id"),
@NamedQuery(name="Contact.findAllWithDetail",
query="select distinct c from Contact c left join fetch c.contactTelDetails t left join fetch
c.hobbies h")
})
public class Contact implements Serializable {
    private Long id;
    private int version;
    private String firstName;
    private String lastName;
    private Date birthDate;
    private Set<ContactTelDetail> contactTelDetails = new HashSet<ContactTelDetail>();
    private Set<Hobby> hobbies = new HashSet<Hobby>();

    @Id
    @GeneratedValue(strategy = IDENTITY)
    @Column(name = "ID")
    public Long getId() {
        return this.id;
    }
```

```java
    public void setId(Long id) {
        this.id = id;
    }

    @Version
    @Column(name = "VERSION")
    public int getVersion() {
        return this.version;
    }

    public void setVersion(int version) {
        this.version = version;
    }

    @Column(name = "FIRST_NAME")
    public String getFirstName() {
        return this.firstName;
    }

    public void setFirstName(String firstName) {
        this.firstName = firstName;
    }

    @Column(name = "LAST_NAME")
    public String getLastName() {
        return this.lastName;
    }

    public void setLastName(String lastName) {
        this.lastName = lastName;
    }

    @Temporal(TemporalType.DATE)
    @Column(name = "BIRTH_DATE")
    public Date getBirthDate() {
        return this.birthDate;
    }

    public void setBirthDate(Date birthDate) {
        this.birthDate = birthDate;
    }

    @OneToMany(mappedBy = "contact", cascade=CascadeType.ALL,
        orphanRemoval=true)
    public Set<ContactTelDetail> getContactTelDetails() {
        return this.contactTelDetails;
    }

    public void setContactTelDetails(Set<ContactTelDetail> contactTelDetails) {
     this.contactTelDetails = contactTelDetails;
    }
```

```java
    public void addContactTelDetail(ContactTelDetail contactTelDetail) {
        contactTelDetail.setContact(this);
        getContactTelDetails().add(contactTelDetail);
    }

    public void removeContactTelDetail(ContactTelDetail contactTelDetail) {
        getContactTelDetails().remove(contactTelDetail);
    }

    @ManyToMany
    @JoinTable(name = "contact_hobby_detail",
        joinColumns = @JoinColumn(name = "CONTACT_ID"),
        inverseJoinColumns = @JoinColumn(name = "HOBBY_ID"))
    public Set<Hobby> getHobbies() {
        return this.hobbies;
    }

    public void setHobbies(Set<Hobby> hobbies) {
        this.hobbies = hobbies;
    }

    @Override
    public String toString() {
        return "Contact - Id: " + id + ", First name: " + firstName
            + ", Last name: " + lastName + ", Birthday: " + birthDate;
    }
}
```

From the named query with the name Contact.findById, we declare a named parameter :id. Listing 7-19 shows the implementation of the findById() in ContactDaoImpl.

Listing 7-19. Implementing the findById Method

```java
package com.apress.prospring4.ch7;

import org.springframework.transaction.annotation.Transactional;
import org.springframework.stereotype.Repository;
import org.apache.commons.logging.Log;
import org.apache.commons.logging.LogFactory;
import org.hibernate.SessionFactory;
import javax.annotation.Resource;
import java.util.List;

@Transactional
@Repository("contactDao")
public class ContactDaoImpl implements ContactDao {
    private static final Log LOG = LogFactory.getLog(ContactDaoImpl.class);

    private SessionFactory sessionFactory;
```

```java
    @Override
    @Transactional(readOnly=true)
    public List<Contact> findAll() {
        return sessionFactory.getCurrentSession().createQuery("from Contact c").list();
    }

    @Override
    @Transactional(readOnly=true)
    public List<Contact> findAllWithDetail() {
        return sessionFactory.getCurrentSession().
            getNamedQuery("Contact.findAllWithDetail").list();
    }

    @Override
    @Transactional(readOnly=true)
    public Contact findById(Long id) {
        return (Contact) sessionFactory.getCurrentSession().
            getNamedQuery("Contact.findById").
            setParameter("id", id).uniqueResult();
    }

    @Override
    public Contact save(Contact contact) {
        return null;
    }

    @Override
    public void delete(Contact contact) {

    }

    public SessionFactory getSessionFactory() {
        return sessionFactory;
    }

    @Resource(name="sessionFactory")
    public void setSessionFactory(SessionFactory sessionFactory) {
        this.sessionFactory = sessionFactory;
    }
}
```

In this listing, we use the same Session.getNameQuery() method. But then we also call the setParameter() method, passing in the named parameter with its value. For multiple parameters, you can use the setParameterList() or setParameters() method of the Query interface.

There are also some more-advanced query methods, such as native query and criteria query, which we discuss in the next chapter when we talk about JPA.

To test the method, Listing 7-20 shows the modified SpringHibernateSample class.

Listing 7-20. Testing the findById Method

```
package com.apress.prospring4.ch7;

import java.util.List;

import org.springframework.context.support.GenericXmlApplicationContext;

public class SpringHibernateSample {
    public static void main(String[] args) {
        GenericXmlApplicationContext ctx = new GenericXmlApplicationContext();
        ctx.load("classpath:META-INF/spring/app-context-annotation.xml");
        ctx.refresh();

        ContactDao contactDao = ctx.getBean("contactDao", ContactDao.class);

        Contact contact = contactDao.findById(1l);
        System.out.println("");
        System.out.println("Contact with id 1:" + contact);
        System.out.println("");
    }
}
```

Running the program produces the following output (other output was omitted):

```
Contact with id 1:Contact - Id: 1, First name: Chris, Last name: Schaefer, Birthday: 1981-05-03
```

Inserting Data

Inserting data in Hibernate is very simple. One other fancy thing is retrieving the database-generated primary key. In the previous chapter on JDBC, we needed to explicitly declare that we wanted to retrieve the generated key, pass in the KeyHolder, and get the key back from it after executing the insert statement. With Hibernate, all those actions are not required. Hibernate will retrieve the generated key and populate the domain object after insert. Listing 7-21 shows the implementation of the save() method.

Listing 7-21. Implementing the save Method

```
package com.apress.prospring4.ch7;

import org.springframework.transaction.annotation.Transactional;
import org.springframework.stereotype.Repository;
import org.apache.commons.logging.Log;
import org.apache.commons.logging.LogFactory;
import org.hibernate.SessionFactory;
import javax.annotation.Resource;
import java.util.List;

@Transactional
@Repository("contactDao")
```

```java
public class ContactDaoImpl implements ContactDao {
    private static final Log LOG = LogFactory.getLog(ContactDaoImpl.class);

    private SessionFactory sessionFactory;

    @Override
    @Transactional(readOnly=true)
    public List<Contact> findAll() {
        return sessionFactory.getCurrentSession().createQuery("from Contact c").list();
    }

    @Override
    @Transactional(readOnly=true)
    public List<Contact> findAllWithDetail() {
        return sessionFactory.getCurrentSession().
            getNamedQuery("Contact.findAllWithDetail").list();
    }

    @Override
    @Transactional(readOnly=true)
    public Contact findById(Long id) {
        return (Contact) sessionFactory.getCurrentSession().
            getNamedQuery("Contact.findById").
            setParameter("id", id).uniqueResult();
    }

    @Override
    public Contact save(Contact contact) {
        sessionFactory.getCurrentSession().saveOrUpdate(contact);
        LOG.info("Contact saved with id: " + contact.getId());
        return contact;
    }

    @Override
    public void delete(Contact contact) {

    }

    public SessionFactory getSessionFactory() {
        return sessionFactory;
    }

    @Resource(name="sessionFactory")
    public void setSessionFactory(SessionFactory sessionFactory) {
        this.sessionFactory = sessionFactory;
    }
}
```

We just need to invoke the Session.saveOrUpdate() method, which can be used for both insert and update operations. We also log the ID of the saved contact object that will be populated by Hibernate after the object is persisted. Listing 7-22 shows the code for inserting a new contact record in the SpringHibernateSample class.

Listing 7-22. Testing Insert Operation

```java
package com.apress.prospring4.ch7;

import java.util.List;
import java.util.Date;

import org.springframework.context.support.GenericXmlApplicationContext;

public class SpringHibernateSample {
    public static void main(String[] args) {
        GenericXmlApplicationContext ctx = new GenericXmlApplicationContext();
        ctx.load("classpath:META-INF/spring/app-context-annotation.xml");
        ctx.refresh();

        ContactDao contactDao = ctx.getBean("contactDao", ContactDao.class);

        Contact contact = new Contact();
        contact.setFirstName("Michael");
        contact.setLastName("Jackson");
        contact.setBirthDate(new Date());

        ContactTelDetail contactTelDetail =
            new ContactTelDetail("Home", "1111111111");

        contact.addContactTelDetail(contactTelDetail);

        contactTelDetail = new ContactTelDetail("Mobile", "2222222222");

        contact.addContactTelDetail(contactTelDetail);

        contactDao.save(contact);

        listContactsWithDetail(contactDao.findAllWithDetail());
    }

    private static void listContactsWithDetail(List<Contact> contacts) {
        System.out.println("");
        System.out.println("Listing contacts with details:");

        for (Contact contact: contacts) {
            System.out.println(contact);

            if (contact.getContactTelDetails() != null) {
                for (ContactTelDetail contactTelDetail:
                        contact.getContactTelDetails()) {
                    System.out.println(contactTelDetail);
                }
            }
```

```
            if (contact.getHobbies() != null) {
                for (Hobby hobby: contact.getHobbies()) {
                    System.out.println(hobby);
                }
            }

            System.out.println();
        }
    }
}
```

As shown in Listing 7-22, we create a new contact, add two telephone details, and save the object. Afterward, we list all the contacts again. Running the program yields the following output:

```
Hibernate: insert into contact_tel_detail (ID, CONTACT_ID, TEL_NUMBER, TEL_TYPE, VERSION) values
(null, ?, ?, ?, ?)
18:04:00,240  INFO com.apress.prospring4.ch7.ContactDaoImpl:  38 - Contact saved with id: 4

Listing contacts with details:
Contact - Id: 1, First name: Chris, Last name: Schaefer, Birthday: 1981-05-03
Contact Tel Detail - Id: 1, Contact id: 1, Type: Mobile, Number: 1234567890
Contact Tel Detail - Id: 2, Contact id: 1, Type: Home, Number: 1234567890
Hobby :Movies
Hobby :Swimming

Contact - Id: 4, First name: Michael, Last name: Jackson, Birthday: 2013-07-25
Contact Tel Detail - Id: 4, Contact id: 4, Type: Mobile, Number: 2222222222
Contact Tel Detail - Id: 5, Contact id: 4, Type: Home, Number: 1111111111

Contact - Id: 3, First name: John, Last name: Smith, Birthday: 1964-02-28

Contact - Id: 2, First name: Scott, Last name: Tiger, Birthday: 1990-11-02
Contact Tel Detail - Id: 3, Contact id: 2, Type: Home, Number: 1234567890
Hobby :Swimming
```

From the INFO log record, you can see that the id of the newly saved contact was populated correctly. Hibernate will also show all the SQL statements being executed against the database so you know what is happening behind the scenes.

Updating Data

Updating a contact is as easy as inserting data. Suppose for the contact with an ID of 1, we want to update its first name and remove the home telephone record. To test the update operation, Listing 7-23 shows the required modifications to the SpringHibernateSample class.

Listing 7-23. Testing Update Operation

```
package com.apress.prospring4.ch7;

import java.util.List;
import java.util.Date;
import java.util.Set;
```

```java
import org.springframework.context.support.GenericXmlApplicationContext;

public class SpringHibernateSample {
    public static void main(String[] args) {
        GenericXmlApplicationContext ctx = new GenericXmlApplicationContext();
        ctx.load("classpath:META-INF/spring/app-context-annotation.xml");
        ctx.refresh();

        ContactDao contactDao = ctx.getBean("contactDao", ContactDao.class);

        Contact contact = contactDao.findById(1l);
        contact.setFirstName("Kim Fung");

        Set<ContactTelDetail> contactTels = contact.getContactTelDetails();

        ContactTelDetail toDeleteContactTel = null;

        for (ContactTelDetail contactTel: contactTels) {
            if (contactTel.getTelType().equals("Home")) {
                toDeleteContactTel = contactTel;
            }
        }

        contact.removeContactTelDetail(toDeleteContactTel);

        contactDao.save(contact);

        listContactsWithDetail(contactDao.findAllWithDetail());
    }

    private static void listContactsWithDetail(List<Contact> contacts) {
        System.out.println("");
        System.out.println("Listing contacts with details:");

        for (Contact contact: contacts) {
            System.out.println(contact);

            if (contact.getContactTelDetails() != null) {
                for (ContactTelDetail contactTelDetail:
                        contact.getContactTelDetails()) {
                    System.out.println(contactTelDetail);
                }
            }

            if (contact.getHobbies() != null) {
                for (Hobby hobby: contact.getHobbies()) {
                    System.out.println(hobby);
                }
            }

            System.out.println();
        }
    }
}
```

As shown in the previous listing, we first retrieve the record with an ID of 1. Afterward, the first name is changed. We then loop through the telephone objects, retrieve the one with type "Home", and remove it from the contact's telephone detail property. Finally, we call the ContactDao.save() method again. When you run the program, you will see the following output:

```
Listing contacts with details:
Contact - Id: 1, First name: Kim Fung, Last name: Schaefer, Birthday: 1981-05-03
Contact Tel Detail - Id: 1, Contact id: 1, Type: Mobile, Number: 1234567890
Hobby :Movies
Hobby :Swimming

Contact - Id: 3, First name: John, Last name: Smith, Birthday: 1964-02-28

Contact - Id: 2, First name: Scott, Last name: Tiger, Birthday: 1990-11-02
Contact Tel Detail - Id: 3, Contact id: 2, Type: Home, Number: 1234567890
Hobby :Swimming
```

You will see the first name is updated, and the home telephone is removed. The telephone can be removed because of the orphanRemoval=true attribute we pass into the one-to-many association, which instructs Hibernate to remove all orphan records that exist in the database but are no longer found in the object when persisted.

Deleting Data

Deleting data is simple as well. Just call the Session.delete() method and pass in the contact object. Listing 7-24 shows the code for deletion.

Listing 7-24. Implementing the delete Method

```java
package com.apress.prospring4.ch7;

import org.springframework.transaction.annotation.Transactional;
import org.springframework.stereotype.Repository;
import org.apache.commons.logging.Log;
import org.apache.commons.logging.LogFactory;
import org.hibernate.SessionFactory;
import javax.annotation.Resource;
import java.util.List;

@Transactional
@Repository("contactDao")
public class ContactDaoImpl implements ContactDao {
    private static final Log LOG = LogFactory.getLog(ContactDaoImpl.class);

    private SessionFactory sessionFactory;

    @Override
    @Transactional(readOnly=true)
    public List<Contact> findAll() {
        return sessionFactory.getCurrentSession().createQuery("from Contact c").list();
    }
```

```
    @Override
    @Transactional(readOnly=true)
    public List<Contact> findAllWithDetail() {
        return sessionFactory.getCurrentSession().
            getNamedQuery("Contact.findAllWithDetail").list();
    }

    @Override
    @Transactional(readOnly=true)
    public Contact findById(Long id) {
        return (Contact) sessionFactory.getCurrentSession().
            getNamedQuery("Contact.findById").
            setParameter("id", id).uniqueResult();
    }

    @Override
    public Contact save(Contact contact) {
        sessionFactory.getCurrentSession().saveOrUpdate(contact);
        LOG.info("Contact saved with id: " + contact.getId());
        return contact;
    }

    @Override
    public void delete(Contact contact) {
        sessionFactory.getCurrentSession().delete(contact);
        LOG.info("Contact deleted with id: " + contact.getId());
    }

    public SessionFactory getSessionFactory() {
        return sessionFactory;
    }

    @Resource(name="sessionFactory")
    public void setSessionFactory(SessionFactory sessionFactory) {
        this.sessionFactory = sessionFactory;
    }
}
```

The delete operation will delete the contact record, together with all its associated information, including telephone details and hobbies, as we defined cascade=CascadeType.ALL in the mapping. Listing 7-25 shows the code for testing the delete method in the SpringHibernateSample class.

Listing 7-25. Testing Delete Operation

```
package com.apress.prospring4.ch7;

import java.util.List;
import java.util.Date;
import java.util.Set;

import org.springframework.context.support.GenericXmlApplicationContext;
```

341

```java
public class SpringHibernateSample {
    public static void main(String[] args) {
        GenericXmlApplicationContext ctx = new GenericXmlApplicationContext();
        ctx.load("classpath:META-INF/spring/app-context-annotation.xml");
        ctx.refresh();

        ContactDao contactDao = ctx.getBean("contactDao", ContactDao.class);

        Contact contact = contactDao.findById(1l);

        contactDao.delete(contact);

        listContactsWithDetail(contactDao.findAllWithDetail());
    }

    private static void listContactsWithDetail(List<Contact> contacts) {
        System.out.println("");
        System.out.println("Listing contacts with details:");

        for (Contact contact: contacts) {
            System.out.println(contact);

            if (contact.getContactTelDetails() != null) {
                for (ContactTelDetail contactTelDetail:
                        contact.getContactTelDetails()) {
                    System.out.println(contactTelDetail);
                }
            }

            if (contact.getHobbies() != null) {
                for (Hobby hobby: contact.getHobbies()) {
                    System.out.println(hobby);
                }
            }

            System.out.println();
        }
    }
}
```

The previous listing retrieves the contact with an ID of 1 and then calls the delete method to delete the contact information. Running the program will produce the following output:

```
Listing contacts with details:
Contact - Id: 3, First name: John, Last name: Smith, Birthday: 1964-02-28
Contact - Id: 2, First name: Scott, Last name: Tiger, Birthday: 1990-11-02
Contact Tel Detail - Id: 3, Contact id: 2, Type: Home, Number: 1234567890
Hobby :Swimming
```

You can see that the contact with an ID of 1 was deleted.

Considerations When Using Hibernate

As shown in the examples of this chapter, once all the object-to-relational mapping, associations, and queries are properly defined, Hibernate can provide an environment for you to focus on programming with the object model, rather than composing SQL statements for each operation. In the past few years, Hibernate has been evolving quickly and has been widely adopted by Java developers as the data access layer library, both in the open source community and in enterprises.

However, there are some points you need to bear in mind. First, because you don't have control over the generated SQL, you should be very careful when defining the mappings, especially the associations and their fetching strategy. Then observe the SQL statements generated by Hibernate to verify that all perform as you expect.

Understanding the internal mechanism of how Hibernate manages its session is also very important, especially in batch job operations. Hibernate will keep the managed objects in session and will flush and clear them regularly. Poorly designed data access logic may cause Hibernate to flush the session too frequently and greatly impact the performance. If you want absolute control over the query, you can use a native query, which we discuss in next chapter.

Finally, the settings (batch size, fetch size, and so forth) also play an important role in tuning Hibernate's performance. You should define them in your session factory and adjust them while load testing your application to identify the optimal value.

After all, Hibernate, and its excellent JPA support that we discuss in next chapter, is a natural decision for Java developers looking for an OO way to implement data access logic.

Summary

In this chapter, we discussed the basic concepts of Hibernate and how to configure it within a Spring application. Then we covered common techniques for defining ORM mappings, and we covered associations and how to use the HibernateTemplate class to perform various database operations.

With regards to Hibernate, we covered only a small piece of its functionality and features. For those interested in using Hibernate with Spring, we highly recommend you study Hibernate's standard documentation. Also, numerous books discuss Hibernate in detail. I recommend *Beginning Hibernate, Third Edition* by Joseph Ottinger, Jeff Linwood, and Dave Minter (Apress, 2014), and *Pro JPA 2* by Mike Keith and Merrick Schincariol (Apress, 2013).

In the next chapter, we take a look at the JPA and how to use it when using Spring. Hibernate provides excellent support for JPA, and we continue to use Hibernate as the persistence provider for the examples in the next chapter. For query and update operations, JPA act likes Hibernate. In the next chapter, we discuss advanced topics including native and criteria query and how we can use Hibernate as well as its JPA support.

■ ■ ■

CHAPTER 8

Data Access in Spring with JPA2

In the previous chapter, we discussed how to use Hibernate with Spring when implementing data access logic with the ORM approach. We demonstrated how to configure Hibernate's `SessionFactory` in Spring's configuration and how to use the `Session` interface for various data access operations. However, that is just one way Hibernate can be used. Another way of adopting Hibernate in a Spring application is to use Hibernate as a persistence provider of the standard Java Persistence API (JPA).

Hibernate's POJO mapping and its powerful query language (HQL) have gained great success and also influenced the development of data access technology standards in the Java world. After Hibernate, the JCP developed the Java Data Objects (JDO) standard and then JPA.

At the time of this writing, JPA has reached version 2.1 and provides concepts that were standardized such as `PersistenceContext`, `EntityManager`, and the Java Persistence Query Language (JPQL). These standardizations provide a way for developers to switch between JPA persistence providers such as Hibernate, EclipseLink, Oracle TopLink, and Apache OpenJPA. As a result, most new JEE applications are adopting JPA as the data access layer.

Spring also provides excellent support for JPA. For example, a number of `EntityManagerFactoryBeans` are provided for bootstrapping a JPA entity manager with support for all of the JPA providers mentioned earlier. The Spring Data project also provides a subproject called Spring Data JPA, which provides advanced support for using JPA in Spring applications. The main features of the Spring Data JPA project include concepts of a `Repository` and `Specification` and support for the Query Domain-Specific Language, also known as QueryDSL.

This chapter covers how to use JPA 2.1 with Spring, using Hibernate as the underlying persistence provider. You will learn how to implement various database operations by using JPA's `EntityManager` interface and JPQL. Then you will see how Spring Data JPA can further help simplify JPA development. Finally, we present advanced topics related to ORM, including native queries and criteria queries.

Specifically, we discuss the following topics:

- *Core concepts of Java Persistence API (JPA)*: We cover some of the major concepts of JPA.

- *Configuring the JPA entity manager*: We discuss the types of `EntityManagerFactory` that Spring supports and how to configure the most commonly used one, `LocalContainerEntityManagerFactoryBean`, in Spring's XML configuration.

- *Data operations*: We show how to implement basic database operations in JPA, which is much like the concepts when using Hibernate on its own.

- *Advanced query operations*: We discuss how to use native queries in JPA and the strongly typed criteria API in JPA for more-flexible query operations.

- *Introducing Spring Data Java Persistence API (JPA)*: We discuss the Spring Data JPA project and demonstrate how it can help simplify the development of data access logic.

- • *Tracking entity changes and auditing:* In database update operations, it's a common requirement to keep track of the date an entity was created or last updated and who made the change. Also, for critical information such as a customer, a history table that stores each version of the entity is usually required. We discuss how Spring Data JPA and Hibernate Envers (Hibernate Entity Versioning System) can help ease the development of such logic.

■ **Note**   Like Hibernate, JPA supports the definition of mappings either in XML or in Java annotations. This chapter focuses on the annotation type of mapping, because its usage tends to be much more popular than the XML style.

Introducing JPA 2.1

Like other Java Specification Requests (JSRs), the objective of the JPA 2.1 specification (JSR-338) is to standardize the ORM programming model in both the JSE and JEE environments. It defines a common set of concepts, annotations, interfaces, and other services that a JPA persistence provider should implement. When programming to the JPA standard, developers have the option of switching the underlying provider at will, just like switching to another JEE-compliant application server for applications developed on the JEE standards.

Within JPA, the core concept is the EntityManager interface, which comes from factories of the type EntityManagerFactory. The main job of EntityManager is to maintain a persistence context, in which all the entity instances managed by it will be stored. The configuration of EntityManager is defined as a persistence unit, and there can be more than one persistence unit in an application. If you are using Hibernate, you can think of the persistence context in the same way as the Session interface, while EntityManagerFactory is the same as SessionFactory. In Hibernate, the managed entities are stored in the session, which you can directly interact with via Hibernate's SessionFactory or Session interface. In JPA, however, you can't interact with the persistence context directly. Instead, you need to rely on EntityManager to do the work for you.

JPQL is very similar to HQL, so if you have used HQL before, JPQL should be easy to pick up. However, in JPA 2, a strongly typed criteria API was introduced, which relies on the mapped entities' metadata to construct the query. Given this, any errors will be discovered at compile time rather than runtime.

For a detailed discussion of JPA 2, we recommend the book *Pro JPA 2* by Mike Keith and Merrick Schincariol (Apress, 2013).

In this section, we discuss the basic concepts of JPA, the sample data model that will be used in this chapter, and how to configure Spring's ApplicationContext to support JPA.

Using the Sample Data Model for Example Code

In this chapter, we use the same data model as used in Chapter 7. However, when we discuss how to implement the auditing features, we will add a few columns and a history table for demonstration. To get started, we will begin with the same database creation scripts used in the previous chapter. If you skipped Chapter 7, take a look at the data model presented in that chapter's "Sample Data Model for Example Code" section, which can help you understand the sample code in this chapter.

Configuring JPA EntityManagerFactory

As mentioned earlier in this chapter, to use JPA in Spring, we need to configure EntityManagerFactory, just like the SessionFactory used in Hibernate. Spring supports three types of EntityManagerFactory configurations.

The first one uses the LocalEntityManagerFactoryBean class. It's the simplest one, which requires only the persistence unit name. However, since it doesn't support the injection of DataSource and hence isn't able to participate in global transactions, it's suitable only for simple development purposes.

The second option is for use in a JEE-compliant container, in which the application server bootstraps the JPA persistence unit based on the information in the deployment descriptors. This allows Spring to look up the entity manager via JNDI lookup. Listing 8-1 shows a code snippet for looking up an entity manager via JNDI.

Listing 8-1. Looking Up Entity Manager via JNDI

```
<beans>
    <jee:jndi-lookup id="prospring4Emf"
        jndi-name="persistence/prospring4PersistenceUnit"/>
</beans>
```

In the JPA specification, a persistence unit should be defined in the configuration file `META-INF/persistence.xml`. However, as of Spring 3.1, a new feature has been added that eliminates this need; we show you how to use it later in this chapter.

The third option, which is the most common and is used in this chapter, is the `LocalContainerEntityManagerFactoryBean` class. It supports the injection of `DataSource` and can participate in both local and global transactions. Listing 8-2 shows the corresponding XML configuration file (`app-context-annotation.xml`).

Listing 8-2. Spring Configuration for `LocalContainerEntityManagerFactoryBean`

```xml
<?xml version="1.0" encoding="UTF-8"?>

<beans xmlns="http://www.springframework.org/schema/beans"
    xmlns:xsi=http://www.w3.org/2001/XMLSchema-instance
    xmlns:context="http://www.springframework.org/schema/context"
    xmlns:jdbc=http://www.springframework.org/schema/jdbc
    xmlns:tx="http://www.springframework.org/schema/tx"
    xsi:schemaLocation="http://www.springframework.org/schema/jdbc
        http://www.springframework.org/schema/jdbc/spring-jdbc.xsd
        http://www.springframework.org/schema/beans
        http://www.springframework.org/schema/beans/spring-beans.xsd
        http://www.springframework.org/schema/tx
        http://www.springframework.org/schema/tx/spring-tx.xsd
        http://www.springframework.org/schema/context
        http://www.springframework.org/schema/context/spring-context.xsd">

    <jdbc:embedded-database id="dataSource" type="H2">
        <jdbc:script location="classpath:META-INF/sql/schema.sql"/>
        <jdbc:script location="classpath:META-INF/sql/test-data.sql"/>
    </jdbc:embedded-database>

    <bean id="transactionManager" class="org.springframework.orm.jpa.JpaTransactionManager">
        <property name="entityManagerFactory" ref="emf"/>
    </bean>

    <tx:annotation-driven transaction-manager="transactionManager" />

    <bean id="emf" class="org.springframework.orm.jpa.LocalContainerEntityManagerFactoryBean">
        <property name="dataSource" ref="dataSource" />
        <property name="jpaVendorAdapter">
            <bean class="org.springframework.orm.jpa.vendor.HibernateJpaVendorAdapter" />
        </property>
```

```xml
            <property name="packagesToScan" value="com.apress.prospring4.ch8"/>
            <property name="jpaProperties">
                <props>
                    <prop key="hibernate.dialect">org.hibernate.dialect.H2Dialect</prop>
                    <prop key="hibernate.max_fetch_depth">3</prop>
                    <prop key="hibernate.jdbc.fetch_size">50</prop>
                    <prop key="hibernate.jdbc.batch_size">10</prop>
                    <prop key="hibernate.show_sql">true</prop>
                </props>
            </property>
        </bean>

        <context:component-scan base-package="com.apress.prospring4.ch8" />
</beans>
```

In the previous configuration, several beans are declared in order to be able to support the configuration of LocalContainerEntityManagerFactoryBean with Hibernate as the persistence provider. The main configurations are as follows:

- *The* dataSource *bean*: We declared the data source with an embedded database using H2. Because it's an embedded database, the database name is not required.

- *The* transactionManager *bean*: EntityManagerFactory requires a transaction manager for transactional data access. Spring provides a transaction manager specifically for JPA (org. springframework.orm.jpa.JpaTransactionManager). The bean is declared with an ID of transactionManager assigned. We discuss transactions in detail in Chapter 9. We declare the tag <tx:annotation-driven> to support a declaration of the transaction demarcation requirements using annotations.

- *Component scan*: The tag should be familiar to you. We instruct Spring to scan the components under the package com.apress.prospring4.ch8.

- *JPA* EntityManagerFactory *bean*: The emf bean is the most important part. First, we declare the bean to use the LocalContainerEntityManagerFactoryBean. Within the bean, several properties are provided. First, as you might have expected, we need to inject the DataSource bean. Second, we configure the property jpaVendorAdapter with the class HibernateJpaVendorAdapter, because we are using Hibernate. Third, we instruct the entity factory to scan for the domain objects with ORM annotations under the package com.apress. prospring4.ch8 (specified by the <property name="packagesToScan"> tag). Note that this feature has been available only since Spring 3.1, and with the support of domain class scanning, you can skip the definition of the persistence unit in the META-INF/persistence. xml file. Finally, the jpaProperties property provides configuration details for the persistence provider, Hibernate. You will see that the configuration options are the same as those we used in Chapter 7, so we can skip the explanation here.

Using JPA Annotations for ORM Mapping

Hibernate influenced the design of JPA in many ways. For the mapping annotations, they are so close that the annotations we used in Chapter 7 for mapping the domain objects to the database are the same in JPA. If you take a look at the domain classes' source code in Chapter 7, you will see that all mapping annotations are under the package javax.persistence, which means those annotations are already JPA compatible.

Once EntityManagerFactory has been properly configured, injecting it into your classes is very simple. Listing 8-3 shows the code for the ContactServiceImpl class, which we will use as the sample for performing database operations using JPA.

Listing 8-3. Injection of EntityManager

```
package com.apress.prospring4.ch8;

import org.springframework.stereotype.Repository;
import org.springframework.stereotype.Service;
import org.springframework.transaction.annotation.Transactional;

import java.util.List;

import javax.persistence.PersistenceContext;
import javax.persistence.EntityManager;

import org.apache.commons.logging.Log;
import org.apache.commons.logging.LogFactory;

@Service("jpaContactService")
@Repository
@Transactional
public class ContactServiceImpl implements ContactService {
    private Log log = LogFactory.getLog(ContactServiceImpl.class);

    @PersistenceContext
    private EntityManager em;

    @Override
    public List<Contact> findAll() {
        return null;
    }

    @Override
    public List<Contact> findAllWithDetail() {
        return null;
    }

    @Override
    public Contact findById(Long id) {
        return null;
    }

    @Override
    public Contact save(Contact contact) {
        return null;
    }
```

```
    @Override
    public void delete(Contact contact) {

    }
}
```

Several annotations are applied to the class. The @Service annotation is used to identify the class as being a Spring component that provides business services to another layer and assigns the Spring bean the name jpaContactService. The @Repository annotation indicates that the class contains data access logic and instructs Spring to translate the vendor-specific exceptions to Spring's DataAccessException hierarchy. As you are already familiar with, the @Transactional annotation is used for defining transaction requirements.

To inject EntityManager, we use the @PersistenceContext annotation, which is the standard JPA annotation for entity manager injection. It may be questionable as to why we're using the name @PersistenceContext to inject an entity manager, but if you consider that the persistence context itself is managed by EntityManager, the annotation naming makes perfect sense. If you have multiple persistence units in your application, you can also add the unitName attribute to the annotation to specify which persistence unit you want to be injected. Typically, a persistence unit represents an individual back-end DataSource.

Performing Database Operations with JPA

This section covers how to perform database operations in JPA. Listing 8-4 shows the ContactService interface, which indicates the contact information services we are going to provide.

Listing 8-4. The ContactService Interface

```
package com.apress.prospring4.ch8;

import java.util.List;

public interface ContactService {
    List<Contact> findAll();
    List<Contact> findAllWithDetail();
    Contact findById(Long id);
    Contact save(Contact contact);
    void delete(Contact contact);
}
```

The interface is very simple; it has just three finder methods, one save method, and one delete method. The save method will serve both the insert and update operations.

Using the Java Persistence Query Language to Query Data

The syntax for JPQL and HQL is very similar, and in fact, all the HQL queries that we used in Chapter 7 are reusable to implement the three finder methods within the ContactService interface. In order to use JPA and Hibernate, you need to add the dependencies as outlined in Table 8-1 to your project.

Table 8-1. *Dependencies for Hibernate and JPA*

Group ID	Artifact ID	Version	Description
org.hibernate	hibernate-entitymanager	4.2.3.Final	Hibernate 4 library
org.hibernate.javax.persistence	hibernate-jpa-2.1-api	1.0.0.Final	JPA library

Listing 8-5 recaps the code for the domain object model classes from Chapter 7.

Listing 8-5. Domain Model Objects

```
package com.apress.prospring4.ch8;

import static javax.persistence.GenerationType.IDENTITY;

import java.io.Serializable;
import java.util.Date;
import java.util.HashSet;
import java.util.Set;
import javax.persistence.Entity;
import javax.persistence.Table;
import javax.persistence.Id;
import javax.persistence.GeneratedValue;
import javax.persistence.Column;
import javax.persistence.Version;
import javax.persistence.Temporal;
import javax.persistence.TemporalType;
import javax.persistence.OneToMany;
import javax.persistence.ManyToMany;
import javax.persistence.JoinTable;
import javax.persistence.JoinColumn;
import javax.persistence.CascadeType;
import javax.persistence.NamedQueries;
import javax.persistence.NamedQuery;

@Entity
@Table(name = "contact")
@NamedQueries({
    @NamedQuery(name="Contact.findAll", query="select c from Contact c"),
    @NamedQuery(name="Contact.findById",
        query="select distinct c from Contact c left join fetch c.contactTelDetails t left join
fetch c.hobbies h where c.id = :id"),
    @NamedQuery(name="Contact.findAllWithDetail",
        query="select distinct c from Contact c left join fetch c.contactTelDetails t left join
fetch c.hobbies h")
})
public class Contact implements Serializable {
    private Long id;
    private int version;
    private String firstName;
    private String lastName;
```

```java
private Date birthDate;
private Set<ContactTelDetail> contactTelDetails = new HashSet<ContactTelDetail>();
private Set<Hobby> hobbies = new HashSet<Hobby>();

@Id
@GeneratedValue(strategy = IDENTITY)
@Column(name = "ID")
public Long getId() {
    return this.id;
}

public void setId(Long id) {
    this.id = id;
}

@Version
@Column(name = "VERSION")
public int getVersion() {
    return this.version;
}

public void setVersion(int version) {
    this.version = version;
}

@Column(name = "FIRST_NAME")
public String getFirstName() {
    return this.firstName;
}

public void setFirstName(String firstName) {
    this.firstName = firstName;
}

@Column(name = "LAST_NAME")
public String getLastName() {
    return this.lastName;
}

public void setLastName(String lastName) {
    this.lastName = lastName;
}

@Temporal(TemporalType.DATE)
@Column(name = "BIRTH_DATE")
public Date getBirthDate() {
    return this.birthDate;
}

public void setBirthDate(Date birthDate) {
    this.birthDate = birthDate;
}
```

```java
    @OneToMany(mappedBy = "contact", cascade=CascadeType.ALL,
        orphanRemoval=true)
    public Set<ContactTelDetail> getContactTelDetails() {
        return this.contactTelDetails;
    }

    public void setContactTelDetails(Set<ContactTelDetail> contactTelDetails) {
     this.contactTelDetails = contactTelDetails;
    }

    public void addContactTelDetail(ContactTelDetail contactTelDetail) {
        contactTelDetail.setContact(this);
        getContactTelDetails().add(contactTelDetail);
    }

    public void removeContactTelDetail(ContactTelDetail contactTelDetail) {
        getContactTelDetails().remove(contactTelDetail);
    }

    @ManyToMany
    @JoinTable(name = "contact_hobby_detail",
        joinColumns = @JoinColumn(name = "CONTACT_ID"),
        inverseJoinColumns = @JoinColumn(name = "HOBBY_ID"))
    public Set<Hobby> getHobbies() {
        return this.hobbies;
    }

    public void setHobbies(Set<Hobby> hobbies) {
        this.hobbies = hobbies;
    }

    @Override
    public String toString() {
        return "Contact - Id: " + id + ", First name: " + firstName
            + ", Last name: " + lastName + ", Birthday: " + birthDate;
    }
}

package com.apress.prospring4.ch8;

import static javax.persistence.GenerationType.IDENTITY;

import java.io.Serializable;
import javax.persistence.Entity;
import javax.persistence.Table;
import javax.persistence.Id;
import javax.persistence.GeneratedValue;
import javax.persistence.Column;
import javax.persistence.Version;
import javax.persistence.ManyToOne;
import javax.persistence.JoinColumn;
```

```java
@Entity
@Table(name = "contact_tel_detail")
public class ContactTelDetail implements Serializable {
    private Long id;
    private int version;
    private String telType;
    private String telNumber;
    private Contact contact;

    public ContactTelDetail() {
    }

    public ContactTelDetail(String telType, String telNumber) {
        this.telType = telType;
        this.telNumber = telNumber;
    }

    @Id
    @GeneratedValue(strategy = IDENTITY)
    @Column(name = "ID")
    public Long getId() {
        return this.id;
    }

    public void setId(Long id) {
        this.id = id;
    }

    @Version
    @Column(name = "VERSION")
    public int getVersion() {
        return this.version;
    }

    public void setVersion(int version) {
        this.version = version;
    }

    @Column(name = "TEL_TYPE")
    public String getTelType() {
        return this.telType;
    }

    public void setTelType(String telType) {
        this.telType = telType;
    }

    @Column(name = "TEL_NUMBER")
    public String getTelNumber() {
        return this.telNumber;
    }
}
```

```java
    public void setTelNumber(String telNumber) {
        this.telNumber = telNumber;
    }

    @ManyToOne
    @JoinColumn(name = "CONTACT_ID")
    public Contact getContact() {
        return this.contact;
    }

    public void setContact(Contact contact) {
        this.contact = contact;
    }

    @Override
    public String toString() {
        return "Contact Tel Detail - Id: " + id + ", Contact id: "
            + getContact().getId() + ", Type: "
            + telType + ", Number: " + telNumber;
    }
}
package com.apress.prospring4.ch8;

import java.io.Serializable;
import javax.persistence.Entity;
import javax.persistence.Table;
import javax.persistence.Column;
import javax.persistence.Id;
import javax.persistence.ManyToMany;
import javax.persistence.JoinTable;
import javax.persistence.JoinColumn;
import java.util.Set;
import java.util.HashSet;

@Entity
@Table(name = "hobby")
public class Hobby implements Serializable {
    private String hobbyId;
    private Set<Contact> contacts = new HashSet<Contact>();

    @Id
    @Column(name = "HOBBY_ID")
    public String getHobbyId() {
        return this.hobbyId;
    }

    public void setHobbyId(String hobbyId) {
        this.hobbyId = hobbyId;
    }
```

```
    @ManyToMany
    @JoinTable(name = "contact_hobby_detail",
        joinColumns = @JoinColumn(name = "HOBBY_ID"),
        inverseJoinColumns = @JoinColumn(name = "CONTACT_ID"))
    public Set<Contact> getContacts() {
        return this.contacts;
    }

    public void setContacts(Set<Contact> contacts) {
        this.contacts = contacts;
    }

    @Override
    public String toString() {
        return "Hobby :" + getHobbyId();
    }
}
```

When you compare the queries with those in Chapter 7, you will find no difference at all. So, if you are using Hibernate, migrating to JPA is relatively easy.

Let's begin with the findAll() method, which simply retrieves all the contacts from the database. Listing 8-6 shows the updated code.

Listing 8-6. Implementing the findAll() Method

```
package com.apress.prospring4.ch8;

import org.springframework.stereotype.Repository;
import org.springframework.stereotype.Service;
import org.springframework.transaction.annotation.Transactional;

import java.util.List;

import javax.persistence.PersistenceContext;
import javax.persistence.EntityManager;

import org.apache.commons.logging.Log;
import org.apache.commons.logging.LogFactory;

@Service("jpaContactService")
@Repository
@Transactional
public class ContactServiceImpl implements ContactService {
    private Log log = LogFactory.getLog(ContactServiceImpl.class);

    @PersistenceContext
    private EntityManager em;

    @Transactional(readOnly=true)
    @Override
```

```
    public List<Contact> findAll() {
        List<Contact> contacts = em.createNamedQuery("Contact.findAll",
            Contact.class).getResultList();
        return contacts;
    }

    @Override
    public List<Contact> findAllWithDetail() {
        return null;
    }

    @Override
    public Contact findById(Long id) {
        return null;
    }

    @Override
    public Contact save(Contact contact) {
        return null;
    }
    @Override
    public void delete(Contact contact) {

    }
}
```

As shown in this listing, we use the EntityManager.createNamedQuery() method, passing in the name of the query and the expected return type. In this case, EntityManager will return a TypedQuery<X> interface. The method TypedQuery.getResultList() is then called to retrieve the contacts.

Listing 8-7 shows a simple testing program for ContactServiceImpl.

Listing 8-7. Testing the ContactServiceImpl Class

```
package com.apress.prospring4.ch8;

import java.util.List;

import org.springframework.context.support.GenericXmlApplicationContext;

public class SpringJPASample {
    public static void main(String[] args) {
        GenericXmlApplicationContext ctx = new GenericXmlApplicationContext();
        ctx.load("classpath:META-INF/spring/app-context-annotation.xml");
        ctx.refresh();

        ContactService contactService = ctx.getBean(
            "jpaContactService", ContactService.class);

        listContacts(contactService.findAll());
    }
```

```
        private static void listContacts(List<Contact> contacts) {
            System.out.println("");
            System.out.println("Listing contacts without details:");
            for (Contact contact: contacts) {
                System.out.println(contact);
                System.out.println();
            }
        }
    }
```

Running the previous class yields the following output:

```
Listing contacts without details:
Contact - Id: 1, First name: Chris, Last name: Schaefer, Birthday: 1981-05-03

Contact - Id: 2, First name: Scott, Last name: Tiger, Birthday: 1990-11-02

Contact - Id: 3, First name: John, Last name: Smith, Birthday: 1964-02-28
```

■ **Note** For associations, the JPA specification states that, by default, the persistence providers must fetch the association eagerly. However, for Hibernate's JPA implementation, the default fetching strategy is still lazy. So, when using Hibernate's JPA implementation, you don't need to explicitly define an association as lazy fetching. The default fetching strategy of Hibernate is different from the JPA specification.

Now let's implement the findAllWithDetail() method, which will fetch all the associated telephone details and hobbies. Listing 8-8 shows the updated ContactServiceImpl class.

Listing 8-8. Implementing the FindAllWithDetail() Method

```
package com.apress.prospring4.ch8;

import org.springframework.stereotype.Repository;
import org.springframework.stereotype.Service;
import org.springframework.transaction.annotation.Transactional;

import java.util.List;

import javax.persistence.PersistenceContext;
import javax.persistence.EntityManager;

import org.apache.commons.logging.Log;
import org.apache.commons.logging.LogFactory;

@Service("jpaContactService")
@Repository
@Transactional
public class ContactServiceImpl implements ContactService {
    private Log log = LogFactory.getLog(ContactServiceImpl.class);
```

```java
@PersistenceContext
private EntityManager em;

@Transactional(readOnly=true)
@Override
public List<Contact> findAll() {
    List<Contact> contacts = em.createNamedQuery("Contact.findAll",
        Contact.class).getResultList();
    return contacts;
}

@Transactional(readOnly=true)
@Override
public List<Contact> findAllWithDetail() {
    List<Contact> contacts = em.createNamedQuery(
        "Contact.findAllWithDetail", Contact.class).getResultList();
    return contacts;
}

@Override
public Contact findById(Long id) {
    return null;
}

@Override
public Contact save(Contact contact) {
    return null;
}

@Override
public void delete(Contact contact) {

}
}
```

findAllWithDetail() is the same as the findAll() method, but it uses a different named query with left join fetch enabled. Listing 8-9 shows the revised testing program to list the contact details.

Listing 8-9. Testing the ContactServiceImpl Class

```java
package com.apress.prospring4.ch8;

import java.util.List;

import org.springframework.context.support.GenericXmlApplicationContext;

public class SpringJPASample {
    public static void main(String[] args) {
        GenericXmlApplicationContext ctx = new GenericXmlApplicationContext();
        ctx.load("classpath:META-INF/spring/app-context-annotation.xml");
        ctx.refresh();
```

```
        ContactService contactService = ctx.getBean(
            "jpaContactService", ContactService.class);

        List<Contact> contacts = contactService.findAllWithDetail();
        listContactsWithDetail(contacts);
    }

    private static void listContactsWithDetail(List<Contact> contacts) {
        System.out.println("");
        System.out.println("Listing contacts with details:");
        for (Contact contact: contacts) {
            System.out.println(contact);
            if (contact.getContactTelDetails() != null) {
                for (ContactTelDetail contactTelDetail:
                        contact.getContactTelDetails()) {
                    System.out.println(contactTelDetail);
                }
            }
            if (contact.getHobbies() != null) {
                for (Hobby hobby: contact.getHobbies()) {
                    System.out.println(hobby);
                }
            }
            System.out.println();
        }
    }
}
```

If you run the program again, you will see the following output:

```
Listing contacts with details:
Contact - Id: 1, First name: Chris, Last name: Schaefer, Birthday: 1981-05-03
Contact Tel Detail - Id: 2, Contact id: 1, Type: Home, Number: 1234567890
Contact Tel Detail - Id: 1, Contact id: 1, Type: Mobile, Number: 1234567890
Hobby :Movies
Hobby :Swimming

Contact - Id: 3, First name: John, Last name: Smith, Birthday: 1964-02-28

Contact - Id: 2, First name: Scott, Last name: Tiger, Birthday: 1990-11-02
Contact Tel Detail - Id: 3, Contact id: 2, Type: Home, Number: 1234567890
Hobby :Swimming
```

Now let's see the findById() method, which demonstrates how to use a named query with named parameters in JPA. The associations will be fetched as well. Listing 8-10 shows the updated implementation.

Listing 8-10. Implementing the findById() Method

```java
package com.apress.prospring4.ch8;

package com.apress.prospring4.ch8;

import org.springframework.stereotype.Repository;
import org.springframework.stereotype.Service;
import org.springframework.transaction.annotation.Transactional;

import java.util.List;

import javax.persistence.PersistenceContext;
import javax.persistence.EntityManager;
import javax.persistence.TypedQuery;

import org.apache.commons.logging.Log;
import org.apache.commons.logging.LogFactory;

@Service("jpaContactService")
@Repository
@Transactional
public class ContactServiceImpl implements ContactService {
    private Log log = LogFactory.getLog(ContactServiceImpl.class);

    @PersistenceContext
    private EntityManager em;

    @Transactional(readOnly=true)
    @Override
    public List<Contact> findAll() {
        List<Contact> contacts = em.createNamedQuery("Contact.findAll",
            Contact.class).getResultList();
        return contacts;
    }

    @Transactional(readOnly=true)
    @Override
    public List<Contact> findAllWithDetail() {
        List<Contact> contacts = em.createNamedQuery(
            "Contact.findAllWithDetail", Contact.class).getResultList();
        return contacts;
    }

    @Transactional(readOnly=true)
    @Override
    public Contact findById(Long id) {
        TypedQuery<Contact> query = em.createNamedQuery(
            "Contact.findById", Contact.class);
        query.setParameter("id", id);

        return query.getSingleResult();
    }
```

```
    @Override
    public Contact save(Contact contact) {
        return null;
    }

    @Override
    public void delete(Contact contact) {

    }
}
```

EntityManager.createNamedQuery(java.lang.String name, java.lang.Class<T> resultClass) was called to get an instance of the TypedQuery<T> interface, which ensures that the result of the query must be of type Contact. Then the TypedQuery<T>.setParameter() method was used to set the values of the named parameters within the query and then to invoke the getSingleResult() method, since the result should contain only a single Contact object with the specified ID. We will leave the testing of the method as an exercise for you.

Query with Untyped Results

In many cases, you would like to submit a query to the database and manipulate the results at will, instead of storing them in a mapped entity class. One typical example is a web-based report that lists only a certain number of columns across multiple tables.

For example, say you have a web page that shows the summary information of all the contact information. The summary information contains each contact's first name, last name, and home telephone number only. Those contacts without home telephone numbers will not be listed. In this case, we can implement this use case with a query and then manually manipulate ResultSet.

Let's create a new class called ContactSummaryUntypeImpl and name the method displayAllContactSummary(). Listing 8-11 shows a typical implementation of the method.

Listing 8-11. Implementing displayAllContactSummary() in the ContactSummaryUntypeImpl Class

```
package com.apress.prospring4.ch8;

import org.springframework.stereotype.Service;
import org.springframework.stereotype.Repository;
import org.springframework.transaction.annotation.Transactional;

import javax.persistence.PersistenceContext;
import javax.persistence.EntityManager;

import java.util.List;
import java.util.Iterator;

@Service("contactSummaryUntype")
@Repository
@Transactional
public class ContactSummaryUntypeImpl {
    @PersistenceContext
    private EntityManager em;
```

```java
    @Transactional(readOnly=true)
    public void displayAllContactSummary() {
        List result = em
                .createQuery("select c.firstName, c.lastName, t.telNumber "
                    + "from Contact c left join c.contactTelDetails t "
                    + " where t.telType='Home'").getResultList();
        int count = 0;

        for (Iterator i = result.iterator(); i.hasNext();) {
            Object[] values = (Object[]) i.next();

            System.out.println(++count + ": " + values[0] + ", "
                + values[1] + ", " + values[2]);
        }
    }
}
```

As shown in this listing, we use the EntityManager.createQuery() method to create Query, passing in the JPQL statement, and then get the result list.

When we explicitly specify the columns to be selected within JPQL, JPA will return an iterator, and each item within the iterator is an array of objects. We loop through the iterator, and for each element in the object array, the value is displayed. Each object array corresponds to a record within the ResultSet. Listing 8-12 shows the testing program.

Listing 8-12. Testing the displayAllContactSummary() Method

```java
package com.apress.prospring4.ch8;

import java.util.List;

import org.springframework.context.support.GenericXmlApplicationContext;

public class SpringJPASample {
    public static void main(String[] args) {
        GenericXmlApplicationContext ctx = new GenericXmlApplicationContext();
        ctx.load("classpath:META-INF/spring/app-context-annotation.xml");
        ctx.refresh();

        ContactSummaryUntypeImpl contactSummaryUntype =
            ctx.getBean("contactSummaryUntype",
                ContactSummaryUntypeImpl.class);

        contactSummaryUntype.displayAllContactSummary();
    }
}
```

Running the testing program produces the following output:

```
1: Chris, Schaefer, 1234567890
2: Scott, Tiger, 1234567890
```

In JPA, there is a more elegant solution, rather than playing around with the object array returned from the query, which is discussed in next section.

Query for a Custom Result Type with a Constructor Expression

In JPA, when querying for a custom result like the one in the previous section, you can instruct JPA to directly construct a POJO from each record for you. For the example in the previous section, let's create a POJO called ContactSummary that stores the results of the query for the contact summary. Listing 8-13 shows the class.

Listing 8-13. The ContactSummary Class

```java
package com.apress.prospring4.ch8;

import java.io.Serializable;

public class ContactSummary implements Serializable {
    private String firstName;
    private String lastName;
    private String homeTelNumber;

    public ContactSummary(String firstName, String lastName,
            String homeTelNumber) {
        this.firstName = firstName;
        this.lastName = lastName;
        this.homeTelNumber = homeTelNumber;
    }

    public String getFirstName() {
        return firstName;
    }

    public String getLastName() {
        return lastName;
    }

    public String getHomeTelNumber() {
        return homeTelNumber;
    }

    public String toString() {
        return "First name: " + firstName + " Last Name: " + lastName
            + " Home Phone: " + homeTelNumber;
    }
}
```

The previous ContactSummary class has the properties for each contact summary, with a constructor method that accepts all the properties.

Having the ContactSummary class in place, we can revise the findAll() method and use a constructor expression within the query to instruct the JPA provider to map the ResultSet to the ContactSummary class. Let's create an interface for the ContactSummary service first. Listing 8-14 shows the interface.

Listing 8-14. The ContactSummaryService Interface

```
package com.apress.prospring4.ch8;

import java.util.List;

public interface ContactSummaryService {
    List<ContactSummary> findAll();
}
```

Listing 8-15 shows the implementation of the ContactSummaryService.findAll() method, using the constructor expression for ResultSet mapping.

Listing 8-15. Implementation of the findAll() Method Using the Constructor Expression

```
package com.apress.prospring4.ch8;

import org.springframework.stereotype.Service;
import org.springframework.stereotype.Repository;
import org.springframework.transaction.annotation.Transactional;

import javax.persistence.PersistenceContext;
import javax.persistence.EntityManager;

import java.util.List;

@Service("contactSummaryService")
@Repository
@Transactional
public class ContactSummaryServiceImpl implements ContactSummaryService {
    @PersistenceContext
    private EntityManager em;

    @Transactional(readOnly=true)
    @Override
    public List<ContactSummary> findAll() {
        List<ContactSummary> result = em.createQuery(
            "select new com.apress.prospring4.ch8.ContactSummary("
            + "c.firstName, c.lastName, t.telNumber) "
            + "from Contact c left join c.contactTelDetails t "
            + "where t.telType='Home'",
            ContactSummary.class).getResultList();

        return result;
    }
}
```

In the JPQL statement, the new keyword was specified, together with the fully qualified name of the POJO class that will store the results and pass in the selected attributes as the constructor argument of each ContactSummary class. Finally, the ContactSummary class was passed into the createQuery() method to indicate the result type.

To test the findAll() method, let's update the SpringJPASample class as shown in Listing 8-16.

Listing 8-16. Testing the findAll() Method by Using the Constructor Expression

```
package com.apress.prospring4.ch8;

import java.util.List;

import org.springframework.context.support.GenericXmlApplicationContext;

public class SpringJPASample {
    public static void main(String[] args) {
        GenericXmlApplicationContext ctx = new GenericXmlApplicationContext();
        ctx.load("classpath:META-INF/spring/app-context-annotation.xml");
        ctx.refresh();

        ContactSummaryService contactSummaryService =
            ctx.getBean("contactSummaryService",ContactSummaryService.class);

        List<ContactSummary> contacts = contactSummaryService.findAll();

        for (ContactSummary contactSummary: contacts) {
            System.out.println(contactSummary);
        }
    }
}
```

Executing the ContactSummarySample class again produces the output for each ContactSummary object within the list, as shown here (other output was omitted):

```
First name: Chris Last Name: Schaefer Home Phone: 1234567890
First name: Scott Last Name: Tiger Home Phone: 1234567890
```

As you can see, the constructor expression is very useful for mapping the result of a custom query into POJOs for further application processing.

Inserting Data

Inserting data by using JPA is very simple. Like Hibernate, JPA also supports retrieving a database-generated primary key. Listing 8-17 shows updated code to support the implementation of the save() method.

Listing 8-17. Implementing the save() Method

```
package com.apress.prospring4.ch8;

import org.springframework.stereotype.Service;
import org.springframework.stereotype.Repository;
import org.springframework.transaction.annotation.Transactional;

import java.util.List;

import javax.persistence.PersistenceContext;
import javax.persistence.EntityManager;
import javax.persistence.TypedQuery;
```

```java
import org.apache.commons.logging.Log;
import org.apache.commons.logging.LogFactory;

@Service("jpaContactService")
@Repository
@Transactional
public class ContactServiceImpl implements ContactService {
    private Log log = LogFactory.getLog(ContactServiceImpl.class);

    @PersistenceContext
    private EntityManager em;

    @Transactional(readOnly=true)
    @Override
    public List<Contact> findAll() {
        List<Contact> contacts = em.createNamedQuery("Contact.findAll",
            Contact.class).getResultList();
        return contacts;
    }

    @Transactional(readOnly=true)
    @Override
    public List<Contact> findAllWithDetail() {
        List<Contact> contacts = em.createNamedQuery(
            "Contact.findAllWithDetail", Contact.class).getResultList();
        return contacts;
    }

    @Transactional(readOnly=true)
    @Override
    public Contact findById(Long id) {
        TypedQuery<Contact> query = em.createNamedQuery(
            "Contact.findById", Contact.class);
        query.setParameter("id", id);

        return query.getSingleResult();
    }

    @Override
    public Contact save(Contact contact) {
        if (contact.getId() == null) {
            log.info("Inserting new contact");
            em.persist(contact);
        } else {
            em.merge(contact);
            log.info("Updating existing contact");
        }

        log.info("Contact saved with id: " + contact.getId());

        return contact;
    }
```

```
    @Override
    public void delete(Contact contact) {

    }
}
```

As shown here, the save() method first checks whether the object is a new entity instance, by checking the id value. If id is null (that is, not yet assigned), the object is a new entity instance, and the EntityManager.persist() method will be invoked. When calling the persist() method, EntityManager persists the entity and makes it a managed instance within the current persistence context. If the id value exists, then we're carrying out an update, and the EntityManager.merge() method will be called instead. When the merge() method is called, the EntityManager merges the state of the entity into the current persistence context.

Listing 8-18 shows the updated code to insert a new contact record.

Listing 8-18. Testing the Insert Operation

```
package com.apress.prospring4.ch8;

import java.util.List;
import java.util.Date;

import org.springframework.context.support.GenericXmlApplicationContext;

public class SpringJPASample {
    public static void main(String[] args) {
        GenericXmlApplicationContext ctx = new GenericXmlApplicationContext();
        ctx.load("classpath:META-INF/spring/app-context-annotation.xml");
        ctx.refresh();

        ContactService contactService = ctx.getBean(
            "jpaContactService", ContactService.class);

        Contact contact = new Contact();
        contact.setFirstName("Michael");
        contact.setLastName("Jackson");
        contact.setBirthDate(new Date());

        ContactTelDetail contactTelDetail =
            new ContactTelDetail("Home", "1111111111");

        contact.addContactTelDetail(contactTelDetail);

        contactTelDetail = new ContactTelDetail("Mobile", "2222222222");

        contact.addContactTelDetail(contactTelDetail);

        contactService.save(contact);

        listContactsWithDetail(contactService.findAllWithDetail());
    }
```

```
    private static void listContactsWithDetail(List<Contact> contacts) {
        System.out.println("");
        System.out.println("Listing contacts with details:");

        for (Contact contact: contacts) {
            System.out.println(contact);
            if (contact.getContactTelDetails() != null) {
                for (ContactTelDetail contactTelDetail:
                    contact.getContactTelDetails()) {
                    System.out.println(contactTelDetail);
                }
            }

            if (contact.getHobbies() != null) {
                for (Hobby hobby: contact.getHobbies()) {
                    System.out.println(hobby);
                }
            }

            System.out.println();
        }
    }
}
```

As shown here, we create a new contact, add two telephone details, and save the object. Then we list all the contacts again. Running the program yields the following output:

```
INFO apress.prospring4.ch8.ContactServiceImpl:  50 - Inserting new contact
Hibernate: insert into contact (ID, BIRTH_DATE, FIRST_NAME, LAST_NAME, VERSION) values (null, ?, ?, ?, ?)
Hibernate: insert into contact_tel_detail (ID, CONTACT_ID, TEL_NUMBER, TEL_TYPE, VERSION) values
(null, ?, ?, ?, ?)
Hibernate: insert into contact_tel_detail (ID, CONTACT_ID, TEL_NUMBER, TEL_TYPE, VERSION) values
(null, ?, ?, ?, ?)
INFO apress.prospring4.ch8.ContactServiceImpl:  57 - Contact saved with id: 4

Listing contacts with details:
Contact - Id: 1, First name: Chris, Last name: Schaefer, Birthday: 1981-05-03
Contact Tel Detail - Id: 2, Contact id: 1, Type: Home, Number: 1234567890
Contact Tel Detail - Id: 1, Contact id: 1, Type: Mobile, Number: 1234567890
Hobby :Movies
Hobby :Swimming

Contact - Id: 4, First name: Michael, Last name: Jackson, Birthday: 2013-08-12
Contact Tel Detail - Id: 4, Contact id: 4, Type: Home, Number: 1111111111
Contact Tel Detail - Id: 5, Contact id: 4, Type: Mobile, Number: 2222222222

Contact - Id: 3, First name: John, Last name: Smith, Birthday: 1964-02-28

Contact - Id: 2, First name: Scott, Last name: Tiger, Birthday: 1990-11-02
Contact Tel Detail - Id: 3, Contact id: 2, Type: Home, Number: 1234567890
Hobby :Swimming
```

From the INFO log record, you can see that the id of the newly saved contact was populated correctly. Hibernate will also show all the SQL statements being fired to the database.

Updating Data

Updating data is as easy as inserting data. Let's go through an example. Suppose for a contact with an ID of 1, we want to update its first name and remove the home telephone record. To test the update operation, Listing 8-19 shows the modifications required to the SpringJPASample class.

Listing 8-19. Testing the Update Operation

```
package com.apress.prospring4.ch8;

import java.util.List;
import java.util.Date;
import java.util.Set;

import org.springframework.context.support.GenericXmlApplicationContext;

public class SpringJPASample {
    public static void main(String[] args) {
        GenericXmlApplicationContext ctx = new GenericXmlApplicationContext();
        ctx.load("classpath:META-INF/spring/app-context-annotation.xml");
        ctx.refresh();

        ContactService contactService = ctx.getBean(
            "jpaContactService", ContactService.class);

        Contact contact = contactService.findById(1l);

        System.out.println("");
        System.out.println("Contact with id 1:" + contact);
        System.out.println("");

        contact.setFirstName("Justin");

        Set<ContactTelDetail> contactTels = contact.getContactTelDetails();
        ContactTelDetail toDeleteContactTel = null;

        for (ContactTelDetail contactTel: contactTels) {
            if (contactTel.getTelType().equals("Home")) {
                toDeleteContactTel = contactTel;
            }
        }
        contactTels.remove(toDeleteContactTel);
        contactService.save(contact);

        listContactsWithDetail(contactService.findAllWithDetail());
    }

    private static void listContactsWithDetail(List<Contact> contacts) {
        System.out.println("");
        System.out.println("Listing contacts with details:");
```

```
    for (Contact contact: contacts) {
        System.out.println(contact);
        if (contact.getContactTelDetails() != null) {
            for (ContactTelDetail contactTelDetail:
                contact.getContactTelDetails()) {
                System.out.println(contactTelDetail);
            }
        }

        if (contact.getHobbies() != null) {
            for (Hobby hobby: contact.getHobbies()) {
                System.out.println(hobby);
            }
        }

        System.out.println();
    }
  }

}
```

We first retrieve the record with an ID of 1 and we change the first name. Then we loop through the telephone objects and retrieve the one with type "Home" and remove it from the contact's telephone detail property. Finally, we call the ContactService.save() method again. When you run the program, you will see the following output (other output was omitted):

```
Listing contacts with details:
Contact - Id: 1, First name: Justin, Last name: Schaefer, Birthday: 1981-05-03
Contact Tel Detail - Id: 1, Contact id: 1, Type: Mobile, Number: 1234567890
Hobby :Swimming
Hobby :Movies

Contact - Id: 3, First name: John, Last name: Smith, Birthday: 1964-02-28

Contact - Id: 2, First name: Scott, Last name: Tiger, Birthday: 1990-11-02
Contact Tel Detail - Id: 3, Contact id: 2, Type: Home, Number: 1234567890
Hobby :Swimming
```

You will see the first name was updated, and the home telephone was removed. The telephone can be removed because of the orphanRemoval=true attribute that was defined in the one-to-many association, which instructs the JPA provider (Hibernate) to remove all orphan records that exist in the database but are no longer found in the object when persisted.

```
@OneToMany(mappedBy = "contact", cascade=CascadeType.ALL, orphanRemoval=true)
```

Deleting Data

Deleting data is just as simple. Simply call the EntityManager.remove() method and pass in the contact object. Listing 8-20 shows the updated code to delete a contact.

Listing 8-20. Implementing the delete() Method

```java
package com.apress.prospring4.ch8;

import org.springframework.stereotype.Service;
import org.springframework.stereotype.Repository;
import org.springframework.transaction.annotation.Transactional;

import java.util.List;

import javax.persistence.PersistenceContext;
import javax.persistence.EntityManager;
import javax.persistence.TypedQuery;

import org.apache.commons.logging.Log;
import org.apache.commons.logging.LogFactory;

@Service("jpaContactService")
@Repository
@Transactional
public class ContactServiceImpl implements ContactService {
    private Log log = LogFactory.getLog(ContactServiceImpl.class);

    @PersistenceContext
    private EntityManager em;

    @Transactional(readOnly=true)
    @Override
    public List<Contact> findAll() {
        List<Contact> contacts = em.createNamedQuery("Contact.findAll",
            Contact.class).getResultList();
        return contacts;
    }

    @Transactional(readOnly=true)
    @Override
    public List<Contact> findAllWithDetail() {
        List<Contact> contacts = em.createNamedQuery(
            "Contact.findAllWithDetail", Contact.class).getResultList();
        return contacts;
    }

    @Transactional(readOnly=true)
    @Override
    public Contact findById(Long id) {
        TypedQuery<Contact> query = em.createNamedQuery(
            "Contact.findById", Contact.class);
        query.setParameter("id", id);

        return query.getSingleResult();
    }
```

```java
    @Override
    public Contact save(Contact contact) {
        if (contact.getId() == null) {
            log.info("Inserting new contact");
            em.persist(contact);
        } else {
            em.merge(contact);
            log.info("Updating existing contact");
        }

        log.info("Contact saved with id: " + contact.getId());

        return contact;
    }
    @Override
    public void delete(Contact contact) {
        Contact mergedContact = em.merge(contact);
        em.remove(mergedContact);

        log.info("Contact with id: " + contact.getId()  + " deleted successfully");
    }
}
```

First the EntityManager.merge() method is invoked to merge the state of the entity into the current persistence context. The merge() method returns the managed entity instance. Then EntityManager.remove() is called, passing in the managed contact entity instance. The remove operation deletes the contact record, together with all its associated information, including telephone details and hobbies, as we defined the cascade=CascadeType.ALL in the mapping. To test the delete operation, Listing 8-21 shows the modifications needed to the SpringJPASample class.

Listing 8-21. Testing the Delete Operation

```java
package com.apress.prospring4.ch8;

import java.util.List;

import org.springframework.context.support.GenericXmlApplicationContext;

public class SpringJPASample {
    public static void main(String[] args) {
        GenericXmlApplicationContext ctx = new GenericXmlApplicationContext();
        ctx.load("classpath:META-INF/spring/app-context-annotation.xml");
        ctx.refresh();

        ContactService contactService = ctx.getBean(
            "jpaContactService", ContactService.class);

        Contact contact = contactService.findById(1l);
        contactService.delete(contact);

        listContactsWithDetail(contactService.findAllWithDetail());
    }
```

```
    private static void listContactsWithDetail(List<Contact> contacts) {
        System.out.println("");
        System.out.println("Listing contacts with details:");

        for (Contact contact: contacts) {
            System.out.println(contact);
            if (contact.getContactTelDetails() != null) {
                for (ContactTelDetail contactTelDetail:
                    contact.getContactTelDetails()) {
                    System.out.println(contactTelDetail);
                }
            }
            if (contact.getHobbies() != null) {
                for (Hobby hobby: contact.getHobbies()) {
                    System.out.println(hobby);
                }
            }

            System.out.println();
        }
    }
}
```

The previous listing retrieves the contact with an ID of 1 and then calls the delete() method to delete the contact information. Running the program produces the following output:

```
Listing contacts with details:
Contact - Id: 3, First name: John, Last name: Smith, Birthday: 1964-02-28

Contact - Id: 2, First name: Scott, Last name: Tiger, Birthday: 1990-11-02
Contact Tel Detail - Id: 3, Contact id: 2, Type: Home, Number: 1234567890
Hobby :Swimming
```

You can see that the contact with an ID of 1 was deleted.

Using a Native Query

Having discussed performing trivial database operations by using JPA, now let's move on to some more-advanced topics. Sometimes you may want to have absolute control over the query that will be submitted to the database. One example is using a hierarchical query in an Oracle database. This kind of query is database-specific and referred to as a *native query*.

JPA supports the execution of native queries; EntityManager will submit the query to the database as is, without any mapping or transformation performed. One main benefit of using JPA native queries is the mapping of ResultSet back to the ORM-mapped entity classes. The following two sections discuss how to use a native query to retrieve all contacts and directly map ResultSet back to the Contact objects.

Simple Native Query

To demonstrate how to use a native query, let's implement a new method to retrieve all the contacts from the database. Listing 8-22 shows the new method to be added in the ContactService interface.

Listing 8-22. The findAllByNativeQuery() Method

```
package com.apress.prospring4.ch8;

import java.util.List;

public interface ContactService {
    List<Contact> findAll();
    List<Contact> findAllWithDetail();
    Contact findById(Long id);
    Contact save(Contact contact);
    void delete(Contact contact);
    List<Contact> findAllByNativeQuery();
}
```

Listing 8-23 shows the implementation of the findAllByNativeQuery() method.

Listing 8-23. Implementing the findAllByNativeQuery() Method

```
package com.apress.prospring4.ch8;

import org.springframework.stereotype.Service;
import org.springframework.stereotype.Repository;
import org.springframework.transaction.annotation.Transactional;

import java.util.List;

import javax.persistence.PersistenceContext;
import javax.persistence.EntityManager;
import javax.persistence.TypedQuery;

import org.apache.commons.logging.Log;
import org.apache.commons.logging.LogFactory;

@Service("jpaContactService")
@Repository
@Transactional
public class ContactServiceImpl implements ContactService {
    final static String ALL_CONTACT_NATIVE_QUERY =
        "select id, first_name, last_name, birth_date, version from contact";

    private Log log = LogFactory.getLog(ContactServiceImpl.class);

    @PersistenceContext
    private EntityManager em;

    @Transactional(readOnly=true)
    @Override
    public List<Contact> findAll() {
        List<Contact> contacts = em.createNamedQuery("Contact.findAll",
            Contact.class).getResultList();
        return contacts;
    }
```

```java
    @Transactional(readOnly=true)
    @Override
    public List<Contact> findAllWithDetail() {
        List<Contact> contacts = em.createNamedQuery(
            "Contact.findAllWithDetail", Contact.class).getResultList();
        return contacts;
    }

    @Transactional(readOnly=true)
    @Override
    public Contact findById(Long id) {
        TypedQuery<Contact> query = em.createNamedQuery(
            "Contact.findById", Contact.class);
        query.setParameter("id", id);

        return query.getSingleResult();
    }

    @Override
    public Contact save(Contact contact) {
        if (contact.getId() == null) {
            log.info("Inserting new contact");
            em.persist(contact);
        } else {
            em.merge(contact);
            log.info("Updating existing contact");
        }

        log.info("Contact saved with id: " + contact.getId());

        return contact;
    }

    @Override
    public void delete(Contact contact) {
        Contact mergedContact = em.merge(contact);
        em.remove(mergedContact);

        log.info("Contact with id: " + contact.getId()  + " deleted successfully");
    }

    @Transactional(readOnly=true)
    @Override
    public List<Contact> findAllByNativeQuery() {
        return em.createNativeQuery(ALL_CONTACT_NATIVE_QUERY,
            Contact.class).getResultList();
    }
}
```

You can see that the native query is just a simple SQL statement to retrieve all the columns from the CONTACT table. To create and execute the query, EntityManager.createNativeQuery() was first called, passing in the query string as well as the result type. The result type should be a mapped entity class (in this case the Contact class). The createNativeQuery() method returns a Query interface, which provides the getResultList() operation to get the result list. The JPA provider will execute the query and transform the ResultSet into the entity instances, based on the JPA mappings defined in the entity class. Executing the previous method produces the same result as the findAll() method.

Native Query with SQL ResultSet Mapping

Besides the mapped domain object, you can pass in a string, which indicates the name of a SQL ResultSet mapping. A SQL ResultSet mapping is defined at the entity-class level by using the @SqlResultSetMapping annotation. A SQL ResultSet mapping can have one or more entity and column mappings.

Let's define a simple SQL ResultSet mapping in the Contact entity class (see Listing 8-24).

Listing 8-24. Using SQL ResultSet Mapping

```
package com.apress.prospring4.ch8;

import static javax.persistence.GenerationType.IDENTITY;

import java.io.Serializable;
import java.util.Date;
import java.util.HashSet;
import java.util.Set;
import javax.persistence.Entity;
import javax.persistence.Table;
import javax.persistence.Id;
import javax.persistence.GeneratedValue;
import javax.persistence.Column;
import javax.persistence.Version;
import javax.persistence.Temporal;
import javax.persistence.TemporalType;
import javax.persistence.OneToMany;
import javax.persistence.ManyToMany;
import javax.persistence.JoinTable;
import javax.persistence.JoinColumn;
import javax.persistence.CascadeType;
import javax.persistence.NamedQueries;
import javax.persistence.NamedQuery;
import javax.persistence.SqlResultSetMapping;
import javax.persistence.EntityResult;

@Entity
@Table(name = "contact")
@NamedQueries({
    @NamedQuery(name="Contact.findAll", query="select c from Contact c"),
    @NamedQuery(name="Contact.findById",
        query="select distinct c from Contact c left join fetch c.contactTelDetails t left join
fetch c.hobbies h where c.id = :id"),
```

```
    @NamedQuery(name="Contact.findAllWithDetail",
        query="select distinct c from Contact c left join fetch c.contactTelDetails t left join
fetch c.hobbies h")
})
@SqlResultSetMapping(
    name="contactResult",
    entities=@EntityResult(entityClass=Contact.class)
)
public class Contact implements Serializable {
    private Long id;
    private int version;
    private String firstName;
    private String lastName;
    private Date birthDate;
    private Set<ContactTelDetail> contactTelDetails = new HashSet<ContactTelDetail>();
    private Set<Hobby> hobbies = new HashSet<Hobby>();

    @Id
    @GeneratedValue(strategy = IDENTITY)
    @Column(name = "ID")
    public Long getId() {
        return this.id;
    }

    public void setId(Long id) {
        this.id = id;
    }

    @Version
    @Column(name = "VERSION")
    public int getVersion() {
        return this.version;
    }

    public void setVersion(int version) {
        this.version = version;
    }

    @Column(name = "FIRST_NAME")
    public String getFirstName() {
        return this.firstName;
    }

    public void setFirstName(String firstName) {
        this.firstName = firstName;
    }

    @Column(name = "LAST_NAME")
    public String getLastName() {
        return this.lastName;
    }
```

```java
    public void setLastName(String lastName) {
        this.lastName = lastName;
    }
    @Temporal(TemporalType.DATE)
    @Column(name = "BIRTH_DATE")
    public Date getBirthDate() {
        return this.birthDate;
    }

    public void setBirthDate(Date birthDate) {
        this.birthDate = birthDate;
    }

    @OneToMany(mappedBy = "contact", cascade=CascadeType.ALL,
        orphanRemoval=true)
    public Set<ContactTelDetail> getContactTelDetails() {
        return this.contactTelDetails;
    }

    public void setContactTelDetails(Set<ContactTelDetail> contactTelDetails) {
     this.contactTelDetails = contactTelDetails;
    }

    public void addContactTelDetail(ContactTelDetail contactTelDetail) {
        contactTelDetail.setContact(this);
        getContactTelDetails().add(contactTelDetail);
    }

    public void removeContactTelDetail(ContactTelDetail contactTelDetail) {
        getContactTelDetails().remove(contactTelDetail);
    }

    @ManyToMany
    @JoinTable(name = "contact_hobby_detail",
        joinColumns = @JoinColumn(name = "CONTACT_ID"),
        inverseJoinColumns = @JoinColumn(name = "HOBBY_ID"))
    public Set<Hobby> getHobbies() {
        return this.hobbies;
    }

    public void setHobbies(Set<Hobby> hobbies) {
        this.hobbies = hobbies;
    }

    @Override
    public String toString() {
        return "Contact - Id: " + id + ", First name: " + firstName
            + ", Last name: " + lastName + ", Birthday: " + birthDate;
    }
}
```

A SQL ResultSet mapping called contactResult is defined for the entity class, with the entityClass attribute in the Contact class itself. JPA supports more-complex mapping for multiple entities and supports mapping down to column-level mapping.

After the SQL ResultSet mapping is defined, the findAllByNativeQuery() method can be invoked using the ResultSet mapping's name. Listing 8-25 shows the updated ContactService code.

Listing 8-25. Implementing the findAllByNativeQuery() Method by Using SQL ResultSet Mapping

```java
package com.apress.prospring4.ch8;

import org.springframework.stereotype.Service;
import org.springframework.stereotype.Repository;
import org.springframework.transaction.annotation.Transactional;

import java.util.List;

import javax.persistence.PersistenceContext;
import javax.persistence.EntityManager;
import javax.persistence.TypedQuery;

import org.apache.commons.logging.Log;
import org.apache.commons.logging.LogFactory;

@Service("jpaContactService")
@Repository
@Transactional
public class ContactServiceImpl implements ContactService {
    final static String ALL_CONTACT_NATIVE_QUERY =
        "select id, first_name, last_name, birth_date, version from contact";

    private Log log = LogFactory.getLog(ContactServiceImpl.class);

    @PersistenceContext
    private EntityManager em;

    @Transactional(readOnly=true)
    @Override
    public List<Contact> findAll() {
        List<Contact> contacts = em.createNamedQuery("Contact.findAll",
            Contact.class).getResultList();
        return contacts;
    }

    @Transactional(readOnly=true)
    @Override
    public List<Contact> findAllWithDetail() {
        List<Contact> contacts = em.createNamedQuery(
            "Contact.findAllWithDetail", Contact.class).getResultList();
        return contacts;
    }
```

```
    @Transactional(readOnly=true)
    @Override
    public Contact findById(Long id) {
        TypedQuery<Contact> query = em.createNamedQuery(
            "Contact.findById", Contact.class);
        query.setParameter("id", id);

        return query.getSingleResult();
    }

    @Override
    public Contact save(Contact contact) {
        if (contact.getId() == null) {
            log.info("Inserting new contact");
            em.persist(contact);
        } else {
            em.merge(contact);
            log.info("Updating existing contact");
        }

        log.info("Contact saved with id: " + contact.getId());

        return contact;
    }

    @Override
    public void delete(Contact contact) {
        Contact mergedContact = em.merge(contact);
        em.remove(mergedContact);

        log.info("Contact with id: " + contact.getId()  + " deleted successfully");
    }

    @Transactional(readOnly=true)
    @Override
    public List<Contact> findAllByNativeQuery() {
        return em.createNativeQuery(ALL_CONTACT_NATIVE_QUERY,
            "contactResult").getResultList();
    }
}
```

As you can see, JPA also provides strong support for executing native queries, with a flexible SQL ResultSet mapping facility provided.

Using the JPA 2 Criteria API for a Criteria Query

Most applications provide a front end for users to search for information. Most likely, a large number of searchable fields are displayed, and the users enter information in only some of them and do the search. It's very difficult to prepare a large number of queries, with each possible combination of parameters that users may choose to enter. In this situation, the criteria API query feature comes to the rescue.

In JPA 2, one major new feature introduced was a strongly typed Criteria API query. In this new Criteria API, the criteria being passed into the query is based on the mapped entity classes' meta-model. As a result, each criteria specified is strongly typed, and errors will be discovered at compile time, rather than runtime.

In the JPA Criteria API, an entity class meta-model is represented by the entity class name with a suffix of an underscore (_). For example, the meta-model class for the Contact entity class is Contact_. Listing 8-26 shows the Contact_ class.

Listing 8-26. JPA 2 Strongly Typed Criteria API: Meta-Model

```
package com.apress.prospring4.ch8;

import java.util.Date;
import javax.persistence.metamodel.SetAttribute;
import javax.persistence.metamodel.SingularAttribute;
import javax.persistence.metamodel.StaticMetamodel;

@StaticMetamodel(Contact.class)
public abstract class Contact_ {
    public static volatile SingularAttribute<Contact, Long> id;
    public static volatile SetAttribute<Contact, ContactTelDetail>
        contactTelDetails;
    public static volatile SingularAttribute<Contact, String> lastName;
    public static volatile SingularAttribute<Contact, Date> birthDate;
    public static volatile SetAttribute<Contact, Hobby> hobbies;
    public static volatile SingularAttribute<Contact, String> firstName;
    public static volatile SingularAttribute<Contact, Integer> version;
}
```

The meta-model class is annotated with @StaticMetamodel, and the attribute is the mapped entity class. Within the class are the declaration of each attribute and its related types.

It would be tedious to code and maintain those meta-model classes. However, tools can help generate those meta-model classes automatically based on the JPA mappings within the entity classes. The one provided by Hibernate is called Hibernate Metamodel Generator (http://www.hibernate.org/subprojects/jpamodelgen.html).

The way you go about generating your meta-model classes depends on what tools you are using to develop and build your project. We recommend reading the Usage section of the documentation (http://docs.jboss.org/hibernate/jpamodelgen/1.3/reference/en-US/html_single/#chapter-usage) for specific details. The sample code that comes as part of this book uses Maven to generate the meta-classes. The required dependency for meta-model class generation is listed in Table 8-2.

Table 8-2. *Dependency for Meta-Model Class Generation*

JAR File	Description
hibernate-jpamodelgen-1.3.0.Final.jar	This is the main library for generating meta-model classes. You can locate the file at hibernate-jpamodelgen-1.3.0.Final after extracting the downloaded package or through a build tool such as Maven.

With our class generation strategy set up, let's define a query that accepts both the first name and last name for searching contacts. Listing 8-27 shows the definition of the new method findByCriteriaQuery() in the ContactService interface.

Listing 8-27. The findByCriteriaQuery() Method

```
package com.apress.prospring4.ch8;

import java.util.List;

public interface ContactService {
    List<Contact> findAll();
    List<Contact> findAllWithDetail();
    Contact findById(Long id);
    Contact save(Contact contact);
    void delete(Contact contact);
    List<Contact> findAllByNativeQuery();
    List<Contact> findByCriteriaQuery(String firstName, String lastName);
}
```

Listing 8-28 shows the implementation of the findByCriteriaQuery() method using a JPA 2 criteria API query.

Listing 8-28. Implementing the findByCriteriaQuery() Method

```
package com.apress.prospring4.ch8;

import org.springframework.stereotype.Service;
import org.springframework.stereotype.Repository;
import org.springframework.transaction.annotation.Transactional;

import java.util.List;

import javax.persistence.PersistenceContext;
import javax.persistence.EntityManager;
import javax.persistence.TypedQuery;
import javax.persistence.criteria.CriteriaBuilder;
import javax.persistence.criteria.CriteriaQuery;
import javax.persistence.criteria.Root;
import javax.persistence.criteria.JoinType;
import javax.persistence.criteria.Predicate;

import org.apache.commons.logging.Log;
import org.apache.commons.logging.LogFactory;

@Service("jpaContactService")
@Repository
@Transactional
public class ContactServiceImpl implements ContactService {
    final static String ALL_CONTACT_NATIVE_QUERY =
        "select id, first_name, last_name, birth_date, version from contact";

    private Log log = LogFactory.getLog(ContactServiceImpl.class);

    @PersistenceContext
    private EntityManager em;
```

```java
@Transactional(readOnly=true)
@Override
public List<Contact> findAll() {
    List<Contact> contacts = em.createNamedQuery("Contact.findAll",
        Contact.class).getResultList();
    return contacts;
}

@Transactional(readOnly=true)
@Override
public List<Contact> findAllWithDetail() {
    List<Contact> contacts = em.createNamedQuery(
        "Contact.findAllWithDetail", Contact.class).getResultList();
    return contacts;
}

@Transactional(readOnly=true)
@Override
public Contact findById(Long id) {
    TypedQuery<Contact> query = em.createNamedQuery(
        "Contact.findById", Contact.class);
    query.setParameter("id", id);

    return query.getSingleResult();
}

@Override
public Contact save(Contact contact) {
    if (contact.getId() == null) {
        log.info("Inserting new contact");
        em.persist(contact);
    } else {
        em.merge(contact);
        log.info("Updating existing contact");
    }

    log.info("Contact saved with id: " + contact.getId());

    return contact;
}

@Override
public void delete(Contact contact) {
    Contact mergedContact = em.merge(contact);
    em.remove(mergedContact);

    log.info("Contact with id: " + contact.getId()  + " deleted successfully");
}

@Transactional(readOnly=true)
@Override
```

```
public List<Contact> findAllByNativeQuery() {
    return em.createNativeQuery(ALL_CONTACT_NATIVE_QUERY,
        "contactResult").getResultList();
}

@Transactional(readOnly=true)
@Override
public List<Contact> findByCriteriaQuery(String firstName, String lastName) {
    log.info("Finding contact for firstName: " + firstName
                + " and lastName: " + lastName);

    CriteriaBuilder cb = em.getCriteriaBuilder();
    CriteriaQuery<Contact> criteriaQuery = cb.createQuery(Contact.class);
    Root<Contact> contactRoot = criteriaQuery.from(Contact.class);
    contactRoot.fetch(Contact_.contactTelDetails, JoinType.LEFT);
    contactRoot.fetch(Contact_.hobbies, JoinType.LEFT);

    criteriaQuery.select(contactRoot).distinct(true);

    Predicate criteria = cb.conjunction();

    if (firstName != null) {
        Predicate p = cb.equal(contactRoot.get(Contact_.firstName),
            firstName);
         criteria = cb.and(criteria, p);
    }
    if (lastName != null) {
        Predicate p = cb.equal(contactRoot.get(Contact_.lastName),
            lastName);
        criteria = cb.and(criteria, p);
    }

    criteriaQuery.where(criteria);

    return em.createQuery(criteriaQuery).getResultList();
}
}
```

Listing 8-28 is breaks down the criteria API usage:

- EntityManager.getCriteriaBuilder() is called to retrieve an instance of CriteriaBuilder.

- A typed query is created using CriteriaBuilder.createQuery(), passing in Contact as the result type.

- The CriteriaQuery.from() method is invoked, passing in the entity class. The result is a query root object (the Root<Contact> interface) corresponding to the specified entity. The query root object forms the basis for path expressions within the query.

- The two Root.fetch() method calls enforce the eager fetching of the associations relating to telephone details and hobbies. The JoinType.LEFT argument specifies an outer join. Calling the Root.fetch() method with JoinType.LEFT as the second argument is equivalent to specifying the left join fetch join operation in JPQL.

385

- The CriteriaQuery.select() method is called and passes the root query object as the result type. The distinct() method with true means that duplicate records should be eliminated.

- A Predicate instance is obtained by calling the CriteriaBuilder.conjunction() method, which means that a conjunction of one or more restrictions is made. A Predicate can be a simple or compound predicate, and a predicate is a restriction that indicates the selection criteria defined by an expression.

- The first- and last-name arguments are checked. If the argument is not null, a new Predicate will be constructed using the CriteriaBuilder() method (that is, the CriteriaBuilder. and() method). The method equal() is to specify an equal restriction, within which Root. get() was called, passing in the corresponding attribute of the entity class meta-model to which the restriction applies. The constructed predicate is then "conjunct" with the existing predicate (stored by the variable criteria) by calling the CriteriaBuilder.and() method.

- The Predicate is constructed with all the criteria and restrictions and passed as the where clause to the query by calling the CriteriaQuery.where() method.

- Finally, CriteriaQuery is passed to the EntityManager. The EntityManager then constructs the query based on the CriteriaQuery passed in, executes the query, and returns the result.

To test the criteria query operation, Listing 8-29 shows the updated SpringJPASample class.

Listing 8-29. Testing the findByCriteriaQuery() Method

```
package com.apress.prospring4.ch8;

import java.util.List;
import java.util.Date;
import java.util.Set;

import org.springframework.context.support.GenericXmlApplicationContext;

public class SpringJPASample {
    public static void main(String[] args) {
        GenericXmlApplicationContext ctx = new GenericXmlApplicationContext();
        ctx.load("classpath:META-INF/spring/app-context-annotation.xml");
        ctx.refresh();

        ContactService contactService = ctx.getBean(
            "jpaContactService", ContactService.class);

        List<Contact> contacts = contactService.findByCriteriaQuery("John", "Smith");
        listContactsWithDetail(contacts);
    }

    private static void listContactsWithDetail(List<Contact> contacts) {
        System.out.println("");
        System.out.println("Listing contacts with details:");

        for (Contact contact: contacts) {
            System.out.println(contact);
```

```
        if (contact.getContactTelDetails() != null) {
            for (ContactTelDetail contactTelDetail:
                contact.getContactTelDetails()) {
                System.out.println(contactTelDetail);
            }
        }

        if (contact.getHobbies() != null) {
            for (Hobby hobby: contact.getHobbies()) {
                System.out.println(hobby);
            }
        }

        System.out.println();
    }
  }
}
```

Running the program produces the following output (other output was omitted):

```
INFO apress.prospring4.ch8.ContactServiceImpl:  91 - Finding contact for firstName: John and
lastName: Smith
...

Listing contacts with details:
Contact - Id: 3, First name: John, Last name: Smith, Birthday: 1964-02-28
```

You can try a different combination or pass a null value to either of the arguments to observe the output.

Introducing Spring Data JPA

The Spring Data JPA project is a subproject under the Spring Data umbrella project. The main objective of the project is to provide additional features for simplifying application development with JPA.

Spring Data JPA provides several main features. In this section, we discuss two. The first one is the Repository abstraction, and the other one is the entity listener for keeping track of basic audit information of entity classes.

Adding Spring Data JPA Library Dependencies

To use Spring Data JPA, we need to add the dependency to the project. Table 8-3 describes the Maven dependency information.

Table 8-3. *Maven Dependency for Spring Data JPA*

Group ID	Artifact ID	Version	Description
org.springframework.data	spring-data-jpa	1.3.0.RELEASE	The Spring Data JPA library
com.google.guava	guava	14.0.1	Helpful utility classes for handling collections, etc
org.springframework	spring-aop	4.0.2.RELEASE	The Spring AOP package for aspect-oriented programming support

Using Spring Data JPA Repository Abstraction for Database Operations

One of the main concepts of Spring Data and all its subprojects is the Repository abstraction, which belongs to the Spring Data Commons project (https://github.com/spring-projects/spring-data-commons). At the time of this writing, it's at version 1.5.2.RELEASE. In Spring Data JPA, the repository abstraction wraps the underlying JPA EntityManager and provides a simpler interface for JPA-based data access. The central interface within Spring Data is the org.springframework.data.repository.Repository<T,ID extends Serializable> interface, which is a marker interface belonging to the Spring Data Commons distribution. Spring Data provides various extensions of the Repository interface; one of them is the org.springframework.data.repository.CrudRepository interface (which also belongs to the Spring Data Commons project), which we discuss in this section.

The CrudRepository interface provides a number of commonly used methods. Listing 8-30 shows the interface declaration, which is extracted from Spring Data Commons project source code.

Listing 8-30. The CrudRepository Interface

```
package org.springframework.data.repository;

import java.io.Serializable;

@NoRepositoryBean
public interface CrudRepository<T, ID extends Serializable> extends Repository<T, ID> {
    long count();
    void delete(ID id);
    void delete(Iterable<? extends T> entities);
    void delete(T entity);
    void deleteAll();
    boolean exists(ID id);
    Iterable<T> findAll();
    T findOne(ID id);
    Iterable<T> save(Iterable<? extends T> entities);
    T save(T entity);
}
```

Although the method naming is self-explanatory, it's better to show how the Repository abstraction works by going through a simple example. Let's revise the ContactService interface a bit, down to just three finder methods. Listing 8-31 shows the revised ContactService interface. After the ContactService interface is revised, the JpaSample and ContactServiceImpl classes will have errors. Just delete these two classes and proceed with the implementation of the interface by using Spring Data JPA.

Listing 8-31. The Revised ContactService Interface

```
package com.apress.prospring4.ch8;

import java.util.List;

public interface ContactService {
    List<Contact> findAll();
    List<Contact> findByFirstName(String firstName);
    List<Contact> findByFirstNameAndLastName(String firstName, String lastName);
}
```

The next step is to prepare the ContactRepository interface, which extends the CrudRepository interface. Listing 8-32 shows the ContactRepository interface.

Listing 8-32. The ContactRepository Interface

```
package com.apress.prospring4.ch8;

import java.util.List;

import org.springframework.data.repository.CrudRepository;

public interface ContactRepository extends CrudRepository<Contact, Long> {
    List<Contact> findByFirstName(String firstName);
    List<Contact> findByFirstNameAndLastName(String firstName, String lastName);
}
```

We just need to declare two methods in this interface, as the findAll() method is already provided by the CrudRepository.findAll() method. As shown in the preceding listing, the ContactRepository interface extends the CrudRepository interface, passing in the entity class (Contact) and the ID type (Long). One fancy aspect of Spring Data's Repository abstraction is that when you use the common naming convention such as findByFirstName and findByFirstNameAndLastName, you don't need to provide Spring Data JPA with the named query. Instead, Spring Data JPA will "infer" and construct the query for you based on the method name. For example, for the findByFirstName() method, Spring Data JPA will automatically prepare the query select c from Contact c where c.firstName = :firstName for you and set the named parameter firstName from the argument.

To use the Repository abstraction, we have to define it in Spring's configuration. Listing 8-33 shows the configuration file (app-context-annotation.xml).

Listing 8-33. JPA Repository Configuration in Spring

```
<?xml version="1.0" encoding="UTF-8"?>

<beans xmlns="http://www.springframework.org/schema/beans"
    xmlns:xsi="http://www.w3.org/2001/XMLSchema-instance"
    xmlns:context="http://www.springframework.org/schema/context"
    xmlns:jdbc="http://www.springframework.org/schema/jdbc"
    xmlns:jpa="http://www.springframework.org/schema/data/jpa"
    xmlns:tx="http://www.springframework.org/schema/tx"
    xsi:schemaLocation="http://www.springframework.org/schema/beans
        http://www.springframework.org/schema/beans/spring-beans.xsd
        http://www.springframework.org/schema/context
        http://www.springframework.org/schema/context/spring-context.xsd
        http://www.springframework.org/schema/jdbc
        http://www.springframework.org/schema/jdbc/spring-jdbc.xsd
        http://www.springframework.org/schema/data/jpa
        http://www.springframework.org/schema/data/jpa/spring-jpa.xsd
        http://www.springframework.org/schema/tx
        http://www.springframework.org/schema/tx/spring-tx.xsd">

    <jdbc:embedded-database id="dataSource" type="H2">
        <jdbc:script location="classpath:META-INF/sql/schema.sql"/>
        <jdbc:script location="classpath:META-INF/sql/test-data.sql"/>
    </jdbc:embedded-database>
```

```xml
<bean id="transactionManager"
    class="org.springframework.orm.jpa.JpaTransactionManager">
    <property name="entityManagerFactory" ref="emf"/>
</bean>

<tx:annotation-driven transaction-manager="transactionManager" />
<bean id="emf" class="org.springframework.orm.jpa.LocalContainerEntityManagerFactoryBean">
    <property name="dataSource" ref="dataSource" />
    <property name="jpaVendorAdapter">
        <bean class="org.springframework.orm.jpa.vendor.HibernateJpaVendorAdapter" />
    </property>
    <property name="packagesToScan"
         value="com.apress.prospring4.ch8"/>
    <property name="jpaProperties">
        <props>
            <prop key="hibernate.dialect">
                org.hibernate.dialect.H2Dialect
            </prop>
            <prop key="hibernate.max_fetch_depth">3</prop>
            <prop key="hibernate.jdbc.fetch_size">50</prop>
            <prop key="hibernate.jdbc.batch_size">10</prop>
            <prop key="hibernate.show_sql">true</prop>
        </props>
    </property>
</bean>

<context:component-scan base-package="com.apress.prospring4.ch8"/>

<jpa:repositories base-package="com.apress.prospring4.ch8"
                  entity-manager-factory-ref="emf"
                  transaction-manager-ref="transactionManager"/>
</beans>
```

First, we need to add the jpa namespace in the configuration file. Then, the `<jpa:repositories>` tag is used to configure Spring Data JPA's Repository abstraction. We instruct Spring to scan the package `com.apress.prospring4.ch8` for repository interfaces and to pass in `EntityManagerFactory` and the transaction manager, respectively.

Listing 8-34 shows the implementation of the three finder methods of the `ContactService` interface.

Listing 8-34. The `ContactServiceImpl` Class

```java
package com.apress.prospring4.ch8;

import org.springframework.stereotype.Service;
import org.springframework.stereotype.Repository;
import org.springframework.transaction.annotation.Transactional;

import org.springframework.beans.factory.annotation.Autowired;

import java.util.List;
import java.util.Lists;
```

```
@Service("springJpaContactService")
@Repository
@Transactional
public class ContactServiceImpl implements ContactService {
    @Autowired
    private ContactRepository contactRepository;

    @Transactional(readOnly=true)
    public List<Contact> findAll() {
        return Lists.newArrayList(contactRepository.findAll());
    }

    @Transactional(readOnly=true)
    public List<Contact> findByFirstName(String firstName) {
        return contactRepository.findByFirstName(firstName);
    }

    @Transactional(readOnly=true)
    public List<Contact> findByFirstNameAndLastName(
        String firstName, String lastName) {
        return contactRepository.findByFirstNameAndLastName(
            firstName, lastName);
    }
}
```

You can see that instead of EntityManager, we just need to inject the ContactRepository interface into the service class, and Spring Data JPA will do all the low-level work for us. Listing 8-35 shows the updated testing program.

Listing 8-35. The SpringJpaSample Class

```
package com.apress.prospring4.ch8;

import java.util.List;
import java.util.Date;
import java.util.Set;

import org.springframework.context.support.GenericXmlApplicationContext;

public class SpringJPASample {
    public static void main(String[] args) {
        GenericXmlApplicationContext ctx = new GenericXmlApplicationContext();
        ctx.load("classpath:META-INF/spring/app-context-annotation.xml");
        ctx.refresh();

        ContactService contactService = ctx.getBean(
            "springJpaContactService", ContactService.class);

        listContacts("Find all:", contactService.findAll());
        listContacts("Find by first name:", contactService.findByFirstName("Chris"));
        listContacts("Find by first and last name:",
            contactService.findByFirstNameAndLastName("Chris", "Schaefer"));
    }
```

```
    private static void listContacts(String message, List<Contact> contacts) {
        System.out.println("");
        System.out.println(message);
        for (Contact contact: contacts) {
            System.out.println(contact);
            System.out.println();
        }
    }
}
```

Running the program yields the contact listing as expected.

You have seen how Spring Data JPA can help simplify the development. We don't need to prepare a named query, don't need to call the EntityManager.createQuery() method, and so on.

What we covered were only the simplest examples. The Repository abstraction supports a lot of features, including defining custom queries with the @Query annotation, the Specification feature (belonging to the Spring Data JPA project as of version 1.4.4.RELEASE), and so on. For more information, please refer to the reference documentation listed here:

- *Spring Data Commons project*: http://static.springsource.org/spring-data/data-commons/docs/current/reference/html/

- *Spring Data JPA project*: http://static.springsource.org/spring-data/data-jpa/docs/current/reference/html/

Keeping Track of Changes on the Entity Class

In most applications, we need to keep track of basic audit activities for the business data being maintained by users. The audit information typically includes the user who creates the data, the date it was created, the date it was last modified, and the user who last modified it.

The Spring Data JPA project provides this function in the form of a JPA entity listener, which helps you keep track of the audit information automatically. To use the feature, the entity class needs to implement the org.springframework.data.domain.Auditable<U,ID extends Serializable> interface (belonging to Spring Data Commons) or extend any class that implemented the interface. Listing 8-36 shows the Auditable interface that was extracted from Spring Data's reference documentation.

Listing 8-36. The Auditable Interface

```
package org.springframework.data.domain;

import java.io.Serializable;

import org.joda.time.DateTime;

public interface Auditable<U, ID extends Serializable>
    extends Persistable<ID> {

    U getCreatedBy();
    void setCreatedBy(final U createdBy);

    DateTime getCreatedDate();
    void setCreated(final DateTime creationDate);
```

```
    U getLastModifiedBy();
    void setLastModifiedBy(final U lastModifiedBy);

    DateTime getLastModifiedDate();
    void setLastModified(final DateTime lastModifiedDate);
}
```

To show how it works, let's create a new table called CONTACT_AUDIT in our database schema, which is based on the CONTACT table, with four audit-related columns added. Listing 8-37 shows the table creation script (schema.sql).

Listing 8-37. The CONTACT_AUDIT Table

```
CREATE TABLE CONTACT_AUDIT (
        ID INT NOT NULL AUTO_INCREMENT
    , FIRST_NAME VARCHAR(60) NOT NULL
    , LAST_NAME VARCHAR(40) NOT NULL
    , BIRTH_DATE DATE
    , VERSION INT NOT NULL DEFAULT 0
    , CREATED_BY VARCHAR(20)
    , CREATED_DATE TIMESTAMP
    , LAST_MODIFIED_BY VARCHAR(20)
    , LAST_MODIFIED_DATE TIMESTAMP
    , UNIQUE UQ_CONTACT_AUDIT_1 (FIRST_NAME, LAST_NAME)
    , PRIMARY KEY (ID)
);
```

The four columns with bold characters indicate the audit-related columns. The next step is to create the entity class called ContactAudit. Listing 8-38 shows the ContactAudit class.

Listing 8-38. The ContactAudit Class

```
package com.apress.prospring4.ch8;

import static javax.persistence.GenerationType.IDENTITY;

import java.io.Serializable;
import java.util.Date;
import javax.persistence.Entity;
import javax.persistence.Table;
import javax.persistence.Id;
import javax.persistence.GeneratedValue;
import javax.persistence.Column;
import javax.persistence.Version;
import javax.persistence.Temporal;
import javax.persistence.TemporalType;
import javax.persistence.Transient;
import org.hibernate.annotations.Type;
import org.springframework.data.domain.Auditable;
import org.joda.time.DateTime;
```

```java
@Entity
@Table(name = "contact_audit")
public class ContactAudit implements Auditable<String, Long>, Serializable {
    private Long id;
    private int version;
    private String firstName;
    private String lastName;
    private Date birthDate;
    private String createdBy;
    private DateTime createdDate;
    private String lastModifiedBy;
    private DateTime lastModifiedDate;

    @Id
    @GeneratedValue(strategy = IDENTITY)
    @Column(name = "ID")
    public Long getId() {
        return this.id;
    }

    public void setId(Long id) {
        this.id = id;
    }

    @Version
    @Column(name = "VERSION")
    public int getVersion() {
        return this.version;
    }

    public void setVersion(int version) {
        this.version = version;
    }
    @Column(name = "FIRST_NAME")
    public String getFirstName() {
        return this.firstName;
    }

    public void setFirstName(String firstName) {
        this.firstName = firstName;
    }

    @Column(name = "LAST_NAME")
    public String getLastName() {
        return this.lastName;
    }

    public void setLastName(String lastName) {
        this.lastName = lastName;
    }
```

```java
@Temporal(TemporalType.DATE)
@Column(name = "BIRTH_DATE")
public Date getBirthDate() {
    return this.birthDate;
}

public void setBirthDate(Date birthDate) {
    this.birthDate = birthDate;
}

@Column(name="CREATED_BY")
public String getCreatedBy() {
    return createdBy;
}

public void setCreatedBy(String createdBy) {
    this.createdBy = createdBy;
}
@Column(name="CREATED_DATE")
@Type(type="org.jadira.usertype.dateandtime.joda.PersistentDateTime")
public DateTime getCreatedDate() {
    return createdDate;
}

public void setCreatedDate(DateTime createdDate) {
    this.createdDate = createdDate;
}

@Column(name="LAST_MODIFIED_BY")
public String getLastModifiedBy() {
    return lastModifiedBy;
}

public void setLastModifiedBy(String lastModifiedBy) {
    this.lastModifiedBy = lastModifiedBy;
}

@Column(name="LAST_MODIFIED_DATE")
@Type(type="org.jadira.usertype.dateandtime.joda.PersistentDateTime")
public DateTime getLastModifiedDate() {
    return lastModifiedDate;
}

public void setLastModifiedDate(DateTime lastModifiedDate) {
    this.lastModifiedDate = lastModifiedDate;
}

@Transient
public boolean isNew() {
    if (id == null) {
        return true;
```

```
        } else {
            return false;
        }
    }

    public String toString() {
        return "Contact - Id: " + id + ", First name: " + firstName
            + ", Last name: " + lastName + ", Birthday: " + birthDate
            + ", Create by: " + createdBy + ", Create date: " + createdDate
            + ", Modified by: " + lastModifiedBy + ", Modified date: "
            + lastModifiedDate;
    }
}
```

The ContactAudit entity class implements the Auditable interface and its methods by mapping the four auditing columns. The @Column annotations are applied to map to the actual column in the table. For the two date attributes (createdDate and lastModifiedDate), the Hibernate custom user type annotation @Type is applied with the implementation class set to org.joda.time.contrib.hibernate.PersistentDateTime. As the Spring Data JPA's Auditable interface uses the Joda-time library's DateTime type, the joda-time-hibernate library provides this custom user type for use with Hibernate when persisting the attribute into the TIMESTAMP column in the database. The isNew() method of the Auditable interface (inherited from the org.springframework.data.domain.Persistable<ID extends Serializable> interface) is also implemented. The annotation @Transient means that the field doesn't need to persist. Spring Data JPA uses this function to identify whether it's a new entity in order to determine whether we need to set the createdBy and createdDate attributes. In the implementation, we just check the ID, and if the value is null, we return true, which it means it's a new entity instance.

Listing 8-39 shows the ContactAuditService interface, where we define only a few methods to demonstrate the auditing feature.

Listing 8-39. The ContactAuditService Interface

```java
package com.apress.prospring4.ch8;

import java.util.List;

public interface ContactAuditService {
    List<ContactAudit> findAll();
    ContactAudit findById(Long id);
    ContactAudit save(ContactAudit contact);
}
```

The next step is to create the ContactAuditRepository interface, which is shown in Listing 8-40.

Listing 8-40. The ContactAuditRepository Interface

```java
package com.apress.prospring4.ch8;

import org.springframework.data.repository.CrudRepository;

public interface ContactAuditRepository extends CrudRepository<ContactAudit, Long> {
}
```

The ContactAuditRepository interface just extends CrudRepository, which has already implemented all the methods that we are going to use for ContactAuditService. The findById() method is implemented by the CrudRepository.findOne() method.

Listing 8-41 shows the service implementation class ContactAuditServiceImpl.

Listing 8-41. The ContactAuditServiceImpl Class

```
package com.apress.prospring4.ch8;

import org.springframework.stereotype.Service;
import org.springframework.stereotype.Repository;
import org.springframework.transaction.annotation.Transactional;
import org.springframework.beans.factory.annotation.Autowired;

import java.util.List;
import com.google.common.collect.Lists;

@Service("contactAuditService")
@Repository
@Transactional
public class ContactAuditServiceImpl implements ContactAuditService {
    @Autowired
    private ContactAuditRepository contactAuditRepository;

    @Transactional(readOnly=true)
    public List<ContactAudit> findAll() {
        return Lists.newArrayList(contactAuditRepository.findAll());
    }

    public ContactAudit findById(Long id) {
        return contactAuditRepository.findOne(id);
    }

    public ContactAudit save(ContactAudit contact) {
        return contactAuditRepository.save(contact);
    }
}
```

We also need to do a little configuration work. The first task is to declare AuditingEntityListener<T>, which is a JPA entity listener that provides the auditing service. To declare the listener, create a file called /src/main/resources/ META-INF/orm.xml (it's mandatory to use this file name, which is indicated by JPA specification) under the project root folder and declare the listener, like the one in Listing 8-42.

Listing 8-42. Declaring the Entity Listener

```
<?xml version="1.0" encoding="UTF-8" ?>

<entity-mappings xmlns="http://java.sun.com/xml/ns/persistence/orm"
    xmlns:xsi="http://www.w3.org/2001/XMLSchema-instance"
    xsi:schemaLocation="http://java.sun.com/xml/ns/persistence/orm
        http://java.sun.com/xml/ns/persistence/orm_2_0.xsd"
        version="2.0">
    <description>JPA</description>
```

```
        <persistence-unit-metadata>
            <persistence-unit-defaults>
                <entity-listeners>
                    <entity-listener
class="org.springframework.data.jpa.domain.support.AuditingEntityListener" />
                </entity-listeners>
            </persistence-unit-defaults>
        </persistence-unit-metadata>
</entity-mappings>
```

The JPA provider will discover this listener during persistence operations (save and update events) for audit fields processing.

We also need to define the listener in Spring's configuration. Listing 8-43 shows the required configuration (app-context-annotation.xml).

Listing 8-43. Declaring the Entity Listener in Spring

```xml
<?xml version="1.0" encoding="UTF-8"?>

<beans xmlns="http://www.springframework.org/schema/beans"
    xmlns:xsi="http://www.w3.org/2001/XMLSchema-instance"
    xmlns:context="http://www.springframework.org/schema/context"
    xmlns:jdbc="http://www.springframework.org/schema/jdbc"
    xmlns:jpa="http://www.springframework.org/schema/data/jpa"
    xmlns:tx="http://www.springframework.org/schema/tx"
    xsi:schemaLocation="http://www.springframework.org/schema/beans
        http://www.springframework.org/schema/beans/spring-beans.xsd
        http://www.springframework.org/schema/context
        http://www.springframework.org/schema/context/spring-context.xsd
        http://www.springframework.org/schema/jdbc
        http://www.springframework.org/schema/jdbc/spring-jdbc.xsd
        http://www.springframework.org/schema/data/jpa
        http://www.springframework.org/schema/data/jpa/spring-jpa.xsd
        http://www.springframework.org/schema/tx
        http://www.springframework.org/schema/tx/spring-tx.xsd">

    <jdbc:embedded-database id="dataSource" type="H2">
        <jdbc:script location="classpath:META-INF/sql/schema.sql"/>
        <jdbc:script location="classpath:META-INF/sql/test-data.sql"/>
    </jdbc:embedded-database>

    <bean id="transactionManager"
        class="org.springframework.orm.jpa.JpaTransactionManager">
        <property name="entityManagerFactory" ref="emf"/>
    </bean>

    <tx:annotation-driven transaction-manager="transactionManager" />
```

```xml
<bean id="emf" class="org.springframework.orm.jpa.LocalContainerEntityManagerFactoryBean">
    <property name="dataSource" ref="dataSource" />
    <property name="jpaVendorAdapter">
        <bean class="org.springframework.orm.jpa.vendor.HibernateJpaVendorAdapter" />
    </property>
    <property name="packagesToScan"
        value="com.apress.prospring4.ch8"/>
    <property name="jpaProperties">
        <props>
            <prop key="hibernate.dialect">
                org.hibernate.dialect.H2Dialect
            </prop>
            <prop key="hibernate.max_fetch_depth">3</prop>
            <prop key="hibernate.jdbc.fetch_size">50</prop>
            <prop key="hibernate.jdbc.batch_size">10</prop>
            <prop key="hibernate.show_sql">true</prop>
        </props>
    </property>
</bean>

<context:component-scan base-package="com.apress.prospring4.ch8"/>

<jpa:repositories base-package="com.apress.prospring4.ch8"
                  entity-manager-factory-ref="emf"
                  transaction-manager-ref="transactionManager"/>

<jpa:auditing auditor-aware-ref="auditorAwareBean"/>

<bean id="auditorAwareBean" class="com.apress.prospring4.ch8.AuditorAwareBean"/>
</beans>
```

The tag <Spring Data JPA project:audit information:auditing> is to enable the Spring Data JPA auditing feature, while the bean auditorAwareBean is the bean providing the user information. Listing 8-44 shows the AuditorAwareBean class.

Listing 8-44. The AuditorAwareBean Class

```java
package com.apress.prospring4.ch8;

import org.springframework.data.domain.AuditorAware;

public class AuditorAwareBean implements AuditorAware<String> {
    public String getCurrentAuditor() {
        return "prospring4";
    }
}
```

The AuditorAwareBean implements the AuditorAware<T> interface, passing in the type String. In real situations, this should be an instance of user information—for example, a User class, which represents the logged-in user who is performing the data update action. We use String here just for simplicity. In the AuditorAwareBean class, the method getCurrentAuditor() is implemented, and the value is hard-coded to prospring4. In real situations, the user should be obtained from the underlying security infrastructure. For example, in Spring Security, the user information can be retrieved from the SecurityContextHolder class.

Now all the implementation work is completed. Listing 8-45 shows the SpringJPASample testing program.

Listing 8-45. Testing the Spring Data JPA Auditing Feature

```java
package com.apress.prospring4.ch8;

import java.util.List;
import java.util.Date;
import java.util.Set;

import org.springframework.context.support.GenericXmlApplicationContext;

public class SpringJPASample {
    public static void main(String[] args) {
        GenericXmlApplicationContext ctx = new GenericXmlApplicationContext();
        ctx.load("classpath:META-INF/spring/app-context-annotation.xml");
        ctx.refresh();

        ContactAuditService contactService = ctx.getBean(
            "contactAuditService", ContactAuditService.class);

        List<ContactAudit> contacts = contactService.findAll();
        listContacts(contacts);

        System.out.println("Add new contact");
        ContactAudit contact = new ContactAudit();
        contact.setFirstName("Michael");
        contact.setLastName("Jackson");
        contact.setBirthDate(new Date());
        contactService.save(contact);
        contacts = contactService.findAll();
        listContacts(contacts);

        contact = contactService.findById(1l);
        System.out.println("");
        System.out.println("Contact with id 1:" + contact);
        System.out.println("");

        System.out.println("Update contact");
        contact.setFirstName("Tom");
        contactService.save(contact);
        contacts = contactService.findAll();
        listContacts(contacts);
    }

    private static void listContacts(List<ContactAudit> contacts) {
        System.out.println("");
        System.out.println("Listing contacts without details:");
        for (ContactAudit contact: contacts) {
            System.out.println(contact);
            System.out.println();
        }
    }
}
```

In Listing 8-45, we list the contact audit information both after a new contact is inserted and after it's later updated. Running the program produces the following output:

```
Add new contact
Listing contacts without details:
Contact - Id: 1, First name: Michael, Last name: Jackson, Birthday: 2013-08-11, Create by:
prospring4, Create date: 2013-08-11T05:29:37.660-04:00, Modified by: prospring4, Modified date:
2013-08-11T05:29:37.660-04:00

Update contact
Listing contacts without details:
Contact - Id: 1, First name: Tom, Last name: Jackson, Birthday: 2013-08-11, Create by: prospring4,
Create date: 2013-08-11T05:29:37.660-04:00, Modified by: prospring4, Modified date: 2013-08-
11T05:29:37.864-04:00
```

In the previous output, you can see that after the new contact is created, the create date and last-modified dates are the same. However, after the update, the last-modified date is updated. Auditing is another handy feature that Spring Data JPA provides so that you don't need to implement the logic yourself.

Keeping Entity Versions by Using Hibernate Envers

In an enterprise application, for business-critical data, it is always a requirement to keep *versions* of each entity. For example, in a customer relationship management (CRM) system, each time a customer record is inserted, updated, or deleted, the previous version should be kept in a history or auditing table to fulfill the firm's auditing or other compliance requirements.

To accomplish this, there are two common options. The first one is to create database triggers that will clone the pre-update record into the history table before any update operations. The second is to develop the logic in the data access layer (for example, by using AOP). However, both options have their drawbacks. The trigger approach is tied to the database platform, while implementing the logic manually is quite clumsy and error prone.

Hibernate Envers (Entity Versioning System) is a Hibernate module specifically designed to automate the versioning of entities. In this section, we discuss how to use Envers to implement the versioning of the ContactAudit entity.

■ **Note** Hibernate Envers is not a feature of JPA. We mention it here because we believe it's more appropriate to cover this after we have discussed some basic auditing features that you can use with Spring Data JPA.

Envers supports two auditing strategies, which are shown in Table 8-4.

Table 8-4. Envers Auditing Strategies

Auditing Strategy	Description
Default	Envers maintains a column for the revision of the record. Every time a record is inserted or updated, a new record will be inserted into the history table with the revision number retrieved from a database sequence or table.
Validity audit	This strategy stores both the start and end revisions of each history record. Every time a record is inserted or updated, a new record will be inserted into the history table with the start revision number. At the same time, the previous record will be updated with the end revision number. It's also possible to configure Envers to record the timestamp at which the end revision was updated into the previous history record.

In this section, we demonstrate the validity audit strategy. Although it will trigger more database updates, retrieving the history records becomes much faster. Because the end revision timestamp is also written to the history records, it will be easier to identify the snapshot of a record at a specific point in time when querying the data.

Adding Tables for Entity Versioning

To support entity versioning, we need to add a few tables. First, for each table that the entity (in this case, the ContactAudit entity class) will be versioning, we need to create the corresponding history table. For the versioning of records in the CONTACT_AUDIT table, let's create a history table called CONTACT_AUDIT_H. Listing 8-46 shows the table creation script (schema.sql).

Listing 8-46. The CONTACT_AUDIT_H Table

```
CREATE TABLE CONTACT_AUDIT_H (
    ID INT NOT NULL
    , FIRST_NAME VARCHAR(60) NOT NULL
    , LAST_NAME VARCHAR(40) NOT NULL
    , BIRTH_DATE DATE
    , VERSION INT NOT NULL DEFAULT 0
    , CREATED_BY VARCHAR(20)
    , CREATED_DATE TIMESTAMP
    , LAST_MODIFIED_BY VARCHAR(20)
    , LAST_MODIFIED_DATE TIMESTAMP
    , AUDIT_REVISION INT NOT NULL
    , ACTION_TYPE INT
    , AUDIT_REVISION_END INT
    , AUDIT_REVISION_END_TS TIMESTAMP
    , UNIQUE UQ_CONTACT_AUDIT_H_1 (FIRST_NAME, LAST_NAME)
    , PRIMARY KEY (ID, AUDIT_REVISION)
);
```

To support the validity audit strategy, we need to add four columns for each history table (as shown in Listing 8-46). Table 8-5 shows the columns and their purposes.

Table 8-5. Columns Required for History Table

Column Type	Data Type	Description
AUDIT_REVISION	INT	The start revision of the history record
AUDIT_TYPE	INT	The action type, with these possible values: 0 – Add, 1 – Modify, 2 – Delete
AUDIT_REVISION_END	INT	The end revision of the history record
AUDIT_REVISION_END_TS	TIMESTAMP	The timestamp at which the end revision was updated

Hibernate Envers requires another table for keeping track of the revision number and the timestamp at which each revision was created. The table name should be REVINFO. Listing 8-47 shows the table creation script (schema.sql).

Listing 8-47. The REVINFO Table

```
CREATE TABLE REVINFO (
    REVTSTMP BIGINT NOT NULL
    , REV INT NOT NULL AUTO_INCREMENT
    , PRIMARY KEY (REVTSTMP, REV)
);
```

The REV column is for storing each revision number, which will be auto-incremented when a new history record is created. The REVTSTMP column stores the timestamp (in a number format) when the revision was created.

Configuring EntityManagerFactory for Entity Versioning

Hibernate Envers is implemented in the form of EJB listeners. We can configure those listeners in the LocalContainerEntityManagerFactory bean. Listing 8-48 shows the bean configuration (app-context-annotation.xml).

Listing 8-48. Configuring Hibernate Envers in Spring

```xml
<?xml version="1.0" encoding="UTF-8"?>

<beans xmlns="http://www.springframework.org/schema/beans"
    xmlns:xsi="http://www.w3.org/2001/XMLSchema-instance"
    xmlns:context="http://www.springframework.org/schema/context"
    xmlns:jdbc="http://www.springframework.org/schema/jdbc"
    xmlns:jpa="http://www.springframework.org/schema/data/jpa"
    xmlns:tx="http://www.springframework.org/schema/tx"
    xsi:schemaLocation="http://www.springframework.org/schema/beans
        http://www.springframework.org/schema/beans/spring-beans.xsd
        http://www.springframework.org/schema/context
        http://www.springframework.org/schema/context/spring-context.xsd
        http://www.springframework.org/schema/jdbc
        http://www.springframework.org/schema/jdbc/spring-jdbc.xsd
        http://www.springframework.org/schema/data/jpa
        http://www.springframework.org/schema/data/jpa/spring-jpa.xsd
        http://www.springframework.org/schema/tx
        http://www.springframework.org/schema/tx/spring-tx.xsd">

    <jdbc:embedded-database id="dataSource" type="H2">
        <jdbc:script location="classpath:META-INF/sql/schema.sql"/>
        <jdbc:script location="classpath:META-INF/sql/test-data.sql"/>
    </jdbc:embedded-database>

    <bean id="transactionManager"
        class="org.springframework.orm.jpa.JpaTransactionManager">
        <property name="entityManagerFactory" ref="emf"/>
    </bean>

    <tx:annotation-driven transaction-manager="transactionManager" />

    <bean id="emf" class="org.springframework.orm.jpa.LocalContainerEntityManagerFactoryBean">
        <property name="dataSource" ref="dataSource" />
        <property name="jpaVendorAdapter">
            <bean class="org.springframework.orm.jpa.vendor.HibernateJpaVendorAdapter" />
        </property>
```

```xml
        <property name="packagesToScan"
            value="com.apress.prospring4.ch8"/>
        <property name="jpaProperties">
            <props>
                <prop key="hibernate.dialect">
                    org.hibernate.dialect.H2Dialect
                </prop>
                <prop key="hibernate.max_fetch_depth">3</prop>
                <prop key="hibernate.jdbc.fetch_size">50</prop>
                <prop key="hibernate.jdbc.batch_size">10</prop>
                <prop key="hibernate.show_sql">true</prop>

                <!-- Properties for Hibernate Envers -->
                <prop key="org.hibernate.envers.audit_table_suffix">_H</prop>
                <prop key="org.hibernate.envers.revision_field_name">
                    AUDIT_REVISION
                </prop>
                <prop key="org.hibernate.envers.revision_type_field_name">
                    ACTION_TYPE
                </prop>
                <prop key="org.hibernate.envers.audit_strategy">
                    org.hibernate.envers.strategy.ValidityAuditStrategy
                </prop>
                <prop key="org.hibernate.envers.audit_strategy_validity_end_rev_field_name">
                    AUDIT_REVISION_END
                </prop>
                <prop key="org.hibernate.envers.audit_strategy_validity_store_revend_timestamp">
                    True
                </prop>
                <prop key="org.hibernate.envers.audit_strategy_validity_revend_timestamp_field_name">
                    AUDIT_REVISION_END_TS
                </prop>
            </props>
        </property>
    </bean>

    <context:component-scan base-package="com.apress.prospring4.ch8"/>

    <jpa:repositories base-package="com.apress.prospring4.ch8"
                      entity-manager-factory-ref="emf"
                      transaction-manager-ref="transactionManager"/>

    <jpa:auditing auditor-aware-ref="auditorAwareBean"/>

    <bean id="auditorAwareBean" class="com.apress.prospring4.ch8.AuditorAwareBean"/>
</beans>
```

The Envers audit event listener (org.hibernate.envers.event.AuditEventListener) is attached to various persistence events. The listener intercepts the events post-insert, post-update, or post-delete and clones the pre-update snapshot of the entity class into the history table. The listener is also attached to those association update events (pre-collection-update, pre-collection-remove, and pre-collection-recreate) for handling the update operations of the entity class's associations. Envers is capable of keeping the history of the entities within an association (for example one-to-many or many-to-many).

404

A few properties are also defined for Hibernate Envers, which are summarized in Table 8-6 (the prefix of the properties, `org.hibernate.envers`, is omitted for clarity).

Table 8-6. *Properties for Hibernate Envers*

Column Type	Description
`audit_table_suffix`	The table name suffix for the versioned entity. For example, for the entity class `ContactAudit`, which is mapped to the `CONTACT_AUDIT` table, Envers will keep the history in the table `CONTACT_AUDIT_H`, since we defined the value `_H` for the property.
`revision_field_name`	The history table's column for storing the revision number for each history record.
`revision_type_field_name`	The history table's column for storing the update action type.
`audit_strategy`	The audit strategy to use for entity versioning.
`audit_strategy_validity_end_rev_field_name`	The history table's column for storing the end revision number for each history record. Required only when using the validity audit strategy.
`audit_strategy_validity_store_revend_timestamp`	Whether to store the timestamp when the end revision number for each history record is updated. Required only when using the validity audit strategy.
`audit_strategy_validity_revend_timestamp_field_name`	The history table's column for storing the timestamp when the end revision number for each history record is updated. Required only when using the validity audit strategy and the previous property is set to `true`.

Enabling Entity Versioning and History Retrieval

To enable versioning of an entity, just annotate the entity class with `@Audited`. Listing 8-49 shows the `ContactAudit` entity class with the annotation applied.

Listing 8-49. The `ContactAudit` Class

```
package com.apress.prospring4.ch8;

import static javax.persistence.GenerationType.IDENTITY;

import java.io.Serializable;
import java.util.Date;
import javax.persistence.Entity;
import javax.persistence.Table;
import javax.persistence.Id;
import javax.persistence.GeneratedValue;
import javax.persistence.Column;
import javax.persistence.Version;
```

```java
import javax.persistence.Temporal;
import javax.persistence.TemporalType;
import javax.persistence.Transient;
import org.hibernate.annotations.Type;
import org.springframework.data.domain.Auditable;
import org.joda.time.DateTime;
import org.hibernate.envers.Audited;

@Entity
@Audited
@Table(name = "contact_audit")
public class ContactAudit implements Auditable<String, Long>, Serializable {
    private Long id;
    private int version;
    private String firstName;
    private String lastName;
    private Date birthDate;
    private String createdBy;
    private DateTime createdDate;
    private String lastModifiedBy;
    private DateTime lastModifiedDate;

    @Id
    @GeneratedValue(strategy = IDENTITY)
    @Column(name = "ID")
    public Long getId() {
        return this.id;
    }

    public void setId(Long id) {
        this.id = id;
    }

    @Version
    @Column(name = "VERSION")
    public int getVersion() {
        return this.version;
    }

    public void setVersion(int version) {
        this.version = version;
    }

    @Column(name = "FIRST_NAME")
    public String getFirstName() {
        return this.firstName;
    }

    public void setFirstName(String firstName) {
        this.firstName = firstName;
    }
```

```java
@Column(name = "LAST_NAME")
public String getLastName() {
    return this.lastName;
}

public void setLastName(String lastName) {
    this.lastName = lastName;
}

@Temporal(TemporalType.DATE)
@Column(name = "BIRTH_DATE")
public Date getBirthDate() {
    return this.birthDate;
}

public void setBirthDate(Date birthDate) {
    this.birthDate = birthDate;
}

@Column(name="CREATED_BY")
public String getCreatedBy() {
    return createdBy;
}

public void setCreatedBy(String createdBy) {
    this.createdBy = createdBy;
}

@Column(name="CREATED_DATE")
@Type(type="org.jadira.usertype.dateandtime.joda.PersistentDateTime")
public DateTime getCreatedDate() {
    return createdDate;
}

public void setCreatedDate(DateTime createdDate) {
    this.createdDate = createdDate;
}

@Column(name="LAST_MODIFIED_BY")
public String getLastModifiedBy() {
    return lastModifiedBy;
}

public void setLastModifiedBy(String lastModifiedBy) {
    this.lastModifiedBy = lastModifiedBy;
}
```

```
    @Column(name="LAST_MODIFIED_DATE")
    @Type(type="org.jadira.usertype.dateandtime.joda.PersistentDateTime")
    public DateTime getLastModifiedDate() {
        return lastModifiedDate;
    }

    public void setLastModifiedDate(DateTime lastModifiedDate) {
        this.lastModifiedDate = lastModifiedDate;
    }

    @Transient
    public boolean isNew() {
        if (id == null) {
            return true;
        } else {
            return false;
        }
    }

    public String toString() {
        return "Contact - Id: " + id + ", First name: " + firstName
            + ", Last name: " + lastName + ", Birthday: " + birthDate
            + ", Create by: " + createdBy + ", Create date: " + createdDate
            + ", Modified by: " + lastModifiedBy + ", Modified date: "
            + lastModifiedDate;
    }
}
```

The entity class is annotated with @Audited, which Envers listeners will check for and perform versioning of the updated entities. By default, Envers will also try to keep a history of the associations.

To retrieve the history records, Envers provides the org.hibernate.envers.AuditReader interface, which can be obtained from the AuditReaderFactory class. Let's add a new method called findAuditByRevision() into the ContactAuditService interface for the retrieving the ContactAudit history record by the revision number. Listing 8-50 shows the ContactAuditService interface.

Listing 8-50. The findAuditByRevision() Method

```
package com.apress.prospring4.ch8;

import java.util.List;

public interface ContactAuditService {
    List<ContactAudit> findAll();
    ContactAudit findById(Long id);
    ContactAudit save(ContactAudit contact);
    ContactAudit findAuditByRevision(Long id, int revision);
}
```

To retrieve a history record, one option is to pass in the entity's ID and the revision number. Listing 8-51 shows the implementation of the method.

Listing 8-51. Implementing the findAuditByRevision() Method

```
package com.apress.prospring4.ch8;

import org.springframework.stereotype.Service;
import org.springframework.stereotype.Repository;
import org.springframework.transaction.annotation.Transactional;
import org.springframework.beans.factory.annotation.Autowired;

import java.util.List;
import com.google.common.collect.Lists;

import org.hibernate.envers.AuditReader;
import org.hibernate.envers.AuditReaderFactory;

import javax.persistence.PersistenceContext;
import javax.persistence.EntityManager;

@Service("contactAuditService")
@Repository
@Transactional
public class ContactAuditServiceImpl implements ContactAuditService {
    @Autowired
    private ContactAuditRepository contactAuditRepository;

    @PersistenceContext
    private EntityManager entityManager;

    @Transactional(readOnly=true)
    public List<ContactAudit> findAll() {
        return Lists.newArrayList(contactAuditRepository.findAll());
    }

    public ContactAudit findById(Long id) {
        return contactAuditRepository.findOne(id);
    }

    public ContactAudit save(ContactAudit contact) {
        return contactAuditRepository.save(contact);
    }

    @Transactional(readOnly=true)
    @Override
    public ContactAudit findAuditByRevision(Long id, int revision) {
        AuditReader auditReader = AuditReaderFactory.get(entityManager);
        return auditReader.find(ContactAudit.class, id, revision);
    }
}
```

The EntityManager is injected into the class, which is passed to the AuditReaderFactory to retrieve an instance of AuditReader. Then we can call the AuditReader.find() method to retrieve the instance of the ContactAudit entity at a particular revision.

Testing Entity Versioning

Let's take a look at how entity versioning works. Listing 8-52 shows the testing code snippet; the code for bootstrapping ApplicationContext and the listContacts() function is the same as the code in the SpringJpaSample class.

Listing 8-52. Testing Entity Versioning

```java
package com.apress.prospring4.ch8;

import java.util.List;
import java.util.Date;
import java.util.Set;

import org.springframework.context.support.GenericXmlApplicationContext;

public class SpringJPASample {
    public static void main(String[] args) {
        GenericXmlApplicationContext ctx = new GenericXmlApplicationContext();
        ctx.load("classpath:META-INF/spring/app-context-annotation.xml");
        ctx.refresh();

        ContactAuditService contactService = ctx.getBean(
            "contactAuditService", ContactAuditService.class);

        System.out.println("Add new contact");
        ContactAudit contact = new ContactAudit();
        contact.setFirstName("Michael");
        contact.setLastName("Jackson");
        contact.setBirthDate(new Date());
        contactService.save(contact);
        listContacts(contactService.findAll());

        System.out.println("Update contact");
        contact.setFirstName("Tom");
        contactService.save(contact);
        listContacts(contactService.findAll());

        ContactAudit oldContact = contactService.findAuditByRevision(1l, 1);
        System.out.println("");
        System.out.println("Old Contact with id 1 and rev 1:" + oldContact);
        System.out.println("");
        oldContact = contactService.findAuditByRevision(1l, 2);
        System.out.println("");
        System.out.println("Old Contact with id 1 and rev 2:" + oldContact);
        System.out.println("");
    }

    private static void listContacts(List<ContactAudit> contacts) {
        System.out.println("");
        System.out.println("Listing contacts without details:");
```

```
        for (ContactAudit contact: contacts) {
            System.out.println(contact);
            System.out.println();
        }
    }
}
```

We first create a new contact and then update it. Then we retrieve the `ContactAudit` entities with revisions 1 and 2, respectively. Running the code produces the following output:

```
Listing contacts without details:
Contact - Id: 1, First name: Tom, Last name: Jackson, Birthday: 2013-08-11, Create by: prospring4,
Create date: 2013-08-11T06:06:21.216-04:00, Modified by: prospring4, Modified date: 2013-08-
11T06:06:21.556-04:00

Old Contact with id 1 and rev 1:Contact - Id: 1, First name: Michael, Last name: Jackson, Birthday:
2013-08-11, Create by: prospring4, Create date: 2013-08-11T06:06:21.216-04:00, Modified by:
prospring4, Modified date: 2013-08-11T06:06:21.216-04:00

Old Contact with id 1 and rev 2:Contact - Id: 1, First name: Tom, Last name: Jackson, Birthday:
2013-08-11, Create by: prospring4, Create date: 2013-08-11T06:06:21.216-04:00, Modified by:
prospring4, Modified date: 2013-08-11T06:06:21.556-04:00
```

From the previous output, you can see that after the update operation, the `ContactAudit`'s first name is changed to Tom. However, when looking at the history, at revision 1, the first name is Michael. At revision 2, the first name becomes Tom. Also notice that the last-modified date of revision 2 reflects the updated date-time correctly.

Considerations When Using JPA

Although we covered a fair amount, this chapter dives into only a small portion of JPA. For example, using JPA to call a database stored procedure is not covered. JPA is a complete and powerful ORM data access standard, and with the help of third-party libraries such as Spring Data JPA and Hibernate Envers, you can implement various crosscutting concerns relatively easily.

JPA is a JEE standard that is supported by most major open source communities as well as commercial vendors (JBoss, GlassFish, WebSphere, WebLogic, and so on). So, it's a compelling choice for adopting JPA as the data access standard. If you require absolute control over the query, you can use JPA's native query support instead of using JDBC directly.

In conclusion, for developing JEE applications with Spring, we recommend using JPA to implement the data access layer. When desired, you can still mix in JDBC for some special data access needs. Always remember that Spring allows you to mix and match data access technologies easily, with the transaction management transparently handled for you.

Summary

In this chapter, we covered the basic concepts of JPA and how to configure JPA's `EntityManagerFactory` in Spring by using Hibernate as the persistence service provider. Then we discussed using JPA to perform basic database operations. Advanced topics included native queries and the strongly typed JPA criteria API.

Additionally, we demonstrated how Spring Data JPA's `Repository` abstraction can help simplify JPA application development, as well as how to use its entity listener to keep track of basic auditing information for entity classes. For full versioning of entity classes, using Hibernate Envers to fulfill the requirement was also covered.

In the next chapter, we discuss transaction management in Spring.

CHAPTER 9

■ ■ ■

Transaction Management

Transactions are one of the most critical parts of building a reliable enterprise application. The most common type of transaction is a database operation. In a typical database update operation, a database transaction begins, data is updated, and then the transaction is committed or rolled back, depending on the result of the database operation. However, in many cases, depending on the application requirements and the back-end resources that the application needs to interact with (such as an RDBMS, message-oriented middleware, an ERP system, and so on), transaction management can be much more complicated.

In the early days of Java application development (after JDBC was created, but before the JEE standard or an application framework like Spring was available), developers programmatically controlled and managed transactions within application code. When JEE and, more specifically, the EJB standard became available, developers were able to use container-managed transactions (CMTs) to manage transactions in a declarative way. But the complicated transaction declaration in the EJB deployment descriptor was difficult to maintain and introduced unnecessary complexity for transaction processing. Some developers favored having more control over the transaction and chose bean-managed transactions (BMTs) to manage transactions in a programmatic way. However, the complexity of programming with the Java Transaction API (JTA) also hindered developers' productivity.

As discussed in Chapter 5 on AOP, transaction management is a cross-cutting concern and should not be coded within the business logic. The most appropriate way to implement transaction management is to allow developers to define transaction requirements in a declarative way and have frameworks such as Spring, JEE, or AOP weave in the transaction processing logic on our behalf. In this chapter, we discuss how Spring helps simplify the implementation of transaction-processing logic. Spring provides support for both declarative and programmatic transaction management.

Spring offers excellent support for declarative transactions, which means you do not need to clutter your business logic with transaction management code. All you have to do is declare those methods (within classes or layers) that must participate in a transaction, together with the details of the transaction configuration, and Spring will take care of handling the transaction management. To be more specific, this chapter covers the following:

- *Spring transaction abstraction layer*: We discuss the base components of Spring transaction abstraction classes and explain how to use these classes to control the properties of the transactions.

- *Declarative transaction management*: We show you how to use Spring and just plain Java objects to implement declarative transactional management. We offer examples for declarative transaction management using the XML configuration files as well as Java annotations.

- *Programmatic transaction management*: Even though programmatic transaction management is not used very often, we explain how to use the Spring-provided TransactionTemplate class, which gives you full control over the transaction management code.

- *Global transactions with JTA*: For global transactions that need to span multiple back-end resources, we show how to configure and implement global transactions in Spring by using JTA.

Exploring the Spring Transaction Abstraction Layer

When developing your applications, no matter whether you choose to use Spring or not, you have to make a fundamental choice when using transactions about whether to use global or local transactions. *Local transactions* are specific to a single transactional resource (a JDBC connection, for example), whereas *global transactions* are managed by the container and can span multiple transactional resources.

Transaction Types

Local transactions are easy to manage, and if all operations in your application need to interact with just one transactional resource (such as a JDBC transaction), using local transactions will be sufficient. However, if you are not using an application framework such as Spring, you have a lot of transaction management code to write, and if in the future the scope of the transaction needs to be extended across multiple transactional resources, you have to drop the local transaction management code and rewrite it to use global transactions.

In the Java world, global transactions were implemented with the JTA. In this scenario, a JTA-compatible transaction manager connects to multiple transactional resources via respective resource managers, which are capable of communicating with the transaction manager over the XA protocol (an open standard defining distributed transactions), and the 2 Phase Commit (2PC) mechanism was used to ensure that all back-end data sources were updated or rolled back altogether. If either of the back-end resources fails, the entire transaction will roll back, and hence the updates to other resources will be rolled back too.

Figure 9-1 shows a high-level view of global transactions with JTA.

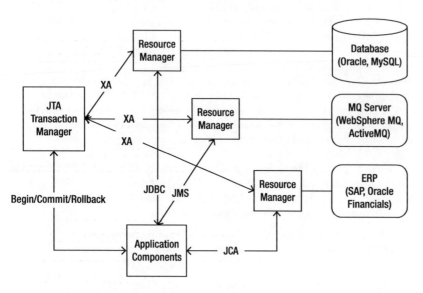

Figure 9-1. *Overview of global transactions with JTA*

As shown in Figure 9-1, four main parties participate in a global transaction (also generally referred to as a *distributed transaction*). The first party is the back-end resource, such as an RDBMS, messaging middleware, an enterprise resource planning (ERP) system, and so on.

The second party is the resource manager, which is generally provided by the back-end resource vendor and is responsible for interacting with the back-end resource. For example, when connecting to a MySQL database, we need to interact with the MysqlXADataSource class provided by MySQL's Java connector. Other back-end resources (for example, MQ, ERP, and so on) provide their resource managers too.

The third party is the JTA transaction manager, which is responsible for managing, coordinating, and synchronizing the transaction status with all resource managers that are participating in the transaction. The XA protocol is used, which is an open standard widely used for distributed transaction processing. The JTA transaction manager also supports 2PC so that all changes will be committed together, and if any resource update fails, the entire transaction will be rolled back, resulting in none of the resources being updated. The entire mechanism was specified by the Java Transaction Service (JTS) specification.

The final component is the application. Either the application itself or the underlying container or Spring framework that the application runs on manages the transaction (begin, commit, roll back a transaction, and so on). At the same time, the application interacts with the underlying back-end resources via various standards defined by JEE. As shown in Figure 9-1, the application connects to the RDBMS via JDBC, MQ via JMS, and an ERP system via Java EE Connector Architecture (JCA).

JTA is supported by all full-blown JEE-compliant application servers (for example, JBoss, WebSphere, WebLogic, and GlassFish), within which the transaction is available via JNDI lookup. As for stand-alone applications or web containers (for example, Tomcat and Jetty), there also exist open source and commercial solutions that provide support for JTA/XA in those environments (for example, Atomikos, Java Open Transaction Manager (JOTM), and Bitronix).

Implementations of the PlatformTransactionManager

In Spring, the `PlatformTransactionManager` interface uses the `TransactionDefinition` and `TransactionStatus` interfaces to create and manage transactions. The actual implementation of these interfaces must have detailed knowledge of the transaction manager. Figure 9-2 shows the implementations of `PlatformTransactionManager` in Spring.

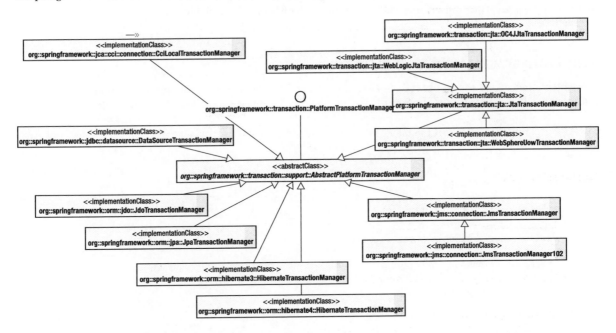

Figure 9-2. `PlatformTransactionManager` *implementations as of Spring*

Spring provides a rich set of implementations for the `PlatformTransactionManager` interface. The `CciLocalTransactionManager` class supports JEE, JCA, and the Common Client Interface (CCI). The `DataSourceTransactionManager` class is for generic JDBC connections. For the ORM side, there are a number of implementations, including JDO (`JdoTransactionManager` class), JPA (`JpaTransactionManager` class), and Hibernate 3 and Hibernate 4 (`HibernateTransactionManager` with different package names). For JMS, the implementations include JMS 1.1 or newer (`JmsTransactionManager` class). For JTA, the generic implementation class is `JtaTransactionManager`. Spring also provides several JTA transaction manager classes that are specific to particular application servers. Those classes provide native support for WebSphere (`WebSphereUowTransactionManager` class), WebLogic (`WebLogicJtaTransactionManager` class), and Oracle OC4J (`OC4JJtaTransactionManager` class).

Analyzing Transaction Properties

In this section, we discuss the transaction properties that Spring supports, focusing on interacting with RDBMS as the back-end resource.

Transactions have the four notoriously known ACID properties—atomicity, consistency, isolation, and durability—and it is up to the transactional resources to maintain these aspects of a transaction. You cannot control the atomicity, consistency, and durability of a transaction. However, you can control the transaction propagation and time-out, as well as configure whether the transaction should be read-only and specify the isolation level.

Spring encapsulates all these settings in a `TransactionDefinition` interface. This interface is used in the core interface of the transaction support in Spring, the `PlatformTransactionManager` interface, whose implementations perform transaction management on a specific platform, such as JDBC or JTA. The core method, `PlatformTransactionManager.getTransaction()`, takes a `TransactionDefinition` interface as an argument and returns a `TransactionStatus` interface. The `TransactionStatus` interface is used to control the transaction execution, more specifically to set the transaction result and to check whether the transaction is completed or whether it is a new transaction.

The TransactionDefinition Interface

As we mentioned earlier, the `TransactionDefinition` interface controls the properties of a transaction. Let's take a more detailed look at the `TransactionDefinition` interface (see Listing 9-1) and describe its methods.

Listing 9-1. `TransactionDefinition` Interface

```
package org.springframework.transaction;

import java.sql.Connection;

public interface TransactionDefinition {

    // Variable declaration statements omitted

    int getPropagationBehavior();

    int getIsolationLevel();

    int getTimeout();

    boolean isReadOnly();

    String getName();

}
```

The simple and obvious methods of this interface are getTimeout(), which returns the time (in seconds) in which the transaction must complete, and isReadOnly(), which indicates whether the transaction is read-only. The transaction manager implementation can use this value to optimize the execution and check to make sure that the transaction is performing only read operations. The getName() method returns the name of the transaction.

The other two methods, getPropagationBehavior() and getIsolationLevel(), need to be discussed in more detail. We begin with getIsolationLevel(), which controls what changes to the data other transactions see. Table 9-1 lists the transaction isolation levels you can use and explains what changes made in the current transaction other transactions can access.

Table 9-1. *Transaction Isolation Levels*

Isolation Level	Description
TransactionDefinition.ISOLATION_DEFAULT	Default isolation level of the underlying datastore.
TransactionDefinition.ISOLATION_READ_UNCOMMITTED	Lowest level of isolation; it is barely a transaction at all because it allows this transaction to see data modified by other uncommitted transactions.
TransactionDefinition.ISOLATION_READ_COMMITTED	Default level in most databases; it ensures that other transactions are not able to read data that has not been committed by other transactions. However, the data that was read by one transaction can be updated by other transactions.
TransactionDefinition.ISOLATION_REPEATABLE_READ	Stricter than ISOLATION_READ_COMMITTED; it ensures that once you select data, you can select at least the same set again. However, if other transactions insert new data, you can still select the newly inserted data.
TransactionDefinition.ISOLATION_SERIALIZABLE	The most expensive and reliable isolation level; all transactions are treated as if they were executed one after another.

Choosing the appropriate isolation level is very important for the consistency of the data, but making these choices can have a great impact on performance. The highest isolation level, TransactionDefinition.ISOLATION_SERIALIZABLE, is particularly expensive to maintain.

The getPropagationBehavior() method specifies what happens to a transactional call, depending on whether there is an active transaction. Table 9-2 describes the values for this method.

Table 9-2. *Propagation Behavior Values*

Isolation Level	Description
TransactionDefinition.PROPAGATION_REQUIRED	Supports a transaction if one already exists. If there is no transaction, it starts a new one.
TransactionDefinition.PROPAGATION_SUPPORTS	Supports a transaction if one already exists. If there is no transaction, it executes nontransactionally.
TransactionDefinition.PROPAGATION_MANDATORY	Supports a transaction if one already exists. Throws an exception if there is no active transaction.
TransactionDefinition.PROPAGATION_REQUIRES_NEW	Always starts a new transaction. If an active transaction already exists, it is suspended.
TransactionDefinition.PROPAGATION_NOT_SUPPORTED	Does not support execution with an active transaction. Always executes nontransactionally and suspends any existing transaction.
TransactionDefinition.PROPAGATION_NEVER	Always executes nontransactionally even if an active transaction exists. Throws an exception if an active transaction exists.
TransactionDefinition.PROPAGATION_NESTED	Runs in a nested transaction if an active transaction exists. If there is no active transaction, the execution is executed as if Transaction Definition.PROPAGATION_ REQUIRED is set.

The TransactionStatus Interface

The TransactionStatus interface, shown in Listing 9-2, allows a transactional manager to control the transaction execution. The code can check whether the transaction is a new one or whether it is a read-only transaction and it can initiate a rollback.

Listing 9-2. TransactionStatus Declaration

```
package org.springframework.transaction;

public interface TransactionStatus extends SavepointManager {

    boolean isNewTransaction();

    boolean hasSavepoint();

    void setRollbackOnly();

    boolean isRollbackOnly();

    void flush();

    boolean isCompleted();

}
```

The methods of the `TransactionStatus` interface are fairly self-explanatory; the most notable one is `setRollbackOnly()`, which causes a rollback and ends the active transaction.

The `hasSavePoint()` method returns whether the transaction internally carries a save point (that is, the transaction was created as a nested transaction based on a save point). The `flush()` method flushes the underlying session to a datastore if applicable (for example, when using with Hibernate). The `isCompleted()` method returns whether the transaction has ended (that is, committed or rolled back).

Sample Data Model and Infrastructure for Example Code

This section provides an overview of the data model and the infrastructure used in our examples of transaction management. We use JPA with Hibernate as the persistence layer for implementing data access logic. In addition, the Spring Data JPA and its repository abstraction are used to simplify development of basic database operations.

Creating a Simple Spring JPA Project with Dependencies

Let's start by creating the project. Because we are using JPA, we also need to add the required dependencies to the project for the examples in this chapter. Table 9-3 shows the additional dependencies required.

Table 9-3. *Maven Dependencies for Spring Data JPA*

Group ID	Artifact ID	Version	Description
org.springframework.data	spring-data-jpa	1.5.0.RELEASE	Spring Data JPA library
org.springframework	spring-core	4.0.2.RELEASE	The core Spring module
org.springframework	spring-context	4.0.2.RELEASE	The Spring context module
org.hibernate.javax.persistence	hibernate-jpa-2.1-api	1.0.0.Final	The Hibernate JPA API
org.hibernate	hibernate-entitymanager	4.2.3.Final	The Hibernate entity manager
com.google.guava	guava	14.0.1	Contains useful helper classes
log4j	log4j	1.2.17	The log4j logging implementation
com.h2database	h2	1.3.172	The H2 embedded database
org.slf4j	slf4j-log4j12	1.7.6	The library that bridges the SLF4J logging to the log4j library
org.aspectj	aspectjrt	1.7.2 (1.8.0.M1 for Java 8)	The AspectJ runtime library
org.aspectj	aspectjweaver	1.7.2 (1.8.0.M1 for Java 8)	The AspectJ weaver library

To observe the detailed behavior of the example code as we modify the transaction attributes, let's also turn on the DEBUG-level logging in log4j. Listing 9-3 shows the log4j.properties file.

Listing 9-3. Turning on DEBUG Logging in log4j.properties

```
log4j.rootCategory=DEBUG, stdout

log4j.appender.stdout=org.apache.log4j.ConsoleAppender
log4j.appender.stdout.layout=org.apache.log4j.PatternLayout
log4j.appender.stdout.layout.ConversionPattern=%d %p [%c] - <%m>%n

log4j.category.org.springframework.transaction=INFO
log4j.category.org.hibernate.SQL=DEBUG
```

Sample Data Model and Common Classes

To keep things simple, we will use just one table, the CONTACT table that we used throughout the chapters about data access. Listings 9-4 and 9-5 show the data creation script (schema.sql) and test data population script, respectively (test-data.sql).

Listing 9-4. Table Creation Script

```
DROP TABLE IF EXISTS CONTACT;

CREATE TABLE CONTACT (
    ID INT NOT NULL AUTO_INCREMENT
    , FIRST_NAME VARCHAR(60) NOT NULL
    , LAST_NAME VARCHAR(40) NOT NULL
    , BIRTH_DATE DATE
    , VERSION INT NOT NULL DEFAULT 0
    , UNIQUE UQ_CONTACT_1 (FIRST_NAME, LAST_NAME)
    , PRIMARY KEY (ID)
);
```

Listing 9-5. Test Data Population Script

```
insert into contact (first_name, last_name, birth_date)
    values ('Chris', 'Schaefer', '1981-05-03');
insert into contact (first_name, last_name, birth_date)
    values ('Scott', 'Tiger', '1990-11-02');
insert into contact (first_name, last_name, birth_date)
    values ('John', 'Smith', '1964-02-28');
```

The entity class is simple too; Listing 9-6 shows the Contact class.

Listing 9-6. The Contact Class

```
package com.apress.prospring4.ch9;

import javax.persistence.Column;
import javax.persistence.Entity;
import javax.persistence.GeneratedValue;
import javax.persistence.GenerationType;
import javax.persistence.Id;
import javax.persistence.NamedQueries;
import javax.persistence.NamedQuery;
import javax.persistence.Table;
import javax.persistence.Temporal;
import javax.persistence.TemporalType;
import javax.persistence.Version;
import java.io.Serializable;
import java.util.Date;

@Entity
@Table(name = "contact")
@NamedQueries({
        @NamedQuery(name="Contact.findAll", query="select c from Contact c"),
        @NamedQuery(name="Contact.countAll", query="select count(c) from Contact c")
})
public class Contact implements Serializable {

    private Long id;
    private int version;
    private String firstName;
    private String lastName;
    private Date birthDate;

    public Contact() {
    }

    @Id
    @GeneratedValue(strategy = GenerationType.IDENTITY)
    @Column(name = "ID")
    public Long getId() {
        return this.id;
    }

    public void setId(Long id) {
        this.id = id;
    }

    @Version
    @Column(name = "VERSION")
    public int getVersion() {
        return this.version;
    }
```

```java
    public void setVersion(int version) {
        this.version = version;
    }

    @Column(name = "FIRST_NAME")
    public String getFirstName() {
        return this.firstName;
    }

    public void setFirstName(String firstName) {
        this.firstName = firstName;
    }

    @Column(name = "LAST_NAME")
    public String getLastName() {
        return this.lastName;
    }

    public void setLastName(String lastName) {
        this.lastName = lastName;
    }

    @Temporal(TemporalType.DATE)
    @Column(name = "BIRTH_DATE")
    public Date getBirthDate() {
        return this.birthDate;
    }

    public void setBirthDate(Date birthDate) {
        this.birthDate = birthDate;
    }

    @Override
    public String toString() {
        return "Contact - Id: " + id + ", First name: " + firstName
                + ", Last name: " + lastName + ", Birthday: " + birthDate;
    }
}
```

To use Spring Data JPA's repository abstraction, we also need to define the ContactRepository interface, which extends Spring Data Common's CrudRepository<T,ID extends Serializable> interface. Listing 9-7 shows the ContactRepository interface.

Listing 9-7. The ContactRepository Class

```java
package com.apress.prospring4.ch9;

import org.springframework.data.repository.CrudRepository;

public interface ContactRepository extends CrudRepository<Contact, Long> {

}
```

As shown in Listing 9-7, no additional method is required, because those methods provided by the `CrudRepository` interface already are sufficient for the examples in this chapter.

Finally, let's take a look at the `ContactService` interface, which defines all the business logic in relation to the Contact entity class. Listing 9-8 shows the `ContactService` interface.

Listing 9-8. The `ContactService` Interface

```
package com.apress.prospring4.ch9;

import java.util.List;

public interface ContactService {
    List<Contact> findAll();
    Contact findById(Long id);
    Contact save(Contact contact);
    long countAll();
}
```

All methods are self-explanatory. In the next section, we discuss how to implement transaction management in various ways by implementing the `ContactService` interface.

Declarative and Programmatic Transactions with Spring

Spring has three options for transaction management. Two of them are for declarative transaction management, with one using Java annotations and the other using XML configuration. The third option is managing transactions programmatically. We will go through the three of them, one by one, in the following sections.

Using Annotations for Transaction Management

Currently, using annotations is the most common way to define transaction requirements in Spring. The main benefit is that the transaction requirement together with the detail transaction properties (time-out, isolation level, propagation behavior, and so on), are defined within the code itself, which makes the application easier to trace and maintain.

To enable annotation support for transaction management in Spring, we need to add the `<tx:annotation-driven>` tag in the XML configuration file. Listing 9-9 shows the configuration file (`tx-annotation-app-context.xml`).

Listing 9-9. Spring Configuration for Annotation Transaction Support

```
<?xml version="1.0" encoding="UTF-8"?>
<beans xmlns="http://www.springframework.org/schema/beans"
    xmlns:xsi="http://www.w3.org/2001/XMLSchema-instance"
    xmlns:context="http://www.springframework.org/schema/context"
    xmlns:jdbc="http://www.springframework.org/schema/jdbc"
    xmlns:tx="http://www.springframework.org/schema/tx"
    xmlns:jpa="http://www.springframework.org/schema/data/jpa"
    xsi:schemaLocation="http://www.springframework.org/schema/jdbc
        http://www.springframework.org/schema/jdbc/spring-jdbc.xsd
        http://www.springframework.org/schema/beans
        http://www.springframework.org/schema/beans/spring-beans.xsd
        http://www.springframework.org/schema/tx
        http://www.springframework.org/schema/tx/spring-tx.xsd
        http://www.springframework.org/schema/data/jpa
        http://www.springframework.org/schema/data/jpa
```

```
                http://www.springframework.org/schema/data/jpa/spring-jpa.xsd
                http://www.springframework.org/schema/context
                http://www.springframework.org/schema/context/spring-context.xsd">

    <jdbc:embedded-database id="dataSource" type="H2">
        <jdbc:script location="classpath:META-INF/config/schema.sql"/>
        <jdbc:script location="classpath:META-INF/config/test-data.sql"/>
    </jdbc:embedded-database>

    <bean id="transactionManager" class="org.springframework.orm.jpa.JpaTransactionManager">
        <property name="entityManagerFactory" ref="emf"/>
    </bean>

    <tx:annotation-driven/>

    <bean id="emf" class="org.springframework.orm.jpa.LocalContainerEntityManagerFactoryBean">
        <property name="dataSource" ref="dataSource" />
        <property name="jpaVendorAdapter">
            <bean class="org.springframework.orm.jpa.vendor.HibernateJpaVendorAdapter" />
        </property>
        <property name="packagesToScan" value="com.apress.prospring4.ch9 "/>
        <property name="jpaProperties">
            <props>
                <prop key="hibernate.dialect">
                    org.hibernate.dialect.H2Dialect
                </prop>
                <prop key="hibernate.max_fetch_depth">3</prop>
                <prop key="hibernate.jdbc.fetch_size">50</prop>
                <prop key="hibernate.jdbc.batch_size">10</prop>
                <prop key="hibernate.show_sql">true</prop>
            </props>
        </property>
    </bean>

    <context:component-scan
        base-package="com.apress.prospring4.ch9" />

    <jpa:repositories base-package="com.apress.prospring4.ch9"
        entity-manager-factory-ref="emf"
        transaction-manager-ref="transactionManager"/>
</beans>
```

First, an embedded H2 database is defined with the database creation and data population scripts. Then, because we are using JPA, the JpaTransactionManager bean is defined. The <tx:annotation-driven> specifies that we are using annotations for transaction management. The EntityManagerFactory bean is then defined, followed by the <context:component-scan> to scan the service-layer classes. Finally, the <jpa:repositories> tag is used to enable Spring Data JPA's repository abstraction.

For the implementation of the ContactService interface, we begin by creating the class with an empty implementation of all the methods in the ContactService interface.

Let's implement the ContactService.findAll() method first. Listing 9-10 shows the ContactServiceImpl class with the findAll() method implemented.

Listing 9-10. The ContactServiceImpl Class with the findAll() Method Implemented

```
package com.apress.prospring4.ch9;

import com.google.common.collect.Lists;
import org.springframework.beans.factory.annotation.Autowired;
import org.springframework.stereotype.Repository;
import org.springframework.stereotype.Service;
import org.springframework.transaction.annotation.Transactional;

import java.util.List;

@Service("contactService")
@Repository
@Transactional
public class ContactServiceImpl implements ContactService {
    private ContactRepository contactRepository;

    @Override
    @Transactional(readOnly=true)
    public List<Contact> findAll() {
        return Lists.newArrayList(contactRepository.findAll());
    }

    @Autowired
    public void setContactRepository(ContactRepository contactRepository) {
        this.contactRepository = contactRepository;
    }
}
```

When using annotation-based transaction management, the only annotation that we need to deal with is @Transactional. In Listing 9-10, the @Transactional annotation is applied at the class level, which means that, by default, Spring will ensure that a transaction is present before the execution of each method within the class. The @Transactional annotation supports a number of attributes that you can provide to override the default behavior. Table 9-4 shows the available attributes, together with the possible and default values.

Table 9-4. *Attributes for the @Transactional Annotation*

Attribute Name	Default Value	Possible Values
propagation	Propagation.REQUIRED	Propagation.REQUIRED Propagation.SUPPORTS Propagation.MANDATORY Propagation.REQUIRES_NEW Propagation.NOT_SUPPORTED Propagation.NEVER Propagation.NESTED
isolation	Isolation.DEFAULT (Default isolation level of the underlying resource)	Isolation.DEFAULT Isolation.READ_UNCOMMITTED Isolation.READ_COMMITTED Isolation.REPEATABLE_READ Isolation.SERIALIZABLE

(continued)

Table 9-4. (*continued*)

Attribute Name	Default Value	Possible Values
timeout	TransactionDefinition.TIMEOUT_DEFAULT (Default transaction time-out in seconds of the underlying resource)	An integer value larger than zero; indicates the number in seconds for transaction time-out
readOnly	false	True false
rollbackFor	Exception classes for which the transaction will be rolled back	N/A
rollbackForClassName	Exception class names for which the transaction will be rolled back	N/A
noRollbackFor	Exception classes for which the transaction will not be rolled back	N/A
noRollbackForClassName	Exception class names for which the transaction will not be rolled back	N/A
value	"" (A qualifier value for the specified transaction)	N/A

As a result, based on Table 9-4, the @Transactional annotation without any attribute means that the transaction propagation is required, the isolation is the default, the time-out is the default, and the mode is read-write.

For the findAll() method in Listing 9-10, the method is annotated with @Transactional(readOnly=true). This will override the default annotation applied at the class level, with all other attributes unchanged, but the transaction is set to read-only.

Listing 9-11 shows the testing program for the findAll() method.

Listing 9-11. Testing the findAll() Method

```
package com.apress.prospring4.ch9;

import java.util.List;

import org.springframework.context.support.GenericXmlApplicationContext;

public class TxAnnotationSample {
    public static void main(String[] args) {
        GenericXmlApplicationContext ctx = new GenericXmlApplicationContext();
        ctx.load("classpath:META-INF/spring/tx-annotation-app-context.xml");
        ctx.refresh();

        ContactService contactService = ctx.getBean("contactService",
            ContactService.class);

        List<Contact> contacts = contactService.findAll();

        for (Contact contactTemp: contacts) {
            System.out.println(contactTemp);
        }
    }
}
```

Running the program produces the following reduced output (see the debug log in your console for full details):

```
Contact - Id: 1, First name: Chris, Last name: Schaefer, Birthday: 1981-05-03
Contact - Id: 2, First name: Scott, Last name: Tiger, Birthday: 1990-11-02
Contact - Id: 3, First name: John, Last name: Smith, Birthday: 1964-02-28
```

As shown in the previous output, the irrelevant output statements were removed for clarity. First, before the findAll() method is run, Spring's JpaTransactionManager creates a new transaction (the name is equal to the fully qualified class name with the method name) with default attributes, but the transaction is set to read-only, as defined at the method-level @Transactional annotation. Then, the query is submitted, and upon completion and without any errors, the transaction is committed. The JpaTransactionManager handles the creation and commit operations of the transaction.

Let's proceed to the implementation of the update operation. We need to implement both the findById() and save() methods in the ContactService interface. Listing 9-12 shows the implementation.

Listing 9-12. The ContactServiceImpl Class with the findById() and save() Methods Implemented

```
package com.apress.prospring4.ch9;

import com.google.common.collect.Lists;
import org.springframework.beans.factory.annotation.Autowired;
import org.springframework.stereotype.Repository;
import org.springframework.stereotype.Service;
import org.springframework.transaction.annotation.Transactional;

import java.util.List;

@Service("contactService")
@Repository
@Transactional
public class ContactServiceImpl implements ContactService {
    private ContactRepository contactRepository;

    @Override
    @Transactional(readOnly=true)
    public List<Contact> findAll() {
        return Lists.newArrayList(contactRepository.findAll());
    }

    @Override
    @Transactional(readOnly=true)
    public Contact findById(Long id) {
        return contactRepository.findOne(id);
    }

    @Override
    public Contact save(Contact contact) {
        return contactRepository.save(contact);
    }
```

```
    @Override
    public long countAll() {
        return 0;
    }

    @Autowired
    public void setContactRepository(ContactRepository contactRepository) {
        this.contactRepository = contactRepository;
    }
}
```

The findById() method is also annotated with @Transactional(readOnly=true). Generally, the readOnly=true attribute should be applied to all finder methods. The main reason is that most persistence providers will perform a certain level of optimization on read-only transactions. For example, Hibernate will not maintain the snapshots of the managed instances retrieved from the database with read-only turned on.

For the save() method, we simply invoke the CrudRepository.save() method and don't provide any annotation. This means the class-level annotation will be used, which is a read-write transaction.

Let's modify the TxAnnotationSample class for testing the save() method, as shown in Listing 9-13.

Listing 9-13. Testing the save() Method

```
package com.apress.prospring4.ch9;

import java.util.List;

import org.springframework.context.support.GenericXmlApplicationContext;

public class TxAnnotationSample {
    public static void main(String[] args) {
        GenericXmlApplicationContext ctx = new GenericXmlApplicationContext();
        ctx.load("classpath:META-INF/spring/tx-annotation-app-context.xml");
        ctx.refresh();

        ContactService contactService = ctx.getBean("contactService",
                ContactService.class);

        List<Contact> contacts = contactService.findAll();

        for (Contact contactTemp: contacts) {
            System.out.println(contactTemp);
        }

        Contact contact = contactService.findById(1L);
        contact.setFirstName("Peter");
        contactService.save(contact);
        System.out.println("Contact saved successfully: " + contact);

    }
}
```

The Contact object with id 1 is retrieved, and then the first name is updated and saved to the database. Running the code produces the following relevant output:

```
Contact saved successfully: Contact – Id: 1, First name: Peter, Last name: Schaefer,
Birthdate: 1981-05-03
```

The save() method gets the default attributes that are inherited from the class-level @Transactional annotation. Upon completion of the update operation, Spring's JpaTransactionManager fires a transaction commit, which causes Hibernate to flush the persistence context and commit the underlying JDBC connection to the database.

Finally, let's take a look at the countAll() method. We will investigate two transaction configurations for this method. Although the CrudRepository.count() method can fulfill the purpose, we will not use that method. Instead, we will implement another method for demonstration purposes, mainly because the methods defined by the CrudRepository interface in Spring Data are already marked with the appropriate transaction attributes.

Listing 9-14 shows the new method countAllContacts() defined in the ContactRepository interface.

Listing 9-14. The ContactRepository Interface with the countAllContacts() Method

```
package com.apress.prospring4.ch9;

import org.springframework.data.jpa.repository.Query;
import org.springframework.data.repository.CrudRepository;

public interface ContactRepository extends CrudRepository<Contact, Long> {
    @Query("select count(c) from Contact c")
    Long countAllContacts();
}
```

For the new countAllContacts() method, the @Query annotation is applied, with the value equaling the JPQL statement that counts the number of contacts. Listing 9-15 shows the implementation of the countAll() method in the ContactServiceImpl class.

Listing 9-15. The ContactServiceImpl Class with the countAll() Method Implemented

```
package com.apress.prospring4.ch9;

import com.google.common.collect.Lists;
import org.springframework.beans.factory.annotation.Autowired;
import org.springframework.stereotype.Repository;
import org.springframework.stereotype.Service;
import org.springframework.transaction.annotation.Transactional;

import java.util.List;

@Service("contactService")
@Repository
@Transactional
public class ContactServiceImpl implements ContactService {
    private ContactRepository contactRepository;
```

```java
    @Override
    @Transactional(readOnly=true)
    public List<Contact> findAll() {
        return Lists.newArrayList(contactRepository.findAll());
    }

    @Override
    @Transactional(readOnly=true)
    public Contact findById(Long id) {
        return contactRepository.findOne(id);
    }

    @Override
    public Contact save(Contact contact) {
        return contactRepository.save(contact);
    }

    @Override
    @Transactional(readOnly=true)
    public long countAll() {
        return contactRepository.countAllContacts();
    }

    @Autowired
    public void setContactRepository(ContactRepository contactRepository) {
        this.contactRepository = contactRepository;
    }
}
```

The annotation is the same as other finder methods. Listing 9-16 shows the testing code snippet.

Listing 9-16. Testing the countAll() Method

```java
package com.apress.prospring4.ch9;

import java.util.List;

import org.springframework.context.support.GenericXmlApplicationContext;

public class TxAnnotationSample {
    public static void main(String[] args) {
        GenericXmlApplicationContext ctx = new GenericXmlApplicationContext();
        ctx.load("classpath:META-INF/spring/tx-annotation-app-context.xml");
        ctx.refresh();

        ContactService contactService = ctx.getBean("contactService",
                ContactService.class);

        List<Contact> contacts = contactService.findAll();

        for (Contact contactTemp: contacts) {
            System.out.println(contactTemp);
        }
```

```
        Contact contact = contactService.findById(1L);
        contact.setFirstName("Peter");
        contactService.save(contact);
        System.out.println("Contact saved successfully: " + contact);
        System.out.println("Contact count: " + contactService.countAll());
    }
}
```

Running the program produces the following output:

```
Contact count: 3
```

In this output, you can see that the transaction for countAll() was created with read-only equaling true, as expected.

But for the countAll() function, we don't want it to be enlisted in a transaction at all. We don't need the result to be managed by the underlying JPA EntityManager. Instead, we just want to get the count and forget about it. In this case, we can override the transaction propagation behavior to Propagation.NEVER. Listing 9-17 shows the revised countAll() method.

Listing 9-17. The ContactServiceImpl Class with Revised countAll() Implemented

```java
package com.apress.prospring4.ch9;

import com.google.common.collect.Lists;
import org.springframework.beans.factory.annotation.Autowired;
import org.springframework.stereotype.Repository;
import org.springframework.stereotype.Service;
import org.springframework.transaction.annotation.Propagation;
import org.springframework.transaction.annotation.Transactional;

import java.util.List;

@Service("contactService")
@Repository
@Transactional
public class ContactServiceImpl implements ContactService {
    private ContactRepository contactRepository;

    @Override
    @Transactional(readOnly=true)
    public List<Contact> findAll() {
        return Lists.newArrayList(contactRepository.findAll());
    }

    @Override
    @Transactional(readOnly=true)
    public Contact findById(Long id) {
        return contactRepository.findOne(id);
    }

    @Override
    public Contact save(Contact contact) {
        return contactRepository.save(contact);
    }
```

```
    @Override
    @Transactional(propagation= Propagation.NEVER)
    public long countAll() {
        return contactRepository.countAllContacts();
    }

    @Autowired
    public void setContactRepository(ContactRepository contactRepository) {
        this.contactRepository = contactRepository;
    }
}
```

Run the testing code in Listing 9-16 again, and you will find that the transaction will not be created for the countAll() method in the debug output.

This section covered some major configurations that you will deal with when processing transactions on a day-to-day basis. For special cases, you may need to define the time-out, isolation level, rollback (or not) for specific exceptions, and so on.

■ **Note**   Spring's JpaTransactionManager doesn't support a custom isolation level. Instead, it always uses the default isolation level for the underlying datastore. If you are using Hibernate as the JPA service provider, you can use a work-around: extend the HibernateJpaDialect class to support a custom isolation level.

Using XML Configuration for Transaction Management

Another common approach of declarative transaction management is to use Spring's AOP support. Before Spring version 2, we needed to use the TransactionProxyFactoryBean class to define transaction requirements for Spring beans. However, ever since version 2, Spring provides a much simpler way by introducing aop-namespace and using the common AOP configuration technique for defining transaction requirements.

In this section, the example we will use is the same as the annotation one. We will just modify it to the XML configuration style. Listing 9-18 shows the XML configuration file for transaction management (tx-declarative-app-context.xml).

Listing 9-18. XML Configuration for Transaction Management

```
<?xml version="1.0" encoding="UTF-8"?>
<beans xmlns="http://www.springframework.org/schema/beans"
    xmlns:xsi="http://www.w3.org/2001/XMLSchema-instance"
    xmlns:context="http://www.springframework.org/schema/context"
    xmlns:jdbc="http://www.springframework.org/schema/jdbc"
    xmlns:tx="http://www.springframework.org/schema/tx"
    xmlns:jpa="http://www.springframework.org/schema/data/jpa"
    xmlns:aop="http://www.springframework.org/schema/aop"
    xsi:schemaLocation="http://www.springframework.org/schema/jdbc
        http://www.springframework.org/schema/jdbc/spring-jdbc.xsd
        http://www.springframework.org/schema/beans
        http://www.springframework.org/schema/beans/spring-beans.xsd
        http://www.springframework.org/schema/tx
        http://www.springframework.org/schema/tx/spring-tx.xsd
        http://www.springframework.org/schema/data/jpa
```

```
        http://www.springframework.org/schema/data/jpa/spring-jpa.xsd
        http://www.springframework.org/schema/context
        http://www.springframework.org/schema/context/spring-context.xsd
        http://www.springframework.org/schema/aop
        http://www.springframework.org/schema/aop/spring-aop.xsd">

    <aop:config>
        <aop:pointcut id="serviceOperation" expression=
            "execution(* com.apress.prospring4.ch9.*ServiceImpl.*(..))"/>
        <aop:advisor pointcut-ref="serviceOperation" advice-ref="txAdvice"/>
    </aop:config>

    <tx:advice id="txAdvice">
        <tx:attributes>
            <tx:method name="find*" read-only="true"/>
            <tx:method name="count*" propagation="NEVER"/>
            <tx:method name="*"/>
        </tx:attributes>
    </tx:advice>

    <jdbc:embedded-database id="dataSource" type="H2">
        <jdbc:script location="classpath:META-INF/config/schema.sql"/>
        <jdbc:script location="classpath:META-INF/config/test-data.sql"/>
    </jdbc:embedded-database>

    <bean id="transactionManager" class="org.springframework.orm.jpa.JpaTransactionManager">
        <property name="entityManagerFactory" ref="emf"/>
    </bean>

    <bean id="emf" class="org.springframework.orm.jpa.LocalContainerEntityManagerFactoryBean">
        <property name="dataSource" ref="dataSource" />
        <property name="jpaVendorAdapter">
            <bean class="org.springframework.orm.jpa.vendor.HibernateJpaVendorAdapter" />
        </property>
        <property name="packagesToScan" value="com.apress.prospring4 "/>
        <property name="jpaProperties">
            <props>
                <prop key="hibernate.dialect">
                    org.hibernate.dialect.H2Dialect
                </prop>
                <prop key="hibernate.max_fetch_depth">3</prop>
                <prop key="hibernate.jdbc.fetch_size">50</prop>
                <prop key="hibernate.jdbc.batch_size">10</prop>
                <prop key="hibernate.show_sql">true</prop>
            </props>
        </property>
    </bean>

    <context:component-scan
        base-package="com.apress.prospring4.ch9"/>

    <jpa:repositories base-package="com.apress.prospring4.ch9 "
        entity-manager-factory-ref="emf"
        transaction-manager-ref="transactionManager"/>
</beans>
```

The configuration is quite similar to the annotation one in Listing 9-9. Basically, the <tx:annotation-driven> tag is removed, and the <context:component-scan> tag is modified for the package name we used for declarative transaction management. The most important tags are <aop:config> and <tx:advice>.

Under the <aop:config> tag, a pointcut is defined for all operations within the service layer (that is, all implementation classes under the com.apress.prospring4.ch9 package). The advice is referencing the bean with an ID of txAdvice, which is defined by the <tx:advice> tag. In the <tx:advice> tag, we configure the transaction attributes for various methods that we want to participate in a transaction. As shown in the tag, we specify that all finder methods (methods with the prefix find) will be read-only, and we specify that the count methods (methods with the prefix count) will not participate in the transaction. For the rest of the methods, the default transaction behavior will be applied. This configuration is the same as the one in the annotation example. Listing 9-19 shows the implementation class for XML declarative transaction management.

Listing 9-19. ContactServiceImpl Class for XML Transaction Configuration

```
package com.apress.prospring4.ch9;

import com.google.common.collect.Lists;
import org.springframework.beans.factory.annotation.Autowired;
import org.springframework.stereotype.Repository;
import org.springframework.stereotype.Service;

import java.util.List;

@Service("contactService")
@Repository
public class ContactServiceImpl implements ContactService {
    private ContactRepository contactRepository;

    @Override
    public List<Contact> findAll() {
        return Lists.newArrayList(contactRepository.findAll());
    }

    @Override
    public Contact findById(Long id) {
        return contactRepository.findOne(id);
    }

    @Override
    public Contact save(Contact contact) {
        return contactRepository.save(contact);
    }

    @Override
    public long countAll() {
        return contactRepository.countAllContacts();
    }

    @Autowired
    public void setContactRepository(ContactRepository contactRepository) {
        this.contactRepository = contactRepository;
    }
}
```

This is basically the same as the annotation example, but with just the @Transactional annotations removed, because now Spring AOP, based on the XML configuration, will do the weaving of transactions. Listing 9-20 shows the testing program.

Listing 9-20. Testing the XML Transaction Configuration

```
package com.apress.prospring4.ch9;

import java.util.List;

import org.springframework.context.support.GenericXmlApplicationContext;

import com.apress.prospring4.ch9.domain.Contact;
import com.apress.prospring4.ch9.service.ContactService;

public class TxDeclarativeSample {

    public static void main(String[] args) {
        GenericXmlApplicationContext ctx = new GenericXmlApplicationContext();
        ctx.load("classpath:tx-declarative-app-context.xml");
        ctx.refresh();

        ContactService contactService = ctx.getBean("contactService",
            ContactService.class);

        // Testing findAll() method
        List<Contact> contacts = contactService.findAll();

        for (Contact contact: contacts) {
            System.out.println(contact);
        }

        // Testing save() method
        Contact contact = contactService.findById(1l);
        contact.setFirstName("Peter");
        contactService.save(contact);
        System.out.println("Contact saved successfully");

        // Testing countAll() method
        System.out.println("Contact count: " + contactService.countAll());

    }

}
```

We will leave you to test the program and observe the output for transaction-related operations that Spring and Hibernate have performed. Basically, they are the same as the annotation example.

Using Programmatic Transactions

The third option is to control the transaction behavior programmatically. In this case, we have two options. The first one is to inject an instance of `PlatformTransactionManager` into the bean and interact with the transaction manager directly. Another option is to use the Spring-provided `TransactionTemplate` class, which simplifies your work a lot. In this section, we demonstrate using the `TransactionTemplate` class. To make it simple, we focus on implementing the `ContactService.countAll()` method.

Listing 9-21 shows the XML configuration for using programmatic transaction (`tx-programmatic-app-context.xml`).

Listing 9-21. Spring Configuration for Programmtic Transaction Management

```xml
<?xml version="1.0" encoding="UTF-8"?>
<beans xmlns="http://www.springframework.org/schema/beans"
    xmlns:xsi="http://www.w3.org/2001/XMLSchema-instance"
    xmlns:context="http://www.springframework.org/schema/context"
    xmlns:jdbc="http://www.springframework.org/schema/jdbc"
    xmlns:tx="http://www.springframework.org/schema/tx"
    xmlns:jpa="http://www.springframework.org/schema/data/jpa"
    xsi:schemaLocation="http://www.springframework.org/schema/jdbc
        http://www.springframework.org/schema/jdbc/spring-jdbc.xsd
        http://www.springframework.org/schema/beans
        http://www.springframework.org/schema/beans/spring-beans.xsd
        http://www.springframework.org/schema/tx
        http://www.springframework.org/schema/tx/spring-tx.xsd
        http://www.springframework.org/schema/data/jpa
        http://www.springframework.org/schema/data/jpa/spring-jpa.xsd
        http://www.springframework.org/schema/context
        http://www.springframework.org/schema/context/spring-context.xsd">

    <jdbc:embedded-database id="dataSource" type="H2">
        <jdbc:script location="classpath:META-INF/config/schema.sql"/>
        <jdbc:script location="classpath:META-INF/config/test-data.sql"/>
    </jdbc:embedded-database>

    <bean id="transactionTemplate"
        class="org.springframework.transaction.support.TransactionTemplate">
        <property name="propagationBehaviorName" value="PROPAGATION_NEVER"/>
        <property name="timeout" value="30"/>
        <property name="transactionManager" ref="transactionManager"/>
    </bean>

    <bean id="transactionManager" class="org.springframework.orm.jpa.JpaTransactionManager">
        <property name="entityManagerFactory" ref="emf"/>
    </bean>

    <bean id="emf" class="org.springframework.orm.jpa.LocalContainerEntityManagerFactoryBean">
        <property name="dataSource" ref="dataSource" />
        <property name="jpaVendorAdapter">
            <bean class="org.springframework.orm.jpa.vendor.HibernateJpaVendorAdapter" />
        </property>
        <property name="packagesToScan"
            value="com.apress.prospring4.ch9"/>
```

```xml
            <property name="jpaProperties">
                <props>
                    <prop key="hibernate.dialect">
                        org.hibernate.dialect.H2Dialect
                    </prop>
                    <prop key="hibernate.max_fetch_depth">3</prop>
                    <prop key="hibernate.jdbc.fetch_size">50</prop>
                    <prop key="hibernate.jdbc.batch_size">10</prop>
                    <prop key="hibernate.show_sql">true</prop>
                </props>
            </property>
        </bean>

        <context:component-scan
            base-package="com.apress.prospring4.ch9"/>

        <jpa:repositories base-package="com.apress.prospring4.ch9"
            entity-manager-factory-ref="emf"
            transaction-manager-ref="transactionManager"/>
</beans>
```

Here the AOP transaction advice is removed. In addition, a transactionTemplate bean is defined, using the org.springframework.transaction.support.TransactionTemplate class, with the transaction attributes defined in the properties section. Let's take a look at the implementation of the countAll() method, which is shown in Listing 9-22.

Listing 9-22. Programmatic Transaction Management Implementation

```java
package com.apress.prospring4.ch9;

import com.google.common.collect.Lists;
import org.springframework.beans.factory.annotation.Autowired;
import org.springframework.stereotype.Repository;
import org.springframework.stereotype.Service;
import org.springframework.transaction.TransactionStatus;
import org.springframework.transaction.support.TransactionCallback;
import org.springframework.transaction.support.TransactionTemplate;

import javax.persistence.EntityManager;
import javax.persistence.PersistenceContext;
import java.util.List;

@Service("contactService")
@Repository
public class ContactServiceImpl implements ContactService {
    private ContactRepository contactRepository;
    private TransactionTemplate transactionTemplate;

    @PersistenceContext
    private EntityManager em;

    @Override
    public List<Contact> findAll() {
        return Lists.newArrayList(contactRepository.findAll());
    }
```

```java
    @Override
    public Contact findById(Long id) {
        return contactRepository.findOne(id);
    }

    @Override
    public Contact save(Contact contact) {
        return contactRepository.save(contact);
    }

    @Override
    public long countAll() {
        return transactionTemplate.execute(new TransactionCallback<Long>() {
            public Long doInTransaction(TransactionStatus transactionStatus) {
                return em.createNamedQuery("Contact.countAll",
                        Long.class).getSingleResult();
            }

        });
    }

    @Autowired
    public void setContactRepository(ContactRepository contactRepository) {
        this.contactRepository = contactRepository;
    }

    @Autowired
    public void setTransactionTemplate(TransactionTemplate transactionTemplate) {
        this.transactionTemplate = transactionTemplate;
    }
}
```

Here the TransactionTemplate class is injected from Spring. And then in the countAll() method, the TransactionTemplate.execute() method is invoked, passing in a declaration of an inner class that implements the TransactionCallback<T> interface. Then the doInTransaction() is overridden with the desired logic. The logic will run within the attributes as defined by the transactionTemplate bean. Listing 9-23 shows the testing program.

Listing 9-23. Testing Programmatic Transaction

```java
package com.apress.prospring4.ch9;

import org.springframework.context.support.GenericXmlApplicationContext;

public class TxProgrammaticSample {
    public static void main(String[] args) {
        GenericXmlApplicationContext ctx = new GenericXmlApplicationContext();
        ctx.load("classpath:META-INF/spring/tx-programmatic-app-context.xml");
        ctx.refresh();
```

```
        ContactService contactService = ctx.getBean("contactService",
            ContactService.class);

        System.out.println("Contact count: " + contactService.countAll());
    }
}
```

We will leave it to you to run the program and observe the result. Try to tweak the transaction attributes and see what happens in the transaction processing of the countAll() method.

Considerations on Transaction Management

So, having discussed the various ways for implementing transaction management, which one should you use? The declarative approach is recommended in all cases, and you should avoid implementing transaction management within your code as far as possible. Most of the time, when you find it necessary to code transaction control logic in the application, it is because of bad design, and in this case, you should consider refactoring your logic into manageable pieces and have the transaction requirements defined on those pieces declaratively.

For the declarative approach, using XML and using annotations both have their own pros and cons. Some developers prefer not to declare transaction requirements in code, while others prefer using annotations for easy maintenance, because you can see all the transaction requirement declarations within the code. Again, let the application requirements drive your decision, and once your team or company has standardized on the approach, stay consistent with the configuration style.

Global Transactions with Spring

Many enterprise Java applications need to access multiple back-end resources. For example, a piece of customer information received from an external business partner may need to update the databases for multiple systems (CRM, ERP, and so on). Some may even need to produce a message and send it to an MQ server via JMS for all other applications within the company that are interested in customer information. Transactions that span multiple back-end resources are referred to as *global* (or distributed) transactions.

A main characteristic of a global transaction is the guarantee of atomicity, which means that involved resources are all updated, or none is updated. This includes complex coordination and synchronization logic that should be handled by the transaction manager. In the Java world, JTA is the de facto standard for implementing global transactions.

Spring supports JTA transactions equally well as local transactions and hides that logic from the business code. In this section, we demonstrate how to implement global transactions by using JTA with Spring.

Infrastructure for Implementing the JTA Sample

We are using the same table as for the previous samples in this chapter. However, the embedded H2 database doesn't fully support XA (at least at the time of writing), so in this example, we use MySQL as the back-end database.

We also want to show how to implement global transactions with JTA in a stand-alone application or web container environment. So, in this example, we use Atomikos (http://www.atomikos.com/Main/TransactionsEssentials), which is a widely used open source JTA transaction manager for use in a non-JEE environment.

To show how global transactions work, we need at least two back-end resources. To make things simple, we will use one MySQL database but two JPA entity managers to simulate the use case. The effect is the same, because you have multiple JPA persistence units to distinct back-end databases.

In the MySQL database, we create two schemas, as shown in Table 9-5.

Table 9-5. *MySQL Database Schemas*

Schema Name	Connection Information	Data Population Scripts
prospring4_ch9a	User: prospring4_ch9a Password: prospring4_ch9a	schema.sql test-data.sql
prospring4_ch9b	User: prospring4_ch9b Password: prospring4_ch9b	schema.sql test-data.sql

Then, we need to add the required dependencies on MySQL and Atomikos to the project. Table 9-6 shows the dependencies required.

Table 9-6. *Maven Dependencies for MySQL and Atomikos*

Group ID	Artifact ID	Version	Description
mysql	mysql-connector-java	5.1.29	The Java library for MySQL 5
com.atomikos	transactions-jdbc	3.9.3	The JTA transaction library for Atomikos

After the setup has completed, we can proceed to the Spring configuration and implementation.

Implementing Global Transactions with JTA

First let's take a look at Spring's configuration. Listing 9-24 shows the file content (tx-jta-app-context.xml).

Listing 9-24. Spring Configuration with JTA

```xml
<?xml version="1.0" encoding="UTF-8"?>
<beans xmlns="http://www.springframework.org/schema/beans"
      xmlns:xsi="http://www.w3.org/2001/XMLSchema-instance"
      xmlns:context="http://www.springframework.org/schema/context"
      xmlns:tx="http://www.springframework.org/schema/tx"
      xsi:schemaLocation="http://www.springframework.org/schema/beans
       http://www.springframework.org/schema/beans/spring-beans.xsd
       http://www.springframework.org/schema/tx
       http://www.springframework.org/schema/tx/spring-tx.xsd
       http://www.springframework.org/schema/context
       http://www.springframework.org/schema/context/spring-context.xsd">

    <bean id="dataSourceA" class="com.atomikos.jdbc.AtomikosDataSourceBean"
        init-method="init" destroy-method="close">
        <property name="uniqueResourceName" value="XADBMSA"/>
        <property name="xaDataSourceClassName" value="com.mysql.jdbc.jdbc2.optional.MysqlXADataSource"/>
        <property name="xaProperties">
            <props>
                <prop key="databaseName">prospring4_ch9a</prop>
                <prop key="user">prospring4_ch9a</prop>
                <prop key="password">prospring4_ch9a</prop>
            </props>
        </property>
        <property name="poolSize" value="1"/>
    </bean>
```

```xml
<bean id="dataSourceB" class="com.atomikos.jdbc.AtomikosDataSourceBean"
      init-method="init" destroy-method="close">
    <property name="uniqueResourceName" value="XADBMSB"/>
    <property name="xaDataSourceClassName" value="com.mysql.jdbc.jdbc2.optional.MysqlXADataSource"/>
    <property name="xaProperties">
        <props>
            <prop key="databaseName">prospring4_ch9b</prop>
            <prop key="user">prospring4_ch9b</prop>
            <prop key="password">prospring4_ch9b</prop>
        </props>
    </property>
    <property name="poolSize" value="1"/>
</bean>

<bean id="emfBase" class="org.springframework.orm.jpa.LocalContainerEntityManagerFactoryBean"
      abstract="true">
    <property name="jpaVendorAdapter">
        <bean class="org.springframework.orm.jpa.vendor.HibernateJpaVendorAdapter"/>
    </property>
    <property name="packagesToScan" value="com.apress.prospring4.ch9"/>
    <property name="jpaProperties">
        <props>
            <prop key="hibernate.transaction.factory_class">
                org.hibernate.engine.transaction.internal.jta.CMTTransactionFactory</prop>
            <prop key="hibernate.transaction.manager_lookup_class">
                com.atomikos.icatch.jta.hibernate3.TransactionManagerLookup</prop>
            <prop key="hibernate.dialect">
                org.hibernate.dialect.MySQL5Dialect</prop>
            <prop key="hibernate.max_fetch_depth">3</prop>
            <prop key="hibernate.jdbc.fetch_size">50</prop>
            <prop key="hibernate.jdbc.batch_size">10</prop>
            <prop key="hibernate.show_sql">true</prop>
        </props>
    </property>
</bean>

<bean id="emfA" parent="emfBase">
    <property name="dataSource" ref="dataSourceA"/>
    <property name="persistenceUnitName" value="emfA"/>
</bean>

<bean id="emfB" parent="emfBase">
    <property name="dataSource" ref="dataSourceB"/>
    <property name="persistenceUnitName" value="emfB"/>
</bean>

<tx:annotation-driven transaction-manager="transactionManager" />

<bean id="atomikosTransactionManager" class="com.atomikos.icatch.jta.UserTransactionManager"
      init-method="init" destroy-method="close">
    <property name="forceShutdown" value="true"/>
</bean>
```

```xml
<bean id="atomikosUserTransaction" class="com.atomikos.icatch.jta.UserTransactionImp">
    <property name="transactionTimeout" value="300"/>
</bean>

<bean id="transactionManager" class="org.springframework.transaction.jta.JtaTransactionManager">
    <property name="transactionManager" ref="atomikosTransactionManager"/>
    <property name="userTransaction" ref="atomikosUserTransaction"/>
</bean>

<context:component-scan base-package="com.apress.prospring4.ch9 " />
</beans>
```

The configuration is long but not too complex. First, two DataSource beans are defined to indicate the two database resources. The bean names are dataSourceA and dataSourceB, which connect to the schemas prospring4_ch9a and prospring4_ch9b, respectively. Both DataSource beans use the class com.atomikos.jdbc. AtomikosDataSourceBean, which supports an XA-compliant DataSource, and within the two beans' definitions, MySQL's XA DataSource implementation class is defined (com.mysql.jdbc.jdbc2.optional.MysqlXADataSource), which is the resource manager for MySQL. Then, the database connection information is provided. Note that the poolSize attribute defines the number of connections within the connection pool that Atomikos needs to maintain. It's not mandatory. However, if the attribute is not provided, Atomikos will use the default value 1.

For the Atomikos part, two beans, the atomikosTransactionManager and atomikosUserTransaction beans, are defined. The implementation classes are provided by Atomikos, which implements the standard JEE's TransactionManager and UserTransaction interfaces, respectively. Those beans provide the transaction coordination and synchronization services required by JTA and communicate with the resource managers over the XA protocol in supporting 2PC. Then, Spring's transactionManager bean (with JtaTransactionManager as the implementation class) is defined, injecting the two transaction beans provided by Atomikos. This instructs Spring to use Atomikos JTA for transaction management.

Then, three EntityManagerFactory beans are defined, named emfBase, emfA, and emfB. The emfBase bean is an abstract parent bean, which wraps the common JPA properties. The emfBase bean is implemented with Spring's LocalContainerEntityManagerFactoryBean class. The emfA and emfB beans both inherit the configuration from the parent bean emfBase, and the only difference between the two beans is that they were injected with the corresponding data source (that is, dataSourceA injected into emfA, and dataSourceB injected into emfB). Consequently, emfA will connect to MySQL's prospring4_ch9a schema via the dataSourceA bean, while emfB will connect to the prospring4_ch9b schema via the dataSourceB bean. Take a look at the properties hibernate.transaction.factory_ class and hibernate.transaction.manager_lookup_class in the emfBase bean. These two properties are very important, because they are used by Hibernate to look up the underlying UserTransaction and TransactionManager interfaces in order to participate in the persistence context that it's managing into the global transaction.

Listing 9-25 shows the ContactServiceImpl class for JTA. Note that for simplicity only the save() method is implemented.

Listing 9-25. JTA ContactService Implementation Class

```java
package com.apress.prospring4.ch9;

import java.util.List;

import javax.persistence.EntityManager;
import javax.persistence.PersistenceContext;
import javax.persistence.PersistenceException;

import org.springframework.orm.jpa.JpaSystemException;
import org.springframework.stereotype.Repository;
import org.springframework.stereotype.Service;
import org.springframework.transaction.annotation.Transactional;
```

```java
@Service("contactService")
@Repository
@Transactional
public class ContactServiceImpl implements ContactService {
    @PersistenceContext(unitName="emfA")
    private EntityManager emA;

    @PersistenceContext(unitName="emfB")
    private EntityManager emB;

    @Override
    @Transactional(readOnly=true)
    public List<Contact> findAll() {
        return null;
    }
    @Override
    @Transactional(readOnly=true)
    public Contact findById(Long id) {
        return null;
    }

    @Override
    public Contact save(Contact contact) {
        Contact contactB = new Contact();
        contactB.setFirstName(contact.getFirstName());
        contactB.setLastName(contact.getLastName());
        if (contact.getId() == null) {
            emA.persist(contact);
            emB.persist(contactB);
            // throw new JpaSystemException(new PersistenceException());
        } else {
            emA.merge(contact);
            emB.merge(contact);
        }

        return contact;
    }

    @Override
    public long countAll() {
        return 0;
    }
}
```

The two entity managers defined are injected into the `ContactServiceImpl` class. In the `save()` method, we persist the contact object to the two schemas, respectively. Ignore the throw exception statement at the moment; we will use it later to verify that the transaction was rolled back when saving to the schema `prospring4_ch9b` fails. Listing 9-26 shows the testing program.

Listing 9-26. Testing JTA

```
package com.apress.prospring4.ch9;

import org.springframework.context.support.GenericXmlApplicationContext;

public class TxJtaSample {
    public static void main(String[] args) {
        GenericXmlApplicationContext ctx = new GenericXmlApplicationContext();
        ctx.load("classpath:META-INF/spring/tx-jta-app-context.xml");
        ctx.refresh();

        ContactService contactService = ctx.getBean("contactService",
            ContactService.class);

        Contact contact = new Contact();
        contact.setFirstName("Jta");
        contact.setLastName("Manager");
        contactService.save(contact);
        System.out.println("Contact saved successfully");
    }
}
```

The program creates a new contact object and calls the `ContactService.save()` method. The implementation will try to persist the same object to two databases. Providing all went well, running the program produces the following output (the other output was omitted):

```
Contact saved successfully
```

Atomikos creates a composite transaction, communicates with the XA DataSource (MySQL, in this case), performs synchronization, commits the transaction, and so on.

From the database, you will see that the new contact is persisted to both schemas of the database, respectively.

Now let's see how the rollback works. As shown in Listing 9-25, instead of calling `emB.persist()`, we just throw an exception. Listing 9-27 shows the code snippet.

Listing 9-27. Testing JTA Transaction Rollback

```
//emB.persist(contactB);
throw new JpaSystemException(new PersistenceException());
```

To test the rollback scenario, delete the new records inserted by the previous example from the two MySQL databases first (that is, the contact record with `FIRST_NAME` Jta and `LAST_NAME` Manager). Running the program again produces the following results:

```
Exception in thread "main" org.springframework.orm.jpa.JpaSystemException: nested exception is
javax.persistence.PersistenceException
...
Caused by: javax.persistence.PersistenceException
```

As shown in the previous output, the first contact is persisted (note the `insert` statement). However, when saving to the second `DataSource`, because an exception is thrown, Atomikos will roll back the entire transaction. You can take a look at the schema `prospring4_ch9a` to check that the new contact was not saved.

Considerations on Using JTA Transaction Manager

Whether to use JTA for global transaction management is under hot debate. For example, the Spring development team generally does not recommend using JTA for global transactions.

As a general principle, when your application is deployed to a full-blown JEE application server, there is no point in not using JTA, because all the vendors of the popular JEE application servers have optimized their JTA implementation for their platforms. That's one major feature that you are paying for.

For stand-alone or web container deployment, let the application requirements drive your decision. Perform load testing as early as possible to verify that performance is not being impaired by using JTA.

One piece of good news is that Spring works seamlessly with both local and global transactions in most major web and JEE containers, so code modification is generally not required when you switch from one transaction management strategy to another. In case you decide to use JTA within your application, make sure you use Spring's `JtaTransactionManager`.

Summary

Transaction management is a key part of ensuring data integrity in almost any type of application. In this chapter, we discussed how to use Spring to manage transactions with almost no impact on your source code. You also learned how to use local and global transactions.

We provided various examples of transaction implementation, including declarative ways of using XML configuration and annotation, as well as the programmatic approach.

Local transactions are supported inside/outside a JEE application server, and only simple configuration is required to enable local transaction support in Spring. However, setting up a global transaction environment involves more work and greatly depends on which JTA provider and corresponding back-end resources your application needs to interact with.

CHAPTER 10

■ ■ ■

Validation with Type Conversion and Formatting

In an enterprise application, *validation* is critical. The purpose of validation is to verify that the data being processed fulfills all predefined business requirements as well as to ensure the data integrity and usefulness in other layers of the application.

In application development, data validation is always mentioned alongside conversion and formatting. The reason is that the format of the source of data most likely is different from the format being used in the application. For example, in a web application, a user enters information in the web browser front end. When the user saves that data, it is sent to the server (after the local validation has completed). On the server side, a data-binding process is performed, in which the data from the HTTP request is extracted, converted, and bound to corresponding domain objects (for example, a user enters contact information in an HTML form that is then bound to a Contact object in the server), based on the formatting rules defined for each attribute (for example, the date format pattern is yyyy-MM-dd). When the data binding is complete, validation rules are applied to the domain object to check for any constraint violation. If everything runs fine, the data is persisted, and a success message is displayed to the user. Otherwise, validation error messages are populated and displayed to the user.

In the first part of this chapter, you will learn how Spring provides sophisticated support for type conversion, field formatting, and validation. Specifically, this chapter covers the following topics:

- *The Spring type conversion system and the Formatter service provider interface (SPI)*: We present the generic type conversion system and Formatter SPI. We cover how the new services can be used to replace the previous PropertyEditor support and how they convert between any Java types.

- *Validation in Spring*: We discuss how Spring supports domain object validation. First, we provide a short introduction to Spring's own Validator interface. Then, we focus on the JSR-349 Bean Validation support.

Dependencies

As in prior chapters, the samples presented in this chapter require some dependencies, which are shown in Table 10-1. One dependency you may notice is joda-time. If you are running Java 8, Spring 4 also supports JSR-310, which is the javax.time API.

Table 10-1. *Maven Dependencies for Validation*

Group ID	Artifact ID	Version	Description
javax.validation	validation-api	1.1.0.Final	JSR-349 API library.
org.hibernate	hibernate-validator	5.1.0.Final	Hibernate Validator library that supports JSR-349, "Bean Validation."
joda-time	joda-time	2.3	A date-time API intended to simplify the built-in Java date and time libraries. In this chapter, we use it in our domain objects.

Spring Type Conversion System

In Spring 3, a new type conversion system was introduced, providing a powerful way to convert between any Java types within Spring-powered applications. This section shows how this new service can perform the same functionality provided by the previous PropertyEditor support, as well as how it supports the conversion between any Java types. We also demonstrate how to implement a custom type converter by using the Converter SPI.

Conversion from a String Using PropertyEditors

Chapter 3 covered how Spring handles the conversion from a String in the properties files into the properties of POJOs by supporting PropertyEditors. Let's do a quick review here, and then cover how Spring's Converter SPI (available since 3.0) provides a more powerful alternative.

Consider a Contact class with a couple of attributes, as in Listing 10-1.

Listing 10-1. The Contact Class

```
package com.apress.prospring4.ch10;

import java.net.URL;
import org.joda.time.DateTime;

public class Contact {
    private String firstName;
    private String lastName;
    private DateTime birthDate;
    private URL personalSite;

    public String getFirstName() {
        return firstName;
    }

    public void setFirstName(String firstName) {
        this.firstName = firstName;
    }

    public String getLastName() {
        return lastName;
    }
```

```
    public void setLastName(String lastName) {
        this.lastName = lastName;
    }

    public DateTime getBirthDate() {
        return birthDate;
    }

    public void setBirthDate(DateTime birthDate) {
        this.birthDate = birthDate;
    }

    public URL getPersonalSite() {
        return personalSite;
    }

    public void setPersonalSite(URL personalSite) {
        this.personalSite = personalSite;
    }

    public String toString() {
        return "First name: " + getFirstName()
                + " - Last name: " + getLastName()
                + " - Birth date: " + getBirthDate()
                + " - Personal site: " + getPersonalSite();
    }
}
```

For the birth date attribute, we use JodaTime's `DateTime` class. In addition, there is a URL type field that indicates the contact's personal web site, if applicable.

Now suppose we want to construct `Contact` objects in Spring's `ApplicationContext`, with values stored either in Spring's configuration file or in a properties file. Listing 10-2 shows the Spring XML configuration file (`prop-editor-app-context.xml`).

Listing 10-2. Spring Configuration for Property Editor

```
<?xml version="1.0" encoding="UTF-8"?>
<beans xmlns="http://www.springframework.org/schema/beans"
       xmlns:xsi="http://www.w3.org/2001/XMLSchema-instance"
       xmlns:context="http://www.springframework.org/schema/context"
       xmlns:util="http://www.springframework.org/schema/util"
       xmlns:p="http://www.springframework.org/schema/p"
       xsi:schemaLocation="http://www.springframework.org/schema/beans
        http://www.springframework.org/schema/beans/spring-beans.xsd
        http://www.springframework.org/schema/context
        http://www.springframework.org/schema/context/spring-context.xsd
        http://www.springframework.org/schema/util
        http://www.springframework.org/schema/util/spring-util.xsd">

    <context:annotation-config/>

    <context:property-placeholder location="classpath:application.properties"/>
```

```xml
<bean id="customEditorConfigurer"
    class="org.springframework.beans.factory.config.CustomEditorConfigurer"
    p:propertyEditorRegistrars-ref="propertyEditorRegistrarsList"/>

<util:list id="propertyEditorRegistrarsList">
    <bean class="com.apress.prospring4.ch10.DateTimeEditorRegistrar">
        <constructor-arg value="${date.format.pattern}"/>
    </bean>
</util:list>

<bean id="chris" class="com.apress.prospring4.ch10.Contact"
    p:firstName="Chris"
    p:lastName="Schaefer"
    p:birthDate="1981-05-03"
    p:personalSite="http://www.dtzq.com"/>

<bean id="myContact" class="com.apress.prospring4.ch10.Contact"
    p:firstName="${myContact.firstName}"
    p:lastName="${myContact.lastName}"
    p:birthDate="${myContact.birthDate}"
    p:personalSite="${myContact.personalSite}"/>
</beans>
```

Here we construct two different beans of the Contact class. The chris bean is constructed with values provided in the configuration file, while for the myContact bean, the attributes are externalized into a properties file. In addition, a custom editor is defined for converting from a String to JodaTime's DateTime type, and the date-time format pattern is externalized in the properties file too. Listing 10-3 shows the properties file (application.properties).

Listing 10-3. The application.properties File

```
date.format.pattern=yyyy-MM-dd

myContact.firstName=Scott
myContact.lastName=Tiger
myContact.birthDate=1984-6-30
myContact.personalSite=http://www.somedomain.com
```

Listing 10-4 shows the custom editor for converting String values into the JodaTime DateTime type.

Listing 10-4. Custom Editor for JodaTime DateTime

```java
package com.apress.prospring4.ch10;

import org.joda.time.DateTime;
import org.joda.time.format.DateTimeFormat;
import org.joda.time.format.DateTimeFormatter;
import org.springframework.beans.PropertyEditorRegistrar;
import org.springframework.beans.PropertyEditorRegistry;

import java.beans.PropertyEditorSupport;
```

```java
public class DateTimeEditorRegistrar implements PropertyEditorRegistrar {
    private DateTimeFormatter dateTimeFormatter;

    public DateTimeEditorRegistrar(String dateFormatPattern) {
        dateTimeFormatter = DateTimeFormat.forPattern(dateFormatPattern);
    }

    @Override
    public void registerCustomEditors(PropertyEditorRegistry registry) {
        registry.registerCustomEditor(DateTime.class, new DateTimeEditor(dateTimeFormatter));
    }

    private static class DateTimeEditor extends PropertyEditorSupport {
        private DateTimeFormatter dateTimeFormatter;

        public DateTimeEditor(DateTimeFormatter dateTimeFormatter) {
            this.dateTimeFormatter = dateTimeFormatter;
        }

        @Override
        public void setAsText(String text) throws IllegalArgumentException {
            setValue(DateTime.parse(text, dateTimeFormatter));
        }
    }
}
```

Listing 10-4 implements the PropertyEditorRegister interface to register our custom PropertyEditor. We then create an inner class called DateTimeEditor that handles the conversion of the String to a DateTime. We use an inner class in this sample, as it's accessed by only our PropertyEditorRegistrar implementation. Now let's test it. Listing 10-5 shows the testing program.

Listing 10-5. Testing Property Editor

```java
package com.apress.prospring4.ch10;

import org.springframework.context.support.GenericXmlApplicationContext;

public class PropEditorExample {
    public static void main(String[] args) {
        GenericXmlApplicationContext ctx = new GenericXmlApplicationContext();
        ctx.load("classpath:META-INF/spring/prop-editor-app-context.xml");
        ctx.refresh();

        Contact chris = ctx.getBean("chris", Contact.class);
        System.out.println("Chris info: " + chris);

        Contact myContact = ctx.getBean("myContact", Contact.class);
        System.out.println("My contact info: " + myContact);
    }
}
```

As you can see, the two `Contact` beans are retrieved from `ApplicationContext` and printed. Running the program produces the following output:

```
Chris info: First name: Chris - Last name: Schaefer - Birth date: 1981-05-03T00:00:00.000-04:00 -
Personal site: http://www.dtzq.com
My contact info: First name: Scott - Last name: Tiger - Birth date: 1984-06-30T00:00:00.000-04:00 -
Personal site: http://www.somedomain.com
```

As shown in the output, the properties are converted and applied to the `Contact` beans.

Introducing Spring Type Conversion

Since Spring 3.0, a general type conversion system was introduced, which resides under the package `org.springframework.core.convert`. In addition to providing an alternative to `PropertyEditor` support, the type conversion system can be configured to convert between any Java types and POJOs (while `PropertyEditor` is focused on converting `String` representations in the properties file into Java types).

Implementing a Custom Converter

To see the type conversion system in action, let's revisit the previous example and use the same `Contact` class. Suppose this time we want to use the type conversion system to convert the date in `String` format into the `Contact`'s `birthDate` property, which is of JodaTime's `DateTime` type. To support the conversion, instead of creating a custom `PropertyEditor`, we create a custom converter by implementing the `org.springframework.core.convert.converter.Converter<S,T>` interface. Listing 10-6 shows the custom converter.

Listing 10-6. Custom DateTime Converter

```java
package com.apress.prospring4.ch10;

import javax.annotation.PostConstruct;

import org.joda.time.DateTime;
import org.joda.time.format.DateTimeFormat;
import org.joda.time.format.DateTimeFormatter;
import org.springframework.beans.factory.annotation.Autowired;
import org.springframework.core.convert.converter.Converter;

public class StringToDateTimeConverter implements Converter<String, DateTime> {
    private static final String DEFAULT_DATE_PATTERN = "yyyy-MM-dd";
    private DateTimeFormatter dateFormat;

    private String datePattern = DEFAULT_DATE_PATTERN;

    public String getDatePattern() {
        return datePattern;
    }

    @Autowired(required=false)
    public void setDatePattern(String datePattern) {
        this.datePattern = datePattern;
    }
```

```
@PostConstruct
public void init() {
    dateFormat = DateTimeFormat.forPattern(datePattern);
}

@Override
public DateTime convert(String dateString) {
    return dateFormat.parseDateTime(dateString);
}
}
```

We implement the interface Converter<String, DateTime>, which means the converter is responsible for converting a String (the source type S) to a DateTime type (the target type T). The injection of the date-time pattern is optional, by annotating it with @Autowired(required=false). If not injected, the default pattern yyyy-MM-dd is used. Then, in the initialization method (the init() method annotated with @PostConstruct), an instance of JodaTime's DateTimeFormat class is constructed, which will perform the conversion based on the specified pattern. Finally, the convert() method is implemented to provide the conversion logic.

Configuring ConversionService

To use the conversion service instead of PropertyEditor, we need to configure an instance of the org.springframework.core.convert.ConversionService interface in Spring's ApplicationContext. Listing 10-7 shows the configuration file (conv-service-app-context.xml).

Listing 10-7. Configuration of ConversionService

```xml
<?xml version="1.0" encoding="UTF-8"?>
<beans xmlns="http://www.springframework.org/schema/beans"
    xmlns:xsi="http://www.w3.org/2001/XMLSchema-instance"
    xmlns:context="http://www.springframework.org/schema/context"
    xmlns:p="http://www.springframework.org/schema/p"
    xsi:schemaLocation="http://www.springframework.org/schema/beans
        http://www.springframework.org/schema/beans/spring-beans.xsd
        http://www.springframework.org/schema/context
        http://www.springframework.org/schema/context/spring-context.xsd">

    <context:annotation-config/>

    <bean id="conversionService" class="org.springframework.context.support.
ConversionServiceFactoryBean">
        <property name="converters">
            <list>
                <bean class="com.apress.prospring4.ch10.StringToDateTimeConverter"/>
            </list>
        </property>
    </bean>

    <bean id="chris" class="com.apress.prospring4.ch10.Contact"
        p:firstName="Chris"
        p:lastName="Schaefer"
        p:birthDate="1981-05-03"
        p:personalSite="http://www.dtzq.com"/>
</beans>
```

453

Here we instruct Spring to use the type conversion system by declaring a conversionService bean with the class ConversionServiceFactoryBean. If no conversion service bean is defined, Spring will use the PropertyEditor-based system.

By default, the type conversion service supports conversion between common types including strings, numbers, enums, collections, maps, and so on. In addition, the conversion from Strings to Java types within the PropertyEditor-based system is supported.

For the conversionService bean, a custom converter is configured for conversion from a String to DateTime. Listing 10-8 shows a testing program.

Listing 10-8. Testing ConversionService

```
package com.apress.prospring4.ch10;

import org.springframework.context.support.GenericXmlApplicationContext;

public class ConvServExample {
    public static void main(String[] args) {
        GenericXmlApplicationContext ctx = new GenericXmlApplicationContext();
        ctx.load("classpath:META-INF/spring/conv-service-app-context.xml");
        ctx.refresh();

        Contact chris = ctx.getBean("chris", Contact.class);

        System.out.println("Contact info: " + chris);
    }
}
```

Running the testing program produces the following output:

```
Contact info: First name: Chris - Last name: Schaefer - Birth date: 1981-05-03T00:00:00.000-04:00 -
Personal site: http://www.dtzq.com
```

As you can see, the chris bean's property conversion result is the same as when we use PropertyEditors.

Converting Between Arbitrary Types

The real strength of the type conversion system is the ability to convert between arbitrary types. To see it in action, suppose we have another class, called AnotherContact, that is the same as the Contact class. Listing 10-9 shows the class.

Listing 10-9. The AnotherContact Class

```
package com.apress.prospring4.ch10;

import java.net.URL;

import org.joda.time.DateTime;

public class AnotherContact {
    private String firstName;
    private String lastName;
    private DateTime birthDate;
    private URL personalSite;
```

```java
    public String getFirstName() {
        return firstName;
    }

    public void setFirstName(String firstName) {
        this.firstName = firstName;
    }

    public String getLastName() {
        return lastName;
    }

    public void setLastName(String lastName) {
        this.lastName = lastName;
    }

    public DateTime getBirthDate() {
        return birthDate;
    }

    public void setBirthDate(DateTime birthDate) {
        this.birthDate = birthDate;
    }

    public URL getPersonalSite() {
        return personalSite;
    }

    public void setPersonalSite(URL personalSite) {
        this.personalSite = personalSite;
    }

    public String toString() {
        return "First name: " + getFirstName()
                + " - Last name: " + getLastName()
                + " - Birth date: " + getBirthDate()
                + " - Personal site: " + getPersonalSite();
    }
}
```

We want to be able to convert any instance of the Contact class to the AnotherContact class. When converted, the firstName and lastName of Contact will become lastName and firstName of AnotherContact, respectively. Let's implement another custom converter to perform the conversion. Listing 10-10 shows the custom converter.

Listing 10-10. The ContactToAnotherContactConverter Class

```java
package com.apress.prospring4.ch10;

import org.springframework.core.convert.converter.Converter;

public class ContactToAnotherContactConverter
    implements Converter<Contact, AnotherContact> {
```

```
    @Override
    public AnotherContact convert(Contact contact) {
        AnotherContact anotherContact = new AnotherContact();
        anotherContact.setFirstName(contact.getLastName());
        anotherContact.setLastName(contact.getFirstName());
        anotherContact.setBirthDate(contact.getBirthDate());
        anotherContact.setPersonalSite(contact.getPersonalSite());

        return anotherContact;
    }
}
```

The class is simple; just swap the firstName and lastName attributes between the Contact and AnotherContact classes. To register the custom converter into ApplicationContext, replace the definition of the conversionService bean in the file (conv-service-app-context.xml) with the code snippet in Listing 10-11.

Listing 10-11. Adding the Converter to the Conversion Service

```xml
<?xml version="1.0" encoding="UTF-8"?>
<beans xmlns="http://www.springframework.org/schema/beans"
       xmlns:xsi="http://www.w3.org/2001/XMLSchema-instance"
       xmlns:context="http://www.springframework.org/schema/context"
       xmlns:p="http://www.springframework.org/schema/p"
       xsi:schemaLocation="http://www.springframework.org/schema/beans
        http://www.springframework.org/schema/beans/spring-beans.xsd
        http://www.springframework.org/schema/context
        http://www.springframework.org/schema/context/spring-context.xsd">

    <context:annotation-config/>

    <bean id="conversionService" class="org.springframework.context.support.
ConversionServiceFactoryBean">
        <property name="converters">
            <list>
                <bean class="com.apress.prospring4.ch10.StringToDateTimeConverter"/>
                <bean class="com.apress.prospring4.ch10.ContactToAnotherContactConverter"/>
            </list>
        </property>
    </bean>

    <bean id="chris" class="com.apress.prospring4.ch10.Contact"
          p:firstName="Chris"
          p:lastName="Schaefer"
          p:birthDate="1981-05-03"
          p:personalSite="http://www.dtzq.com"/>
</beans>
```

The order of the beans within the converters property is not important.

To test the conversion, we use the same testing program as the previous sample, which is the ConvServExample class. Listing 10-12 shows the revised main() method.

Listing 10-12. Testing ConversionService

```
package com.apress.prospring4.ch10;

import org.springframework.context.support.GenericXmlApplicationContext;
import org.springframework.core.convert.ConversionService;

import java.util.ArrayList;
import java.util.HashSet;
import java.util.List;
import java.util.Set;

public class ConvServExample {
    public static void main(String[] args) {
        GenericXmlApplicationContext ctx = new GenericXmlApplicationContext();
        ctx.load("classpath:META-INF/spring/conv-service-app-context.xml");
        ctx.refresh();

        Contact chris = ctx.getBean("chris", Contact.class);

        System.out.println("Contact info: " + chris);

        ConversionService conversionService = ctx.getBean(ConversionService.class);

        AnotherContact anotherContact =
            conversionService.convert(chris, AnotherContact.class);
        System.out.println("Another contact info: " + anotherContact);

        String[] stringArray = conversionService.convert("a,b,c", String[].class);

        System.out.println("String array: " + stringArray[0] +
            stringArray[1] + stringArray[2]);

        List<String> listString = new ArrayList<String>();
        listString.add("a");
        listString.add("b");
        listString.add("c");

        Set<String> setString = conversionService.convert(listString, HashSet.class);

        for (String string: setString)
            System.out.println("Set: " + string);
    }
}
```

A handle to the ConversionService interface is obtained from ApplicationContext. Because we already registered ConversionService in ApplicationContext with our custom converters, we can use it to convert the Contact object, as well as convert between other types that the conversion service already supports. As shown in the listing, examples of converting from a String (delimited by a comma character) to an Array and from a List to a Set were also added for demonstration purposes.

Running the program produces the following output:

```
Contact info: First name: Chris - Last name: Schaefer - Birth date: 1981-05-03T00:00:00.000-04:00 -
Personal site: http://www.dtzq.com
Another contact info: First name: Schaefer - Last name: Chris - Birth date: 1981-05-03T00:00:00.000-
04:00 - Personal site: http://www.dtzq.com
String array: abc
Set: a
Set: b
Set: c
```

In the output, you will see that Contact and AnotherContact are converted correctly, as well as the String to Array and the List to Set. With Spring's type conversion service, you can create custom converters easily and perform conversion at any layer within your application. One possible use case is that you have two systems with the same contact information that you need to update. However, the database structure is different (for example, the last name in system A means the first name in system B, and so on). You can use the type conversion system to convert the objects before persisting to each individual system.

Starting with Spring 3.0, Spring MVC makes heavy use of the conversion service (as well as the Formatter SPI that we discuss in the next section). In the web application context configuration, the declaration of the tag <mvc:annotation-driven/>will automatically register all default converters (for example, StringToArrayConverter, StringToBooleanConverter, and StringToLocaleConverter, all residing under the org.springframework.core. convert.support package) and formatters (for example, CurrencyFormatter, DateFormatter, and NumberFormatter, all residing under various subpackages within the org.springframework.format package). More is covered in Chapter 16, when we discuss web application development in Spring.

Field Formatting in Spring

Besides the type conversion system, another great feature that Spring brings to developers is the Formatter SPI. As you might expect, this SPI can help configure the field-formatting aspects.

In the Formatter SPI, the main interface for implementing a formatter is the org.springframework. format.Formatter<T> interface. Spring provides a few implementations of commonly used types, including CurrencyFormatter, DateFormatter, NumberFormatter, and PercentFormatter.

Implementing a Custom Formatter

Implementing a custom formatter is easy too. We will use the same Contact class and implement a custom formatter for converting the DateTime type of the birthDate attribute to and from a String.

However, this time we will take a different approach; we will extend Spring's org.springframework. format.support.FormattingConversionServiceFactoryBean class and provide our custom formatter. The FormattingConversionServiceFactoryBean class is a factory class that provides convenient access to the underlying FormattingConversionService class, which supports the type conversion system, as well as field formatting according to the formatting rules defined for each field type.

Listing 10-13 shows a custom class that extends the FormattingConversionServiceFactoryBean class, with a custom formatter defined for formatting JodaTime's DateTime type.

Listing 10-13. The ApplicationConversionServiceFactoryBean Class

```java
package com.apress.prospring4.ch10;

import java.text.ParseException;
import java.util.HashSet;
import java.util.Locale;
import java.util.Set;

import javax.annotation.PostConstruct;

import org.joda.time.DateTime;
import org.joda.time.format.DateTimeFormat;
import org.joda.time.format.DateTimeFormatter;
import org.springframework.beans.factory.annotation.Autowired;
import org.springframework.format.Formatter;
import org.springframework.format.support.FormattingConversionServiceFactoryBean;

public class ApplicationConversionServiceFactoryBean extends
    FormattingConversionServiceFactoryBean {

    private static final String DEFAULT_DATE_PATTERN = "yyyy-MM-dd";

    private DateTimeFormatter dateFormat;

    private String datePattern = DEFAULT_DATE_PATTERN;

    private Set<Formatter<?>>formatters = new HashSet<Formatter<?>>();

    public String getDatePattern() {
        return datePattern;
    }

    @Autowired(required=false)
    public void setDatePattern(String datePattern) {
        this.datePattern = datePattern;
    }

    @PostConstruct
    public void init() {
        dateFormat = DateTimeFormat.forPattern(datePattern);
        formatters.add(getDateTimeFormatter());
        setFormatters(formatters);
    }

    public Formatter<DateTime> getDateTimeFormatter() {
        return new Formatter<DateTime>() {
            @Override
            public DateTime parse(String dateTimeString, Locale locale) throws ParseException {
                System.out.println("Parsing date string: " + dateTimeString);
                return dateFormat.parseDateTime(dateTimeString);
            }
```

```
        @Override
        public String print(DateTime dateTime, Locale locale) {
            System.out.println("Formatting datetime: " + dateTime);
            return dateFormat.print(dateTime);
        }
    };
    }
}
```

In the preceding listing, the custom formatter is in bold. It implements the Formatter<DateTime> interface and implements two methods defined by the interface. The parse() method parses the String format into the DateTime type (the locale was also passed for localization support), while the print() method is to format a DateTime instance into a String. The date pattern can be injected into the bean (or the default will be yyyy-MM-dd). Also, in the init() method, the custom formatter is registered by calling the setFormatters() method. You can add as many formatters as required.

Configuring ConversionServiceFactoryBean

To configure the ApplicationConversionServiceFactoryBean in Spring's ApplicationContext, we just need to declare a bean with that class as the provider. Listing 10-14 shows the configuration (conv-format-service-app-context.xml).

Listing 10-14. The conv-format-service-app-context.xml File

```xml
<?xml version="1.0" encoding="UTF-8"?>
<beans xmlns="http://www.springframework.org/schema/beans"
    xmlns:xsi="http://www.w3.org/2001/XMLSchema-instance"
    xmlns:context="http://www.springframework.org/schema/context"
    xmlns:p="http://www.springframework.org/schema/p"
    xsi:schemaLocation="http://www.springframework.org/schema/beans
        http://www.springframework.org/schema/beans/spring-beans.xsd
        http://www.springframework.org/schema/context
        http://www.springframework.org/schema/context/spring-context.xsd">

    <context:annotation-config/>

    <bean id="conversionService"
class="com.apress.prospring4.ch10.ApplicationConversionServiceFactoryBean"/>

    <bean id="chris" class="com.apress.prospring4.ch10.Contact"
        p:firstName="Chris"
        p:lastName="Schaefer"
        p:birthDate="1981-05-03"
        p:personalSite="http://www.dtzq.com"/>
</beans>
```

Listing 10-15 shows the testing program.

Listing 10-15. Testing the Custom Formatter

```
package com.apress.prospring4.ch10;

import org.springframework.context.support.GenericXmlApplicationContext;
import org.springframework.core.convert.ConversionService;

public class ConvFormatServExample {
    public static void main(String[] args) {
        GenericXmlApplicationContext ctx = new GenericXmlApplicationContext();
        ctx.load("classpath:META-INF/spring/conv-format-service-app-context.xml");
        ctx.refresh();

        Contact chris = ctx.getBean("chris", Contact.class);

        System.out.println("Contact info: " + chris);

        ConversionService conversionService = ctx.getBean("conversionService",
ConversionService.class);
        System.out.println("Birthdate of contact is : " +
            conversionService.convert(chris.getBirthDate(), String.class));
    }
}
```

Running the program produces the following output:

```
Parsing date string: 1981-05-03
Contact info: First name: Chris - Last name: Schaefer - Birth date: 1981-05-03T00:00:00.000-04:00 -
Personal site: http://www.dtzq.com
Formatting datetime: 1981-05-03T00:00:00.000-04:00
Birthdate of contact is : 1981-05-03
```

In the output, you can see that Spring uses our custom formatter's parse() method to convert the property from a String to the DateTime type of the birthDate attribute. When we call the ConversionService.convert() method and pass in the birthDate attribute, Spring will call the print() method to format the output.

Validation in Spring

Validation is a critical part of any application. Validation rules applied on domain objects ensure that all business data is well structured and fulfills all the business definitions. The ideal case is that all validation rules are maintained in a centralized location, and the same set of rules are applied to the same type of data, no matter which source the data comes from (for example, from user input via a web application, from a remote application via web services, from a JMS message, or from a file).

When talking about validation, conversion and formatting are important too, because before a piece of data can be validated, it should be converted to the desired POJO according to the formatting rules defined for each type. For example, a user enters some contact information via a web application within a browser and then submits that data to a server. On the server side, if the web application was developed in Spring MVC, Spring will extract the data from the HTTP request and perform the conversion from a String to the desired type based on the formatting rule (for example, a String representing a date will be converted into a Date field, with the formatting rule yyyy-MM-dd). The process is called *data binding*. When the data binding is complete and the domain object constructed, validation will then be applied to the object, and any errors will be returned and displayed to the user. If validation succeeds, the object will be persisted to the database.

461

Spring supports two main types of validation. The first one is provided by Spring, within which custom validators can be created by implementing the `org.springframework.validation.Validator` interface. The other one is via Spring's support of JSR-349, the Bean Validation API. We present both of them in the coming sections.

Using the Spring Validator Interface

Using Spring's `Validator` interface, we can develop some validation logic by creating a class to implement the interface. Let's see how it works. For the `Contact` class that we've worked with so far, suppose the first name cannot be empty. To validate `Contact` objects against this rule, we can create a custom validator. Listing 10-16 shows the validator class.

Listing 10-16. The `ContactValidator` Class

```
package com.apress.prospring4.ch10;

import org.springframework.stereotype.Component;
import org.springframework.validation.Errors;
import org.springframework.validation.ValidationUtils;
import org.springframework.validation.Validator;

@Component("contactValidator")
public class ContactValidator implements Validator {
    @Override
    public boolean supports(Class<?> clazz) {
        return Contact.class.equals(clazz);
    }

    @Override
    public void validate(Object obj, Errors e) {
        ValidationUtils.rejectIfEmpty(e, "firstName", "firstName.empty");
    }
}
```

The validator class implements the `Validator` interface and implements two methods. The `supports()` method indicates whether validation of the passed-in class type is supported by the validator. The `validate()` method performs validation on the passed-in object. The result will be stored in an instance of the `org.springframework.validation.Errors` interface. In the `validate()` method, we perform a check only on the `firstName` attribute and use the convenient `ValidationUtils.rejectIfEmpty()` method to ensure that the first name of the contact is not empty. The last argument is the error code, which can be used for looking up validation messages from resource bundles to display localized error messages.

Listing 10-17 shows the Spring configuration file (`spring-validator-app-context.xml`).

Listing 10-17. Configuration for Spring Validator

```
<?xml version="1.0" encoding="UTF-8"?>
<beans xmlns="http://www.springframework.org/schema/beans"
    xmlns:xsi="http://www.w3.org/2001/XMLSchema-instance"
    xmlns:context="http://www.springframework.org/schema/context"
    xsi:schemaLocation="http://www.springframework.org/schema/beans
        http://www.springframework.org/schema/beans/spring-beans.xsd
```

```
        http://www.springframework.org/schema/context
        http://www.springframework.org/schema/context/spring-context.xsd">

    <context:component-scan base-package="com.apress.prospring4.ch10"/>
</beans>
```

Listing 10-18 shows the testing program for the validator class.

Listing 10-18. Testing Spring Validator

```
package com.apress.prospring4.ch10;

import java.util.List;

import org.springframework.context.support.GenericXmlApplicationContext;
import org.springframework.validation.BeanPropertyBindingResult;
import org.springframework.validation.ObjectError;
import org.springframework.validation.ValidationUtils;
import org.springframework.validation.Validator;

public class SpringValidatorSample {
    public static void main(String[] args) {
        GenericXmlApplicationContext ctx = new GenericXmlApplicationContext();
        ctx.load("classpath:META-INF/spring/spring-validator-app-context.xml");
        ctx.refresh();

        Contact contact = new Contact();
        contact.setFirstName(null);
        contact.setLastName("Schaefer");

        Validator contactValidator = ctx.getBean("contactValidator", Validator.class);

        BeanPropertyBindingResult result =
            new BeanPropertyBindingResult(contact, "Chris");

        ValidationUtils.invokeValidator(contactValidator, contact, result);

        List<ObjectError> errors = result.getAllErrors();
        System.out.println("No of validation errors: " + errors.size());

        for (ObjectError error: errors) {
            System.out.println(error.getCode());
        }
    }
}
```

A Contact object is constructed with the first name set to null. Then, the validator is retrieved from ApplicationContext. To store the validation result, an instance of the BeanPropertyBindingResult class is constructed. To perform the validation, the ValidationUtils.invokeValidator() method is called. Then we check for validation errors.

Running the program produces the following output:

```
No of validation errors: 1
firstName.empty
```

The validation produces one error, and the error code is displayed correctly.

Using JSR-349 Bean Validation

As of Spring 4, full support for the JSR-349 Bean Validation API has been supported. The Bean Validation API defines a set of constraints in the form of Java annotations (for example, @NotNull) under the package javax.validation. constraints that can be applied to the domain objects. In addition, custom validators (for example, class-level validators) can be developed and applied by using annotation.

Using the Bean Validation API frees you from coupling to a specific validation service provider. By using the Bean Validation API, you can use standard annotations and the API for implementing validation logic to your domain objects, without knowing the underlying validation service provider. For example, the Hibernate Validator version 5 (http://hibernate.org/subprojects/validator) is the JSR-349 reference implementation.

Spring provides seamless support for the Bean Validation API. The main features include support for JSR-349 standard annotations for defining validation constraints, custom validators, and configuration of JSR-349 validation within Spring's ApplicationContext. Let's go through them one by one in the following sections. Spring still seamlessly provides support for JSR-303 when using Hibernate Validator version 4 and the 1.0 version of the validation API on your classpath.

Defining Validation Constraints on Object Properties

Let's begin with applying validation constraints to domain object properties. Listing 10-19 shows a Customer class with validation constraints applied to the firstName and customerType attributes.

Listing 10-19. The Customer Class

```java
package com.apress.prospring4.ch10;

import javax.validation.constraints.NotNull;
import javax.validation.constraints.Size;

public class Customer {
    @NotNull
    @Size(min=2, max=60)
    private String firstName;

    private String lastName;

    @NotNull
    private CustomerType customerType;

    private Gender gender;

    public String getFirstName() {
        return firstName;
    }
```

```java
public void setFirstName(String firstName) {
    this.firstName = firstName;
}

public String getLastName() {
    return lastName;
}

public void setLastName(String lastName) {
    this.lastName = lastName;
}

public CustomerType getCustomerType() {
    return customerType;
}

public void setCustomerType(CustomerType customerType) {
    this.customerType = customerType;
}

public Gender getGender() {
    return gender;
}

public void setGender(Gender gender) {
    this.gender = gender;
}

public boolean isIndividualCustomer() {
    return this.customerType.equals(CustomerType.INDIVIDUAL);
}
}
```

Here the validation constraints applied are shown in bold. For the firstName attribute, two constraints are applied. The first one is governed by the @NotNull annotation, which indicates that the value should not be null. Moreover, the @Size annotation governs the length of the firstName attribute. The @NotNull constraint is applied to the customerType attribute too. Listings 10-20 and 10-21 show the CustomerType and Gender classes, respectively.

Listing 10-20. The CustomerType Class

```java
package com.apress.prospring4.ch10;

public enum CustomerType {
    INDIVIDUAL("I"), CORPORATE("C");

    private String code;

    private CustomerType(String code) {
        this.code = code;
    }
```

```
    @Override
    public String toString() {
        return this.code;
    }
}
```

Listing 10-21. The Gender Class

```
package com.apress.prospring4.ch10;

public enum Gender {
    MALE("M"), FEMALE("F");

    private String code;

    private Gender(String code) {
        this.code = code;
    }

    @Override
    public String toString() {
        return this.code;
    }
}
```

The customer type indicates whether a customer is an individual or a company, while the gender should be applied for only individual customers. For companies, the gender should be `null`.

Configuring Bean Validation Support in Spring

To configure the support of the Bean Validation API in Spring's `ApplicationContext`, we define an instance of the class `org.springframework.validation.beanvalidation.LocalValidatorFactoryBean` in Spring's configuration. Listing 10-22 shows the configuration (`jsr349-app-context.xml`).

Listing 10-22. Configuring Bean Validation API in Spring

```xml
<?xml version="1.0" encoding="UTF-8"?>
<beans xmlns="http://www.springframework.org/schema/beans"
    xmlns:xsi="http://www.w3.org/2001/XMLSchema-instance"
    xmlns:context="http://www.springframework.org/schema/context"
    xsi:schemaLocation="http://www.springframework.org/schema/beans
        http://www.springframework.org/schema/beans/spring-beans.xsd
        http://www.springframework.org/schema/context
        http://www.springframework.org/schema/context/spring-context.xsd">

    <context:component-scan
        base-package="com.apress.prospring4.ch10"/>

    <bean id="validator" class="org.springframework.validation.beanvalidation.
LocalValidatorFactoryBean"/>
</beans>
```

The declaration of a bean with the class LocalValidatorFactoryBean is all that is required. By default, Spring will search for the existence of the Hibernate Validator library in the classpath. Now, let's create a service class that provides a validation service for the Customer class. Listing 10-23 shows the content.

Listing 10-23. The MyBeanValidationService Class

```
package com.apress.prospring4.ch10;

import java.util.Set;

import javax.validation.ConstraintViolation;
import javax.validation.Validator;

import org.springframework.beans.factory.annotation.Autowired;
import org.springframework.stereotype.Service;

@Service("myBeanValidationService")
public class MyBeanValidationService {
    @Autowired
    private Validator validator;

    public Set<ConstraintViolation<Customer>>validateCustomer(Customer customer) {
        return validator.validate(customer);
    }
}
```

An instance of the javax.validation.Validator was injected (note the difference from the Spring-provided Validator interface, which is org.springframework.validation.Validator). Once the LocalValidatorFactoryBean is defined, you can create a handle to the Validator interface anywhere in your application. To perform validation on a POJO, the Validator.validate() method is called. The validation results will be returned as a List of the ConstraintViolation<T> interface.

Listing 10-24 shows the testing program.

Listing 10-24. The Jsr349Sample Class

```
package com.apress.prospring4.ch10;

import java.util.HashSet;
import java.util.Set;

import javax.validation.ConstraintViolation;

import org.springframework.context.support.GenericXmlApplicationContext;

public class Jsr349Sample {
    public static void main(String[] args) {
        GenericXmlApplicationContext ctx = new GenericXmlApplicationContext();
        ctx.load("classpath:META-INF/spring/jsr349-app-context.xml");
        ctx.refresh();

        MyBeanValidationService myBeanValidationService =
            ctx.getBean("myBeanValidationService", MyBeanValidationService.class);
```

```
        Customer customer = new Customer();
        customer.setFirstName("C");
        customer.setLastName("Schaefer");
        customer.setCustomerType(null);
        customer.setGender(null);

        validateCustomer(customer, myBeanValidationService);
    }

    private static void validateCustomer(Customer customer,
        MyBeanValidationService myBeanValidationService) {

        Set<ConstraintViolation<Customer>>violations =
            new HashSet<ConstraintViolation<Customer>>();
        violations = myBeanValidationService.validateCustomer(customer);

        listViolations(violations);
    }

    private static void listViolations(Set<ConstraintViolation<Customer>>violations) {
        System.out.println("No. of violations: " + violations.size());

        for (ConstraintViolation<Customer> violation: violations) {
            System.out.println("Validation error for property: " +
                violation.getPropertyPath()
                + " with value: " + violation.getInvalidValue()
                + " with error message: " + violation.getMessage());
        }
    }
}
```

As shown in this listing, a Customer object is constructed with firstName and customerType violating the constraints. In the validateCustomer() method, the MyBeanValidationService.validateCustomer() method is called, which in turn will invoke the JSR-349 Bean Valiadation API.

Running the program produces the following output:

```
No. of violations: 2
Validation error for property: customerType with value: null with error message: may not be null
Validation error for property: firstName with value: C with error message: size must be between
2 and 60
```

As you can see, there are two violations, and the messages are shown. In the output, you will also see that Hibernate Validator had already constructed default validation error messages based on the annotation. You can also provide your own validation error message, which we demonstrate in the next section.

Creating a Custom Validator

Besides attribute-level validation, we can apply class-level validation. For example, for the Customer class, for individual customers, we want to make sure that the lastName and gender attributes are not null. In this case, we can develop a custom validator to perform the check. In the Bean Validation API, developing a custom validator is a two-step process. First create an Annotation type for the validator, as shown in Listing 10-25. The second step is to develop the class that implements the validation logic.

Listing 10-25. The CheckIndividualCustomer Annotation

```
package com.apress.prospring4.ch10;

import java.lang.annotation.Documented;
import java.lang.annotation.ElementType;
import java.lang.annotation.Retention;
import java.lang.annotation.RetentionPolicy;
import java.lang.annotation.Target;

import javax.validation.Constraint;
import javax.validation.Payload;

@Retention(RetentionPolicy.RUNTIME)
@Target(ElementType.TYPE)
@Constraint(validatedBy=IndividualCustomerValidator.class)
@Documented
public @interface CheckIndividualCustomer {
    String message() default "Individual customer should have gender and last name defined";
    Class<?>[] groups() default {};
    Class<? extends Payload>[] payload() default {};
}
```

The @Target(ElementType.TYPE) means that the annotation should be applied only at the class level. The @Constraint annotation indicates that it's a validator, and the validatedBy attribute specifies the class providing the validation logic. Within the body, three attributes are defined (in the form of a method), as follows:

- The message attribute defines the message (or error code) to return when the constraint is violated. A default message can also be provided in the annotation.

- The groups attribute specifies the validation group if applicable. It's possible to assign validators to different groups and perform validation on a specific group.

- The payload attribute specifies additional payload objects (of the class implementing the javax.validation.Payload interface). It allows you to attach additional information to the constraint (for example, a payload object can indicate the severity of a constraint violation).

Listing 10-26 shows the IndividualCustomerValidator class that provides the validation logic.

Listing 10-26. The IndividualCustomerValidator Class

```
package com.apress.prospring4.ch10;

import javax.validation.ConstraintValidator;
import javax.validation.ConstraintValidatorContext;

public class IndividualCustomerValidator implements
    ConstraintValidator<CheckIndividualCustomer, Customer> {

    @Override
    public void initialize(CheckIndividualCustomer constraintAnnotation) {
    }
```

```
@Override
public boolean isValid(Customer customer,
    ConstraintValidatorContext context) {

    boolean result = true;

    if (customer.getCustomerType() != null &&
        (customer.isIndividualCustomer() && (customer.getLastName() == null ||
            customer.getGender() == null))) {
        result = false;
    }

    return result;
}
}
```

The IndividualCustomerValidator implements the ConstraintValidator<CheckIndividualCustomer, Customer> interface, which means that the validator checks the CheckIndividualCustomer annotation on the Customer classes. The isValid() method is implemented, and the underlying validation service provider (for example, Hibernate Validator) will pass the instance under validation to the method. In the method, we verify that if the customer is an individual, the lastName and gender properties should not be null. The result is a Boolean value that indicates the validation result.

To enable the validation, apply the @CheckIndividualCustomer annotation to the Customer class, as shown in Listing 10-27.

Listing 10-27. Applying Custom Validation to the Customer Class

```
package com.apress.prospring4.ch10;

@CheckIndividualCustomer
public class Customer {
    ...
}
```

To test the custom validation, add the code snippet in Listing 10-28 to the main() method of the testing class (Jsr349Sample) in Listing 10-24.

Listing 10-28. Applying Custom Validation to the Customer Class

```
customer.setFirstName("Chris");
customer.setLastName("Schaefer");
customer.setCustomerType(CustomerType.INDIVIDUAL);
customer.setGender(null);

validateCustomer(customer, myBeanValidationService);
```

Running the program produces the following output (the other output was omitted):

```
No. of violations: 1
Validation error for property:  with value: com.apress.prospring4.ch10.Customer@5ae50ce6 with error
message: Individual customer should have gender and last name defined
```

In the output, you can see that the value being checked (which is the `Customer` object) violates the validation rule for individual customers, because the gender attribute is null. Note also that in the output, the property path is empty, because it's a class-level validation error.

Using AssertTrue for Custom Validation

Besides implementing a custom validator, another way to apply custom validation in the Bean Validation API is to use the `@AssertTrue` annotation. Let's see how it works.

For the `Customer` class, remove the `@CheckIndividualCustomer` annotation and modify the code snippet from Listing 10-29 to the `Customer` class.

Listing 10-29. Applying `@AssertTrue` to the `Customer` Class

```
public class Customer {
...
    @AssertTrue(message="ERROR! Individual customer should have gender and last name defined")
    public boolean isIndividualCustomer() {
        boolean result = true;

        if (getCustomerType() != null &&
                (this.customerType.equals(CustomerType.INDIVIDUAL) && (gender == null ||
lastName == null))) {
            result = false;
        }

        return result;
    }
...
}
```

The `isValidIndividualCustomer()` method is added to the `Customer` class and annotated with `@AssertTrue` (which is under the package `javax.validation.constraints`). When invoking validation, the provider will invoke the checking and make sure that the result is true. JSR-349 also provides the `@AssertFalse` annotation to check for some condition that should be false. Now run the testing program (`Jsr349Sample`) again, and you will get the same output as produced by the custom validator.

Considerations for Custom Validation

So, for custom validation in JSR-349, which approach should you use: the custom validator or the `@AssertTrue` annotation? Generally, the `@AssertTrue` method is simpler to implement, and you can see the validation rules right in the code of the domain objects. However, for validators with more-complicated logic (for example, say you need to inject a service class, access a database, and check for valid values), then implementing a custom validator is the way to go, because you never want to inject service-layer objects into your domain objects. Also, custom validators can be reused across similar domain objects.

Deciding Which Validation API to Use

Having discussed Spring's own `Validator` interface and the Bean Validation API, which one should you use in your application? JSR-349 is definitely the way to go. The following are the major reasons:

- JSR-349 is a JEE standard and is broadly supported by many front-end/back-end frameworks (for example, Spring, JPA 2, Spring MVC, and GWT).

- JSR-349 provides a standard validation API that hides the underlying provider, so you are not tied to a specific provider.

- Spring tightly integrates with JSR-349 starting with version 4. For example, in the Spring MVC web controller, you can annotate the argument in a method with the `@Valid` (under the package `javax.validation`) annotation, and Spring will invoke JSR-349 validation automatically during the data-binding process. Moreover, in a Spring MVC web application context configuration, a simple tag called `<mvc:annotation-driven/>` will configure Spring to automatically enable the Spring type conversion system and field formatting, as well as support of JSR-349 Bean Validation.

- If you are using JPA 2, the provider will automatically perform JSR-349 validation to the entity before persisting, providing another layer of protection.

For detailed information about using JSR-349 Bean Validation with Hibernate Validator as the implementation provider, please refer to Hibernate Validator's documentation page (`http://docs.jboss.org/hibernate/validator/5.1/reference/en-US/html`).

Summary

In this chapter, we covered the Spring type conversion system as well as the field Formatter SPI. You saw how the new type conversion system could be used for arbitrary type conversion, in addition to the `PropertyEditors` support.

We also covered validation support in Spring, Spring's `Validator` interface, and the recommended JSR-349 Bean Validation support in Spring.

CHAPTER 11

■ ■ ■

Task Scheduling in Spring

Task scheduling is a common feature in enterprise applications. Task scheduling is composed mainly of three parts: the task (which is the piece of business logic needed to run at a specific time or on a regular basis), the trigger (which specifies the condition under which the task should be executed), and the scheduler (which executes the task based on the information from the trigger).

Specifically, this chapter covers the following topics:

- *Task scheduling in Spring:* We discuss how Spring supports task scheduling, focusing on the TaskScheduler abstraction introduced in Spring 3. We also cover scheduling scenarios such as fixed-interval scheduling and cron expressions.

- *Asynchronous task execution:* We show how to use the @Async annotation in Spring to execute tasks asynchronously.

- *Task execution in Spring:* We briefly discuss Spring's TaskExecutor interface and how tasks are executed.

Dependencies for the Task Scheduling Samples

Table 11-1 shows the dependencies that are needed for the task scheduling samples in this chapter.

Table 11-1. *Maven Dependencies for Task Scheduling*

Group ID	Artifact ID	Version	Description
org.springframework.data	spring-data-jpa	1.5.0.RELEASE	Spring Data JPA library.
joda-time	joda-time	2.3	JodaTime (http://joda-time.sourceforge.net/).
org.jadira.usertype	usertype.core	3.0.0.GA	Library for integration with Hibernate for date-time data persistence.
com.google.guava	guava	14.0.1	Contains useful helper classes for working with collections, concurrency, string processing, and so on.
org.slf4j	slf4j-log4j12	1.7.6	The SLF4J logging library (www.slf4j.org) is used as the logging library for the samples in this chapter. This library helps chain the SLF4J logger to the underlying log4j library for logging purposes.

Task Scheduling in Spring

Enterprise applications often need to schedule tasks. In many applications, various tasks (such as sending e-mail notifications to customers, running day-end jobs, doing data housekeeping, and updating data in batches) need to be scheduled to run on a regular basis, either in a fixed interval (for example, every hour) or at a specific schedule (for example, at 8 p.m. every night, from Monday to Friday). As mentioned, task scheduling consists of three parts: the schedule definition (trigger), the task execution (scheduler), and the task itself.

There are many ways to trigger the execution of a task in a Spring application. One way is to trigger a job externally from a scheduling system that already exists in the application deployment environment. For example, many enterprises use commercial systems, such as Control-M or CA AutoSys, for scheduling tasks. If the application is running on a Linux/Unix platform, the crontab scheduler can be used. The job triggering can be done by sending a RESTful-WS request to the Spring application and having Spring's MVC controller trigger the task.

Another way is to use the task scheduling support in Spring. Spring provides three options in terms of task scheduling:

- *Support of JDK Timer*: Spring supports JDK's Timer object for task scheduling.

- *Integrates with Quartz*: The Quartz Scheduler (`www.quartz-scheduler.org`) is a popular open source scheduling library.

- *Spring's own* `Spring TaskScheduler Abstraction`: Spring 3 introduces the `TaskScheduler` abstraction, which provides a simple way to schedule tasks and supports most typical requirements.

This section focuses on using Spring's `TaskScheduler` abstraction for task scheduling.

Introducing the Spring TaskScheduler Abstraction

Spring's `TaskScheduler` abstraction has mainly three participants:

- *The* `Trigger` *interface*: The `org.springframework.scheduling.Trigger` interface provides support for defining the triggering mechanism. Spring provides two `Trigger` implementations. The `CronTrigger` class supports triggering based on a `cron` expression, while the `PeriodicTrigger` class supports triggering based on an initial delay and then a fixed interval.

- *The task*: The task is the piece of business logic that needs to be scheduled. In Spring, a task can be specified as a method within any Spring bean.

- *The* `TaskScheduler` *interface*: The `org.springframework.scheduling.TaskScheduler` interface provides support for task scheduling. Spring provides three implementation classes of the `TaskScheduler` interface. The `TimerManagerTaskScheduler` class (under the package `org.springframework.scheduling.commonj`) wraps CommonJ's `commonj.timers.TimerManager` interface, which is commonly used in commercial JEE application servers such as WebSphere and WebLogic. The `ConcurrentTaskScheduler` and `ThreadPoolTaskScheduler` classes (both under the package `org.springframework.scheduling.concurrent`) wrap the `java.util.concurrent.ScheduledThreadPoolExecutor` class. Both classes support task execution from a shared thread pool.

Figure 11-1 shows the relationships between the `Trigger` interface, the `TaskScheduler` interface, and the task (which implements the `java.lang.Runnable` interface).

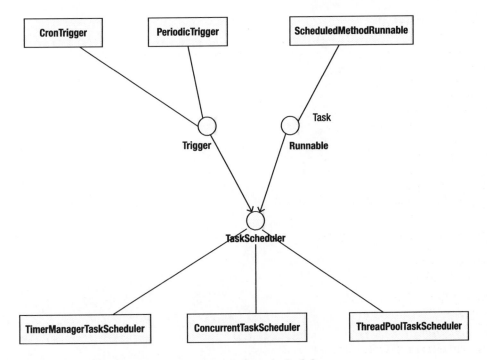

Figure 11-1. *Relationship between trigger, task, and scheduler*

To schedule tasks by using Spring's TaskScheduler abstraction, you have two options. One is to use task-namespace in Spring's XML configuration, and the other is to use annotations. Let's go through each of them.

Exploring a Sample Task

To demonstrate task scheduling in Spring, let's implement a simple job first, namely, an application maintaining a database of car information. Listing 11-1 shows the Car class, which is implemented as a JPA entity class.

Listing 11-1. The Car Class

```
package com.apress.prospring4.ch11;

import static javax.persistence.GenerationType.IDENTITY;

import javax.persistence.Column;
import javax.persistence.Entity;
import javax.persistence.GeneratedValue;
import javax.persistence.Id;
import javax.persistence.Table;
import javax.persistence.Version;

import org.hibernate.annotations.Type;
import org.joda.time.DateTime;
```

```java
@Entity
@Table(name="car")
public class Car {
    private Long id;
    private String licensePlate;
    private String manufacturer;
    private DateTime manufactureDate;
    private int age;
    private int version;

    @Id
    @GeneratedValue(strategy = IDENTITY)
    @Column(name = "ID")
    public Long getId() {
        return id;
    }

    @Column(name="LICENSE_PLATE")
    public String getLicensePlate() {
        return licensePlate;
    }

    @Column(name="MANUFACTURER")
    public String getManufacturer() {
        return manufacturer;
    }

    @Column(name="MANUFACTURE_DATE")
    @Type(type="org.jadira.usertype.dateandtime.joda.PersistentDateTime")
    public DateTime getManufactureDate() {
        return manufactureDate;
    }

    @Column(name="AGE")
    public int getAge() {
        return age;
    }

    @Version
    public int getVersion() {
        return version;
    }

    public void setId(Long id) {
        this.id = id;
    }

    public void setLicensePlate(String licensePlate) {
        this.licensePlate = licensePlate;
    }

    public void setManufacturer(String manufacturer) {
        this.manufacturer = manufacturer;
    }
```

```
    public void setManufactureDate(DateTime manufactureDate) {
        this.manufactureDate = manufactureDate;
    }

    public void setAge(int age) {
        this.age = age;
    }

    public void setVersion(int version) {
        this.version = version;
    }

    @Override
    public String toString() {
        return "License: " + licensePlate + " - Manufacturer: " + manufacturer
                + " - Manufacture Date: " + manufactureDate + " - Age: " + age;
    }
}
```

Listings 11-2 and 11-3 show the table creation script (schema.sql) and testing data population script (test-data.sql) for the Car entity class, respectively.

Listing 11-2. The Table Creation Script

```
DROP TABLE IF EXISTS CONTACT;

CREATE TABLE CAR (
    ID INT NOT NULL AUTO_INCREMENT
    , LICENSE_PLATE VARCHAR(20) NOT NULL
    , MANUFACTURER VARCHAR(20) NOT NULL
    , MANUFACTURE_DATE DATE NOT NULL
    , AGE INT NOT NULL DEFAULT 0
    , VERSION INT NOT NULL DEFAULT 0
    , UNIQUE UQ_CAR_1 (LICENSE_PLATE)
    , PRIMARY KEY (ID)
);
```

Listing 11-3. The Testing Data Population Script

```
insert into car (license_plate, manufacturer, manufacture_date) values ('LICENSE-1001', 'Ford',
'1980-07-30');
insert into car (license_plate, manufacturer, manufacture_date) values ('LICENSE-1002', 'Toyota',
'1992-12-30');
insert into car (license_plate, manufacturer, manufacture_date) values ('LICENSE-1003', 'BMW',
'2003-1-6');
```

Let's define a service layer for the Car entity. We will use Spring Data's JPA and its repository abstraction support. Listing 11-4 shows the CarRepository interface.

Listing 11-4. The CarRepository Interface

```
package com.apress.prospring4.ch11;

import org.springframework.data.repository.CrudRepository;

public interface CarRepository extends CrudRepository<Car, Long> {
}
```

It's nothing special; we just implemented the CrudRepository<Car,Long> interface. Listings 11-5 and 11-6 show the CarService interface and the implementation CarServiceImpl class, respectively.

Listing 11-5. The CarService Interface

```
package com.apress.prospring4.ch11;

import java.util.List;

public interface CarService {
    List<Car> findAll();
    Car save(Car car);
    void updateCarAgeJob();
}
```

Listing 11-6. The CarServiceImpl Class

```
package com.apress.prospring4.ch11;

import com.google.common.collect.Lists;
import org.joda.time.DateTime;
import org.joda.time.Years;
import org.slf4j.Logger;
import org.slf4j.LoggerFactory;
import org.springframework.beans.factory.annotation.Autowired;
import org.springframework.stereotype.Repository;
import org.springframework.stereotype.Service;
import org.springframework.transaction.annotation.Transactional;

import java.util.List;

@Service("carService")
@Repository
@Transactional
public class CarServiceImpl implements CarService {
    final Logger logger = LoggerFactory.getLogger(CarServiceImpl.class);

    @Autowired
    CarRepository carRepository;
```

```java
@Override
@Transactional(readOnly=true)
public List<Car> findAll() {
    return Lists.newArrayList(carRepository.findAll());
}

@Override
public Car save(Car car) {
    return carRepository.save(car);
}

@Override
public void updateCarAgeJob() {
    List<Car> cars = findAll();

    DateTime currentDate = DateTime.now();
    logger.info("Car age update job started");

    for (Car car: cars) {
        int age =
            Years.yearsBetween(car.getManufactureDate(), currentDate).getYears();

        car.setAge(age);
        save(car);
        logger.info("Car age update--- " + car);
    }

    logger.info("Car age update job completed successfully");
}
}
```

Two methods were provided; one retrieves the information about all cars, and the other persists an updated Car object. The third method, updateCarAgeJob(), is the job that needs to be run regularly to update the age of the car based on the manufacture date of the car and the current date.

Listing 11-7 shows the Spring configuration to support the car application (car-job-app-context.xml).

Listing 11-7. The car-job-app-context.xml File

```xml
<?xml version="1.0" encoding="UTF-8"?>
<beans xmlns="http://www.springframework.org/schema/beans"
       xmlns:context="http://www.springframework.org/schema/context"
       xmlns:jdbc="http://www.springframework.org/schema/jdbc"
       xmlns:tx="http://www.springframework.org/schema/tx"
       xmlns:jpa="http://www.springframework.org/schema/data/jpa"
       xmlns:xsi="http://www.w3.org/2001/XMLSchema-instance"
       xsi:schemaLocation="http://www.springframework.org/schema/beans
        http://www.springframework.org/schema/beans/spring-beans.xsd
        http://www.springframework.org/schema/context
        http://www.springframework.org/schema/context/spring-context.xsd
        http://www.springframework.org/schema/jdbc
        http://www.springframework.org/schema/jdbc/spring-jdbc.xsd
```

```
            http://www.springframework.org/schema/tx
            http://www.springframework.org/schema/tx/spring-tx.xsd
            http://www.springframework.org/schema/data/jpa
            http://www.springframework.org/schema/data/jpa/spring-jpa.xsd">

    <jdbc:embedded-database id="dataSource" type="H2">
        <jdbc:script location="classpath:META-INF/config/schema.sql"/>
        <jdbc:script location="classpath:META-INF/config/test-data.sql"/>
    </jdbc:embedded-database>

    <bean id="transactionManager" class="org.springframework.orm.jpa.JpaTransactionManager">
        <property name="entityManagerFactory" ref="emf"/>
    </bean>

    <tx:annotation-driven transaction-manager="transactionManager"/>

    <bean id="emf" class="org.springframework.orm.jpa.LocalContainerEntityManagerFactoryBean">
        <property name="dataSource" ref="dataSource"/>
        <property name="jpaVendorAdapter">
            <bean class="org.springframework.orm.jpa.vendor.HibernateJpaVendorAdapter"/>
        </property>
        <property name="packagesToScan" value="com.apress.prospring4.ch11"/>
        <property name="jpaProperties">
            <props>
                <prop key="hibernate.dialect">
                    org.hibernate.dialect.H2Dialect
                </prop>
                <prop key="hibernate.max_fetch_depth">3</prop>
                <prop key="hibernate.jdbc.fetch_size">50</prop>
                <prop key="hibernate.jdbc.batch_size">10</prop>
                <prop key="hibernate.show_sql">true</prop>
            </props>
        </property>
    </bean>

    <jpa:repositories base-package="com.apress.prospring4.ch11"
                      entity-manager-factory-ref="emf"
                      transaction-manager-ref="transactionManager"/>

    <context:component-scan base-package="com.apress.prospring4.ch11"/>
</beans>
```

The configuration should be familiar to you. Now let's proceed to schedule the car age update job in Spring.

Using task-namespace for Task Scheduling

Like the support for other namespaces in Spring, task-namespace provides a simplified configuration for scheduling tasks by using Spring's TaskScheduler abstraction.

Using task-namespace for task scheduling is very simple. Listing 11-8 shows the configuration file (task-namespace-app-context.xml).

Listing 11-8. Spring Configuration Using `task-namespace`

```xml
<?xml version="1.0" encoding="UTF-8"?>
<beans xmlns="http://www.springframework.org/schema/beans"
       xmlns:task="http://www.springframework.org/schema/task"
       xmlns:xsi="http://www.w3.org/2001/XMLSchema-instance"
       xsi:schemaLocation="http://www.springframework.org/schema/beans
        http://www.springframework.org/schema/beans/spring-beans.xsd
        http://www.springframework.org/schema/task
        http://www.springframework.org/schema/task/spring-task.xsd">

    <import resource="car-job-app-context.xml"/>

    <task:scheduler id="myScheduler" pool-size="10"/>

    <task:scheduled-tasks scheduler="myScheduler">
        <task:scheduled ref="carService" method="updateCarAgeJob" fixed-delay="10000"/>
    </task:scheduled-tasks>
</beans>
```

The context for the car application is imported. When it encounters the `<task:scheduler>` tag, Spring instantiates an instance of the `ThreadPoolTaskScheduler` class, while the attribute `pool-size` specifies the size of the thread pool that the scheduler can use. Within the `<task:scheduled-tasks>` tag, one or more tasks can be scheduled. In the `<task:scheduled>` tag, a task can reference a Spring bean (the `carService` bean, in this case) and a specific method within the bean (in this case, the `updateCarAgeJob()` method). The attribute `fixed-delay` instructs Spring to instantiate `PeriodicTrigger` as the `Trigger` implementation for `TaskScheduler`.

Listing 11-9 shows the testing program for task scheduling.

Listing 11-9. Testing Task Scheduling in Spring

```java
package com.apress.prospring4.ch11;

import org.springframework.context.support.GenericXmlApplicationContext;

public class ScheduleTaskSample {
    public static void main(String[] args) {
        GenericXmlApplicationContext ctx = new GenericXmlApplicationContext();
        ctx.load("classpath:META-INF/spring/task-namespace-app-context.xml");
        ctx.refresh();
        while (true) {
        }
    }
}
```

The class is simple; just bootstrap `ApplicationContext` and then keep looping. Running the program produces the following batch job output every 10 seconds:

```
<Car age update job started>
<Car age update--- License: LICENSE-1001 - Manufacturer: Ford - Manufacture Date: 1980-07-
29T20:00:00.000-04:00 - Age: 33>
<Car age update--- License: LICENSE-1002 - Manufacturer: Toyota - Manufacture Date: 1992-12-
29T19:00:00.000-05:00 - Age: 21>
<Car age update--- License: LICENSE-1003 - Manufacturer: BMW - Manufacture Date: 2003-01-
05T19:00:00.000-05:00 - Age: 11>
<Car age update job completed successfully>
```

From the output, you can see that the cars' age attributes are updated.

Besides a fixed interval, a more flexible scheduling mechanism is to use a `cron` expression. In Listing 11-8, change the line from this:

```
<task:scheduled ref="carService" method="updateCarAgeJob" fixed-delay="10000"/>
```

To the following:

```
<task:scheduled ref="carService" method="updateCarAgeJob" cron="0 * * * * *"/>
```

After the change, run the `ScheduleTaskSample` class again, and you will see the job will run every minute.

Using Annotations for Task Scheduling

Another option for scheduling tasks with Spring's `TaskScheduler` abstraction is to use an annotation. Spring provides the `@Scheduled` annotation for this purpose.

To enable annotation support for task scheduling, we need to provide the `<task:annotation-driven>` tag in Spring's XML configuration. Listing 11-10 shows the configuration (`task-annotation-app-context.xml`).

Listing 11-10. Spring Configuration for Annotation-Based Scheduling

```xml
<?xml version="1.0" encoding="UTF-8"?>
<beans xmlns="http://www.springframework.org/schema/beans"
    xmlns:task="http://www.springframework.org/schema/task"
    xmlns:xsi="http://www.w3.org/2001/XMLSchema-instance"
    xsi:schemaLocation="http://www.springframework.org/schema/beans
        http://www.springframework.org/schema/beans/spring-beans.xsd
        http://www.springframework.org/schema/task
        http://www.springframework.org/schema/task/spring-task.xsd">

    <import resource="car-job-app-context.xml"/>

    <task:scheduler id="myScheduler" pool-size="10"/>

    <task:annotation-driven scheduler="myScheduler"/>
</beans>
```

Here the `<task:annotation-driven>` tag enables support for annotation-based scheduling, with the scheduler attribute referencing the `myScheduler` bean.

To schedule a specific method in a Spring bean, just annotate the method with `@Scheduled` and pass in the scheduling requirements. Listing 11-11 shows the code snippet of the revised `CarServiceImpl` `updateCarAgeJob()` method.

Listing 11-11. Revised `CarServiceImpl` Class

```java
@Scheduled(fixedDelay=10000)
public void updateCarAgeJob() {
    ...
}
```

Listing 11-12 shows the testing program.

Listing 11-12. Testing Annotation-Based Scheduling

```
package com.apress.prospring4.ch11;

import org.springframework.context.support.GenericXmlApplicationContext;

public class ScheduleTaskAnnotationSample {
    public static void main(String[] args) {
        GenericXmlApplicationContext ctx = new GenericXmlApplicationContext();
        ctx.load("classpath:META-INF/spring/task-annotation-app-context.xml");
        ctx.refresh();

        while (true) {
        }
    }
}
```

Running the program produces the same output as using task-namespace. You can try different triggering mechanisms by changing the attribute within the @Scheduled annotation (that is, fixedDelay, fixedRate, cron). Feel free to test it yourself.

Asynchronous Task Execution in Spring

Since version 3.0, Spring also supports using annotations to execute a task asynchronously. To do this, you just need to annotate the method with @Async.

Let's go through a simple example to see it in action. Listing 11-13 and Listing 11-14 show the AsyncService interface and its implementation class AsyncServiceImpl, respectively.

Listing 11-13. The AsyncService Interface

```
package com.apress.prospring4.ch11;

import java.util.concurrent.Future;

public interface AsyncService {
    void asyncTask();
    Future<String> asyncWithReturn(String name);
}
```

Listing 11-14. The AsyncServiceImpl Class

```
package com.apress.prospring4.ch11;

import java.util.concurrent.Future;

import org.slf4j.Logger;
import org.slf4j.LoggerFactory;
import org.springframework.scheduling.annotation.Async;
import org.springframework.scheduling.annotation.AsyncResult;
import org.springframework.stereotype.Service;
```

```java
@Service("asyncService")
public class AsyncServiceImpl implements AsyncService {
    final Logger logger = LoggerFactory.getLogger(AsyncServiceImpl.class);

    @Async
    @Override
    public void asyncTask() {
        logger.info("Start execution of async. task");

        try {
            Thread.sleep(10000);
        } catch (Exception ex) {
            ex.printStackTrace();
        }

        logger.info("Complete execution of async. task");
    }

    @Async
    @Override
    public Future<String> asyncWithReturn(String name) {
        logger.info("Start execution of async. task with return");

        try {
            Thread.sleep(5000);
        } catch (Exception ex) {
            ex.printStackTrace();
        }

        logger.info("Complete execution of async. task with return");

        return new AsyncResult<String>("Hello: " + name);
    }
}
```

AsyncService defines two methods. The asyncTask() method is a simple task that logs information to the logger. The method asyncWithReturn() accepts a String argument and returns an instance of the java.util.concurrent. Future<V> interface. Upon completion of asyncWithReturn(), the result is stored in an instance of the org. springframework.scheduling.annotation.AsyncResult<V> class, which implements the Future<V> interface and can be used by the caller to retrieve the result of the execution later.

Listing 11-15 shows the Spring configuration file (async-app-context.xml).

Listing 11-15. Spring Configuration for Async Task

```xml
<?xml version="1.0" encoding="UTF-8"?>
<beans xmlns="http://www.springframework.org/schema/beans"
    xmlns:xsi="http://www.w3.org/2001/XMLSchema-instance"
    xmlns:context="http://www.springframework.org/schema/context"
    xmlns:task="http://www.springframework.org/schema/task"
    xsi:schemaLocation="http://www.springframework.org/schema/beans
        http://www.springframework.org/schema/beans/spring-beans.xsd
        http://www.springframework.org/schema/context
```

```
            http://www.springframework.org/schema/context/spring-context.xsd
            http://www.springframework.org/schema/task
            http://www.springframework.org/schema/task/spring-task.xsd">

    <context:component-scan base-package="com.apress.prospring4.ch11"/>

    <task:annotation-driven />
</beans>
```

From Listing 11-15, we need the `<task:annotation-driven/>` tag for support of the @Async annotation. Listing 11-16 shows the testing program.

Listing 11-16. Testing AsyncTask

```java
package com.apress.prospring4.ch11;

import java.util.concurrent.Future;

import org.springframework.context.support.GenericXmlApplicationContext;

public class AsyncTaskSample {
    public static void main(String[] args) {
        GenericXmlApplicationContext ctx = new GenericXmlApplicationContext();
        ctx.load("classpath:META-INF/spring/async-app-context.xml");
        ctx.refresh();

        AsyncService asyncService = ctx.getBean("asyncService", AsyncService.class);

        for (int i = 0; i < 5; i++) {
            asyncService.asyncTask();
        }

        Future<String> result1 = asyncService.asyncWithReturn("Chris");
        Future<String> result2 = asyncService.asyncWithReturn("John");
        Future<String> result3 = asyncService.asyncWithReturn("Robert");

        try {
            Thread.sleep(6000);

            System.out.println("Result1: " + result1.get());
            System.out.println("Result2: " + result2.get());
            System.out.println("Result3: " + result3.get());
        } catch (Exception ex) {
            ex.printStackTrace();
        }
    }
}
```

We call the `asyncTask()` method five times and then `asyncWithReturn()` three times with different arguments, and then retrieve the result after sleeping for 6 seconds.

Running the program produces the following output:

```
2014-03-13 12:40:06,474 INFO [com.apress.prospring4.ch11.AsyncServiceImpl] - <Start execution of
async. task>
2014-03-13 12:40:06,474 INFO [com.apress.prospring4.ch11.AsyncServiceImpl] - <Start execution of
async. task>
2014-03-13 12:40:06,475 INFO [com.apress.prospring4.ch11.AsyncServiceImpl] - <Start execution of
async. task>
2014-03-13 12:40:06,475 INFO [com.apress.prospring4.ch11.AsyncServiceImpl] - <Start execution of
async. task>
2014-03-13 12:40:06,475 INFO [com.apress.prospring4.ch11.AsyncServiceImpl] - <Start execution of
async. task>
2014-03-13 12:40:06,475 INFO [com.apress.prospring4.ch11.AsyncServiceImpl] - <Start execution of
async. task with return>
2014-03-13 12:40:06,475 INFO [com.apress.prospring4.ch11.AsyncServiceImpl] - <Start execution of
async. task with return>
2014-03-13 12:40:06,475 INFO [com.apress.prospring4.ch11.AsyncServiceImpl] - <Start execution of
async. task with return>
2014-03-13 12:40:11,477 INFO [com.apress.prospring4.ch11.AsyncServiceImpl] - <Complete execution of
async. task with return>
2014-03-13 12:40:11,477 INFO [com.apress.prospring4.ch11.AsyncServiceImpl] - <Complete execution of
async. task with return>
2014-03-13 12:40:11,477 INFO [com.apress.prospring4.ch11.AsyncServiceImpl] - <Complete execution of
async. task with return>
Result1: Hello: Chris
Result2: Hello: John
Result3: Hello: Robert
2014-03-13 12:40:16,477 INFO [com.apress.prospring4.ch11.AsyncServiceImpl] - <Complete execution of
async. task>
2014-03-13 12:40:16,477 INFO [com.apress.prospring4.ch11.AsyncServiceImpl] - <Complete execution of
async. task>
2014-03-13 12:40:16,477 INFO [com.apress.prospring4.ch11.AsyncServiceImpl] - <Complete execution of
async. task>
2014-03-13 12:40:16,477 INFO [com.apress.prospring4.ch11.AsyncServiceImpl] - <Complete execution of
async. task>
2014-03-13 12:40:16,477 INFO [com.apress.prospring4.ch11.AsyncServiceImpl] - <Complete execution of
async. task>
```

From the output, you can see that all the calls were started at the same time. The three calling with return values complete first and are displayed on the console output. Finally, the five asyncTask() methods called are completed too.

Task Execution in Spring

Since Spring 2.0, the framework provided an abstraction for executing tasks by way of the TaskExecutor interface. A TaskExecutor does as exactly as it sounds: it executes a task represented by a Java Runnable implementation. Out of the box, Spring provides a number of TaskExecutor implementations suited for different needs. A full list of TaskExecutor implementations can be found at

```
http://docs.spring.io/spring/docs/4.0.2.RELEASE/javadoc-api/org/springframework/core/task/
TaskExecutor.html.
```

Some commonly used TaskExecutor implementations are listed here:

- SimpleAsyncTaskExecutor: Creates new threads on each invocation; does not reuse existing threads.

- SyncTaskExecutor: Does not execute asynchronously, and invocation occurs in the calling thread.

- SimpleThreadPoolTaskExecutor: Subclass of Quartz's SimpleThreadPool and used when you need to share a thread pool by both Quartz and non-Quartz components.

- ThreadPoolTaskExecutor: TaskExecutor implementation providing the ability to configure ThreadPoolExecutor via bean properties and expose it as a Spring TaskExecutor.

Each TaskExecutor implementation serves its own purpose, and the calling convention is the same. The only variation is in the configuration, when defining which TaskExecutor implementation you want to use and its properties, if any. Let's take a look at a simple example that prints out a number of messages. The TaskExecutor that we will use is SimpleAsyncTaskExecutor. First let's create a bean class that holds the task execution logic, as shown in Listing 11-17.

Listing 11-17. TaskToExecute Bean Example

```
package com.apress.prospring4.ch11;

import org.springframework.core.task.TaskExecutor;

public class TaskToExecute {
    private TaskExecutor taskExecutor;

    public void executeTask() {
        for(int i=0; i < 10; i++) {
            taskExecutor.execute(new Runnable() {
                @Override
                public void run() {
                    System.out.println("Hello from thread: "
                            + Thread.currentThread().getName());
                }
            });
        }
    }

    public void setTaskExecutor(TaskExecutor taskExecutor) {
        this.taskExecutor = taskExecutor;
    }
}
```

This class is just a regular POJO that takes TaskExecutor as a property and defines a method executeTask(). The executeTask() method calls the execute method of the provided TaskExecutor by creating a new Runnable instance containing the logic we would like to execute for this task. Next let's create the bean configuration (app-context.xml), as shown in Listing 11-18.

Listing 11-18. Bean Configuration for Task Execution

```xml
<?xml version="1.0" encoding="UTF-8"?>
<beans xmlns="http://www.springframework.org/schema/beans"
    xmlns:xsi="http://www.w3.org/2001/XMLSchema-instance"
    xmlns:p="http://www.springframework.org/schema/p"
    xsi:schemaLocation="http://www.springframework.org/schema/beans
        http://www.springframework.org/schema/beans/spring-beans.xsd">

    <bean id="taskExecutorSample" class="com.apress.prospring4.ch11.TaskToExecute"
        p:taskExecutor-ref="taskExecutor"/>

    <bean id="taskExecutor" class="org.springframework.core.task.SimpleAsyncTaskExecutor"/>
</beans>
```

Here we define a new bean called taskExecutor by using the SimpleAsyncTaskExecutor implementation of the TaskExecutor interface. Then we inject that into our TaskToExecute bean. Now let's test it out, as shown in Listing 11-19.

Listing 11-19. Task Execution Test Driver

```java
package com.apress.prospring4.ch11;

import org.springframework.context.support.GenericXmlApplicationContext;

public class TaskExecutorSample {
    public static void main(String[] args) {
        GenericXmlApplicationContext ctx = new GenericXmlApplicationContext();
        ctx.load("classpath:META-INF/spring/app-context.xml");
        ctx.refresh();

        TaskToExecute taskToExecute = ctx.getBean(TaskToExecute.class);
        taskToExecute.executeTask();
    }
}
```

Now let's run the example, and it should print output similar to the following:

```
Hello from thread: SimpleAsyncTaskExecutor-1
Hello from thread: SimpleAsyncTaskExecutor-3
Hello from thread: SimpleAsyncTaskExecutor-2
Hello from thread: SimpleAsyncTaskExecutor-5
Hello from thread: SimpleAsyncTaskExecutor-4
Hello from thread: SimpleAsyncTaskExecutor-6
Hello from thread: SimpleAsyncTaskExecutor-7
Hello from thread: SimpleAsyncTaskExecutor-8
Hello from thread: SimpleAsyncTaskExecutor-9
Hello from thread: SimpleAsyncTaskExecutor-10
```

As you can see from the output, each task (the message we are printing) is displayed as it's executed. We print out the message plus the thread name, which is by default the class name (SimpleAsyncTaskExecutor), and the thread number.

Summary

In this chapter, we covered Spring's support for task scheduling. We focused on Spring's built-in TaskScheduler abstraction and demonstrated how to use it to fulfill task scheduling needs with a sample batch data update job. We also covered how Spring supports annotation for executing tasks asynchronously. Additionally, we briefly covered Spring's TaskExecutor and common implementations.

CHAPTER 12

■ ■ ■

Using Spring Remoting

An enterprise application typically needs to communicate with other applications. Take, for example, a company selling products; when a customer places an order, an order-processing system processes that order and generates a transaction. During order processing, an inquiry is made to the inventory system to check whether the product is in stock. Upon order confirmation, a notification is sent to the fulfillment system to deliver the product to the customer. Finally, the information is sent to the accounting system; an invoice is generated, and the payment is processed.

Most of the time, this business process is not fulfilled by a single application but by a number of applications working together. Some of the applications may be developed in-house, and others may be purchased from external vendors. Moreover, the applications may be running on different machines in different locations and implemented with different technologies and programming languages (for example, Java, .NET, or C++). Performing the handshaking between applications in order to build an efficient business process is always a critical task when architecting and implementing an application. As a result, remoting support via various protocols and technologies is needed for an application to participate well in an enterprise environment.

In the Java world, remoting support has existed since Java was first created. In the early days (Java 1.*x*), most remoting requirements were implemented by using traditional TCP sockets or Java Remote Method Invocation (RMI). After J2EE came on the scene, EJB and JMS became common choices for inter-application server communications. The rapid evolution of XML and the Internet gave rise to remote support using XML over HTTP, including the Java API for XML-based RPC (JAX-RPC), the Java API for XML Web Services (JAX-WS), and HTTP-based technologies (for example, Hessian, and Burlap). Spring also offers its own HTTP-based remoting support, called the Spring HTTP invoker. In recent years, to cope with the explosive growth of the Internet and more-responsive web application requirements (for example, via Ajax), more lightweight and efficient remoting support of applications has become critical for the success of an enterprise. Consequently, the Java API for RESTful Web Services (JAX-RS) was created and quickly gained popularity. Other protocols, such as Comet and HTML5 WebSocket, also attracted a lot of developers. Needless to say, remoting technologies keep evolving at a rapid pace.

In terms of remoting, as mentioned, Spring provides its own support (via the Spring HTTP invoker), as well as supporting a lot of technologies mentioned earlier (for example, RMI, EJB, JMS, Hessian, Burlap, JAX-RPC, JAX-WS, and JAX-RS). It's not possible to cover all of them in this chapter. So, here we focus on those that are most commonly used. Specifically, this chapter covers the following topics:

- *Spring HTTP invoker*: If both applications that need to communicate are Spring based, the Spring HTTP invoker provides a simple and efficient way to invoke the services exposed by other applications. We show you how to use the Spring HTTP invoker to expose a service within its service layer, as well as invoking the services provided by a remote application.

- *Using JMS in Spring*: The Java Message Service (JMS) provides another asynchronous and loosely coupled way of exchanging messages between applications. We show you how Spring simplifies application development with JMS.

- *Using RESTful web services in Spring*: Designed specifically around HTTP, RESTful web services are the most commonly used technology for providing remote support for an application, as well as supporting highly interactive web application front ends using Ajax. We show how Spring MVC provides comprehensive support for exposing services using JAX-RS and how to invoke services by using the RestTemplate class. We also discuss how to secure the services from unauthorized access.

- *Using AMQP in Spring*: The sister project Spring Advanced Message Queuing Protocol (AMQP) provides a typical Spring-like abstraction around AMQP along with a RabbitMQ implementation. This project offers a rich set of capabilities, but in this chapter we focus on its remoting capabilities through the projects RPC supports.

Adding Required Dependencies for the JPA Back End

We need to add the required dependencies to the project. Table 12-1 shows the dependencies required for implementing a service layer with JPA 2 and Hibernate as the persistence provider. Also, Spring Data JPA will be used.

Table 12-1. *Maven Dependencies for Service Layer*

Group ID	Artifact ID	Version	Description
org.springframework	spring-context	4.0.2.RELEASE	Spring context module.
org.springframework	spring-orm	4.0.2.RELEASE	Spring ORM module.
org.springframework	spring-tx	4.0.2.RELEASE	Spring transaction support module.
org.springframework	spring-web	4.0.2.RELEASE	Spring web module.
org.springframework	spring-webmvc	4.0.2.RELEASE	Spring web MVC module.
org.springframework.data	spring-data-jpa	1.5.0.RELEASE	Spring Data JPA library.
org.springframework	spring-oxm	4.0.2.RELEASE	Spring OXM module.
org.hibernate	hibernate-entitymanager	4.2.3.Final	Hibernate entity manager with JPA 2 support.
org.hibernate.javax.persistence	hibernate-jpa-2.1-api	1.0.0.Final	Hibernate's JPA API.
com.h2database	h2	1.3.172	H2 database for embedded JDBC access.
joda-time	joda-time	2.3	JodaTime is a date-time API aimed to ease the built-in date-time library included in Java. If you are using Java 8, Spring also provides full support for the javax.time API. In this chapter, we use it in our domain objects too.
org.jadira.usertype	usertype.core	3.0.0.GA	JodaTime library for integration with Hibernate for date-time data persistence.
com.google.guava	guava	14.0.1	Contains useful helper classes.
log4j	log4j	1.2.17	The Log4j logging framework.

(*continued*)

Table 12-1. (*continued*)

Group ID	Artifact ID	Version	Description
org.codehaus.castor	castor-xml	1.3.3	Castor OXM mapping framework.
com.fasterxml.jackson.core	jackson-core	2.3.2	The Jackson core library.
com.fasterxml.jackson.core	jackson-databind	2.3.2	The Jackson DataBind library.
org.springframework.security	spring-security-web	3.2.1.RELEASE	The Spring Security web module.
org.springframework.security	spring-security-config	3.2.1.RELEASE	The Spring Security config module.
org.apache.httpcomponents	httpclient	4.3	The Apache HTTPClient library.

Using a Data Model for Samples

In the samples in this chapter, we use a simple data model, which contains only a single CONTACT table for storing contact information. Listing 12-1 shows the script for schema creation (schema.sql).

Listing 12-1. Sample Database Schema

```
DROP TABLE IF EXISTS CONTACT;

CREATE TABLE CONTACT (
    ID INT NOT NULL AUTO_INCREMENT
    , FIRST_NAME VARCHAR(60) NOT NULL
    , LAST_NAME VARCHAR(40) NOT NULL
    , BIRTH_DATE DATE
    , VERSION INT NOT NULL DEFAULT 0
    , UNIQUE UQ_CONTACT_1 (FIRST_NAME, LAST_NAME)
    , PRIMARY KEY (ID)
);
```

As you can see, the CONTACT table stores only a few basic fields of a contact's information. Listing 12-2 shows the testing data population script (test-data.sql).

Listing 12-2. Sample Data Population Script

```
insert into contact (first_name, last_name, birth_date) values ('Chris', 'Schaefer', '1981-05-03');
insert into contact (first_name, last_name, birth_date) values ('Scott', 'Tiger', '1990-11-02');
insert into contact (first_name, last_name, birth_date) values ('John', 'Smith', '1964-02-28');
```

Implementing and Configuring ContactService

With our dependencies outlined, we can start to implement and configure the service layer for our samples in this chapter. In the following sections, we discuss the implementation of the ContactService using JPA 2, Spring Data JPA, and Hibernate as the persistence service provider. Then, we cover how to configure the service layer in the Spring project.

Implementing ContactService

In the samples, we expose the services for various operations on the contact information to remote clients. First we need to create the Contact entity class, which is shown in Listing 12-3.

Listing 12-3. The Contact Entity Class

```
package com.apress.prospring4.ch12;

import static javax.persistence.GenerationType.IDENTITY;

import java.io.Serializable;

import org.hibernate.annotations.Type;
import org.joda.time.DateTime;

import javax.persistence.Column;
import javax.persistence.Entity;
import javax.persistence.GeneratedValue;
import javax.persistence.Id;
import javax.persistence.Table;
import javax.persistence.Version;

@Entity
@Table(name = "contact")
public class Contact implements Serializable {
    private Long id;
    private int version;
    private String firstName;
    private String lastName;
    private DateTime birthDate;

    @Id
    @GeneratedValue(strategy = IDENTITY)
    @Column(name = "ID")
    public Long getId() {
        return id;
    }

    @Version
    @Column(name = "VERSION")
    public int getVersion() {
        return version;
    }

    @Column(name = "FIRST_NAME")
    public String getFirstName() {
        return firstName;
    }

    @Column(name = "LAST_NAME")
    public String getLastName() {
        return lastName;
    }
```

```
@Column(name = "BIRTH_DATE")
@Type(type="org.jadira.usertype.dateandtime.joda.PersistentDateTime")
public DateTime getBirthDate() {
    return birthDate;
}

public void setId(Long id) {
    this.id = id;
}

public void setVersion(int version) {
    this.version = version;
}

public void setFirstName(String firstName) {
    this.firstName = firstName;
}

public void setLastName(String lastName) {
    this.lastName = lastName;
}

public void setBirthDate(DateTime birthDate) {
    this.birthDate = birthDate;
}

@Override
public String toString() {
    return "Contact - Id: " + id + ", First name: " + firstName
            + ", Last name: " + lastName + ", Birthday: " + birthDate;
}
}
```

As shown in this listing, standard JPA annotations are used. We also use JodaTime's DateTime class for the birthDate attribute.

Let's proceed to the service layer; Listing 12-4 shows the ContactService interface, with the services we want to expose.

Listing 12-4. The ContactService Interface

```
package com.apress.prospring4.ch12;

import java.util.List;

public interface ContactService {
    List<Contact> findAll();
    List<Contact> findByFirstName(String firstName);
    Contact findById(Long id);
    Contact save(Contact contact);
    void delete(Contact contact);
}
```

The methods should be self-explanatory. Because we will use Spring Data JPA's repository support, we implement the ContactRepository interface, as shown in Listing 12-5.

Listing 12-5. *The ContactRepository Interface*

```
package com.apress.prospring4.ch12;

import java.util.List;

import org.springframework.data.repository.CrudRepository;

public interface ContactRepository extends CrudRepository<Contact, Long> {
    List<Contact> findByFirstName(String firstName);
}
```

By extending the CrudRepository<T,ID extends Serializable> interface, for the methods in ContactService, we need to explicitly declare only the findByFirstName() method.

Listing 12-6 shows the implementation class of the ContactService interface.

Listing 12-6. *The ContactServiceImpl Class*

```
package com.apress.prospring4.ch12;

import java.util.List;

import org.springframework.beans.factory.annotation.Autowired;
import org.springframework.stereotype.Repository;
import org.springframework.stereotype.Service;
import org.springframework.transaction.annotation.Transactional;

import com.google.common.collect.Lists;

@Service("contactService")
@Repository
@Transactional
public class ContactServiceImpl implements ContactService {
    @Autowired
    private ContactRepository contactRepository;

    @Override
    @Transactional(readOnly=true)
    public List<Contact> findAll() {
        return Lists.newArrayList(contactRepository.findAll());
    }

    @Override
    @Transactional(readOnly=true)
    public List<Contact> findByFirstName(String firstName) {
        return contactRepository.findByFirstName(firstName);
    }
```

```java
@Override
@Transactional(readOnly=true)
public Contact findById(Long id) {
    return contactRepository.findOne(id);
}

@Override
public Contact save(Contact contact) {
    return contactRepository.save(contact);
}

@Override
public void delete(Contact contact) {
    contactRepository.delete(contact);
}
```

The implementation is basically completed, and the next step is to configure the service in Spring's `ApplicationContext` within the web project, which is discussed in the next section.

Configuring ContactService

For JPA access, we create an individual configuration file called `datasource-tx-jpa.xml`. Listing 12-7 shows the configuration file.

Listing 12-7. The `datasource-tx-jpa.xml` Configuration File

```xml
<?xml version="1.0" encoding="UTF-8"?>
<beans xmlns="http://www.springframework.org/schema/beans"
    xmlns:xsi="http://www.w3.org/2001/XMLSchema-instance"
    xmlns:context="http://www.springframework.org/schema/context"
    xmlns:jdbc="http://www.springframework.org/schema/jdbc"
    xmlns:jpa="http://www.springframework.org/schema/data/jpa"
    xmlns:tx="http://www.springframework.org/schema/tx"
    xsi:schemaLocation="http://www.springframework.org/schema/beans
        http://www.springframework.org/schema/beans/spring-beans.xsd
        http://www.springframework.org/schema/context
        http://www.springframework.org/schema/context/spring-context.xsd
        http://www.springframework.org/schema/jdbc
        http://www.springframework.org/schema/jdbc/spring-jdbc.xsd
        http://www.springframework.org/schema/data/jpa
        http://www.springframework.org/schema/data/jpa/spring-jpa.xsd
        http://www.springframework.org/schema/tx
        http://www.springframework.org/schema/tx/spring-tx.xsd">

    <jdbc:embedded-database id="dataSource" type="H2">
        <jdbc:script location="classpath:META-INF/config/schema.sql"/>
        <jdbc:script location="classpath:META-INF/config/test-data.sql"/>
    </jdbc:embedded-database>
```

```
<bean id="transactionManager" class="org.springframework.orm.jpa.JpaTransactionManager">
    <property name="entityManagerFactory" ref="emf"/>
</bean>

<tx:annotation-driven transaction-manager="transactionManager" />

<bean id="emf" class="org.springframework.orm.jpa.LocalContainerEntityManagerFactoryBean">
    <property name="dataSource" ref="dataSource" />
    <property name="jpaVendorAdapter">
        <bean class="org.springframework.orm.jpa.vendor.HibernateJpaVendorAdapter" />
    </property>
    <property name="packagesToScan" value="com.apress.prospring4.ch12"/>
    <property name="jpaProperties">
        <props>
            <prop key="hibernate.dialect">org.hibernate.dialect.H2Dialect</prop>
            <prop key="hibernate.max_fetch_depth">3</prop>
            <prop key="hibernate.jdbc.fetch_size">50</prop>
            <prop key="hibernate.jdbc.batch_size">10</prop>
            <prop key="hibernate.show_sql">true</prop>
        </props>
    </property>
</bean>

<context:annotation-config/>

<jpa:repositories base-package="com.apress.prospring4.ch12"
                  entity-manager-factory-ref="emf"
                  transaction-manager-ref="transactionManager"/>
</beans>
```

Since we are exposing the HTTP invoker via Spring MVC, we then need to import the configuration into Spring's root WebApplicationContext. For a Spring MVC project, the file is located at /src/main/webapp/WEB-INF/spring/root-context.xml. Listing 12-8 shows the revised file.

Listing 12-8. The root-context.xml File

```
<?xml version="1.0" encoding="UTF-8"?>
<beans xmlns="http://www.springframework.org/schema/beans"
    xmlns:xsi="http://www.w3.org/2001/XMLSchema-instance"
    xmlns:context="http://www.springframework.org/schema/context"
    xsi:schemaLocation="http://www.springframework.org/schema/beans
        http://www.springframework.org/schema/beans/spring-beans.xsd
        http://www.springframework.org/schema/context
        http://www.springframework.org/schema/context/spring-context.xsd">

    <import resource="classpath:META-INF/spring/datasource-tx-jpa.xml" />

    <context:component-scan base-package="com.apress.prospring4.ch12" />
</beans>
```

First the context namespace is added to the configuration file. Then, the file datasource-tx-jpa.xml is imported into the WebApplicationContext, and finally, we instruct Spring to scan for the specified package for Spring beans. Now, the service layer is completed and ready to be exposed and used by remote clients.

Using the Spring HTTP Invoker

If the application you are going to communicate with is also Spring-powered, using the Spring HTTP invoker is a good choice. It provides an extremely simple way to expose the services within the Spring `WebApplicationContext` to remote clients also using the Spring HTTP invoker to invoke the service. The procedures for exposing and accessing the service are elaborated in the following sections.

Exposing the Service

To expose the service, in the `root-context.xml` configuration file, add the bean definition in Listing 12-9.

Listing 12-9. Bean for Exposing Contact Service Using HTTP Invoker

```
<bean name="contactExporter" class="org.springframework.remoting.httpinvoker.
HttpInvokerServiceExporter">
    <property name="service" ref="contactService" />
    <property name="serviceInterface"
        value="com.apress.prospring4.ch12.ContactService" />
</bean>
```

A `contactExporter` bean is defined with the `HttpInvokerServiceExporter` class, which is for exporting any Spring bean as a service via the HTTP invoker. Within the bean, two properties are defined. The first one is the service property, indicating the bean providing the service. For this property, the `contactService` bean is injected. The second property is the interface type to expose, which is the `com.apress.prospring4.ch12.ContactService` interface.

Next, we need to define a servlet within the web deployment descriptor (`/src/main/webapp/WEB-INF/web.xml`) for the service. Listing 12-10 shows the code snippet to add into the `web.xml` file.

Listing 12-10. Servlet Definition for the HTTP Invoker

```
<web-app xmlns="http://java.sun.com/xml/ns/javaee"
        xmlns:xsi="http://www.w3.org/2001/XMLSchema-instance"
        xsi:schemaLocation="http://java.sun.com/xml/ns/javaee
        http://java.sun.com/xml/ns/javaee/web-app_3_0.xsd"
        version="3.0">

    <display-name>Spring HTTP Invoker Sample</display-name>

    <context-param>
        <param-name>contextConfigLocation</param-name>
        <param-value>/WEB-INF/spring/root-context.xml</param-value>
    </context-param>

    <listener>
        <listener-class>org.springframework.web.context.ContextLoaderListener</listener-class>
    </listener>

    <servlet>
        <servlet-name>contactExporter</servlet-name>
```

```
        <servlet-class>
            org.springframework.web.context.support.HttpRequestHandlerServlet
        </servlet-class>
    </servlet>

    <servlet-mapping>
        <servlet-name>contactExporter</servlet-name>
        <url-pattern>/remoting/ContactService</url-pattern>
    </servlet-mapping>
</web-app>
```

As shown in Listing 12-10, a servlet with the class HttpRequestHandlerServlet is defined, which is used to expose the Spring exporter defined in the WebApplicationContext. Note that the servlet name (contactExporter) should match the bean name of the exporter (see Listing 12-9; the bean name is also contactExporter). Then, the servlet is mapped to the URL /remoting/ContactService under the web context (that is, http://localhost:8080/ch12/remoting/ContactService) of the application.

At this point, the server-side development is complete. As this is a Spring MVC web application, a WAR file needs to be created and deployed to a servlet container. There are multiple ways to do this—for example, a stand-alone container such as Tomcat, an IDE-launched instance of Tomcat, or an embedded Tomcat instance that runs with a build tool such as Maven. Which option you choose is up to your needs, but for a local development environment, an embedded instance launched from your build tool or directly from your IDE is recommended. In the same code for this book, we use the embedded flavor via Maven. See the book source code for more details.

At this point, you should build your web application and deploy via the method of your choice. If you try going to the ContactService URL (http://localhost:8080/ch12/remoting/ContactService) and see a 500 error, don't worry, as you will need the client to make the request.

Invoking the Service

Invoking a service via the Spring HTTP invoker is simple. First we configure a Spring ApplicationContext, as shown in Listing 12-11 (http-invoker-app-context.xml).

Listing 12-11. Spring ApplicationContext for HTTP Invoker Client

```
<?xml version="1.0" encoding="UTF-8"?>
<beans xmlns="http://www.springframework.org/schema/beans"
    xmlns:xsi="http://www.w3.org/2001/XMLSchema-instance"
    xsi:schemaLocation="http://www.springframework.org/schema/beans
        http://www.springframework.org/schema/beans/spring-beans.xsd">

    <bean id="remoteContactService" class="org.springframework.remoting.httpinvoker.
HttpInvokerProxyFactoryBean">
        <property name="serviceUrl"
            value="http://localhost:8080/ch12/remoting/ContactService" />
        <property name="serviceInterface"
            value="com.apress.prospring4.ch12.ContactService" />
    </bean>
</beans>
```

As shown in Listing 12-11, for the client side, a bean of type HttpInvokerProxyFactoryBean is declared. Two properties are set. The serviceUrl specifies the location of the remote service, which is http://localhost:8080/ch12/remoting/ContactService. The second property is the interface of the service (that is, ContactService). If you are developing another project for the client, you need to have the ContactService interface and the Contact entity class within your client application's classpath.

Listing 12-12 shows a main class for invoking the remote service.

Listing 12-12. The HttpInvokerClientSample Class

```
package com.apress.prospring4.ch12;

import java.util.List;

import org.springframework.context.support.GenericXmlApplicationContext;

public class HttpInvokerClientSample {
    public static void main(String[] args) {
        GenericXmlApplicationContext ctx = new GenericXmlApplicationContext();
        ctx.load("classpath:META-INF/spring/http-invoker-app-context.xml");
        ctx.refresh();

        ContactService contactService =
            ctx.getBean("remoteContactService", ContactService.class);

        System.out.println("Finding all contacts");
        List<Contact> contacts = contactService.findAll();
        listContacts(contacts);

        System.out.println("Finding contact with first name equals Chris");
        contacts = contactService.findByFirstName("Chris");
        listContacts(contacts);
    }

    private static void listContacts(List<Contact> contacts) {
        for (Contact contact: contacts) {
            System.out.println(contact);
        }

        System.out.println("");
    }
}
```

As shown in Listing 12-12, the program is just like any other stand-alone Spring application. The ApplicationContext is initialized, and then the contactService bean is retrieved. Then we just call its methods as with a local application. Running the program produces the following output:

```
Finding all contacts
Contact - Id: 1, First name: Chris, Last name: Schaefer, Birthday: 1981-05-02T20:00:00.000-04:00
Contact - Id: 2, First name: Scott, Last name: Tiger, Birthday: 1990-11-01T19:00:00.000-05:00
Contact - Id: 3, First name: John, Last name: Smith, Birthday: 1964-02-27T19:00:00.000-05:00

Finding contact with first name equals Chris
Contact - Id: 1, First name: Chris, Last name: Schaefer, Birthday: 1981-05-02T20:00:00.000-04:00
```

In the previous output, you can see that the findAll() and findByFirstName() methods are called, and the results are returned.

Using JMS in Spring

Using message-oriented middleware (generally referred to as an *MQ server*) is another popular way to support communication between applications. The main benefits of a message queue (MQ) server are that it provides an asynchronous and loosely coupled way for application integration. In the Java world, JMS is the standard for connecting to an MQ server for sending or receiving messages.

An MQ server maintains a list of queues and topics for which applications can connect to and send and receive messages. The following is a brief description of the difference between a queue and a topic:

- *Queue*: A queue is used to support a point-to-point message exchange model. When a producer sends a message to a queue, the MQ server keeps the message within the queue and delivers it to one, and only one, consumer the next time the consumer connects.

- *Topic*: A topic is used to support the publish-subscribe model. Any number of clients can subscribe to the message within a topic. When a message arrives for that topic, the MQ server delivers it to all clients that have subscribed to the message. This model is particularly useful when you have multiple applications that will be interested in the same piece of information (for example, a news feed).

In JMS, a producer connects to an MQ server and sends a message to a queue or topic. A consumer also connects to the MQ server and listens to a queue or topics for messages of interest. In JMS 1.1, the API was unified so the producer and consumer don't need to deal with different APIs for interacting with queues and topics. In this section, we focus on the point-to-point style for using queues, which is a more commonly used pattern within an enterprise.

To develop and test a JMS application, an MQ server is required. In this section, we use the Apache ActiveMQ server (`activemq.apache.org`), which is a popular open source MQ server.

To prepare for the sample, several new Maven dependencies are required, as listed in Table 12-2. Please add them into your project.

Table 12-2. *Maven Dependencies for JMS and ActiveMQ*

Group ID	Artifact ID	Version	Description
org.springframework	spring-jms	4.0.2.RELEASE	Spring JMS module
org.apache.activemq	activemq-core	5.7.0	ActiveMQ Java library
javax.jms	jms	1.1	JMS 1.1 API

Setting Up ActiveMQ

Setting up ActiveMQ for development use is easy. As with Tomcat in the prior sample, ActiveMQ can be run as a stand-alone server or embedded and launched from your build tool (such as Maven). For development purposes, we are using the embedded version as we did with Tomcat. If you would like to set up a stand-alone server, see the ActiveMQ web site download page (`http://activemq.apache.org/download.html`) for more information. Refer to the sample code provided with this book to see how an embedded ActiveMQ instance is configured in the build system.

Implementing a JMS Listener in Spring

To develop a message listener, we need to create a class that implements the `javax.jms.MessageListener` interface and implements its `onMessage()` method. Listing 12-13 shows the class.

Listing 12-13. A JMS Message Listener Class

```
package com.apress.prospring4.ch12;

import javax.jms.JMSException;
import javax.jms.Message;
import javax.jms.MessageListener;
import javax.jms.TextMessage;

import org.slf4j.Logger;
import org.slf4j.LoggerFactory;

public class SimpleMessageListener implements MessageListener {
    private static final Logger logger = LoggerFactory.getLogger(SimpleMessageListener.class);

    @Override
    public void onMessage(Message message) {
        TextMessage textMessage = (TextMessage) message;

        try {
            logger.info("Message received: " + textMessage.getText());
        } catch (JMSException ex) {
            logger.error("JMS error", ex);
        }
    }
}
```

In the onMessage() method, an instance of the javax.jms.Message interface will be passed upon message arrival. Within the method, the message is cast to an instance of the javax.jms.TextMessage interface, and the message body in text is retrieved using the TextMessage.getText() method. For a list of possible message formats, please refer to the current JEE online documentation.

Having the message listener in place, the next step is to define the Spring ApplicationContext configuration. Listing 12-14 shows the file (jms-listener-app-context.xml).

Listing 12-14. JMS Message Listener Configuration

```
<?xml version="1.0" encoding="UTF-8"?>
<beans xmlns="http://www.springframework.org/schema/beans"
    xmlns:xsi="http://www.w3.org/2001/XMLSchema-instance"
    xmlns:jms="http://www.springframework.org/schema/jms"
    xmlns:p="http://www.springframework.org/schema/p"
    xsi:schemaLocation="http://www.springframework.org/schema/beans
        http://www.springframework.org/schema/beans/spring-beans.xsd
        http://www.springframework.org/schema/jms
        http://www.springframework.org/schema/jms/spring-jms.xsd">

    <bean id="connectionFactory"
        class="org.apache.activemq.ActiveMQConnectionFactory"
        p:brokerURL="tcp://localhost:61616" />

    <bean id="simpleMessageListener" class="com.apress.prospring4.ch12.SimpleMessageListener"/>
```

```
    <jms:listener-container container-type="default"
        connection-factory="connectionFactory" acknowledge="auto">
        <jms:listener destination="prospring4" ref="simpleMessageListener" method="onMessage" />
    </jms:listener-container>
</beans>
```

We first declare a javax.jms.ConnectionFactory interface provided by the ActiveMQ Java library (the ActiveMQConnectionFactory class). Then, a bean of type SimpleMessageListener is declared. Finally, we use the handy <jms:listener-container> tag provided by Spring's jms namespace to declare a message listener, providing the destination (that is, the prospring4 queue), the bean reference, and the method to invoke on message arrival.

Now let's see how to send a message to the prospring4 queue.

Sending JMS Messages in Spring

Let's see how to send messages by using JMS in Spring. We will use the handy org.springframework.jms.core. JmsTemplate class for this purpose. First we will develop a MessageSender interface and its implementation class, SimpleMessageSender. Listings 12-15 and 12-16 show the interface and the class, respectively.

Listing 12-15. The MessageSender Interface

```
package com.apress.prospring4.ch12;

public interface MessageSender {
    void sendMessage(String message);
}
```

Listing 12-16. The SimpleMessageSender Class

```
package com.apress.prospring4.ch12;

import javax.jms.JMSException;
import javax.jms.Message;
import javax.jms.Session;

import org.springframework.beans.factory.annotation.Autowired;
import org.springframework.jms.core.JmsTemplate;
import org.springframework.jms.core.MessageCreator;
import org.springframework.stereotype.Component;

@Component("messageSender")
public class SimpleMessageSender implements MessageSender {
    @Autowired
    private JmsTemplate jmsTemplate;

    @Override
    public void sendMessage(final String message) {
        this.jmsTemplate.send(new MessageCreator() {
            @Override
```

```
        public Message createMessage(Session session)
            throws JMSException {
            return session.createTextMessage(message);
        }
    });
  }
}
```

As you can see, an instance of JmsTemplate is injected. In the sendMessage() method, we call the JmsTemplate. send() method, with an in-place construction of an instance of the org.springframework.jms.core.MessageCreator interface. In the MessageCreator instance, the createMessage() method is implemented to create a new instance of TextMessage that will be sent to ActiveMQ.

Listing 12-17 shows the Spring configuration of the JMS sender (jms-sender-app-context.xml).

Listing 12-17. Spring Configuration for Sending Messages

```xml
<?xml version="1.0" encoding="UTF-8"?>
<beans xmlns="http://www.springframework.org/schema/beans"
    xmlns:xsi="http://www.w3.org/2001/XMLSchema-instance"
    xmlns:context="http://www.springframework.org/schema/context"
    xmlns:p="http://www.springframework.org/schema/p"
    xsi:schemaLocation="http://www.springframework.org/schema/beans
        http://www.springframework.org/schema/beans/spring-beans.xsd
        http://www.springframework.org/schema/context
        http://www.springframework.org/schema/context/spring-context.xsd">

    <bean id="connectionFactory"
        class="org.apache.activemq.ActiveMQConnectionFactory"
        p:brokerURL="tcp://localhost:61616" />

    <bean id="jmsTemplate" class="org.springframework.jms.core.JmsTemplate">
        <constructor-arg name="connectionFactory" ref="connectionFactory"/>
        <property name="defaultDestinationName" value="prospring4"/>
    </bean>

    <context:component-scan base-package="com.apress.prospring4.ch12"/>
</beans>
```

The connectionFactory bean is defined as usual. In addition, an instance of JmsTemplate is declared, with connectionFactory as the constructor argument, and defaultDestinationName is set to the prospring4 queue.

Now let's tie both sending and receiving together to see JMS in action. Listing 12-18 shows the main testing program for sending messages and receiving messages.

Listing 12-18. Test Sending and Receiving Messages

```java
package com.apress.prospring4.ch12;

import org.springframework.context.support.GenericXmlApplicationContext;

public class JmsSample {
    public static void main(String[] args) {
        GenericXmlApplicationContext ctx = new GenericXmlApplicationContext();
```

```
        ctx.load("classpath:META-INF/spring/jms-sender-app-context.xml",
                "classpath:META-INF/spring/jms-listener-app-context.xml");
        ctx.refresh();

        MessageSender messageSender = ctx.getBean("messageSender", MessageSender.class);

        for(int i=0; i < 10; i++) {
            messageSender.sendMessage("Test message: " + i);
        }
    }
}
```

The program is simple. Running the program sends messages to the queue. The JmsListenerSample class receives those messages, and the following output can be seen in your console:

```
INFO ss.prospring4.ch12.SimpleMessageListener:  19 - Message received: Test message: 0
INFO ss.prospring4.ch12.SimpleMessageListener:  19 - Message received: Test message: 1
INFO ss.prospring4.ch12.SimpleMessageListener:  19 - Message received: Test message: 2
INFO ss.prospring4.ch12.SimpleMessageListener:  19 - Message received: Test message: 3
INFO ss.prospring4.ch12.SimpleMessageListener:  19 - Message received: Test message: 4
INFO ss.prospring4.ch12.SimpleMessageListener:  19 - Message received: Test message: 5
INFO ss.prospring4.ch12.SimpleMessageListener:  19 - Message received: Test message: 6
INFO ss.prospring4.ch12.SimpleMessageListener:  19 - Message received: Test message: 7
INFO ss.prospring4.ch12.SimpleMessageListener:  19 - Message received: Test message: 8
INFO ss.prospring4.ch12.SimpleMessageListener:  19 - Message received: Test message: 9
```

In real life, the message will most likely be in XML format, representing a piece of business information (for example, an online order, transaction, or booking).

As you can see, sending and receiving messages with Spring JMS is easy. This section covers only the basic usage scenarios of JMS. For details, please refer to the online JEE documentation.

Working with JMS 2.0

As of Spring Framework 4.0, support for JMS 2.0 has been implemented. JMS 2.0 functionality is usable simply by having the JMS 2.0 JAR in your classpath while retaining backward compatibility for 1.x. At the time of this writing, ActiveMQ does not support JMS 2.0, so we will utilize HornetQ (containing JMS 2.0 support starting at 2.4.0.Final) as the message broker in this sample and will use a stand-alone server. Downloading and installing HornetQ is outside the scope of this book; please refer to the documentation at http://docs.jboss.org/hornetq/2.4.0.Final/docs/quickstart-guide/html/index.html.

In this example, we are using the code from our JMS 1.1 / ActiveMQ sample but with some slight configuration modifications for HornetQ. We also need to use the JMS 2.0 dependency rather than JMS 1.1, as shown in Table 12-3.

Table 12-3. *Maven Dependencies for JMS 2.0 Sample*

Group ID	Artifact ID	Version	Description
org.springframework	spring-jms	4.0.2.RELEASE	Spring JMS module
org.slf4j	slf4j-log4j12	1.7.6	The SLF4J logging framework log4j adapter
javax.jms	javax.jms-api	2.0	JMS 2.0 API
org.hornetq	hornet-jms-client	2.4.0.Final	The HornetQ JMS client API

First we need to create a queue within the HornetQ JMS configuration file. This file resides under the directory that you extracted HornetQ in. The location of the file is `config/stand-alone/non-clustered/hornetq-jms.xml`, and we need to add the queue definition as shown in Listing 12-19.

Listing 12-19. HornetQ Queue Definition

```
<configuration xmlns="urn:hornetq"
            xmlns:xsi="http://www.w3.org/2001/XMLSchema-instance"
            xsi:schemaLocation="urn:hornetq /schema/hornetq-jms.xsd">

    ...

    <queue name="prospring4">
        <entry name="/queue/prospring4"/>
    </queue>
</configuration>
```

Now start the HornetQ server by running the `run.sh` (depending on your operating system) script and ensure that the server starts without any errors. Next we need to modify our configuration files to use a HornetQ connection factory rather than an ActiveMQ one. First let's modify the Spring sender configuration (`jms-sender-app-context.xml`) as shown in Listing 12-20.

Listing 12-20. HornetQ Sender Configuration

```
<?xml version="1.0" encoding="UTF-8"?>
<beans xmlns="http://www.springframework.org/schema/beans"
      xmlns:xsi="http://www.w3.org/2001/XMLSchema-instance"
      xmlns:context="http://www.springframework.org/schema/context"
      xsi:schemaLocation="http://www.springframework.org/schema/beans
        http://www.springframework.org/schema/beans/spring-beans.xsd
        http://www.springframework.org/schema/context
        http://www.springframework.org/schema/context/spring-context.xsd">

    <bean id="connectionFactory" class="org.hornetq.jms.client.HornetQJMSConnectionFactory">
        <constructor-arg name="ha" value="false" />
        <constructor-arg>
            <bean class="org.hornetq.api.core.TransportConfiguration">
                <constructor-arg
                    value="org.hornetq.core.remoting.impl.netty.NettyConnectorFactory"/>
```

```
                    <constructor-arg>
                        <map key-type="java.lang.String" value-type="java.lang.Object">
                            <entry key="host" value="127.0.0.1"/>
                            <entry key="port" value="5445"/>
                        </map>
                    </constructor-arg>
                </bean>
            </constructor-arg>
        </bean>

        <bean id="jmsTemplate" class="org.springframework.jms.core.JmsTemplate">
            <constructor-arg name="connectionFactory" ref="connectionFactory"/>
            <property name="defaultDestinationName" value="prospring4"/>
        </bean>

        <context:component-scan base-package="com.apress.prospring4.ch12"/>
    </beans>
```

The only changes are to the connectionFactory bean and specific to HornetQ. For more details, see the documentation URL listed at the start of this section. Now let's modify the Spring client configuration (jms-listener-app-context.xml) as shown in Listing 12-21.

Listing 12-21. HornetQ Client Configuration

```xml
<?xml version="1.0" encoding="UTF-8"?>
<beans xmlns="http://www.springframework.org/schema/beans"
       xmlns:xsi="http://www.w3.org/2001/XMLSchema-instance"
       xmlns:jms="http://www.springframework.org/schema/jms"
       xsi:schemaLocation="http://www.springframework.org/schema/beans
        http://www.springframework.org/schema/beans/spring-beans.xsd
        http://www.springframework.org/schema/jms
        http://www.springframework.org/schema/jms/spring-jms.xsd">

    <bean id="connectionFactory" class="org.hornetq.jms.client.HornetQJMSConnectionFactory">
        <constructor-arg name="ha" value="false" />
        <constructor-arg>
            <bean class="org.hornetq.api.core.TransportConfiguration">
                <constructor-arg
                    value="org.hornetq.core.remoting.impl.netty.NettyConnectorFactory"/>
                <constructor-arg>
                    <map key-type="java.lang.String" value-type="java.lang.Object">
                        <entry key="host" value="127.0.0.1"/>
                        <entry key="port" value="5445"/>
                    </map>
                </constructor-arg>
            </bean>
        </constructor-arg>
    </bean>

    <bean id="simpleMessageListener" class="com.apress.prospring4.ch12.SimpleMessageListener"/>
```

```
<jms:listener-container container-type="default"
                        connection-factory="connectionFactory" acknowledge="auto">
    <jms:listener destination="prospring4" ref="simpleMessageListener" method="onMessage" />
</jms:listener-container>
</beans>
```

Finally, let's modify our SimpleMessageSender class, which has access to the JmsTemplate, as shown in Listing 12-22. We will be setting the Delivery Delay property of JmsTemplate, which is a JMS 2.0 feature. This property sets the minimum length of time in milliseconds that must elapse after a message is sent, before the JMS broker can deliver the message to a consumer. If you don't have the JMS 2.0 JAR but rather a 1.x version, Spring will throw an exception when trying to use this method, indicating that JMS 2.0 is required.

Listing 12-22. Setting the Delivery Delay in a JMS 2.0 Message Producer

```java
package com.apress.prospring4.ch12;

import javax.jms.JMSException;
import javax.jms.Message;
import javax.jms.Session;

import org.springframework.beans.factory.annotation.Autowired;
import org.springframework.jms.core.JmsTemplate;
import org.springframework.jms.core.MessageCreator;
import org.springframework.stereotype.Component;

@Component("messageSender")
public class SimpleMessageSender implements MessageSender {
    @Autowired
    private JmsTemplate jmsTemplate;

    @Override
    public void sendMessage(final String message) {
        jmsTemplate.setDeliveryDelay(5000L);

        this.jmsTemplate.send(new MessageCreator() {
            @Override
            public Message createMessage(Session session)
                    throws JMSException {
                return session.createTextMessage(message);
            }
        });
    }
}
```

Now run the sample again, and you will see the same results, except the message delivery is delayed.

Using RESTful-WS in Spring

Nowadays, RESTful-WS is perhaps the most widely used technology for remote access. From remote service invocation via HTTP to supporting an Ajax-style interactive web front end, RESTful-WS is being adopted intensively.

RESTful web services are popular for several reasons:

- *Easy to understand*: RESTful web services are designed around HTTP. The URL, together with the HTTP method, specifies the intention of the request. For example, the URL http://somedomain.com/restful/customer/1 with an HTTP method of GET means that the client wants to retrieve the customer information, where the customer ID equals 1.

- *Lightweight*: RESTful is much more lightweight when compared to SOAP-based web services, which include a large amount of metadata to describe which service the client wants to invoke. For a RESTful request and response, it's simply an HTTP request and response, as with any other web application.

- *Firewall friendly*: Because RESTful web services are designed to be accessible via HTTP (or HTTPS), the application becomes much more firewall friendly and easily accessed by remote clients.

In this section, we present the basic concepts of RESTful-WS and Spring's support of RESTful-WS through its Spring MVC module.

Introducing RESTful Web Services

The *REST* in RESTful-WS is short for REpresentational State Transfer, which is an architectural style. REST defines a set of architectural constraints that together describe a *uniform interface* for accessing resources.

The main concepts of this uniform interface include the identification of resources and the manipulation of resources through representations.

For the identification of resources, a piece of information should be accessible via a uniform resource identifier (URI). For example, the URL www.somedomain.com/api/contact/1 is a URI that represents a resource, which is a piece of contact information with an identifier of 1. If the contact with an identifier of 1 does not exist, the client will get a 404 HTTP error, just like a page not found in a web site. Another example, www.somedomain.com/api/contacts, is a URI that represents a resource that is a list of contact information.

Those identifiable resources can be managed through various representations, as shown in Table 12-4.

Table 12-4. *Representations for Manipulating Resources*

Representation	Description
GET	GET retrieves a representation of a resource.
HEAD	Identical to GET, without the response body. Typically used for getting a header.
POST	POST creates a new resource.
PUT	PUT updates a resource.
DELETE	DELETE deletes a resource.
OPTIONS	OPTIONS retrieves allowed HTTP methods.

For a detailed description of RESTful web services, we recommend *Ajax and REST Recipes: A Problem-Solution Approach* by Christian Gross (Apress, 2006).

Adding Required Dependencies for Samples

To develop the samples in this section, the dependencies listed in Table 12-5 are required. Add them into your project.

Table 12-5. *Maven Dependencies for RESTful Web Services*

Group ID	Artifact ID	Version	Description
`org.springframework`	`spring-oxm`	4.0.2.RELEASE	Spring object-to-XML mapping module.
`org.codehaus.jackson`	`jackson-mapper-lgpl`	1.9.13	Jackson JSON processor to support data in JSON format.
`org.codehaus.castor`	`castor-xml`	1.3.3	The Castor XML library will be used for marshaling and unmarshaling of XML data.
`org.springframework.security`	`spring-security-core`	3.2.1.RELEASE	Spring Security core module.
`org.springframework.security`	`spring-security-web`	3.2.1.RELEASE	Spring Security web module for securing RESTful-WS.
`org.springframework.security`	`spring-security-config`	3.2.1.RELEASE	Spring Security configuration module.
`org.apache.httpcomponents`	`httpclient`	4.3	Apache HTTP Components project. The HTTP client library will be used for RESTful-WS invocation.

Designing the Contact RESTful Web Service

When developing a RESTful-WS application, the first step is to design the service structure, which includes what HTTP methods will be supported, together with the target URLs for different operations. For our contact RESTful web services, we want to support query, create, update, and delete operations. For querying, we want to support retrieving all contacts or a single contact by ID.

The services will be implemented as a Spring MVC controller. The name is the `ContactController` class, under the package `com.apress.prospring4.ch12`. The URL pattern, HTTP method, description, and corresponding controller methods are shown in Table 12-6. For the URLs, they all use the prefix `http://localhost:8080/ch12/restful`. In terms of data format, both XML and JSON are supported. The corresponding format will be provided according to the accept media type of the client's HTTP request header.

Table 12-6. *Design of RESTful Web Services*

URL	HTTP Method	Description	Controller Method
`/contact/listdata`	GET	To retrieve all contacts	`listData(...)`
`/contact/{id}`	GET	To retrieve a single contact with the specified ID	`findContactById(...)`
`/contact`	POST	To create a new contact	`create(...)`
`/contact/{id}`	PUT	To update an existing contact with the specified ID	`update(...)`
`/contact`	DELETE	To delete a contact with ID	`delete(...)`

Using Spring MVC to Expose RESTful Web Services

In this section, we show you how to use Spring MVC to expose the contact services as RESTful web services, as designed in the previous section. This sample builds upon some of the ContactService classes that were used in the Spring HTTP invoker sample.

First we will create another domain object, the Contacts class. Listing 12-23 shows the Contacts class.

Listing 12-23. The Contacts Class

```java
package com.apress.prospring4.ch12;

import java.io.Serializable;
import java.util.List;

public class Contacts implements Serializable {
    private List<Contact> contacts;

    public Contacts() {
    }

    public Contacts(List<Contact> contacts) {
        this.contacts = contacts;
    }

    public List<Contact> getContacts() {
        return contacts;
    }

    public void setContacts(List<Contact> contacts) {
        this.contacts = contacts;
    }
}
```

The Contacts class has a single property, which is a list of Contact objects. The purpose is to support the transformation from a list of contacts (returned by the listData() method within the ContactController class) into XML or JSON format.

Configuring Castor XML

To support the transformation of the returned contact information into XML format, we will use the Castor XML library (http://castor.codehaus.org). Castor supports several modes between POJO and XML transformation, and in this sample, we use an XML file to define the mapping. Listing 12-24 shows the mapping file (oxm-mapping.xml).

Listing 12-24. Defining Castor XML Mapping

```xml
<mapping>
    <class name="com.apress.prospring4.ch12.Contacts">
        <field name="contacts" type="com.apress.prospring4.ch12.Contact" collection="arraylist">
            <bind-xml name="contact"/>
        </field>
    </class>
</mapping>
```

```
<class name="com.apress.prospring4.ch12.Contact" identity="id">
    <map-to xml="contact" />

    <field name="id" type="long">
        <bind-xml name="id" node="element"/>
    </field>
    <field name="firstName" type="string">
        <bind-xml name="firstName" node="element" />
    </field>
    <field name="lastName" type="string">
        <bind-xml name="lastName" node="element" />
    </field>
    <field name="birthDate" type="string" handler="dateHandler">
        <bind-xml name="birthDate" node="element" />
    </field>
    <field name="version" type="integer">
        <bind-xml name="version" node="element" />
    </field>
</class>

<field-handler name="dateHandler" class="com.apress.prospring4.ch12.DateTimeFieldHandler">
    <param name="date-format" value="yyyy-MM-dd"/>
</field-handler>
</mapping>
```

Two mappings are defined. The first <class> tag maps the Contacts class, within which its contacts property (a List of Contact objects) is mapped using the <bind-xml name="contact"/>tag. The Contact object is then mapped (with the <map-to xml="contact" />tag within the second <class> tag). In addition, to support the transformation from JodaTime's DateTime type (for Contact's birthDate attribute), we implement a custom Castor field handler. Listing 12-25 shows the field handler.

Listing 12-25. Custom Field Handler for DateTime Type in Castor

```
package com.apress.prospring4.ch12;

import java.util.Properties;

import org.exolab.castor.mapping.GeneralizedFieldHandler;
import org.exolab.castor.mapping.ValidityException;
import org.joda.time.DateTime;
import org.joda.time.format.DateTimeFormat;
import org.joda.time.format.DateTimeFormatter;

public class DateTimeFieldHandler extends GeneralizedFieldHandler {
    private static String dateFormatPattern;

    @Override
    public void setConfiguration(Properties config) throws ValidityException {
        dateFormatPattern = config.getProperty("date-format");
    }
```

```
    @Override
    public Object convertUponGet(Object value) {
        DateTime dateTime = (DateTime) value;

        return format(dateTime);
    }

    @Override
    public Object convertUponSet(Object value) {
        String dateTimeString = (String) value;

        return parse(dateTimeString);
    }

    @Override
    public Class<DateTime> getFieldType() {
        return DateTime.class;
    }

    protected static String format(final DateTime dateTime) {
        String dateTimeString = "";

        if (dateTime != null) {
            DateTimeFormatter dateTimeFormatter =
                    DateTimeFormat.forPattern(dateFormatPattern);
            dateTimeString = dateTimeFormatter.print(dateTime);
        }

        return dateTimeString;
    }

    protected static DateTime parse(final String dateTimeString) {
        DateTime dateTime = new DateTime();

        if (dateTimeString != null) {
            DateTimeFormatter dateTimeFormatter =
                    DateTimeFormat.forPattern(dateFormatPattern);
            dateTime = dateTimeFormatter.parseDateTime(dateTimeString);
        }

        return dateTime;
    }
}
```

We extend Castor's org.exolab.castor.mapping.GeneralizedFieldHandler class and implement the convertUponGet(), convertUponSet(), and getFieldType() methods. Within the methods, we implement the logic to perform the transformation between DateTime and String for use by Castor.

In addition, we also define a properties file for use with Castor. Listing 12-26 shows the file (castor.properties).

Listing 12-26. The castor.properties File

```
org.exolab.castor.indent=true
```

The property instructs Castor to generate XML with an indent, which is much easier to read when testing.

Implementing ContactController

The next step is to implement the controller class, ContactController. Listing 12-27 shows the ContactController class, which has all the methods in Table 12-6 implemented.

Listing 12-27. The ContactController Class

```java
package com.apress.prospring4.ch12;

import org.slf4j.Logger;
import org.slf4j.LoggerFactory;
import org.springframework.beans.factory.annotation.Autowired;
import org.springframework.stereotype.Controller;
import org.springframework.web.bind.annotation.PathVariable;
import org.springframework.web.bind.annotation.RequestBody;
import org.springframework.web.bind.annotation.RequestMapping;
import org.springframework.web.bind.annotation.RequestMethod;
import org.springframework.web.bind.annotation.ResponseBody;

@Controller
@RequestMapping(value="/contact")
public class ContactController {
    final Logger logger = LoggerFactory.getLogger(ContactController.class);

    @Autowired
    private ContactService contactService;

    @RequestMapping(value = "/listdata", method = RequestMethod.GET)
    @ResponseBody
    public Contacts listData() {
        return new Contacts(contactService.findAll());
    }

    @RequestMapping(value="/{id}", method=RequestMethod.GET)
    @ResponseBody
    public Contact findContactById(@PathVariable Long id) {
        return contactService.findById(id);
    }

    @RequestMapping(value="/", method=RequestMethod.POST)
    @ResponseBody
    public Contact create(@RequestBody Contact contact) {
        logger.info("Creating contact: " + contact);
        contactService.save(contact);
        logger.info("Contact created successfully with info: " + contact);
        return contact;
    }

    @RequestMapping(value="/{id}", method=RequestMethod.PUT)
    @ResponseBody
    public void update(@RequestBody Contact contact,
        @PathVariable Long id) {
        logger.info("Updating contact: " + contact);
```

```
        contactService.save(contact);
        logger.info("Contact updated successfully with info: " + contact);
    }

    @RequestMapping(value="/{id}", method=RequestMethod.DELETE)
    @ResponseBody
    public void delete(@PathVariable Long id) {
        logger.info("Deleting contact with id: " + id);
        Contact contact = contactService.findById(id);
        contactService.delete(contact);
        logger.info("Contact deleted successfully");
    }
}
```

The main points about Listing 12-27 are as follows:

- The class is annotated with @Controller, indicating that it's a Spring MVC controller.

- The class-level annotation @RequestMapping(value="/contact") indicates that this controller will be mapped to all URLs under the main web context. In this sample, all URLs under http://localhost:8080/ch12/contact will be handled by this controller.

- The ContactService within the service layer implemented earlier in this chapter is autowired into the controller.

- The @RequestMapping annotation for each method indicates the URL pattern and the corresponding HTTP method that it will be mapped to. For example, the listData() method will be mapped to the http://localhost:8080/ch12/contact/listdata URL, with an HTTP GET method. For the update() method, it will be mapped to the URL http://localhost:8080/ch12/contact/{id}, with an HTTP PUT method.

- The @ResponseBody annotation is applied to all methods. This instructs that all the return values from the methods should be written to the HTTP response stream directly.

- For methods that accept path variables (for example, the findContactById() method), the path variable is annotated with @PathVariable. This instructs Spring MVC to bind the path variable within the URL (for example, http://localhost:8080/ch12/contact/1) into the id argument of the findContactById() method. Note that for the id argument, the type is Long, while Spring's type conversion system will automatically handle the conversion from String to Long for us.

- For the create() and update() method, the Contact argument is annotated with @RequestBody. This instructs Spring to automatically bind the content within the HTTP request body into the Contact domain object. The conversion will be done by the declared instances of the HttpMessageConverter<Object> interface (under the package org.springframework. http.converter) for supporting formats, which will be discussed later in this chapter.

Configuring the RESTful Servlet

After the controller is completed, we can define it in Spring MVC. First we need to define a DispatcherServlet (under the package org.springframework.web.servlet) to instruct Spring MVC to dispatch all RESTful requests to the ContactController. To declare the servlet, add the code snippet in Listing 12-28 into the web deployment descriptor file (src/main/webapp/WEB-INF/web.xml).

Listing 12-28. *The Dispatcher Servlet for RESTful-WS*

```
<web-app xmlns="http://java.sun.com/xml/ns/javaee"
         xmlns:xsi="http://www.w3.org/2001/XMLSchema-instance"
         xsi:schemaLocation="http://java.sun.com/xml/ns/javaee
         http://java.sun.com/xml/ns/javaee/web-app_3_0.xsd"
         version="3.0">

    <display-name>Spring REST Sample</display-name>

    <listener>
        <listener-class>org.springframework.web.context.ContextLoaderListener</listener-class>
    </listener>

    <servlet>
        <servlet-name>restful</servlet-name>
        <servlet-class>org.springframework.web.servlet.DispatcherServlet</servlet-class>
        <init-param>
            <param-name>contextConfigLocation</param-name>
            <param-value>/WEB-INF/spring/rest-context.xml</param-value>
        </init-param>
        <load-on-startup>1</load-on-startup>
    </servlet>

    <servlet-mapping>
        <servlet-name>restful</servlet-name>
        <url-pattern>/restful/*</url-pattern>
    </servlet-mapping>
</web-app>
```

A servlet named restful is declared, which is of type DispatcherServlet (details of DispatcherServlet are discussed in Chapter 16). In Spring MVC, each DispatchServlet will have its own WebApplicationContext (however, all service-layer beans defined in the root-context.xml file, which is called the root WebApplicationContext, will be available for each servlet's own WebApplicationContext too).

The <servlet-mapping> tag instructs the web container (for example, Tomcat) that all URLs under the pattern /restful/* (for example, http://localhost:8080/ch12/restful/contact) will be handled by the restful servlet.

As shown in Listing 12-28, for the restful servlet, we also specify that the Spring WebApplicationContext for this DispatcherServlet should be loaded from rest-context.xml. Listing 12-29 shows the configuration file.

Listing 12-29. *The Spring WebApplicationContext for RESTful-WS*

```
<?xml version="1.0" encoding="UTF-8"?>
<beans xmlns="http://www.springframework.org/schema/beans"
       xmlns:xsi="http://www.w3.org/2001/XMLSchema-instance"
       xmlns:context="http://www.springframework.org/schema/context"
       xmlns:mvc="http://www.springframework.org/schema/mvc"
       xsi:schemaLocation="http://www.springframework.org/schema/beans
         http://www.springframework.org/schema/beans/spring-beans.xsd
         http://www.springframework.org/schema/context
         http://www.springframework.org/schema/context/spring-context.xsd
         http://www.springframework.org/schema/mvc
         http://www.springframework.org/schema/mvc/spring-mvc.xsd">
```

```
    <mvc:annotation-driven>
        <mvc:message-converters>
            <bean class="org.springframework.http.converter.json.
MappingJackson2HttpMessageConverter"/>
            <bean class="org.springframework.http.converter.xml.MarshallingHttpMessageConverter">
                <property name="marshaller" ref="castorMarshaller"/>
                <property name="unmarshaller" ref="castorMarshaller"/>
            </bean>
        </mvc:message-converters>
    </mvc:annotation-driven>

    <context:component-scan base-package="com.apress.prospring4.ch12"/>

    <bean id="castorMarshaller" class="org.springframework.oxm.castor.CastorMarshaller">
        <property name="mappingLocation" value="classpath:META-INF/spring/oxm-mapping.xml"/>
    </bean>
</beans>
```

The important points for Listing 12-29 are as follows:

- The `<mvc:annotation-driven>` tag enables the annotation support for Spring MVC (that is, the @Controller annotation), as well as registers Spring's type conversion and formatting system. In addition, JSR-303 validation support is also enabled under the definition of this tag.

- Under `<mvc:annotation-driven>`, the `<mvc:message-converters>` tag declares the instances of HttpMessageConverter that will be used for media conversion for supported formats. Note that the `<mvc:message-converters>` tag was introduced in Spring 3.1. Because we will support both JSON and XML as the data format, two converters are declared. The first one is MappingJackson2HttpMessageConverter, which is Spring's support for the Jackson JSON library (http://jackson.codehaus.org). The other one is MarshallingHttpMessageConverter, which is provided by the spring-oxm module for XML marshaling/unmarshaling. Within the MarshallingHttpMessageConverter, we need to define the marshaler and unmarshaler to use, which is the one provided by Castor in our case.

- For the castorMarshaller bean, we use the Spring-provided class org.springframework. oxm.castor.CastorMarshaller, which integrates with Castor, and we provide the mapping location that Castor requires for its processing.

- The `<context:component-scan>` tag instructs Spring to scan for the specified package for controller classes.

Now, the server-side service is complete. At this point, you should build the WAR file containing the web application, or if you are using an IDE such as STS, launch the Tomcat instance.

Using curl to Test RESTful-WS

Let's do a quick test of the RESTful web services that we implemented. One easy way is to use curl (http://curl.haxx.se), which is a command-line tool for transporting data with URL syntax. To use the tool, just download it from the web site and extract in onto your computer.

For example, to test the retrieval of all contacts, open a command prompt in Windows or a terminal in Unix/Linux, run the sample, and fire the command shown in Listing 12-30.

Listing 12-30. curl Command for Testing RESTful-WS with JSON output

```
curl -v -H "Accept: application/json" http://localhost:8080/ch12/restful/contact/listdata
...
{
  "contacts": [
    {
      "id": 1,
      "version": 0,
      "firstName": "Chris",
      "lastName": "Schaefer",
      "birthDate": {
        "year": 1981,
        "dayOfMonth": 2,
        "dayOfWeek": 6,
        "era": 1,
        "dayOfYear": 122,
        "weekyear": 1981,
        "weekOfWeekyear": 18,
        "monthOfYear": 5,
        "yearOfEra": 1981,
        "yearOfCentury": 81,
        "centuryOfEra": 19,
        "millisOfSecond": 0,
        "millisOfDay": 72000000,
        "secondOfMinute": 0,
        "secondOfDay": 72000,
        "minuteOfHour": 0,
        "minuteOfDay": 1200,
        "hourOfDay": 20,
        "chronology": {
          "zone": {
            "fixed": false,
            "uncachedZone": {
              "fixed": false,
              "cachable": true,
              "id": "America\/New_York"
            },
            "id": "America\/New_York"
          }
        },
        "zone": {
          "fixed": false,
          "uncachedZone": {
            "fixed": false,
            "cachable": true,
            "id": "America\/New_York"
          },
          "id": "America\/New_York"
        },
```

```
        "millis": 357696000000,
        "afterNow": false,
        "beforeNow": true,
        "equalNow": false
      }
    },
    {
      "id": 2,
      "version": 0,
      "firstName": "Scott",
      "lastName": "Tiger",
      "birthDate": {
        "year": 1990,
        "dayOfMonth": 1,
        "dayOfWeek": 4,
        "era": 1,
        "dayOfYear": 305,
        "weekyear": 1990,
        "weekOfWeekyear": 44,
        "monthOfYear": 11,
        "yearOfEra": 1990,
        "yearOfCentury": 90,
        "centuryOfEra": 19,
        "millisOfSecond": 0,
        "millisOfDay": 68400000,
        "secondOfMinute": 0,
        "secondOfDay": 68400,
        "minuteOfHour": 0,
        "minuteOfDay": 1140,
        "hourOfDay": 19,
        "chronology": {
          "zone": {
            "fixed": false,
            "uncachedZone": {
              "fixed": false,
              "cachable": true,
              "id": "America\/New_York"
            },
            "id": "America\/New_York"
          }
        },
        "zone": {
          "fixed": false,
          "uncachedZone": {
            "fixed": false,
            "cachable": true,
            "id": "America\/New_York"
          },
          "id": "America\/New_York"
        },
```

```json
        "millis": 657504000000,
        "afterNow": false,
        "beforeNow": true,
        "equalNow": false
      }
    },
    {
      "id": 3,
      "version": 0,
      "firstName": "John",
      "lastName": "Smith",
      "birthDate": {
        "year": 1964,
        "dayOfMonth": 27,
        "dayOfWeek": 4,
        "era": 1,
        "dayOfYear": 58,
        "weekyear": 1964,
        "weekOfWeekyear": 9,
        "monthOfYear": 2,
        "yearOfEra": 1964,
        "yearOfCentury": 64,
        "centuryOfEra": 19,
        "millisOfSecond": 0,
        "millisOfDay": 68400000,
        "secondOfMinute": 0,
        "secondOfDay": 68400,
        "minuteOfHour": 0,
        "minuteOfDay": 1140,
        "hourOfDay": 19,
        "chronology": {
          "zone": {
            "fixed": false,
            "uncachedZone": {
              "fixed": false,
              "cachable": true,
              "id": "America\/New_York"
            },
            "id": "America\/New_York"
          }
        },
        "zone": {
          "fixed": false,
          "uncachedZone": {
            "fixed": false,
            "cachable": true,
            "id": "America\/New_York"
          },
          "id": "America\/New_York"
        },
```

```
        "millis": -184377600000,
        "afterNow": false,
        "beforeNow": true,
        "equalNow": false
      }
    }
  ]
}
```

This command sends an HTTP request to the server's RESTful web service; in this case, it invokes the listData() method in ContactController to retrieve and return all contact information. Also, the –H option declares an HTTP header attribute, meaning that the client wants to receive data in JSON format. Running the command produces output in JSON format for the initially populated contact information that was returned. Now let's take a look at the XML format; the command is shown in Listing 12-31.

Listing 12-31. curl Command for Testing RESTful-WS with XML output

```
curl -v -H "Accept: application/xml" http://localhost:8080/ch12/restful/contact/listdata
...
<?xml version="1.0" encoding="UTF-8"?>
<contacts>
    <contact>
        <id>1</id>
        <firstName>Chris</firstName>
        <lastName>Schaefer</lastName>
        <birthDate>1981-05-02</birthDate>
        <version>0</version>
    </contact>
    <contact>
        <id>2</id>
        <firstName>Scott</firstName>
        <lastName>Tiger</lastName>
        <birthDate>1990-11-01</birthDate>
        <version>0</version>
    </contact>
    <contact>
        <id>3</id>
        <firstName>John</firstName>
        <lastName>Smith</lastName>
        <birthDate>1964-02-27</birthDate>
        <version>0</version>
    </contact>
</contacts>
```

As you can see, there is only one difference compared to Listing 12-30. The accept media was changed from JSON to XML. Running the command produces XML output instead. This is because of the HttpMessageConverters that were defined in the RESTful servlet's WebApplicationContext, while Spring MVC will invoke the corresponding message converter based on the client's HTTP header's accept media information and will write to the HTTP response accordingly.

Using RestTemplate to Access RESTful-WS

For Spring-based applications, the `RestTemplate` class is designed to access RESTful web services. In this section, we show how to use the class to access the contact service on the server.

First let's take a look at the basic `ApplicationContext` configuration for Spring's `RestTemplate`, as shown in Listing 12-32 (`restful-client-app-context.xml`).

Listing 12-32. The `restful-client-app-context.xml` File

```xml
<?xml version="1.0" encoding="UTF-8"?>
<beans xmlns="http://www.springframework.org/schema/beans"
      xmlns:xsi="http://www.w3.org/2001/XMLSchema-instance"
      xsi:schemaLocation="http://www.springframework.org/schema/beans
       http://www.springframework.org/schema/beans/spring-beans.xsd">

    <bean id="restTemplate" class="org.springframework.web.client.RestTemplate">
        <property name="messageConverters">
            <list>
                <bean class="org.springframework.http.converter.xml.MarshallingHttpMessageConverter">
                    <property name="marshaller" ref="castorMarshaller"/>
                    <property name="unmarshaller" ref="castorMarshaller"/>
                    <property name="supportedMediaTypes">
                        <list>
                            <bean class="org.springframework.http.MediaType">
                                <constructor-arg index="0" value="application"/>
                                <constructor-arg index="1" value="xml"/>
                            </bean>
                        </list>
                    </property>
                </bean>
            </list>
        </property>
    </bean>

    <bean id="castorMarshaller" class="org.springframework.oxm.castor.CastorMarshaller">
        <property name="mappingLocation" value="classpath:META-INF/spring/oxm-mapping.xml"/>
    </bean>
</beans>
```

A `restTemplate` bean is declared using the `RestTemplate` class. The class uses Castor to inject the property `messageConverters` with an instance of `MarshallingHttpMessageConverter`, the same as the one on the server side. The mapping file will be shared between both the server and client sides. In addition, for the `restTemplate` bean, within the anonymous class `MarshallingHttpMessageConverter`, the property `supportedMediaTypes` is injected with an anonymous bean declaration of a `MediaType` instance, indicating that the only supported media is XML. As a result, the client is always expecting XML as the return data format, and Castor will help perform the conversion between POJO and XML.

Let's try the service to get all contacts first. Listing 12-33 shows the main testing program.

Listing 12-33. Testing RestTemplate

```
package com.apress.prospring4.ch12;

import org.springframework.context.support.GenericXmlApplicationContext;
import org.springframework.web.client.RestTemplate;

public class RestfulClientSample {
    private static final String URL_GET_ALL_CONTACTS =
            "http://localhost:8080/ch12/restful/contact/listdata";
    private static final String URL_GET_CONTACT_BY_ID =
            "http://localhost:8080/ch12/restful/contact/{id}";
    private static final String URL_CREATE_CONTACT =
            "http://localhost:8080/ch12/restful/contact/";
    private static final String URL_UPDATE_CONTACT =
            "http://localhost:8080/ch12/restful/contact/{id}";
    private static final String URL_DELETE_CONTACT =
            "http://localhost:8080/ch12/restful/contact/{id}";

    public static void main(String[] args) {
        GenericXmlApplicationContext ctx = new GenericXmlApplicationContext();
        ctx.load("classpath:META-INF/spring/restful-client-app-context.xml");
        ctx.refresh();

        Contact contact;
        RestTemplate restTemplate = ctx.getBean("restTemplate", RestTemplate.class);

        System.out.println("Testing retrieve all contacts:");
        Contacts contacts =
            restTemplate.getForObject(URL_GET_ALL_CONTACTS, Contacts.class);
        listContacts(contacts);
    }

    private static void listContacts(Contacts contacts) {
        for (Contact contact: contacts.getContacts()) {
            System.out.println(contact);
        }

        System.out.println("");
    }
}
```

Here the URLs for accessing various operations are declared, which will be used in later samples. In the main()
method, the instance of RestTemplate is retrieved, and then the RestTemplate.getForObject() is called (which
corresponds to the HTTP GET method), passing in the URL and the expected return type, which is the Contacts class
that contains the full list of contacts.

Make sure the application server is running. Running the program produces the following output:

```
Testing retrieve all contacts:
Contact - Id: 1, First name: Chris, Last name: Schaefer, Birthday: 1981-05-02T00:00:00.000-04:00
Contact - Id: 2, First name: Scott, Last name: Tiger, Birthday: 1990-11-01T00:00:00.000-05:00
Contact - Id: 3, First name: John, Last name: Smith, Birthday: 1964-02-27T00:00:00.000-05:00
```

As you can see, the `MarshallingHttpMessageConverter` registered within the `RestTemplate` converts the message into a POJO automatically.

Next, let's try to retrieve a contact by ID. Add the code snippet in Listing 12-34 into the `main()` method of the `RestfulClientSample` class.

Listing 12-34. *Testing* `RestTemplate` *to Obtain a Contact By ID*

```
System.out.println("Testing retrieve a contact by id :");
contact = restTemplate.getForObject(URL_GET_CONTACT_BY_ID, Contact.class, 1);
System.out.println(contact);
System.out.println("");
```

Here we use a variant of the `RestTemplate.getForObject()` method, which also passes in the ID of the contact we want to retrieve as the path variable within the URL (the `{id}` path variable in the `URL_GET_CONTACT_BY_ID`). If the URL has more than one path variable, you can use an instance of `Map<String,Object>` or use the varargs support of the method to pass in the path variables. With varargs, you need to follow the order of the path variable as declared in the URL. Running the program again produces the following output (other output has been omitted):

```
Testing retrieve a contact by id :
Contact - Id: 1, First name: Chris, Last name: Schaefer, Birthday: 1981-05-02T00:00:00.000-04:00
```

As you can see, the correct contact is retrieved. Now it's update's turn. Add the code snippet in Listing 12-35 into the `main()` method of the `RestfulClientSample` class.

Listing 12-35. *Testing* `RestTemplate` *for Update Operation*

```
contact = restTemplate.getForObject(URL_UPDATE_CONTACT, Contact.class, 1);
contact.setFirstName("John Doe");
System.out.println("Testing update contact by id :");
restTemplate.put(URL_UPDATE_CONTACT, contact, 1);
System.out.println("Contact update successfully: " + contact);
System.out.println("");
```

First we retrieve the contact we want to update. After the contact object is updated, we then use the `RestTemplate.put()` method, which corresponds to the HTTP PUT method, passing in the update URL, the updated contact object, and the ID of the contact to update. Running the program again produces the following output (other output has been omitted):

```
Testing update contact by id :
Contact update successfully: Contact - Id: 1, First name: John Doe, Last name: Schaefer, Birthday:
1981-05-02T00:00:00.000-04:00
```

Next is the delete operation. Add the code snippet in Listing 12-36 into the `main()` method of the `RestfulClientSample` class.

Listing 12-36. *Testing* `RestTemplate` *for the Delete Operation*

```
restTemplate.delete(URL_DELETE_CONTACT, 1);
System.out.println("Testing delete contact by id :");
contacts = restTemplate.getForObject(URL_GET_ALL_CONTACTS, Contacts.class);
listContacts(contacts);
```

The RestTemplate.delete() method is called, which corresponds to the HTTP DELETE method, passing in the URL and the ID. Then, all contacts are retrieved and displayed again to verify the deletion. Running the program again produces the following output (other output has been omitted):

```
Testing delete contact by id :
Contact - Id: 2, First name: Scott, Last name: Tiger, Birthday: 1990-11-01T00:00:00.000-05:00
Contact - Id: 3, First name: John, Last name: Smith, Birthday: 1964-02-27T00:00:00.000-05:00
```

As you can see, the contact with an ID of 1 is deleted. Finally, let's try the insert operation. Add the code snippet in Listing 12-37 into the main() method of the RestfulClientSample class.

Listing 12-37. Testing RestTemplate for Insert Operation

```
System.out.println("Testing create contact :");
Contact contactNew = new Contact();
contactNew.setFirstName("James");
contactNew.setLastName("Gosling");
contactNew.setBirthDate(new DateTime());
contactNew =
    restTemplate.postForObject(URL_CREATE_CONTACT, contactNew, Contact.class);
System.out.println("Contact created successfully: " + contactNew);
```

A new instance of the Contact object is constructed. Then the RestTemplate.postForObject() method is called, which corresponds to the HTTP POST method, passing in the URL, the Contact object we want to create, and the class type. Running the program again produces the following output:

```
Testing create contact :
Contact created successfully: Contact - Id: null, First name: James, Last name: Gosling, Birthday:
2014-03-13T00:00:00.000-04:00
```

The contact is created on the server and returned to the client.

Securing RESTful-WS with Spring Security

Any remoting service requires security to restrict unauthorized parties from accessing the service and retrieving business information or acting on it. RESTful-WS is no exception. In this section, we demonstrate how to use the Spring Security project to secure RESTful-WS on the server. In this example, we are using Spring Security 3.2 (as of this writing, the latest release is 3.2.1.RELEASE), which provides some useful support for RESTful-WS.

Using Spring Security to secure RESTful-WS is a three-step process. First, in the web application deployment descriptor (web.xml), we need to declare a filter; add the code snippet as shown in Listing 12-38.

Listing 12-38. Declaring Spring Security Filter in web.xml

```
<filter>
    <filter-name>springSecurityFilterChain</filter-name>
    <filter-class>org.springframework.web.filter.DelegatingFilterProxy</filter-class>
</filter>

<filter-mapping>
    <filter-name>springSecurityFilterChain</filter-name>
    <url-pattern>/restful/*</url-pattern>
</filter-mapping>
```

A filter is declared to enable Spring Security to intercept the HTTP request for an authentication and authorization check. Because we want to secure only RESTful-WS, the filter is applied only to the URL pattern /restful/* (see the <filter-mapping> tag).

The next step is to create the Spring Security configuration, which will reside in the root WebApplicationContext. Listing 12-39 shows the file (web-security.xml).

Listing 12-39. Spring Security Configuration

```
<?xml version="1.0" encoding="UTF-8"?>
<beans:beans xmlns="http://www.springframework.org/schema/security"
    xmlns:beans="http://www.springframework.org/schema/beans"
    xmlns:xsi="http://www.w3.org/2001/XMLSchema-instance"
    xsi:schemaLocation="http://www.springframework.org/schema/beans
        http://www.springframework.org/schema/beans/spring-beans.xsd
        http://www.springframework.org/schema/security
        http://www.springframework.org/schema/security/spring-security.xsd">

    <http pattern="/restful/**" create-session="stateless">
        <intercept-url pattern='/**' access='ROLE_REMOTE' />
        <http-basic />
    </http>

    <authentication-manager>
        <authentication-provider>
            <user-service>
                <user name="remote" password="remote" authorities="ROLE_REMOTE" />
            </user-service>
        </authentication-provider>
    </authentication-manager>
</beans:beans>
```

We declare the security namespace (note the line xmlns="http://www.springframework.org/schema/security") and use it as the default namespace for the configuration file. In the <http> tag, we declare that the resources under the URL /restful/** should be protected. The attribute create-session, which was new in Spring Security 3.1.0, is introduced to allow us to configure whether the HTTP session will be created upon authentication. Since the RESTful-WS we are using is stateless, we set the value to stateless, which instructs Spring Security not to create an HTTP session for all RESTful requests. This can help improve the performance of the RESTful services.

Next, in the <intercept-url> tag, we set that only users with the ROLE_REMOTE role assigned can access the RESTful service. The <http-basic/>tag specifies that only HTTP basic authentication is supported for RESTful services.

The <authentication-manager> tag defines the authentication information. Here we define a simple authentication provider with a hard-coded user and password (both set to remote) with the ROLE_REMOTE role assigned. In an enterprise environment, most likely the authentication will be done by either a database or an LDAP lookup. Finally, we import the Spring Security configuration in the root WebApplicationContext. Add the following line into the file root-context.xml:

```
<import resource="web-security.xml" />
```

Now the security setup is complete. If you run the RestfulClientSample class again, you will have the following output (other output has been omitted):

```
Exception in thread "main" org.springframework.web.cient.HttpClientErrorException: 401 Unauthorized
```

You will get the HTTP status code 401, which means you are not authorized to access the service. Now let's configure the client's RestTemplate to provide the credential information to the server.

First the configuration for the RESTful client program needs to be revised. Listing 12-40 shows the revised configuration file (restful-client-app-context.xml).

Listing 12-40. Revised restful-client-app-context.xml File

```xml
<?xml version="1.0" encoding="UTF-8"?>
<beans xmlns="http://www.springframework.org/schema/beans"
    xmlns:xsi="http://www.w3.org/2001/XMLSchema-instance"
    xsi:schemaLocation="http://www.springframework.org/schema/beans
        http://www.springframework.org/schema/beans/spring-beans.xsd">

    <bean id="restTemplate"
        class="org.springframework.web.client.RestTemplate">
        <constructor-arg ref="httpRequestFactory"/>
        <property name="messageConverters">
            <!-- Setting same as before and omitted here -->
        </property>
    </bean>

    <bean id="castorMarshaller"
        class="org.springframework.oxm.castor.CastorMarshaller">
        <property name="mappingLocation" value="classpath:META-INF/spring/oxm-mapping.xml"/>
    </bean>

    <bean id="httpRequestFactory"
        class="org.springframework.http.client.HttpComponentsClientHttpRequestFactory">
        <constructor-arg>
            <bean class="org.apache.http.impl.client.DefaultHttpClient">
                <property name="credentialsProvider">
                    <bean class="com.apress.prospring4.ch12.CustomCredentialsProvider">
                        <property name="credentials">
                            <bean class="org.apache.http.auth.UsernamePasswordCredentials">
                                <constructor-arg name="userName" value="remote"/>
                                <constructor-arg name="password" value="remote"/>
                            </bean>
                        </property>
                    </bean>
                </property>
            </bean>
        </constructor-arg>
    </bean>
</beans>
```

In the restTemplate bean, a constructor argument with a reference to the httpRequestFactory bean is injected. For the httpRequestFactory bean, the HttpComponentsClientHttpRequestFactory class is used, which is Spring's support for the Apache HttpComponents HttpClient library, and we need the library to construct an instance of DefaultHttpClient that stores the credentials for our client. To support the injection of credentials, we implement a simple CustomCredentialsProvider class, as shown in Listing 12-41.

Listing 12-41. The `CustomCredentialsProvider` Class

```
package com.apress.prospring4.ch12;

import org.apache.http.auth.AuthScope;
import org.apache.http.auth.Credentials;
import org.apache.http.impl.client.BasicCredentialsProvider;

public class CustomCredentialsProvider extends BasicCredentialsProvider {
    public void setCredentials(Credentials credentials) {
        this.setCredentials(AuthScope.ANY, credentials);
    }
}
```

The class extends the `BasicCredentialsProvider` class within the HttpComponents library, and a new setter method is implemented to support the injection of a credential. Looking back at Listing 12-40, you will see that the credential is injected into this class by using an instance of the `UsernamePasswordCredentials` class. The `UsernamePasswordCredentials` class is constructed with the remote username and password. With the `httpRequestFactory` constructed and injected into the `RestTemplate`, all RESTful requests fired using this template will carry the credential provided. Now we can simply run the `RestfulClientSample` class again, and you will see that the services are invoked as usual.

Using AMQP in Spring

Remoting can also be accomplished by using remote procedure call) RPC style communication via Advanced Message Queuing Protocol (AMQP) as a transport. Similar to using JMS, AMQP also uses a message broker to exchange messages through. In this example, we use RabbitMQ (`www.rabbitmq.org`) as the AMQP server. Spring itself does not provide remoting capabilities in the core framework. Instead, they are handled by a sister project called Spring AMQP (`http://projects.spring.io/spring-amqp`), which we use as the underlying communication API. The Spring AMQP project provides a base abstraction around AMQP and an implementation for communicating with RabbitMQ. In this chapter, we won't cover all of AMQP or Spring AMQP's features, just the remoting functionality via RPC communication.

First, you will need to obtain RabbitMQ from `www.rabbitmq.com/download.html` and start the server. RabbitMQ will work fine out of box for our needs, and no configuration changes are needed.

Once RabbitMQ is running, the next thing we need to do is create a service interface. In this example, we create a simple Weather Service that returns a forecast for the provided state code. Let's get started by creating the `WeatherService` interface shown in Listing 12-42.

Listing 12-42. The `WeatherService` Interface

```
package com.apress.prospring4.ch12;

public interface WeatherService {
    String getForecast(String stateCode);
}
```

Next, let's create an implementation of `WeatherService` that will simply reply with a weather forecast for the provided state, or an unavailable message if no forecast is available, as shown in Listing 12-43.

Listing 12-43. The WeatherService Implementation

```
package com.apress.prospring4.ch12;

public class WeatherServiceImpl implements WeatherService {
    @Override
    public String getForecast(String stateCode) {
        if ("FL".equals(stateCode)) {
            return "Hot";
        } else if ("MA".equals(stateCode)) {
            return "Cold";
        }

        return "Not available at this time";
    }
}
```

With our weather service code in place, let's build our configuration file (`amqp-rpc-app-context.xml`) that will configure our AMQP connection and expose our WeatherService, as shown in Listing 12-44.

Listing 12-44. The WeatherService Configuration

```
<?xml version="1.0" encoding="UTF-8"?>
<beans xmlns="http://www.springframework.org/schema/beans"
       xmlns:xsi="http://www.w3.org/2001/XMLSchema-instance"
       xmlns:rabbit="http://www.springframework.org/schema/rabbit"
       xsi:schemaLocation="http://www.springframework.org/schema/beans
        http://www.springframework.org/schema/beans/spring-beans.xsd
        http://www.springframework.org/schema/rabbit
        http://www.springframework.org/schema/rabbit/spring-rabbit.xsd">

    <rabbit:connection-factory id="connectionFactory" host="localhost" />

    <rabbit:template id="amqpTemplate" connection-factory="connectionFactory"
                    reply-timeout="2000" routing-key="forecasts"
                    exchange="weather" />

    <rabbit:admin connection-factory="connectionFactory" />

    <rabbit:queue name="forecasts" />

    <rabbit:direct-exchange name="weather">
        <rabbit:bindings>
            <rabbit:binding queue="forecasts" key="forecasts" />
        </rabbit:bindings>
    </rabbit:direct-exchange>

    <bean id="weatherServiceProxy"
        class="org.springframework.amqp.remoting.client.AmqpProxyFactoryBean">
        <property name="amqpTemplate" ref="amqpTemplate" />
        <property name="serviceInterface" value="com.apress.prospring4.ch12.WeatherService" />
    </bean>
```

```
<rabbit:listener-container connection-factory="connectionFactory">
    <rabbit:listener ref="weatherServiceExporter" queue-names="forecasts" />
</rabbit:listener-container>

<bean id="weatherServiceExporter"
      class="org.springframework.amqp.remoting.service.AmqpInvokerServiceExporter">
    <property name="amqpTemplate" ref="amqpTemplate" />
    <property name="serviceInterface" value="com.apress.prospring4.ch12.WeatherService" />
    <property name="service">
        <bean class="com.apress.prospring4.ch12.WeatherServiceImpl"/>
    </property>
</bean>
</beans>
```

We configure our RabbitMQ connection along with exchange and queue information. We then create a bean by using the AmqpProxyFactoryBean class, which our client uses as a proxy to make an RPC request. For the response, we use the AmqpInvokerServiceExporter class, which gets wired into a listener container. The listener container is responsible for listening for AMQP messages and handing them off to our weather service. As you can see, the configuration is similar to JMS in terms of connections, queues, listener containers, and so on. While similar in configuration, JMS and AMQP are very different transports, and it's recommended to visit the AMQP web site (www.amqp.org) for full details on the protocol. With our configuration in place, let's create a sample class to execute RPC calls, as shown in Listing 12-45.

Listing 12-45. The AmqpRpcSample Class

```
package com.apress.prospring4.ch12;

import org.springframework.context.support.GenericXmlApplicationContext;

public class AmqpRpcSample {
    public static void main(String[] args) {
        GenericXmlApplicationContext ctx = new GenericXmlApplicationContext();
        ctx.load("classpath:META-INF/spring/amqp-rpc-app-context.xml");
        ctx.refresh();

        WeatherService weatherService = ctx.getBean(WeatherService.class);
        System.out.println("Forecast for FL: " + weatherService.getForecast("FL"));
        System.out.println("Forecast for MA: " + weatherService.getForecast("MA"));
        System.out.println("Forecast for CA: " + weatherService.getForecast("CA"));

        ctx.close();
    }
}
```

Now let's run the sample, and you should get the following output:

```
Forecast for FL: Hot
Forecast for MA: Cold
Forecast for CA: Not available at this time
```

Summary

In this chapter, we covered the most commonly used remoting techniques in Spring-based applications.

If both applications are running Spring, then using the Spring HTTP invoker is a viable option. If an asynchronous mode or loosely coupled mode of integration is required, JMS is a commonly used approach. We discussed how to use RESTful-WS in Spring for exposing services or accessing services with the `RestTemplate` class. Finally, we discussed how to use Spring AMQP for RPC-style remoting via RabbitMQ.

In the next chapter, we discuss using Spring for testing our applications.

CHAPTER 13

■ ■ ■

Spring Testing

When developing applications for enterprise use, testing is an important way to ensure that the completed application performs as expected and fulfills all kinds of requirements (architectural, security, user requirements, and so on). Every time a change is made, you should ensure that the changes that were introduced don't impact the existing logic. Maintaining an ongoing build and test environment is critical for ensuring high-quality applications. Reproducible tests with high coverage for all your code allow you to deploy new applications and changes to applications with a high level of confidence.

In an enterprise development environment, there are many kinds of testing that target each layer within an enterprise application, and each kind of testing has its own characteristics and requirements. In this chapter, we discuss the basic concepts involved in the testing of various application layers, especially in the testing of Spring-powered applications. We also cover the ways in which Spring makes implementing the test cases of various layers easier for developers. Specifically, this chapter covers the following topics:

- *Enterprise testing framework*: We briefly describe an enterprise-testing framework. We discuss various kinds of testing and their purposes. We focus on unit testing, targeting various application layers.

- *Logic unit test*: The finest unit test is to test only the logic of the methods within a class, with all other dependencies being "mocked" with the correct behavior. In this chapter, we discuss the implementation of logic unit testing for the Spring MVC controller classes, with the help of a Java mock library to perform the mocking of a class's dependencies.

- *Integration unit test*: In an enterprise-testing framework, integration testing refers to testing the interaction of a group of classes within different application layers for a specific piece of business logic. Typically, in an integration-testing environment, the service layer should test with the persistence layer, with the back-end database available. However, as application architecture evolves and the maturity of lightweight in-memory databases evolves, it's now a common practice to "unit test" the service layer with the persistence layer and back-end database as a whole. For example, in this chapter, we use JPA 2, with Hibernate and Spring Data JPA as the persistence provider and with H2 as the database. In this architecture, it's of less importance to "mock" Hibernate and Spring Data JPA when testing the service layer. As a result, in this chapter, we discuss testing of the service layer together with the persistence layer and the H2 in-memory database. This kind of testing is generally referred to as *integration unit testing*, which sits in the middle of unit testing and full-blown integration testing.

- *Front-end unit test*: Even if we test every layer of the application, after the application is deployed, we still need to ensure that the entire application works as expected. More specifically, for a web application, upon deployment to the continuous build environment, we should run front-end testing to ensure that the user interface is working properly. For example, for a contact application, we should ensure that each step of the normal functionality works properly, and we also should test exceptional cases (for example, how the application functions when information doesn't pass the validation phase). In this chapter, we briefly discuss a front-end testing framework.

Introducing an Enterprise Testing Framework

An *enterprise-testing framework* refers to testing activities in the entire application's life cycle. In various phases, different testing activities are performed to verify that the functionalities of the application are working as expected, according to the defined business and technical requirements.

In each phase, different test cases are executed. Some are automated, while others are performed manually. In each case, the result is verified by the corresponding personnel (for example, business analysts, application users, and so on).

Table 13-1 describes the characteristics and objectives of each type of testing, as well as common tools and libraries that are used for implementing the test cases.

Table 13-1. *Description of Enterprise Testing Framework*

Test Category	Description	Common Tools
Logic unit test	A logic unit test takes a single object and tests it by itself, without worrying about the role it plays in the surrounding system.	Unit test: JUnit, TestNG Mock object: Mockito, EasyMock
Integration unit test	An integration unit test focuses on testing the interaction between components in a "near real" environment. These tests will exercise the interactions with the container (embedded DB, web container, and so on).	Embedded DB: H2 database DB testing: DbUnit In-memory web container: Jetty
Front-end unit test	A front-end unit test focuses on testing the user interface. The objective is to ensure that each user interface reacts to users' actions and produces output to users as expected.	Selenium
Continuous build and code quality test	The application code base should be built on a regular basis to ensure that the code quality complies with the standard (for example, comments are all in place, no empty exception catch block, and so on). Also, test coverage should be as high as possible to ensure that all developed lines of codes are tested.	Code quality: PMD, Checkstyle, FindBugs, Sonar Test coverage: Cobertura, EclEmma Build tool: Gradle, Maven Continuous build: Hudson, Jenkins

(continued)

Table 13-1. (*continued*)

Test Category	Description	Common Tools
System integration test	The system integration test verifies the accuracy of communication among all programs in the new system and between the new system and all external interfaces. The integration test must also prove that the new system performs according to the functional specifications and functions effectively in the operating environment without adversely affecting other systems.	IBM Rational Systems Tester
Functional test	Use cases and business rules are tested by functional tests. The goals of these tests are to verify that inputs are accepted properly and outputs are generated properly, where *properly* means in accordance both with the use case specifications and with the business rules. This is black-box testing by interacting with the application via the GUI and analyzing the results.	IBM Rational Functional Tester, HP Unified Functional Testing
System quality test	The system quality test is to ensure that the developed application meets those nonfunctional requirements. Most of the time, this tests the performance of the application to ensure that the target requirements for concurrent users of the system and workload are met. Other nonfunctional requirements include security, high-availability features, and so on.	Apache JMeter, HP LoadRunner
User acceptance test	The user acceptance test simulates the actual working conditions of the new system, including the user manuals and procedures. Extensive user involvement in this stage of testing provides the user with invaluable training in operating the new system. It also benefits the programmer or designer to see the user experience with the new programs. This joint involvement encourages the user and operations personnel to approve the system conversion.	IBM Rational TestManager, HP Quality Center

In this chapter, we focus on the implementation of the three kinds of unit test (logic unit test, integration unit test, and front-end unit test) and show how the Spring TestContext framework and other supporting tools and libraries can help in developing those test cases.

Instead of presenting the full details and list of classes that the Spring Framework provides in the testing area, we cover the most commonly used patterns and the supporting interfaces and classes within the Spring TestContext framework as we implement the sample test cases in this chapter.

Using Spring Test Annotations

Before moving on to logic and integration tests, it's worth noting that Spring provides testing-specific annotations in addition to the standard annotations (such as @Autowired and @Resource). These annotations can be used in your logic and unit tests, providing various functionality such as simplified context file loading, profiles, test execution timing, and much more. Table 13-2 outlines the annotations and their uses.

Table 13-2. *Spring Testing Annotations*

Annotation	Description
@ContextConfiguration	Class-level annotation used to determine how to load and configure an ApplicationContext for integration tests.
@WebAppConfiguration	Class-level annotation used to indicate the ApplicationContext loaded should be a WebApplicationContext.
@ContextHierarchy	Class-level annotation providing the ability to define a hierarchy of ApplicationContexts for the given test. This annotation contains one or more @ContextConfiguration annotations representing the configuration files.
@ActiveProfiles	Class-level annotation indicating which bean profile should be active.
@DirtiesContext	Class- and method-level annotation used to indicate that the context has been modified or corrupted in some way during the execution of the test and should be closed and rebuilt for subsequent tests.
@TestExecutionListeners	Class-level annotation for configuring TestExecutionListeners that should be registered with the TestContextManager.
@TransactionConfiguration	Class-level annotation used to indicate transaction configuration such as rollback settings and a transaction manager (if your desired transaction manager does not have a bean name of transactionManager).
@Rollback	Class- and method-level annotation used to indicate whether the transaction should be rolled back for the annotated test method. Class-level annotations are used for testing class default settings.
@BeforeTransaction	Method-level annotation indicating that the annotated method should be called before a transaction is started for test methods marked with the @Transactional annotation.
@AfterTransaction	Method-level annotation indicating that the annotated method should be called after a transaction has ended for test methods marked with the @Transactional annotation.
@IfProfileValue	Class- and method-level annotation used to indicate that the test method should be enabled for a specific set of environmental conditions.
@ProfileValueSourceConfiguration	Class-level annotation used to specify the ProfileValueSource used by @IfProfileValue. If this annotation is not declared on the test, SystemProfileValueSource is used as the default.
@Timed	Method-level annotation used to indicate that the test must finish in the specified time period.
@Repeat	Method-level annotation used to indicate that the annotated test method should be repeated the specified number of times.

Implementing Logic Unit Tests

As previously discussed, a logic unit test is the finest level of testing. The objective is to verify the behavior of an individual class, with all the class's dependencies being "mocked" with expected behavior. In this section, we demonstrate a logic unit test by implementing the test cases for the ContactController class, with the service layer being mocked with expected behavior. To help mock the behavior of the service layer, we will use Mockito (http://code.google.com/p/mockito), which is a popular mocking framework.

Adding Required Dependencies

First we need to add the dependencies into the project, as shown in Table 13-3. We will also be building upon classes and interfaces created in prior chapters such as Contact, ContactService, and so on.

Table 13-3. *Maven Dependencies for Mockito*

Group ID	Artifact ID	Version	Description
org.mockito	mockito-core	1.9.5	Core library of the Mockito mocking framework
org.springframework	spring-context	4.0.2.RELEASE	Spring context module
org.springframework	spring-test	4.0.2.RELEASE	Spring test module
org.springframework	spring-web	4.0.2.RELEASE	Spring web module
junit	junit	4.11	JUnit testing framework
org.slf4j	slf4j-log4j12	1.7.6	SFL4J log4J library
joda-time	joda-time	2.3	JodaTime Date/Time library
org.jadira.usertype	usertype.core	3.0.0.GA	Time/Date user types for Hibernate/JodaTime

Unit Testing Spring MVC Controllers

In the presentation layer, controller classes provide the integration between the user interface and the service layer.

Methods in controller classes will be mapped to the HTTP requests. Within the method, the request will be processed, will bind to model objects, and will interact with the service layer (which was injected into the controller classes via Spring's DI) to process the data. Upon completion, depending on the result, the controller class will update the model and the view state (for example, user messages, objects for REST services, and so on) and return the logical view (or the model with the view together) for Spring MVC to resolve the view to be displayed to the user.

For unit testing controller classes, the main objective is to make sure that the controller methods update the model and other view states properly and return the correct view. As we want to test only the controller classes' behavior, we need to "mock" the service layer with the correct behavior.

For the ContactController class, we would like to develop the test cases for the listData() and create(Contact) methods. In the following sections, we discuss the steps for this.

Testing the listData() Method

Let's create our first test case for the ContactController.listData() method. In this test case, we want to make sure that when the method is called, after the list of contacts is retrieved from the service layer, the information is saved correctly into the model, and the correct objects are returned. Listing 13-1 shows the test case.

Listing 13-1. Testing the listData() Method

```java
package com.apress.prospring4.ch13;

import static org.junit.Assert.assertEquals;
import static org.mockito.Mockito.mock;
import static org.mockito.Mockito.when;

import java.util.ArrayList;
import java.util.List;

import org.junit.Before;
import org.junit.Test;

import org.mockito.invocation.InvocationOnMock;
import org.mockito.stubbing.Answer;

import org.springframework.test.util.ReflectionTestUtils;
import org.springframework.ui.ExtendedModelMap;

public class ContactControllerTest {
    private final List<Contact> contacts = new ArrayList<Contact>();

    @Before
    public void initContacts() {
        Contact contact = new Contact();
        contact.setId(1l);
        contact.setFirstName("Chris");
        contact.setLastName("Schaefer");
        contacts.add(contact);
    }

    @Test
    public void testList() throws Exception {
        ContactService contactService = mock(ContactService.class);
        when(contactService.findAll()).thenReturn(contacts);

        ContactController contactController = new ContactController();

        ReflectionTestUtils.setField(contactController, "contactService", contactService);

        ExtendedModelMap uiModel = new ExtendedModelMap();
        uiModel.addAttribute("contacts", contactController.listData());

        Contacts modelContacts = (Contacts) uiModel.get("contacts");

        assertEquals(1, modelContacts.getContacts().size());
    }
}
```

First, the test case calls the initContacts() method, which is applied with the @Before annotation, which indicates to JUnit that the method should be run before running each test case (in case you want to run some logic before the entire test class, use the @BeforeClass annotation). In the method, a list of contacts is initialized with hard-coded information.

Second, the testList() method is applied with the @Test annotation, which indicates to JUnit that it's a test case that JUnit should run. Within the test case, the private variable contactService (of type ContactService) is mocked by using Mockito's Mockito.mock() method (note the import static statement). The when() method is also provided by Mockito to mock the ContactService.findAll() method, which will be used by the ContactController class.

Third, an instance of the ContactController class is created, and then its contactService variable, which will be injected by Spring in normal situations, is set with the mocked instance by using the Spring-provided ReflectionTestUtils class's setField() method. ReflectionTestUtils provides a collection of reflection-based utility methods for use in unit and integration testing scenarios. In addition, an instance of the ExtendedModelMap class (which implements the org.springframework.ui.Model interface) is constructed.

Next, the ContactController.listData() method is called. Upon invocation, the result is verified by calling the various assert methods (provided by JUnit) to ensure that the list of contact information is saved correctly in the model used by the view.

Now we can run the test case, and it should run successfully. You can verify this via your build system or IDE. We can now proceed with the create() method.

Testing the create() Method

Listing 13-2 shows the code snippet for testing the create() method.

Listing 13-2. Testing the create() Method

```
package com.apress.prospring4.ch13;

...

import org.mockito.stubbing.Answer;
import org.mockito.invocation.InvocationOnMock;

...

public class ContactControllerTests {
    ...

    @Test
    public void testCreate() {
        final Contact newContact = new Contact();
        newContact.setId(999l);
        newContact.setFirstName("Rod");
        newContact.setLastName("Johnson");

        ContactService contactService = mock(ContactService.class);
        when(contactService.save(newContact)).thenAnswer(new Answer<Contact>() {
            public Contact answer(InvocationOnMock invocation) throws Throwable {
                contacts.add(newContact);
                return newContact;
            }
        });
```

```
        ContactController contactController = new ContactController();
        ReflectionTestUtils.setField(contactController, "contactService",
                contactService);

        Contact contact = contactController.create(newContact);
        assertEquals(Long.valueOf(999l), contact.getId());
        assertEquals("Rod", contact.getFirstName());
        assertEquals("Johnson", contact.getLastName());

        assertEquals(2, contacts.size());
    }
}
```

The `ContactService.save()` method is mocked to simulate the addition of a new `Contact` object in the list of contacts. Note the use of the `org.mockito.stubbing.Answer<T>` interface, which mocks the method with the expected logic and returns a value.

Then, the `ContactController.create()` method is called, and assert operations are invoked to verify the result. Run the result again, and note the test case results.

For the `create()` method, we should create more test cases to test various scenarios. For example, we need to test when data access errors are encountered during the save operation.

Implementing an Integration Test

In this section, we will implement the integration test for the service layer. In the contact application, the core service is the class `com.apress.prospring4.ch13.ContactServiceImpl`, which is the JPA implementation of the `com.apress.prospring4.ch13.ContactService` interface.

When unit testing the service layer, we will use the H2 in-memory database to host the data model and testing data, with the JPA providers (Hibernate and Spring Data JPA's repository abstraction) in place. The objective is to ensure that the `ContactServiceImpl` class is performing the business functions correctly.

In the following sections, we show how to test some of the finder methods and the save operation of the `ContactServiceImpl` class.

Adding Required Dependencies

For implementing test cases with the database in place, we need a library that can help populate the desired testing data in the database before executing the test case and that can perform the necessary database operations easily. Moreover, in order to make it easier to prepare the test data, we will support the preparation of test data in Microsoft Excel format.

To fulfill these purposes, additional libraries are required. On the database side, DbUnit (http://dbunit.sourceforge.net) is a common library that can help implement database-related testing. In addition, the Apache POI (http://poi.apache.org) project's library will be used to help parse the test data that was prepared in Microsoft Excel. Table 13-4 shows the required dependencies.

Table 13-4. *Maven Dependencies for Integration Unit Test*

Group ID	Artifact ID	Version	Description
`org.dbunit`	`dbunit`	2.4.9	DbUnit library
`org.apache.poi`	`poi`	3.2-FINAL	Apache POI library that supports reading and writing of files in Microsoft Office format. 3.2-FINAL is used due to incompatibilities with DbUnit.
`org.springframework.data`	`spring-data-jpa`	1.5.0	Spring Data JPA module
`org.springframework`	`spring-orm`	4.0.2.RELEASE	Spring ORM module
`com.h2database`	`h2`	1.3.172	H2 database
`javax.validation`	`validation-api`	1.1.0.Final	JSR-349 validation API
`org.hibernate`	`hibernate-validator`	5.1.0.Final	Hibernate JSR-349 validation API implementation
`javax.el`	`el-api`	2.2	EL library API

Configuring the Profile for Service-Layer Testing

The bean definition profiles feature introduced in Spring 3.1 is very useful for implementing a test case with the appropriate configuration of the testing components. To facilitate the testing of the service layer, we will also use the profile feature for the `ApplicationContext` configuration.

For the contact application, we would like to have two profiles, as follows:

- *Development profile* (dev): Profile with configuration for the development environment. For example, in the development system, the back-end H2 database will have both the database creation and the initial data population scripts executed.

- *Testing profile* (test): Profile with configuration for the testing environment. For example, in the testing environment, the back-end H2 database will have only the database creation script executed, while the data will be populated by the test case.

Let's configure the profile environment for the contact application. For the contact application, the back-end configuration (that is data source, JPA, transaction, and so on) was defined in the configuration XML file `datasource-tx-jpa.xml`. We would like to configure the data source in the file for the dev profile only. To do this, we need to wrap the data source bean with the profile configuration. Listing 13-3 shows the code snippet for the change required.

Listing 13-3. Configure Profile for Data Source

```xml
<?xml version="1.0" encoding="UTF-8"?>
<beans xmlns="http://www.springframework.org/schema/beans"
       xmlns:xsi="http://www.w3.org/2001/XMLSchema-instance"
       xmlns:context="http://www.springframework.org/schema/context"
       xmlns:jdbc="http://www.springframework.org/schema/jdbc"
       xmlns:jpa="http://www.springframework.org/schema/data/jpa"
       xmlns:tx="http://www.springframework.org/schema/tx"
       xsi:schemaLocation="http://www.springframework.org/schema/beans
        http://www.springframework.org/schema/beans/spring-beans.xsd
        http://www.springframework.org/schema/context
```

```
            http://www.springframework.org/schema/context/spring-context.xsd
            http://www.springframework.org/schema/jdbc
            http://www.springframework.org/schema/jdbc/spring-jdbc.xsd
            http://www.springframework.org/schema/data/jpa
            http://www.springframework.org/schema/data/jpa/spring-jpa.xsd
            http://www.springframework.org/schema/tx
            http://www.springframework.org/schema/tx/spring-tx.xsd">

    <bean id="transactionManager" class="org.springframework.orm.jpa.JpaTransactionManager">
        <property name="entityManagerFactory" ref="emf"/>
    </bean>

    <tx:annotation-driven transaction-manager="transactionManager" />

    <bean id="emf" class="org.springframework.orm.jpa.LocalContainerEntityManagerFactoryBean">
        <property name="dataSource" ref="dataSource" />
        <property name="jpaVendorAdapter">
            <bean class="org.springframework.orm.jpa.vendor.HibernateJpaVendorAdapter" />
        </property>
        <property name="packagesToScan" value="com.apress.prospring4.ch13"/>
        <property name="jpaProperties">
            <props>
                <prop key="hibernate.dialect">org.hibernate.dialect.H2Dialect</prop>
                <prop key="hibernate.max_fetch_depth">3</prop>
                <prop key="hibernate.jdbc.fetch_size">50</prop>
                <prop key="hibernate.jdbc.batch_size">10</prop>
                <prop key="hibernate.show_sql">true</prop>
            </props>
        </property>
    </bean>

    <context:annotation-config/>

    <jpa:repositories base-package="com.apress.prospring4.ch13"
                      entity-manager-factory-ref="emf"
                      transaction-manager-ref="transactionManager"/>

    <beans profile="dev">
        <jdbc:embedded-database id="dataSource" type="H2">
            <jdbc:script location="classpath:META-INF/config/schema.sql"/>
            <jdbc:script location="classpath:META-INF/config/test-data.sql"/>
        </jdbc:embedded-database>
    </beans>
</beans>
```

As shown in the code snippet, the dataSource bean is wrapped with the <beans> tag and given the profile attribute with the value dev, which indicates that the data source is applicable only for the development system. Remember, profiles can be activated by, for example, passing –Dspring.profiles.active=dev to the JVM as a system parameter.

Implementing the Infrastructure Classes

Before implementing the individual test case, we need to implement some classes to support the population of test data in the Excel file. Moreover, to ease the development of the test case, we want to introduce a custom annotation called @DataSets, which accepts the Excel file name as the argument. We will develop a custom test execution listener (a feature supported by the Spring testing framework) to check for the existence of the annotation and load the data accordingly.

In the following sections, we discuss how to implement the various infrastructure classes and the custom listener that loads data from the Excel file.

Implementing Custom TestExecutionListener

In the spring-test module, the org.springframework.test.context.TestExecutionListener interface defines a listener API that can intercept the events in the various phases of the test case execution (for example, before and after the class under test, before and after the method under test, and so on). In testing the service layer, we will implement a custom listener for the newly introduced @DataSets annotation. The objective is to support the population of test data with a simple annotation on the test case. For example, to test the ContactService.findAll() method, we would like to have the code look like the code snippet in Listing 13-4.

Listing 13-4. Usage of the @DataSets Annotation

```
@DataSets(setUpDataSet="/com/apress/prospring4/ch13/ContactServiceImplTest.xls")
@Test
public void testFindAll() throws Exception {
    List<Contact> result = contactService.findAll();

    ...
}
```

The application of the @DataSets annotation to the test case indicates that before running the test, testing data needs to be loaded into the database from the specified Excel file.

First we need to define the custom annotation, which is shown in Listing 13-5.

Listing 13-5. The Custom Annotation (@DataSets)

```
package com.apress.prospring4.ch13;

import java.lang.annotation.ElementType;
import java.lang.annotation.Retention;
import java.lang.annotation.RetentionPolicy;
import java.lang.annotation.Target;

@Retention(RetentionPolicy.RUNTIME)
@Target(ElementType.METHOD)
public @interface DataSets {
    String setUpDataSet() default "";
}
```

The custom annotation @DataSets is a method-level annotation. In addition, implementing the TestExecutionListener interface, which is shown in Listing 13-6, will develop the custom test listener class.

Listing 13-6. The Custom Test Execution Listener

```
package com.apress.prospring4.ch13;

import org.dbunit.IDatabaseTester;
import org.dbunit.dataset.IDataSet;
import org.dbunit.util.fileloader.XlsDataFileLoader;
import org.springframework.test.context.TestContext;
import org.springframework.test.context.TestExecutionListener;

public class ServiceTestExecutionListener implements TestExecutionListener {
    private IDatabaseTester databaseTester;

    @Override
    public void afterTestClass(TestContext arg0) throws Exception {
    }

    @Override
    public void afterTestMethod(TestContext arg0) throws Exception {
        if (databaseTester != null) {
            databaseTester.onTearDown();
        }
    }

    @Override
    public void beforeTestClass(TestContext arg0) throws Exception {
    }

    @Override
    public void beforeTestMethod(TestContext testCtx) throws Exception {
        DataSets dataSetAnnotation = testCtx.getTestMethod().getAnnotation(DataSets.class);

        if (dataSetAnnotation == null ) {
            return;
        }

        String dataSetName = dataSetAnnotation.setUpDataSet();

        if (!dataSetName.equals("") ) {
            databaseTester = (IDatabaseTester)
                    testCtx.getApplicationContext().getBean("databaseTester");
            XlsDataFileLoader xlsDataFileLoader = (XlsDataFileLoader)
                    testCtx.getApplicationContext().getBean("xlsDataFileLoader");
            IDataSet dataSet = xlsDataFileLoader.load(dataSetName);

            databaseTester.setDataSet(dataSet);
            databaseTester.onSetup();
        }
    }

    @Override
    public void prepareTestInstance(TestContext arg0) throws Exception {
    }
}
```

After implementing the TestExecutionListener interface, a number of methods need to be implemented. However, in our case, we are interested only in the methods beforeTestMethod() and afterTestMethod(), in which the population and cleanup of the testing data before and after the execution of each test method will be performed. Note that within each method, Spring will pass in an instance of the TestContext class so the method can access the underlying testing ApplicationContext bootstrapped by the Spring Framework.

The method beforeTestMethod() is of particular interest. First, it checks for the existence of the @DataSets annotation for the test method. If the annotation exists, the test data will be loaded from the specified Excel file. In this case, the IDatabaseTester interface (with the implementation class org.dbunit.DataSourceDatabaseTester, which we will discuss later) is obtained from the TestContext. The IDatabaseTester interface is provided by DbUnit and supports database operations based on a given database connection or data source.

Second, an instance of the XlsDataFileLoader class is obtained from TestContext. The XlsDataFileLoader class is DbUnit's support of loading data from the Excel file. It uses the Apache POI library behind the scenes for reading files in Microsoft Office format. Then, the XlsDataFileLoader.load() method is called to load the data from the file, which returns an instance of the IDataSet interface, representing the set of data loaded.

Finally, the IDatabaseTester.setDataSet() is called to set the testing data, and the IDatabaseTester.onSetup() method is called to trigger the population of data.

In the afterTestMethod() method, the IDatabaseTester.onTearDown() method is called to clean up the data.

Implementing the Configuration Class

Let's proceed to implement the configuration class for the testing environment. Listing 13-7 shows the code using Java Config style configuration.

Listing 13-7. The ServiceTestConfig Class

```
package com.apress.prospring4.ch13;

import javax.sql.DataSource;

import org.dbunit.DataSourceDatabaseTester;
import org.dbunit.util.fileloader.XlsDataFileLoader;
import org.springframework.context.annotation.Bean;
import org.springframework.context.annotation.ComponentScan;
import org.springframework.context.annotation.Configuration;
import org.springframework.context.annotation.ImportResource;
import org.springframework.context.annotation.Profile;
import org.springframework.jdbc.datasource.embedded.EmbeddedDatabaseBuilder;
import org.springframework.jdbc.datasource.embedded.EmbeddedDatabaseType;

@Configuration
@ImportResource("classpath:META-INF/spring/datasource-tx-jpa.xml")
@ComponentScan(basePackages={"com.apress.prospring4.ch13"})
@Profile("test")
public class ServiceTestConfig {
    @Bean
    public DataSource dataSource() {
        return new EmbeddedDatabaseBuilder().setType(EmbeddedDatabaseType.H2)
            .addScript("classpath:schema.sql").build();
    }
```

```
@Bean(name="databaseTester")
    public DataSourceDatabaseTester dataSourceDatabaseTester() {
    DataSourceDatabaseTester databaseTester =
        new DataSourceDatabaseTester(dataSource());
    return databaseTester;
}

@Bean(name="xlsDataFileLoader")
public XlsDataFileLoader xlsDataFileLoader() {
    return new XlsDataFileLoader();
}
}
```

The ServiceTestConfig class defines the ApplicationContext for service-layer testing. First, the XML configuration file datasource-tx-jpa.xml is imported, which defines the transaction and JPA configuration that is reusable for testing. Then the @ComponentScan annotation is applied to instruct Spring to scan the service-layer beans that we want to test. The @Profile annotation specifies that the beans defined in this class belong to the test profile.

Second, within the class, another dataSource bean is declared that executes only the schema.sql script to the H2 database without any data. The custom test execution listener for loading test data from the Excel file used the databaseTester and xlsDataFileLoader beans. Note that the dataSourceDatabaseTester bean was constructed using the dataSource bean defined for the testing environment.

Unit Testing the Service Layer

Let's begin with unit testing the finder methods, including the ContactService.findAll() and ContactService.findByFirstNameAndLastName() methods. First we need to prepare the testing data in Excel format. A common practice is to put the file into the same folder as the test case class, with the same name. So, in this case, the file name is /src/test/java/com/apress/prospring4/ch13/data/ContactServiceImplTest.xls.

The testing data is prepared in a worksheet. The worksheet's name is the table's name (CONTACT), while the first row is the column names within the table. Starting with the second row, data is entered for the first and last name along with the birthdate. We specify the ID column, but no value is provided. This is because the ID will be populated by the database. See the book source code for an example Excel file.

Listing 13-8 shows the test class with test cases for the two finder methods.

Listing 13-8. Testing the Finder Methods

```
package com.apress.prospring4.ch13;

import static org.junit.Assert.assertEquals;
import static org.junit.Assert.assertNotNull;
import static org.junit.Assert.assertNull;

import java.util.List;

import org.junit.Test;
import org.junit.runner.RunWith;
import org.springframework.beans.factory.annotation.Autowired;
import org.springframework.test.context.ActiveProfiles;
import org.springframework.test.context.ContextConfiguration;
import org.springframework.test.context.TestExecutionListeners;
```

```
import org.springframework.test.context.junit4.AbstractTransactionalJUnit4SpringContextTests;
import org.springframework.test.context.junit4.SpringJUnit4ClassRunner;

@RunWith(SpringJUnit4ClassRunner. class)
@ContextConfiguration(classes = {ServiceTestConfig.class})
@TestExecutionListeners({ServiceTestExecutionListener.class})
@ActiveProfiles("test")
public class ContactServiceImplTest extends AbstractTransactionalJUnit4SpringContextTests {
    @Autowired
    ContactService contactService;

    @DataSets(setUpDataSet= "/com/apress/prospring4/ch13/ContactServiceImplTest.xls")
    @Test
    public void testFindAll() throws Exception {
        List<Contact> result = contactService.findAll();

        assertNotNull(result);
        assertEquals(1, result.size());
    }

    @DataSets(setUpDataSet="/com/apress/prospring4/ch13/ContactServiceImplTest.xls")
    @Test
    public void testFindByFirstNameAndLastName_1() throws Exception {
        Contact result = contactService.findByFirstNameAndLastName("Chris", "Schaefer");
        assertNotNull(result);
    }

    @DataSets(setUpDataSet="/com/apress/prospring4/ch13/ContactServiceImplTest.xls")
    @Test
    public void testFindByFirstNameAndLastName_2() throws Exception {
        Contact result = contactService.findByFirstNameAndLastName("Peter", "Chan");
        assertNull(result);
    }
}
```

The @RunWith annotation is the same as testing the controller class. The @ContextConfiguration specifies that the ApplicationContext configuration should be loaded from the ServiceTestConfig class. The @TestExecutionListeners annotation indicates that the ServiceTestExecutionListener class should be used for intercepting the test case execution life cycle. The @ActiveProfiles annotation specifies the profile to use. So, in this case, the dataSource bean defined in the ServiceTestConfig class will be loaded, instead of the one defined in the datasource-tx-jpa.xml file, since it belongs to the dev profile.

In addition, the class extends Spring's AbstractTransactionalJUnit4SpringContextTests class, which is Spring's support for JUnit, with Spring's DI and transaction management mechanism in place. Note that in Spring's testing environment, Spring will roll back the transaction upon execution of each test method so that all database update operations will be rolled back. To control the rollback behavior, you can use the @Rollback annotation at the method level.

There is one test case for the findAll() method and two test cases for the testFindByFirstNameAndLastName() method (one retrieves a result and one doesn't). All the finder methods are applied with the @DataSets annotation with the contact test data file in Excel. In addition, the ContactService is autowired into the test case from ApplicationContext. The rest of the code should be self-explanatory. Various assert statements are applied in each test case to make sure that the result is as expected.

Run the test case and ensure that it passes. Next, let's test the save operation. In our case, we would like to test two scenarios. One is the normal situation in which a valid contact is saved successfully, and the other is a contact error that should cause the correct exception to be thrown. Listing 13-9 shows the additional snippet for the two test cases.

Listing 13-9. Testing the Save Operation

```
package com.apress.prospring4.ch13;

...

import javax.persistence.EntityManager;
import javax.persistence.PersistenceContext;

import javax.validation.ConstraintViolationException;
...

public class ContactServiceImplTest extends AbstractServiceImplTest {
    @PersistenceContext
    private EntityManager em;

    ...

    @Test
    public void testAddContact() throws Exception {
        deleteFromTables("CONTACT");

        Contact contact = new Contact();
        contact.setFirstName("Rod");
        contact.setLastName("Johnson");

        contactService.save(contact);
        em.flush();

        List<Contact> contacts = contactService.findAll();
        assertEquals(1, contacts.size());
    }

    @Test(expected=ConstraintViolationException.class)
    public void testAddContactWithJSR349Error() throws Exception {
        deleteFromTables("CONTACT");

        Contact contact = new Contact();

        contactService.save(contact);
        em.flush();

        List<Contact> contacts = contactService.findAll();
        assertEquals(0, contacts.size());
    }
}
```

In the preceding listing, take a look at the testAddContact() method. Within the method, to ensure that no data exists in the CONTACT table, we call the convenient method deleteFromTables() provided by the AbstractTransactionalJUnit4SpringContextTests class to clean up the table. Note that after calling the save operation, we need to explicitly call the EntityManager.flush() method to force Hibernate to flush the persistence context to the database so that the findAll() method can retrieve the information from the database correctly.

In the second test method, the testAddContactWithJSR349Error() method, we test the save operation of a contact with a validation error. Note that in the @Test annotation, an expected attribute is passed, which specifies that this test case is expected to throw an exception with the specified type, which in this case is the ConstraintViolationException class.

Run the test class again and verify that the result is successful.

Note that we covered only the most commonly used classes within Spring's testing framework. Spring's testing framework provides a lot of support classes and annotations that allow us to apply fine control during the execution of the test case life cycle. For example, the @BeforeTransaction and @AfterTransaction annotations allow certain logic to be executed before Spring initiates a transaction or after a transaction is completed for the test case. For a more detailed description of the various aspects of Spring's testing framework, kindly refer to Spring's reference documentation.

Implementing a Front-End Unit Test

Another testing area of particular interest is testing the front-end behavior as a whole, upon the deployment of the web application to a web container like Apache Tomcat.

The main reason is that even though we test every layer within the application, we still need to make sure that the views behave correctly with different actions from users. Automating front-end testing is very important in saving time for developers and users when repeating the actions on the front end for a test case.

However, developing a test case for a front end is a challenging task, especially for those web applications with a lot of interactive, rich, and Ajax-based components.

Introducing Selenium

Selenium is a powerful and comprehensive tool and framework target for automating web-based front-end testing. The main feature is that by using Selenium, we can "drive" the browsers, simulating user interactions with the application, and perform verification of the view status.

Selenium supports common browsers including Firefox, IE, and Chrome. In terms of languages, Java, C#, PHP, Perl, Ruby, and Python are supported. Selenium is also designed with Ajax and rich Internet applications (RIAs) in mind, making automated testing of modern web applications possible.

In case your application has a lot of front-end user interfaces and needs to run a large number of front-end tests, the selenium-server module provides built-in grid functionality that supports the execution of front-end tests among a group of computers.

The Selenium IDE is a Firefox plug-in that can help "record" user interactions with the web application. It also supports replay and exports the scripts into various formats that can help simplify the development of test cases.

Starting from version 2.0, Selenium integrates the WebDriver API, which addresses a number of limitations and provides an alternative, and simpler, programming interface. The result is a comprehensive object-oriented API that provides additional support for a larger number of browsers along with improved support for modern advanced web application testing problems.

Front-end web testing is a complex subject and beyond the scope of this book. From this brief overview, you can see how Selenium can help automate the user interaction with the web application front end with cross-browser compatibility. For more details, please refer to Selenium's online documentation (http://seleniumhq.org/docs).

Summary

In this chapter, we covered how to develop various kinds of unit testing in Spring-based applications with the help of commonly used frameworks, libraries, and tools including JUnit, DbUnit, and Mockito.

First, we presented a high-level description of an enterprise-testing framework, which shows what tests should be executed in each phase of the application development life cycle. Second, we developed two types of tests, including a logic unit test and integration unit test. We then briefly touched on the front-end testing framework Selenium.

Testing an enterprise application is a huge topic, and if you want to have a more detailed understanding of the JUnit library, we recommend the book *JUnit in Action*, by Petar Tahchiev et al (Manning, 2010).

CHAPTER 14

■ ■ ■

Scripting Support in Spring

In previous chapters, you saw how the Spring Framework can help Java developers create JEE applications. By using the Spring Framework's DI mechanism and its integration with each layer (via libraries within the Spring Framework's own modules or via integration with third-party libraries), you can simplify implementing and maintaining business logic.

However, all the logic we have developed so far was with the Java language. Although Java is one of the most successful programming languages in history, it is still criticized for some weaknesses, including its language structure and its lack of comprehensive support in areas such as massive parallel processing.

For example, one feature of the Java language is that all variables are statically typed. In other words, in a Java program, each variable declared should have a static type associated with it (`String`, `int`, `Object`, `ArrayList`, and so on). However, in some scenarios, dynamic typing may be preferred, which is supported by dynamic languages such as JavaScript.

To address those requirements, many scripting languages have been developed. Some of the most popular include JavaScript, Groovy, Scala, Ruby, and Erlang. Almost all of these languages support dynamic typing and were designed to provide the features that are not available in Java, as well as targeting other specific purposes. For example, Scala (`www.scala-lang.org`) combines functional programming patterns with OO patterns and supports a more comprehensive and scalable concurrent programming model with concepts of actors and message passing. In addition, Groovy (`http://groovy.codehaus.org`) provides a simplified programming model and supports the implementation of domain-specific languages (DSLs) that make the application code easier to read and maintain.

One other important concept that these scripting languages bring to Java developers is closures (which we discuss in more detail later in this chapter). Simply speaking, a *closure* is a piece (or block) of code wrapped in an object. Like a Java method, it's executable and can receive parameters and return objects and values. In addition, it's a normal object that can be passed with a reference around your application, like any POJO in Java.

In this chapter, we cover some of the main concepts behind scripting languages, with the primary focus on Groovy; you'll see how the Spring Framework can work with scripting languages seamlessly to provide specific functionality to Spring-based applications. Specifically, this chapter covers the following topics:

- *Scripting support in Java*: In JCP, JSR-223 ("Scripting for the Java Platform") enables the support of scripting languages in Java; it has been available in Java since SE 6. We provide an overview of scripting support in Java.

- *Groovy*: We present a high-level introduction to the Groovy language, which is one of the most popular scripting languages being used with Java.

- *Using Groovy with Spring*: The Spring Framework provides comprehensive support for scripting languages. Since version 3.1, out-of-the-box support for Groovy, JRuby, and BeanShell is provided.

This chapter is not intended to serve as a detailed reference on using scripting languages. Each language has one or more books of their own that discuss their design and usage in detail. The main objective of this chapter is to describe how the Spring Framework supports scripting languages, with a sound example showing the benefits of using a scripting language in addition to Java in a Spring-based application.

Working with Scripting Support in Java

Starting with Java 6, the Scripting for the Java Platform API (JSR-223) is bundled into the JDK. Its objective is to provide a standard mechanism for running logic written in other scripting languages on the JVM. Out of the box, JDK 6 comes bundled with the engine called Mozilla Rhino, which is able to evaluate JavaScript programs. This section introduces you to the JSR-223 support in JDK 6.

In JDK 6, the scripting support classes reside in the javax.script package. First let's develop a simple program to retrieve the list of script engines. Listing 14-1 shows the class content.

Listing 14-1. Listing Scripting Engines

```
package com.apress.prospring4.ch14;

import javax.script.ScriptEngineFactory;
import javax.script.ScriptEngineManager;

public class ListScriptEngines {
    public static void main(String[] args) {
        ScriptEngineManager mgr = new ScriptEngineManager();

        for (ScriptEngineFactory factory : mgr.getEngineFactories()) {
            String engineName= factory.getEngineName();
            String languageName = factory.getLanguageName();
            String version = factory.getLanguageVersion();
            System.out.println("Engine name: " + engineName + " Language: " + languageName  +
                                "version: " + version);
        }
    }
}
```

An instance of the ScriptEngineManager class is created, which will discover and maintain a list of engines (in other words, classes implementing the javax.script.ScriptEngine interface) from the classpath. Then, a list of ScriptEngineFactory interfaces is retrieved by calling the ScriptEngineManager.getEngineFactories() method. The ScriptEngineFactory interface is used to describe and instantiate script engines. From each ScriptEngineFactory interface, information about the scripting language support can be retrieved. Running the program may produce varied output, depending on your setup, and you should see something similar to the following in your console:

```
Engine name: AppleScriptEngine Language: AppleScript Version: 2.3.1
Engine name: Oracle Nashorn Language: ECMAScript Version: ECMA - 262 Edition 5.1
```

Let's write a simple program to evaluate a basic JavaScript expression. .The program is shown in Listing 14-2.

Listing 14-2. Evaluates a JavaScript Expression

```
package com.apress.prospring4.ch14;

import javax.script.ScriptEngine;
import javax.script.ScriptEngineManager;
import javax.script.ScriptException;
```

```
public class JavaScriptTest {
    public static void main(String[] args) {
        ScriptEngineManager mgr = new ScriptEngineManager();
        ScriptEngine jsEngine = mgr.getEngineByName("JavaScript");

        try {
            jsEngine.eval("print('Hello JavaScript in Java')");
        } catch (ScriptException ex) {
            ex.printStackTrace();
        }
    }
}
```

Here an instance of the `ScriptEngine` interface is retrieved from the `ScriptEngineManager` class, using the name `JavaScript`. Then, the `ScriptEngine.eval()`method is called, passing in a `String` argument, which contains a JavaScript expression. Note that the argument can also be a `java.io.Reader` class, which can read JavaScript from a file. Running the program produces the following result:

```
Hello JavaScript in Java
```

This should give you an idea of how to run scripts in Java. However, it's not of much interest to just dump some output using another language. In the next section, we introduce Groovy, a powerful and comprehensive scripting language.

Introducing Groovy

Started by James Strachan in 2003, the main objective of Groovy is to provide an agile and dynamic language for the JVM, with features inspired from other popular scripting languages including Python, Ruby, and Smalltalk. Groovy is built on top of Java, extends Java, and addresses some of the shortcomings in Java.

In the following sections, we discuss some main features and concepts behind Groovy and how it supplements Java to address specific application needs. Note that many features mentioned here also are available in other scripting languages (for example, Scala, Erlang, Python, and Clojure).

Dynamic Typing

One main difference between Groovy (and many other scripting languages) and Java is the support of dynamic typing of variables. In Java, all properties and variables should be statically typed. In other words, the type should be provided with the `declare` statement. However, Groovy supports the dynamic typing of variables. In Groovy, dynamic typing variables are declared with the keyword `def`.

Let's see this in action by developing a simple Groovy script. The file suffix of a Groovy class or script is `groovy`. Listing 14-3 shows a simple Groovy script with dynamic typing in action.

Listing 14-3. Dynamic Typing in Groovy

```
class Contact {
    def firstName
    def lastName
    def birthDate
```

```
    String toString() {
        "($firstName,$lastName,$birthDate)"
    }
}

Contact contact = new Contact(firstName: 'Chris', lastName: 'Schaefer', birthDate: new Date())
Contact anotherContact =
    new Contact(firstName: 42, lastName: 'Schaefer', birthDate: new Date())

println contact
println anotherContact

println contact.firstName + 42
println anotherContact.firstName + 42
```

This Groovy script can be run directly in an IDE, executed without compilation (Groovy provides a command-line tool called groovy that can execute Groovy scripts directly) or can be compiled to Java bytecode and then executed just like other Java classes. Groovy scripts don't require a main() method for execution. Also, a class declaration that matches the file name is not required.

In this example, a class Contact is defined, with the properties set to dynamic typing with the def keyword. Three properties are declared. Then, the toString() method is overridden with a closure that returns a string.

Next, two instances of the Contact object are constructed, with shorthand syntax provided by Groovy to define the properties. For the first Contact object, the firstName attribute is supplied with a String, while an integer is provided for the second Contact object. Finally, the println statement (the same as calling System.out.println() method) is used for printing the two contact objects. To show how Groovy handles dynamic typing, two println statements are defined to print the output for the operation firstName + 42. Note that in Groovy, when passing an argument to a method, the parentheses are optional.

Running the program produces the following output:

```
(Chris,Schaefer,Thu Mar 13 14:01:38 EDT 2014)
(42,Schaefer,Thu Mar 13 14:01:38 EDT 2014)
Chris42
84
```

From the output, you can see that since firstName is defined with dynamic typing, the object constructs successfully when passing in either a String or an integer as the type. In addition, in the last two println statements, the add operation was correctly applied to the firstName property of both objects. In the first scenario, since firstName is a String, the string 42 is appended to it. For the second scenario, since firstName is an integer, the integer 42 is added to it, resulting in 84.

Dynamic typing support of Groovy provides greater flexibility for manipulating class properties and variables in application logic.

Simplified Syntax

Groovy also provides simplified syntax so that the same logic in Java can be implemented in Groovy with less code. Some of the basic syntax is as follows:

- A semicolon is not required for ending a statement.

- In methods, the return keyword is optional.

- All methods and classes are `public` by default. So you don't need to declare the `public` keyword for method declaration, unless required.

- Within a class, Groovy will automatically generate the getter/setter methods for the declared properties. So in a Groovy class, you just need to declare the type and name (for example, `String firstName` or `def firstName`), and you can access the properties in any other Groovy/Java classes by using the getter/setter methods automatically. In addition, you can simply access the property without the get/set prefix (for example, `contact.firstName = 'Chris'`). Groovy will handle them for you intelligently.

Groovy also provides simplified syntax and many useful methods to the Java Collection API. Listing 14-4 shows some of the commonly used Groovy operations for list manipulation.

Listing 14-4. Groovy for Managing Lists

```
def list = ['This', 'is', 'Chris']
assert list.size() == 3
assert list.class == ArrayList

assert list.reverse() == ['Chris', 'is', 'This']

assert list.sort{ it.size() } == ['is', 'This', 'Chris']

assert list[0..1] == ['is', 'This']
```

The listing shows only a very small portion of the features that Groovy offers. For a more detailed description, please refer to the Groovy online documentation at `http://groovy.codehaus.org/JN1015-Collections`.

Closure

One of the most important features that Groovy adds to Java is the support of closures. A *closure* allows a piece of code to be wrapped as an object and to be passed freely within the application. Closure is a powerful feature that enables smart and dynamic behavior. The addition of closure support to the Java language has been requested for a long time. JSR-335, "Lambda Expressions for the Java Programming Language," which aims to support programming in a multicore environment by adding closures and related features to the Java language, has been added to Java 8 and supported by the new Spring Framework 4.

Listing 14-5 shows a simple example of using closures (the file name is `SimpleClosure.groovy`) in Groovy.

Listing 14-5. A Simple Closure Example

```
def names = ['Chris', 'Johnny', 'Mary']

names.each {println 'Hello: ' + it}
```

Here a list is declared. Then, the convenient each() method is used for an operation that will iterate through each item in the list. The argument to the each() method is a closure, which is enclosed in curly braces in Groovy. As a result, the logic in the closure will be applied to each item within the list. Within the closure, it is a special variable used by Groovy to represent the item currently in context. So, the closure will prefix each item in the list with the `String` "Hello: " and then print it. Running the script produces the following output:

```
Hello: Chris
Hello: Johnny
Hello: Mary
```

As mentioned, a closure can be declared as a variable and used when required. Another example is shown in Listing 14-6.

Listing 14-6. Define a Closure as Variable

```
def map = ['a': 10, 'b': 50]

Closure square = {key, value -> map[key] = value * value}

map.each square

println map
```

In this example, a map is defined. Then, a variable of type `Closure` is declared. The closure accepts the key and value of a map's entry as its arguments, and the logic calculates the square of the value of the key. Running the program produces the following output:

```
[a:100, b:2500]
```

This is just a simple introduction to closures. In the next section, we develop a simple rule engine by using Groovy and Spring; closures are used also. For a more detailed description of using closures in Groovy, please refer to the online documentation at `http://groovy.codehaus.org/JN2515-Closures`.

Using Groovy with Spring

The main benefit that Groovy and other scripting languages bring to Java-based applications is the support of dynamic behavior. By using a closure, business logic can be packaged as an object and passed around the application like any other variables.

Another main feature of Groovy is the support for developing DSLs by using its simplified syntax and closures. As the name implies, a DSL is a language targeted for a particular domain with very specific goals in design and implementation. The objective is to build a language that is understandable not only by the developers but the business analysts and users as well. Most of the time, the domain is a business area. For example, DSLs can be defined for customer classification, sales charge calculation, salary calculation, and so on.

In this section, we demonstrate using Groovy to implement a simple rule engine with Groovy's DSL support. The implementation is referencing the sample from the excellent article on this topic at `www.pleus.net/articles/grules/grules.pdf`, with modifications. In addition, we discuss how Spring's support of refreshable beans enables the update of the underlying rules on the fly without the need to compile, package, and deploy the application.

In this sample, we implement a rule used for classifying a specific contact into different categories based on their age, which is calculated based on their date-of-birth property.

Adding Required Dependencies

In the sample, we will use Groovy and the JodaTime library, so we need to add the required dependencies in Table 14-1 to our project.

Table 14-1. *Maven Dependencies for Groovy and JodaTime*

Group ID	Artifact ID	Version	Description
org.codehaus.groovy	groovy-all	2.2.2	Groovy library
joda-time	joda-time	2.3	JodaTime date-time type library

Developing the Contact Domain

As mentioned, a DSL targets a specific domain, and most of the time the domain is referring to some kind of business data. For the rule we are going to implement, it was designed to be applied to the domain of contact information.

So, the first step is to develop the domain object model we want the rule to apply to. This sample is very simple and contains only one Contact entity class, as shown in Listing 14-7. Note that it's a POJO class, like those we used in previous chapters.

Listing 14-7. The Contact Domain

```
package com.apress.prospring4.ch14;

import org.joda.time.DateTime;

public class Contact {
    private Long id;
    private String firstName;
    private String lastName;
    private DateTime birthDate;
    private String ageCategory;

    public Long getId() {
        return id;
    }

    public void setId(Long id) {
        this.id = id;
    }

    public String getFirstName() {
        return firstName;
    }

    public void setFirstName(String firstName) {
        this.firstName = firstName;
    }

    public String getLastName() {
        return lastName;
    }

    public void setLastName(String lastName) {
        this.lastName = lastName;
    }
```

```
    public DateTime getBirthDate() {
        return birthDate;
    }

    public void setBirthDate(DateTime birthDate) {
        this.birthDate = birthDate;
    }

    public String getAgeCategory() {
        return ageCategory;
    }

    public void setAgeCategory(String ageCategory) {
        this.ageCategory = ageCategory;
    }

    @Override
    public String toString() {
        return "Contact - Id: " + id + ", First name: " + firstName
                + ", Last name: " + lastName + ", Birthday: " + birthDate
                + ", Age category: " + ageCategory;
    }
}
```

Here the Contact class is simple contact information. For the ageCategory property, we want to develop a dynamic rule that can be used to perform classification. The rule will calculate the age based on the birthDate property and then assign the ageCategory property (for example, kid, youth, or adult) based on the rule.

Implementing the Rule Engine

The next step is to develop a simple rule engine for applying the rules on the domain object. First we need to define what information a rule needs to contain. Listing 14-8 shows the Rule class, which is a Groovy class (the file name is Rule.groovy).

Listing 14-8. The Rule Class

```
package com.apress.prospring4.ch14

class Rule {
    private boolean singlehit = true
    private conditions = new ArrayList()
    private actions = new ArrayList()
    private parameters = new ArrayList()
}
```

Each rule has several properties. The conditions property defines the various conditions that the rule engine should check for with the domain object under processing. The actions property defines the actions to take when a match on the condition is hit. The parameters property defines the behavior of the rule, which is the outcome of the action for different conditions. Finally, the singlehit property defines whether the rule should end its execution immediately whenever a match of condition is found.

The next step is the engine for rule execution. Listing 14-9 shows the RuleEngine interface (note it's a Java interface).

Listing 14-9. The RuleEngine Interface

```
package com.apress.prospring4.ch14;

public interface RuleEngine {
    void run(Rule rule, Object object);
}
```

The interface defines only a method run( ), which is to apply the rule to the domain object argument.

We will provide the implementation of the rule engine in Groovy. Listing 14-10 shows the Groovy class RuleEngineImpl (the file name is RuleEngineImpl.groovy).

Listing 14-10. The RuleEngineImpl Groovy Class

```
package com.apress.prospring4.ch14

import org.springframework.stereotype.Component

@Component("ruleEngine")
class RuleEngineImpl implements RuleEngine {
    public void run(Rule rule, Object object) {
        println "Executing rule"

        def exit=false

        rule.parameters.each{ArrayList params ->
            def paramIndex=0
            def success=true

            if(!exit){
                rule.conditions.each{
                    println "Condition Param index: " + paramIndex
                    success = success && it(object,params[paramIndex])
                    println "Condition success: " + success
                    paramIndex++
                }

                if(success && !exit){
                    rule.actions.each{
                        println "Action Param index: " + paramIndex
                        it(object,params[paramIndex])
                        paramIndex++
                    }
                    if (rule.singlehit){
                        exit=true
                    }
                }
            }
        }
    }
}
```

First RuleEngineImpl implements the RuleEngine Java interface, and Spring's annotation is applied like any other POJO. Within the run() method, the parameters defined in the rule are passed into a closure for processing one by one. For each parameter (which is a list of values), the conditions (each condition is a closure) are checked one by one with the corresponding item within the parameter's list and the domain object. The success indicator becomes true only when all the conditions result in a positive match. In this case, the actions (each action is a closure too) defined in the rule will be performed on the object, with the corresponding value within the parameter's list. Finally, if a match is found for a specific parameter and the singlehit variable is true, the rule execution will be stopped and will exit immediately.

To allow the retrieval of a rule in a more flexible way, let's define a RuleFactory interface, as shown in Listing 14-11. Note that it's a Java interface.

Listing 14-11. The RuleFactory Interface

```
package com.apress.prospring4.ch14;

public interface RuleFactory {
    Rule getAgeCategoryRule();
}
```

Since there is only one rule for an age category classification for contacts, the interface defines only a single method for retrieving the rule.

To make our rule engine transparent to the consumer, let's develop a simple service layer to wrap it up. Listing 14-12 and Listing 14-13 show the ContactService interface and the ContactServiceImpl class, respectively. Note that they are Java implementations.

Listing 14-12. The ContactService Interface

```
package com.apress.prospring4.ch14;

public interface ContactService {
    void applyRule(Contact contact);
}
```

Listing 14-13. The ContactServiceImpl Class

```
package com.apress.prospring4.ch14;

import org.springframework.beans.factory.annotation.Autowired;
import org.springframework.context.ApplicationContext;
import org.springframework.stereotype.Service;

@Service("contactService")
public class ContactServiceImpl implements ContactService {
    @Autowired
    ApplicationContext ctx;

    @Autowired
    private RuleFactory ruleFactory;

    @Autowired
    private RuleEngine ruleEngine;
```

```
    public void applyRule(Contact contact) {
        Rule ageCategoryRule = ruleFactory.getAgeCategoryRule();
        ruleEngine.run(ageCategoryRule, contact);
    }
}
```

In Listing 14-13, the required Spring beans are autowired into the service implementation class. In the applyRule() method, the rule is obtained from the rule factory and then applied to the Contact object. The result is that the ageCategory property for the Contact will be derived based on the rule's defined conditions, actions, and parameters.

Implementing the Rule Factory as a Spring Refreshable Bean

Now we can implement the rule factory and the rule for age category classification. We want to be able to update the rule on the fly and have Spring check for its changes and pick it up to apply the latest logic. The Spring Framework provides wonderful support for Spring beans written in scripting languages, called *refreshable beans*. We will see how to configure a Groovy script as a Spring bean and instruct Spring to refresh the bean on a regular interval later. First let's see the implementation of the rule factory in Groovy. To allow dynamic refresh, we put the class into an external folder so it can be modified. We will call this folder rules. The RuleFactoryImpl class (which is a Groovy class, with the name RuleFactoryImpl.groovy) will be placed into this folder. Listing 14-14 shows the class content.

Listing 14-14. The RuleFactoryImpl Class

```
package com.apress.prospring4.ch14

import org.joda.time.DateTime
import org.joda.time.Years
import org.springframework.stereotype.Component;

@Component
class RuleFactoryImpl implements RuleFactory {
    Closure age =
        { birthDate -> return Years.yearsBetween(birthDate, new DateTime()).getYears() }

    public Rule getAgeCategoryRule() {
        Rule rule = new Rule()

        rule.singlehit=true

        rule.conditions=[ {object, param -> age(object.birthDate) >=param},
                {object, param -> age(object.birthDate) <= param}]

        rule.actions=[{object, param -> object.ageCategory = param}]

        rule.parameters=[
                [0,10,'Kid'],
                [11,20,'Youth'],
                [21,40,'Adult'],
```

```
            [41,60,'Middle-aged'],
            [61,120,'Old']
        ]

        return rule
    }
}
```

The class implements the RuleFactory interface, and the getAgeCategoryRule() method is implemented to provide the rule. Within the rule, a Closure called age is defined to calculate the age based on the birthDate property (which is of JodaTime's DateTime type) of a Contact object.

Within the rule, two conditions are defined. The first one is to check whether the age of a contact is larger than or equal to the provided parameter value, while the second check is for the smaller-than or equal-to condition.

Then, one action is defined to assign the value provided in the parameter to the ageCategory property of the Contact object.

The parameters define the values for both condition checking and action. For example, in the first parameter, it means that when the age is between 0 and 10, then the value Kid will be assigned to the ageCategory property of the Contact object, and so on. So, for each parameter, the first two values will be used by the two conditions to check for age range, while the last value will be used for assigning the ageCategory property.

The next step is to define the Spring ApplicationContext. Listing 14-15 shows the configuration file (app-context.xml).

Listing 14-15. The Spring Configuration

```xml
<?xml version="1.0" encoding="UTF-8"?>
<beans xmlns="http://www.springframework.org/schema/beans"
       xmlns:xsi="http://www.w3.org/2001/XMLSchema-instance"
       xmlns:context="http://www.springframework.org/schema/context"
       xmlns:lang="http://www.springframework.org/schema/lang"
       xsi:schemaLocation="http://www.springframework.org/schema/beans
        http://www.springframework.org/schema/beans/spring-beans.xsd
        http://www.springframework.org/schema/context
        http://www.springframework.org/schema/context/spring-context.xsd
        http://www.springframework.org/schema/lang
        http://www.springframework.org/schema/lang/spring-lang.xsd">

    <context:component-scan base-package="com.apress.prospring4.ch14" />

    <lang:groovy id="ruleFactory" refresh-check-delay="5000"
                 script-source="file:rules/RuleFactoryImpl.groovy"/>
</beans>
```

The configuration is simple. For defining Spring beans in a scripting language, we need to use lang-namespace. Then, the <lang:groovy> tag is used to declare a Spring bean with a Groovy script. The script-source attribute defines the location of the Groovy script that Spring will load from. For the refreshable bean, the attribute refresh-check-delay should be provided. In this case, we supplied the value of 5000 ms, which instructs Spring to check for file changes if the elapsed time from the last invocation is greater than 5 seconds. Note that Spring will not check the file every 5 seconds. Instead, it will check the file only when the corresponding bean is invoked.

Testing the Age Category Rule

Now we are ready to test the rule. The testing program is shown in Listing 14-16, which is a Java class.

Listing 14-16. Testing the Rule Engine

```
package com.apress.prospring4.ch14;

import org.joda.time.format.DateTimeFormat;
import org.springframework.context.support.GenericXmlApplicationContext;

public class RuleEngineTest {
    public static void main(String[] args) {
        GenericXmlApplicationContext ctx = new GenericXmlApplicationContext();
        ctx.load("classpath:META-INF/spring/app-context.xml");
        ctx.refresh();

        ContactService contactService = ctx.getBean("contactService", ContactService.class);

        Contact contact = new Contact();
        contact.setId(1l);
        contact.setFirstName("Chris");
        contact.setLastName("Schaefer");
        contact.setBirthDate(DateTimeFormat.forPattern("yyyy-MM-dd").parseDateTime("1981-05-03"));

        contactService.applyRule(contact);
        System.out.println("Contact: " + contact);

        try {
            System.in.read();
        } catch (Exception ex) {
            ex.printStackTrace();
        }

        contactService.applyRule(contact);
        System.out.println("Contact: " + contact);
    }
}
```

Upon initialization of Spring's GenericXmlApplicationContext, an instance of the Contact object is constructed. Then, the instance of the ContactService interface is obtained to apply the rule onto the Contact object and then output the result to the console. The program will be paused for user input, before the second application of the rule. During the pause, we can then modify the RuleFactoryImpl.groovy class so that Spring will refresh the bean and we can see the changed rule in action.

Running the testing program produces the following output:

```
Executing rule
Condition Param index: 0
Condition success: true
Condition Param index: 1
Condition success: false
Condition Param index: 0
Condition success: true
Condition Param index: 1
Condition success: false
Condition Param index: 0
```

```
Condition success: true
Condition Param index: 1
Condition success: true
Action Param index: 2
Contact: Contact - Id: 1, First name: Chris, Last name: Schaefer,
Birthday: 1981-05-03T00:00:00.000-04:00, Age category: Adult
```

From the logging statement in the output, since the age of the contact is 32, you can see that the rule will find a matching in the third parameter (in other words, [21,40,'Adult']). As a result, the ageCategory is set to Adult.

Now the program is paused, so let's change the parameters within the RuleFactoryImpl.groovy class. Listing 14-17 shows the code snippet.

Listing 14-17. Modify Rule Parameters

```
rule.parameters=[
[0,10,'Kid'],
[11,20,'Youth'],
[21,30,'Adult'],
[31,60,'Middle-aged'],
[61,120,'Old']
]
```

Change and save the file as indicated. Now press the Enter key in the console area to trigger the second application of the rule to the same object. After the program continues, the following output is produced:

```
Executing rule
Condition Param index: 0
Condition success: true
Condition Param index: 1
Condition success: false
Condition Param index: 0
Condition success: true
Condition Param index: 1
Condition success: false
Condition Param index: 0
Condition success: true
Condition Param index: 1
Condition success: false
Condition Param index: 0
Condition success: true
Condition Param index: 1
Condition success: false
Condition Param index: 0
Condition success: true
Condition Param index: 1
Condition success: true
Action Param index: 2
Contact: Contact - Id: 1, First name: Chris, Last name: Schaefer,
Birthday: 1981-05-03T00:00:00.000-04:00, Age category: Middle-aged
```

In the previous output, you can see that the rule execution stops at the fourth parameter (in other words, [31,60,'Middle-aged']), and as a result, the value Middle-aged is assigned to the ageCategory property.

If you take a look at the article that was referred to when we prepared this sample (www.pleus.net/articles/grules/grules.pdf), it also shows how the rule parameter can be externalized into a Microsoft Excel file, so users can prepare and update the parameter file by themselves.

Of course, this rule is a simple one, but it shows how a scripting language such as Groovy can help supplement Spring-based Java EE applications in specific areas—for example, using a rule engine with DSL.

You may be asking, "Is it possible to go one step further by storing the rule into the database and then have Spring's refreshable bean feature detect the change from the database?" This can help further simplify the maintenance of the rule by providing a front end for users (or administrator) to update the rule into the database on the fly, instead of uploading the file. Actually, there is a JIRA issue in the Spring Framework that discusses this (https://jira.springsource.org/browse/SPR-5106). Stay tuned with this feature. In the meantime, providing a user front end to upload the rule class is also a workable solution. Of course, extreme care should be taken in this case, and the rule should be tested thoroughly before you upload it to the production environment.

Inlining Dynamic Language Code

Not only can dynamic language code be executed from external source files, but you can also inline this code directly into your bean configuration. While this practice may be useful in some scenarios such as quick proof of concepts and so on, from a maintainability standpoint, it would not be good practice to build an entire application by using this method. Using our previous Rule engine as an example, let's delete the file `RuleEngineImpl.groovy` and move that code into an inline bean definition (in file `app-context.xml`), as shown in Listing 14-18.

Listing 14-18. Inlined `RuleEngineImpl.groovy` code into `app-context.xml`

```xml
<?xml version="1.0" encoding="UTF-8"?>
<beans xmlns="http://www.springframework.org/schema/beans"
       xmlns:xsi="http://www.w3.org/2001/XMLSchema-instance"
       xmlns:context="http://www.springframework.org/schema/context"
       xmlns:lang="http://www.springframework.org/schema/lang"
       xsi:schemaLocation="http://www.springframework.org/schema/beans
        http://www.springframework.org/schema/beans/spring-beans.xsd
        http://www.springframework.org/schema/context
        http://www.springframework.org/schema/context/spring-context.xsd
        http://www.springframework.org/schema/lang
        http://www.springframework.org/schema/lang/spring-lang.xsd">

    <context:component-scan base-package="com.apress.prospring4.ch14" />

    <lang:groovy id="ruleFactory" refresh-check-delay="5000"
                 script-source="file:rules/RuleFactoryImpl.groovy"/>

    <lang:groovy id="ruleEngine">
        <lang:inline-script>
            <![CDATA[
package com.apress.prospring4.ch14

import org.springframework.stereotype.Component

class RuleEngineImpl implements RuleEngine {
    public void run(Rule rule, Object object) {
        println "Executing rule"

        def exit=false
```

```
        rule.parameters.each{ArrayList params ->
            def paramIndex=0
            def success=true

        if(!exit){
            rule.conditions.each{
                println "Condition Param index: " + paramIndex
                success = success && it(object,params[paramIndex])
                println "Condition success: " + success
                paramIndex++
            }

            if(success && !exit){
                rule.actions.each{
                    println "Action Param index: " + paramIndex
                    it(object,params[paramIndex])
                    paramIndex++
                }
                if (rule.singlehit){
                    exit=true
                }
            }
        }
    }
}
}
}
        ]]>
    </lang:inline-script>
  </lang:groovy>
</beans>
```

As you can see, we added the lang:groovy tag with an ID of ruleEngine representing the bean name. We then used the lang:inline-script tag to encapsulate our Groovy code from RuleEngineImpl.groovy. Surrounding our Groovy code is a CDATA tag to avoid our code being parsed by the XML parser. Now with that in place, go ahead and run the rule engine sample again. As you can see, it works the same way, except we inlined the Groovy code directly into the bean definition rather than having it reside in an external file. Using the code from RuleEngineImpl.groovy was also done intentionally to show how unwieldy an application can become when inlining large amounts of code.

Summary

In this chapter, we covered how to use scripting languages in Java applications and demonstrated how the Spring Framework's support of scripting languages can help provide dynamic behavior to the application.

First we discussed JSR-223, the Scripting for the Java Platform API, which was built into Java 6 and supports the execution of JavaScript out of the box. Then, we introduced Groovy, a popular scripting language within the Java developer communities. We also demonstrated some of its main features when compared to the traditional Java language.

Finally, we discussed the support of scripting languages in the Spring Framework. We saw it in action by designing and implementing a very simple rule engine using Groovy's DSL support. We also discussed how the rule can be modified and have the Spring Framework pick up the changes automatically by using its refreshable bean feature, without the need to compile, package, and deploy the application. Additionally, we showed how to inline Groovy code directly into a configuration file to define a bean's implementation code.

CHAPTER 15

■ ■ ■

Spring Application Monitoring

A typical JEE application contains a number of layers and components, such as the presentation layer, service layer, persistence layer, and back-end data source. During the development stage, or after the application had been deployed to the quality assurance (QA) or production environment, we want to ensure that the application is in a healthy state without any potential problems or bottlenecks.

In a Java application, various areas may cause performance problems or overload server resources (such as CPU, memory, or I/O). Examples are inefficient Java code, memory leaks (for example, Java code keeps allocating new objects without releasing the reference and prevents the underlying JVM from freeing up the memory during the garbage collection process), JVM parameters, thread pool parameters, data source configurations (for example, the number of concurrent database connections allowed), database setup, and long-running SQL queries.

Consequently, we need to understand an application's runtime behavior and identify whether any potential bottlenecks or problems exist. In the Java world, a lot of tools can help monitor the detailed runtime behavior of JEE applications. Most of them are built on top of the Java Management Extensions (JMX) technology.

In this chapter, we present common techniques for monitoring Spring-based JEE applications. Specifically, this chapter covers the following topics:

- *Spring support of JMX*: We discuss Spring's comprehensive support of JMX and demonstrate how to expose Spring beans for monitoring with JMX tools. In this chapter, we use VisualVM (http://visualvm.java.net/index.html) as the application-monitoring tool.

- *Monitoring Hibernate statistics*: Hibernate and many other packages provide support classes and infrastructure for exposing the operational status and performance metrics using JMX. We take a look at how to enable the JMX monitoring of those commonly used components in Spring-powered JEE applications.

Remember that this chapter is not intended to be an introduction to JMX, and a basic understanding of JMX is assumed. For detailed information, please refer to Oracle's online resource at www.oracle.com/technetwork/java/javase/tech/javamanagement-140525.html.

JMX Support in Spring

In JMX, the classes that are exposed for JMX monitoring and management are called *managed beans* (generally referred to as *MBeans*). The Spring Framework supports several mechanisms for exposing MBeans. This chapter focuses on exposing Spring beans (which were developed as simple POJOs) as MBeans for JMX monitoring.

In the following sections, we discuss the procedure for exposing a bean containing application-related statistics as an MBean for JMX monitoring. Topics include implementing the Spring bean, exposing the Spring bean as an MBean in Spring ApplicationContext, and using VisualVM to monitor the MBean.

Exporting a Spring Bean to JMX

As an example, we will use the "rest" sample from Chapter 12. Review that chapter for the sample application code, or jump directly to the book's source companion, which provides the source code we will use to build upon. With our JMX additions, we would like to expose the count of the contacts in the database for JMX monitoring purposes. So, let's implement the interface and the class, which are shown in Listings 15-1 and 15-2, respectively.

Listing 15-1. The AppStatistics Interface

```
package com.apress.prospring4.ch15;

public interface AppStatistics {
    int getTotalContactCount();
}
```

Listing 15-2. The AppStatisticsImpl Class

```
package com.apress.prospring4.ch15;

import org.springframework.beans.factory.annotation.Autowired;

public class AppStatisticsImpl implements AppStatistics {
    @Autowired
    private ContactService contactService;

    @Override
    public int getTotalContactCount() {
        return contactService.findAll().size();
    }
}
```

In this example, a method is defined to retrieve the total count of contact records in the database. To expose the Spring bean as JMX, we need to add configuration in Spring's ApplicationContext. Listing 15-3 shows the code snippet needed to expose a Spring bean to JMX in the configuration file (rest-context.xml).

Listing 15-3. Expose Spring Bean to JMX

```
<?xml version="1.0" encoding="UTF-8"?>
<beans xmlns="http://www.springframework.org/schema/beans"
       xmlns:xsi="http://www.w3.org/2001/XMLSchema-instance"
       xmlns:context="http://www.springframework.org/schema/context"
       xmlns:mvc="http://www.springframework.org/schema/mvc"
       xsi:schemaLocation="http://www.springframework.org/schema/beans
         http://www.springframework.org/schema/beans/spring-beans.xsd
         http://www.springframework.org/schema/context
         http://www.springframework.org/schema/context/spring-context.xsd
         http://www.springframework.org/schema/mvc
         http://www.springframework.org/schema/mvc/spring-mvc.xsd">

    <mvc:annotation-driven>
        <mvc:message-converters>
```

```
            <bean class="org.springframework.http.converter.json.
MappingJackson2HttpMessageConverter"/>
                <bean class="org.springframework.http.converter.xml.MarshallingHttpMessageConverter">
                    <property name="marshaller" ref="castorMarshaller"/>
                    <property name="unmarshaller" ref="castorMarshaller"/>
                </bean>
        </mvc:message-converters>
    </mvc:annotation-driven>

    <context:component-scan base-package="com.apress.prospring4.ch15"/>

    <bean id="castorMarshaller" class="org.springframework.oxm.castor.CastorMarshaller">
        <property name="mappingLocation" value="classpath:META-INF/spring/oxm-mapping.xml"/>
    </bean>

    <bean id="appStatisticsBean" class="com.apress.prospring4.ch15.AppStatisticsImpl"/>

    <bean id="jmxExporter" class="org.springframework.jmx.export.MBeanExporter">
        <property name="beans">
            <map>
                <entry key="bean:name=ProSpring4ContactApp" value-ref="appStatisticsBean"/>
            </map>
        </property>
    </bean>
</beans>
```

First, the bean for the POJO with statistics (AppStatisticsImpl) that we want to expose is declared. Second, the jmxExporter bean with the implementation class MBeanExporter is declared.

The MBeanExporter class is the core class within the Spring Framework's support for JMX. It's responsible for registering Spring beans with a JMX MBean server (a server that implements JDK's javax.management.MBeanServer interface, which exists in most commonly used web and JEE containers, such as Tomcat and WebSphere). When exposing a Spring bean as an MBean, Spring will attempt to locate a running MBeanServer instance within the server and register the MBean with it. For example, with Tomcat, an MBeanServer will be created automatically, so no additional configuration is required.

Within the jmxExporter bean, the property beans defines the Spring beans we want to expose. It's a Map, and any number of MBeans can be specified here. In our case, we would like to expose the appStatisticsBean bean, which contains information about the contact application we want to show to administrators. For the MBean definition, the key will be used as the ObjectName (the javax.management.ObjectName class in JDK) for the Spring bean referenced by the corresponding entry value. In the previous configuration, the appStatisticsBean will be exposed under the ObjectName bean:name=Prospring4ContactApp. By default, all public properties of the bean are exposed as attributes, and all public methods are exposed as operations.

Now the MBean is available for monitoring via JMX. Let's proceed to set up VisualVM and use its JMX client for monitoring purposes.

Setting Up VisualVM for JMX Monitoring

VisualVM is a very useful tool that can help in monitoring Java applications in various aspects. It's a free tool and resides under the bin folder in the JDK installation folder. A stand-alone version can also be downloaded from the project web site (http://visualvm.java.net/download.html). We use the stand-alone version in this chapter; at the time of this writing, the version is 1.3.7.

VisualVM uses a plug-in system to support various monitoring functions. To support monitoring MBeans of Java applications, we need to install the MBeans plug-in. To install the plug-in, follow these steps:

1. From VisualVM's menu, choose Tools ➤ Plug-ins.

2. Click the Available Plug-ins tab.

3. Click the Check for Newest button.

4. Select the plug-in VisualVM-MBeans and then click the Install button.

After completing the installation, verify that Tomcat is up and that the sample application is running. Then in VisualVM's left Applications view, you should be able to see that the Tomcat process is running.

By default, VisualVM scans for the Java applications that are running on the JDK platform. Double-clicking the desired node brings up the monitoring screen.

After the installation of the VisualVM-MBeans plug-in, you will able to see the MBeans tab. Clicking this tab shows the available MBeans. You should see the node called bean. When you expand it, it will show the Prospring4ContactApp MBean that was exposed.

On the right side, you will see the method that we implemented in the bean, with the attribute TotalContactCount (which was automatically derived by the getTotalContactCount() method within the bean). The value is 3, corresponding to the number of records we added in the database at application startup. In a regular application, this number would change based on the number of contacts added during the application runtime.

Monitoring Hibernate Statistics

Hibernate also supports the maintenance and exposure of persistence-related metrics to JMX. To enable this, in the JPA configuration (the file datasource-tx-jpa.xml file), add two more Hibernate properties, as shown in Listing 15-4.

Listing 15-4. Enable Hibernate Statistics

```
<?xml version="1.0" encoding="UTF-8"?>
<beans xmlns="http://www.springframework.org/schema/beans"
       xmlns:xsi="http://www.w3.org/2001/XMLSchema-instance"
       xmlns:context="http://www.springframework.org/schema/context"
       xmlns:jdbc="http://www.springframework.org/schema/jdbc"
       xmlns:jpa="http://www.springframework.org/schema/data/jpa"
       xmlns:tx="http://www.springframework.org/schema/tx"
       xsi:schemaLocation="http://www.springframework.org/schema/beans
         http://www.springframework.org/schema/beans/spring-beans.xsd
         http://www.springframework.org/schema/context
         http://www.springframework.org/schema/context/spring-context.xsd
         http://www.springframework.org/schema/jdbc
         http://www.springframework.org/schema/jdbc/spring-jdbc.xsd
         http://www.springframework.org/schema/data/jpa
         http://www.springframework.org/schema/data/jpa/spring-jpa.xsd
         http://www.springframework.org/schema/tx
         http://www.springframework.org/schema/tx/spring-tx.xsd">

    <jdbc:embedded-database id="dataSource" type="H2">
        <jdbc:script location="classpath:META-INF/config/schema.sql"/>
        <jdbc:script location="classpath:META-INF/config/test-data.sql"/>
    </jdbc:embedded-database>
```

```
<bean id="transactionManager" class="org.springframework.orm.jpa.JpaTransactionManager">
    <property name="entityManagerFactory" ref="emf"/>
</bean>

<tx:annotation-driven transaction-manager="transactionManager" />

<bean id="emf" class="org.springframework.orm.jpa.LocalContainerEntityManagerFactoryBean">
    <property name="dataSource" ref="dataSource" />
    <property name="jpaVendorAdapter">
        <bean class="org.springframework.orm.jpa.vendor.HibernateJpaVendorAdapter" />
    </property>
    <property name="packagesToScan" value="com.apress.prospring4.ch15"/>
    <property name="jpaProperties">
        <props>
            <prop key="hibernate.dialect">org.hibernate.dialect.H2Dialect</prop>
            <prop key="hibernate.max_fetch_depth">3</prop>
            <prop key="hibernate.jdbc.fetch_size">50</prop>
            <prop key="hibernate.jdbc.batch_size">10</prop>
            <prop key="hibernate.show_sql">true</prop>
            <!-- Hibernate statistics properties -->
            <prop key="hibernate.generate_statistics">true</prop>
            <prop key="hibernate.session_factory_name">sessionFactory</prop>
        </props>
    </property>
</bean>

<context:annotation-config/>

<jpa:repositories base-package="com.apress.prospring4.ch15"
                  entity-manager-factory-ref="emf"
                  transaction-manager-ref="transactionManager"/>
</beans>
```

The property `hibernate.generate_statistics` instructs Hibernate to generate statistics for its JPA persistence provider, while the property `hibernate.session_factory_name` defines the name of the session factory required by the Hibernate statistics MBean. Both of these additions can be seen under the "Hibernate statistics properties" comment.

Finally, we need to add the MBean into Spring's `MBeanExporter` configuration. Listing 15-5 shows the updated MBean configuration that we created earlier in the file `rest-context.xml`.

Listing 15-5. MBean for Hibernate Statistics

```
<?xml version="1.0" encoding="UTF-8"?>
<beans xmlns="http://www.springframework.org/schema/beans"
       xmlns:xsi="http://www.w3.org/2001/XMLSchema-instance"
       xmlns:context="http://www.springframework.org/schema/context"
       xmlns:mvc="http://www.springframework.org/schema/mvc"
       xsi:schemaLocation="http://www.springframework.org/schema/beans
        http://www.springframework.org/schema/beans/spring-beans.xsd
        http://www.springframework.org/schema/context
        http://www.springframework.org/schema/context/spring-context.xsd
        http://www.springframework.org/schema/mvc
        http://www.springframework.org/schema/mvc/spring-mvc.xsd">
```

```
    <mvc:annotation-driven>
        <mvc:message-converters>
            <bean class="org.springframework.http.converter.json.
MappingJackson2HttpMessageConverter"/>
            <bean class="org.springframework.http.converter.xml.MarshallingHttpMessageConverter">
                <property name="marshaller" ref="castorMarshaller"/>
                <property name="unmarshaller" ref="castorMarshaller"/>
            </bean>
        </mvc:message-converters>
    </mvc:annotation-driven>

    <context:component-scan base-package="com.apress.prospring4.ch15"/>

    <bean id="castorMarshaller" class="org.springframework.oxm.castor.CastorMarshaller">
        <property name="mappingLocation" value="classpath:META-INF/spring/oxm-mapping.xml"/>
    </bean>

    <bean id="appStatisticsBean" class="com.apress.prospring4.ch15.AppStatisticsImpl"/>

    <bean id="jmxExporter" class="org.springframework.jmx.export.MBeanExporter">
        <property name="beans">
            <map>
                <entry key="bean:name=ProSpring4ContactApp" value-ref="appStatisticsBean"/>
                <entry key="bean:name=Prospring4ContactApp-hibernate" value-ref="statisticsBean"/>
            </map>
        </property>
    </bean>

    <bean id="statisticsBean" class="org.hibernate.jmx.StatisticsService">
        <property name="statisticsEnabled" value="true"/>
        <property name="sessionFactoryJNDIName" value="sessionFactory"/>
    </bean>
</beans>
```

A new statisticsBean is declared, with Hibernate's StatisticsService class as the implementation. This is how Hibernate supports exposing statistics to JMX. Note the property sessionFactoryJNDIName, which should match the one defined in Listing 15-4(hibernate.session_factory_name). Then within the jmxExporter bean, another bean with ObjectName bean:name=Prospring4ContactApp-hibernate is declared that references the statisticsBean bean.

Now the Hibernate statistics are enabled and available via JMX. Reload the application, and after VisualVM is refreshed, you will be able to see the Hibernate statistics MBean. Clicking the node displays the detail statistics on the right side. Note that for the information that is not of a Java primitive type (for example, a List), you can click in the field to expand it and show the content.

In VisualVM, you can see many other metrics, such as EntityNames, SessionOpenCount, SecondCloseCount, and QueryExecutionMaxTime. Those figures are useful for you to understand the persistence behavior within your application and can assist you in troubleshooting and performance-tuning exercises.

Summary

In this chapter, we covered high-level topics of monitoring a Spring-powered JEE application.

First, we discussed Spring's support of JMX, the standard in monitoring Java applications. Then we discussed implementing custom MBeans for exposing application-related information, as well as exposing statistics of common components such as Hibernate.

CHAPTER 16

■ ■ ■

Web Applications with Spring

In an enterprise application, the presentation layer critically affects the level of acceptance that users give the application. The presentation layer is the front door into your application. It lets users perform business functions provided by the application, as well as presenting a view of the information that is being maintained by the application. How the user interface performs greatly contributes to the success of the application.

Because of the explosive growth of the Internet (especially these days, and the rise of different kinds of devices that people are using), developing an application's presentation layer is a challenging task. The following are some of the major considerations when developing web applications:

- *Performance*: Performance is always the top requirement of a web application. If users choose a function or click a link and it takes a long time to execute (in the world of the Internet, 3 seconds is like a century), users will definitely not be happy with the application.

- *User-friendliness*: The application should be easy to use and easy to navigate, with clear instructions that don't confuse the user.

- *Interactivity and richness*: The user interface should be highly interactive and responsive. In addition, the presentation should be rich in terms of visual presentation, such as charting, dashboard type of interface, and so on.

- *Accessibility*: Nowadays, users require that the application is accessible from anywhere via any device. In the office, they will use their desktop for accessing the application. On the road, users will use various mobile devices (including laptops, tablets and smartphones) to access the application.

Developing a web application to fulfill the previous requirements is not easy, but they are considered mandatory for business users. Fortunately, many new technologies and frameworks have also been developed to address those needs. Many web application frameworks and libraries—such as Spring MVC, Struts, Tapestry, Java Server Faces (JSF), Google Web Toolkit (GWT), jQuery, and Dojo, to name a few—provide tools and rich component libraries that can help you develop highly interactive web front ends. In addition, many frameworks provide tools or corresponding widget libraries targeting mobile devices including smartphones and tablets. The rise of the HTML5 and CSS3 standards and the support of these latest standards by most web browsers and mobile device manufacturers also helps ease the development of web applications that need to be available anywhere, from any device.

In terms of web application development, Spring provides comprehensive and intensive support. The Spring MVC module provides a solid infrastructure and Model View Controller (MVC) framework for web application development. When using Spring MVC, you can use various view technologies (for example, JSP or Velocity). In addition, Spring MVC integrates with many common web frameworks and toolkits (for example, Struts and GWT). Other Spring projects help address specific needs for web applications. For example, Spring MVC, when combined with the Spring Web Flow project and its Spring Faces module, provides comprehensive support for developing web applications with complex flows and using JSF as the view technology. Simply speaking, there are so many choices out there in terms of presentation layer development.

This chapter focuses on Spring MVC and discusses how we can use the powerful features provided by Spring MVC to develop highly performing web applications. Specifically, this chapter covers the following topics:

- *Spring MVC*: We discuss the main concepts of the MVC pattern and introduce Spring MVC. We present Spring MVC's core concepts, including its WebApplicationContext hierarchy and the request-handling life cycle.

- *i18n, locale, and theming*: Spring MVC provides comprehensive support for common web application requirements including i18n (internationalization), locale, and theming. We discuss how to use Spring MVC to develop web applications that support those requirements.

- *View and Ajax support*: Spring MVC supports many view technologies. In this chapter, we focus on using JavaServer Pages (JSP) and Tiles as the view part of the web application. On top of JSP, JavaScript will be used to provide the richness part. There are many outstanding and popular JavaScript libraries, such as jQuery and Dojo. In this chapter, we focus on using jQuery, with its subproject jQuery UI library that supports the development of highly interactive web applications.

- *Pagination and file upload support*: When developing the samples in this chapter, we discuss how we can use Spring Data JPA and the front-end jQuery component to provide pagination support when browsing grid-based data. In addition, how to implement file upload in Spring MVC is covered. Instead of integration with Apache Commons File Upload, we discuss how we can use Spring MVC with the Servlet 3.1 container's built-in multipart support for file upload.

- *Security*: Security is a big topic in web applications. We discuss how we can use Spring Security to help protect the application and handle logins and logouts.

Implementing the Service Layer for Samples

In the service layer for this chapter, we will still use the contact application as the sample. In this section, we discuss the data model and the implementation of the service layer that will be used throughout this chapter.

Using a Data Model for Samples

For the data model in the samples in this chapter, we will use a very simple one, which contains only a single CONTACT table for storing contact information. Listing 16-1 shows the script for schema creation (schema.sql).

Listing 16-1. Sample Database Schema

```
DROP TABLE IF EXISTS CONTACT;

CREATE TABLE CONTACT (
        ID INT NOT NULL AUTO_INCREMENT
    , FIRST_NAME VARCHAR(60) NOT NULL
    , LAST_NAME VARCHAR(40) NOT NULL
    , BIRTH_DATE DATE
    , DESCRIPTION VARCHAR(2000)
    , PHOTO BLOB
    , VERSION INT NOT NULL DEFAULT 0
    , UNIQUE UQ_CONTACT_1 (FIRST_NAME, LAST_NAME)
    , PRIMARY KEY (ID)
);
```

As you can see, the CONTACT table stores only a few basic fields of a contact's information. One thing worth mentioning is the PHOTO column, of the BLOB (binary large object) data type, which will be used to store the photo of a contact using file upload. Listing 16-2 shows the testing data population script (test-data.sql).

Listing 16-2. Sample Data Population Script

```
insert into contact (first_name, last_name, birth_date) values ('Chris', 'Schaefer', '1981-05-03');
insert into contact (first_name, last_name, birth_date) values ('Scott', 'Tiger', '1990-11-02');
insert into contact (first_name, last_name, birth_date) values ('John', 'Smith', '1964-02-28');
insert into contact (first_name, last_name, birth_date) values ('Peter', 'Jackson', '1944-1-10');
insert into contact (first_name, last_name, birth_date) values ('Jacky', 'Chan', '1955-10-31');
insert into contact (first_name, last_name, birth_date) values ('Susan', 'Boyle', '1970-05-06');
insert into contact (first_name, last_name, birth_date) values ('Tinner', 'Turner', '1967-04-30');
insert into contact (first_name, last_name, birth_date) values ('Lotus', 'Notes', '1990-02-28');
insert into contact (first_name, last_name, birth_date) values ('Henry', 'Dickson', '1997-06-30');
insert into contact (first_name, last_name, birth_date) values ('Sam', 'Davis', '2001-01-31');
insert into contact (first_name, last_name, birth_date) values ('Max', 'Beckham', '2002-02-01');
insert into contact (first_name, last_name, birth_date) values ('Paul', 'Simon', '2002-02-28');
```

This time, more testing data was populated in order to show you the pagination support later.

Implementing and Configuring ContactService

In the following sections, we first discuss the implementation of the ContactService by using JPA 2, Spring Data JPA, and Hibernate as the persistence service provider. Then will cover the configuration of the service layer in the Spring project.

Implementing ContactService

In the samples, we will expose the services for various operations on the contact information to the presentation layer. First we need to create the Contact entity class, which is shown in Listing 16-3.

Listing 16-3. The Contact Entity Class

```
package com.apress.prospring4.ch16;

import static javax.persistence.GenerationType.IDENTITY;

import java.io.Serializable;

import org.hibernate.annotations.Type;
import org.joda.time.DateTime;
import org.springframework.format.annotation.DateTimeFormat;
import org.springframework.format.annotation.DateTimeFormat.ISO;

import javax.persistence.Basic;
import javax.persistence.Column;
import javax.persistence.Entity;
import javax.persistence.FetchType;
import javax.persistence.GeneratedValue;
import javax.persistence.Id;
```

575

```java
import javax.persistence.Lob;
import javax.persistence.Table;
import javax.persistence.Transient;
import javax.persistence.Version;

@Entity
@Table(name = "contact")
public class Contact implements Serializable {
    private Long id;
    private int version;
    private String firstName;
    private String lastName;
    private DateTime birthDate;
    private String description;
    private byte[] photo;

    @Id
    @GeneratedValue(strategy = IDENTITY)
    @Column(name = "ID")
    public Long getId() {
        return id;
    }

    public void setId(Long id) {
        this.id = id;
    }

    @Version
    @Column(name = "VERSION")
    public int getVersion() {
        return version;
    }

    public void setVersion(int version) {
        this.version = version;
    }

    @Column(name = "FIRST_NAME")
    public String getFirstName() {
        return firstName;
    }

    public void setFirstName(String firstName) {
        this.firstName = firstName;
    }

    @Column(name = "LAST_NAME")
    public String getLastName() {
        return lastName;
    }
```

```java
    public void setLastName(String lastName) {
        this.lastName = lastName;
    }


    @Column(name = "BIRTH_DATE")
    @Type(type="org.jadira.usertype.dateandtime.joda.PersistentDateTime")
    @DateTimeFormat(iso=ISO.DATE)
    public DateTime getBirthDate() {
        return birthDate;
    }

    public void setBirthDate(DateTime birthDate) {
        this.birthDate = birthDate;
    }

    @Column(name = "DESCRIPTION")
    public String getDescription() {
        return description;
    }

    public void setDescription(String description) {
        this.description = description;
    }

    @Basic(fetch= FetchType.LAZY)
    @Lob
    @Column(name = "PHOTO")
    public byte[] getPhoto() {
        return photo;
    }

    public void setPhoto(byte[] photo) {
        this.photo = photo;
    }

    @Transient
    public String getBirthDateString() {
        String birthDateString = "";
        if (birthDate != null)
            birthDateString = org.joda.time.format.DateTimeFormat
                    .forPattern("yyyy-MM-dd").print(birthDate);
        return birthDateString;
    }

    @Override
    public String toString() {
        return "Contact - Id: " + id + ", First name: " + firstName
                + ", Last name: " + lastName + ", Birthday: " + birthDate
                + ", Description: " + description;
    }
}
```

As shown in Listing 16-3, standard JPA annotations are used. We also use JodaTime's `DateTime` class for the birthDate attribute. Please also note the following:

- A new transient property (by applying the `@Transient` annotation to the getter method) called `birthDateString` is added, which will be used for front-end presentation in later samples.

- For the photo attribute, we use a byte array as the Java data type, which corresponds to the BLOB data type in the RDBMS. In addition, the getter method is annotated with `@Lob` and `@Basic(fetch=FetchType.LAZY)`. The former annotation indicates to the JPA provider that it's a large object column, while the latter indicates that the attribute should be fetched lazily in order to avoid a performance impact when loading a class that does not require photo information.

Let's proceed to the service layer. Listing 16-4 shows the `ContactService` interface with the services we would like to expose.

Listing 16-4. The `ContactService` Interface

```
package com.apress.prospring4;

import java.util.List;

public interface ContactService {
    List<Contact> findAll();
    Contact findById(Long id);
    Contact save(Contact contact);
}
```

The methods should be self-explanatory. Because we will use Spring Data JPA's repository support, we will implement the `ContactRepository` interface, as shown in Listing 16-5.

Listing 16-5. The `ContactRepository` Interface

```
package com.apress.prospring4.ch16;

import org.springframework.data.repository.CrudRepository;

public interface ContactRepository extends CrudRepository<Contact, Long> {
}
```

Listing 16-6 shows the implementation class of the `ContactService` interface.

Listing 16-6. The `ContactServiceImpl` Class

```
package com.apress.prospring4.ch16;

import java.util.List;

import org.springframework.beans.factory.annotation.Autowired;
import org.springframework.stereotype.Repository;
import org.springframework.stereotype.Service;
import org.springframework.transaction.annotation.Transactional;

import com.google.common.collect.Lists;
```

```java
@Repository
@Transactional
@Service("contactService")
public class ContactServiceImpl implements ContactService {
    private ContactRepository contactRepository;

    @Override
    @Transactional(readOnly=true)
    public List<Contact> findAll() {
        return Lists.newArrayList(contactRepository.findAll());
    }

    @Override
    @Transactional(readOnly=true)
    public Contact findById(Long id) {
        return contactRepository.findOne(id);
    }

    @Override
    public Contact save(Contact contact) {
        return contactRepository.save(contact);
    }

    @Autowired
    public void setContactRepository(ContactRepository contactRepository) {
        this.contactRepository = contactRepository;
    }
}
```

The implementation is basically completed, and the next step is to configure the service in Spring's ApplicationContext within the web project, which is discussed in next section.

Configuring ContactService

To set up the service layer within the Spring MVC project, first we create an individual configuration file called datasource-tx-jpa.xml. Listing 16-7 shows the configuration file.

Listing 16-7. The datasource-tx-jpa.xml Configuration File

```xml
<?xml version="1.0" encoding="UTF-8"?>
<beans xmlns="http://www.springframework.org/schema/beans"
       xmlns:xsi="http://www.w3.org/2001/XMLSchema-instance"
       xmlns:context="http://www.springframework.org/schema/context"
       xmlns:jdbc="http://www.springframework.org/schema/jdbc"
       xmlns:jpa="http://www.springframework.org/schema/data/jpa"
       xmlns:tx="http://www.springframework.org/schema/tx"
       xsi:schemaLocation="http://www.springframework.org/schema/beans
         http://www.springframework.org/schema/beans/spring-beans.xsd
         http://www.springframework.org/schema/context
         http://www.springframework.org/schema/context/spring-context.xsd
         http://www.springframework.org/schema/jdbc
```

```
        http://www.springframework.org/schema/jdbc/spring-jdbc.xsd
        http://www.springframework.org/schema/data/jpa
        http://www.springframework.org/schema/data/jpa/spring-jpa.xsd
        http://www.springframework.org/schema/tx
        http://www.springframework.org/schema/tx/spring-tx.xsd">

    <jdbc:embedded-database id="dataSource" type="H2">
        <jdbc:script location="classpath:META-INF/sql/schema.sql"/>
        <jdbc:script location="classpath:META-INF/sql/test-data.sql"/>
    </jdbc:embedded-database>

    <bean id="transactionManager" class="org.springframework.orm.jpa.JpaTransactionManager">
        <property name="entityManagerFactory" ref="emf"/>
    </bean>

    <tx:annotation-driven transaction-manager="transactionManager" />

    <bean id="emf" class="org.springframework.orm.jpa.LocalContainerEntityManagerFactoryBean">
        <property name="dataSource" ref="dataSource" />
        <property name="jpaVendorAdapter">
            <bean class="org.springframework.orm.jpa.vendor.HibernateJpaVendorAdapter" />
        </property>
        <property name="packagesToScan" value="com.apress.prospring4"/>
        <property name="jpaProperties">
            <props>
                <prop key="hibernate.dialect">
                    org.hibernate.dialect.H2Dialect
                </prop>
                <prop key="hibernate.max_fetch_depth">3</prop>
                <prop key="hibernate.jdbc.fetch_size">50</prop>
                <prop key="hibernate.jdbc.batch_size">10</prop>
                <prop key="hibernate.show_sql">true</prop>
            </props>
        </property>
    </bean>

    <context:annotation-config/>

    <jpa:repositories base-package="com.apress.prospring4.ch16"
                      entity-manager-factory-ref="emf"
                      transaction-manager-ref="transactionManager"/>
</beans>
```

Next we need to import the configuration into Spring's root `WebApplicationContext`. Listing 16-8 shows the configuration file.

Listing 16-8. The root-context.xml File

```
<?xml version="1.0" encoding="UTF-8"?>
<beans xmlns="http://www.springframework.org/schema/beans"
    xmlns:xsi="http://www.w3.org/2001/XMLSchema-instance"
    xmlns:context="http://www.springframework.org/schema/context"
    xsi:schemaLocation="http://www.springframework.org/schema/beans
        http://www.springframework.org/schema/beans/spring-beans.xsd
        http://www.springframework.org/schema/context
        http://www.springframework.org/schema/context/spring-context.xsd">

    <import resource="classpath:META-INF/spring/datasource-tx-jpa.xml" />

    <context:component-scan base-package="com.apress.prospring4.ch16" />
</beans>
```

First the context namespace is added to the configuration file. Then the file datasource-tx-jpa.xml is imported into the WebApplicationContext, and finally, we instruct Spring to scan for the specified package for Spring beans.

Now the service layer is completed and ready to be exposed and used by remote clients.

Introducing MVC and Spring MVC

Before we move on to implement the presentation layer, let's go through some major concepts of MVC as a pattern in web applications and how Spring MVC provides comprehensive support in this area.

In the following sections, we present these high-level concepts one by one. First, we give a brief introduction to MVC. Second, we present a high-level view of Spring MVC and its WebApplicationContext hierarchy. Finally, we discuss the request life cycle within Spring MVC.

Introducing MVC

MVC is a commonly used pattern in implementing the presentation layer of an application. The main principle of the MVC pattern is to define an architecture with clear responsibilities for different components. As its name implies, there are three participants within the MVC pattern:

- *Model*: A model represents the business data as well as the "state" of the application within the context of the user. For example, in an e-commerce web site, the model will include the user profile information, shopping cart data, and order data if users purchase goods on the site.

- *View*: This presents the data to the user in the desired format, supports interaction with users, and supports client-side validation, i18n, styles, and so on.

- *Controller*: The controller handles requests for actions performed by users in the front end, interacting with the service layer, updating the model, and directing users to the appropriate view based on the result of execution.

Because of the rise of Ajax-based web applications, the MVC pattern has been enhanced to provide a more responsive and rich user experience. For example, when using JavaScript, the view can "listen" to events or actions performed by the user and then submit an XMLHttpRequest to the server. On the controller side, instead of returning the view, the raw data (for example, in XML or JSON format) is returned, and the JavaScript application performs "partial" updates of the view with the received data. Figure 16-1 shows this concept.

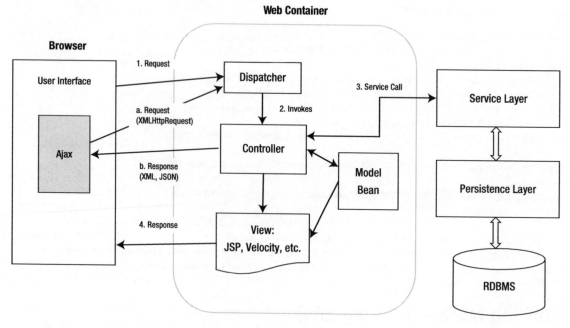

Figure 16-1. *The MVC pattern*

Figure 16-1 illustrates a commonly used web application pattern, which can be treated as an enhancement to the traditional MVC pattern. A normal view request is handled as follows:

1. *Request*: A request is submitted to the server. On the server side, most frameworks (for example, Spring MVC or Struts) have a dispatcher (in the form of a servlet) to handle the request.

2. *Invokes*: The dispatcher dispatches the request to the appropriate controller based on the HTTP request information and the web application configuration.

3. *Service call*: The controller interacts with the service layer.

4. *Response*: The controller updates the model and, based on the execution result, returns the corresponding view to the user.

In addition, within a view, Ajax calls will happen. For example, say the user is browsing data within a grid. When the user clicks the next page, instead of a full-page refresh, the following flow will happen:

1. *Request*: An XMLHttpRequest is prepared and submitted to the server. The dispatcher will dispatch the request to the corresponding controller.

2. *Response*: The controller interacts with the service layer, and the response data will be formatted and sent to the browser. No view is involved in this case. The browser receives the data and performs a partial update of the existing view.

Introducing Spring MVC

In the Spring Framework, the Spring MVC module provides comprehensive support for the MVC pattern, with support for other features (for example, theming, i18n, validation, and type conversion and formatting) that ease the implementation of the presentation layer.

In the following sections, we discuss the main concepts of Spring MVC. Topics include Spring MVC's WebApplicationContext hierarchy, a typical request-handling life cycle, and configuration.

Spring MVC WebApplicationContext Hierarchy

In Spring MVC, the DispatcherServlet is the central servlet that receives requests and dispatches them to the appropriate controllers. In a Spring MVC application, there can be any number of DispatcherServlets for various purposes (for example, handling user interface requests and RESTful-WS requests), and each DispatcherServlet has its own WebApplicationContext configuration, which defines the servlet-level characteristics, such as controllers supporting the servlet, handler mapping, view resolving, i18n, theming, validation, and type conversion and formatting.

Underneath the servlet-level WebApplicationContext configurations, Spring MVC also maintains a root WebApplicationContext, which includes the application-level configurations such as back-end data source, security, and service and persistence layer configuration. The root WebApplicationContext will be available to all servlet-level WebApplicationContexts.

Let's look at an example. Say we have two DispatcherServlets in an application. One servlet is to support the user interface (we call it the application servlet), and the other is to provide services in the form of RESTful-WS to other applications (we call it the RESTful servlet). In Spring MVC, we will define the configurations for both the root WebApplicationContext and the WebApplicationContext for the two DispatcherServlets. Figure 16-2 shows the WebApplicationContext hierarchy that will be maintained by Spring MVC for this scenario.

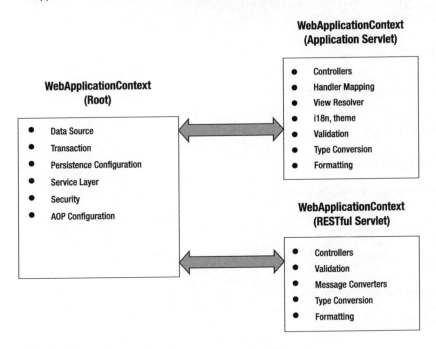

Figure 16-2. Spring MVC WebApplicationContext hierarchy

Spring MVC Request Life Cycle

Let's see how Spring MVC handles a request. Figure 16-3 shows the main components involved in handling a request in Spring MVC.

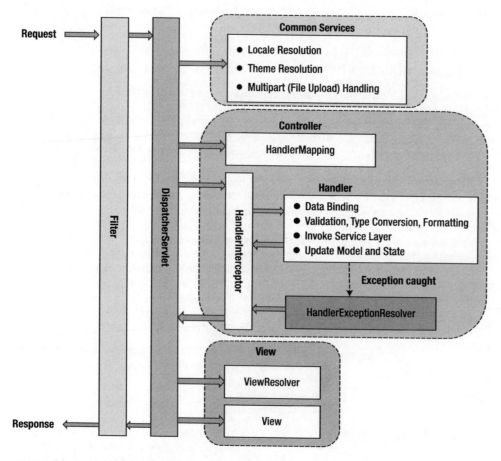

Figure 16-3. *Spring MVC request life cycle*

The main components and their purposes are as follows:

- *Filter*: The filter applies to every request. Several commonly used filters and their purposes are described in the next section.

- *Dispatcher servlet*: The servlet analyzes the requests and dispatches them to the appropriate controller for processing.

- *Common services*: The common services will apply to every request to provide supports including i18n, theme, and file upload. Their configuration is defined in the DispatcherServlet's WebApplicationContext.

- *Handler mapping*: This maps the request to the handler (a method within a Spring MVC controller class). Since Spring 2.5, in most situations the configuration is not required because Spring MVC will automatically register the `org.springframework.web.servlet.mvc.annotation.DefaultAnnotationHandlerMapping` class that maps handlers based on HTTP paths expressed through the `@RequestMapping` annotation at the type or method level within controller classes.

- *Handler interceptor*: In Spring MVC, you can register interceptors for the handlers for implementing common checking or logic. For example, a handler interceptor can check to ensure that only the handlers can be invoked during office hours.

- *Handler exception resolver*: In Spring MVC, the `HandlerExceptionResolver` interface (under the package `org.springframework.web.servlet`) is designed to deal with unexpected exceptions thrown during request processing by handlers. By default, the `DispatcherServlet` registers the `DefaultHandlerExceptionResolver` class (under the package `org.springframework.web.servlet.mvc.support`). This resolver handles certain standard Spring MVC exceptions by setting a specific response status code. You can also implement your own exception handler by annotating a controller method with the `@ExceptionHandler` annotation and passing in the exception type as the attribute.

- *View Resolver*: Spring MVC's `ViewResolver` interface (under the package `org.springframework.web.servlet`) supports view resolution based on a logical name returned by the controller. There are many implementation classes to support various view resolving mechanisms. For example, the `UrlBasedViewResolver` class supports direct resolution of logical names to URLs. The `ContentNegotiatingViewResolver` class supports dynamic resolving of views depending on the media type supported by the client (such as XML, PDF, and JSON). There also exist a number of implementations to integrate with different view technologies, such as FreeMarker (`FreeMarkerViewResolver`), Velocity (`VelocityViewResolver`), and JasperReports (`JasperReportsViewResolver`).

These descriptions cover only a few commonly used handlers and resolvers. For a full description, please refer to the Spring Framework reference documentation and its Javadoc.

Spring MVC Configuration

To enable Spring MVC within a web application, some initial configuration is required, especially for the web deployment descriptor `web.xml`. Since Spring 3.1, support has been available for code-based configuration within a Servlet 3.0 web container, which we discuss in "Supporting Servlet 3 Code-Based Configuration" later in this chapter.

To configure Spring MVC support for web applications, we need to perform the following configurations in the web deployment descriptor:

- Configuring the root `WebApplicationContext`

- Configuring the servlet filters required by Spring MVC

- Configuring the dispatcher servlets within the application

First, let's create our `web.xml` file utilizing Servlet 3.0. Listing 16-9 shows the configuration.

Listing 16-9. The Web Deployment Description for Spring MVC

```xml
<?xml version="1.0" encoding="UTF-8"?>
<web-app version="3.0" xmlns="http://java.sun.com/xml/ns/javaee"
    xmlns:xsi="http://www.w3.org/2001/XMLSchema-instance"
    xsi:schemaLocation="http://java.sun.com/xml/ns/javaee
        http://java.sun.com/xml/ns/javaee/web-app_3_0.xsd">

  <context-param>
      <param-name>contextConfigLocation</param-name>
      <param-value>/WEB-INF/spring/root-context.xml</param-value>
  </context-param>

  <filter>
      <filter-name>CharacterEncodingFilter</filter-name>
      <filter-class>org.springframework.web.filter.CharacterEncodingFilter</filter-class>
      <init-param>
          <param-name>encoding</param-name>
          <param-value>UTF-8</param-value>
      </init-param>
      <init-param>
          <param-name>forceEncoding</param-name>
          <param-value>true</param-value>
      </init-param>
  </filter>

  <filter>
      <filter-name>HttpMethodFilter</filter-name>
      <filter-class>org.springframework.web.filter.HiddenHttpMethodFilter</filter-class>
  </filter>

  <filter>
      <filter-name>Spring OpenEntityManagerInViewFilter</filter-name>
      <filter-class>org.springframework.orm.jpa.support.OpenEntityManagerInViewFilter
</filter-class>
  </filter>

  <filter-mapping>
      <filter-name>CharacterEncodingFilter</filter-name>
      <url-pattern>/*</url-pattern>
  </filter-mapping>

  <filter-mapping>
      <filter-name>HttpMethodFilter</filter-name>
      <url-pattern>/*</url-pattern>
  </filter-mapping>

  <filter-mapping>
      <filter-name>Spring OpenEntityManagerInViewFilter</filter-name>
      <url-pattern>/*</url-pattern>
  </filter-mapping>
```

```
<listener>
    <listener-class>org.springframework.web.context.ContextLoaderListener</listener-class>
    </listener>

<servlet>
    <servlet-name>appServlet</servlet-name>
    <servlet-class>org.springframework.web.servlet.DispatcherServlet</servlet-class>
    <init-param>
        <param-name>contextConfigLocation</param-name>
        <param-value>/WEB-INF/spring/appServlet/servlet-context.xml</param-value>
    </init-param>
    <load-on-startup>1</load-on-startup>
</servlet>

<servlet-mapping>
    <servlet-name>appServlet</servlet-name>
    <url-pattern>/</url-pattern>
</servlet-mapping>
</web-app>
```

The main points for Listing 16-9 are as follows:

- In the `<web-app>` tag, the `version` attribute and the corresponding URL are used to indicate to the web container that the web application will use Servlet 3.0.

- In the `<context-param>` tag, the `contextConfigLocation` param is provided, which defines the location of Spring's root `WebApplicationContext` configuration file.

- A number of servlet filters provided by Spring MVC are defined, and all filters are mapped to the web application root context URL. Those filters are commonly used in web applications. Table 16-1 shows the filters configured and their purpose.

Table 16-1. *Commonly Used Spring MVC Servlet Filters*

Filter Class Name	Description
org.springframework.web.filter. CharacterEncodingFilter	This filter is used to specify the character encoding for the request.
org.springframework.web.filter. HiddenHttpMethodFilter	This filter provides support for HTTP methods other than GET and POST (for example, PUT).
org.springframework.orm.jpa.support. OpenEntityManagerInViewFilter	This filter binds the JPA EntityManager to the thread for the entire processing of the request. It can help restore the same EntityManager for subsequent requests of the same user so that JPA features such as lazy fetching will be able to work.

- A listener of class `org.springframework.web.context.ContextLoaderListener` is defined. This is for Spring to bootstrap and shut down the root `WebApplicationContext`.

- One dispatcher servlet (called `appServlet`) is defined. The `WebApplicationContext` for the dispatcher servlet is located at `/src/main/webapp/WEB-INF/spring/appServlet/servlet-context.xml`.

Creating the First View in Spring MVC

Having the service layer and Spring MVC configuration in place, we can start to implement our first view. In this section, we will implement a simple view to display all contacts that were initially populated by the test data script (test-data.sql).

As mentioned earlier, we will use JSPX to implement the view. JSPX is JSP in well-formed XML format. The main advantages of JSPX over JSP are as follows:

- JSPX forces the separation of code from the view layer more strictly. For example, you can't place Java "scriptlets" in a JSPX document.

- Tools might perform instant validation (on the XML syntax), so mistakes can be caught earlier.

We need to configure our project with the dependencies listed in Table 16-2.

Table 16-2. *Maven Dependencies for Spring MVC View*

Group ID	Artifact ID	Version	Description
org.springframework	spring-webmvc	4.0.2.RELEASE	The Spring Web MVC module for MVC support
org.hibernate.javax. persistence	hibernate-jpa-2.1-api	1.0.0.Final	The Hibernate JPA implementation
joda-time	joda-time	2.2	The JodaTime Date/Time API
org.jadira.usertype	usertype.core	3.0.0.GA	Usertype helper API for working with persistence Date/Time
org.springframework.data	spring-data-jpa	1.5.0.RELEASE	Spring Data JPA API
com.google.guava	guava	14.0.1	Helper API for working with collections and so on
com.h2database	h2	1.3.172	The H2 embedded database
joda-time	joda-time-jsptags	1.1.1	JSP tag library that support formatting of JodaTime types in views

Configuring the DispatcherServlet

The next step is to configure the DispatcherServlet. Listing 16-10 shows the revised configuration (/src/main/webapp/WEB-INF/spring/appServlet/servlet-context.xml).

Listing 16-10. The DispatcherServlet Configuration

```xml
<?xml version="1.0" encoding="UTF-8"?>
<beans:beans xmlns="http://www.springframework.org/schema/mvc"
    xmlns:xsi="http://www.w3.org/2001/XMLSchema-instance"
    xmlns:beans="http://www.springframework.org/schema/beans"
    xmlns:context="http://www.springframework.org/schema/context"
    xsi:schemaLocation="http://www.springframework.org/schema/mvc
        http://www.springframework.org/schema/mvc/spring-mvc.xsd
        http://www.springframework.org/schema/beans
        http://www.springframework.org/schema/beans/spring-beans.xsd
```

```
            http://www.springframework.org/schema/context
            http://www.springframework.org/schema/context/spring-context.xsd">

    <annotation-driven />

    <resources mapping="/resources/**" location="/resources/" />

    <beans:bean class="org.springframework.web.servlet.view.InternalResourceViewResolver">
        <beans:property name="prefix" value="/WEB-INF/views/" />
        <beans:property name="suffix" value=".jspx" />
    </beans:bean>

    <context:component-scan base-package="com.apress.prospring4.ch16" />
</beans:beans>
```

The mvc namespace is declared as the default namespace. The `<annotation-driven>` tag enables the support of annotation configuration for Spring MVC controllers, as well as enabling Spring type conversion and formatting support. Also, support for JSR-349, "Bean Validation" is enabled by this tag. The `<resources>` tag defines the static resources (for example, CSS, JavaScript, and images) and their locations so Spring MVC can improve the performance in serving those files. The `<context:component-scan>` tag should be familiar to you.

For the ViewResolver interface, we will keep on using the InternalResourceViewResolver class as the implementation. However, we will change the suffix to `.jspx`.

Implementing the ContactController

Having the DispatcherServlet's WebApplicationContext configured, the next step is to implement the controller class. Listing 16-11 shows the ContactController class.

Listing 16-11. The ContactController Class

```java
package com.apress.prospring4.ch16;

import java.util.List;

import org.slf4j.Logger;
import org.slf4j.LoggerFactory;
import org.springframework.beans.factory.annotation.Autowired;
import org.springframework.stereotype.Controller;
import org.springframework.ui.Model;
import org.springframework.web.bind.annotation.RequestMapping;
import org.springframework.web.bind.annotation.RequestMethod;

@RequestMapping("/contacts")
@Controller
public class ContactController {
    private final Logger logger = LoggerFactory.getLogger(ContactController.class);

    private ContactService contactService;

    @RequestMapping(method = RequestMethod.GET)
    public String list(Model uiModel) {
        logger.info("Listing contacts");
```

```
            List<Contact> contacts = contactService.findAll();
            uiModel.addAttribute("contacts", contacts);

            logger.info("No. of contacts: " + contacts.size());

            return "contacts/list";
        }

        @Autowired
        public void setContactService(ContactService contactService) {
            this.contactService = contactService;
        }
}
```

The annotation @Controller is applied to the class, indicating that it's a Spring MVC controller. The @RequestMapping annotation at the class level indicates the root URL that will be handled by the controller. In this case, all URLs with the prefix /ch16/contacts will be dispatched to this controller. In the list() method, the @RequestMapping annotation is also applied, but this time the method is mapped to the HTTP GET method. This means that the URL /ch16/contacts with the HTTP GET method will be handled by this method. Within the list() method, the list of contacts are retrieved and saved into the Model interface passed in to the method by Spring MVC. Finally, the logical view name contacts/list is returned. In the DispatcherServlet configuration, the InternalResourceViewResolver is configured as the view resolver, and the file has the prefix /WEB-INF/views/ and the suffix .jspx. As a result, Spring MVC will pick up the file /WEB-INF/views/contacts/list.jspx as the view.

Implementing the Contact List View

The next step is to implement the view page for displaying the contact information, which is the file /src/main/webapp/WEB-INF/views/contacts/list.jspx. Listing 16-12 shows the page content.

Listing 16-12. The Contact List View

```xml
<?xml version="1.0" encoding="UTF-8" standalone="no"?>
<div xmlns:jsp="http://java.sun.com/JSP/Page"
    xmlns:c="http://java.sun.com/jsp/jstl/core"
    xmlns:joda="http://www.joda.org/joda/time/tags"
    version="2.0">
    <jsp:directive.page contentType="text/html;charset=UTF-8"/>
    <jsp:output omit-xml-declaration="yes"/>

    <h1>Contact Listing</h1>

    <c:if test="${not empty contacts}">
        <table>
            <thead>
                <tr>
                    <th>First Name</th>
                    <th>Last Name</th>
                    <th>Birth Date</th>
                </tr>
            </thead>
```

```
        <tbody>
            <c:forEach items="${contacts}" var="contact">
                <tr>
                    <td>${contact.firstName}</td>
                    <td>${contact.lastName}</td>
                    <td><joda:format value="${contact.birthDate}" pattern="yyyy-MM-dd"/></td>
                </tr>
            </c:forEach>
        </tbody>
    </table>
  </c:if>
</div>
```

If you have developed JSP before, Listing 16-12 should be familiar to you. But since this is a JSPX page, the page content is embedded under the `<div>` tag. In addition, the tag libraries being used are declared as XML namespaces.

First, the `<jsp:directive.page>` tag defines the attributes that apply to the entire JSPX page, while the `<jsp:output>` tag controls the properties of the output of the JSPX document.

Second, the tag `<c:if>` detects whether the model attribute `contacts` is empty. Because we already populated some contact information in the database, the `contacts` attribute should contain data. As a result, the `<c:forEach>` tag will render the contact information in the table within the page. Note the use of the `<joda:format>` tag to format the `birthDate` attribute, which is of JodaTime's `DateTime` type.

Testing the Contact List View

Now we are ready to test the contact list view. First build and deploy the application, then to test the contact list view, open a web browser and visit the URL `http://localhost:8080/contact-webapp/contacts`. You should be able to see the contact listing page.

Now we have our first view working. In the upcoming sections, we will enrich the application with more views and enable support of i18n, themes, and so on.

Understanding Spring MVC Project Structure

Before we dive into the implementation of the various aspects of a web application, let's take a look at what the project structure in our sample web application developed in this chapter looks like.

Typically, in a web application, a lot of files are required to support various features. For example, there are a lot of static resource files, such as style sheets, JavaScript files, images, and component libraries. Then there are files that support presenting the interface in various languages. And of course, there are the view pages that will be parsed and rendered by the web container, as well as the layout and definition files that will be used by the templating framework (for example, Apache Tiles) for providing a consistent look and feel of the application.

It's always a good practice to store files that serve different purposes in a well-structured folder hierarchy to give you a clear picture of the various resources being used by the application and ease ongoing maintenance work.

Table 16-3 lists the folder structure of the web application that will be developed in this chapter along with the purpose of each folder. Note that the structure presented here is not mandatory but is commonly used in the developer community for web application development.

Table 16-3. Sample Web Project Folder Structure Description

Folder Name	Purpose	Note
ckeditor	CKEditor (http://ckeditor.com) is a JavaScript component library that provides a rich-text editor in input form. We will use it to enable rich-text editing of a contact's description.	Copy the folder from the sample source code into the folder of your project.
jqgrid	jqGrid (www.trirand.com/blog) is a component built on top of jQuery that provides various grid-based components for data presentation. We will use this library for implementing the grid in order to display contacts, as well as to support Ajax-style pagination.	Copy the folder from the sample source code into the folder of your project.
scripts	This is the folder for all generic JavaScript files. For the samples in this chapter, jQuery (http://jquery.org) and jQuery UI (http://jqueryui.com) JavaScript libraries will be used to implement a rich user interface. The scripts will be placed in this folder. In-house JavaScript libraries should be put here too.	Copy the folder from the sample source code into the folder of your project.
styles	Stores the style sheet files and related images in supporting the styles.	Copy the folder from the sample source code into the folder of your project.
WEB-INF/i18n	Files for supporting i18n. The file application*.properties stores the layout-related text (for example, page titles, field labels, and menu titles). The message*.properties file stores various messages (for example, success and error messages, and validation messages). In the sample, we will support both English (US) and Chinese (HK).	Copy the folder from the sample source code into the folder of your project.
WEB-INF/layouts	This folder stores the layout view and definitions. Those files will be used by the Apache Tiles (http://tiles.apache.org) templating framework.	
WEB-INF/spring	This folder stores the Spring MVC WebApplicationContext configurations. Both the root-level and dispatcher servlet–level context configurations are stored here.	
WEB-INF/views	This folder stores the views (in our case, JSPX files) that will be used by the application.	

In the upcoming sections, we will need various files (for example, CSS files, JavaScript files, and images) to support the implementation. The source code of the CSS and JavaScript will not be shown here. Given that, we recommend you download a copy of the source code for this chapter and extract it to a temporary folder so that you can copy the files required into the project directly.

Enabling i18n (Internationalization)

When developing web applications, it's always good practice to enable i18n in the early stage. The main work is to externalize the user interface text and messages into properties files.

Even though you may not have i18n requirements on day one, it's good to externalize the language-related settings so that it will be easier later when you need to support more languages.

With Spring MVC, enabling i18n is very simple. First, externalize the language-related user interface settings into various properties files within the /WEB-INF/i18n folder, as described in Table 16-3. Because we will support both English (US) and Chinese (HK), we will need four files. The application.properties and message.properties files store the settings for the default locale, which in our case is English (US). In addition, the application_zh_HK.properties and message_zh_HK.properties files store the settings in the Chinese (HK) language.

Configuring i18n in DispatcherServlet Configuration

Having the language settings in place, the next step is to configure the DispatcherServlet's WebApplicationContext for i18n support.

Listing 16-13 shows the revised configuration file with i18n support (servlet-context.xml).

Listing 16-13. Revised Servlet Context Configuration

```xml
<?xml version="1.0" encoding="UTF-8"?>
<beans:beans xmlns="http://www.springframework.org/schema/mvc"
    xmlns:xsi="http://www.w3.org/2001/XMLSchema-instance"
    xmlns:beans="http://www.springframework.org/schema/beans"
    xmlns:p="http://www.springframework.org/schema/p"
    xmlns:context="http://www.springframework.org/schema/context"
    xsi:schemaLocation="http://www.springframework.org/schema/mvc
        http://www.springframework.org/schema/mvc/spring-mvc.xsd
        http://www.springframework.org/schema/beans
        http://www.springframework.org/schema/beans/spring-beans.xsd
        http://www.springframework.org/schema/context
        http://www.springframework.org/schema/context/spring-context.xsd">

    <annotation-driven />

    <resources location="/, classpath:/META-INF/web-resources/" mapping="/resources/**"/>

    <default-servlet-handler/>

    <beans:bean class="org.springframework.web.servlet.view.InternalResourceViewResolver">
        <beans:property name="prefix" value="/WEB-INF/views/" />
        <beans:property name="suffix" value=".jspx" />
    </beans:bean>

    <context:component-scan base-package="com.apress.prospring4.ch16" />

    <interceptors>
        <beans:bean class="org.springframework.web.servlet.i18n.LocaleChangeInterceptor"
            p:paramName="lang"/>
    </interceptors>

    <beans:bean class="org.springframework.context.support.ReloadableResourceBundleMessageSource"
        id="messageSource" p:basenames="WEB-INF/i18n/messages,WEB-INF/i18n/application"
        p:fallbackToSystemLocale="false"/>

    <beans:bean class="org.springframework.web.servlet.i18n.CookieLocaleResolver"
        id="localeResolver" p:cookieName="locale"/>
</beans:beans>
```

In Listing 16-13, first the p namespace is added, and the resource definition is revised to reflect the new folder structure as presented in Table 16-3. The <resources> tag belongs to the mvc namespace and was introduced in Spring 3. This tag defines the locations of the static resource files, which enable Spring MVC to handle the files within those folders efficiently. Within the tag, the location attribute defines the folders for the static resources. The first path, /, indicates the root folder for the web application, which is /src/main/webapp, while the second path, classpath:/META-INF/web-resources/, indicates the resource files for the included library. It will be useful if you include the Spring JavaScript module, which includes the supporting resource files within the /META-INF/web-resources folder. The mapping attribute defines the URL for mapping to static resources; as an example, for the URL http://localhost:8080/contact-webapp/resources/styles/standard.css, Spring MVC will retrieve the file standard.css from the folder /src/main/webapp/styles. The <default-servlet-handler/>tag enables the mapping of the DispatcherServlet to the web application's root context URL, while still allowing static resource requests to be handled by the container's default servlet.

Second, a Spring MVC interceptor with class LocaleChangeInterceptor is defined, which intercepts all the requests to the DispatcherServlet. The interceptor supports locale switching with a configurable request parameter. From the interceptor configuration, the URL param with the name lang is defined for changing the locale for the application.

Then, a bean with class ReloadableResourceBundleMessageSource is defined. The ReloadableResourceBundleMessageSource class implements the MessageSource interface, which loads the messages from the defined files (in this case, it's the messages*.properties and application*.properties in the /WEB-INF/i18n folder) in supporting i18n. Note the property fallbackToSystemLocale. This property instructs Spring MVC whether to fall back to the locale of the system that the application is running on when a special resource bundle for the client locale isn't found.

Finally, a bean with the CookieLocaleResolver class is defined. This class supports the storage and retrieval of locale settings from the user browser's cookie.

Modifying the Contact List View for i18n Support

Now we can change the JSPX page to display i18n messages. Listing 16-14 shows the revised contact list view (list.jspx).

Listing 16-14. Revised Contact List View for i18n

```
<?xml version="1.0" encoding="UTF-8" standalone="no"?>
<div xmlns:jsp="http://java.sun.com/JSP/Page"
    xmlns:c="http://java.sun.com/jsp/jstl/core"
    xmlns:joda="http://www.joda.org/joda/time/tags"
    xmlns:spring="http://www.springframework.org/tags"
    version="2.0">
    <jsp:directive.page contentType="text/html;charset=UTF-8"/>
    <jsp:output omit-xml-declaration="yes"/>

    <spring:message code="label_contact_list" var="labelContactList"/>
    <spring:message code="label_contact_first_name" var="labelContactFirstName"/>
    <spring:message code="label_contact_last_name" var="labelContactLastName"/>
    <spring:message code="label_contact_birth_date" var="labelContactBirthDate"/>

    <h1>${labelContactList}</h1>
```

```
    <c:if test="${not empty contacts}">
        <table>
            <thead>
                <tr>
                    <th>${labelContactFirstName}</th>
                    <th>${labelContactLastName}</th>
                    <th>${labelContactBirthDate}</th>
                </tr>
            </thead>
            <tbody>
                <c:forEach items="${contacts}" var="contact">
                    <tr>
                        <td>${contact.firstName}</td>
                        <td>${contact.lastName}</td>
                        <td><joda:format value="${contact.birthDate}" pattern="yyyy-MM-dd"/></td>
                    </tr>
                </c:forEach>
            </tbody>
        </table>
    </c:if>
</div>
```

As shown in Listing 16-14, first the `spring` namespace is added into the page. Then, the `<spring:message>` tag is used to load the messages required by the view in the corresponding variables. Finally, the page title and the labels are changed to use the i18n messages.

Now build and redeploy the project, open your browser, and point to the URL `http://localhost:8080/contact-webapp/contacts?lang=zh_HK`. You will see the page in the Chinese (HK) locale.

Because we defined `localeResolver` in the `DispatcherServlet`'s `WebApplicationContext`, Spring MVC will store the locale setting in your browser's cookie (with the name `locale`), and by default, the cookie will be kept for the user session. If you want to persist the cookie for a longer time, in the `localeResolver` bean definition in Listing 16-13, you can override the property `cookieMaxAge`, which is inherited from the class `org.springframework.web.util.CookieGenerator`.

To switch to English (US), you can change the URL in your browser to reflect `?lang=en_US`, and the page will switch back to English (US). Although we don't provide the properties file named `application_en_US.properties`, Spring MVC will fall back to use the file `application.properties`, which stores the properties in the default language of English.

Using Theming and Templating

Besides i18n, a web application requires an appropriate look and feel (for example, a business web site needs a professional look and feel, while a social web site needs a more vivid style), as well as a consistent layout so that users will not get confused while using the web application.

In a web application, the styles should be externalized in style sheets, instead of hard-coded into the view page. In addition, the style names should be consistent so that various *themes* can be prepared by simply switching the style sheet file. Spring MVC provides comprehensive support for the theming of web applications.

In addition, in order to provide a consistent layout, a templating framework is required. In this section, we will use Apache Tiles (`http://tiles.apache.org`), a popular page templating framework, for view templating support. Spring MVC tightly integrates with Apache Tiles in this aspect. Spring also supports Velocity and FreeMarker out of the box, which are more-general templating systems and useful outside a web application as well for e-mail templates and so on.

In the following sections, we discuss how to enable theming support in Spring MVC, as well as how to use Apache Tiles to define our page layout.

Theming Support

Spring MVC provides comprehensive support for theming, and enabling it in web applications is easy. For example, in the sample contact application in this chapter, we want to create a theme and name it standard. First, in the folder /src/main/resources, create a file named standard.properties with the content in Listing 16-15.

Listing 16-15. The standard.properties File

```
styleSheet=resources/styles/standard.css
```

This properties file contains a property named styleSheet, which points to the style sheet to use for the standard theme. This properties file is the ResourceBundle for the theme, and you can add as many components for your theme as you want (for example, the logo image location and background image location).

The next step is to configure the DispatcherServlet's WebApplicationContext for theming support by modifying the configuration file (servlet-context.xml). First, within the <interceptors> definition, we need to add one more interceptor bean, as shown in Listing 16-16.

Listing 16-16. Configure the Theme Interceptor

```
<interceptors>
    <beans:bean class="org.springframework.web.servlet.theme.ThemeChangeInterceptor"/>
    <beans:bean class="org.springframework.web.servlet.i18n.LocaleChangeInterceptor"
        p:paramName="lang"/>
</interceptors>
```

The new interceptor ThemeChangeInterceptor is added, and this class intercepts every request for changing the theme.

Second, add the bean definitions in Listing 16-17 into the configuration file (servlet-context.xml).

Listing 16-17. Configure Theme Support

```
<beans:bean class="org.springframework.ui.context.support.ResourceBundleThemeSource"
id="themeSource"/>

<beans:bean class="org.springframework.web.servlet.theme.CookieThemeResolver"
id="themeResolver" p:cookieName="theme" p:defaultThemeName="standard"/>
```

Here, two beans are defined. The first bean, implemented by the ResourceBundleThemeSource class, is responsible for loading the ResourceBundle of the active theme. For example, if the active theme is called standard, the bean will look for the file standard.properties as the ResourceBundle of the theme. The second bean, implemented by the CookieThemeResolver class, is used to resolve the active theme for users. The property defaultThemeName defines the default theme to use, which is the standard theme. Note that as its name implies, the CookieThemeResolver class uses cookies to store the theme for the user. There also exists the SessionThemeResolver class that stores the theme attribute in a user's session.

Now the standard theme is configured and ready for use in our views. Listing 16-18 shows the revised contact list view (/WEB-INF/views/contacts/list.jspx) with theme support.

Listing 16-18. Contact List View with Theme Support

```xml
<?xml version="1.0" encoding="UTF-8" standalone="no"?>
<div xmlns:jsp="http://java.sun.com/JSP/Page"
    xmlns:c="http://java.sun.com/jsp/jstl/core"
    xmlns:joda="http://www.joda.org/joda/time/tags"
    xmlns:spring="http://www.springframework.org/tags"
    version="2.0">
    <jsp:directive.page contentType="text/html;charset=UTF-8"/>
    <jsp:output omit-xml-declaration="yes"/>

    <spring:message code="label_contact_list" var="labelContactList"/>
    <spring:message code="label_contact_first_name" var="labelContactFirstName"/>
    <spring:message code="label_contact_last_name" var="labelContactLastName"/>
    <spring:message code="label_contact_birth_date" var="labelContactBirthDate"/>

    <head>
        <spring:theme code="styleSheet" var="app_css" />
        <spring:url value="/${app_css}" var="app_css_url" />
        <link rel="stylesheet" type="text/css" media="screen" href="${app_css_url}" />
    </head>

    <h1>${labelContactList}</h1>

    <c:if test="${not empty contacts}">
        <table>
            <thead>
            <tr>
                <th>${labelContactFirstName}</th>
                <th>${labelContactLastName}</th>
                <th>${labelContactBirthDate}</th>
            </tr>
            </thead>
            <tbody>
            <c:forEach items="${contacts}" var="contact">
                <tr>
                    <td>${contact.firstName}</td>
                    <td>${contact.lastName}</td>
                    <td><joda:format value="${contact.birthDate}" pattern="yyyy-MM-dd"/></td>
                </tr>
            </c:forEach>
            </tbody>
        </table>
    </c:if>
</div>
```

A <head> section is added in the view, and the <spring:theme> tag is used to retrieve the styleSheet property from the theme's ResourceBundle, which is the style sheet file standard.css. Finally, the link to the style sheet is added into the view.

After rebuilding and redeploying the application to the server, open the browser and point to the contact list view's URL again (http://localhost:8080/contact-webapp/contacts), and you will see that the style defined in standard.css file was applied.

Using Spring MVC's theme support, you can easily add new themes or change the existing theme within your application.

View Templating with Apache Tiles

For view templating using JSP technology, Apache Tiles (http://tiles.apache.org) is the most popular framework in use. Spring MVC tightly integrates with Tiles.

In order to use Tiles and validation on data, we need to add the required dependencies in the project, as shown in Table 16-4.

Table 16-4. *Maven Dependencies for Apache Tiles*

Group ID	Artifact ID	Version	Description
org.apache.tiles	tiles-core	3.0.4	The core library for Apache Tiles
org.apache.tiles	tiles-jsp	3.0.4	Apache Tiles support for JSP view files
javax.validation	validation-api	1.1.0.Final	JSR-349 validation API
org.hibernate	hibernate-validator	5.1.0.Final	JSR-349 validation implementation

In the following sections, we discuss how to implement page templates, including page layout design, definition, and implementation of the components within the layout.

Template Layout Design

First we need to define the number of templates required in our application and the layout for each template.

In the contact sample in this chapter, we require only one template. The layout is rather trivial, as shown in Figure 16-4.

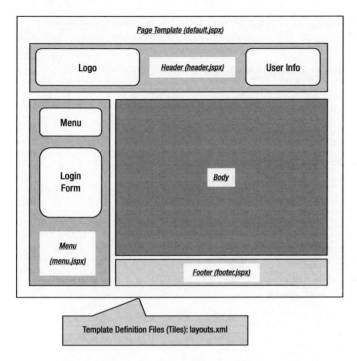

Figure 16-4. *Page template with layout components*

As you can see, the template requires the following page components:

- /WEB-INF/views/header.jspx: This page provides the header area.

- /WEB-INF/views/menu.jspx: This page provides the left menu area, as well as the login form that will be implemented later in this chapter.

- /WEB-INF/views/footer.jspx: This page provides the footer area.

We will use Apache Tiles to define the template, and we need to develop the page template file as well as the layout definitions file, as listed here:

- /WEB-INF/layouts/default.jspx: This page provides the overall page layout for a specific template.

- /WEB-INF/layouts/layouts.xml: This file stores the page layout definitions required by Apache Tiles.

Implement Page Layout Components

Having the layout defined, we can implement the page components. First we will develop the page template file and the layout definition files required by Apache Tiles.

Listing 16-19 shows the Apache Tiles definition file (src/main/webapp/WEB-INF/layouts/layouts.xml).

Listing 16-19. Apache Tiles Definition File

```xml
<?xml version="1.0" encoding="UTF-8"?>
<!DOCTYPE tiles-definitions PUBLIC
        "-//Apache Software Foundation//DTD Tiles Configuration 2.1//EN"
        "http://tiles.apache.org/dtds/tiles-config_3_0.dtd">

<tiles-definitions>
  <definition name="default" template="/WEB-INF/layouts/default.jspx">
    <put-attribute name="header" value="/WEB-INF/views/header.jspx" />
    <put-attribute name="menu" value="/WEB-INF/views/menu.jspx" />
    <put-attribute name="footer" value="/WEB-INF/views/footer.jspx" />
  </definition>
</tiles-definitions>
```

The file should be easy to understand. There is one page template definition, with the name `default`. The template code is in the file `default.jspx`. Within the page, three components are defined, named header, menu, and footer. The content of the components will be loaded from the file provided by the `value` attribute. For a detailed description of the Tiles definition, please refer to the project documentation page (`http://tiles.apache.org/`).

Listing 16-20 shows the default page template (`default.jspx`).

Listing 16-20. The Default Template File

```jsp
<html xmlns:jsp="http://java.sun.com/JSP/Page"
      xmlns:c="http://java.sun.com/jsp/jstl/core"
      xmlns:fn="http://java.sun.com/jsp/jstl/functions"
      xmlns:tiles="http://tiles.apache.org/tags-tiles"
      xmlns:spring="http://www.springframework.org/tags">

    <jsp:output doctype-root-element="HTML" doctype-system="about:legacy-compat" />

    <jsp:directive.page contentType="text/html;charset=UTF-8" />
    <jsp:directive.page pageEncoding="UTF-8" />

    <head>
        <meta http-equiv="Content-Type" content="text/html; charset=UTF-8" />
        <meta http-equiv="X-UA-Compatible" content="IE=8" />

        <spring:theme code="styleSheet" var="app_css" />
        <spring:url value="/${app_css}" var="app_css_url" />
        <link rel="stylesheet" type="text/css" media="screen" href="${app_css_url}" />

        <!-- Get the user locale from the page context (it was set by Spring MVC's locale resolver) -->
        <c:set var="userLocale">
            <c:set var="plocale">${pageContext.response.locale}</c:set>
            <c:out value="${fn:replace(plocale, '_', '-')}" default="en" />
        </c:set>

        <spring:message code="application_name" var="app_name" htmlEscape="false"/>
        <title><spring:message code="welcome_h3" arguments="${app_name}" /></title>
    </head>
```

```
    <body class="tundra spring">
        <div id="headerWrapper">
            <tiles:insertAttribute name="header" ignore="true" />
        </div>
        <div id="wrapper">
            <tiles:insertAttribute name="menu" ignore="true" />
            <div id="main">
                <tiles:insertAttribute name="body"/>
                <tiles:insertAttribute name="footer" ignore="true"/>
            </div>
        </div>
    </body>
</html>
```

The page is basically a JSP page. The highlights are as follows:

- The `<spring:theme>` tag is placed in the template, which supports theming at the template level.

- The `<tiles:insertAttribute>` tag is used to indicate the page components that need to be loaded from other files, as indicated in the layouts.xml file.

Now let's implement the header, menu, and footer components. The contents are shown in Listings 16-21, 16-22, and 16-23, respectively.

Listing 16-21. The Header Component (header.jspx)

```
<div id="header" xmlns:jsp="http://java.sun.com/JSP/Page"
    xmlns:spring="http://www.springframework.org/tags"
    version="2.0">
    <jsp:directive.page contentType="text/html;charset=UTF-8" />
    <jsp:output omit-xml-declaration="yes" />

    <spring:message code="header_text" var="headerText"/>

    <div id="appname">
        <h1>${headerText}</h1>
    </div>
</div>
```

Listing 16-22. The Menu Component (menu.jspx)

```
<?xml version="1.0" encoding="UTF-8" standalone="no"?>
<div id="menu" xmlns:jsp="http://java.sun.com/JSP/Page"
    xmlns:c="http://java.sun.com/jsp/jstl/core"
    xmlns:spring="http://www.springframework.org/tags"
    version="2.0">
        <jsp:directive.page contentType="text/html;charset=UTF-8" />
        <jsp:output omit-xml-declaration="yes" />
```

```
        <spring:message code="menu_header_text" var="menuHeaderText"/>
        <spring:message code="menu_add_contact" var="menuAddContact"/>
        <spring:url value="/contacts?form" var="addContactUrl"/>

    <h3>${menuHeaderText}</h3>
    <a href="${addContactUrl}"><h3>${menuAddContact}</h3></a>
</div>
```

Listing 16-23. The Footer Component (footer.jspx)

```
<?xml version="1.0" encoding="UTF-8" standalone="no"?>
<div id="footer" xmlns:jsp="http://java.sun.com/JSP/Page"
    xmlns:spring="http://www.springframework.org/tags" version="2.0">
    <jsp:directive.page contentType="text/html;charset=UTF-8" />
    <jsp:output omit-xml-declaration="yes" />

    <spring:message code="home_text" var="homeText"/>
    <spring:message code="label_en_US" var="labelEnUs"/>
    <spring:message code="label_zh_HK" var="labelZhHk"/>
    <spring:url value="/contacts" var="homeUrl"/>

    <a href="${homeUrl}">${homeText}</a> |
    <a href="${homeUrl}?lang=en_US">${labelEnUs}</a> |
    <a href="${homeUrl}?lang=zh_HK">${labelZhHk}</a>
</div>
```

Now for contact list view, we can modify it to fit into the template. Basically, we just need to remove the <head> section, because it's now in the template page (default.jspx). Listing 16-24 shows the revised contact list view.

Listing 16-24. The Revised Contact List View (/views/contacts/list.jspx)

```
<?xml version="1.0" encoding="UTF-8" standalone="no"?>
<div xmlns:jsp="http://java.sun.com/JSP/Page"
    xmlns:c="http://java.sun.com/jsp/jstl/core"
    xmlns:joda="http://www.joda.org/joda/time/tags"
    xmlns:spring="http://www.springframework.org/tags"
    version="2.0">
    <jsp:directive.page contentType="text/html;charset=UTF-8"/>
    <jsp:output omit-xml-declaration="yes"/>

    <spring:message code="label_contact_list" var="labelContactList"/>
    <spring:message code="label_contact_first_name" var="labelContactFirstName"/>
    <spring:message code="label_contact_last_name" var="labelContactLastName"/>
    <spring:message code="label_contact_birth_date" var="labelContactBirthDate"/>

    <h1>${labelContactList}</h1>

    <c:if test="${not empty contacts}">
        <table>
            <thead>
                <tr>
                    <th>${labelContactFirstName}</th>
                    <th>${labelContactLastName}</th>
```

```
            <th>${labelContactBirthDate}</th>
        </tr>
    </thead>
    <tbody>
        <c:forEach items="${contacts}" var="contact">
            <tr>
                <td>${contact.firstName}</td>
                <td>${contact.lastName}</td>
                <td><joda:format value="${contact.birthDate}" pattern="yyyy-MM-dd"/></td>
            </tr>
        </c:forEach>
    </tbody>
</table>
</c:if>
</div>
```

Now the template, definition, and components are ready; the next step is to configure Spring MVC to integrate with Apache Tiles.

Configure Tiles in Spring MVC

Configuring Tiles support in Spring MVC is simple. In the DispatcherServlet configuration (servlet-context.xml), we need to make a modification to replace the InternalResourceViewResolver with the UrlBasedViewResolver class. Listing 16-25 shows the revisions that need to be made to the configuration file.

Listing 16-25. Configure Tiles Support in Spring MVC

```
<?xml version="1.0" encoding="UTF-8"?>

    <!-- Other code omitted -->
    <!-- Remove the following bean -->
    <beans:bean class="org.springframework.web.servlet.view.InternalResourceViewResolver">
        <beans:property name="prefix" value="/WEB-INF/views/" />
        <beans:property name="suffix" value=".jspx" />
    </beans:bean>

    <!-- Other code omitted -->

    <!-- Add the following beans -->
    <!-- Tiles Configuration -->
    <beans:bean class="org.springframework.web.servlet.view.UrlBasedViewResolver"
        id="tilesViewResolver">
        <beans:property name="viewClass" value="org.springframework.web.servlet.view.tiles3.TilesView"/>
    </beans:bean>
```

```
    <beans:bean class="org.springframework.web.servlet.view.tiles3.TilesConfigurer"
id="tilesConfigurer">
        <beans:property name="definitions">
            <beans:list>
                <beans:value>/WEB-INF/layouts/layouts.xml</beans:value>
                <beans:value>/WEB-INF/views/**/views.xml</beans:value>
            </beans:list>
        </beans:property>
    </beans:bean>

</beans:beans>
```

The bean you need to remove is indicated by a comment, while the new bean definitions follow. First, the original `ViewResolver` bean (with the `InternalResourceViewResolver` class) is removed. Then, a `ViewResolver` bean with the class `UrlBasedViewResolver` is defined, with the property `viewClass` set to the `TilesView` class, which is Spring MVC's support for Tiles. Finally, a `tilesConfigurer` bean is defined that provides the layout configurations required by Tiles.

One final configuration file we need to prepare is the `/WEB-INF/views/contacts/views.xml` file, which defines the views for the contact application in our sample. Listing 16-26 shows the file content.

Listing 16-26. The `views.xml` File

```
<?xml version="1.0" encoding="UTF-8" standalone="no"?>
<!DOCTYPE tiles-definitions PUBLIC "-//Apache Software Foundation//DTD Tiles Configuration 3.0//EN"
"http://tiles.apache.org/dtds/tiles-config_3_0.dtd">
<tiles-definitions>
    <definition extends="default" name="contacts/list">
        <put-attribute name="body" value="/WEB-INF/views/contacts/list.jspx" />
    </definition>
</tiles-definitions>
```

As shown in Listing 16-26, the logical view name is mapped to the corresponding body attribute of the view to display. As in the `ContactController` class in Listing 16-11, the `list()` method returns the logical view name `contacts/list`, so Tiles will be able to map the view name to the correct template and the view body to display.

We can now test the page. Make sure that the project was rebuilt and deployed to the server. Load the contact list view again (`http://localhost:8080/contact-webapp/contacts`), and the view based on the template will be displayed.

Implementing the Views for Contact Information

Now we can proceed to implement the views that allow users to view the details of a contact, create new contacts, or update existing contact information.

In the following sections, we discuss the mapping of URLs to the various views, as well as how the views are implemented. We also discuss how to enable JSR-349 validation support in Spring MVC for the edit view.

Mapping URLs to the Views

First we need to design how the various URLs are to be mapped to the corresponding views. In Spring MVC, one of the best practices is to follow the RESTful-style URL for mapping views. Table 16-5 shows the URLs-to-views mapping, as well as the controller method name that will handle the action.

Table 16-5. *Mapping of URLs to Views*

URL	HTTP Method	Controller Method	Description
/contacts	GET	list()	List the contact information.
/contacts/{id}	GET	show()	Display a single contact's information.
/contacts/{id}?form	GET	updateForm()	Display the edit form for updating an existing contact.
/contacts/{id}?form	POST	update()	Users update the contact information and submit the form. Data will be processed here.
/contacts?form	GET	createForm()	Display the edit form for creating a new contact.
/contacts?form	POST	create()	Users enter contact information and submit the form. Data will be processed here.
/contacts/photo/{id}	GET	downloadPhoto()	Download the photo of a contact.

Implementing the Show Contact View

Now we implement the view for showing a contact's information. Implementing the show view is a three-step process:

- Implement the controller method.
- Implement the show contact view (/views/contacts/show.jspx).
- Modify the view definition file for the view (/views/contacts/views.xml).

Listing 16-27 shows the show() method implementation of the ContactController class for displaying a contact's information.

Listing 16-27. The show() Method of the ContactController Class

```
package com.apress.prospring4.ch16;

import java.util.List;

import org.slf4j.Logger;
import org.slf4j.LoggerFactory;
import org.springframework.beans.factory.annotation.Autowired;
import org.springframework.stereotype.Controller;
import org.springframework.ui.Model;
import org.springframework.web.bind.annotation.PathVariable;
import org.springframework.web.bind.annotation.RequestMapping;
import org.springframework.web.bind.annotation.RequestMethod;

@RequestMapping("/contacts")
@Controller
public class ContactController {
    private final Logger logger = LoggerFactory.getLogger(ContactController.class);

    private ContactService contactService;
```

```
    @RequestMapping(method = RequestMethod.GET)
    public String list(Model uiModel) {
        logger.info("Listing contacts");

        List<Contact> contacts = contactService.findAll();
        uiModel.addAttribute("contacts", contacts);

        logger.info("No. of contacts: " + contacts.size());

        return "contacts/list";
    }

    @RequestMapping(value = "/{id}", method = RequestMethod.GET)
    public String show(@PathVariable("id") Long id, Model uiModel) {
        Contact contact = contactService.findById(id);
        uiModel.addAttribute("contact", contact);

        return "contacts/show";
    }

    @Autowired
    public void setContactService(ContactService contactService) {
        this.contactService = contactService;
    }
}
```

In the show() method, the @RequestMapping annotation applied to the method indicates that the method is to handle the URL /contacts/{id} with the HTTP GET method. In the method, the @PathVariable annotation is applied to the argument id, which instructs Spring MVC to extract the id from the URL into the argument. Then the contact is retrieved and added to the Model, and the logical view name contacts/show is returned. The next step is to implement the show contact view (/views/contacts/show.jspx), which is shown in Listing 16-28.

Listing 16-28. The Show Contact View

```
<?xml version="1.0" encoding="UTF-8" standalone="no"?>
<div xmlns:jsp="http://java.sun.com/JSP/Page"
    xmlns:c="http://java.sun.com/jsp/jstl/core"
    xmlns:spring="http://www.springframework.org/tags"
    xmlns:form="http://www.springframework.org/tags/form"
    xmlns:joda="http://www.joda.org/joda/time/tags"
    version="2.0">
    <jsp:directive.page contentType="text/html;charset=UTF-8"/>
    <jsp:output omit-xml-declaration="yes"/>

    <spring:message code="label_contact_info" var="labelContactInfo"/>
    <spring:message code="label_contact_first_name" var="labelContactFirstName"/>
    <spring:message code="label_contact_last_name" var="labelContactLastName"/>
    <spring:message code="label_contact_birth_date" var="labelContactBirthDate"/>
    <spring:message code="label_contact_description" var="labelContactDescription"/>
    <spring:message code="label_contact_update" var="labelContactUpdate"/>
    <spring:message code="date_format_pattern" var="dateFormatPattern"/>
```

```
<spring:url value="/contacts" var="editContactUrl"/>

<h1>${labelContactInfo}</h1>

<div id="contactInfo">

    <c:if test="${not empty message}">
        <div id="message" class="${message.type}">${message.message}</div>
    </c:if>

    <table>
        <tr>
            <td>${labelContactFirstName}</td>
            <td>${contact.firstName}</td>
        </tr>
        <tr>
            <td>${labelContactLastName}</td>
            <td>${contact.lastName}</td>
        </tr>
        <tr>
            <td>${labelContactBirthDate}</td>
            <td><joda:format value="${contact.birthDate}" pattern="${dateFormatPattern}"/></td>
        </tr>
        <tr>
            <td>${labelContactDescription}</td>
            <td>${contact.description}</td>
        </tr>
    </table>

    <a href="${editContactUrl}/${contact.id}?form">${labelContactUpdate}</a>
</div>
</div>
```

The page is simple; it simply displays the model attribute contact within the page.

The final step is to modify the view definition file (/views/contacts/views.xml) for mapping the logical view name contacts/show. Simply append the code snippet in Listing 16-29 into the file, under the <tiles-definitions> tag.

Listing 16-29. The Show Contact View Mapping

```
<definition extends="default" name="contacts/show">
    <put-attribute name="body" value="/WEB-INF/views/contacts/show.jspx" />
</definition>
```

The show contact view is complete. Now we need to add an anchor link into the contact list view (/views/contacts/list.jspx) for each contact to the show contact view. Listing 16-30 shows the revised file.

Listing 16-30. Add the Anchor Link in the List Contact View

```
<?xml version="1.0" encoding="UTF-8" standalone="no"?>
<div xmlns:jsp="http://java.sun.com/JSP/Page"
    xmlns:c="http://java.sun.com/jsp/jstl/core"
    xmlns:joda="http://www.joda.org/joda/time/tags"
```

```
        xmlns:spring="http://www.springframework.org/tags"
        version="2.0">
    <jsp:directive.page contentType="text/html;charset=UTF-8"/>
    <jsp:output omit-xml-declaration="yes"/>

    <spring:message code="label_contact_list" var="labelContactList"/>
    <spring:message code="label_contact_first_name" var="labelContactFirstName"/>
    <spring:message code="label_contact_last_name" var="labelContactLastName"/>
    <spring:message code="label_contact_birth_date" var="labelContactBirthDate"/>

    <spring:url value="/contacts" var="showContactUrl"/>

    <h1>${labelContactList}</h1>

    <c:if test="${not empty contacts}">
        <table>
            <thead>
            <tr>
                <th>${labelContactFirstName}</th>
                <th>${labelContactLastName}</th>
                <th>${labelContactBirthDate}</th>
            </tr>
            </thead>
            <tbody>
            <c:forEach items="${contacts}" var="contact">
                <tr>
                    <td><a href="${showContactUrl}/${contact.id}">${contact.firstName}</a></td>
                    <td>${contact.lastName}</td>
                    <td><joda:format value="${contact.birthDate}" pattern="yyyy-MM-dd"/></td>
                </tr>
            </c:forEach>
            </tbody>
        </table>
    </c:if>
</div>
```

As shown in Listing 16-30, we declare an URL variable by using the `<spring:url>` tag and add an anchor link for the `firstName` attribute. To test the show contact view, upon rebuild and deploy, open the contact list view again. The list should now include the hyperlink to the show contact view. Clicking any link will bring you to the show contact information view.

Implementing the Edit Contact View

Let's implement the view for editing a contact. It's the same as the show view; first we add the methods `updateForm()` and `update()` to the `ContactController` class. Listing 16-31 shows the revised controller for the two methods.

Listing 16-31. Revised Controller for Update Contact

```java
package com.apress.prospring4.ch16;

import java.util.List;
import java.util.Locale;

import org.slf4j.Logger;
import org.slf4j.LoggerFactory;
import org.springframework.beans.factory.annotation.Autowired;
import org.springframework.context.MessageSource;
import org.springframework.stereotype.Controller;
import org.springframework.ui.Model;
import org.springframework.validation.BindingResult;
import org.springframework.web.bind.annotation.PathVariable;
import org.springframework.web.bind.annotation.RequestMapping;
import org.springframework.web.bind.annotation.RequestMethod;
import org.springframework.web.servlet.mvc.support.RedirectAttributes;

import javax.servlet.http.HttpServletRequest;

@RequestMapping("/contacts")
@Controller
public class ContactController {
    private final Logger logger = LoggerFactory.getLogger(ContactController.class);

    private ContactService contactService;
    private MessageSource messageSource;

    @RequestMapping(method = RequestMethod.GET)
    public String list(Model uiModel) {
        logger.info("Listing contacts");

        List<Contact> contacts = contactService.findAll();
        uiModel.addAttribute("contacts", contacts);

        logger.info("No. of contacts: " + contacts.size());

        return "contacts/list";
    }

    @RequestMapping(value = "/{id}", method = RequestMethod.GET)
    public String show(@PathVariable("id") Long id, Model uiModel) {
        Contact contact = contactService.findById(id);
        uiModel.addAttribute("contact", contact);

        return "contacts/show";
    }
```

```
@RequestMapping(value = "/{id}", params = "form", method = RequestMethod.POST)
public String update(Contact contact, BindingResult bindingResult, Model uiModel,
                     HttpServletRequest httpServletRequest, RedirectAttributes redirectAttributes,
                     Locale locale) {
    logger.info("Updating contact");
    if (bindingResult.hasErrors()) {
        uiModel.addAttribute("message", new Message("error",
                messageSource.getMessage("contact_save_fail", new Object[]{}, locale)));
        uiModel.addAttribute("contact", contact);
        return "contacts/update";
    }
    uiModel.asMap().clear();
    redirectAttributes.addFlashAttribute("message", new Message("success",
            messageSource.getMessage("contact_save_success", new Object[]{}, locale)));
    contactService.save(contact);
    return "redirect:/contacts/" + UrlUtil.encodeUrlPathSegment(contact.getId().toString(),
            httpServletRequest);
}

@RequestMapping(value = "/{id}", params = "form", method = RequestMethod.GET)
public String updateForm(@PathVariable("id") Long id, Model uiModel) {
    uiModel.addAttribute("contact", contactService.findById(id));
    return "contacts/update";
}

@Autowired
public void setContactService(ContactService contactService) {
    this.contactService = contactService;
}

@Autowired
public void setMessageSource(MessageSource messageSource) {
    this.messageSource = messageSource;
}
}
```

In Listing 16-31, the highlights are as follows:

- The MessageSource interface is autowired into the controller for retrieving messages with i18n support.

- For the updateForm() method, the contact is retrieved and saved into the Model, and then the logical view contacts/update is returned, which will display the edit contact view.

- The update() method will be triggered when the user updates contact information and clicks the Save button. This method needs a bit of explanation. First, Spring MVC will try to bind the submitted data to the Contact domain object and perform the type conversion and formatting automatically. If binding errors are found (for example, the birth date was entered in the wrong format), the errors will be saved into the BindingResult interface (under the package org.springframework.validation), and an error message will be saved into the Model, redisplaying the edit view. If the binding is successful, the data will be saved, and the logical view name will be returned for the display contact view by using redirect: as the prefix. Note that we want to display the message after the redirect, so we need to use the RedirectAttributes.addFlashAttribute() method (an interface under the package org.springframework.web.servlet.mvc.support) for displaying the success message in the show contact view. In Spring MVC, flash attributes are saved temporarily before the redirect (typically in the session) to be made available to the request after the redirect and removed immediately.

- The Message class is a custom class that stores the message retrieved from MessageSource and the type of message (that is, success or error) for the view to display in the message area. Listing 16-32 shows the content of the Message class.

- UrlUtil is a utility class for encoding the URL for redirect. Listing 16-33 shows its content.

Listing 16-32. The Message Class

```
package com.apress.prospring4.ch16;

public class Message {
    private String type;
    private String message;

    public Message(String type, String message) {
        this.type = type;
        this.message = message;
    }

    public String getType() {
        return type;
    }

    public String getMessage() {
        return message;
    }
}
```

Listing 16-33. The UrlUtil Class

```
package com.apress.prospring4.ch16;

import java.io.UnsupportedEncodingException;

import javax.servlet.http.HttpServletRequest;

import org.springframework.web.util.UriUtils;
import org.springframework.web.util.WebUtils;
```

```
        public class UrlUtil {
            public static String encodeUrlPathSegment(String pathSegment,
    HttpServletRequest httpServletRequest) {
                String enc = httpServletRequest.getCharacterEncoding();

                if (enc == null) {
                    enc = WebUtils.DEFAULT_CHARACTER_ENCODING;
                }

                try {
                    pathSegment = UriUtils.encodePathSegment(pathSegment, enc);
                } catch (UnsupportedEncodingException uee) {
                    //
                }

                return pathSegment;
            }
        }
```

Next is the edit contact view (/views/contacts/edit.jspx), and we will use it for both updating and creating a new contact. Listing 16-34 shows the content.

Listing 16-34. The Edit Contact View

```
<?xml version="1.0" encoding="UTF-8" standalone="no"?>
<div xmlns:jsp="http://java.sun.com/JSP/Page"
    xmlns:c="http://java.sun.com/jsp/jstl/core"
    xmlns:spring="http://www.springframework.org/tags"
    xmlns:form="http://www.springframework.org/tags/form"
    version="2.0">
    <jsp:directive.page contentType="text/html;charset=UTF-8"/>
    <jsp:output omit-xml-declaration="yes"/>

    <spring:message code="label_contact_new" var="labelContactNew"/>
    <spring:message code="label_contact_update" var="labelContactUpdate"/>
    <spring:message code="label_contact_first_name" var="labelContactFirstName"/>
    <spring:message code="label_contact_last_name" var="labelContactLastName"/>
    <spring:message code="label_contact_birth_date" var="labelContactBirthDate"/>
    <spring:message code="label_contact_description" var="labelContactDescription"/>
    <spring:message code="label_contact_photo" var="labelContactPhoto"/>

    <spring:eval expression="contact.id == null ? labelContactNew:labelContactUpdate"
        var="formTitle"/>

    <h1>${formTitle}</h1>

    <div id="contactUpdate">
    <form:form modelAttribute="contact" id="contactUpdateForm" method="post">

        <c:if test="${not empty message}">
            <div id="message" class="${message.type}">${message.message}</div>
        </c:if>
```

```
        <form:label path="firstName">
            ${labelContactFirstName}*
        </form:label>
        <form:input path="firstName" />
        <div>
            <form:errors path="firstName" cssClass="error" />
        </div>
        <p/>

        <form:label path="lastName">
            ${labelContactLastName}*
        </form:label>
        <form:input path="lastName" />
        <div>
            <form:errors path="lastName" cssClass="error" />
        </div>
        <p/>

        <form:label path="birthDate">
            ${labelContactBirthDate}
        </form:label>
        <form:input path="birthDate" id="birthDate"/>
        <div>
            <form:errors path="birthDate" cssClass="error" />
        </div>
        <p/>

        <form:label path="description">
            ${labelContactDescription}
        </form:label>
        <form:textarea cols="60" rows="8" path="description" id="contactDescription"/>
        <div>
            <form:errors path="description" cssClass="error" />
        </div>
        <p/>

        <form:hidden path="version" />

        <button type="submit">Save</button>
        <button type="reset">Reset</button>

    </form:form>
    </div>
</div>
```

The highlights for Listing 16-34 are as follows:

- The <spring:eval> tag is used, which uses the Spring Expression Language to test whether the contact ID is null. If yes, then it's a new contact; otherwise, it's an update. The corresponding form title will be displayed.

- Various Spring MVC <form> tags are used within the form for displaying the label, the input field, and errors in case binding was not successful on form submission.

Next, add the view mapping to the view definition file (/views/contacts/views.xml). Listing 16-35 shows the code snippet.

Listing 16-35. The Edit Contact View Mapping

```
<definition extends="default" name="contacts/update">
    <put-attribute name="body" value="/WEB-INF/views/contacts/edit.jspx" />
</definition>
```

The edit view is now completed. Let's rebuild and deploy the project. Upon clicking the edit link, the edit view will be displayed. Update the information and click the Save button. If binding was success, then you will see the success message, and the show contact view will be displayed.

Implementing the Add Contact View

Implementing the add contact view is much like the edit view. Because we will reuse the edit.jspx page, we only need to add the methods in the ContactController class and the view definition.

Listing 16-36 shows the revised contact controller functionality in the ContactController class.

Listing 16-36. The Revised ContactController for the Add Contact Methods

```
package com.apress.prospring4.ch16;

import java.util.List;
import java.util.Locale;

import org.slf4j.Logger;
import org.slf4j.LoggerFactory;
import org.springframework.beans.factory.annotation.Autowired;
import org.springframework.context.MessageSource;
import org.springframework.stereotype.Controller;
import org.springframework.ui.Model;
import org.springframework.validation.BindingResult;
import org.springframework.web.bind.annotation.PathVariable;
import org.springframework.web.bind.annotation.RequestMapping;
import org.springframework.web.bind.annotation.RequestMethod;
import org.springframework.web.servlet.mvc.support.RedirectAttributes;

import javax.servlet.http.HttpServletRequest;

@RequestMapping("/contacts")
@Controller
public class ContactController {
    private final Logger logger = LoggerFactory.getLogger(ContactController.class);

    private ContactService contactService;
    private MessageSource messageSource;

    @RequestMapping(method = RequestMethod.GET)
    public String list(Model uiModel) {
        logger.info("Listing contacts");
```

```java
        List<Contact> contacts = contactService.findAll();
        uiModel.addAttribute("contacts", contacts);

        logger.info("No. of contacts: " + contacts.size());

        return "contacts/list";
    }

    @RequestMapping(value = "/{id}", method = RequestMethod.GET)
    public String show(@PathVariable("id") Long id, Model uiModel) {
        Contact contact = contactService.findById(id);
        uiModel.addAttribute("contact", contact);

        return "contacts/show";
    }

    @RequestMapping(value = "/{id}", params = "form", method = RequestMethod.POST)
    public String update(Contact contact, BindingResult bindingResult, Model uiModel,
                         HttpServletRequest httpServletRequest, RedirectAttributes
redirectAttributes, Locale locale) {
        logger.info("Updating contact");
        if (bindingResult.hasErrors()) {
            uiModel.addAttribute("message", new Message("error",
                    messageSource.getMessage("contact_save_fail", new Object[]{}, locale)));
            uiModel.addAttribute("contact", contact);
            return "contacts/update";
        }
        uiModel.asMap().clear();
        redirectAttributes.addFlashAttribute("message", new Message("success",
                messageSource.getMessage("contact_save_success", new Object[]{}, locale)));
        contactService.save(contact);
        return "redirect:/contacts/" + UrlUtil.encodeUrlPathSegment(contact.getId().toString(),
                httpServletRequest);
    }

    @RequestMapping(value = "/{id}", params = "form", method = RequestMethod.GET)
    public String updateForm(@PathVariable("id") Long id, Model uiModel) {
        uiModel.addAttribute("contact", contactService.findById(id));
        return "contacts/update";
    }

    @RequestMapping(params = "form", method = RequestMethod.POST)
    public String create(Contact contact, BindingResult bindingResult, Model uiModel,
HttpServletRequest httpServletRequest, RedirectAttributes redirectAttributes, Locale locale) {

        logger.info("Creating contact");
```

```java
        if (bindingResult.hasErrors()) {
            uiModel.addAttribute("message", new Message("error",
                    messageSource.getMessage("contact_save_fail", new Object[]{}, locale)));
            uiModel.addAttribute("contact", contact);
            return "contacts/create";
        }

        uiModel.asMap().clear();
        redirectAttributes.addFlashAttribute("message", new Message("success",
                messageSource.getMessage("contact_save_success", new Object[]{}, locale)));

        logger.info("Contact id: " + contact.getId());

        contactService.save(contact);

        return "redirect:/contacts/" + UrlUtil.encodeUrlPathSegment(contact.getId().toString(),
                httpServletRequest);
    }

    @RequestMapping(params = "form", method = RequestMethod.GET)
    public String createForm(Model uiModel) {
        Contact contact = new Contact();
        uiModel.addAttribute("contact", contact);

        return "contacts/create";
    }

    @Autowired
    public void setContactService(ContactService contactService) {
        this.contactService = contactService;
    }

    @Autowired
    public void setMessageSource(MessageSource messageSource) {
        this.messageSource = messageSource;
    }
}
```

Next, add the view mapping to the view definition file (/views/contacts/views.xml). Listing 16-37 shows the code snippet.

Listing 16-37. The Add Contact View Mapping

```xml
<definition extends="default" name="contacts/create">
    <put-attribute name="body" value="/WEB-INF/views/contacts/edit.jspx" />
</definition>
```

The add view is now complete. After you rebuild and deploy the project, click the New Contact link in the menu area. The add contact view will be displayed, allowing you to enter new contact details.

Enabling JSR-349 Bean Validation

Let's configure JSR-349, "Bean Validation," support for creation and update contact actions. First, apply the validation constraints to the Contact domain object. In this sample, we define constraints only for the firstName and lastName attributes. Listing 16-38 shows the revised Contact class with the annotations applied to the firstName and lastName attributes.

Listing 16-38. Applying Constraints to the Contact Domain Object

```
package com.apress.prospring4.ch16;

import static javax.persistence.GenerationType.IDENTITY;

import java.io.Serializable;

import org.hibernate.annotations.Type;
import org.hibernate.validator.constraints.NotEmpty;
import org.joda.time.DateTime;
import org.springframework.format.annotation.DateTimeFormat;
import org.springframework.format.annotation.DateTimeFormat.ISO;

import javax.persistence.Basic;
import javax.persistence.Column;
import javax.persistence.Entity;
import javax.persistence.FetchType;
import javax.persistence.GeneratedValue;
import javax.persistence.Id;
import javax.persistence.Lob;
import javax.persistence.Table;
import javax.persistence.Transient;
import javax.persistence.Version;
import javax.validation.constraints.Size;

@Entity
@Table(name = "contact")
public class Contact implements Serializable {
    private Long id;
    private int version;
    private String firstName;
    private String lastName;
    private DateTime birthDate;
    private String description;
    private byte[] photo;

    @Id
    @GeneratedValue(strategy = IDENTITY)
    @Column(name = "ID")
    public Long getId() {
        return id;
    }
```

```java
public void setId(Long id) {
    this.id = id;
}

@Version
@Column(name = "VERSION")
public int getVersion() {
    return version;
}

public void setVersion(int version) {
    this.version = version;
}

@NotEmpty(message="{validation.firstname.NotEmpty.message}")
@Size(min=3, max=60, message="{validation.firstname.Size.message}")
@Column(name = "FIRST_NAME")
public String getFirstName() {
    return firstName;
}

public void setFirstName(String firstName) {
    this.firstName = firstName;
}

@NotEmpty(message="{validation.lastname.NotEmpty.message}")
@Size(min=1, max=40, message="{validation.lastname.Size.message}")
@Column(name = "LAST_NAME")
public String getLastName() {
    return lastName;
}

public void setLastName(String lastName) {
    this.lastName = lastName;
}

@Column(name = "BIRTH_DATE")
@Type(type="org.jadira.usertype.dateandtime.joda.PersistentDateTime")
@DateTimeFormat(iso=ISO.DATE)
public DateTime getBirthDate() {
    return birthDate;
}

public void setBirthDate(DateTime birthDate) {
    this.birthDate = birthDate;
}

@Column(name = "DESCRIPTION")
public String getDescription() {
    return description;
}
```

```
    public void setDescription(String description) {
        this.description = description;
    }

    @Basic(fetch= FetchType.LAZY)
    @Lob
    @Column(name = "PHOTO")
    public byte[] getPhoto() {
        return photo;
    }

    public void setPhoto(byte[] photo) {
        this.photo = photo;
    }

    @Transient
    public String getBirthDateString() {
        String birthDateString = "";
        if (birthDate != null)
            birthDateString = org.joda.time.format.DateTimeFormat
                    .forPattern("yyyy-MM-dd").print(birthDate);
        return birthDateString;
    }

    @Override
    public String toString() {
        return "Contact - Id: " + id + ", First name: " + firstName
                + ", Last name: " + lastName + ", Birthday: " + birthDate
                + ", Description: " + description;
    }
}
```

The constraints are applied to their respective methods. Note that for the validation message, we use a code by using the curly braces. This will cause the validation messages to retrieve from the ResourceBundle and hence support i18n.

To enable JSR-349 validation during the web data binding process, we just need to apply the @Valid annotation to the argument of the create() and update() methods in the ContactController class. Listing 16-39 shows the code snippet for both methods.

Listing 16-39. Enable JSR-349 Validation in Controller

```
public String update(@Valid Contact contact, ...

public String create(@Valid Contact contact, ...
```

We also want the JSR-349 validation message to use the same ResourceBundle as for the views. To do this, we need to configure the validator in the DispatcherServlet configuration (servlet-context.xml). Listing 16-40 shows the code snippet for the change.

Listing 16-40. Configure JSR-349 Support in Spring MVC

```xml
<?xml version="1.0" encoding="UTF-8"?>

    <!-- Other code omitted -->

    <annotation-driven validator="validator"/>
    <!-- Other code omitted -->

    <beans:bean id="validator" class="org.springframework.validation.beanvalidation.
LocalValidatorFactoryBean">
        <beans:property name="validationMessageSource" ref="messageSource"/>
    </beans:bean>
</beans:beans>
```

First, a `validator` bean is defined, with the class `LocalValidatorFactoryBean`, for JSR-349 support. Note that we set the `validationMessageSource` property to reference the `messageSource` bean defined, which instructs the JSR-349 validator to look up the messages by the codes from the `messageSource` bean. Then for the `<annotation-driven>` tag, the `validator` attribute is explicitly defined to reference the `validator` bean we defined.

That's all, and we can test the validation now. Bring up the add contact view and just click the Save button. The returned page will now show us a validation error.

Switch to the Chinese (HK) language, and do the same thing. This time, the messages will be displayed in Chinese.

Now the views are basically complete, except the delete action. We leave that one to you as an exercise. Next, we will start to give our application more richness.

Using jQuery and jQuery UI

Although the views for our contact application work well, the user interface is quite raw. For example, for the birth date field, it would be much better if we could add a date picker for entering the birth date of the contact, instead of having the user input the date string manually.

To provide a richer interface to the users of a web application, unless you are using rich Internet application (RIA) technologies that require special runtimes on the web browser client (for example, Adobe Flex requires Flash, JavaFX requires JRE, and Microsoft Silverlight requires Silverlight), you need to use JavaScript to implement the features.

However, developing web front ends with raw JavaScript is not easy. The syntax is very different from Java, and you also need to deal with cross-browser compatibility issues. As a result, a lot of open source JavaScript libraries are available that can make the process easier, such as jQuery and Dojo Toolkit.

In the following sections, we discuss how to use jQuery and jQuery UI to develop more-responsive and interactive user interfaces. We also discuss some commonly used jQuery plug-ins for specific purposes, such as rich-text editing support, and discuss some grid-based components for browsing data.

Introducing jQuery and jQuery UI

jQuery (`http://jquery.org`) is one of the most popular JavaScript libraries being used for web front-end development. jQuery provides comprehensive support for main features including a robust "selector" syntax for selecting DOM elements within the document, a sophisticated event model, and powerful Ajax support.

Built on top of jQuery, the jQuery UI library (`http://jqueryui.com`) provides a rich set of widgets and effects. Main features include widgets for commonly used user interface components (a date picker, autocomplete, accordion, and so on), drag and drop, effects and animation, theming, and more.

There exists a wealth of jQuery plug-ins developed by the jQuery community for specific purposes, and we discuss two of them in this chapter.

What we cover here only scratches the surface of jQuery. For more details on using jQuery, we recommend the books *jQuery Recipes: A Problem-Solution Approach* by B.M. Harwani (Apress, 2010) and *jQuery in Action*, Second Edition by Bear Bibeault and Yehuda Katz (Manning, 2010).

Enabling jQuery and jQuery UI in a View

To be able to use jQuery and jQuery UI components in our view, we need to include the required style sheets and JavaScript files.

If you read the section "Understanding Spring MVC Project Structure" earlier in this chapter, the required files should have been already copied into the project. The main files that we need to include in our view are as follows:

- `/src/main/webapp/scripts/jquery-1.11.1.js`: This is the core jQuery JavaScript library. The version we use in this chapter is 1.11.1. Note that it's the full source version. In production, you should use the minified version (that is, `jquery-1.11.1.min.js`), which is optimized and compressed to improve download and execution performance.

- `/src/main/webapp/scripts/jquery-ui-1.10.4.custom.min.js`: This is the jQuery UI library bundled with a theme style sheet that can be customized and downloaded from the jQuery UI Themeroller page (`http://jqueryui.com/themeroller`). The jQuery UI version we are using is 1.10.4. Note that it's the minified version of JavaScript.

- `/src/main/webapp/styles/custom-theme/jquery-ui-1.10.4.custom.css`: This is the style sheet for the custom theme that will be used by jQuery UI for theming support.

To include the previous files, we only need to include them in our template page (that is, `/layouts/default.jspx`). Listing 16-41 shows the code snippet that needs to be added to the page.

Listing 16-41. Include jQuery in Template Page

```
<html xmlns:jsp="http://java.sun.com/JSP/Page">

    <!-- Other code omitted -->

    <head>
        <meta http-equiv="Content-Type" content="text/html; charset=UTF-8" />
        <meta http-equiv="X-UA-Compatible" content="IE=8" />

        <spring:theme code="styleSheet" var="app_css" />
        <spring:url value="/${app_css}" var="app_css_url" />
        <link rel="stylesheet" type="text/css" media="screen" href="${app_css_url}" />

        <!-- jQuery and jQuery UI -->
        <spring:url value="/resources/scripts/jquery-1.11.1.js" var="jquery_url" />
        <spring:url value="/resources/scripts/jquery-ui-1.10.4.custom.min.js"
            var="jquery_ui_url" />
        <spring:url value="/resources/styles/custom-theme/jquery-ui-1.10.4.custom.css"
            var="jquery_ui_theme_css" />
        <link rel="stylesheet" type="text/css" media="screen" href="${jquery_ui_theme_css}" />
        <script src="${jquery_url}" type="text/javascript"><jsp:text/></script>
        <script src="${jquery_ui_url}" type="text/javascript"><jsp:text/></script>

    <!-- Other code omitted -->
</html>
```

First, the `<spring:url>` tag is used to define the URLs for the files and store them in variables. Then, in the `<head>` section, the reference to the CSS and JavaScript files is added. Note the use of the `<jsp:text/>`tag within the `<script>` tag. This is because JSPX will autocollapse tags without a body. So, the tag `<script ...></script>` in the file will end up as `<script .../>`in the browser, which will cause undetermined behavior in the page. The addition of `<jsp:text/>`ensures that the `<script>` tag will not render in the page because it avoids unexpected issues.

With these scripts included, we can add some fancier stuff into our view. For the edit contact view, let's make our buttons look a bit better and enable the date picker component for the birth date field. Listing 16-42 shows the change that we need to add to the view (/views/contacts/edit.jspx) for the button and date field.

Listing 16-42. Decorate the Button and Date Picker in the Edit Contact View

```
<?xml version="1.0" encoding="UTF-8" standalone="no"?>

<div xmlns:jsp="http://java.sun.com/JSP/Page"
     xmlns:c="http://java.sun.com/jsp/jstl/core"
     xmlns:spring="http://www.springframework.org/tags"
     xmlns:form="http://www.springframework.org/tags/form"
     version="2.0">

    <script type="text/javascript">
    $(function(){
        $('#birthDate').datepicker({
            dateFormat: 'yy-mm-dd',
            changeYear: true
        });
    });
    </script>

    <!-- Other code omitted -->

    <button type="submit" class="ui-button ui-widget ui-state-default ui-corner-all
ui-button-text-only">
        <span class="ui-button-text">Save</span>
    </button>
    <button type="reset" class="ui-button ui-widget ui-state-default ui-corner-all
ui-button-text-only">
        <span class="ui-button-text">Reset</span>
    </button>

    <!-- Other code omitted -->
</div>
```

The `$(function(){})` syntax instructs jQuery to execute the script when the document is ready. Within the function, the birth date input field (with ID `birthDate`) is decorated using jQuery UI's `datepicker()` function. Second, various style classes are added to the buttons.

Now redeploy the application, and you will see the new button style, and when you click the birth date field, the date picker component will be displayed.

Rich-Text Editing with CKEditor

For the description field of the contact information, we use the Spring MVC <form:textarea> tag to support multiline input. Suppose we want to enable rich-text editing, which is a common requirement for long text inputs such as user comments.

To support this feature, we will use the rich-text component library CKEditor (http://ckeditor.com), which is a common rich-text JavaScript component, with integration with jQuery UI. The files are in the folder /src/main/webapp/ckeditor of the sample source code.

First we need to include the required JavaScript files into the template page (default.jspx). Listing 16-43 shows the code snippet you need to add to the page.

Listing 16-43. Add CKEditor to Page Template

```
<html xmlns:jsp="http://java.sun.com/JSP/Page"
      xmlns:c="http://java.sun.com/jsp/jstl/core"
      xmlns:fn="http://java.sun.com/jsp/jstl/functions"
      xmlns:tiles="http://tiles.apache.org/tags-tiles"
      xmlns:spring="http://www.springframework.org/tags">

        <!-- Other code omitted -->

        <!-- jQuery and jQuery UI -->

        <!-- CKEditor -->
        <spring:url value="/resources/ckeditor/ckeditor.js" var="ckeditor_url" />
        <spring:url value="/resources/ckeditor/adapters/jquery.js" var="ckeditor_jquery_url" />
        <script type="text/javascript" src="${ckeditor_url}"><jsp:text/></script>
        <script type="text/javascript" src="${ckeditor_jquery_url}"><jsp:text/></script>

        <!-- Other code omitted -->
</html>
```

In Listing 16-43, we included two scripts: the core CKEditor script and the adapter with jQuery.

The next step is to enable the CKEditor in the edit contact view. Listing 16-44 shows the change required for the page (edit.jspx).

Listing 16-44. Add CKEditor to Edit Contact View

```
<?xml version="1.0" encoding="UTF-8" standalone="no"?>

    <!-- Other code omitted -->

    <script type="text/javascript">
    $(function(){
        $('#birthDate').datepicker({
            dateFormat: 'yy-mm-dd',
            changeYear: true
        });
```

```
        $("#contactDescription").ckeditor(
            {
                toolbar : 'Basic',
                uiColor : '#CCCCCC'
            }
        );
    });
    </script>

    <!-- Other code omitted -->

</div>
```

The contact description field is decorated with CKEditor when the document is ready. Redeploy the application and go to the add contact page, and the description field will be enabled with rich-text editing support.

For complete documentation on using and configuring CKEditor, please refer to the project documentation site (http://docs.cksource.com/).

Using jqGrid for a Data Grid with Pagination

The current contact list view is fine if only a few contacts exist in the system. However, as the data grows to thousands and even more records, performance will become a problem.

A common solution is to implement a data grid component, with pagination support, for data browsing so that the user browses only a certain number of records, which avoids a large amount of data transfer between the browser and the web container. This section demonstrates the implementation of a data grid with jqGrid (www.trirand.com/blog), a popular JavaScript-based data grid component. The version we are using is 4.6.0.

For the pagination support, we will use jqGrid's built-in Ajax pagination support, which fires an XMLHttpRequest for each page and accepts JSON data format for page data. So, we need to add the JSON library dependency into our project, as shown in Table 16-6.

Table 16-6. *Maven Dependencies for JSON*

Group ID	Artifact ID	Version	Description
org.codehaus.jackson	jackson-mapper-lgpl	1.9.13	Jackson JSON processor to support data in JSON format

In the following sections, we discuss how to implement the pagination support on both the server and client sides. First, we cover implementing the jqGrid component in the contact list view. Then, we discuss how to implement pagination on the server side by using the Spring Data Commons module's comprehensive pagination support.

Enable jqGrid in the Contact List View

To enable jqGrid in our views, first we need to include the required JavaScript and style sheet files in the template page (default.jspx). Listing 16-45 shows the code snippet required.

Listing 16-45. Add jqGrid to Page Template

```
<html xmlns:jsp="http://java.sun.com/JSP/Page"

    <!-- Other code omitted -->

        <!-- CKEditor -->

        <!-- jqGrid -->
        <spring:url value="/resources/jqgrid/css/ui.jqgrid.css" var="jqgrid_css" />
        <spring:url value="/resources/jqgrid/js/i18n/grid.locale-en.js"
        var="jqgrid_locale_url" />
        <spring:url value="/resources/jqgrid/js/jquery.jqGrid.min.js" var="jqgrid_url" />
        <link rel="stylesheet" type="text/css" media="screen" href="${jqgrid_css}" />
        <script type="text/javascript" src="${jqgrid_locale_url}"><jsp:text/></script>
    <script type="text/javascript" src="${jqgrid_url}"><jsp:text/></script>

    <!-- Other code omitted -->

</html>
```

First, the grid-specific CSS file is loaded. Then, two JavaScript files are required. The first one is the locale script (in this case, we use English), and the second one is the jqGrid core library file (`jquery.jqGrid.min.js`).

The next step is to modify the contact list view (`list.jspx`) to use jqGrid. Listing 16-46 shows the revised page.

Listing 16-46. Contact List Page with jqGrid

```
<?xml version="1.0" encoding="UTF-8" standalone="no"?>
<div xmlns:jsp="http://java.sun.com/JSP/Page"
    xmlns:c="http://java.sun.com/jsp/jstl/core"
    xmlns:spring="http://www.springframework.org/tags"
    version="2.0">
    <jsp:directive.page contentType="text/html;charset=UTF-8"/>
    <jsp:output omit-xml-declaration="yes"/>

    <spring:message code="label_contact_list" var="labelContactList"/>
    <spring:message code="label_contact_first_name" var="labelContactFirstName"/>
    <spring:message code="label_contact_last_name" var="labelContactLastName"/>
    <spring:message code="label_contact_birth_date" var="labelContactBirthDate"/>
    <spring:url value="/contacts/" var="showContactUrl"/>

    <script type="text/javascript">
    $(function(){
      $("#list").jqGrid({
        url:'${showContactUrl}/listgrid',
        datatype: 'json',
        mtype: 'GET',
        colNames:['${labelContactFirstName}', '${labelContactLastName}',
            '${labelContactBirthDate}'],
```

```
      colModel :[
        {name:'firstName', index:'firstName', width:150},
        {name:'lastName', index:'lastName', width:100},
        {name:'birthDateString', index:'birthDate', width:100}
      ],
      jsonReader : {
          root:"contactData",
          page: "currentPage",
          total: "totalPages",
          records: "totalRecords",
          repeatitems: false,
          id: "id"
      },
      pager: '#pager',
      rowNum:10,
      rowList:[10,20,30],
      sortname: 'firstName',
      sortorder: 'asc',
      viewrecords: true,
      gridview: true,
      height: 250,
      width: 500,
      caption: '${labelContactList}',
      onSelectRow: function(id){
          document.location.href ="${showContactUrl}/" + id;
      }
    });
  });
  </script>

  <c:if test="${not empty message}">
      <div id="message" class="${message.type}">${message.message}</div>
  </c:if>

  <h2>${labelContactList}</h2>

  <div>
  <table id="list"><tr><td/></tr></table>
  </div>
  <div id="pager"></div>
</div>
```

We declare a `<table>` tag with an ID of list for displaying the grid data. Under the table, a `<div>` section with an ID of pager is defined, which is the pagination part for jqGrid.

Within the JavaScript, when the document is ready, we instruct jqGrid to decorate the table with an ID of list into a grid and provide detail configuration information. Some main highlights of the scripts are as follows:

- The url attribute specifies the link for sending XMLHttpRequest, which gets the data for the current page.

- The datatype attribute specifies the data format, in this case JSON. jqGrid also supports XML format.

- The mtype attribute defines the HTTP method to use, which is GET.

- The colNames attribute defines the column header for the data to be displayed in the grid, while the colModel attribute defines the detail for each data column.

- The jsonReader attribute defines the JSON data format that the server will be returning.

- The pager attribute enables pagination support.

- The onSelectRow attribute defines the action to take when a row was selected. In our case, we will direct the user to the show contact view with the contact ID.

For a detailed description on the configuration and usage of jqGrid, please refer to the project's documentation site (www.trirand.com/jqgridwiki/doku.php?id=wiki:jqgriddocs).

Enable Pagination on the Server Side

On the server side, there are several steps to take to implement pagination. First we will use the Spring Data Commons module's pagination support. To enable this, we need only to modify the ContactRepository interface to extend the PagingAndSortingRepository<T,ID extends Serializable> interface instead of the CrudRepository<T,ID extends Serializable> interface. Listing 16-47 shows the revised interface.

Listing 16-47. The Revised ContactRepository Interface

```
package com.apress.prospring4;

import org.springframework.data.repository.PagingAndSortingRepository;

public interface ContactRepository extends PagingAndSortingRepository<Contact, Long> {
}
```

The next step is to add a new method in the ContactService interface to support retrieving the data by page. Listing 16-48 shows the revised interface.

Listing 16-48. The Revised ContactService Interface

```
package com.apress.prospring4.ch16;

import java.util.List;

import org.springframework.data.domain.Page;
import org.springframework.data.domain.Pageable;

public interface ContactService {
    List<Contact> findAll();
    Contact findById(Long id);
    Contact save(Contact contact);
    Page<Contact> findAllByPage(Pageable pageable);
}
```

As shown in Listing 16-48, a new method findAllByPage() is added, taking an instance of the Pageable interface as an argument. Listing 16-49 shows the implementation of the findAllByPage() method in the ContactServiceImpl class. The method returns an instance of the Page<T> interface (belonging to Spring Data Commons and under the package org.springframework.data.domain).

Listing 16-49. The Revised ContactServiceImpl Class

```java
package com.apress.prospring4.ch16;

import java.util.List;

import org.springframework.beans.factory.annotation.Autowired;
import org.springframework.data.domain.Page;
import org.springframework.data.domain.Pageable;
import org.springframework.stereotype.Repository;
import org.springframework.stereotype.Service;
import org.springframework.transaction.annotation.Transactional;

import com.google.common.collect.Lists;

@Repository
@Transactional
@Service("contactService")
public class ContactServiceImpl implements ContactService {
    private ContactRepository contactRepository;

    @Override
    @Transactional(readOnly=true)
    public List<Contact> findAll() {
        return Lists.newArrayList(contactRepository.findAll());
    }

    @Override
    @Transactional(readOnly=true)
    public Contact findById(Long id) {
        return contactRepository.findOne(id);
    }

    @Override
    public Contact save(Contact contact) {
        return contactRepository.save(contact);
    }

    @Autowired
    public void setContactRepository(ContactRepository contactRepository) {
        this.contactRepository = contactRepository;
    }

    @Override
    @Transactional(readOnly=true)
    public Page<Contact> findAllByPage(Pageable pageable) {
        return contactRepository.findAll(pageable);
    }

}
```

In Listing 16-49, in the method, we simply call the `findAll(Pageable)` method, which was provided by the `PagingAndSortingRepository<T,ID extends Serializable>` interface.

The next step is to implement the method in the `ContactController` class to take the Ajax request from jqGrid for page data. Listing 16-50 shows the implementation.

Listing 16-50. The Revised `ContactController` Class

```
package com.apress.prospring4;

// Import statements omitted

@RequestMapping("/contacts")
@Controller
public class ContactController {

    // Other code omitted

    @RequestMapping(value = "/listgrid", method = RequestMethod.GET,
        produces="application/json")
    @ResponseBody
    public ContactGrid listGrid(@RequestParam(value = "page", required = false) Integer page,
        @RequestParam(value = "rows", required = false) Integer rows,
        @RequestParam(value = "sidx", required = false) String sortBy,
        @RequestParam(value = "sord", required = false) String order) {

        logger.info("Listing contacts for grid with page: {}, rows: {}", page, rows);
        logger.info("Listing contacts for grid with sort: {}, order: {}", sortBy, order);

        // Process order by
        Sort sort = null;
        String orderBy = sortBy;
        if (orderBy != null && orderBy.equals("birthDateString"))
            orderBy = "birthDate";

        if (orderBy != null && order != null) {
            if (order.equals("desc")) {
                sort = new Sort(Sort.Direction.DESC, orderBy);
            } else
                sort = new Sort(Sort.Direction.ASC, orderBy);
        }

        // Constructs page request for current page
        // Note: page number for Spring Data JPA starts with 0, while jqGrid starts with 1
        PageRequest pageRequest = null;

        if (sort != null) {
            pageRequest = new PageRequest(page - 1, rows, sort);
        } else {
            pageRequest = new PageRequest(page - 1, rows);
        }
```

```
        Page<Contact> contactPage = contactService.findAllByPage(pageRequest);

        // Construct the grid data that will return as JSON data
        ContactGrid contactGrid = new ContactGrid();

        contactGrid.setCurrentPage(contactPage.getNumber() + 1);
        contactGrid.setTotalPages(contactPage.getTotalPages());
        contactGrid.setTotalRecords(contactPage.getTotalElements());

        contactGrid.setContactData(Lists.newArrayList(contactPage.iterator()));

        return contactGrid;
    }
}
```

The method handles the Ajax request, reads the parameters (page number, records per page, sort by, sort order) from the request (the parameter names in the code sample are jqGrid's defaults), constructs an instance of the PageRequest class that implements the Pageable interface, and then invokes the ContactService.findAllByPage() method to get the page data. Then, an instance of the ContactGrid class is constructed and returned to jqGrid in JSON format. Listing 16-51 shows the ContactGrid class.

Listing 16-51. The ContactGrid Class

```
package com.apress.prospring4.ch16;

import java.util.List;

public class ContactGrid {
    private int totalPages;
    private int currentPage;
    private long totalRecords;
    private List<Contact> contactData;

    public int getTotalPages() {
        return totalPages;
    }

    public void setTotalPages(int totalPages) {
        this.totalPages = totalPages;
    }

    public int getCurrentPage() {
        return currentPage;
    }

    public void setCurrentPage(int currentPage) {
        this.currentPage = currentPage;
    }

    public long getTotalRecords() {
        return totalRecords;
    }
}
```

```java
    public void setTotalRecords(long totalRecords) {
        this.totalRecords = totalRecords;
    }

    public List<Contact> getContactData() {
        return contactData;
    }

    public void setContactData(List<Contact> contactData) {
        this.contactData = contactData;
    }
}
```

Now we are ready to test the new contact list view. Make sure the project is rebuilt and deployed, and then invoke the contact list view. You should now see an enhanced grid view of the contact listing.

You can play around with the grid, browse the pages, change the number of records per page, change the sort order by clicking the column headers, and so on. i18n is also supported, and you can try to see the grid with Chinese labels.

jqGrid also supports data filtering. For example, we can filter data by first names containing "Chris" or when the birth date is between date ranges.

Handling File Upload

The contact information has a field of BLOB type to store a photo, which can be uploaded from the client. This section shows how to implement file upload in Spring MVC.

For a long time, the standard servlet specification didn't support file upload. As a result, Spring MVC worked with other libraries (the most common one being the Apache Commons FileUpload library, http://commons.apache.org/fileupload) to serve this purpose. Spring MVC has built-in support for Commons FileUpload. However, starting from Servlet 3.0, file upload has become a built-in feature of the web container. Tomcat 7 supports Servlet 3.0, and Spring has also supported Servlet 3.0 file upload since version 3.1.

In the following sections, we discuss how to implement the file upload using Spring MVC and Servlet 3.0. Table 16-7 shows the dependencies required.

Table 16-7. *Maven Dependencies for File Upload*

Group ID	Artifact ID	Version	Description
javax	javaee-web-api	7.0	JEE 7.0 Web Profile API, which contains the library for Servlet 3.1. Please use the provided scope for this dependency in your build configuration.
commons-io	commons-io	2.4	The Apache Commons IO module provides a lot of useful functions to ease I/O handling in Java.

Configuring File Upload Support

In a Servlet 3.0–compatible web container with Spring MVC, configuring file upload support is a two-step process.

First, in the web deployment descriptor (web.xml) for the DispatchServlet definition, we need to add a <multipart-config> section. Listing 16-52 shows the code snippet for this change.

Listing 16-52. Add File Upload Support in `web.xml`

```xml
<?xml version="1.0" encoding="UTF-8"?>
<web-app version="3.0" xmlns="http://java.sun.com/xml/ns/javaee"

    <!-- Other code omitted -->

    <!-- Processes application requests -->
    <servlet>
        <servlet-name>appServlet</servlet-name>
        <servlet-class>org.springframework.web.servlet.DispatcherServlet</servlet-class>
        <init-param>
            <param-name>contextConfigLocation</param-name>
            <param-value>/WEB-INF/spring/appServlet/servlet-context.xml</param-value>
        </init-param>
        <load-on-startup>1</load-on-startup>
        <multipart-config>
            <max-file-size>5000000</max-file-size>
        </multipart-config>
    </servlet>

    <!-- Other code omitted -->

</web-app>
```

In Servlet 3.0, the servlet that supports file upload should be provided with a `<multipart-config>` tag to configure the support. The `<max-file-size>` tag controls the maximum file size allowed for upload, which is 5 MB.

Second, we need to configure a bean that implements the `MultipartResolver` interface in the DispatcherServlet's `WebApplicationContext`. Listing 16-53 shows the bean definition that you need to add to the file (`servlet-context.xml`).

Listing 16-53. Configure the MultipartResolver Support in Spring MVC

```xml
<beans:bean
    class="org.springframework.web.multipart.support.StandardServletMultipartResolver"
    id="multipartResolver"/>
```

Note the implementation class `StandardServletMultipartResolver`, which is used to support native file upload in the Servlet 3.0 container.

Modifying Views for File Upload Support

We need to modify two views for file upload support. The first one is the edit view (`edit.jspx`) to support photo upload for a contact, and the second one is the show view (`show.jspx`) for displaying the photo.

Listing 16-54 shows the changes required for the edit view.

Listing 16-54. Edit Contact View for File Upload Support

```
<?xml version="1.0" encoding="UTF-8" standalone="no"?>

    <!-- Other code omitted -->

    <form:form modelAttribute="contact" id="contactUpdateForm" method="post"
        enctype="multipart/form-data">

        <!-- Other code omitted -->

        <form:label path="description">
            ${labelContactDescription}
        </form:label>
        <form:textarea cols="60" rows="8" path="description" id="contactDescription"/>
        <div>
            <form:errors path="description" cssClass="error" />
        </div>
        <p/>

        <label for="file">
            ${labelContactPhoto}
        </label>
        <input name="file" type="file"/>
        <p/>

    <!-- Other code omitted -->

</div>
```

In Listing 16-54, within the `<form:form>` tag, we need to enable the multipart file upload support by specifying the attribute enctype. Next, the file upload field is added to the form.

We also need to modify the show view to display the photo for a contact. Listing 16-55 shows the changes required to the view (`show.jspx`).

Listing 16-55. Show Contact View for Display File

```
<?xml version="1.0" encoding="UTF-8" standalone="no"?>

    <!-- Other code omitted -->

    <spring:message code="label_contact_photo" var="labelContactPhoto"/>
    <spring:url value="/contacts/photo" var="contactPhotoUrl"/>

    <!-- Other code omitted -->
        <tr>
            <td>${labelContactDescription}</td>
            <td>${contact.description}</td>
        </tr>
```

```
        <tr>
            <td>${labelContactPhoto}</td>
            <td><img src="${contactPhotoUrl}/${contact.id}"></img></td>
        </tr>
    <!-- Other code omitted -->
</div>
```

In Listing 16-55, a new row is added to the table for displaying the photo by pointing to the URL for photo download.

Modifying Controller for File Upload Support

The final step is to modify the controller. We need to make two changes. The first change is to the create() method to accept the upload file as a request parameter. The second change is to implement a new method for photo download based on the supplied contact ID. Listing 16-56 shows the revised ContactController class.

Listing 16-56. Revised Controller Class with File Upload and Download Support

```
package com.apress.prospring4.ch16;

import javax.servlet.http.Part;

// Other import statements omitted
@RequestMapping("/contacts")
@Controller
public class ContactController {

    @RequestMapping(method = RequestMethod.POST)
    public String create(@Valid Contact contact, BindingResult bindingResult, Model uiModel,
HttpServletRequest httpServletRequest, RedirectAttributes redirectAttributes, Locale locale,
@RequestParam(value="file", required=false) Part file) {
        logger.info("Creating contact");
        if (bindingResult.hasErrors()) {
            uiModel.addAttribute("message", new Message("error",
                messageSource.getMessage("contact_save_fail", new Object[]{}, locale)));
            uiModel.addAttribute("contact", contact);
            return "contacts/create";
        }
        uiModel.asMap().clear();
        redirectAttributes.addFlashAttribute("message", new Message("success",
            messageSource.getMessage("contact_save_success", new Object[]{}, locale)));

        logger.info("Contact id: " + contact.getId());

        // Process upload file
        if (file != null) {
            logger.info("File name: " + file.getName());
            logger.info("File size: " + file.getSize());
            logger.info("File content type: " + file.getContentType());
            byte[] fileContent = null;
```

```
        try {
            InputStream inputStream = file.getInputStream();
            if (inputStream == null) logger.info("File inputstream is null");
                fileContent = IOUtils.toByteArray(inputStream);
                contact.setPhoto(fileContent);
            } catch (IOException ex) {
                logger.error("Error saving uploaded file");
            }
        contact.setPhoto(fileContent);
    }

    contactService.save(contact);
    return "redirect:/contacts/" + UrlUtil.encodeUrlPathSegment(contact.getId().toString(),
httpServletRequest);
}

@RequestMapping(value = "/photo/{id}", method = RequestMethod.GET)
@ResponseBody
public byte[] downloadPhoto(@PathVariable("id") Long id) {

    Contact contact = contactService.findById(id);

    if (contact.getPhoto() != null) {
        logger.info("Downloading photo for id: {} with size: {}", contact.getId(),
            contact.getPhoto().length);
    }

    return contact.getPhoto();
}
}
```

First, in the create() method, a new request parameter of interface type javax.servlet.http.Part is added as an argument, which Spring MVC will provide based on the uploaded content in the request. Then the method will get the content saved into the photo property of the Contact object.

Next, a new method downloadPhoto() is added to handle the file download. The method just retrieves the photo field from the contact object and directly writes into the response stream, which corresponds to the <img> tag in the show view.

To test the file upload function, redeploy the application and add a new contact with a photo. Upon completion, you will be able to see the photo in the show view.

We also need to modify the edit function for changing the photo, but we will skip it here and leave it as an exercise for you.

Securing a Web Application with Spring Security

Suppose now we want to secure our contact application. Only those users who logged into the application with a valid user ID can add a new contact or update existing contacts. Other users, known as anonymous users, can only view contact information.

Spring Security is the best choice for securing Spring-based applications. Although mostly used in the presentation layer, Spring Security can help secure all layers within the application, including the service layer. In the following sections, we demonstrate how to use Spring Security to secure the contact application.

Table 16-8 lists the dependencies required for Spring Security.

Table 16-8. *Maven Dependencies for Spring Security*

Group ID	Artifact ID	Version	Description
org.springframework.security	spring-security-core	3.2.1.RELEASE	Spring Security core module
org.springframework.security	spring-security-web	3.2.1.RELEASE	Spring Security web module
org.springframework.security	spring-security-config	3.2.1.RELEASE	Spring Security configuration module
org.springframework.security	spring-security-taglibs	3.2.1.RELEASE	Spring Security JSP tag library

Configuring Spring Security

To configure Spring Security, first we need to configure a filter in the web deployment descriptor (web.xml). Listing 16-57 shows the code snippet you need to add to the web.xml file.

Listing 16-57. Configure Spring Security Filter

```xml
<?xml version="1.0" encoding="UTF-8"?>
<web-app version="3.0" xmlns="http://java.sun.com/xml/ns/javaee"

    <!-- Other code omitted -->

    <!-- Spring Security Configuration -->
    <filter>
        <filter-name>springSecurityFilterChain</filter-name>
        <filter-class>org.springframework.web.filter.DelegatingFilterProxy</filter-class>
    </filter>

    <filter-mapping>
        <filter-name>springSecurityFilterChain</filter-name>
        <url-pattern>/*</url-pattern>
    </filter-mapping>

    <!-- Other code omitted -->
</web-app>
```

In Listing 16-57, the filter for Spring Security is shown. The next step is to define the Spring Security context, which will be imported by the root WebApplicationContext configuration file. Listing 16-58 shows the configuration file (/META-INF/spring/security-context.xml).

Listing 16-58. Spring Security Context Configuration

```xml
<?xml version="1.0" encoding="UTF-8"?>
<beans:beans xmlns="http://www.springframework.org/schema/security"
    xmlns:beans="http://www.springframework.org/schema/beans"
    xmlns:xsi="http://www.w3.org/2001/XMLSchema-instance"
    xsi:schemaLocation="http://www.springframework.org/schema/beans
        http://www.springframework.org/schema/beans/spring-beans.xsd
        http://www.springframework.org/schema/security
        http://www.springframework.org/schema/security/spring-security.xsd">
```

```
<http use-expressions="true">
    <intercept-url pattern='/*' access='permitAll' />
    <form-login login-page="/contacts" authentication-failure-url="/security/loginfail"
        default-target-url="/contacts" />
    <logout logout-success-url="/contacts"/>
</http>

<authentication-manager>
    <authentication-provider>
        <user-service>
            <user name="user" password="user" authorities="ROLE_USER" />
        </user-service>
    </authentication-provider>
</authentication-manager>
</beans:beans>
```

First, the `<http>` tag defines the security configuration for HTTP requests. The attribute `use-expressions` means that we want to use Spring Expression Language (SpEL) for the expressions. The `<intercept-url>` tag specifies that all users are allowed to enter the application. We will see how we can protect the function by hiding the editing options in the view using Spring Security's tag library and controller method security. Then the `<form-login>` defines the support for form login. As we discussed in the layout, the login form will display on the left. We provide a logout link as well.

The `<authentication-manager>` tag defines the authentication mechanism. In the configuration, we hard-code a single user with the role ROLE_USER assigned. In a production environment, the user should be authenticated against the database, LDAP, or an SSO mechanism.

Listing 16-59 shows the revised `root-context.xml` file to import the security configuration file.

Listing 16-59. Spring Security Context Configuration

```
<?xml version="1.0" encoding="UTF-8"?>
<beans xmlns="http://www.springframework.org/schema/beans"
    xmlns:xsi="http://www.w3.org/2001/XMLSchema-instance"
    xmlns:context="http://www.springframework.org/schema/context"
    xsi:schemaLocation="http://www.springframework.org/schema/beans
      http://www.springframework.org/schema/beans/spring-beans.xsd
      http://www.springframework.org/schema/context
      http://www.springframework.org/schema/context/spring-context.xsd">

    <import resource="classpath:META-INF/spring/datasource-tx-jpa.xml" />
    <import resource="classpath:META-INF/spring/security-context.xml"/>

    <context:component-scan base-package="com.apress.prospring4.ch16" />
</beans>
```

Adding Login Functions to the Application

We need to modify two page components: the header (`header.jspx`) and the menu (`menu.jspx`).

Listing 16-60 shows the revised `header.jspx` file to display the user information if the user is logged in.

Listing 16-60. Display Login User Information

```
<div id="header" xmlns:jsp="http://java.sun.com/JSP/Page"
        xmlns:spring="http://www.springframework.org/tags"
        xmlns:sec="http://www.springframework.org/security/tags"
        version="2.0">
        <jsp:directive.page contentType="text/html;charset=UTF-8" />
        <jsp:output omit-xml-declaration="yes" />

    <spring:message code="header_text" var="headerText"/>
    <spring:message code="label_logout" var="labelLogout"/>
    <spring:message code="label_welcome" var="labelWelcome"/>
    <spring:url var="logoutUrl" value="/j_spring_security_logout" />

    <div id="appname">
        <h1>${headerText}</h1>
    </div>

    <div id="userinfo">
        <sec:authorize access="isAuthenticated()">${labelWelcome}
            <sec:authentication property="principal.username" />
            <br/>
            <a href="${logoutUrl}">${labelLogout}</a>
        </sec:authorize>
    </div>
</div>
```

First, the tag library with the prefix `sec` is added for the Spring Security tag library. Then, a `<div>` section with the `<sec:authorize>` tag is added to detect whether the user is logged in. If yes (that is, the `isAuthenticated()` expression returns `true`), the username will be displayed, as well as a logout link.

Listing 16-61 shows the revised `menu.jspx` file, which has the login form added; the New Contact option will display only if the user is logged in.

Listing 16-61. Display Login Form

```
<?xml version="1.0" encoding="UTF-8" standalone="no"?>
<div id="menu" xmlns:jsp="http://java.sun.com/JSP/Page"
    xmlns:c="http://java.sun.com/jsp/jstl/core"
    xmlns:spring="http://www.springframework.org/tags"
    xmlns:sec="http://www.springframework.org/security/tags"
    version="2.0">
        <jsp:directive.page contentType="text/html;charset=UTF-8" />
        <jsp:output omit-xml-declaration="yes" />

        <spring:message code="menu_header_text" var="menuHeaderText"/>
        <spring:message code="menu_add_contact" var="menuAddContact"/>
        <spring:url value="/contacts?form" var="addContactUrl"/>
```

```
<spring:message code="label_login" var="labelLogin"/>
<spring:url var="loginUrl" value="/j_spring_security_check" />


<h3>${menuHeaderText}</h3>
<sec:authorize access="hasRole('ROLE_USER')">
    <a href="${addContactUrl}"><h3>${menuAddContact}</h3></a>
</sec:authorize>


<sec:authorize access="isAnonymous()">
<div id="login">
    <form name="loginForm" action="${loginUrl}" method="post">
        <table>
            <caption align="left">Login:</caption>
            <tr>
                <td>User Name:</td>
                <td><input type="text" name="j_username"/></td>
            </tr>
            <tr>
                <td>Password:</td>
                <td><input type="password" name="j_password"/></td>
            </tr>
            <tr>
                <td colspan="2" align="center"><input name="submit" type="submit"
                    value="Login"/></td>
            </tr>
        </table>
    </form>
</div>
</sec:authorize>
</div>
```

The Add Contact menu item will render only when the user is logged in and has the role ROLE_USER granted (as specified in the <sec:authorized> tag). Second, if the user is not logged in (the second <sec:authorized> tag, when the expression isAnonymous() returns true), then the login form will be displayed.

Redeploy the application, and it will display the login form, noting the new contact link is not shown.

Enter **user** in both the username and password fields and click the Login button. The user information will be displayed in the header area. The new contact link is also shown.

We also need to modify the show view (show.jspx) to show the edit contact link for only logged-in users, but we will skip that here and leave that as an exercise for you.

As defined in Listing 16-58, when the login information is incorrect, the URL to handle this will be at /security/loginfail. So, we need to implement a controller to handle this login fail scenario. Listing 16-62 shows the SecurityController class.

Listing 16-62. The SecurityController Class

```
package com.apress.prospring4.ch16;

import org.slf4j.Logger;
import org.slf4j.LoggerFactory;
import org.springframework.beans.factory.annotation.Autowired;
import org.springframework.context.MessageSource;
```

```
import org.springframework.stereotype.Controller;
import org.springframework.ui.Model;
import org.springframework.web.bind.annotation.RequestMapping;

import java.util.Locale;

@Controller
@RequestMapping("/security")
public class SecurityController {
    private final Logger logger = LoggerFactory.getLogger(SecurityController.class);

    private MessageSource messageSource;

    @RequestMapping("/loginfail")
    public String loginFail(Model uiModel, Locale locale) {
        logger.info("Login failed detected");
        uiModel.addAttribute("message", new Message("error",
                messageSource.getMessage("message_login_fail", new Object[]{}, locale)));
        return "contacts/list";
    }

    @Autowired
    public void setMessageSource(MessageSource messageSource) {
        this.messageSource = messageSource;
    }
}
```

The controller class will handle all URLs with the prefix security, while the method loginFail() will handle the login fail scenario. In the method, we store the login fail message in the Model and then redirect to the home page. Now redeploy the application and enter the wrong user information; the home page will be displayed again with the login fail message.

Using Annotations to Secure Controller Methods

Hiding the new contact link in the menu is not enough. For example, if you enter the URL in the browser directly (http://localhost:8080/contact-webapp/contacts?form), you can still see the add contact page, even though you are not logged in yet. The reason is that we haven't protected the application at the URL level. One method for protecting the page is to configure the Spring Security filter chain (in the file security-context.xml) to intercept the URL for only authenticated users. However, doing this will block all other users from seeing the contact list view.

An alternative for solving the problem is to apply security at the controller method level, using Spring Security's annotation support.

To enable method-level security, we need to modify the DispatcherServlet configuration (servlet-context.xml), as shown in Listing 16-63.

Listing 16-63. Enable Method-Level Security

```
<?xml version="1.0" encoding="UTF-8"?>
<beans:beans xmlns="http://www.springframework.org/schema/mvc"
    xmlns:xsi="http://www.w3.org/2001/XMLSchema-instance"
    xmlns:beans="http://www.springframework.org/schema/beans"
    xmlns:p="http://www.springframework.org/schema/p"
```

```
xmlns:context="http://www.springframework.org/schema/context"
xmlns:security="http://www.springframework.org/schema/security"
xsi:schemaLocation="http://www.springframework.org/schema/mvc
    http://www.springframework.org/schema/mvc/spring-mvc.xsd
    http://www.springframework.org/schema/beans
    http://www.springframework.org/schema/beans/spring-beans.xsd
    http://www.springframework.org/schema/context
    http://www.springframework.org/schema/context/spring-context.xsd
    http://www.springframework.org/schema/security
    http://www.springframework.org/schema/security/spring-security.xsd">

<!-- Enables the Spring MVC @Controller programming model -->
<annotation-driven validator="validator"/>

<!-- Enable controller method level security -->
<security:global-method-security pre-post-annotations="enabled"/>

<!-- Other code omitted -->

</beans:beans>
```

As shown in Listing 16-63, the security namespace is added. Then, the `<security:global-method-security>` tag is used to enable Spring Security's method-level security, and the `pre-post-annotations` attribute enables the support of annotations.

Now we can use the `@PreAuthorize` annotation for the controller method we want to protect. Listing 16-64 shows an example of protecting the `createForm()` method.

Listing 16-64. Applying Spring Security Annotations to `ContactController`

```
@PreAuthorize("isAuthenticated()")
@RequestMapping(params = "form", method = RequestMethod.GET)
public String createForm(Model uiModel) {
    Contact contact = new Contact();
    uiModel.addAttribute("contact", contact);
    return "contacts/create";
}
```

We use the `@PreAuthorize` annotation (under the package `org.springframework.security.access.prepost`) to secure the `createForm()` method, with an argument being the expression for security requirements.

Now you can try to directly enter the new contact URL in the browser, and if you are not logged in, Spring Security will redirect you to the login page, which is the contact list view as configured in the `security-context.xml` file.

Supporting Servlet 3 Code-Based Configuration

Spring also supports Servlet 3.0's code-based configuration, which provides an alternative to the XML configuration required in the web deployment descriptor file (`web.xml`). In this section, we show you how to use Java code to bootstrap the `DispatcherServlet` `WebApplicationContext` instead of configuring it in the `web.xml` file.

To use code-based configuration, we just need to develop a class that implements the `org.springframework.web.WebApplicationInitializer` interface. All classes implementing this interface will be automatically detected by the `org.springframework.web.SpringServletContainerInitializer` class (which implements Servlet 3.0's `javax.servlet.ServletContainerInitializer` interface), which bootstraps automatically in any Servlet 3.0 containers.

Let's see a simple example of using code-based configuration to bootstrap the `DispatcherServlet` `WebApplicationContext`, instead of declaring it in the `web.xml` file.

First, remove the following servlet and servlet mapping definition in Listing 16-65 from the `web.xml` file.

Listing 16-65. Remove the Following Servlet Definition from `web.xml`

```xml
<servlet>
    <servlet-name>appServlet</servlet-name>
    <servlet-class>org.springframework.web.servlet.DispatcherServlet</servlet-class>
    <init-param>
        <param-name>contextConfigLocation</param-name>
        <param-value>/WEB-INF/spring/appServlet/servlet-context.xml</param-value>
    </init-param>
    <load-on-startup>1</load-on-startup>
    <multipart-config>
        <max-file-size>5000000</max-file-size>
    </multipart-config>
</servlet>

<servlet-mapping>
    <servlet-name>appServlet</servlet-name>
    <url-pattern>/</url-pattern>
</servlet-mapping>
```

Second, create a class that implements the `WebApplicationInitializer` interface. Here we called it `MyWebAppInitializer`, and its content is shown in Listing 16-66.

Listing 16-66. The `MyWebAppInitializer` Class

```java
package com.apress.prospring4.ch16;

import javax.servlet.MultipartConfigElement;
import javax.servlet.ServletContext;
import javax.servlet.ServletException;
import javax.servlet.ServletRegistration;

import org.springframework.web.WebApplicationInitializer;
import org.springframework.web.context.support.XmlWebApplicationContext;
import org.springframework.web.servlet.DispatcherServlet;

public class MyWebAppInitializer implements WebApplicationInitializer {
    @Override
    public void onStartup(ServletContext container) throws ServletException {
        XmlWebApplicationContext appContext = new XmlWebApplicationContext();

        appContext.setConfigLocation("/WEB-INF/spring/appServlet/servlet-context.xml");

        ServletRegistration.Dynamic dispatcher =
            container.addServlet("appServlet", new DispatcherServlet(appContext));
```

```
    MultipartConfigElement multipartConfigElement =
        new MultipartConfigElement(null, 5000000, 5000000, 0);
    dispatcher.setMultipartConfig(multipartConfigElement);

    dispatcher.setLoadOnStartup(1);
    dispatcher.addMapping("/");
    }
}
```

As shown here, the `WebApplicationInitializer.onStartup()` method is overridden, with the logic to load the `WebApplicationContext` for the `DispatcherServlet` implemented. By calling the method `ServletContext.addServlet()`, we can add the servlet to the underlying web container. The method will return an instance of the `javax.servlet.ServletRegistration.Dynamic` interface, and via this interface, we can configure various attributes for the servlet, such as the `loadOnStartup` servlet-to-URL mapping, as well as the multipart support for file uploading, and so on. Rebuild and deploy the project, and the `DispatcherServlet`'s `WebApplicationContext` will be bootstrapped like the one defined in the `web.xml` file.

Using this approach, when combined with the Java code-based configuration of Spring, it's possible to implement a pure Java code-based configuration of a Spring-based web application, without the need to declare any Spring configuration in `web.xml` or other Spring XML configuration files.

Summary

In this chapter, we covered many topics related to web development using Spring MVC.

First we discussed the high-level concepts of the MVC pattern. Then we covered Spring MVC's architecture, including its `WebApplicationContext` hierarchy, request-handling life cycle, and configuration.

Next we developed a sample contact application using Spring MVC, with JSPX as the view technology. During the course of developing the samples, we elaborated on different areas. Main topics included i18n, theming, and template support with Apache Tiles. Moreover, we used jQuery, jQuery UI, and other JavaScript libraries to enrich the interface. Samples included the date picker, rich-text editor, and data grid with pagination support. How to secure a web application with Spring Security was discussed too.

We also went through some functionality of Servlet 3.0–compatible web containers such as code-based configuration rather than a `web.xml` file. We demonstrated how to handle file upload within a Servlet 3.0 environment.

In the next chapter, we cover more features that Spring brings us in terms of web application development by introducing WebSocket.

CHAPTER 17

■ ■ ■

WebSocket

Traditionally, web applications have utilized the standard request/response HTTP functionality to provide communication between client and server. As the web has evolved, more interactive abilities have been required, some of which demand push/pull or real-time updates from the server. Over time, various methods have been implemented, such as continuous polling, long polling, and Comet. Each has its pros and cons, and the WebSocket protocol is an attempt to learn from those needs and deficiencies, creating a simpler and more robust way to build interactive applications.

This chapter covers a high-level overview of the WebSocket protocol and the main functionality provided by the Spring Framework. Specifically, this chapter covers the following topics:

- *Introduction to WebSocket*: We provide a general introduction of the WebSocket protocol. This section is not intended to serve as a detailed reference of the WebSocket protocol, but rather as a high-level overview. For details on the protocol, refer to RFC-6455 at `http://tools.ietf.org/html/rfc6455`.

- *Using WebSocket with Spring*: In this section, we dive into some of the details of using WebSocket with the Spring Framework—specifically, using Spring's WebSocket API, utilizing SockJS as a fallback option for non-WebSocket-enabled browsers, and sending messages using Simple (or Streaming) Text Oriented Message Protocol (STOMP) over SockJS/WebSocket.

Introducing WebSocket

WebSocket is a specification developed as part of the HTML5 initiative, allowing for a full-duplex single-socket connection in which messages can be sent between a client and a server. In the past, web applications requiring the functionality of real-time updates would poll a server-side component periodically to obtain this data, opening multiple connections or using long polling.

Using WebSocket for bidirectional communication avoids the need to perform HTTP polling for two-way communications between a client (for example, a web browser) and an HTTP server. The WebSocket protocol is meant to supersede all existing bidirectional communication methods utilizing HTTP as a transport. The single-socket model of WebSocket results in a simpler solution, avoiding the need for multiple connections for each client and less overhead—for example, not needing to send an HTTP header with each message.

WebSocket utilizes HTTP during its initial handshake, which in turn allows it to be used over standard HTTP (80) and HTTPS (443) ports. The WebSocket specification defines a `ws://` and a `wss://` scheme to indicate nonsecure and secure connections.

The WebSocket protocol has two parts: a handshake between client and server, and then data transfer. A WebSocket connection is established by making an upgrade request from HTTP to the WebSocket protocol during the initial handshake between the client and the server, over the same underlying TCP/IP connection. During the data transfer portion of the communication, both client and server can send messages to each other simultaneously, which as you can imagine opens the door to add more-robust real-time communication functionality to your applications.

Using WebSocket with Spring

As of version 4.0, the Spring Framework supports WebSocket-style messaging as well as STOMP as an application-level subprotocol. Within the framework, support for WebSocket can be found in the `spring-websocket` module, which is compatible with the Java WebSocket API standard (JSR-356).

Application developers must also recognize that although WebSocket brings new and exciting opportunities, not all web browsers support the protocol. Given this, the application must continue to work for the user and utilize some sort of fallback technology to simulate the intended functionality as best as possible. To handle this case, the Spring Framework provides transparent fallback options via the SockJS protocol, which will we go into later in this chapter.

Unlike REST-based applications, where services are represented by different URLs, WebSocket uses a single URL to establish the initial handshake, and data flows over that same connection. This type of message-passing functionality is more along the lines of traditional messaging systems. As of Spring Framework 4, core message-based interfaces such as Message have been migrated from the Spring Integration project into a new module called `spring-messaging` to support WebSocket-style messaging applications.

When we refer to using STOMP as an application-level subprotocol, we are talking about the protocol that is transported via WebSocket. WebSocket itself is a low-level protocol that simply transforms bytes into messages. The application needs to understand what is being sent across the wire, which is where a subprotocol such as STOMP comes into play. During the initial handshake, the client and server can use the `Sec-WebSocket-Protocol` header to define what subprotocol to use. While the Spring Framework provides support for STOMP, WebSocket does not mandate anything specific.

Now that we have an understanding of what WebSocket is and the support Spring provides, where might we use this technology? Given the single-socket nature of WebSocket and its ability to provide a continuous bidirectional data flow, WebSocket lends itself well to applications that have a high frequency of message passing and require low-latency communications. Applications that may be good candidates for WebSocket could include gaming, real-time group-collaboration tools, messaging systems, time-sensitive pricing information such as financial updates, and so on. When designing your application with the consideration of using WebSocket, you must take into account both the frequency of messages as well as latency requirements. This will help determine whether to use WebSocket or, for example, HTTP long polling.

Using the WebSocket API

As mentioned earlier in this chapter, WebSocket simply transforms bytes into messages and transports them between client and server. Those messages still need to be understood by the application itself, which is where subprotocols such as STOMP come into play. In the event you would like to work with the lower-level WebSocket API directly, the Spring Framework provides an API that you can interact with to do so. When working with Spring's WebSocket API, you would typically implement the `WebSocketHandler` interface, or use convenience subclasses such as `BinaryWebSocketHandler` for handling binary messages, `SockJsWebSocketHandler` for SockJS messages, or `TextWebSocketHandler` for working with `String`-based messages. In our example, for simplicity we will use a `TextWebSocketHandler` to pass `String` messages via WebSocket. Let's start by taking a look at how we can receive and work with WebSocket messages at a low level, utilizing the Spring WebSocket API.

Each sample in this chapter can also be configured via Java Configuration if that is your preference. It is the author's view that the XML namespace represents the configuration aspects in a succinct fashion, and it will be used throughout the chapter. Please consult the reference manual for more information on Java Configuration.

First let's start by adding the required dependencies as shown in Table 17-1.

Table 17-1. *Maven Dependencies for WebSocket API Sample*

Group ID	Artifact ID	Version	Description
org.springframework	spring-context	4.0.2	Spring Context module.
org.springframework	spring-websocket	4.0.2	Spring WebSocket module.
org.springframework	spring-webmvc	4.0.2	Spring Web MVC module.
org.apache.tomcat	tomcat-websocket-api	7.0.54	Apache Tomcat WebSocket API. As we are using Tomcat in this sample, this is a container requirement.
org.apache.tomcat.embed	tomcat-embed-websocket	7.0.54	Apache Tomcat WebSocket API for embedded Tomcat, which we use to run the sample.

Listing 17-1 shows our web.xml (src/main/webapp/WEB-INF/web.xml) that we need to configure so we can use WebSocket with a standard Spring MVC dispatcher servlet.

Listing 17-1. web.xml Configuration for the DispatcherServlet

```
<web-app xmlns="http://java.sun.com/xml/ns/javaee"
         xmlns:xsi="http://www.w3.org/2001/XMLSchema-instance"
         xsi:schemaLocation="http://java.sun.com/xml/ns/javaee
         http://java.sun.com/xml/ns/javaee/web-app_3_0.xsd"
         version="3.0">

    <display-name>Spring WebSocket API Sample</display-name>

    <servlet>
        <servlet-name>websocket</servlet-name>
        <servlet-class>org.springframework.web.servlet.DispatcherServlet</servlet-class>
        <init-param>
            <param-name>contextConfigLocation</param-name>
            <param-value>/WEB-INF/spring/root-context.xml</param-value>
        </init-param>
        <load-on-startup>1</load-on-startup>
    </servlet>

    <servlet-mapping>
        <servlet-name>websocket</servlet-name>
        <url-pattern>/*</url-pattern>
    </servlet-mapping>
</web-app>
```

This configuration should look familiar to you by now. We first create our servlet definition utilizing Spring's DispatcherServlet, providing it a configuration file (/WEB-INF/spring/root-context.xml). We then provide servlet-mapping, indicating all requests should go through the DispatcherServlet.

Now let's move on and create our root-context file, which contains our WebSocket configuration as shown in Listing 17-2.

Listing 17-2. web.xml Configuration for the DispatcherServlet

```xml
<beans xmlns="http://www.springframework.org/schema/beans"
       xmlns:xsi="http://www.w3.org/2001/XMLSchema-instance"
       xmlns:websocket="http://www.springframework.org/schema/websocket"
       xmlns:mvc="http://www.springframework.org/schema/mvc"
       xsi:schemaLocation="
        http://www.springframework.org/schema/beans
        http://www.springframework.org/schema/beans/spring-beans.xsd
        http://www.springframework.org/schema/websocket
        http://www.springframework.org/schema/websocket/spring-websocket.xsd
        http://www.springframework.org/schema/mvc
        http://www.springframework.org/schema/mvc/spring-mvc.xsd">

    <mvc:resources mapping="/index.html" location="/static/" />

    <websocket:handlers>
        <websocket:mapping path="/echoHandler" handler="echoHandler"/>
    </websocket:handlers>

    <bean id="echoHandler" class="com.apress.prospring4.ch17.EchoHandler"/>
</beans>
```

First, we configure a static resource called index.html. This file contains static HTML and JavaScript that is used to communicate with the back-end WebSocket service. Then, using the websocket namespace, we configure our handlers and corresponding bean to handle the request. We define a single handler mapping in this example, which receives requests at /echoHandler and uses the bean by the ID of echoHandler to receive a message and respond by echoing the provided message back to the client.

Now we are ready to implement a subclass of TextWebSocketHandler (src/main/java/com/apress/prospring4/ch17/EchoHandler.java) to help us deal with String-based messages in a convenient way, as shown in Listing 17-3.

Listing 17-3. Subclass Implementation of TextWebSocketHandler to process String-Based WebSocket Messages

```java
package com.apress.prospring4.ch17;

import org.springframework.web.socket.TextMessage;
import org.springframework.web.socket.WebSocketSession;
import org.springframework.web.socket.handler.TextWebSocketHandler;

import java.io.IOException;

public class EchoHandler extends TextWebSocketHandler {
    @Override
    public void handleTextMessage(WebSocketSession session, TextMessage textMessage)
      throws IOException {
        session.sendMessage(new TextMessage(textMessage.getPayload()));
    }
}
```

As you can see, this is a basic handler that takes the provided message and simply echoes it back to the client. The content of the received WebSocket message is contained in the getPayload() method.

That's pretty much all that is needed on the back end. Given that the EchoHandler is a typical Spring bean, you can do anything you would in a normal Spring application, such as inject services, to carry out any functions this handler may need to do.

Now let's create a simple front-end client where we can interact with the back-end WebSocket service. Our front end is a simple HTML page with a bit of JavaScript that uses the browser's API to make the WebSocket connection, and some jQuery to handle button-click events and data display. Our front-end application will have the ability to connect, disconnect, send a message, and display status updates to the screen. Listing 17-4 shows the code for our front-end client page (src/main/webapp/static/index.html).

Listing 17-4. HTML and JavaScript Code for Our Front-End Client Page

```html
<html>
<head>
    <meta charset="UTF-8">
    <title>WebSocket Tester</title>
    <script language="javascript" type="text/javascript"
src="http://code.jquery.com/jquery-2.1.1.min.js"></script>
    <script language="javascript" type="text/javascript">
        var ping;
        var websocket;

        jQuery(function ($) {
            function writePing(message) {
                $('#pingOutput').append(message + '\n');
            }

            function writeStatus(message) {
                $("#statusOutput").val($("#statusOutput").val() + message + '\n');
            }

            function writeMessage(message) {
                $('#messageOutput').append(message + '\n')
            }

            $('#connect')
                    .click(function doConnect() {
                        websocket = new WebSocket($("#target").val());

                        websocket.onopen = function (evt) {
                            writeStatus("CONNECTED");

                            var ping = setInterval(function () {
                                if (websocket != "undefined") {
                                    websocket.send("ping");
                                }
                            }, 3000);
                        };

                        websocket.onclose = function (evt) {
                            writeStatus("DISCONNECTED");
                        };
```

```
                    websocket.onmessage = function (evt) {
                        if (evt.data === "ping") {
                            writePing(evt.data);
                        } else {
                            writeMessage('ECHO: ' + evt.data);
                        }
                    };

                    websocket.onerror = function (evt) {
                        onError(writeStatus('ERROR:' + evt.data))
                    };
                });

        $('#disconnect')
                .click(function () {
                    if(typeof websocket != 'undefined') {
                        websocket.close();
                        websocket = undefined;
                    } else {
                        alert("Not connected.");
                    }
                });

        $('#send')
                .click(function () {
                    if(typeof websocket != 'undefined') {
                        websocket.send($('#message').val());
                    } else {
                        alert("Not connected.");
                    }
                });
    });
    </script>
</head>

<body>
<h2>WebSocket Tester</h2>
Target:
<input type="text" id="target" size="40" value="ws://localhost:8080/websocket-api/echoHandler"/>
<br/>
<button id="connect">Connect</button>
<button id="disconnect">Disconnect</button>
<br/>
<br/>Message:
<input type="text" id="message" value=""/>
<button id="send">Send</button>
<br/>
<p>Status output:</p>
<pre><textarea id="statusOutput" rows="10" cols="50"></textarea></pre>
<p>Message output:</p>
<pre><textarea id="messageOutput" rows="10" cols="50"></textarea></pre>
```

```
<p>Ping output:</p>
<pre><textarea id="pingOutput" rows="10" cols="50"></textarea></pre>
</body>
</html>
```

Listing 17-4 provides a UI that allows us to call back into our WebSocket API and watch real-time results appear on the screen.

Build the project and deploy it into your web container. Then navigate to `http://localhost:8080/websocket-api/index.html` to bring up the UI. After pressing the Connect button, you will notice a CONNECTED message in the Status Output text area, and every 3 seconds a ping message will display in the Ping Output text area. Go ahead and type a message in the Message text box and then hit the Send button. This message will be sent to the back-end WebSocket service and displayed in the Message Output box. When you have finished sending messages, feel free to press the Disconnect button, and you will see a DISCONNECTED message in the Status Output text area. You will not be able to send any further messages nor disconnect again until you reconnect to the WebSocket service.

While this example utilizes the Spring abstraction on top of the low-level WebSocket API, you can clearly see the exciting possibilities this technology can bring to your applications. Now let's take a look at how to handle this functionality when the browser does not support WebSocket and a fallback option is required. You can test your browser for compatibility by using a site such as `www.websocket.org/echo.html`.

Using SockJS

Because all browsers may not support WebSocket and applications still need to function correctly for end users, the Spring Framework provides a fallback option utilizing SockJS. Using SockJS will provide WebSocket-like behavior as close as possible during runtime without the need for changes to application-side code.

The SockJS protocol is used on the client side via JavaScript libraries. The Spring Framework `spring-websocket` module contains the relevant SockJS server-side components. When using SockJS to provide a seamless fallback option, the client will first send a GET request to the server by using a path of `/info` to obtain transport information from the server. SockJS will first try to use WebSocket, and then HTTP streaming, and finally HTTP long polling as a last resort. To learn more about SockJS and its various projects, see `https://github.com/sockjs`.

Enabling SockJS via the `websocket` namespace support is simple and requires only an additional directive inside the `<websocket:handlers>` block. Let's build a similar application as with the raw WebSocket API, but using SockJS. First we need to add a dependency, as shown in Table 17-2.

Table 17-2. *Maven Dependencies for SockJS Sample*

Group ID	Artifact ID	Version	Description
`com.fasterxml.jackson.core`	`jackson-databind`	2.4.1.1	The Jackson data-binding library

Then let's create our `src/main/webapp/WEB-INF/spring/root-context.xml` file, as shown in Listing 17-5.

Listing 17-5. Modifying `root-context.xml` to Enable SockJS Support

```
<beans xmlns="http://www.springframework.org/schema/beans"
       xmlns:xsi="http://www.w3.org/2001/XMLSchema-instance"
       xmlns:websocket="http://www.springframework.org/schema/websocket"
       xmlns:mvc="http://www.springframework.org/schema/mvc"
       xsi:schemaLocation="
        http://www.springframework.org/schema/beans
        http://www.springframework.org/schema/beans/spring-beans.xsd
```

```
                http://www.springframework.org/schema/websocket
                http://www.springframework.org/schema/websocket/spring-websocket.xsd
                http://www.springframework.org/schema/mvc
                http://www.springframework.org/schema/mvc/spring-mvc.xsd">

    <mvc:resources mapping="/index.html" location="/static/" />

    <websocket:handlers>
        <websocket:mapping path="/echoHandler" handler="echoHandler"/>
        <websocket:sockjs/>
    </websocket:handlers>

    <bean id="echoHandler" class="com.apress.prospring4.ch17.EchoHandler"/>
</beans>
```

Notice that the `<websocket:sockjs>` tag has been added. At the most basic level, this is all that is needed to enable SockJS. We can reuse the EchoHandler class from the WebSocket API example, as we will be providing the same functionality.

This `<websocket:sockjs/>` namespace tag also provides other attributes to set configuration options such as handling session cookies (enabled by default), custom client library loading locations (at the time of this writing, the default is `https://d1fxtkz8shb9d2.cloudfront.net/sockjs-0.3.4.min.js`), heartbeat configuration, message size limits, and so on. These options should be reviewed and configured appropriately, depending on your application needs and transport types.

Next let's create the `web.xml` to reflect our SockJS servlet, as shown in Listing 17-6.

Listing 17-6. web.xml for SockJS

```
<web-app xmlns="http://java.sun.com/xml/ns/javaee"
         xmlns:xsi="http://www.w3.org/2001/XMLSchema-instance"
         xsi:schemaLocation="http://java.sun.com/xml/ns/javaee
         http://java.sun.com/xml/ns/javaee/web-app_3_0.xsd"
         version="3.0">

    <display-name>Spring SockJS API Sample</display-name>

    <servlet>
        <servlet-name>sockjs</servlet-name>
        <servlet-class>org.springframework.web.servlet.DispatcherServlet</servlet-class>
        <init-param>
            <param-name>contextConfigLocation</param-name>
            <param-value>/WEB-INF/spring/root-context.xml</param-value>
        </init-param>
        <load-on-startup>1</load-on-startup>
        <async-supported>true</async-supported>
    </servlet>

    <servlet-mapping>
        <servlet-name>sockjs</servlet-name>
        <url-pattern>/*</url-pattern>
    </servlet-mapping>
</web-app>
```

Next we will need to create an HTML page as we did in the WebSocket API sample, but this time utilizing SockJS to take care of the transport negotiation. The most notable differences are that we use the SockJS library rather than WebSocket directly and utilize a typical http:// scheme rather than ws:// to connect to the endpoint. Our simple HTML client code is shown in Listing 17-7.

Listing 17-7. Front-End HTML Page Used to Send Messages via SockJS

```html
<html>
<head>
    <meta charset="UTF-8">
    <title>SockJS Tester</title>
    <script language="javascript" type="text/javascript"
src="https://d1fxtkz8shb9d2.cloudfront.net/sockjs-0.3.4.min.js"></script>
    <script language="javascript" type="text/javascript"
src="http://code.jquery.com/jquery-2.1.1.min.js"></script>
    <script language="javascript" type="text/javascript">
        var ping;
        var sockjs;

        jQuery(function ($) {
            function writePing(message) {
                $('#pingOutput').append(message + '\n');
            }

            function writeStatus(message) {
                $("#statusOutput").val($("#statusOutput").val() + message + '\n');
            }

            function writeMessage(message) {
                $('#messageOutput').append(message + '\n')
            }

            $('#connect')
                    .click(function doConnect() {
                        sockjs = new SockJS($("#target").val());

                        sockjs.onopen = function (evt) {
                            writeStatus("CONNECTED");

                            var ping = setInterval(function () {
                                if (sockjs != "undefined") {
                                    sockjs.send("ping");
                                }
                            }, 3000);
                        };

                        sockjs.onclose = function (evt) {
                            writeStatus("DISCONNECTED");
                        };

                        sockjs.onmessage = function (evt) {
                            if (evt.data === "ping") {
                                writePing(evt.data);
```

653

```
                        } else {
                            writeMessage('ECHO: ' + evt.data);
                        }
                    };

                    sockjs.onerror = function (evt) {
                        onError(writeStatus('ERROR:' + evt.data))
                    };
                });

        $('#disconnect')
                .click(function () {
                    if(typeof sockjs != 'undefined') {
                        sockjs.close();
                        sockjs = undefined;
                    } else {
                        alert("Not connected.");
                    }
                });

        $('#send')
                .click(function () {
                    if(typeof sockjs != 'undefined') {
                        sockjs.send($('#message').val());
                    } else {
                        alert("Not connected.");
                    }
                });
        });
    </script>
</head>

<body>
<h2>SockJS Tester</h2>
Target:
<input type="text" id="target" size="40" value="http://localhost:8080/sockjs/echoHandler"/>
<br/>
<button id="connect">Connect</button>
<button id="disconnect">Disconnect</button>
<br/>
<br/>Message:
<input type="text" id="message" value=""/>
<button id="send">Send</button>
<br/>
<p>Status output:</p>
<pre><textarea id="statusOutput" rows="10" cols="50"></textarea></pre>
<p>Message output:</p>
<pre><textarea id="messageOutput" rows="10" cols="50"></textarea></pre>
<p>Ping output:</p>
<pre><textarea id="pingOutput" rows="10" cols="50"></textarea></pre>
</body>
</html>
```

With our new SockJS code implemented, build and deploy the project to the container and navigate to the UI located at `http://localhost:8080/sockjs/index.html`, which has all the same features and functionality of the WebSocket sample. To test the SockJS fallback functionality, try disabling WebSocket support in your browser. In Firefox, for example, navigate to the `about:config` page and then search for `network.websocket.enabled`. Toggle this setting to `false`, reload the sample UI, and reconnect. Utilizing a tool such as Live HTTP Headers will allow you to inspect the traffic going from browser to server for verification purposes. After verifying the behavior, toggle the Firefox setting `network.websocket.enabled` back to `true`, reload the page, and reconnect. Watching the traffic via Live HTTP Headers will now show you the WebSocket handshake. In our simple example, everything should work just as with the WebSocket API.

Sending Messages with STOMP

When working with WebSocket, typically a subprotocol such as STOMP will be used as a common format between client and server so both ends know what to expect and react accordingly. STOMP is supported out of the box by the Spring Framework, and we will use this protocol in our sample.

STOMP, a simple, frame-based messaging protocol modeled on HTTP, can be used over any reliable bidirectional streaming network protocol such as WebSocket. STOMP has a standard protocol format; JavaScript client-side support exists for sending and receiving messages in a browser and optionally for plugging into traditional message brokers that support STOMP such as RabbitMQ and ActiveMQ. Out of the box, the Spring Framework supports a simple broker that handles subscription requests and message broadcasting to connected clients in memory. In this sample, we will utilize the simple broker and leave the full-featured broker setup as an exercise for you. See `http://docs.spring.io/spring/docs/current/spring-framework-reference/html/websocket.html#websocket-stomp-handle-broker-relay-configure` for more details.

■ **Note**   For a full description of the STOMP protocol, see `http://stomp.github.io/stomp-specification-1.2.html`.

In our STOMP sample, we will create a simple stock-ticker application that displays a few predefined stock symbols, their current price, and timestamp upon price change. New stock symbols and starting prices can also be added through the UI. Any connecting clients (that is, other browsers in tabs or totally new clients on other networks) will see the same data as they are subscribed to the message broadcasts. Every second, each stock price will be updated to a new random amount and the timestamp updated.

To ensure that our clients will be able to use the stock ticker application, even if their browser does not support WebSocket, we will utilize SockJS again to transparently handle any transport switching. Let's dive into some code. First we need to add a dependency, as shown in Table 17-3.

Table 17-3. *Maven Dependencies for STOMP Sample*

Group ID	Artifact ID	Version	Description
`org.springframework`	`spring-messaging`	4.0.2	The `spring-messaging` module to support message sending in the STOMP sample

Now let's first create our Stock domain object, which holds information about the stock such as its code and price, as shown in Listing 17-8.

Listing 17-8. Stock Domain Object

```java
package com.apress.prospring4.ch17;

import java.util.Date;
import java.io.Serializable;
import java.text.DateFormat;
import java.text.SimpleDateFormat;

public class Stock implements Serializable {
    private static final long serialVersionUID = 1L;
    private static final String DATE_FORMAT = "MMM dd yyyy HH:mm:ss";

    private String code;
    private double price;
    private Date date = new Date();
    private DateFormat dateFormat = new SimpleDateFormat(DATE_FORMAT);

    public Stock() { }

    public Stock(String code, double price) {
        this.code = code;
        this.price = price;
    }

    public String getCode() {
        return code;
    }

    public void setCode(String code) {
        this.code = code;
    }

    public double getPrice() {
        return price;
    }

    public void setPrice(double price) {
        this.price = price;
    }

    public Date getDate() {
        return date;
    }

    public void setDate(Date date) {
        this.date = date;
    }
```

```
    public String getDateFormatted() {
        return dateFormat.format(date);
    }
}
```

Now we need to add an MVC controller to handle the incoming requests, as shown in Listing 17-9.

Listing 17-9. MVC Controller to Handle Incoming Stock Requests

```
package com.apress.prospring4.ch17;

import org.springframework.beans.factory.annotation.Autowired;
import org.springframework.messaging.handler.annotation.MessageMapping;
import org.springframework.messaging.simp.SimpMessagingTemplate;
import org.springframework.scheduling.TaskScheduler;
import org.springframework.stereotype.Controller;

import javax.annotation.PostConstruct;
import java.util.ArrayList;
import java.util.Date;
import java.util.List;
import java.util.Random;

@Controller
public class StockController {
    private TaskScheduler taskScheduler;
    private SimpMessagingTemplate simpMessagingTemplate;

    private List<Stock> stocks = new ArrayList<Stock>();
    private Random random = new Random(System.currentTimeMillis());

    public StockController() {
        stocks.add(new Stock("VMW", 1.00d));
        stocks.add(new Stock("EMC", 1.00d));
        stocks.add(new Stock("GOOG", 1.00d));
        stocks.add(new Stock("IBM", 1.00d));
    }

    @MessageMapping("/addStock")
    public void addStock(Stock stock) throws Exception {
        stocks.add(stock);
        broadcastUpdatedPrices();
    }

    @Autowired
    public void setSimpMessagingTemplate(SimpMessagingTemplate simpMessagingTemplate) {
        this.simpMessagingTemplate = simpMessagingTemplate;
    }

    @Autowired
    public void setTaskScheduler(TaskScheduler taskScheduler) {
        this.taskScheduler = taskScheduler;
    }
```

```java
    private void broadcastUpdatedPrices() {
        for(Stock stock : stocks) {
            stock.setPrice(stock.getPrice() + (getUpdatedStockPrice() * stock.getPrice()));
            stock.setDate(new Date());
        }

        simpMessagingTemplate.convertAndSend("/topic/price", stocks);
    }

    private double getUpdatedStockPrice() {
        double priceChange = random.nextDouble() * 5.0;

        if (random.nextInt(2) == 1) {
            priceChange = -priceChange;
        }

        return priceChange / 100.0;
    }

    @PostConstruct
    private void broadcastTimePeriodically() {
        taskScheduler.scheduleAtFixedRate(new Runnable() {
            @Override
            public void run() {
                broadcastUpdatedPrices();
            }
        }, 1000);
    }
}
```

Our controller does a couple of things here. First, we add a few predefined stock symbols to the list and their starting prices for demonstration purposes. We then define a method addStock, which takes a Stock object, adds it to the list of stocks, and then broadcasts the stocks to all subscribers. When broadcasting the stocks, we iterate through all the stocks that have been added, updating the price for each, and then send them out to all subscribers of /topic/price by using the wired SimpMessagingTemplate. We also use a TaskExecutor to continuously broadcast the updated list of stock prices to all subscribed clients every second.

With our controller in place, let's now create the HTML UI for display to clients (src/main/webapp/static/index.html), as shown in Listing 17-10.

Listing 17-10. HTML UI to Display Stock Prices

```html
<html>
<head>
    <title>Stock Ticker</title>
    <script src="https://d1fxtkz8shb9d2.cloudfront.net/sockjs-0.3.4.min.js"></script>
    <script src="http://cdnjs.cloudflare.com/ajax/libs/stomp.js/2.3.2/stomp.min.js"></script>
    <script src="http://code.jquery.com/jquery-2.1.1.min.js"></script>
    <script>
        var stomp = Stomp.over(new SockJS("/stomp/ws"));
```

```
        function displayStockPrice(frame) {
            var prices = JSON.parse(frame.body);

            $('#price').empty();

            for (var i in prices) {
                var price = prices[i];

                $('#price').append(
                        $('<tr>').append(
                                $('<td>').html(price.code),
                                $('<td>').html(price.price.toFixed(2)),
                                $('<td>').html(price.dateFormatted)
                        )
                );
            }
        }

        var connectCallback = function () {
            stomp.subscribe('/topic/price', displayStockPrice);
        };

        var errorCallback = function (error) {
            alert(error.headers.message);
        };

        stomp.connect("guest", "guest", connectCallback, errorCallback);

        $(document).ready(function () {
            $('.addStockButton').click(function (e) {
                e.preventDefault();

                var jsonstr = JSON.stringify({ 'code': $('.addStock .code').val(),
                    'price': Number($('.addStock .price').val()) });

                stomp.send("/app/addStock", {}, jsonstr);

                return false;
            });
        });
    </script>
</head>
<body>
<b>Stock Ticker</b></h1>
<table border="1">
    <thead>
    <tr>
        <th>Code</th>
        <th>Price</th>
        <th>Time</th>
    </tr>
    </thead>
    <tbody id="price"></tbody>
</table>
```

```
<p class="addStock">
    Code: <input type="text" class="code"/><br/>
    Price: <input type="text" class="price"/><br/>
    <button class="addStockButton">Add Stock</button>
</p>
</body>
</html>
```

Similar to past examples, we have some HTML mixed in with JavaScript to update the display. We utilize jQuery to update HTML data, SockJS to provide transport selection, and the STOMP JavaScript library stomp.js for communication with the server. Data sent via STOMP messages are encoded in JSON format, which we extract on events. Upon STOMP connection, we subscribe to /topic/price to receive stock-price updates.

Now let's configure our built-in STOMP broker in root-context.xml (src/main/webapp/WEB-INF/spring/root-context.xml), as shown in Listing 17-11.

Listing 17-11. STOMP Broker Configuration

```
<beans xmlns="http://www.springframework.org/schema/beans"
       xmlns:xsi="http://www.w3.org/2001/XMLSchema-instance"
       xmlns:websocket="http://www.springframework.org/schema/websocket"
       xmlns:mvc="http://www.springframework.org/schema/mvc"
       xmlns:context="http://www.springframework.org/schema/context"
       xsi:schemaLocation="
        http://www.springframework.org/schema/beans
        http://www.springframework.org/schema/beans/spring-beans.xsd
        http://www.springframework.org/schema/websocket
        http://www.springframework.org/schema/websocket/spring-websocket.xsd
        http://www.springframework.org/schema/mvc
        http://www.springframework.org/schema/mvc/spring-mvc.xsd
        http://www.springframework.org/schema/context
        http://www.springframework.org/schema/context/spring-context.xsd">

    <mvc:annotation-driven />

    <mvc:resources mapping="/index.html" location="/static/" />

    <context:component-scan base-package="com.apress.prospring4.ch17" />

    <websocket:message-broker application-destination-prefix="/app">
        <websocket:stomp-endpoint path="/ws">
            <websocket:sockjs/>
        </websocket:stomp-endpoint>
        <websocket:simple-broker prefix="/topic"/>
    </websocket:message-broker>

    <bean id="taskExecutor" class="org.springframework.core.task.SimpleAsyncTaskExecutor"/>
</beans>
```

For the most part, this configuration should look familiar. In this example, we configure `message-broker` by using the `websocket` namespace, define a STOMP endpoint, and enable SockJS. We also configure the prefix that subscribers will use to receive messages from. The configured `TaskExecutor` is used to provide stock quotes on the defined interval in our controller class. When using the namespace support, the `SimpMessagingTemplate` is automatically created for you and available to inject into your beans.

Now all that's left to do is configure our `web.xml` (`src/main/webapp/WEB-INF/web.xml`), as shown in Listing 17-12.

Listing 17-12. `web.xml` Configuration for STOMP Sample

```xml
<web-app xmlns="http://java.sun.com/xml/ns/javaee"
        xmlns:xsi="http://www.w3.org/2001/XMLSchema-instance"
        xsi:schemaLocation="http://java.sun.com/xml/ns/javaee
        http://java.sun.com/xml/ns/javaee/web-app_3_0.xsd"
        version="3.0">

    <display-name>Spring STOMP Sample</display-name>

    <servlet>
        <servlet-name>stomp</servlet-name>
        <servlet-class>org.springframework.web.servlet.DispatcherServlet</servlet-class>
        <init-param>
            <param-name>contextConfigLocation</param-name>
            <param-value>/WEB-INF/spring/root-context.xml</param-value>
        </init-param>
        <load-on-startup>1</load-on-startup>
        <async-supported>true</async-supported>
    </servlet>

    <servlet-mapping>
        <servlet-name>stomp</servlet-name>
        <url-pattern>/*</url-pattern>
    </servlet-mapping>
</web-app>
```

Now with our code in place, build the project and deploy it to your web container, and then navigate your browser to `http://localhost:8080/stomp/index.html`. When the page loads, you will see a list of predefined stock symbols as well as their prices fluctuating and the timestamp for the updated price. You will also see a section on the page to add a new stock code and price. Go ahead and add a new stock code and price, and the page will immediately start updating. You will see the stock prices changing in real time not only on the current page, but also in any other browser you may open. No validation on the form is performed and is left as an exercise for you.

That's all it takes to create the foundation of a SockJS/STOMP-driven WebSocket application!

Summary

In this chapter, we covered the general concepts of WebSocket. We discussed the Spring Framework's support for the low-level WebSocket API and then moved on to using SockJS as a fallback option to select the appropriate transport, depending on the client browser. Finally, we introduced STOMP as a WebSocket subprotocol for passing messages between client and server.

In the next chapter, we will discuss Spring subprojects, which you can mix into your applications to provide even more robust functionality.

CHAPTER 18

Spring Projects: Batch, Integration, XD, and Boot

This chapter presents a high-level overview of a few projects that are part of the Spring portfolio, notably Spring Batch, Integration, XD, and Boot. This chapter is not intended to cover each project in detail, but to provide just enough information and a sample to get you started. The Spring portfolio contains many more projects than the ones listed in this chapter, but we feel the ones presented here are widely used, and some are new and upcoming projects. You can always view the full list of Spring projects at http://spring.io/projects. This chapter covers the following topics:

- *Spring Batch*: This section covers core concepts of the Spring batch-processing framework, including what it provides you as a developer, and touches on the new JSR-352 support as of Spring Batch 3.0.

- *Spring Integration*: Integration patterns are used in many enterprise applications, and Spring Integration provides a robust framework for implementing these patterns. We will build upon the batch example to show how Spring Integration can be used as part of a workflow to initiate a batch job.

- *Spring XD*: Spring XD ties together many of the existing Spring projects to provide a unified and extensible system for big data applications. Spring XD is a distributed system focusing on data ingestion, real-time analytics, batch processing, and data export. This section shows how to implement the applications from the Batch and Integration samples by utilizing Spring XD via simple DSL in the shell interface.

- *Spring Boot*: Spring Boot aims to simplify application development, enabling developers to create applications with minimal configuration and setup without any code generation. This section introduces Spring Boot with a typical "Hello World!" web application and takes a peek at what it provides your application out of the box without any effort on your part.

As each of these topics could have their own chapter or even books, covering every detail of each project and its various offerings would be impossible. We hope the introductions and basic samples will capture your interest to explore further into each of the frameworks.

Spring Batch

Spring Batch, a framework for batch processing, is part of the Spring portfolio of projects. It's lightweight, flexible, and designed to provide developers with the ability to create robust batch applications with minimal effort. Spring Batch comes with a number of off-the-shelf components for a variety of technologies, and in most cases you may even be able to build your batch application by solely using the provided components.

Typical batch applications include daily invoice generation, payroll systems, and ETL (Extract, Transform, Load) processes. While these are typical examples people may think of up front, Spring Batch can be used for any process that needs to run unattended, not just for these scenarios. As with all other Spring projects, Spring Batch builds upon the core Spring framework, and you have full access to all its capabilities.

At a high level, a batch job contains one or more Steps. Each Step can provide the ability to either execute a single unit of work, which is represented by a Tasklet implementation, or it can participate in what's called *chunk-oriented processing*. With chunk-oriented processing, a Step utilizes an ItemReader to read some form of data, an optional ItemProcessor to do any transformations required on that data, and finally an ItemWriter to write the data out. A Step also has various configuration attributes such as the ability to configure a chunk size (the amount of data to process per transaction), enable multithreaded execution, skip limits, and so on. Listeners can be used at the Step level as well as the Job level to receive notifications of various events that occur during the batch job life cycle—for example, before a Step starts, when a Step ends, hooks into various read/process/write failures during a chunk-oriented processing scenario, and so on.

While most jobs can run perfectly fine in a single-threaded, single-process manner, Spring Batch also provides options for scaling and parallel processing of jobs. Currently, Spring Batch provides the following scalability options out of the box:

- *Multithreaded steps*: This is the simplest way to make a Step multithreaded. Simply add a TaskExecutor of your choice to the Step configuration, and each chunk of items in a chunk-oriented processing setup will be processed in its own thread of execution.

- *Parallel steps*: Let's say, for example, you need to read in two large files with different data at the start of your job. At first you may create two steps, and one will execute after the other. If both of these data file loads do not depend on each other, why not process them both at the same time? For this case, Spring Batch allows you to define a Split that contains Flow elements encapsulating these tasks that should be executed in parallel.

- *Remote chunking*: This scalability option allows you to take a step and remotely distribute the work to a number of remote workers and communicate via some sort of durable middleware such as AMQP or JMS. Remote chunking is typically used when the reading of data is not the bottleneck in the process, yet the writing and optionally processing of chunk data is. *Chunks* of data are sent through the middleware for slave nodes to pick up and process, which then communicate back to the master about the status of their processing of that chunk.

- *Partitioning*: This scalability option is generally used when you want to process a range of data, utilizing threads for each range. A typical scenario is a database table filled with data that has a numerical identifier column. With partitioning, you can "partition" the data to be processed in separate threads with a certain number of records. Spring Batch provides the ability for you as the developer to hook into this partitioning scheme, as it's highly dependent on the use case at hand. Partitioning can be done in local threads or farmed out to remote workers (similar to the remote chunking option).

One basic yet common use case of batch processing is reading in a file of some sort, usually a flat file in a delimited format (for example, comma separated), which then needs to be loaded into a database, with each record optionally processed prior to writing to the database. Let's take a look at how we would implement this use case in Spring Batch.

First we need to add the required dependencies, as shown in Table 18-1.

Table 18-1. *Dependencies for Batch Job*

Group ID	Artifact ID	Version	Description
org.springframework	spring-jdbc	4.0.2.RELEASE	Spring JDBC library
org.springframework	spring-context	4.0.2.RELEASE	Spring Context library
org.springframework.batch	spring-batch-core	3.0.1.RELEASE	Spring Batch Core library
org.springframework.batch	spring-batch-infrastructure	3.0.1.RELEASE	Spring Batch Infrastructure library
commons-dbcp	commons-dbcp	1.4	Commons DBCP database connection pool library
commons-io	commons-io	2.4	Commons IO package for IO helper classes
com.h2database	h2	1.3.172	H2 embedded database library
log4j	log4j	1.2.17	log4j logging framework library

With our dependencies in place, let's dive into the code. First we create a domain object that represents a person based on the data in the file we will read, as shown in Listing 18-1.

Listing 18-1. Person Domain Object

```java
package com.apress.prospring4.ch18;

public class Person {
    private String firstName;
    private String lastName;

    public void setFirstName(String firstName) {
        this.firstName = firstName;
    }

    public String getFirstName() {
        return firstName;
    }

    public void setLastName(String lastName) {
        this.lastName = lastName;
    }

    public String getLastName() {
        return lastName;
    }

    @Override
    public String toString() {
        return "firstName: " + firstName + ", lastName: " + lastName;
    }
}
```

Next, let's create an implementation of an ItemProcessor used to transform the first and last name of each person represented by the Person object to uppercase, as shown in Listing 18-2. Please note that ItemProcessors are not required in a chunk-oriented processing scenario; only an ItemReader and ItemWriter are. We use an ItemProcessor here to serve as an example of how you can transform data prior to writing.

Listing 18-2. ItemProcessor Implementation to Change a Person's First and Last Name to Uppercase

```
package com.apress.prospring4.ch18;

import org.apache.commons.logging.Log;
import org.apache.commons.logging.LogFactory;
import org.springframework.batch.item.ItemProcessor;

public class PersonItemProcessor implements ItemProcessor<Person, Person> {
    private static Log LOG = LogFactory.getLog(PersonItemProcessor.class);

    @Override
    public Person process(Person person) throws Exception {
        String firstName = person.getFirstName().toUpperCase();
        String lastName = person.getLastName().toUpperCase();

        Person transformedPerson = new Person();
        transformedPerson.setFirstName(firstName);
        transformedPerson.setLastName(lastName);

        LOG.info("Transformed person: " + person + " Into: " + transformedPerson);

        return transformedPerson;
    }
}
```

Next up, we will create a StepExecutionListener implementation that resides at the Step level and will tell us how many records were written after the step has completed, as shown in Listing 18-3. A StepExecutionListener also allows us to modify the returned ExitStatus if needed; otherwise, simply return null to keep it unchanged.

Listing 18-3. StepExecutionListener Implementation for Write Counts

```
package com.apress.prospring4.ch18;

import org.springframework.batch.core.ExitStatus;
import org.springframework.batch.core.StepExecution;
import org.springframework.batch.core.listener.StepExecutionListenerSupport;

public class StepExecutionStatsListener extends StepExecutionListenerSupport {
    @Override
    public ExitStatus afterStep(StepExecution stepExecution) {
        System.out.println("Wrote: " + stepExecution.getWriteCount()
                + " items in step: " + stepExecution.getStepName());

        return null;
    }
}
```

At this point, we have our core components assembled, but before moving on to the configuration and invocation code, let's take a look at the data model and the data itself. The data model for our job is very simple (`src/main/resources/META-INF/spring/jobs/personJob/support/person.sql`) and is shown in Listing 18-4.

Listing 18-4. Data Model for Person Job

```
DROP TABLE people IF EXISTS;

CREATE TABLE people (
        person_id BIGINT IDENTITY NOT NULL PRIMARY KEY,
        first_name VARCHAR(20),
        last_name VARCHAR(20)
);
```

And the corresponding data that we will load for the sample (`src/main/resources/META-INF/spring/jobs/personJob/support/test-data.csv`) is shown in Listing 18-5.

Listing 18-5. Data for Person Job

```
Jill,Doe
Joe,Doe
Justin,Matthews
Jane,Matthews
```

Now let's do some configuration to define the job, and set up the embedded database and related job components as shown in Listing 18-6. The file in Listing 18-6 is located at `src/main/resources/META-INF/spring/jobs/personJob/personJob.xml`.

Listing 18-6. Configuration for the Person Job

```xml
<?xml version="1.0" encoding="UTF-8"?>

<beans xmlns="http://www.springframework.org/schema/beans"
        xmlns:xsi="http://www.w3.org/2001/XMLSchema-instance"
        xmlns:batch="http://www.springframework.org/schema/batch"
        xmlns:jdbc="http://www.springframework.org/schema/jdbc"
        xmlns:p="http://www.springframework.org/schema/p"
        xsi:schemaLocation="
        http://www.springframework.org/schema/batch
        http://www.springframework.org/schema/batch/spring-batch.xsd
        http://www.springframework.org/schema/jdbc
        http://www.springframework.org/schema/jdbc/spring-jdbc.xsd
        http://www.springframework.org/schema/beans
        http://www.springframework.org/schema/beans/spring-beans.xsd">

    <batch:job id="personJob">
        <batch:step id="step1">
            <batch:tasklet>
                <batch:chunk reader="itemReader" processor="itemProcessor" writer="itemWriter"
                            commit-interval="10"/>
                <batch:listeners>
                    <batch:listener ref="stepExecutionStatsListener"/>
```

```xml
                </batch:listeners>
            </batch:tasklet>
            <batch:fail on="FAILED"/>
            <batch:end on="*"/>
        </batch:step>
    </batch:job>


    <jdbc:embedded-database id="dataSource" type="H2">
        <jdbc:script location="classpath:/org/springframework/batch/core/schema-h2.sql"/>
        <jdbc:script location="classpath:/META-INF/spring/jobs/personJob/support/person.sql"/>
    </jdbc:embedded-database>


    <bean id="transactionManager"
        class="org.springframework.jdbc.datasource.DataSourceTransactionManager"
            p:dataSource-ref="dataSource"/>


    <batch:job-repository id="jobRepository"/>


    <bean id="jobLauncher"
        class="org.springframework.batch.core.launch.support.SimpleJobLauncher"
            p:jobRepository-ref="jobRepository"/>


    <bean id="stepExecutionStatsListener"
        class="com.apress.prospring4.ch18.StepExecutionStatsListener"/>


    <bean id="itemReader" class="org.springframework.batch.item.file.FlatFileItemReader">
        <property name="resource"
            value="classpath:/META-INF/spring/jobs/personJob/support/test-data.csv"/>
        <property name="lineMapper">
            <bean class="org.springframework.batch.item.file.mapping.DefaultLineMapper">
                <property name="lineTokenizer">
                    <bean

                        class="org.springframework.batch.item.file.transform.DelimitedLineTokenizer">
                        <property name="names" value="firstName,lastName"/>
                    </bean>
                </property>
                <property name="fieldSetMapper">
                    <bean class="org.springframework.batch.item.file.mapping.BeanWrapperFieldSetMapper">
                        <property name="targetType" value="com.apress.prospring4.ch18.Person"/>
                    </bean>
                </property>
            </bean>
        </property>
    </bean>


    <bean id="itemProcessor" class="com.apress.prospring4.ch18.PersonItemProcessor"/>


    <bean id="itemWriter" class="org.springframework.batch.item.database.JdbcBatchItemWriter">
        <property name="itemSqlParameterSourceProvider">
            <bean
```

```
                      class="org.springframework.batch.item.database.BeanPropertyItemSqlParameterSourceProvider"/>
            </property>
            <property name="sql"
      value="INSERT INTO people (first_name, last_name) VALUES (:firstName, :lastName)"/>
            <property name="dataSource" ref="dataSource"/>
      </bean>
</beans>
```

In the configuration, first we define our batch job by using the batch schema. We create a Step, configure it for chunk-oriented processing, and define our ItemReader, ItemProcessor, and ItemWriter along with our listener. We set up an embedded database, define core batch-related beans, and then configure our processing beans.

Finally, last but not least, we need a driver program to launch the job, as shown in Listing 18-7.

Listing 18-7. Driver Program to Launch Job

```
package com.apress.prospring4.ch18;

import org.springframework.batch.core.Job;
import org.springframework.batch.core.JobParameters;
import org.springframework.batch.core.JobParametersBuilder;
import org.springframework.batch.core.launch.JobLauncher;
import org.springframework.context.ApplicationContext;
import org.springframework.context.support.ClassPathXmlApplicationContext;

import java.util.Date;

public class PersonJob {
    public static void main(String[] args) throws Exception {
        ApplicationContext applicationContext
                = new ClassPathXmlApplicationContext("/META-INF/spring/jobs/personJob/personJob.xml");

        Job job = applicationContext.getBean(Job.class);
        JobLauncher jobLauncher = applicationContext.getBean(JobLauncher.class);

        JobParameters jobParameters = new JobParametersBuilder()
                .addDate("date", new Date())
                .toJobParameters();

        jobLauncher.run(job, jobParameters);
    }
}
```

This code should be familiar to you, as for the most part we are creating our context, obtaining a few beans, and calling methods on them. One thing you may notice is the JobParameters object. This object encapsulates parameters that are used to distinguish one instance of a job from another. Job identity is important in determining the last state of the job, if any, which also plays into other things such as the ability to restart a job. In our example, we simply use the current date as our Job parameter. JobParameters can be of many types, and these parameters can be accessed in your Job as reference data.

At this point, we are ready to test out our new job. Compile the code and run the `PersonJob` class. You will see some log statements display on the screen, and the ones of interest are as follows:

```
[org.springframework.batch.core.launch.support.SimpleJobLauncher] - <Job: [FlowJob:
[name=personJob]] launched with the following parameters: [{date=1406078297879}]>
[org.springframework.batch.core.job.SimpleStepHandler] - <Executing step: [step1]>
[com.apress.prospring4.ch18.PersonItemProcessor] - <Transformed person: firstName: Jill, lastName:
Doe Into: firstName: JILL, lastName: DOE>
[com.apress.prospring4.ch18.PersonItemProcessor] - <Transformed person: firstName: Joe, lastName:
Doe Into: firstName: JOE, lastName: DOE>
[com.apress.prospring4.ch18.PersonItemProcessor] - <Transformed person: firstName: Justin, lastName:
Matthews Into: firstName: JUSTIN, lastName: MATTHEWS>
[com.apress.prospring4.ch18.PersonItemProcessor] - <Transformed person: firstName: Jane, lastName:
Matthews Into: firstName: JANE, lastName: MATTHEWS>
Wrote: 4 items in step: step1
[org.springframework.batch.core.launch.support.SimpleJobLauncher] - <Job: [FlowJob:
[name=personJob]] completed with the following parameters: [{date=1406078297879}] and the following
status: [COMPLETED]>
```

And that's all there is to it. You have now built a simple batch job that reads data from a CSV file, transforms the data via an `ItemProcessor` to change the person's first and last name to uppercase, and then writes the results out to a database. You also used a `StepListener` to output the number of items that were written in the step.

For more information on Spring Batch, please see its project page at `http://projects.spring.io/spring-batch/`.

JSR-352

JSR-352 is a specification for "Batch Applications for the Java Platform" and was heavily influenced by Spring Batch. If you choose to utilize JSR-352 for your jobs, you will notice more and more similarities between the two and should feel comfortable if you are already a Spring Batch user. For the most part, Spring Batch and JSR-352 have similar constructs, and Spring Batch has fully supported this JSR as of Spring Batch 3.0. Like Spring Batch, JSR-352 jobs are configured via an XML schema in what is referred to as the Job Specification Language (JSL). Because JSR-352 defines a spec and an API, no off-the-shelf infrastructure components are provided as you may be used to when working with Spring Batch. If you strictly adhere to the JSR-352 API, this means implementing JSR-352 interfaces and writing all of the infrastructure components such as `ItemReaders` and `ItemWriters` on your own.

In this example, we will convert the previous batch example to utilize the JSR-352 JSL, but rather than rolling our own infrastructure components, we will utilize the same `ItemReader`, `ItemProcessor`, and `ItemWriter` as well as taking advantage of Spring for dependency injection and so on. Implementing your job 100 percent to JSR-352 spec compliance will be left as an exercise for you.

In this sample, as mentioned, we will reuse most of the code from the pure Spring Batch sample, with a few minor changes that we will go through here. If you haven't yet, this would be a good time to get the Spring Batch example working and then go forward with applying the changes in this section.

First let's replace the H2 database with HSQLDB; the dependency is shown in Table 18-2.

Table 18-2. *Dependency for JSR-352 Job*

Group ID	Artifact ID	Version	Description
org.hsqldb	hsqldb	2.3.1	The HSQLDB-embedded database library

Now that we have updated the dependency, we need to move `personJob.xml` into a new directory under `src/main/resources/META-INF/batch-jobs/`. This is a requirement per the JSR-352 spec, and when starting a job, all that is needed is the file name without the `.xml` extension. No path is required because it's located in a standard directory. Next we will modify the configuration file a bit, as shown in Listing 18-8.

Listing 18-8. Modified Person Job Configuration for JSR-352

```xml
<?xml version="1.0" encoding="UTF-8"?>

<beans xmlns="http://www.springframework.org/schema/beans"
       xmlns:xsi="http://www.w3.org/2001/XMLSchema-instance"
       xmlns:jdbc="http://www.springframework.org/schema/jdbc"
       xmlns:p="http://www.springframework.org/schema/p"
       xsi:schemaLocation="
       http://www.springframework.org/schema/jdbc
       http://www.springframework.org/schema/jdbc/spring-jdbc.xsd
       http://www.springframework.org/schema/beans
       http://www.springframework.org/schema/beans/spring-beans.xsd
       http://xmlns.jcp.org/xml/ns/javaee http://xmlns.jcp.org/xml/ns/javaee/jobXML_1_0.xsd">

    <job id="personJob" xmlns="http://xmlns.jcp.org/xml/ns/javaee" version="1.0">
        <step id="step1">
            <listeners>
                <listener ref="stepExecutionStatsListener"/>
            </listeners>
            <chunk item-count="10">
                <reader ref="itemReader"/>
                <processor ref="itemProcessor"/>
                <writer ref="itemWriter"/>
            </chunk>
            <fail on="FAILED"/>
            <end on="*"/>
        </step>
    </job>

    <jdbc:embedded-database id="dataSource" type="HSQL">
        <jdbc:script location="classpath:/META-INF/spring/jobs/personJob/support/person.sql"/>
    </jdbc:embedded-database>

    <bean id="stepExecutionStatsListener"
        class="com.apress.prospring4.ch18.StepExecutionStatsListener"/>

    <bean id="itemReader" class="org.springframework.batch.item.file.FlatFileItemReader">
        <property name="resource"
            value="classpath:/META-INF/spring/jobs/personJob/support/test-data.csv"/>
        <property name="lineMapper">
            <bean class="org.springframework.batch.item.file.mapping.DefaultLineMapper">
                <property name="lineTokenizer">
                    <bean

                        class="org.springframework.batch.item.file.transform.DelimitedLineTokenizer">
                        <property name="names" value="firstName,lastName"/>
                    </bean>
```

```
                </property>
                <property name="fieldSetMapper">
                    <bean class="org.springframework.batch.item.file.mapping.
BeanWrapperFieldSetMapper">
                        <property name="targetType" value="com.apress.prospring4.ch18.Person"/>
                    </bean>
                </property>
            </bean>
        </property>
    </bean>

    <bean id="itemProcessor" class="com.apress.prospring4.ch18.PersonItemProcessor"/>

    <bean id="itemWriter" class="org.springframework.batch.item.database.JdbcBatchItemWriter">
        <property name="itemSqlParameterSourceProvider">
            <bean
  class="org.springframework.batch.item.database.BeanPropertyItemSqlParameterSourceProvider"/>
        </property>
        <property name="sql"
  value="INSERT INTO people (first_name, last_name) VALUES (:firstName, :lastName)"/>
        <property name="dataSource" ref="dataSource"/>
    </bean>
</beans>
```

As you can tell, this configuration looks pretty much like the pure Spring Batch example, except the job definition uses the JSR-352 JSL and we are able to remove a few beans (transactionManager, jobRepository, jobLauncher) as they are already provided for us in one way or another. You will also notice an additional schema definition using jobXML_1.0.xsd. Support for this schema is obtained via the JSR-352 API JAR and brought down automatically as a transitive dependency when using a build tool such as Maven. If you need to obtain the dependency manually, see the project page listed at the end of this section. The second part that we need to modify is the PersonJob class, as we are now using JSR-352-specific code to invoke the job, as shown in Listing 18-9.

Listing 18-9. JSR-352 PersonJob Driver Class

```
package com.apress.prospring4.ch18;

import org.springframework.batch.core.jsr.launch.JsrJobOperator;

import javax.batch.runtime.BatchStatus;
import javax.batch.runtime.JobExecution;
import java.util.Properties;

public class PersonJob {
    public static void main(String[] args) throws Exception {
        JsrJobOperator jobOperator = new JsrJobOperator();

        long executionId = jobOperator.start("personJob", new Properties());
        JobExecution jobExecution = jobOperator.getJobExecution(executionId);

        waitForJob(jobOperator, jobExecution);
    }
```

```
private static void waitForJob(JsrJobOperator jobOperator, JobExecution jobExecution) {
    BatchStatus batchStatus = jobExecution.getBatchStatus();

    while(true) {
        if(batchStatus == BatchStatus.STOPPED || batchStatus == BatchStatus.COMPLETED
                || batchStatus == BatchStatus.FAILED) {
            return;
        }

        jobExecution = jobOperator.getJobExecution(jobExecution.getExecutionId());
        batchStatus = jobExecution.getBatchStatus();
    }
}
}
```

This is a bit different from other examples, where we work with the ApplicationContext and beans directly. When creating a JSR-352 job, we use the JsrJobOperator to start and control jobs. Rather than taking a JobParameters object to provide parameters to the job, a Properties object is used instead. The Properties object used is a standard java.util.Properties class, and job parameters should be created with both a String key and value. Another interesting change you may notice is the waitForJob() method. JSR-352 by default launches all jobs asynchronously. Thus, in our stand-alone program, as shown, we need to wait for the job to be in an acceptable state before the program terminates. If your code is running in a container such as an application server of some sort, this code may not be needed. Now let's compile and run the PersonJob class, which will yield the following relevant log statements:

```
[org.springframework.batch.core.job.SimpleStepHandler] - <Executing step: [step1]>
[com.apress.prospring4.ch18.PersonItemProcessor] - <Transformed person: firstName: Jill, lastName:
Doe Into: firstName: JILL, lastName: DOE>
[com.apress.prospring4.ch18.PersonItemProcessor] - <Transformed person: firstName: Joe, lastName:
Doe Into: firstName: JOE, lastName: DOE>
[com.apress.prospring4.ch18.PersonItemProcessor] - <Transformed person: firstName: Justin, lastName:
Matthews Into: firstName: JUSTIN, lastName: MATTHEWS>
[com.apress.prospring4.ch18.PersonItemProcessor] - <Transformed person: firstName: Jane, lastName:
Matthews Into: firstName: JANE, lastName: MATTHEWS>
Wrote: 4 items in step: step1
```

The log output looks pretty much the same, and you have now utilized JSR-352 to define and run your job along with using Spring's functionality for dependency injection and infrastructure components from Spring Batch rather than writing your own.

For more information on JSR-352, please see its project page at https://jcp.org/en/jsr/detail?id=352.

Spring Integration

The *Spring Integration* project provides out-of-the box implementations of the well-known Enterprise Integration Patterns (EIP). Spring Integration focuses on message-driven architectures; provides a simple model for integration solutions, asynchronous abilities, and loosely coupled components; and is designed for extension as well as testability.

At its core, a Message plays a central role in the framework. This generic wrapper around a Java object is combined with metadata used by the framework, more specifically the payload and headers, and is used to determine how to handle that object.

A Message Channel is the *pipe* in a pipes-and-filters architecture in which producers send messages to this channel and consumers receive from it. Message Endpoints, on the other hand, represent the *filter* of the pipes-and-filters architecture and they connect application code to the messaging framework. Some Message Endpoints that are provided out of the box by Spring Integration are Transformers, Filters, Routers, and Splitters—each providing its own roles and responsibilities.

Spring Integration also provides a plethora of integration endpoints (20+ at the time of this writing), which can be located in the documentation section "Endpoint Quick Reference Table" at http://docs.spring.io/spring-integration/reference/htmlsingle/#endpoint-summary. These endpoints provide the ability to connect various resources such as AMQP, files, HTTP, JMX, Syslog, and Twitter. Going even beyond what is provided out of the box by Spring Integration, another project named Spring Integration Extensions is a community-based contribution model located at https://github.com/spring-projects/spring-batch-extensions that contains even more integration possibilities, including AWS (Amazon Web Services), Apache Kafka, SMPP (Short Message Peer-to-Peer), and Voldemort. Between the out-of-the-box and extension project components, Spring Integration provides a wealth of off-the-shelf components, which means the likelihood of having to write your own is greatly reduced.

In this example, we are going to build upon the previous batch examples, but this time introduce Spring Integration to show how we can use it to monitor a directory on a given interval. When a file arrives, we detect that file and kick off the batch job for processing.

In this sample, we are again going to build on the initial "pure" Spring Batch project that we started with in this chapter. Please be sure to take a look and have that running before proceeding, as we will be reviewing only the new classes and configuration modifications here.

First we need to add a few new dependencies for Spring Integration itself, as shown in Table 18-3.

Table 18-3. *Dependencies for Spring Integration*

Group ID	Artifact ID	Version	Description
org.springframework.batch	spring-batch-integration	3.0.1.RELEASE	Spring Batch Integration library
org.springframework.integration	spring-integration-file	4.0.3.RELEASE	Spring Integration File library

With our new dependencies in place, first let's create a class that acts as a Spring Integration *transformer*. This Transformer will receive a Message from an inbound channel that represents a found file and launch the batch job with it, as shown in Listing 18-10.

Listing 18-10. Spring Integration Transformer

```
package com.apress.prospring4.ch18;

import org.springframework.batch.core.Job;
import org.springframework.batch.core.JobParametersBuilder;
import org.springframework.batch.integration.launch.JobLaunchRequest;
import org.springframework.messaging.Message;

import java.io.File;

public class MessageToJobLauncher {
    private Job job;
    private String fileNameKey;

    public MessageToJobLauncher(Job job, String fileNameKey) {
        this.job = job;
        this.fileNameKey = fileNameKey;
    }
```

```java
public JobLaunchRequest toRequest(Message<File> message) {
    JobParametersBuilder jobParametersBuilder = new JobParametersBuilder();
    jobParametersBuilder.addString(fileNameKey, message.getPayload().getAbsolutePath());

    return new JobLaunchRequest(job, jobParametersBuilder.toJobParameters());
}
}
```

Now let's modify our configuration file (src/main/resources/META-INF/spring/jobs/personJob/personJob.xml) to add the integration-specific pieces, as shown in Listing 18-11.

Listing 18-11. Updated Configuration for Spring Integration File Integration

```xml
<?xml version="1.0" encoding="UTF-8"?>

<beans xmlns="http://www.springframework.org/schema/beans"
       xmlns:xsi="http://www.w3.org/2001/XMLSchema-instance"
       xmlns:batch="http://www.springframework.org/schema/batch"
       xmlns:batch-int="http://www.springframework.org/schema/batch-integration"
       xmlns:jdbc="http://www.springframework.org/schema/jdbc"
       xmlns:int="http://www.springframework.org/schema/integration"
       xmlns:int-file="http://www.springframework.org/schema/integration/file"
       xmlns:p="http://www.springframework.org/schema/p"
       xsi:schemaLocation="
       http://www.springframework.org/schema/batch
       http://www.springframework.org/schema/batch/spring-batch.xsd
       http://www.springframework.org/schema/batch-integration
       http://www.springframework.org/schema/batch-integration/spring-batch-integration.xsd
       http://www.springframework.org/schema/jdbc
       http://www.springframework.org/schema/jdbc/spring-jdbc.xsd
       http://www.springframework.org/schema/beans
       http://www.springframework.org/schema/beans/spring-beans.xsd
       http://www.springframework.org/schema/integration
       http://www.springframework.org/schema/integration/spring-integration.xsd
       http://www.springframework.org/schema/integration/file
       http://www.springframework.org/schema/integration/file/spring-integration-file.xsd">

    <batch:job id="personJob">
        <batch:step id="step1">
            <batch:tasklet>
                <batch:chunk reader="itemReader" processor="itemProcessor" writer="itemWriter"
                             commit-interval="10"/>
                <batch:listeners>
                    <batch:listener ref="stepExecutionStatsListener"/>
                </batch:listeners>
            </batch:tasklet>
            <batch:fail on="FAILED"/>
            <batch:end on="*"/>
        </batch:step>
    </batch:job>
```

```xml
    <jdbc:embedded-database id="dataSource" type="H2">
        <jdbc:script location="classpath:/org/springframework/batch/core/schema-h2.sql"/>
        <jdbc:script location="classpath:/META-INF/spring/jobs/personJob/support/person.sql"/>
    </jdbc:embedded-database>

    <bean id="transactionManager" class="org.springframework.jdbc.datasource.
DataSourceTransactionManager"
                p:dataSource-ref="dataSource"/>


    <batch:job-repository id="jobRepository"/>


    <bean id="jobLauncher" class="org.springframework.batch.core.launch.support.SimpleJobLauncher"
                p:jobRepository-ref="jobRepository"/>

    <bean id="stepExecutionStatsListener" class="com.apress.prospring4.ch18.
StepExecutionStatsListener"/>


    <bean id="itemReader" class="org.springframework.batch.item.file.FlatFileItemReader"
        scope="step">
        <property name="resource" value="file://#{jobParameters['file.name']}"/>
        <property name="lineMapper">
            <bean class="org.springframework.batch.item.file.mapping.DefaultLineMapper">
                <property name="lineTokenizer">
                    <bean

                      class="org.springframework.batch.item.file.transform.DelimitedLineTokenizer">
                        <property name="names" value="firstName,lastName"/>
                    </bean>
                </property>
                <property name="fieldSetMapper">
                    <bean

                      class="org.springframework.batch.item.file.mapping.BeanWrapperFieldSetMapper">
                        <property name="targetType" value="com.apress.prospring4.ch18.Person"/>
                    </bean>
                </property>
            </bean>
        </property>
    </bean>


    <bean id="itemProcessor" class="com.apress.prospring4.ch18.PersonItemProcessor"/>


    <bean id="itemWriter" class="org.springframework.batch.item.database.JdbcBatchItemWriter">
        <property name="itemSqlParameterSourceProvider">
            <bean
  class="org.springframework.batch.item.database.BeanPropertyItemSqlParameterSourceProvider"/>
        </property>
        <property name="sql"
  value="INSERT INTO people (first_name, last_name) VALUES (:firstName, :lastName)"/>
        <property name="dataSource" ref="dataSource"/>
    </bean>
```

```xml
<int:channel id="inbound"/>
<int:channel id="outbound"/>

<int:channel id="loggingChannel"/>
<int-file:inbound-channel-adapter id="inboundFileChannelAdapater" channel="inbound"
                                directory="file:/tmp/people/" filename-pattern="*.csv">
    <int:poller fixed-rate="1000"/>
</int-file:inbound-channel-adapter>

<int:transformer input-channel="inbound"
                 output-channel="outbound">
    <bean class="com.apress.prospring4.ch18.MessageToJobLauncher">
        <constructor-arg ref="personJob"/>
        <constructor-arg value="file.name"/>
    </bean>
</int:transformer>

<batch-int:job-launching-gateway request-channel="outbound" reply-channel="loggingChannel"/>

<int:logging-channel-adapter channel="loggingChannel"/>
</beans>
```

The main additions to the configuration are the sections that are prefixed with the int: and batch-int: namespaces. First we create a few named channels to pass data through. We then configure an inbound-channel-adapter specifically for watching the specified directory on a given interval of 1 second. We then configure our Transformer bean, which receives files as standard java.io.File objects wrapped in a Message. Next we configure a job-launching-gateway, which receives job-launch requests from our Transformer to actually invoke the batch job. Last but not least, we create a logging-channel-adapter, which will print out informational notices after the job completes. As you can see by following the configured Channel attributes, each component either consumes messages or produces messages, or both, via Channel's.

Now let's create a simple driver class that loads our configuration file. All this driver class does is load the application context with our configuration and remain running until you kill the process as it continuously polls the specified directory. Create a class called FileWatcher, as shown in Listing 18-12.

Listing 18-12. Driver Class to Watch for Files

```java
package com.apress.prospring4.ch18;

import org.springframework.context.ApplicationContext;
import org.springframework.context.support.ClassPathXmlApplicationContext;

public class FileWatcher {
    public static void main(String[] args) throws Exception {
        ApplicationContext applicationContext
                = new ClassPathXmlApplicationContext("/META-INF/spring/jobs/personJob/personJob.
xml");
    }
}
```

Now compile the code and run the FileWatcher class. When the application starts, you may notice that some log messages are printed to the screen, but eventually nothing else happens. This is because the Spring Integration file adapter is waiting for files to be placed in the configured location on a polling interval, and nothing will happen until it detects a file in that location. Create a simple CSV file such as the following, containing only a single line:

```
Chris, Schaefer
```

Then move this file into our configured location (/tmp/people/) under any file name, as long as it uses the .csv extension (for example, people.csv). Once you have moved that file to the appropriate location, flip back to the console where you have the FileWatcher application running and you will now see output displayed similar to the following:

```
[org.springframework.integration.file.FileReadingMessageSource] - <Created message:
[[Payload File content=/tmp/people/b.csv][Headers={id=0c407bf8-d16d-adbc-c8d7-af3023d404a9,
timestamp=1406080790546}]]>
[org.springframework.batch.core.launch.support.SimpleJobLauncher] - <Job: [FlowJob:
[name=personJob]] launched with the following parameters: [{file.name=/tmp/people/b.csv}]>
[org.springframework.batch.core.job.SimpleStepHandler] - <Executing step: [step1]>
[com.apress.prospring4.ch18.PersonItemProcessor] - <Transformed person: firstName: Chris, lastName:
Schaefer Into: firstName: CHRIS, lastName: SCHAEFER>
Wrote: 1 items in step: step1
[org.springframework.batch.core.launch.support.SimpleJobLauncher] - <Job: [FlowJob:
[name=personJob]] completed with the following parameters: [{file.name=/tmp/people/b.csv}] and the
following status: [COMPLETED]>
[org.springframework.integration.handler.LoggingHandler] - <JobExecution: id=1, version=2,
startTime=Tue Jul 22 21:59:50 EDT 2014, endTime=Tue Jul 22 21:59:50 EDT 2014, lastUpdated=Tue
Jul 22 21:59:50 EDT 2014, status=COMPLETED, exitStatus=exitCode=COMPLETED;exitDescription=,
job=[JobInstance: id=1, version=0, Job=[personJob]], jobParameters=[{file.name=/tmp/people/b.csv}]>
```

As you can see from the log statements, Spring Integration detected the file, created a Message from it, invoked the batch job that transformed the contents of the CSV file, and then wrote the contents to the in-memory database. While this is a simple example, it demonstrates how you can build complex and decoupled workflows between various types of applications by using Spring Integration.

For more information on Spring Integration, please see its project page at http://projects.spring.io/spring-integration/.

Spring XD

Spring XD is an extensible runtime service designed for distributed data ingestion, real-time analytics, batch processing, and data export. Spring XD builds upon many of the existing Spring portfolio projects—most notably from this chapter, the Spring Framework itself, Batch, and Integration. The goal of Spring XD is to provide a unified way to integrate many systems into a cohesive big data solution that helps solve the complexity of many common use cases.

Spring XD can run in a single stand-alone mode, typically for development and testing purposes, as well as in a full-distributed mode providing the ability to have high-availability master nodes along with any number of worker nodes. Spring XD enables you to manage these services via a shell interface (utilizing the Spring shell) as well as through a graphical web interface. These interfaces allow you to define how to assemble various components to accomplish your data processing needs through either a DSL-type syntax via the shell application or by entering data into the web interface, which will build the definitions for you.

The Spring XD DSL is based around a few concepts, notably streams, modules, sources, processors, sinks, and jobs. By combining these components together via concise syntax, it is easy to create flows to connect various technologies to ingest data, process it, and eventually output the data to an external source, or even run a batch job for further processing. Let's take a quick look at these concepts:

- A *stream* defines how data will flow from a source to a sink and may pass through any number of processors. A DSL is used to define a stream—for example, a basic source-to-sink definition may look like `http | file`.

- A *module* encapsulates a reusable unit of work that streams are composed of. Modules are categorized by type based on their role. At the time of this writing, Spring XD contains modules of type source, processor, sink, and job.

- *Sources* in Spring XD either poll an external resource or are triggered by some sort of event. Sources provide output only to downstream components, and the first module in a stream must be a source.

- *Processors* are similar in nature to what we saw in Spring Batch. The role of a processor is to take an input, perform transformation or business logic on the provided object, and return an output.

- On the flip side of a source, a *sink* takes an input source and outputs that data to its destination resource. A sink is the final stop in the stream.

- *Jobs* are modules that define a Spring Batch job. These jobs are defined in the same way as we described at the start of this chapter and are deployed into Spring XD to provide batch-processing capabilities.

- *Taps*, as indicated by their name, listen to data flowing through the stream and also allow you to process that tapped data in a separate stream. The tap concept is similar to the WireTap Enterprise Integration Patterns.

As you would expect, Spring XD provides a number of out-of-the-box sources, processors, sinks, jobs, and taps. As a developer, you are also not limited just to what's provided out of the box, but free to build your own modules and components as well. For more details on creating your own modules and components, see the reference manual on the customization point of interest:

- *Modules*: `http://docs.spring.io/spring-xd/docs/current/reference/html/#_creating_a_ module`

- *Sources*: `http://docs.spring.io/spring-xd/docs/current/reference/html/#creating-a- source-module`

- *Processors*: `http://docs.spring.io/spring-xd/docs/current/reference/html/#creating- a-processor-module`

- *Sinks*: `http://docs.spring.io/spring-xd/docs/current/reference/html/#creating-a- sink-module`

- *Jobs*: `http://docs.spring.io/spring-xd/docs/current/reference/html/#creating-a- job-module`

In this example, we will show you how to use Spring XD's off-the-shelf components to replicate what we created with the Batch and Integration examples, and all through a simple command-line configuration utilizing the XD shell and DSL.

Before you can begin, you must install Spring XD. Refer to the user manual section "Getting Started" at `http://docs.spring.io/spring-xd/docs/current/reference/html/#getting-started`, which provides details on the various ways of installing XD on your machine. The method of installation you choose is a matter of preference and does not impact the sample. Once you have XD installed, start the runtime in single-node mode as described in the documentation.

In order to replicate what we created in the Batch and Integration samples in XD, we need to do only a few basic tasks. First we need to create a CSV file to import, such as the contents listed next and place that in `/tmp/people.csv`:

```
Jill,Doe
Joe,Doe
Justin,Matthews
Jane,Matthews
```

In your Spring XD shell console, type the following command:

```
job create myjob --definition "filejdbc --resources=file:///tmp/people.csv
--names=firstname,lastname --tableName=people --initializeDatabase=true" --deploy
```

Upon hitting Enter in the console, you should see a message stating, "Successfully created and deployed job 'myjob.'" If not, inspect the console output in the terminal where you launched the single-node XD container for more details.

At this point, you have created a new job definition, but nothing has happened yet, as it has not been launched. In the shell, type the following command to launch the job:

```
job launch myjob
```

The shell should now respond with a message indicating that a launch request for myJob has been successfully submitted.

Breaking down the DSL we typed, Spring XD knew that we wanted to create a batch job that reads from a file and outputs to a database via JDBC by the `job create` statement and the `filejdbc` source. It also automatically created the table for us by using the `tableName` parameter, obtained the column names from the `names` parameter, and read our data by the `resources` parameter in which we provided the file path to our CSV file.

If you would like to inspect the imported data, use your favorite database tool and connect to the database you used during setup (either embedded or a real RDBMS) and select the records from the People table to verify. If you do not see data, check the log statements in the console that the single-node container is running in.

At this point, we have typed two commands into the shell, but have not written any code or complex configuration. Yet we have imported the contents of our CSV file into the database with minimal effort. We accomplished this by utilizing Spring XD's prebuilt batch job, defining it with simple command-line DSL syntax, and then launched the job from the shell.

As you can see, Spring XD provides a lot of functionality out of the box that removes the need for the developer to create some of the more common use-case scenarios. While we did some transformation to change the person's first and last name to uppercase in prior samples, we will leave that as an exercise for you to explore Spring XD further!

For more information on Spring XD, please see its project page at `http://projects.spring.io/spring-xd/`.

Spring Boot

The *Spring Boot* project aims to simplify the getting-started experience of building an application by using Spring. Spring Boot takes the guesswork out of manually gathering dependencies and provides some of the most common features needed by most applications, such as metrics and health checks.

Spring Boot takes an "opinionated" approach to achieve the goal of developer simplification by way of providing starter POMs for various types of applications that already contain the proper dependencies and versions, which means less time spent to get started. For those who may be looking to get away from XML completely, Spring Boot does not require any configuration to be written in XML.

In this example, we will create the traditional "Hello World!" web application. You may be surprised to see the minimal amount of code required to do so as compared to your typical Java web application setup.

Typically, we have started off samples by defining the dependencies we need to add to our project. Part of Spring Boot's simplification model is to prepare all the dependencies for you, and when using Maven, for example, you as the developer utilize a parent POM to obtain this functionality.

To get started, let's create the actual project POM file itself, as shown in Listing 18-13.

Listing 18-13. Spring Boot Web POM

```xml
<?xml version="1.0" encoding="UTF-8"?>

<project xmlns="http://maven.apache.org/POM/4.0.0"
         xmlns:xsi="http://www.w3.org/2001/XMLSchema-instance"
         xsi:schemaLocation="http://maven.apache.org/POM/4.0.0
            http://maven.apache.org/xsd/maven-4.0.0.xsd">
    <modelVersion>4.0.0</modelVersion>
    <groupId>com.apress.prospring4.ch18</groupId>
    <artifactId>boot</artifactId>
    <version>4.0-SNAPSHOT</version>
    <name>boot</name>
    <parent>
        <groupId>org.springframework.boot</groupId>
        <artifactId>spring-boot-starter-parent</artifactId>
        <version>1.1.4.RELEASE</version>
    </parent>
    <dependencies>
        <dependency>
            <groupId>org.springframework.boot</groupId>
            <artifactId>spring-boot-starter-web</artifactId>
        </dependency>
        <dependency>
            <groupId>org.springframework.boot</groupId>
            <artifactId>spring-boot-starter-actuator</artifactId>
        </dependency>
    </dependencies>
    <properties>
        <start-class>com.apress.prospring4.ch18.Application</start-class>
    </properties>
    <build>
        <plugins>
            <plugin>
                <groupId>org.springframework.boot</groupId>
                <artifactId>spring-boot-maven-plugin</artifactId>
            </plugin>
        </plugins>
    </build>
</project>
```

With our POM file in place, that takes care of resolving all the dependencies we need for our web project. All we need now is to create two simple classes. First let's create our web controller class, as shown in Listing 18-14.

Listing 18-14. HelloWorldController Class

```
package com.apress.prospring4.ch18;

import org.springframework.web.bind.annotation.RequestMapping;
import org.springframework.web.bind.annotation.RestController;

@RestController
public class HelloWorldController {
    @RequestMapping("/")
    public String helloWorld() {
        return "Hello world";
    }
}
```

This is a typical Spring MVC controller class that you learned about in Chapter 16 and that should be familiar to you already. You may notice the usage of @RestController rather than @Controller. The @RestController annotation is used for convenience, as it is already a @Controller stereotype, in addition the @RequestMapping methods assume @ResponseBody semantics by default. Next we create our bootstrap class by using a simple main() method, as shown in Listing 18-15.

Listing 18-15. Application Bootstrap Class

```
package com.apress.prospring4.ch18;

import org.springframework.boot.SpringApplication;
import org.springframework.boot.autoconfigure.EnableAutoConfiguration;
import org.springframework.context.annotation.ComponentScan;
import org.springframework.context.annotation.Configuration;

@Configuration
@EnableAutoConfiguration
@ComponentScan
public class Application {
    public static void main(String[] args) {
        SpringApplication.run(Application.class, args);
    }
}
```

At this point, you may be asking yourself, where is the web.xml, configuration file, and all the other components I must create for a basic web application? You already defined everything needed in the previous listings! Don't believe it? Compile the project and run the Application class until you see the log message indicating that the application has been started.

If you look at the generated log files, you see a lot going on with such little code. Most notably, it looks like Tomcat is running, and various endpoints such as health checks, environment output information, and metrics are already defined for you. First navigate to http://localhost:8080 and you will see the "Hello World!" web page displayed as expected. Next take a look at some of the preconfigured endpoints (for example, http://localhost:8080/health), which return a JSON representation of the application status. Going further, load http://localhost:8080/metrics to get a better understanding of various metrics that are being collected such as heap size, garbage collection, and so on.

As you may be able to tell already from this one sample alone, Spring Boot radically simplifies the way you go about creating web applications (or any type of application, for that matter). Gone are the days of having to configure numerous files to get a simple web application going, and with an embedded servlet container ready to serve your web application, everything "just works."

While we have shown you a very simple example, keep in mind that Spring Boot does not lock you into using what it chooses; it simply takes the "opinionated" approach and chooses defaults for you. If you don't want to use embedded Tomcat but Jetty instead, simply modify the POM to exclude the Tomcat starter module from the `spring-boot-starter-web` dependency. Utilizing a tool such as Maven's dependency tree is one way to help you visualize what dependencies are being brought into your project. Spring Boot also provides many other starter dependencies for other types of applications, and you are encouraged to read through the documentation for more details.

For more information on Spring Boot, please see its project page at `http://projects.spring.io/spring-boot/`.

Summary

In this chapter, we provided high-level overviews of a few projects in the Spring portfolio. We took a look at Spring Batch, JSR-352, Integration, XD, and Boot, each providing its own unique capabilities aimed at simplifying specific tasks at hand for you as the developer. Some of these projects are new, and some have been proven stable and solid, serving as ideal foundations for other frameworks. We do encourage you to take a look at these projects in deeper detail, as we feel they will greatly simplify your Java projects in general.

Index

■ B

Get the eBook for only $10!

Now you can take the weightless companion with you anywhere, anytime. Your purchase of this book entitles you to 3 electronic versions for only $10.

This Apress title will prove so indispensible that you'll want to carry it with you everywhere, which is why we are offering the eBook in 3 formats for only $10 if you have already purchased the print book.

Convenient and fully searchable, the PDF version enables you to easily find and copy code—or perform examples by quickly toggling between instructions and applications. The MOBI format is ideal for your Kindle, while the ePUB can be utilized on a variety of mobile devices.

Go to www.apress.com/promo/tendollars to purchase your companion eBook.

Apress®
THE EXPERT'S VOICE™

Druck: KN Digital Printforce GmbH · Schockenriedstraße 37 · 70565 Stuttgart